The Devī Gītā

Frontispiece: The Goddess Bhuvaneśvarī, Supreme Ruler of the Universe and revealer of the *Devī Gītā*. Pencil drawing by Dr. Bala Viswanathan. (This illustration also appears in the cover design.)

The Devī Gītā

The Song of the Goddess: A Translation, Annotation, and Commentary

C. Mackenzie Brown

State University of New York Press

Published by
State University of New York Press, Albany

Printed in the United States of America

For information, address State University of New York Press,
State University Plaza, Albany, NY, 12246

Production by Marilyn P. Semerad
Marketing by Nancy Farrell

Library of Congress Cataloging-in-Publication Data

Puranas. Devībhāgavatapurāṇa. Devīgītā. English.
The Devī Gītā : the song of the Goddess ; a translation, annotation, and commentary / C. Mackenzie Brown.
p. cm.
Includes bibliographical references and index.
ISBN 0-7914-3939-9 (hardcover : alk. paper). — ISBN 0-7914-3940-2 (pbk. : alk. paper)
I. Brown, Cheever Mackenzie. II. Title.
BL1140.4.D4742D4813 1998
294.5'925—dc21 98-15227
CIP

10 9 8 7 6 5 4 3 2 1

For Cynthia Ann Humes

Contents

Preface *ix*

Introduction *1*

A Note on the Translation *31*

Navaślokī Devī Gītā: The Essential *Devī Gītā* in Nine Verses *41*

Chapter 1
The Appearance of the Great Goddess Before the Mountain King Himālaya and the Gods *45*

Chapter 2
The Goddess as the Supreme Cause of Creation *85*

Chapter 3
The Goddess Reveals Her Cosmic Body (The Virāj) *111*

Chapter 4
Instruction in the Yoga of Knowledge *137*

Chapter 5
Instruction in the Eight-limbed/Kuṇḍalinī Yoga *161*

Chapter 6
The Goal of the Yogas: Knowledge of Brahman 203

Chapter 7
Instruction in the Yoga of Devotion 219

Chapter 8
Further Instruction in the Yoga of Devotion:
The Sacred Sites, Rites, and Festivals of the Goddess 237

Chapter 9
Vedic and Internal Forms of Goddess Worship 263

Chapter 10
The Tantric Form of Goddess Worship and
the Disappearance of the Great Goddess 285

Afterword 319

Appendix: Verse Index of the Epithets
and Names of the Goddess 325

Sanskrit Text 335

Bibliography 357

Index 375

Preface

I was a college freshman when I read for the first time (in English translation) the *Bhagavad Gītā* with its famous dialogue between Kṛṣṇa and his disciple Arjuna. This text was for me, as it is for many Westerners, a primary initiation into Hindu philosophy and metaphysics. When I eventually chose to go into Hindu studies in graduate school, the *Bhagavad Gītā* and its teachings played an important role in that decision. My views about the *Bhagavad Gītā*, and about the role of texts in general, especially texts of the elite Brahmanical class, have changed radically since my early graduate school days. But back then the *Bhagavad Gītā* was central to me and provided direction for many of my preliminary queries into the Hindu tradition. This orientation was further bolstered when, as a second year Sanskrit student at Harvard, I read the *Bhagavad Gītā* in its original language, under Daniel H. H. Ingalls. I thought, at the time, of someday doing my own translation of the *Bhagavad Gītā*, but, of course, there were already dozens in existence.

Midway through my graduate studies I learned about the existence of other, later *gītā*s, representing the metaphysical and spiritual teachings of various Hindu gods and goddesses and assorted sages. These other *gītā*s were little known in the West and seemed to have little prestige in India, compared to the renown of Kṛṣṇa's *Gītā* with Arjuna. It is perhaps understandable, then, that I initially assumed, without knowing much about these later *gītā*s and not having read them even in translation, that they must be poor imitations of the "real" *Gītā*, by which I meant the *Bhagavad Gītā*.

By dismissing these other *gītās*, I was committing an all too common historicist fallacy, defining in my own mind the most genuine and authoritative text or teaching by its age: the most ancient must be the most authentic. Such a historicist perspective soon changed, however, as I became more and more fascinated by the rich mythological traditions contained in the Hindu Purāṇic literature, almost all of which was composed after the time of the *Bhagavad Gītā*. In the Purāṇas I found a lively and ongoing tradition of mythic and theological reinterpretation that reflected, and inspired, major transformations within the Hindu tradition. It became obvious to me that what came later in the tradition was often more interesting, more illuminating, and more significant for the actual religious lives of Hindus today, than some of the more ancient and formally revered texts.

It was this new perspective that led me to undertake for my doctoral dissertation a critical analysis of the *Brahmavaivarta Purāṇa*, a late medieval Kṛṣṇaite text detailing the amorous exploits of Kṛṣṇa with his favorite female companion Rādhā. I became more and more intrigued by the role of Rādhā in this work, for here she becomes much more than a human paramour, achieving the status of Kṛṣṇa's divine consort and chief mediatrix of salvation. It was through this text that I began to take a deep interest in goddess traditions in India. Such a fascination on my part coincided with a general upsurge of scholarly interest in the role of women in religion. Among the gender issues being discussed were the nature and significance of feminine symbolism and imagery, especially as utilized in envisioning the divine, that occurred in various religious traditions throughout the world.

My study of the *Brahmavaivarta Purāṇa* introduced me to another Purāṇic text, which borrowed from it significant portions of its goddess myths and feminine theological views. This other text, the *Devī-Bhāgavata*, focuses precisely on the divine as feminine. It was quite natural, then, that my next major research project was an analysis of the *Devī-Bhāgavata Purāṇa* (published under the title *The Triumph of the Goddess: The Canonical Models and Theological Visions of the Devī-Bhāgavata Purāṇa*, by the State University of New York Press, 1990). The theological consummation of this *Purāṇa* is undoubtedly the final ten chapters (31-40) of the seventh book, and has come to be generally known as the *Devī Gītā*. In the *Triumph of the Goddess*, I devote a chapter to a historical and theological analysis of the *Devī Gītā*, showing among other things its textual and thematic relation to the *Bhagavad Gītā*. (That analysis has been incorporated in part into the Introduction to this book.) The author of the *Devī Gītā* is clearly indebted to the *Bhagavad Gītā* for many of his themes and motifs. Yet he also brought to his work a broad knowledge of many other important texts of the tradition and a familiarity with major philosophical, theological, ritual, and devotional developments that had occurred since the time of composition of the *Bhagavad Gītā*, possibly some fifteen hundred years earlier.

The *Devī Gītā* struck me at once as an important text from the goddess traditions of India, yet it has been largely ignored by scholars both western and Indian. This very neglect, however, provided me with the opportunity to fulfill, in an unexpected way, my earlier desire to translate "the *Gītā*." Unlike the *Bhagavad Gītā*, the *Devī Gītā* had been translated, to the best of my knowledge, just once into English when I commenced the project in 1990. That earlier rendition, by Hari Prasanna Chatterji, made in the early part of this century, was included in a translation of the whole of the *Devī-Bhāgavata Purāṇa*, making it a bit cumbersome and inaccessible. And the translation suffered innumerable shortcomings, not the least of which was its confusion of the text itself with the one printed Sanskrit commentary on it, by Nīlakaṇṭha the Śaiva. Since 1990, another translation has appeared, by Swami Satyananda Saraswati, inspired by devotion to the Divine Mother Goddess, but showing little concern for the historical and philosophical context of the poem, and frequently misrendering even the most basic and straightforward Sanskrit phrases. (Another translation of the *Devī Gītā*, as part of the *Devī-Bhāgavata Purāṇa*, is planned for the Purāṇic translations being published by Motilal Banarsidass in its Ancient Indian and Mythology Series. No date of publication for this text has yet been announced.)

In undertaking the translation of the *Devī Gītā*, I have tried to let the text speak for itself as much as possible. But I soon realized that some sort of annotation and commentary would be essential for introducing the text to those readers not thoroughly familiar with Hindu theology and myth. To hear fully what the text is saying, it is necessary to know and understand its various mythic references, technical terms, underlying assumptions, and parallel or contrasting schools of thought. Not even a traditional audience in India would necessarily have been familiar with all these matters, and thus there arose the need for commentaries, such as Nīlakaṇṭha's. In one sense, then, I am extending the commentarial tradition represented by Nīlakaṇṭha himself, doing for an English-speaking audience what this traditional pandit did for his own disciples. At the same time, as an empathetic but critical scholar of religion, I offer various comments on the history and development of the text that would probably not be accepted by a traditional commentator.

Originally I had intended to deal at some length with the living context of the *Devī Gītā* in India today, to examine how the text is currently understood and utilized. As the length of the commentary sections expanded, I realized that I would have to curtail such an inquiry. References relevant to the contemporary practice of Hindus and to present understandings of the *Devī Gītā* are for the most part simply scattered throughout the comments and notes. However, in the introductory comment on the "Navaśloki Devī Gītā" and in the Afterword, some of these issues are directly addressed.

Much of the information that I do have on the contemporary usage of the *Devī Gītā* was provided to me by Cynthia Ann Humes. In the late 1980s she carried out extensive field work in Vindhyācal, a historic and important center of goddess worship in north-central India, home of the Devī Vindhyavāsinī. This pilgrimage center is famous for the recitation of goddess texts, especially the *Devī Māhātmya,* but also including the *Devī-Bhāgavata Purāṇa.* Humes interviewed hundreds of pilgrims regarding their textual preferences and recitation practices. In writing *The Triumph of the Goddess,* I queried her frequently about the contemporary attitudes toward and usages of the *Devī-Bhāgavata.* In the course of these and later conversations, she indicated considerable interest in my doing a translation of the *Devī Gītā.* The successful completion of this book owes a great deal to her inspiration and encouragement.

I am indebted to many other individuals for their help in this work. William Eastman, former Director of the State University of New York Press, evinced considerable enthusiasm for the project when I first suggested it to him. Paul Müller-Ortega and Thomas B. Coburn provided early feedback and helpful advice, especially on how to organize the commentary and notes. Andrew O. Fort carefully read and critiqued the sections dealing with Advaita philosophy. David Kinsley furnished me with important background material on the goddess Bhuvaneśvarī. David Gordon White and Cynthia Humes assisted with the translation of the Hindi prefaces to current printed editions of the *Devī Gītā.* Paula M. Cooey and Rita Gross offered valuable insights into issues of gender, including problems relating to the translation of ancient, androcentric texts. Randall L. Nadeau, Deborah Reason, and Maria Cedargren reviewed portions of the text for overall readability. Patricia Atnip perused the entire manuscript, raising many questions from the perspective of a nonacademic but interested reader that helped me to clarify several of my general interpretive comments. Readers for the State University of New York Press included Paul Müller-Ortega, Thomas B. Coburn, Cynthia Humes, and Tracy Pintchman, whose corrections and suggestions for the final revisions of the text I greatly appreciate.

Special thanks are due to Nagaraja Sharma, associate priest at the Hindu Temple of San Antonio, and devotee of the Goddess. Quite fortuitously for me, Mr. Sharma's teacher and father-in-law is the author of a multivolume commentary, in Kannada, on the *Devī-Bhāgavata.* Nagaraja and I sat together many hours in the temple discussing the grammar, style, mythic background, and theology of the *Devī Gītā,* his father-in-law's commentary close at hand for consultation. I am also greatly indebted to Bala Viswanathan, a member of the Hindu Temple of San Antonio, whose three fine pencil drawings of Bhuvaneśvarī, made at my request, grace this book.

My gratitude is also due to Andrea Kanten, former Sanskrit student of mine, who entered the Sanskrit text of the *Devī Gītā* into electronic form for reproduction in this book. Maria G. McWilliams, of the interlibrary loan staff at Trinity University, is to be commended for her patience and perseverance in securing obscure texts and articles. Gretta Small and Pat Atnip rendered considerable assistance in proofreading the galleys. I thank Kay Bolton, copyeditor, and Marilyn P. Semerad, production editor at the State University of New York Press, for their fine help and suggestions. Trinity University's Department of Religion assisted with grants to expedite various stages of my research, and Trinity University provided a semester's leave and a summer stipend to work on this project.

Introduction

The Goddess and Her Song

The *Devī Gītā*, or *Song of the Goddess*, presents a grand vision of the universe created, pervaded, and protected by a supremely powerful, all-knowing, and wholly compassionate divine female. She is Mahā-Devī or the Great Goddess, known to her most devoted followers as the auspicious Mother-of-the-World (*jagad-ambikā, jagan-mātṛ*). Unlike the ferocious and horrific Hindu goddesses such as Kālī and Durgā, the World-Mother of the *Devī Gītā* is benign and beautiful, though some of her lesser manifestations may take on terrifying forms. And unlike other beneficent female divinities such as Pārvatī and Lakṣmī, she is subject to no male consort.

This World-Mother is formally addressed as Bhuvaneśvarī, the "Ruler of the Universe." She resides in her celestial paradise known as Maṇidvīpa, the Jeweled Island, situated at the topmost point of the universe. From there, ever wakeful and alert, she observes the troubles of the world, eager to intervene on behalf of her devotees.

While resting in her island home, she reclines on a sacred throne or couch of remarkable design, composed of five *preta*s, ghosts or corpses. The four legs are the lifeless bodies of Brahmā, Viṣṇu, Rudra, and Īśāna (the latter two being forms or aspects of Śiva), and the seat is the stretched-out corpse of Sadāśiva (the eternal Śiva). This conception of Bhuvaneśvarī seated on her Pañca-Pretāsana (Seat of Five Corpses), marvellously illustrated in Figure 10.1, page 286, reveals her supreme sovereignty, especially over masculine pretensions to cosmic power. Brahmā, Viṣṇu, and Śiva are the three male deities traditionally associated with creating, overseeing, and destroying the universe. But here, as elements of Bhuvaneśvarī's throne, they represent her latent cosmic energies, unconscious and inert, residing under her feet until aroused by her desire. While lounging on this couch at the beginning of creation, the Goddess splits herself into two for the sake of her own pleasure or sport—one half of her body becoming Maheśvara (Śiva).[1] In such manner she dramatically demonstrates her superiority to all the male gods.

The Great Goddess is both wholly transcendent and fully immanent: beyond space and time, she is yet embodied within all existent beings; without form as pure, infinite consciousness (*cit*), she yet dwells each month in the sacred shrine of Kāmākhyā in Assam during her menses. She is the universal, cosmic energy known as Śakti, and the psychophysical, guiding force designated as the Kuṇḍalinī (Serpent Power) resident within each indiviudal. She is eternal, without origin or birth, yet she is born in this world in age after age, to support those who seek her assistance. Precisely to provide comfort and guidance to her devotees, she presents herself in the *Devī Gītā* to reveal the truths leading both to worldly happiness and to the supreme spiritual goals: dwelling in her Jeweled Island and mergence into her own perfect being.

Less well known than the *Bhagavad Gītā* (*The Song of the Lord*) both in India and the West, the *Devī Gītā* nonetheless serves, for certain Hindus who see ultimate reality primarily in terms of a divine and beneficent mother, as the supreme scripture, complementing and completing all others. Indeed, the Goddess herself in the *Devī Gītā* frequently quotes from the *Bhagavad Gītā*, as well as from other Hindu scriptures, but with the understanding that all such passages ultimately point to her as the Absolute.

The *gītā*s of the Goddess and of the Lord are songs in a rather special sense: as philosophical and devotional poems in the form of dialogues between a divine teacher and her or his disciple(s). In the *Bhagavad Gītā*, it is the Lord Kṛṣṇa who responds to the queries of the dejected and reluctant warrior Arjuna as he is about to enter an internecine struggle with a rival family clan. This struggle between the Pāṇḍavas (Arjuna's clan) and the Kauravas is the subject of the great Hindu epic, the *Māhābhārata*, of which the *Bhagavad Gītā* is a small part. The *Bhagavad Gītā*, placed in the tension-filled moments just prior to the beginning of battle, focuses on the various moral and spiritual dilemmas faced by Arjuna. Kṛṣṇa, serving as Arjuna's charioteer, surveys with his despondent student the two armies drawn up for battle and reveals the necessity of the war and of Arjuna's participation in it. In the process Kṛṣṇa explains the nature of existence, human nature, and the solution to human suffering, summarizing in due course the major religious ideals of Hindu culture.

In the *Devī Gītā*, it is the World-Mother Bhuvaneśvarī who expounds similar metaphysical truths to her devotee, the Mountain King Himālaya, in the midst of an assembly of gods. While the occasion for the Devī's revelations is ostensibly prompted by a crisis in the fortunes of the gods, their celestial home being overrun by the demon Tāraka and his army (briefly described in chapter 1), the dramatic, epic context of the *Bhagavad Gītā* is largely missing. The real motivations behind Himālaya's questions to the Goddess are simply his own devotion to her and his desire for liberating knowledge. His thirst for spiritual wisdom is quite disconnected from any specific impending worldly (or celestial) catastrophe.

The revelations of the Goddess in the *Devī Gītā*, like those of Kṛṣṇa in the *Bhagavad Gītā*, take two complementary forms: the disclosure of her primary visual or iconic manifestations (*darśana*), recounted in chapters 1 and 3, and her teaching (*upadeśa*), constituting the bulk of chapters 2 through 10. Her explanations of creation and other cosmological matters are the focus of chapters 2 and 3. Her exposition of the various spiritual disciplines, such as the paths of knowledge (Jñāna Yoga), psychophysical training (the Eight-limbed Yoga of Patañjali and Kuṇḍalinī Yoga) and devotion (Bhakti Yoga), are the concerns of chapters 4 through 10. These teachings elucidating the human predicament are themselves illuminated by the iconic displays, which serve to reveal various aspects of the divine personality of the Goddess and her relationship to the world and humankind.

The manifestation of the Goddess in her highest iconic form, as the lovely, four-armed Bhuvaneśvarī, clearly emphasizes her benign nature. The most detailed visual description of Bhuvaneśvarī in the *Devī Gītā* (1.31–41) stresses her divine beauty and charm, her compassionate face, and her gracious disposition. She is dressed in red, the color of auspiciousness and life. Prominent among her identifying marks are her three playful eyes and her four hands, two of which carry a noose and goad, the other two gesturing her beneficence and granting of fearlessness. A modern devotee affirms that these "four hands represent *dharma, artha, kama* and *moksha*," that is, her eagerness and power to bestow the four chief ends of human existence (virtue, wealth, pleasure, and liberation).[2]

A lower but rather more awesome iconic form of the Goddess revealed in the *Devī Gītā* (3.22–38) is her manifestation as the Virāj, the brilliant Cosmic Body of the world, in which the whole universe appears as parts of her majestic, lordly body. Such a cosmotheistic vision emphasizes the ultimate unity of the Goddess and the manifest world.[3]

In addition to the iconic manifestations and their interrelated teachings, the *Devī Gītā* includes two brief but important hymns of praise (*stotras*). Each is offered to the Goddess by the gods as they behold her two most magnificent forms, as Bhuvaneśvarī and as the Virāj, in awe-struck response to receiving these gracious visions of the Devī. The hymns draw heavily from other scriptural sources, including Arjuna's own wonder-filled praise of Kṛṣṇa after viewing the latter's terrifying cosmic form in the *Bhagavad Gītā*. The hymns of the *Devī Gītā*, praising and describing the supreme reality, summarize and affirm the central revelations of the Goddess herself.

The Historical, Religious, and Literary Background of the Devī Gītā

The *Devī Gītā*, like the *Bhagavad Gītā*, is part of a much larger work but frequently circulates as an independent text. The *Devī Gītā* is a brief section (507 verses) of the rather lengthy *Devī-Bhāgavata Purāṇa* (ca. 18,000 verses), constituting the last ten chapters (31–40) of its seventh book. The bulk of the *Devī-Bhāgavata* may have been composed as early as the twelfth century of the Common Era, though a later date cannot be ruled out. Whether or not the *Devī Gītā* was part of the original composition of the *Devī-Bhāgavata* or a later interpolation is difficult to say. Given the specific philosophical ideas and literary works with which it is familiar (see below), it is difficult to place the *Devī Gītā* earlier than the thirteenth century, and it may be as late as the sixteenth.

The *Devī-Bhāgavata* belongs to a genre of Sanskrit texts known as Purāṇas, a class of works purportedly dealing with ancient (*purāṇa*) events and happenings, both divine and human. For understanding the historical and cultural background of the *Devī Gītā*, a brief consideration of the larger literary context in which it is embedded, including the Purāṇic tradition as a whole, will prove useful.

The Devī Gītā *and the* Devī-Bhāgavata Purāṇa

In formal terms, the *Devī Gītā* is part of an ongoing conversation between a despondent king, Janamejaya, and his spiritual counselor, the venerable sage Vyāsa. This conversation constitutes the great bulk of the *Devī-Bhāgavata* as a whole, and is intended to console Janamejaya following the untimely death of his father, King Parīkṣit. The latter, the grandson of the great epic hero Arjuna, was mortally wounded by snakebite shortly after ascending the throne, and was immediately succeeded by his son Janamejaya. According to the *Devī-Bhāgavata,* when Janamejaya's father met his untimely demise, he descended into hell. Upon learning of his father's miserable fate, the son was left disconsolate. Even after hearing the whole of the *Māhābhārata,* a common therapy for depressed souls in those days, Janamejaya remained grief stricken and inquired of Vyāsa what he should do. Vyāsa is thoroughly qualified to act as spiritual adviser to the king for he is well versed in mystical lore, being credited with composing not only the *Māhābhārata,* but also most of the major Purāṇas.

Vyāsa advises his royal client to build a temple to the Goddess, to perform her worship, and to listen to the *Śrīmad Bhāgavatam*—appropriating here this honorific title of the famous Vaiṣṇava *Bhāgavata Purāṇa* (to be discussed below) for the *Devī Bhāgavata Purāṇa* itself.[4] Vyāsa then recites the greater part of the *Devī-Bhāgavata* to Janamejaya. In this fashion, and duly carrying out the rest of Vyāsa's instructions, the king rescues his father from hell, sending him to the Devī's heaven of the Jeweled Island, and himself attaining peace of mind.[5]

In the course of Vyāsa's recitation, Janamejaya occasionally asks about important points that the sage has previously glossed over rather quickly. One such query, in the first verse of the *Devī Gītā,* concerns the appearance of the Goddess as the supreme lustrous power (*paraṃ mahas*) on the Himālaya Mountain, mentioned by Vyāsa in the preceding chapter.[6] This leads Vyāsa to narrate the events surrounding the manifestation of the Goddess as the supreme light. These events include the instructions of the Devī to Himālaya and constitute the core of the *Devī Gītā.* The Devī's *Song,* while immediately directed to Himālaya, addresses the general situation of humankind, including Janamejaya in his grief.

As indicated above, the Purāṇas recount the great events of old. The Purāṇas focus especially on those events that reveal the constitution of the universe (such as cosmogony) or illustrate in fundamental ways the human condition (such as war or death). Also included among the noteworthy ancient events are those sagely conversations or divine revelations that help to explain the human predicament. The Goddess' *Song,* accordingly, is one of those great happenings, both revealing the nature of finite existence with its attendant sorrows, and prescribing the best ways to deal with it.

The Devī-Bhāgavata Purāṇa *and the Purāṇic Tradition*

The ancient stories of the Purāṇas include myths of creation, histories of ancient dynasties, and the interactions between gods, demons, and human beings. The focus of many of the early myths and legends was the perpetual cycle of conflict between the gods and demons. Victory by the latter threatened the stability of the entire universe and the prosperity of humankind. Retelling of these ancient tales was, in part, to reaffirm the eventual victory of the gods and the reestablishment of cosmic order. The reference to the myth of the demon Tāraka that forms part of the frame story for the *Devī Gītā* (discussed below) is a remnant of this ancient cycle of conflict.

Much of the ancient mythic material precedes the actual composition of any of the extant Purāṇas. The earliest Purāṇas date back to the first centuries of the Common Era, and they often took over and retold stories already found in the great Hindu epics, especially the *Māhābhārata* (itself composed over many centuries, from c. 400 B.C.E. to c. 400 C.E.). The Purāṇas are thus an extension of the epic tradition, but at the same time they radically transformed the early epic world view. The old forms were taken over but filled with new meaning. In particular, the Purāṇic composers (Paurāṇikas) were increasingly inspired by new religious movements of personalistic, theistic devotionalism, known as *bhakti*.

These devotional movements focused their attention on one or another "great god," especially Viṣṇu (and his incarnations such as Kṛṣṇa) and Śiva. The *bhakti* enthusiasts were less and less concerned with the god-demon conflict per se, and more and more with the emotional, devotional attitude that the (minor) gods and demons alike, as well as human beings, might feel toward one of these great gods. Especially noteworthy in this regard are the many stories of pious demons as true devotees of the supreme Lord. Such a motif is reflected in some of the latest compositions of the *Māhābhārata* and signals a moving away from the earlier epic theme of vanquishing the demonic hosts to ensure cosmic order. The *Bhagavad Gītā* (c. first century of the Common Era), also a late addition to the *Māhābhārata*, attests in its own way to the growth of *bhakti* within the most recent layers of the epic.

The Paurāṇikas continued and intensified the *bhakti*c revision of the ancient myths, and also added new types of materials reflective of their devotional concerns. These included, for instance, detailed instructions for ritual worship of the great gods and lists of pilgrimage places often accompanied by prolonged glorifications of these sacred sites. The nature of devotion itself was analyzed, and the characteristics of a true devotee described at length. And of course there developed extensive hymns of praise extolling the virtues of the great gods.

While there are hundreds or even thousands of works known as Purāṇas, and while Purāṇas continue to be composed to the present day, there developed by at least the tenth century the notion of a canon of eighteen major or Mahā-Purāṇas, as well as a set of eighteen minor or Upa-Purāṇas. Most of the so-called major Purāṇas extol the glories either of Viṣṇu in one or another of his incarnations, or of Śiva. Notably absent among the earlier major Purāṇas are any dedicated to the Goddess. Only in the *Mārkaṇḍeya Purāṇa* do we find a brief section, consisting of thirteen chapters (81–93), that describe three great mythic events in the career of the Goddess and glorify her mighty deeds. This famous section, known as the *Devī Māhātmya* (*Glorification of the Goddess*), composed around the sixth century C.E., marks the emergence of the Great Goddess in the Sanskritic, Purāṇic tradition.

Over the next several centuries, other passages glorifying the Goddess were inserted into a number of the major Purāṇas, such as the "*devī māhātmya*" found in the *Kūrma Purāṇa* (1.11). In addition, a few "minor" Purāṇas such as the *Devī* and the *Kālikā*, were dedicated to one or another form of the Goddess. In all these works the Goddess is presented in a somewhat limited aspect, for instance, as primarily a war goddess, and/or as subordinate, to a greater or less extent, to a male deity, usually Śiva. Even in the *Mahābhāgavata Purāṇa*, another Goddess-oriented Upa-Purāṇa, where the Goddess Pārvatī is treated as supreme, there remain implications of subordination, for Pārvatī, according to long-standing tradition, is the dutiful spouse of Śiva.

Sometime after the eleventh century, one ardent follower of the Goddess, or he and a small group of like-minded friends, decided to rectify the situation and compose a great Purāṇa dedicated solely to the object of their devotion, conceived of as the supreme power (*śakti*) of the universe, consort of none, subject to none. The result of their labors is the *Devī-Bhāgavata Purāṇa*. While not all Hindus accept the *Devī-Bhāgavata* as a Mahā-Purāṇa, there are few objective grounds on which to deny it such status. And in the minds of Śāktas (worshipers of Śakti, that is, of the Great Goddess as the supreme power), there is no question at all but that it is a Mahā-Purāṇa.

The *Devī-Bhāgavata* was thus, in part, a response to the growing popularity of the devotional movements centered on the great male gods, and to the increasing prominence of the great Purāṇas extolling Viṣṇu or Śiva. Especially renowned by the beginning of the eleventh century was the *Bhāgavata Purāṇa*, composed by Vaiṣṇavas (followers of Viṣṇu) perhaps a century earlier, and lovingly recounting the boyhood exploits of Kṛṣṇa, one of the prime avataras or incarnations of Viṣṇu. The *Devī-Bhāgavata* is modelled in many ways on the *Bhāgavata*, and substitutes itself in place of the Vaiṣṇava Purāṇa in the traditional list of eighteen Mahā-Purāṇas. It takes over many motifs from the *Bhāgavata*, but reinterprets them in such a way as to belittle Viṣṇu and to glorify the Goddess. It is hardly suprising, then, that the Goddess absorbed, as it were, many of the qualities of Viṣṇu/Kṛṣṇa himself, a process already at work in the *Devī Māhātmya* of the *Mārkaṇḍeya Purāṇa*.

The *Devī-Bhāgavata* was intended not only to show the superiority of the Goddess over various male deities, but also to clarify and elaborate on her nature in her own terms, rather than simply in relation to Viṣṇu. In this reenvisioning of the Goddess, the *Devī-Bhāgavata* relied heavily on earlier Śākta Purāṇic accounts of the great deeds of the Devī, and especially on the *Devī Māhātmya* of the *Mārkaṇḍeya Purāṇa*. In this text, particularly in its hymns, the Goddess is frequently described as both horrific and benign, as the enabling energy in all beings, and as the ultimate creative, controlling, and destructive power in the universe. In the three demon-destroying myths of the *Devī Māhātmya*, her role is that of a deluder and especially of a warrior goddess, often extremely violent and bloodthirsty. The Goddess herself says very little, beyond promising to continue to protect the world in future ages and extolling the virtues of worshiping her and singing her own praises.

The *Devī-Bhāgavata* retells the myths of the *Devī Māhātmya*, twice in fact, but in the process distances the Goddess in her supreme form as the benevolent World-Mother from the lesser forms that are prone to engage in the bloody rampages against the demons. The Goddess in the *Devī-Bhāgavata* becomes less of a warrior goddess, and more a nurturer and comforter of her devotees, and a teacher of wisdom. This development in the character of the Goddess culminates in the *Devī Gītā*.

The Devī Gītā *and the Gītā Tradition*

Just as the *Devī-Bhāgavata* as a whole was intended as a counterpart to the *Bhāgavata Purāṇa*, so the *Devī Gītā*, the philosophical and theological consummation of the text, was intended as a counterpart to the *Bhagavad Gītā*. In both form and content, the *Devī Gītā*, as indicated earlier, often closely resembles the *Bhagavad Gītā*. The latter text, however, was not the only model for the *Devī Gītā*. Long before the composition of the *Devī Gītā*, the *Bhagavad Gītā* had already inspired other "imitations," *gītā*s presenting the teachings of other gods like Śiva, or of certain pious sages.

The earliest of these imitations appear already in the *Māhābhārata*, and are quite common in the Purāṇas. Even the Vaiṣṇavas composed further *gītās*, such as the *Kapila Gītā* found in the *Bhāgavata Purāṇa*. Like the *Bhagavad Gītā*, the *Kapila Gītā* lent many of its themes to the *Devī Gītā*, such as its description of the cosmic form (Virāj) of Kṛṣṇa, and its typology of devotion. The *Devī Gītā*'s ideal of disinterested devotion, in which one surrenders the fruits of one's actions to the supreme, is rooted in the devotional path (Bhakti Yoga) expounded in these Vaiṣṇava *gītās*. Certain cosmological details in the *Devī Gītā* may well have been borrowed from a Śaivite *gītā*, the *Sūta Gītā* from the *Skanda Purāṇa*.

The *Devī Gītā* did not utilize merely the Vaiṣṇava and Śaiva *gītās*, simply substituting the Goddess for Viṣṇu/Kṛṣṇa, or Śiva. The composer of the *Devī Gītā* was clearly acquainted with at least one or two earlier Śākta *gītās*, which had already made significant innovations in adapting the *Bhagavad Gītā* to their own theological vision. They provided a new mythic setting for the revelations of the Goddess, and a different overall structure that emphasized the gracious manifestations of the various forms of the Goddess.

Probably the earliest Śākta *gītā* is the so-called *devī māhātmya* of the *Kūrma Purāṇa*. The line between a *gītā* and a *māhātmya*, incidentally, is far from absolute. The main distinction is that in a *māhātmya*, the perspective is that of the devotee, who listens to the great deeds of the deity and extols the divine majesty, while in a *gītā*, the perspective is largely that of the deity, who instructs the disciple. But since praises of the deity appear in *gītās*, and divine instructions appear in *māhātmyas*, there is considerable overlap. In the case of the *devī māhātmya* of the *Kūrma Purāṇa*, the disciple, the mountain king Himālaya, praises the Goddess with a hymn of her thousand and eight names, and so the text (that is, chapter 11 of the first part of the *Kūrma Purāṇa*) certainly qualifies as a *māhātmya*. At the same time, the rest of this *māhātmya* conforms to the general model of a *gītā*, with its instructions by the Goddess and the revelation of her cosmic forms, often horrific in nature. Accordingly, it is not inappropriate to refer to this text as the *Kūrma Devī Gītā*. In any case, it served as the model for later Śākta *gītās*, such as the one appearing in the *Mahābhāgavata Purāṇa*, which refers to itself as the *Pārvatī Gītā*. And the hymn of one thousand and eight names sung by Himālaya in the *Kūrma Devī Gītā* is alluded to by the Goddess in the *Devī Gītā*.[7]

In both the *Kūrma Devī Gītā* and the *Pārvatī Gītā*, the new mythic setting for the appearance of the Goddess revolves around the birth of Gaurī or Pārvatī, daughter of the Himālaya Mountain. In the former *gītā*, the narrator (Viṣṇu in the form of a tortoise or *kūrma*) makes mention of the famous incarnations of the Goddess as Satī, daughter of Dakṣa, and as Pārvatī, daughter of Himālaya. The assembled sages ask the tortoise who this Devī really is. He responds briefly by describing her nature as Śakti (power) and Māyā (the magical power of creation), and as the helpmate of Śiva. The tortoise then begins an account of the Devī's birth as the daughter of Himālaya, and how the mountain king and his wife performed severe penance to obtain such a child. Upon her birth, the parents are astonished at her splendorous beauty, prompting Himālaya to ask who she is. This provides the opening for the newborn Goddess to begin her spiritual instruction, and to reveal her cosmic forms. While the Goddess is often praised as supreme in the *Kūrma Devī Gītā*, there are nonetheless frequent intimations of her ultimate subordination to Śiva, to whom she is eventually given in marriage in order to benefit the gods.

The *Pārvatī Gītā* adheres closely to the *Kūrma Devī Gītā*'s account of Pārvatī's birth. The *Pārvatī Gītā* adds a few interesting details; for instance, not only do Himālaya and his wife desire the Goddess as their child, but also Śiva, grieving from the loss of his wife Satī, desires the (re)birth of the Goddess so she can once again become his consort. In contrast to the *Kūrma Devī Gītā*, however, the *Pārvatī Gītā* is far more consistent and thoroughgoing in its emphasis on the supreme nature of Pārvatī. She is identified with the ultimate reality, Brahman, and earlier in the *Mahābhāgavata*, she is said to be the source from which arise the three male gods (Brahmā, Viṣṇu, and Śiva) of the cosmic triumvirate. And yet the *Mahābhāgavata* also emphasizes her status as the spouse of Śiva. The *Mahābhāgavata* relates that the three cosmic gods, in order to win the Goddess in marriage, each commenced austerities. The Goddess then assumed a dreadful form to test the concentration of her three suitors. While she readily terrorized Brahmā and Viṣṇu, she was unable to disturb the mind of Śiva and so was pleased to become his wife. Thus, even in the *Pārvatī Gītā*, the wifely status of the Goddess as Pārvatī carries with it, if only implicitly, potential notions of subordination.

The *Devī Gītā* utilizes the by now traditional motif of Pārvatī's birth to introduce the Devī's discourse, but with a twist. Pārvatī herself actually appears only briefly, at the conclusion of the *Song*. For Pārvatī, in the *Devī Gītā*, is merely a lower manifestation of the Goddess, one of her many *śakti*s. The actual teaching is delivered by the Goddess in her highest iconic mode, as the supreme World-Mother Bhuvaneśvarī, beyond birth, beyond marriage, beyond any possible subordination to Śiva.

The Goddess graciously appears before the gods at their request, in a time of great turmoil. The gods are doubly distressed: on the one hand, their celestial homes have been overrun by the demon Tāraka, and on the other, only the legitimate son of Śiva can slay Tāraka, but Śiva is without a wife—his spouse Satī having committed suicide. The gods can see no solution to their predicament, until Viṣṇu suggests that they go the Himālaya mountain and there worship the supreme power of the universe, the Great Goddess. When approached, the Goddess eventually manifests herself before the gods first as a brilliant orb of light, the supreme lustrous power (*paraṃ mahas*) mentioned above. She then emerges from the light as the beautiful and benevolent Bhuvaneśvarī. She promises the gods that her *śakti* Pārvatī will take birth in Himālaya's house, and further indicates that Pārvatī will eventually be given to Śiva to produce Tāraka's slayer. Himālaya is so overwhelmed with devotion at the thought of the Goddess becoming his daughter—admittedly only in one of her lesser forms—that he at once requests to know all about her true nature as explained in the Vedānta (see below), and to learn how to become one with her. It is at this juncture that the Devī's teachings begin.

The emergence of Bhuvaneśvarī from the orb of blazing light clearly elevates the Goddess beyond any hint of inferiority suggested by Pārvatī's association with Śiva. The light represents her supreme form as pure consciousness, transcendent and infinite. While the emergence motif has no counterpart in the *Kūrma Devī Gītā* or *Pārvatī Gītā*, both of these earlier Śākta *gītās* provide the philosophical framework for such a conception. In the *Kūrma Devī Gītā*, Pārvatī states that in addition to her lordly, cosmic form—just displayed to the overwhelmed Himālaya—she has two other forms, composite (*sakala*) and incomposite (*niṣkala*). The incomposite form is supreme, infinite, beyond all limitations, consisting of pure consciousness.[8] Similarly, in the *Pārvatī Gītā*, the Goddess refers to her gross (*sthūla*) and subtle (*sūkṣma*) forms,[9] describing the latter as incomposite (*niṣkala*), beyond speech, pure, without qualities, the supreme light (*paramaṃ jyotis*), and embodying infinite being, consciousness, and bliss (*sac-cid-ānanda*).[10] The *Devī Gītā* has taken these notions of the aniconic (*niṣkala*) and iconic (*sakala*) forms of the Goddess and worked them into the dramatic introduction of Bhuvaneśvarī before the gods.

The emergence of the Goddess out of the orb of light is reminiscent of Śiva's self-manifestation in the famous myth of the origin of his infinite Liṅga ("supreme emblem," often overly interpreted in its phallic aspect, but primarily denoting the ultimate "defining characteristic" of Śiva as consciousness). As told in the *Śiva Purāṇa*, Śiva appears before the quarreling Brahmā and Viṣṇu as a shaft of light (*jyotir-liṅga*), a massive pillar of fire with no top or bottom. Then, as the sacred syllable Oṃ reverberates through space, from out of that blazing column steps forth Śiva in his iconic form as Maheśvara, five-faced and ten-armed.[11] The Jyotir-liṅga represents Śiva as the supreme Brahman without parts (*niṣkala*), without marks (*aliṅga*); the iconic form as with parts (*sakala*), the qualified Brahman that oversees the cosmic processes of creation, and so forth, as well as liberation. The myth serves, among other things, to identify Śiva with the supreme reality of Brahman taught in the ancient Upaniṣads and elaborated upon in the later schools of Vedānta.

The Devī's own myth of emergence functions, on the one hand, as a counterpart to the famous origin myth of the Jyotir-liṅga, belonging to one of her major male rivals, Śiva. On the other hand, in a parallel manner it establishes in dramatic fashion her own identity with the supreme Brahman of the Upaniṣads. Here we see the impact of Vedāntic thought, especially in its Advaitic or nondualist aspect, upon the *Devī Gītā*. The aniconic form of the Goddess as pure consciousness, whose form is formless, clearly reflects the Advaitic view of the ultimate.

Between the time of composition of the *Bhagavad Gītā* and of the *Devī Gītā*, in addition to the arising of Śākta-oriented *bhakti*, there were two other major philosophical and religious developments that directly or indirectly impacted almost all of the subsequent Hindu tradition, and are intricately intertwined in the *Devī Gītā*. First, there emerged in the eighth or ninth century the nondualist school of Advaita Vedānta, just mentioned. Second, and beginning some centuries earlier, there sprang forth a number of movements collectively known as Tantra, representing an alternative nondualistic, ritualized perspective of the universe. Advaitic and Tantric conceptions play a major role in shaping the *Devī Gītā*'s vision of the Goddess, as well as the ways to attain final release from all suffering. Accordingly, we shall next briefly summarize the Vedāntic and Tantric traditions and their literary, philosophical, and practical contributions to the *Devī Gītā*. In addition, we shall look at certain key developments in the particular strand of Tantra known as Śākta Tantrism.

The Devī Gītā *and Advaita Vedānta*

The term *vedānta* literally means "the end (*anta*) of knowledge or wisdom (*veda*)." This knowledge, *veda*, is regarded by Hindus as the blueprint for the whole of creation and the supreme truth of the universe. Such knowledge was discovered through meditation by ancient sages, and was eventually gathered into four collections of sacred lore, known as the four Vedas. Later, other inspired sages explained these Vedas to their disciples, and the transmitted record of their conversations came to constitute a second body of sacred lore known as the Upaniṣads, sometimes also referred to by the general term *veda*, but more often called *vedānta*, the end (*anta*, in the sense of concluding portion) of the Vedas.

The Upaniṣads are not systematic works, as they express various philosophical and theological points of view. Some are quite theistic or cosmotheistic, others more nontheistic. There arose, then, a number of schools that attempted to provide some sort of consistent interpretation for all the teachings contained in the Upaniṣads, often by hierarchically ranking the divergent perspectives. These schools collectively came to call themselves Vedānta, as they based themselves on the *vedānta* (Upaniṣads). They are also appropriately called Vedānta, as they attempt to elucidate the ultimate aim, or end (*anta*), of knowledge (*veda*).

Among the several schools, one in particular stressed the ideal of a single, transpersonal Absolute, the nondual Brahman expounded by many of the Upaniṣadic sages. This nontheistic school, the Advaita, established by Gauḍapāda and his famous disciple Śaṃkara, insisted that Brahman is the sole, full reality, eternal and unchanging. The realm of multiplicity, including the whole of the manifold universe, is regarded as a lower, derivative manifestation, an appearance only, an illusion of sorts. Even God, in the sense of a personal supreme being, is seen as a lower aspect of the Absolute, Brahman partially obscured, or with qualities (*saguṇa*), in contrast to the higher, qualityless (*nirguṇa*) Brahman.

In the Upaniṣads, this *nirguṇa* Brahman is somewhat paradoxically described as infinite being, consciousness, and bliss (*sat*, *cit*, and *ānanda*). These three are regarded not as qualities of Brahman, but as the essence (*svarūpa*) of that which transcends all verbal formulation or conceptualization. The notion of infinite being is further elucidated by the statement that Brahman is "one alone without a second." That is, there is nothing existent anywhere that is not, ultimately, Brahman. Otherwise, if there were a second, Brahman itself would be limited and finite.

Infinite consciousness expresses the idea that Brahman surpasses all limited and individuated mental states of awareness. Brahman is often said to be beyond the three primary states of individual consciousness, waking, dreaming, and deep sleep, being a transcendent state called simply "the fourth" (*turīya*). These four states of consciousness are correlated with four stages of creation (see below), as well as with the four quarters of the primal sonic manifestation of Brahman, the sacred syllable Oṃ (or Auṃ, the three letters *a, u,* and *m* representing the three lower states, and the dot the ensuing silence of "the fourth").

While infinite consciousness transcends all finite consciousness, its very infinitude means that all conscious beings and all states of consciousness are simply manifestations or reflections of the pure consciousness of Brahman. The idea of Brahman as an all-pervading consciousness, according to Advaita, points to the ultimate identity of the individual soul (*jīva*) and the Absolute. The separate, independent existence of the countless *jīva*s in the universe is thus merely an appearance. The *jīva*s are simply the outer manifestation of a deeper, inward reality, the true Self or Ātman. All *jīva*s are refractions of this higher Self, which is identical with Brahman. This ideal is encapsulated in the famous great saying of the Upaniṣads, "You are That" (*tat tvam asi*): that supreme Self identical with the Absolute is your own true nature.

That true Self, our innermost nature, is characterized by infinite bliss and is accordingly the highest object of love. It is the blissful nature of this Self that accounts for our desire to exist forever, to be immortal. The final goal of existence is the full realization of this blissful inner Self and its identity with Brahman.

The suffering we experience in the world is due to the ignorant acceptance of the apparent separateness and multiplicity of *jīva*s. So long as this illusion is accepted, so long will the soul continue circling through the cycle of life and death, known as samsara (*saṃsāra*). The ultimate desire of all souls is liberation (*mokṣa*) from the round of suffering inherent in samsara. But liberation is not just a negative escape from the round of birth, death, and rebirth; it is also the positive attainment of the bliss that is Brahman.

Since the state of suffering, of being bound by samsara, is due to ignorance and nothing more, and since action belongs exclusively to the bound state and not to the nature of pure consciousness, liberation cannot be achieved by any sort of activity. Only knowledge can dispel ignorance, not action, which is itself the product of ignorance. Advaita spells out a step-by-step process by which this knowledge can be attained: (1) listening (*śravaṇa*) to the scriptural teachings from the texts of the Upaniṣads (such as "You are That") as expounded by one's spiritual teacher; (2) reflection (*manana*) on the meaning of such texts; (3) intense meditation (*nididhyāsana*) thereon; and (4) absorption into the Absolute (*samādhi*).

Given its focus on liberation from the realm of samsara, regarded as somewhat illusory, Advaita Vedānta has shown relatively little interest in the process of creation for its own sake. But since liberation involves the undoing or reversing of creation, by which *jīva*s have become enmeshed in delusion, Advaita thinkers have spent no little effort in explaining the cosmogonic process. The final realization depends in part on understanding the true nature of the world, including how the *jīva* came to be self-deluded into thinking of itself as separate and different from Brahman.

Although Brahman is "one alone, without a second," eternal and unchanging, it nonetheless is somehow the source of the world—it brings forth the world through the mysterious creative power of Māyā, neither real nor unreal. When associated with Māyā, Brahman appears in three successive forms or bodies, causal, subtle, and gross, which represent stages of manifestation of the material universe. Interwoven into this scheme is a modified Sāṃkhyan view of creation. According to the Sāṃkhya philosophy, there are two ultimate principles, pure spirit (Puruṣa) and matter (Prakṛti). The former is sentient but inactive, the latter insentient but active. It is from the active Prakṛti that the material universe evolves, through a series of subtle and gross physical and psychological elements, twenty-four in number. The material universe entangles, as it were, the spirit, and yet at the same time Prakṛti works for the emancipation of Puruṣa from its material bonds. The Advaita, with its nondualistic perspective, denies any sort of ultimate dualism such as espoused by the Sāṃkhya. Thus, the Advaita, while fully affirming the ideal of the conscious Puruṣa, identifying it with Brahman, denies full reality to Prakṛti, seeing it as a product of the illusory power of Māyā.

Māyā itself is not fully real, as it is not eternal (since it comes to an end with knowledge) and is subject to change. It is not totally unreal, either, thereby differing from the complete unreality of a barren woman's son, to use a common Advaita analogy (see the Comment on 2.1–11 below). The world, as a product of Māyā, shares in its quality of being neither fully real nor fully unreal. The world may be an illusion, but it is not unreal; it is simply not what it appears to be. It appears manifold and changing. Ultimately, it is none other than Brahman. The exact manner by which the unitary and unchanging Brahman, through the manifestation of Māyā, becomes the manifold and changing universe was a matter of much debate among the later followers of Śaṃkara.

Regardless of the specific details of creation, liberation entails a reversing of the cosmogonic process, through the practice of meditative dissolution. The gross, subtle, and causal bodies are dissolved back into each other, within one's mind. Corresponding to this dissolution is the merging of the twenty-four physical and psychological elements back into their preceding sources, successively, until the final unity or mergence back into Brahman is attained.

These basic ideals of the Advaita Vedānta outlined above also appear in the *Devī Gītā*. Throughout the *Devī Gītā*, the Goddess is identified with various aspects of Brahman, such as *sat*, *cit*, and *ānanda*, and she refers to herself as "the essence or embodiment of Brahman" (*brahma-rūpiṇī*). Indeed, her initial manifestation as the lustrous supreme power (*paraṃ mahas*) is an implicit assimilation of Brahman by the Goddess. In the *Taittirīya Upaniṣad*, the term *mahas*, meaning "greatness, power," as well as "light, lustre," is specifically identified with Brahman (*maha iti brahma*), and as the power by which the various worlds and entities "become great."[12]

The thorough assimilation of Advaita ideals by the *Devī Gītā* is well attested by its familiarity with Vedāntic and Advaitic literature. In describing the nature of the Goddess as Brahman, the *Devī Gītā* relies heavily on the classical Upaniṣads, such as the *Bṛhadāraṇyaka*, *Kaṭha*, and *Muṇḍaka*, frequently quoting brief passages from them. On matters relating to liberation and the path of knowledge, the *Devī Gītā* expresses views very close to those of Śaṃkara and his disciple Sureśvara (ninth century), especially as found in the latter's *Naiṣkarmya Siddhi*. The cosmogonic notions expounded by the Goddess reflect those of the *Pañcīkaraṇa* attributed to Śaṃkara and of the commentary thereon, the *Pañcīkaraṇa-Vārttika* of Sureśvara, as well as of such late Advaita compendia as the *Pañcadaśī* of Vidyāraṇya (thirteenth century) and the *Vedāntasāra* of Sadānanda (fifteenth century).

While the *Devī Gītā* has assimilated many aspects of the Advaita world view, certain basic Advaita ideas, at least as expounded in their classical form, are in tension with other fundamental ideals of the *Devī Gītā*. There are two major areas of difference.

First, the *Devī Gītā*, a theistic work steeped in *bhakti*, sees the ultimate reality as a supreme, personal deity, Bhuvaneśvarī, and not just as the relatively abstract, philosophical Absolute (the *nirguṇa* Brahman). The general perspective of the *Devī Gītā* is simply that Brahman and the Goddess (Bhuvaneśvarī) are identical, but certain practical difficulties remain. For instance, there is some degree of tension (as well as of complementarity) between the path of knowledge, focused on intuiting or recognizing the one single reality, emphasized in Advaita, and the path of devotion, implying some sort of distinction between the worshiper and the worshiped, emphasized in any theistic world view such as Śāktism. Accordingly, the highest goal is perceived in two distinct ways. The supreme aim of Advaita is realization of one's identity with Brahman, while the highest purpose of a devotee of the Goddess is to serve her in her celestial paradise of the Jeweled Island. The *Devī Gītā* bridges the two perspectives in part by affirming the ultimate goal to be realization of one's identity with the Goddess, a goal readily attained while dwelling in her heavenly abode. This sort of synthetic, Advaitic theism is not new in the *Devī Gītā*; the *Bhāgavata Purāṇa* provides a brilliant Vaiṣṇava example of such, and is a model for the *Devī-Bhāgavata*.

The second major difference concerns the attitude toward the world and physical embodiment. The *Devī Gītā*, in accord with the Advaitic theism just discussed, sees the Goddess as the embodiment of Brahman, "one alone, without a second," and associates her creative power of projecting the universe with Māyā. Both ontologically and cosmologically, then, the Great Goddess fully implements her "Brahman nature." Yet, unlike in the more classical Advaita of Śaṃkara, she, as the ultimate reality, not only somehow manifests or wields Māyā, she also *is* Māyā. Thus Māyā, along with all its products—the world with all its embodied beings—has a higher ontological status here than in the view of someone like Śaṃkara. In particular, the physical body is seen primarily not as something disgusting and full of pain, but rather as an exceptionally powerful vehicle for spiritual transformation, a perspective having considerable affinity with the more cosmotheistic teachings of the Upaniṣads, and underlying the Tantric world view with its ritualized contemplative practices.

The Devī Gītā *and Tantra*

The term *tantra* has a wide variety of meanings but most fundamentally refers to a "loom," "thread," or "warp," thereby evoking the notions of weaving and synthesizing. Hindu etymologies emphasize the root *tan*, "to stretch, weave," conjoined to another root, *trā*, "to protect or save." Metaphorically, Tantra thus weaves together and expands various strands or traditions of spiritual practice designed to rescue humankind from the sufferings of samsara.[13] The term is commonly applied to a group of works known as Tantras, which expound the Trantric ideals and practices. It is impossible to define precisely what constitutes such ideals and practices. It is rather a general configuration of multifarious notions, symbol systems, and ritualized spiritual exercises, many of which have their roots or counterparts in non-Tantric Hindu circles and sects.

The specific ideas and practices commonly associated with Tantra will be noted in a moment, but some preliminary observations are in order. One source of confusion in identifying what is Tantric is the frequent contrast, made by many Hindus themselves, between Tantric and Vedic, even though the "Vedic" tradition today is thoroughly pervaded by Tantric elements, and the "Tantric" tradition has assimilated much of the Vedic. The term *Vedic* as used here refers not simply or primarily to the philosophical teachings of the Vedas, but rather to the vision of a society based on the ideals of *varṇāśrama-dharma,* that is, on the proper observance of the rights and responsibilities of well-defined classes and stages of life. This vision is regarded by its promulgators, especially by the Brahmans or priestly class, as embedded in the blueprint of the universe that is the Veda. At times, the Vedic-Brahmanical authorities have been much opposed to the Tantric world view. And certain Tantrics have looked with disdain on the Vedic tradition and its Brahmanical privilege. But there are other Hindus who have seen the two traditions as complementary, in particular those Vaidika Tantrics who see Tantrism as an extension of the Vedic path.

The author or authors of the *Devī Gītā* may be loosely classified as Vaidika Tantrics, though their self-conscious, primary allegiance clearly is to Vedic orthopraxy and Brahmanical authority. The avowed position of the *Devī Gītā* is basically one of accepting Tantric notions, so long as they are not opposed to the Veda. What this means in practice is that the *Devī Gītā* has incorporated many Tantric elements, except for certain antinomian practices associated with those Tantric schools known as Left-Handed (Vāmācāra). Those Left-Handed practices include the ritual consumption of prohibited substances such as meat and wine, and engaging in certain sexual-yogic disciplines involving the union of unmarried partners.

The key Tantric notions and concepts that form part of the general configuration spoken of above, and which play a major role in the *Devī Gītā,* may be considered under two general headings, the theoretical or metaphysical, and the practical. The latter, dealing with the specific techniques of spiritual discipline, are firmly based on the theoretical world view.

Regarding the basic world view, Tantra perceives reality as an interpenetrating set of physical, verbal, mental, psychological, and spiritual elements and forces. These elements and forces, manifesting on both macrocosmic and microcosmic levels, constitute through their interidentification the one absolute reality that is both the nondual Brahman of Advaita and the supreme God or Goddess of the theists. The Absolute is both the One and the Many, spiritual and material. The individual as the microcosm is interidentified in body, speech, and mind, with the body, speech, and mind of God as the macrocosm. Unlike in Advaita, however, the realm of the many and of materiality is not dismissed as merely derivative, secondary, or illusory—in short, something to escape or transcend—but rather is regarded as a powerful expression of nonmaterial energies. Physical embodiment, accordingly, is seen as a prime opportunity for spiritual growth, rather than as an unfortunate predicament requiring withdrawal from, or at least indifference to, the material and sensual realm.

Second, in line with the above world view, Tantric practice focuses on implementing or realizing the whole complex of interidentifications through highly ritualized, psychophysical and contemplative disciplines. These practices include various meditative visualizations aimed at purifying the body and transforming it into the divine body of God or the Goddess, special forms of yoga, most notably the Kuṇḍalinī Yoga, and special forms of worship that emphasize the interpenetrating unity of worshiper, worshiped, and the worship service itself.

Regarding the purification and transformation of the body, two important interrelated and overlapping Tantric techniques are known as *bhūta-śuddhi* ("purification of the bodily elements") and *nyāsa* ("placement, installation, infusion"). The former involves a yogic process similar to Kuṇḍalinī yoga (see below), in which the old body is dissolved and recreated, purged of its sinful tendencies, and infused with divine breath. The latter comprehends a great variety of installations, or infusions of divine energies into one's own body, including the life-breath of the supreme deity.

These energies are often regarded as embedded within, or manifesting themselves in, various sonic forms called mantras, such as the sounds of the letters of the alphabet, and especially in certain mystical syllables known as seed mantras (*bīja-mantras*), in which the sonic energies are highly concentrated. The seed syllables usually have the general form of the ancient Oṃ of the Upaniṣads, beginning with a vowel or consonants and a vowel, and ending in the nasal *ṃ* that tails off into the silence of the Absolute. These syllables, for example Aiṃ and Klīṃ, while having no ordinary semantic meaning, are thought to represent—that is, "re-present" in the sense of remanifesting in the present—the energies that constitute the various gods and other cosmic forces reverberating within the sounds. The seed syllable of the Goddess Bhuvaneśvarī is Hrīṃ, commonly called the Hṛllekhā, and is a counterpart to Oṃ as the sonic emblem of Brahman. And since the Goddess is Brahman, she affirms that her two chief mantras are Oṃ and Hrīṃ.[14]

The installation or *nyāsa* of the mantric syllables in one's body effects an infusion of their cosmic and divine energies into oneself, and an interidentification with the various deities invoked. The process of *nyāsa* involves the use of stylized hand gestures, *mudrās*, which provide a visual counterpart to the sonic forms. Such *mudrās*, while an important aspect of Tantric ritual, are not specifically mentioned in the *Devī Gītā*, though such gestures are assumed. The installation of the letters of the alphabet is referred to as *mātṛkā-nyāsa* ("infusion of the maternal powers"), and of the letters of the Devī's seed syllable, as *hṛllekhā-mātṛkā-nyāsa*. Through these infusions, one attains mastery of the several cosmic forces within this world, as well as union or identity with the Goddess.

Perhaps the best-known feature of Tantric practice that appears in the *Devī Gītā* is Kuṇḍalinī Yoga, summarized in chapter 5 following a description of the classical Eight-limbed Yoga based on Patañjali's *Yoga Sutras.* Kuṇḍalinī Yoga is quite distinct from Patañjali's system, but is thought by many followers of Kuṇḍalinī Yoga to be an extension of the classical forms. The Kuṇḍalinī system presupposes an esoteric or subtle physiology, consisting of several mystic energy channels or arteries (*nāḍīs*) within the body, connecting various psychoenergetic centers (*cakras, padmas*) lying along the central axis or spine.

In the lowermost center, the Base Support (*mūlādhāra*) at the bottom end of the spine, resides the Kuṇḍalinī or "Coiled One," thus referred to as the Serpent Power. The Kuṇḍalinī is none other than the Goddess manifesting within our bodies as the guiding psychospiritual power of our being. In unenlightened, ordinary beings, she lies dormant. The goal of this yoga is to awaken her in the Base Support Center and to cause her to ascend the central axis, breaking through the other centers until she reaches the uppermost center at the top of or slightly above the head, where she unites with her male counterpart, Śiva. Through this nectar-producing union and subsequent descent of the Kuṇḍalinī back to the Base Support, the Tantric practitioner achieves an intensification and reintegration of the various material, psychological, and spiritual forces within the body, a mastery of those elements in the world, and conscious interidentification with the divine Absolute.

All the Tantric practices described above depend for their successful realization on the instructions of a qualified spiritual teacher or guru. And the disciple, in order to obtain initiation into the practices from a guru, must meet certain intellectual, spiritual, and moral qualifications. These ideals give rise to the notion that the spiritual teachings are secret and should not be revealed indiscriminately to just anyone, lest they lose their power, or be misused to the detriment of the practitioner or others. Such emphasis on the guru and the qualifications of the disciple is common to many other Hindu schools or movements, as in the Advaita Vedānta. However, in Tantra the qualifications are less based on gender and class than they are in most Brahmanically orthodox schools.

In the *Devī Gītā,* the stated qualifications for intitiation into the Devī's *Song* reflect to some degree the orthodox bias against women, an ancient bias apparently rooted in the notion that menstruation renders women periodically impure and dangerous, and thus spiritually and ritually less competent than men.[15] Yet the *Devī Gītā*'s underlying attitude toward menstruation is apparently much more positive, or at least ambivalent. In accord with its Tantric perspective commending the body and its processes as powerful spiritual vehicles and manifestations of divine energy, the *Devī Gītā* pays tribute to the sacredness of the menstrual cycle in its reference to the monthly celebration of the menses of the Goddess in Kāmākhyā.[16] In any case, the *Devī Gītā* repeatedly stresses the necessity of love for the Goddess, with no mention of one's gender, as the primary qualification, an emphasis inspired by the devotional ideals of Śāktism. The relationship between Śāktism and Tantrism is an intimate one, and some particular features of Śākta Tantrism are deserving of special attention.

The Devī Gītā *and Śākta Tantrism*

As we have seen, Tantrism may best be described as a general configuration of certain ideals and practices that assume the interpenetration and interidentification of the macrocosmic and microcosmic, the physical and the spiritual. These ideals and practices have been incorporated into various sectarian perspectives, Śaiva, Vaiṣṇava, as well as Śākta. Śaiva and Vaiṣṇava Tantric works, however, usually refer to themselves as Āgamas and Saṃhitās, respectively, while most works called Tantras are Śākta. There is a strong affinity between the Goddess and the Tantric world view, so much so that one scholar refers to the "Śākta forms of Tantrism . . . [as] Hindu Tantrism par excellence."[17] Surely the Śākta identification of the Devī with Māyā and Prakṛti (representing the realm of spiritualized matter), on the one hand, and Tantra's emphasis on the active nature of an inner, salvific agent (manifesting in the role of Śakti as the Kuṇḍalinī), on the other, help to create the special bond between Śāktism and Tantrism.

Within Śākta Tantrism there are several different schools, which may be loosely classified according to two general distinguishing features that characterize their theological perspectives. The first concerns the nature of the Goddess herself, whether she is seen primarily as benign, or horrific, or both. The *Devī Gītā*, like the famous school of Śrī Vidyā that focuses on the gentle Goddess Lalitā, belongs to those Tantric circles emphasizing the benevolent and bountiful aspect of the supreme Śakti.

The second feature involves the relationship of the Devī's aspect as the supreme feminine principle of the universe to the fundamental masculine principle, a relationship usually expressed in terms of the interaction between Śakti and Śiva. The relationship may be one of dependency or codependency (in the strict meaning of the term), or it may be one of radical independence, or something in between. Tantra in general presupposes a bipolar view of ultimate reality, of the One unfolding into Two as the God and Goddess, associated with various other complementary opposites such as spirit and matter, consciousness and energy, passivity and activity. Both creation and liberation are seen as the result of the union or reunion of the two co-ultimate principles/deities.

Śākta Tantrics, focusing on Śakti and her relationship with Śiva, stress to greater or less degree her supremacy, although her effective authority may be limited to a somewhat circumscribed realm. The more moderate Śākta positions preserve a considerable degree of codependency and complementarity. In such moderate perspectives, Śakti often appears as a dominant and forceful mother, aggressively protective of her children, and at the same time, as the submissive and cooperative spouse of Śiva—regardless of however powerful she may be—thereby reflecting and affirming the values of conventional Hindu society. In the conventional view, a woman in control of her own sexuality as a mother is both benevolent and malevolent, fertile and destructive, her unrestrained energy dangerous. If she surrenders control of her sexual energy by submitting herself to a man, she becomes wholly benevolent as a dutiful and obedient wife.[18] Such a conception is manifest in the Śrī Vidyā perception of the benevolent and submissive Lalitā.

More extreme Śākta Tantrics regard the Goddess as inclusive of all the "masculine" qualities and attributes embodied in Śiva, who becomes simply a lower manifestation of the Devī herself. *She* is both male and female, and only in some partial or derivative form, or for the sake of her *own* amusement, does she bring forth out of herself her masculine side as a separate entity, to sport with it in the form of Śiva. Such is the radical position of the *Devī-Bhāgavata* as a whole. This radical view diminishes the significance of the bipolar symbolism that is so characteristic of much Tantra. Thus, while aspects of this bipolar symbolism appear here and there in the *Devī Gītā* (as in its description of the goal of Kuṇḍalinī Yoga), it is generally muted, due to the studied emphasis on Bhuvaneśvarī as the supreme power and independent authority, subordinate to none. Indeed, the primary polar tension in the *Devī Gītā* is not between the masculine Śiva and the feminine Śakti, but between the transpersonal Brahman *and* the personal Bhuvaneśvarī. Defying conventional expectation, however, Bhuvaneśvarī here is both independent and benevolent.

Bhuvaneśvarī herself is an important but not well-known Tantric deity. As she is the basic inspiration underlying the Śākta Tantrism of the *Devī Gītā,* a brief survey of her historical emergence and textual manifestations is in order. Bhuvaneśvarī may well have first appeared in the late Purāṇic and Tantric pantheon not as a separate and individual figure, but as a member of a company of female deities known as the ten Mahāvidyās.[19] The ten represent, on an esoteric level, the various forms of knowledge or wisdom (*vidyā*) and power that constitute the universe. On a more mythological level, they are ten facets or aspects of the Great Goddess. The group in some ways is a late medieval Śākta counterpart of the Vaiṣṇava notion of the ten main avataras of Viṣṇu, whose role frequently is to maintain cosmic order through the destruction of demons.[20] The Mahāvidyās at times function in a similar role, as in the *Śiva Purāṇa* where they come forth from the body of the Great Goddess as she fights against the demon Durgama.[21] But unlike Viṣṇu's avataras, the Mahāvidyās usually work in concert, and their primary role is not necessarily the preservation of cosmic order.[22]

The mythic origin of the ten is recounted in the *Mahābhāgavata Purāṇa,* where they arise out of a fearsome form of Satī in order to frighten Śiva into granting her permission to go and disrupt Dakṣa's sacrifice.[23] In addition, Satī herself portrays these emanations as a means of providing her devotees with various worldly and other-worldly benefits. The ten Mahāvidyās procure these benefits in large part by exercising their terrifying and destructive powers to subdue or defeat enemies. Nonetheless, despite the fierce nature of the Mahāvidyās as indicated by their origin, they also have a more benign potential that is emphasized in later texts, where at least some of them are described as beautiful in appearance.

While the early myths and texts generally do not specify the particular functions of the individual Mahāvidyās, the relatively late *Uddārakośa* expounds the efficacious natures (*guṇas*) of the ten as follows: Tripurā gives liberation (*mukti*), Lakṣmī prosperity (*lakṣmī*), Vāgdevī (Sarasvatī) wisdom (*vidyā*), Tārā knowledge and release (*jñāna and mokṣa*), Bhuvaneśvarī sovereignty (*aiśvarya*), Mātaṅgī freedom from fear of female demons and enemies (*rākṣasīśatrubhīti*), Śārikā happiness (*śam*), Rājñī royal authority (*rājyam*), Bhīḍādevī all-pervading expansiveness (*santati viśvavyāpinī*), and Jvālāmukhī wealth (*dhanam*).[24] These functions are somewhat repetitive and overlapping, but what is noteworthy in the present context is the association of Bhuvaneśvarī with sovereignty.

The word *aiśvarya* (sovereignty), deriving from *īśvara* ("lord"), suggests a supreme, divine power that oversees the universe. It is linked not only with wealth and affluence, but also with omnipotence and omnipresence. *Aiśvarya* is thus a quite natural property of Bhuvaneśvarī, "She who is Lord (Queen, Mistress) of the world." Further, *aiśvarya* subsumes most of the efficacious qualities of the other ten Mahāvidyās, with the exception of those relating to liberation, associated especially with the goddesses Tripurā and Tārā. Bhuvaneśvarī, as we shall see, developed fairly early a certain affinity and synergism with Tripurā (Tripuā-Sundarī or Lalitā, as she is also known) that led to an apparent convergence of the two.

In the *Devī-Bhāgavata,* Bhuvaneśvarī assumes the roles of all the other Mahāvidyās, including those of liberating knowledge and ultimate release. She is the source of all female manifestations or Śaktis, including the Mahāvidyās. In the *Devī-Bhāgavata*'s version of the slaying of Durgama, for instance, various of the traditional Mahāvidyās are named among the Śaktis emanating from her body, but—unlike in the *Śiva Purāṇa*'s version—Bhuvaneśvarī is not included.[25] Emphasizing that she is no longer just one of the ten Mahāvidyās, the *Devī-Bhāgavata* regards her as Mahāvidyā (Great Wisdom) *herself,* whose avataras include many of the earlier members of the famous ten, along with other renowned incarnations of the Goddess. Accordingly, in the story of the slaying of the demon Aruṇa, the gods address the Goddess as Mahāvidyā, who assumes various forms to favor the gods. Among these forms are named several of the usual Mahāvidyās, plus other incarnations such as Śakambharī and Raktadantikā from the *Devī Māhātmya.*[26] As in its story of the slaying of Durgama, the *Devī-Bhāgavata* does not include Bhuvaneśvarī among the forms. Rather, the gods in concluding their hymn of petition use the name Bhuvaneśvarī to refer to the one, supreme World-Mother, who dwells in the Jeweled Island.

The supremacy of Bhuvaneśvarī in the *Devī-Bhāgavata* is marvelously evoked in a detailed description of this paradisial island home of the Goddess, highest of all heavenly realms. The island, lying in the Ocean of Nectar, is forested with a great number of fantastic flowering trees, perfumed with the scent of divine blossoms and resplendent with ornamental lakes and rivers. The palatial structures include a number of walled enclosures, concentrically arranged. Within each enclosure dwell various classes of celestial beings, gods and goddesses, and their incarnations. In the enclosure just outside the central circle reside the closest companions or helpers of the Goddess, her great divisions (*mahā-bhedās*), identified as or associated with her avataras and referred to as Mahāvidyās.[27] In the innermost enclosure dwells Bhuvaneśvarī herself. Her distinctness from, and transcendence over, the Mahāvidyās is hereby amply demonstrated.

Within the final enclosure is the Goddess' own mansion, a magnificent dwelling constructed of wish-fulfilling gems (*cintāmaṇi*). Inside the mansion are situated four *maṇḍapas* (halls), in which she conducts four different sorts of business: indulging in amorous sport, delivering souls from the bondage of rebirth, discoursing on truth, and consulting with her ministers on running the universe.

Within the palace also is the great couch of the five corpses, mentioned earlier. Reclining on this great couch in the midst of her jeweled palace, Bhuvaneśvarī is described in terms similar to that of the goddess Tripurā in the *Tripurā-Rahasya*,[28] and of Lalitā (an alternate name of Tripurā) in the *Brahmāṇḍa Purāṇa*.[29] Indeed, the *Devī Gītā*'s Bhuvaneśvarī seems especially to fuse the characters of her own self as ruling queen with that of Tripurā/Lalitā, who as mentioned above is associated with the giving of liberation. Of all the Mahāvidyās, it is Bhuvaneśvarī and Tripurā/Lalitā who are generally the closest iconographically. Like Bhuvaneśvarī, Tripurā/Lalitā is charmingly beautiful, clothed in red, three-eyed and four-armed, bearing a noose and goad, although her other two hands hold a sugarcane bow and flower arrows rather than gesturing Bhuvaneśvarī's beneficence and assurance of safety. The easy fusion of these two Mahāvidyās reinforces the Tantric ideal that the Goddess is the giver of both *bhukti* and *mukti* (enjoyment and liberation).

The convergence of the two Goddesses is found already, in surprisingly explicit fashion, in the *Devī Upaniṣad* (a text probably composed sometime between the ninth and fourteenth centuries.)[30] It is one of several Śākta Upaniṣads dedicated to one or another particular Goddess conceived as supreme, or to a form of the Goddess. The Goddess in the *Devī Upaniṣad* is addressed in the most general and universal of terms: simply as Mahā-Devī. The Upaniṣad provides two brief iconographic descriptions of this Great Goddess. According to the first, "She is the power of the Self; she is the enchanter of all, holding a noose, a goad, a bow, and arrows; she is the auspicious

Mahāvidyā."[31] Here is a concise description of Tripurā/Lalitā. According to the second depiction, "She resides in the middle of one's lotus heart, shining like the rising sun; auspicious, bearing the noose and the goad while gesturing her beneficence and assurance of safety, she is three-eyed, dressed in red, granting all wishes to her devotees."[32] This, of course, is Bhuvaneśvarī.

The *Devī Upaniṣad* is a Śākta Tantric text that understands itself as fully within the domain of Vedic truth, indicated by the very fact of presenting itself as an Upaniṣad. Its Vedic pedigree is further affirmed by its quoting the famous "Devī Sūkta" from the *Ṛg Veda* (10.125). Its concern with various root or seed mantras of the Goddess, including Hrīṃ, attests to its Tantric nature. This synthesis of the Vedic and Tantric within a Śākta perspective must have had considerable appeal to the composer of the *Devī Gītā.* He clearly was aware of the *Devī Upaniṣad,* as he quotes five verses of its "Devī Stuti" (the hymn offered by the gods in verses 8–13).[33] The *Devī Gītā* shares with the *Devī Upaniṣad* a view of the Goddess that stresses her identity with Brahman and total independence from any male consort. It is no wonder, then, that the Goddess herself mentions the *Devī Upaniṣad* as one of those texts whose recitation is pleasing to her.[34]

The radical Vedicization of the originally Tantric Bhuvaneśvarī is implicitly indicated by the *Devī Gītā* in its classification of Vedic and Tantric types of Goddess worship.[35] This taxonomic scheme designates Bhuvaneśvarī as one of two forms of the Goddess that are the focus of Vedic worship (the other form being that of the Virāj), while the Devī as Kuṇḍalinī is the object of Tantric worship.

The *Devī Gītā* witnesses to the final stage in the remarkable ascent of Bhuvaneśvarī. Beginning as a relatively minor Tantric deity as one of the ten Mahāvidyās, she evolves into the sovereign World-Mother, assimilating and integrating both cosmological supremacy and soteriological proficiency. Finally, in the culmination of her career, she assumes the role of the supreme Vedic feminine principle identified with Brahman.

☙

As the above historical survey indicates, there are few ideas in the *Devī Gītā* that, in themselves, are truly novel. The text is very conservative, rooting its teachings in a wide array of established scriptural works and authoritative religious treatises. This is in harmony with the basic Hindu presupposition that truth is not so much something to be discovered as recovered. From this perspective, the Goddess in her *Song* is merely recovering and revealing the truths that are somewhat obscured in the other sources, setting them in the appropriate theological context of a radical Śāktism. Yet, from a historical point of view, the *Devī Gītā,* almost despite itself, is not lacking in originality of a kind. The way in which it interweaves the various traditions and motifs, ancient and contemporary, and fuses them into a new vision of the Goddess is itself a resourceful and imaginative enterprise, a creative inspiration in its own right.

Notes

1. See *Devī-Bhāgavata Purāṇa* 12.12.13.

2. V. A. K. Ayer, "Mother Bhuvaneswari," *Tattvāloka: The Splendour of Truth,* 11.4 (1988):46. For further interpretation of her iconography, see the Comment on *Devī Gītā* 1.30–41.

3. For a discussion of the cosmotheistic teachings of the *Devī Gītā,*" see the Comments to verses 3.5–12ab and to 3.12cd–19.

4. See my *Triumph of the Goddess,* pp. 18–19, for a brief discussion of this appropriation.

5. See *Devī-Bhāgavata Purāṇa* 2.11–12 and 12.13.

6. *Devī-Bhāgavata Purāṇa* 7.30.38ab.

7. *Devī Gītā* 10.21cd.

8. *Kūrma Purāṇa* 1.11.292–94.

9. *Mahābhāgavata Purāṇa* 18.19–22.

10. *Mahābhāgavata Purāṇa* 18.4–5.

11. *Śiva Purāṇa* 2.1.6–9.

12. *Taittirīya Upaniṣad* 1.5.

13. See Douglas Renfrew Brooks, *The Secret of the Three Cities,* p. 69.

14. *Devī-Bhāgavata Purāṇa* 12.8.64.

15. For a discussion of the Hindu mythological basis for this ancient and orthodox interpretation of menstruation, see Frederick M. Smith, "Indra's Curse, Varuṇa's Noose, and the Suppression of the Woman in the Vedic Śrauta Ritual," in *Roles and Rituals for Hindu Women,* ed. Julia Leslie, pp. 17–45, esp. p. 23.

16. *Devī Gītā* 8.16.

17. Brooks, *Secret of the Three Cities,* p. 72.

18. For a brief and excellent overview of the conception of women in traditional Hindu cosmology, ideology, and religious practice, see Susan S. Wadley, "Women and the Hindu Tradition," in Doranne Jacobson and Susan S. Wadley, *Women in India: Two Perspectives*, pp. 111–35.

19. The specific ten goddesses named vary in different lists, and sometimes there are more than ten. Bhuvaneśvarī appears in most lists, often as the fourth, fifth, or sixth Mahāvidyā. See Chintaharan Chakravarti, *Tantras*, pp. 85–86; Pratapaditya Pal, *Hindu Religion and Iconology According to the Tantrasāra*, pp. 9–10, 57–91; and Narendra Nath Bhattacaryya, *History of the Śākta Religion*, pp. 135–36. For an excellent study of the ten goddesses, see David Kinsley, *Tantric Visions of the Divine Feminine: The Ten Mahāvidyās*. Unfortunately, I received his book too late to utilize in writing the main body of my text, although I did use an early draft of his chapter on Bhuvaneśvarī that now appears in his book.

20. In certain late Tantras, there is an explicit correlation made between the Mahāvidyās and Viṣṇu's ten avataras. See N. Bhattacaryya, *History of the Śākta Religion*, p. 136, and David Kinsley, *Hindu Goddesses*, pp. 161–62.

21. *Śiva Purāṇa*, 5.50.28–29. The ten named here are: (1) Kālī, (2) Tārā, (3) Chinnamastā, (4) Śrīvidyā, (5) Bhuvaneśvarī, (6) Bhairavī, (7) Bagalā, (8) Dhūmra, (9) Tripurasundarī, and (10) Mataṅgī.

22. On the relation of the Mahāvidyās to Viṣṇu's avataras, see Kinsley, *Hindu Goddesses*, pp. 161–64.

23. *Mahābhāgavata Purāṇa* 8.62–71. Dakṣa's sacrifice is briefly discussed in the Comment to *Devī Gītā* 1.3–1.13.

24. *Uddārakośa*, final 5 verses, in *Devī Rahasya with Pariśishṭas*, edited by Ram Chandra Kak and Harabhatta Shastri, p. 531. The text also refers to six other "Daśavidyās," who often appear in other lists: Bhadrakālī, Turī, Chinnamastakā, Dakṣiṇākālikā, Śyāmā, and Kālarātrī. The *Uddārakośa* is a late collection of quotations from forty-seven Tantric works.

25. *Devī-Bhāgavata* 7.28.54–56.

26. *Devī-Bhāgavata* 10.13.87–103.

27. *Devī-Bhāgavata* 12.11.106.

28. *Tripurā-Rahasya (Jñāna Khaṇḍa)* 20.36–42.

29. *Brahmāṇḍa Purāṇa* 3.4.37. See the Comment on *Devī Gītā* 10.8cd–12ab below for further details on the couch of five corpses.

30. See J. N. Faquhar, *An Outline of the Religious Literature of India*, p. 266; Maurice Winternitz, *A History of Indian Literature*, vol. 1, pp. 239–40; Surendranath Dasgupta, *A History of Indian Philosophy*, vol. 1, p. 28; and Brooks, *Secret of the Three Cities*, pp. 12–13.

31. *Devī Upaniṣad* 15.

32. *Devī Upaniṣad* 24.

33. These verses are quoted in *Devī Gītā* 1.44–48.

34. *Devī Gītā* 10.22cd.

35. See chapters 9 and 10.

A Note on the Translation

I have undertaken this translation and interpretation of the *Devī Gītā* with a diverse range of audiences in mind: general readers interested in goddesses and goddess worship but with little prior knowledge of Hindu mythology and philosophy, students familiar with the basic ideas and concepts of Indian thought desiring to learn more about Hindu notions of female divinity, and finally specialists in the fields of Purāṇic studies and the history of Śāktism. The aim, accordingly, is quite ambitious, and for it to succeed it will require careful and patient effort on the part of the reader.

To assist all readers, I have divided the text into sections of a few verses each, introduced by a short summary in brackets [ ]. Following each section is a Comment. These Comments explain key terms, concepts, ritual procedures, and mythic themes appearing in the text. The Comments also offer comparisons with related schools of thought, indicate parallel texts and textual sources of verses in the *Devī Gītā*, and briefly elucidate the historical and religious background, supplementing the remarks of the Introduction. The general reader who wishes simply to deal with the text itself may at first find the Comments intrusive. But the text often does not speak clearly to the uninitiated: its mythic allusions are frequently obscure; its complex philosophical ideas are expressed in a style highly compressed; the religious ideals and values underlying both its general world view and its particular spiritual practices are usually merely assumed. The Comments are thus available for those seeking a more accurate appreciation and understanding of the text.

The notes, both to the text and the Comments, give more detailed information and references that will be of primary interest to specialists. Where material in the notes may be of interest to the general reader, reference to such material is made in the Comments.

In preparing the translation of the *Devī Gītā*, I have consulted several printed editions (listed in the bibliography). Some of these were published as part of the *Devī-Bhāgavata Purāṇa*, others as separate and independent texts. Variations between all the texts are minimal. The only significant difference, occurring in just one edition (the Vārāṇasī 1986 edition of Upendra Pāṇḍeya) was not in the text itself, but in the prefixing to the text a set of nine verses selected from throughout the *Devī Gītā* and representing its mantric essence. Because of their intrinsic interest, and because of the light they shed on changing uses of the *Devī Gītā*, I have included these verses, "The Essential Devī Gītā in Nine Verses," at the beginning of the translation, with commentary.

For the translation as a whole, I eventually chose for my base text the Veṅkaṭeśvara edition of the *Devī-Bhāgavata Purāṇa* (book 7, chapters 31–40), the current Vulgate. (It is also the basis for the Sanskrit text at the end of this book.) It is relatively free of typographical errors, but most important, it includes the only readily available Sanskrit commentary (*devī-bhāgavata-ṭika*) on the text, that of Nīlakaṇṭha the Śaiva.[1] A Mahārāṣṭrian probably living during the last half of the eighteenth century, Nīlakaṇṭha was the author of a number of commentaries on the Purāṇas and Tantras.[2] He offers any translator of the *Devī-Bhāgavata* (or *Devī Gītā*) invaluable assistance, often providing quite plausible explanations of obscure or confusing terms and passages, and insightful interpretations of key theological and philosophical notions (usually from an Advaitic perspective). He was quite fascinated by the *Devī Gītā*, as he refers in a number of places to a "Great Commentary on the *Devī Gītā* composed by me" (*mat-kṛta-devī-gītā-bṛhaṭ-ṭikā*), in which he claims to have explained in greater detail the various teachings of the *Devī Gītā*.[3]

Nīlakaṇṭha is also quite helpful with regard to various text-critical questions, as he cites numerous parallel passages in older works. As noted in the Introduction, the author of the *Devī Gītā* regularly quotes from other texts, or paraphrases them. At times, trying to find the source of these quotations or paraphrases in the vast expanse of Vedic, Upaniṣadic, Purāṇic, Tantric, and Advaitic literature is daunting. As the indefatigable Pandurang Vaman Kane has said regarding his own efforts to trace the Purāṇic source of quotations appearing in works on rites, "I regret that I have not been quite successful [in tracing all sources] owing to several causes such as the vast extent of the Purāṇas, owing to several recensions of the same purāṇa and owing to my inadvertence or sheer weariness. One feels that tracing a verse to its origin is often as difficult as finding a pin in a haystack."[4] Needless to say, Nīlakaṇṭha has saved me much weariness and helped me to find several textual pins. His assistance on all these various matters is gratefully acknowledged in the Comments and notes. Not uncommonly, Nīlakaṇṭha does not give specific references in his citations. Often, for instance, he merely cites: "And thus says scripture" (*tathā ca śrutiḥ*), in referring to a Vedic or Upaniṣadic text. I have supplied, where missing, the more specific reference, including the particular text, chapter, and verse, in brackets { }. I must acknowledge that even with Nīlakaṇṭha's assistance, while I have been able to track down many of the textual sources directly or indirectly used by the author of the *Devī Gītā*, I am sure that some have eluded me.

The early twentieth-century Hindu translator of the first published English translation of the *Devī Gītā* (as part of the *Devī-Bhāgavata*) also found Nīlakaṇṭha quite helpful.[5] As was not uncommon then on the part of Indian translators, some of Nīlakaṇṭha's commentary ended up as part of the translation itself. For this reason alone, a new translation would be quite worthwhile. (Where I have relied on Nīlakaṇṭha for interpreting a word or phrase, I have so noted, but have kept his commentary as such separate from the translation.) There are other reasons as well for retranslating the *Devī Gītā*. Aside from the stilted and awkward style of this earlier translation, its tendency to leave many technical Sanskrit words untranslated (and unexplained) makes the text at times almost unusable by the average English reader. Further, its occasional but serious mistranslations somewhat compromise its scholarly usefulness. (The relatively recent [1991], devotionally inspired translation of the *Devī Gītā* by Swami Satyananda Saraswati provides a more convenient form of the text, but is less reliable and often more confusing, and confused, than its 1920s predecessor.)

The Sanskrit text of the *Devī Gītā* is composed mostly of verses known as *ślokas*, written in the *anuṣṭubh* meter, consisting of four quarters of eight syllables each. The exceptions all seem to be where the author of the *Devī Gītā* is quoting from or paraphrasing non-*śloka* texts, as in 1.45-48, 2.37, 4.32, 4.34, 6.3-14, 7.34, 7.44, and 10.3. Within each *śloka* there is generally a division of the four quarters into two lines of two quarters each. The two lines of a verse tend to represent two integrated semantic subunits, with many exceptions. Not infrequently, a complete unit may consist of only one, or three, or even more lines, resulting in some semantic units not corresponding to the apparent verse numbering.

The translation has rendered all the stanzas (including both the *śloka* and non-*śloka* passages) into free verse of two lines each. The lines of the translation generally correspond quite strictly to the lines of the original text, but little attempt was made to follow the order of quarters within a line. On rare occasions, as when the grammatical subject of a verse occurs only in the second line, strict adherence to the line sequence could at times make for a very awkward word order in English. In such cases, when the ingenuity of the translator failed to find any other solution, the integrity of the lines has been slightly compromised.

A good translation is not simply a literal rendering of the words, grammar, and general style of an original text into another language. Such attempted fidelity may introduce confusion and awkwardness where none existed in the first place, and even lead to basic misunderstandings of the text. A competent and conscientious translator, of course, strives to convey as accurately as possible the meaning of a text. But the task ultimately is one of interpretation. And it is not only the basic semantic meaning that must be interpreted, but also the mood, perspective, and emotional tone of a text. I have thus striven to produce a readable and idiomatic English translation/interpretation that may on occasion sacrifice literalness in order to convey more adequately and compellingly the spirit of the text.[6]

As an example, Sanskrit composers are quite fond of the passive voice, something that often tends to sound quite pedantic, stilted, vague, or archaic in English. Accordingly, I have rendered most passive constructions into the active voice and supplied the active subject, sometimes only implicit in the passive construction. To be sure, the passive voice may be integral to the sense or mood of a given passage, suggesting for instance the absence of an active agent or will. In those cases I have followed the original text. Where the passive voice is integral and where it is merely a compositional convenience, of course, is a judgment call.

Further, the Sanskrit style as mentioned above is at times highly compressed and elliptical. I have generally expanded the translation of such elliptical passages for the sake of clarity, but without bracketing the supplied terms or phrases in order to retain a more friendly looking and readable text (the commentary and annotation already burden the text sufficiently). Most such additions to the literal text are minor, for instance, supplying the specific referent of a pronoun. The few major or significant amplifications have been indicated in the notes to the verses.

One of the most difficult interpretive challenges relates to the androcentric language of the text. While the *Devī Gītā*'s theology is ardently gynocentric, its sociology, so to speak, frequently assumes a traditional male bias. Some might reasonably argue that this androcentric bias has affected the theology as well, resulting in the strong emphasis on the maternal nature of the Goddess. Certainly there can be little doubt that the text was composed by a man, with a traditional male perspective on many issues, as in the admonition that the teachings of the *Devī Gītā* be revealed only to qualified persons beginning with "an eldest son," with no reference of any sort to a daughter. And throughout the text, the author speaks of what a "man" (*nara*) should or should not do, and freely utilizes generic masculine pronouns.

How is a responsible translator, then, to deal with this problem of male-biased language (the "he-man" problem, as some feminist writers have put it). An appeal to cling to "literal accuracy" is not, in my estimation, adequate. A traditional androcentric text that uses the term *man* may not mean the same thing that would be implied in a contemporary text. As Elisabeth Schüssler Fiorenza argues, in relation to biblical texts: "A *historically adequate* translation must take into account the interpretative language in a patriarchal culture. Such androcentric inclusive language mentions women only when their presence has become in any way a problem or when they are 'exceptional,' but it does not mention women in so-called normal situations."[7]

Schüssler Fiorenza's warning, I think, must be heeded in the present case. For instance, the *Devī Gītā* at one point (8.2) has the mountain king Himālaya asking the Goddess: "Tell me all about those matters, O Mother, whereby a man (*nara*) may become completely fulfilled (*kṛta-kṛtya* [a common synonym in Advaita for the *jīvan-mukta* or person who becomes fully liberated while still embodied])." The word *nara* is definitely male, *narī* being "woman." But is the text truly suggesting that only men can be fully liberated in this life by learning about the aforesaid matters?

Some traditional Hindu texts might well answer that question affirmatively. But this hardly seems to be the case in the *Devī Gītā*. Among various evidences, the text elsewhere (6.19) says explicitly that a woman may become completely fulfilled (*kṛta-kṛtya*). The full context, to be sure, is somewhat ambivalent. The text states that when a person attains pure consciousness, that is, merges into the Goddess, then his (*tasya* [but is this intentionally exclusive of "her"?]) mother attains complete fulfillment as well. While a certain androcentric bias is still quite evident in this formulation (the mother seems to have to rely on the efforts of her son [or child?] to attain the final goal, while the lack of reference to the father suggests that he is quite capable of attaining the goal on his own), there is nonetheless the clear assertion that a woman is not excluded from the highest spiritual goal. The use of man in our text, then, may include woman.

In the *Devī Gītā*, women are explicitly mentioned just once. In introducing various rites (*vratas*) that are pleasing to her, the Goddess says, "Both women and men should perform them with diligence."[8] *Vratas* are well known as an integral part of women's religious life. Whether some of the other spiritual practices mentioned in the text, such as certain of the various yogas, are intended for women may be debated. In any case, the teachings of the *Devī Gītā* are clearly addressed to women as well as to men. The actual audience within the text itself is the circle of gods. Among these gods, there is at least one female, Viṣṇu's wife. Further, the whole genre of Purāṇic texts, to which the *Devī Gītā* belongs, is intended for all, men and women, regardless of class. This does not mean the text is egalitarian. At the end of the *Devī-Bhāgavata Purāṇa* (12.12.24-25), the sage Sūta remarks: "Women and Śūdras should never recite this (book), under some sort of delusion. They should hear it from the mouth of a twice-born (male), that is the rule."

Since women clearly are intended to hear the *Devī Gītā*, even if only from the mouth of an upper-caste male, I have chosen to use gender-inclusive language throughout, using "person," "one," "all," "human beings," etc., for the various terms for man. There is, of course, the danger that I will go beyond the intentions of the original, but there is often no sure way to know what those intentions were. For instance, are women to be included in the instructions for practicing the Eight-limbed Yoga? Given the generally sympathetic attitude of the text to Tantric views and practices (at least of the Right-handed sort), which are much more open to women than the traditional Brahmanical stance, it seems probable. And this is so, I feel, despite the fact that among some of the instructions for one of the postures, the practitioner is told to place the heels of the feet under the scrotum (*vṛṣaṇa*). These instructions are almost certainly based on older yogic manuals, manuals which may indeed have meant that those people without scrota are excluded. But there is also the possibility, in a text like the *Devī Gītā*, that "scrotum," like "man," is used more generically. I have thus translated the term as "genitals."

I suspect that at least some of the androcentric language in the *Devī Gītā* is due to the author's heavy appeal to tradition and his predilection to use conventional forms and formulas. Thus, even his statement about giving the text to an eldest son, an ancient and time-honored prescription, seems largely undercut by his much greater emphasis on the necessity for true devotion to the Goddess on the part of the recipient. Nowhere does the author of the *Devī Gītā* suggest that such devotion is restricted to males only.

A reverse kind of gender and language problem confronting the translator revolves around certain androcentric aspects of English. For instance, while Sanskrit easily designates gender with its masculine and feminine inflections and can thus readily transform a noun from one gender to another (e.g., *nara* ["man"] to *narī* ["woman"]), English often lacks an opposite-gender synonym that is truly equivalent. Of particular relevance here is the term "lord." In Sanskrit there is a whole set of names for the supreme deity derived from the root *īś*, "to rule, to be master of, to be able, to own." Among the derived names are *īś, īśa, īśāna, īśitṛ,* and *īśvara,* all rendered by such terms as lord, master, ruler, owner, and often simply used as a name for the supreme being or spirit or lord of the world.

The challenge, then, comes in translating the feminine versions of these terms, terms which occur frequently in the *Devī Gītā*. Often they occur in compound forms, as in the basic name of the Goddess in our text, Bhuvaneśvarī, where *bhuvana* means "universe" or "world." The term *Bhuvaneśvarī,* thus, is literally "Female Lord of the Universe." But "female lord" is a bit awkward, especially in compounds, and can even be misleading. Standard alternative translations for Bhuvaneśvarī include "Queen of the Universe," "Lady of the Universe" (or "Lady-of-the-spheres," in Alain Daniélou's somewhat unconventional rendering), and "Mistress of the Universe." I tested out these, and a variety of other possible translations, on colleagues and students, and serious objections were raised to most of them. One suggested translation received generally positive marks, despite the fact that it does not make clear the gender of the Goddess. The term is *ruler,* a perfectly acceptable rendering of the underlying notion of *īś*. While lord and master are clearly masculine, ruler is rather neutral and can apply to male or female. However, I was at first opposed to the term, for certainly something is lost in not specifying the ruler as female. But I came to see that something is also gained in emphasizing the nongendered power/authority of Bhuvaneśvarī's rulership.

The advantage became clear to me while trying to translate a frequent synonym for Bhuvaneśvarī, *Parameśvarī,* literally, "Supreme Female Ruler." If one uses this literal translation, it immediately raises the question, Who is the supreme, and possibly superior, male ruler? The translations, "Supreme Ruler," and "Ruler of the Universe," leave no doubt about the unique and absolute authority of the Goddess. And as for the possibility that the reader of the *Devī Gītā* might forget her gender, it seems slight given the liberal use of gender-specific terms throughout the text, including Devī, "the Goddess" (seven times in the first chapter of seventy-four verses), and various forms of Mother (eleven times in the first chapter).

Regarding other issues of translation and my interpretive strategies, I have made some attempt to give consistent English equivalents for a given Sanskrit term, but there are many exceptions. These exceptions are often due to the polysemic nature of the Sanskrit terms, but occasionally also to stylistic considerations. For example, the notorious term *dharma* means something like "attribute" or "quality" in verses 2.19–20, but in verses 4.4, 9.14–15, 18, 20, 23, 25, it denotes a moral category or concept. In this latter instance, for partly if not wholly stylistic reasons, the term has been variously translated as "virtue" (4.4), "righteous action" (9.14–15, 18, 20), and "righteousness" (9.23, 25).

Finally, proper names have usually been left untranslated, and the various names of most deities normalized to the forms best known to an English audience (e.g., Śaṃkara [the god, not the teacher] has been rendered as Śiva). The major exception pertains to the Goddess. Her many names and various epithets reveal the complexity of her character and the several diverse aspects of her nature. As the character and nature of the Goddess are one of the central concerns of the *Devī Gītā*, these names and epithets have accordingly been translated, but even here I have felt compelled to make two important exceptions. The two, Śakti ("energy, power") and Māyā ("magical creative power, illusion, power of delusion"), constitute essential features or components of the Goddess. But the two are also extremely complex and multivalent philosophical concepts that in most instances defy easy translation without gross oversimplification. Accordingly, as epithets of the Goddess or as names of her powers, they are usually left untranslated, except where their sense in a given context can be sufficiently conveyed by an English equivalent.

Notes

1. Nīlakaṇṭha's commentary on the *Devī-Bhāgavata* may well be the earliest Sanskrit commentary on the work, and is, as far as I know, the only one printed. Chintaharan Chakravarti points out that Nīlakaṇṭha "was evidently of the opinion that he was the first to comment on the work. But two more commentaries, the dates of which are not known, have been referred to in the *Catalogus Catalogorum* (I.261)" ("Nīlakaṇṭha the Śaiva," *Indian Historical Quarterly* 16 (1940): 579).

2. See Chakravarti, "Nīlakaṇṭa the Śaiva," pp. 574–79. A brief summary of the article is given by Chakravarti in his *Tantras: Studies on Their Religion and Literature,* pp. 70–72.

3. See, for instance, Nīlakaṇṭha's concluding comment on chapter 4 of the *Devī Gītā* (4.50), as well as his comments on 5.46, 5.63, and the final comments to the *Devī Gītā* as a whole (following 10.44). I have been unable to discover whether or not such a commentary still exists. Chakravarti states that of all Nīlakaṇṭa's works, his commentary on the *Devī-Bhāgavata Purāṇa* "appears to be the only work that has so far been printed" (Nīlakaṇṭha the Śaiva," p. 576).

4. Pandurang Vaman Kane, *History of Dharmaśāstra (Ancient and Mediaeval Religious and Civil Law in India),* vol. 5, p. 254.

5. The translator referred to is Hari Prasanna Chatterji [Swami Vijnananda], whose translation of the *Devī-Bhāgavata Purāṇa* was published in 1921–23.

6. Cf. Elisabeth Schüssler Fiorenza, who argues that "a good translation is not a literal transcription but a perceptive interpretation transferring meaning from one lanugage context to another" (*In Memory of Her: A Feminist Theological Reconstruction of Christian Origins,* p. 46).

7. Schüssler Fiorenza, *In Memory of Her,* p. 44.

8. *Devī Gītā* 8.37.

Navaślokī Devī Gītā: The Essential *Devī Gītā* in Nine Verses

The nine verses below, appearing at the beginning of a recent printed edition of the *Devī Gītā*,[1] purport to represent the essential teachings of the text and its most powerful mantric verses. These verses, known as the "Navaślokī Devī Gītā," are regarded in their mantric aspect as concentrated sonic manifestations both of the Goddess and her *Song*. The daily recitation of these nine, for those without time to recite the whole of the *Devī Gītā*, is viewed as a quick and potent means to bring the presence of the Goddess directly into one's own life, providing the same worldly and spiritual benefits as other more complex forms of worshiping and meditating upon the Devī.

The nine also serve as a brief introduction and summary of many of the major themes of the *Song*. These themes are discussed below in the Comment following the Navaślokī. The reader may refer to the main text for additional commentary and notes on these verses. The numbers in brackets at the end of each verse indicate the chapter and verse in the *Devī Gītā* from which the Navaślokī are taken. The Afterword further considers how the attachment of the Navaślokī to the *Devī Gītā* may reflect significant changes in the ways the text has been understood and utilized.

Translation

[The gods sing the praises of the supreme Goddess.]

1. We know you as Mahālakṣmī, we meditate on you as the Śakti of all.
   May the Goddess inspire that knowledge and meditation of ours. [1.48]
2. Hail to her in the form of the Cosmic Body; hail to her in the form of the Cosmic Soul;
   Hail to her in the Unmanifest State; hail to her in the form of the glorious Brahman. [1.49]
3. Through her power of ignorance, she shows herself as the world, like a rope appearing as a serpent, wreath, and the like.
   Through her power of knowledge, she dissolves the world back into herself. We glorify her, Ruler of the Universe. [1.50]

[The Goddess describes her power known as Māyā.]

4. [Māyā is variously called] knowledge, illusion, matter, nature, energy, or the unborn.
   Those versed in Śaiva works call it intelligence. [2.9cd–10ab]
5. From the practical point of view, Māyā is regarded as self-evident.
   In reality, however, it does not exist—only the supreme exists, in an absolute sense. [3.2]

[The Goddess outlines the basic spiritual practices for realizing the supreme unity of Self, the Goddess, and Brahman.]

6. [My sacred syllable Hrīṃ] transcends the distinction of "name" and "named," beyond all dualities.
   It is whole, infinite being, consciousness, and bliss. One should meditate on that reality within the flaming light of consciousness. [4.48]

7. Fixing the mind upon me as the Goddess transcending all space and time,
   One quickly merges with me through realizing the oneness of the soul and Brahman. [5.55cd–56ab]
8. Just this Brahman is immortal; in front is Brahman, behind is Brahman, on the right and the left;
   It extends above and below. The whole universe is just this Brahman, the greatest. [6.14]
9. Like clarified butter hidden in milk, knowledge dwells in every being;
   One should stir continuously, using the mind as the churning stick. [7.44]

Comment

From a devotional and meditational standpoint, the first verse of the "Navaślokī Devī Gītā" provides a fitting introduction to the power of the Goddess inherent in her *Song*. The verse is in the form of the famous Gāyatrī mantra of *Ṛg Veda* 3.62.10, recited daily by devout Hindus to prepare one's mind and heart for spiritual contemplation. At the same time, repetition of the Gāyatrī invokes the deity of the mantra to appear in person before the reciter. The Vedic original invokes the god Savitṛ or the Sun; the *Devī Gītā*'s Gāyatrī invokes a prime manifestation of the Goddess, Mahālakṣmī, identified with the divine power (Śakti) in all beings. This Śakti is thus considered to be directly and immediately present during the rest of the recitation.

While the first Navaślokī verse presents the essence of the Goddess as embodied in the most sacred of Vedic mantras, the second verse identifies her with the ultimate reality of the Upaniṣads, the supreme Brahman in its fourfold aspect, encompassing all levels of consciousness and being. The third verse further explicates this identity utilizing a famous analogy from the Advaita Vedānta, according to which all multiplicity is simply an appearance of the unitary Brahman, like that of a snake in a rope. The appearance is due to the power of ignorance, an aspect of Māyā. This verse, in addition, affirms the identity of the Śākta-Tantric Goddess, Bhuvaneśvarī (Ruler of the Universe), with the nondual Brahman of the Advaita. The first three verses of the Navaślokī, taken from the hymn to the Goddess offered by the gods in chapter 1, clearly attest to the assimilative and synthetic character of the *Devī Gītā* as a whole, affirming from its perspective the basic unity and continuity of the Vedic, Vedāntic, and Tantric traditions.

The remaining verses of the Navaślokī are all spoken by the Goddess herself. In verses four and five, she briefly elaborates on the notion of Māyā implicit in verse three, and hints at the liberating role of knowledge in overcoming the delusions inspired by Māyā. In the last four verses, she stresses the practice of meditation as the means of acquiring the knowledge that culminates in the final realization of the union/identity of the Self, the Goddess, and the Absolute. The Navaślokī thus touch upon the major themes of the *Devī Gītā:* the nature of ultimate reality, its relation to this world, and the means by which we humans can discover and assimilate that reality into our own being.

Note

1. The Vārāṇasī (1986) edition of Upendra Pāṇḍeya (translator and commentator).

Chapter 1

The Appearance of the Great Goddess Before the Mountain King Himālaya and the Gods

Translation

[King Janamejaya inquires of the sage Vyāsa about the appearance of the Goddess on the Himālaya Mountain.]

Janamejaya spoke:

1.1. You said earlier that the supreme lustrous power[1] manifested itself on the crest of Himālaya, the Mountain Lord.
This you mentioned only in passing. Now explain it to me in full detail.

1.2. What thoughtful person would ever tire of drinking the nectarine tales of Śakti?
Death comes even to those who drink divine ambrosia, but not to one who hears[2] this act of hers.

Comment

The *Devī Gītā,* constituting the last ten chapters of the seventh book of the *Devī Bhāgavata Purāṇa,*[3] is part of an ongoing conversation between

King Janamejaya and the sage Vyāsa.[4] In the preceding chapter, Vyāsa had related the story of the goddess Satī, including her suicide by yogic fire. The sage concluded the account of her death by asserting: "And that lustrous power of hers *(tan-mahas)* appeared anew on the crest of Himālaya."[5] Without further elaboration on the manifestation of this lustrous power, Vyāsa then proceeded to tell about the reaction of Satī's spouse, Śiva, to her death (for more on the story of Satī and the aftermath of her death, see the Comment on verses 1.3–13 below). Janamejaya, thoroughly familiar with Vyāsa's tendency to pass quickly over important points, is often compelled to seek fuller explanations. Accordingly, here in the first verse of the *Devī Gītā,* Janamejaya asks for an in-depth account of the appearance of the supreme lustrous power *(paraṃ mahas)* on the Himālaya Mountain.

The *Devī Gītā* thus begins with reference to the reappearance or rebirth of the goddess Satī. By tradition, Satī's next incarnation was as the daughter of the Himālaya Mountain, known as Pārvatī ("She-Who-is-Born-of-a-Mountain *[parvata]*"). The commentator Nīlakaṇṭha[6] immediately identifies the supreme lustrous power as Pārvatī. Yet such an identification is somewhat misleading in terms of the *Devī Gītā*'s own understanding of the Goddess. Satī and Pārvatī (or Gaurī, as she is called in our text) are simply empowered forms or potencies *(śakti*s*),* dynamic manifestations of the supreme Śakti, the highest Power of the Universe. The term *śakti,* feminine in gender, characterizes the essential nature of the Goddess as the energizing force impelling and enlivening the cosmos, and accordingly she herself is called Śakti. The Goddess later in the first chapter (1.63cd) promises Himālaya that her *śakti* Gaurī will be born as his daughter. The Goddess clearly transcends such incarnations as Satī and Gaurī, although in one sense they are identical with her (cf. the Comment on 1.54–65 below). The term *paraṃ mahas,* while connected with Satī's rebirth, more importantly evokes the notion of Brahman, the ultimate reality of the Upaniṣads (see note 1 below). The *Devī Gītā,* then, opens with an implicit affirmation of the Goddess as the supreme Brahman.

Notes

1. *mahas:* literally "light, luster," as well as "greatness, power." In the *Taittirīya Upaniṣad* (1.5), *mahas* is the fourth *(caturthī)* mystic syllable, beyond *bhūḥ, bhuvaḥ,* and *suvaḥ.* The *Taittirīya* specifically identifies this *mahas* with Brahman *(maha iti brahma),* and as the power by which the various worlds and entities "become great." The notion of *mahas* as the fourth also suggests the idea of the fourth state of consciousness *(turīya),* beyond waking, dream, and deep sleep, and thus points to the supreme, aniconic form of the Devī as pure consciousness.

The *Śāradā-Tilaka Tantra*, with which the author of the *Devī Gītā* was almost certainly familiar, begins with an invocation of this supreme reality, *mahas*. There, it is described as having the form of bliss, all-pervading, as being the "sound-Brahman" *(śabda-brahman)*, and as the inner consciousness. (Cf. in the same work 23.37 and 25.56, which give similar descriptions of this supreme power.) Woodroffe, in his summary of the first chapter of the *Śāradā-Tilaka* (p. 5), comments: "The [beginning] verse as it stands . . . refers to the Mahah *[mahas]* (Radiant Energy) in the neuter gender. [The commentator] Rāghava shows how this can be interpreted to apply either to Shiva or Shakti." The *Devī Gītā* applies it exlusively to the Goddess, and affirms in the process that her power *(śakti)* is the same as the lustrous power of Brahman.

2. Hearing or listening *(śravaṇa)* to the stories or virtues of the Goddess is considered one of the main devotional acts that one can offer to her (cf. 7.11, 19 below; cf. also 8.31, where listening to the virtues of the Devī's sacred dwelling places is extolled). The *Bhāgavata Purāṇa* popularized the *bhaktic* ideal of *śravaṇa* with reference to the deeds/virtues of Kṛṣṇa. Thus, the *Bhāgavata* (2.2.37) declares in words similar to the *Devī Gītā*'s above: "Whatever persons drink the nectarine tales of the Lord, the Self, poured into the cups of their ears by the holy, they purify their hearts . . . and attain his lotus feet." Cf. *Bhagavad Gītā* 10.9, where Kṛṣṇa declares that the wise "rejoice in constantly talking about me."

In earlier, non-*bhaktic* Vedānta, in the practice of the yoga of knowledge (Jñāna Yoga), *śravaṇa* refers to hearing the teachings of the Upaniṣads as the first step, along with reflection *(manana)* and intense meditation *(nididhyāsana)*, on the path to self-realization or the realization of the identity of the individual self and Brahman. In the *Devī-Bhāgavata Purāṇa*, *śravaṇa* often serves as a first step to realization of the identity of the self (or Self) and the Goddess. Cf. *Devī Gītā* 2.1 and 4.40.

3. *Devī-Bhāgavata* 7.31–40.

4. Regarding Janamejaya and Vyāsa, see the Introduction, pp. 4–5.

5. *Devī-Bhāgavata* 7.30.38ab.

6. For information on Nīlakaṇṭha, see the Note on the Translation, p. 32.

Translation

[Vyāsa begins the story of Śiva's sorrow following Satī's suicide, and of the ensuing world crisis.]

Vyāsa spoke:

1.3. You are blessed and completely fulfilled;[1] you have been taught by those of great heart;
And you are fortunate, for you possess true devotion to the Goddess.

1.4. Hear, O King, this ancient tale. When the body of Satī was consumed in flames,[2]
The bewildered Śiva wandered about, falling here and there motionless on the ground.[3]

1.5. He was unaware of the manifest world, his mind being fully absorbed.[4]
Regaining his self-composure, he passed the time contemplating the true form[5] of the Goddess.

1.6. Meanwhile, the three-tiered universe,[6] with all that is mobile and immobile, lost its auspicious charm[7]
When the entire world with its oceans, continents, and mountains, was bereft of energy.[8]

1.7. Joy shrivelled up in the heart of each and every being.
All peoples were despondent, their careworn spirits exhausted.

1.8. Then, ever drowning in a sea of misery, they were consumed by disease.
The planets retrogressed ominously; the fortunes of the gods declined.

1.9. Kings, too, suffered misfortune due to material and spiritual forces set in motion by the death of Satī.[9]
Now at that time arose a great demon, Tāraka by name.

1.10. The fiend became master of the three-tiered universe after procuring from Brahmā this boon:
"Only a legitimate son of Śiva shall be your slayer."

1.11. With his death thus fixed by Brahmā, the great demon,
Realizing no lawful son of Śiva existed, roared and rejoiced.

1.12. And all the gods, attacked by Tāraka and driven from their own homes,
Lived in a state of persistent anxiety due to the absence of any legitimate son of Śiva.

The gods thought:

1.13. Śiva has no wife; how shall he engender a son?
How can we prosper, deprived of good fortune?

Comment

The story of Satī's suicide, as Vyāsa says, is indeed ancient, with numerous variations appearing in the *Māhābhārata* and many of the Purāṇas.[10] The basic motive underlying the suicide was an insult by her father Dakṣa directed toward her and her husband Śiva. Dakṣa had refused to invite them to an important sacrificial feast, so Satī sacrificed herself in protest.

The *Devī-Bhāgavata* tells its own version of the story in the chapter immediately preceding the *Devī Gītā.*[11] According to this account, Dakṣa wrongfully indulged his own sexual desire, and as a result of that offense grew hostile to Śiva and Satī. It was due to this enmity (without further explanation) that Satī took her own life. Śiva was devastated by the news of his wife's death and destroyed Dakṣa's sacrifice. He then took the charred remains of Satī onto his shoulders and wandered about in a distracted state of mind. The gods were concerned about Śiva, and so Viṣṇu cut off Satī's body, piece by piece, with his arrows. Wherever the parts of her body fell to the earth from Śiva's shoulder, there he took up residence in various forms, passing the time in practicing recitation, meditation, and absorption (*japa, dhyāna,* and *samādhi*). The dispersal of Satī's body parts underlies the notion of the sacred sites of the Devī (the *śākta-pīṭhas*), dealt with in detail in chapter 8 of the *Devī Gītā.*

Here in the first chapter, after recounting Śiva's distraction, Vyāsa elaborates upon the ensuing chaos on Earth due to the absence of the Devī's energizing power in the form of Satī. Satī represents *saubhāgya:* "good fortune, auspiciousness, beauty or charm." *Saubhāgya* refers particularly to the auspicious state of a married woman whose husband is still living, as opposed to the inauspicious state of widowhood. Here, in something of a reversal, it is the world that endures such an inauspicious state when it loses Satī.

At this point, Vyāsa introduces the story of Tāraka, an archetypal demon who terrorizes and displaces the gods. The traditional accounts of this demon attribute his death to Śiva's son Skanda, whose mother (in the best-known versions at least) is Pārvatī. This tradition is recognized and appropriated into the boon given by Brahmā to Tāraka, which creates the dramatic rationale for the reappearance of the Goddess. The boon necessitates that the widower Śiva procure a new wife, namely Pārvatī/Gaurī.

Brahmā is well known for his granting boons to demons (as a reward for their *tapas* or asceticism) that jeopardize the welfare of the gods. As Brahmā is father of both gods and demons, his generosity to the latter is somewhat understandable. He grants them what they wish—comprehensive invulnerability in the form of a set of conditions seemingly guaranteeing immortality—but always with a loophole, which the gods eventually discover and exploit.

The model for the *Devī Gītā*'s boon to Tāraka appears in the *Matsya Purāṇa.* In its account of the Tāraka myth, the *Matsya* relates that the demon first asks Brahmā for absolute invulnerability, but such a request, as always, is refused. Brahmā instead suggests that Tāraka request that death come only from someone he does not fear. Accordingly, Tāraka asks that he be slain only by a seven-day-old baby.[12] After granting this boon, Brahmā later explains to the gods that the slayer of Tāraka will be born of Śiva, currently without a wife (due to Satī's death), but that the Goddess will soon be born of Himālaya. The son born of her by Śiva, when seven days old, will kill the demon chief.[13]

The *Devī-Bhāgavata* recounts a number of demon tales at great length, frequently emphasizing the clever boons that allow the gods, with the help of the Goddess, finally to overcome their demonic adversaries. But such tales, focusing on the warriorlike aspects of Devī or her *śaktis*, are not the main concern of the *Devī Gītā.* The *Devī Gītā* has little interest in the story of Tāraka as such, using it simply as a means to link together the accounts of Satī and Pārvatī, and thereby providing the traditional Śākta setting for the dialogue between Himālaya and the Goddess (see the Introduction, pp. 9–11, and the Comment on verses 1.66–1.74). The actual Tāraka story, including the birth of Gaurī, her marriage to Śiva, the birth of Skanda, and the slaying of the demon, is told by the *Devī Gītā* in a mere one and a half verses (10.39–40ab).

Notes

1. *kṛta-kṛtya:* literally, "having done what is to be done"; that is, having nothing left to do or accomplish. In the *Devī-Bhāgavata,* it is often a synonym for the person liberated while still living *(jīvan-mukta).* The text affirms, for instance, that after completing the mental worship of the Goddess, "then one becomes liberated while living and attains final release at death; thus, a person is completely fulfilled *(kṛta-kṛtya)* who worships the World-Mother" (3.12.58; cf. 7.30.98). In *Devī Gītā* 6.30, the person who attains knowledge of Brahman is also referred to as *kṛta-kṛtya,* as is the person who performs the various ritual acts of devotion to the Goddess in 8.49. Cf. also 6.19, 8.2, and 10.30.

The term acquired a special, technical meaning in Advaita Vedānta. In *Pañcadaśī* 14.3, the sense of having achieved *kṛta-kṛtya* is one of four aspects of the blissful state of Brahman; the other three are: (1) absence of misery *(duḥkhābhāva)*, (2) attainment of one's desires *(kāmāpti)*, and (3) the sense of having attained what is to be attained *(prāpta-prāpya)*. Cf. *Pañcadaśī* 14.58–62 (and 7.291–95), where a man who has experienced such aspects is repeatedly said to feel "blessed" *(dhanya)*, a term used by Vyāsa earlier in the verse to describe Janamejaya. Cf. also *Vivekacūḍāmaṇi* 488: "I am blessed *(dhanya)*, completely fulfilled *(kṛta-kṛtya)*, and liberated *(vimukta)*."

The term *kṛta-kṛtya* already appears in the *Bhagavad Gītā* and the *Laws of Manu*. In the former (15.20), Kṛṣṇa declares that the person who realizes the truth of his teachings is wise and completely fulfilled. And in the *Laws of Manu* (12.93), the famous law-giver affirms that a person, especially a Brahman, who gives up other activities or duties, concentrating on knowledge of the Self, tranquillity, and study of the Veda, accomplishes all that is to be done (i.e., is completely fulfilled).

2. Satī is so called, according to the *Devī-Bhāgavata* (7.30.23ab), because she is of the nature of truth *(satya-tvāt)*. The term *satī* also refers to the true wife who follows her husband even in death (i.e., on his funeral pyre). In the *Devī-Bhāgavata*, however, Satī's self-immolation precedes her husband's death. To preserve the integrity of a virtuous wife *(satī-dharma-didṛkṣayā)*, she burns her body, not, however, with ordinary fire, but with the fire of yoga *(yogāgninā)* (7.30.37cd).

3. According to the *Kālikā Purāṇa* (18.5), Śiva in his grief for Satī "would fall on the ground one moment, then rising the next would run about; he wandered around one moment, and then would shut his eyes."

4. *samādhi-gata-mānasa:* literally, "his mind gone to a state of absorption." In the traditional eight limbs of yoga, *samādhi* or intense absorption is the final stage and goal. Our text later defines this stage as "constant contemplation on the identity of the individual self and the supreme Self" (5.25). Here, the term is used in a more general sense, as Śiva is apparently absorbed in his grief. Such world-forgetting absorption, however, is clearly therapeutic, for it induces Śiva to meditate on the Goddess.

5. *svarūpa:* "one's own inherent form, or true nature." The Devī's highest nature is pure consciousness, symbolized by light, but the term *svarūpa* is not used in a strict or consistent sense in the *Devī-Bhāgavata* and may well refer here to her beautiful, four-armed form as Bhuvaneśvarī, her supreme iconic form.

6. *trailokya;* the Earth, the heavens above, and the nether worlds.

7. *saubhāgya;* Nīlakaṇṭha glosses the word with *aiśvarya*, "the pervading, sovereign power" of the World-Mother. As noted in the Introduction (p. 24), *aiśvarya* is the primary characteristic traditionally associated with Bhuvaneśvarī.

8. *śakti;* refers both to the Goddess in her form as Satī, and to her energizing power. When Satī was born, described in the preceding chapter of the

Devī-Bhāgavata (7.30.20–22), the reverse occurred: gods and saints rejoiced, the rivers began to flow in their channels, the sun shone brightly, and everything looked auspicious.

9. The text of 1.8cd–1.9ab is highly elliptical. What the text clearly intends is a general parallel and causal connection between the natural, social, and celestial realms in their mutual deterioration. On the material *(adhibhūta)* and spiritual or divine *(adhidaiva)* forces, see R. Nilkantan, *Gītās in the Māhābhārata and the Purāṇas,* p. 74.

10. See D. C. Sircar, *The Śākta Pīṭhas,* pp. 5–7, for a detailed discussion of the variations and development of the myth. Most of the relevant discussion is quoted in Agehananda Bharati, *The Tantric Tradition,* pp. 86–88.

11. *Devī-Bhāgavata* 7.30.26–50.

12. *Matsya Purāṇa* 147.16cd–25.

13. *Matsya Purāṇa* 153.47–54.

Translation

[The gods seek counsel with Viṣṇu, who indicates the solution to their predicament.]

Vyāsa continued:

1.14. Thus afflicted with worry, all the gods journeyed to Viṣṇu's heaven,
Taking counsel with him in private. He then explained their proper recourse:

Viṣṇu spoke:

1.15. Why are you all so worried, for the Auspicious Goddess[1] is a wish-fulfilling tree?[2]
Dwelling in the Jeweled Island[3] as Ruler of the Universe,[4] she is ever attentive.

1.16. She neglects us now only because of our misbehavior.
Such chastisement by the World-Mother[5] is simply for our own instruction.

1.17. As a mother feels no lack of compassion whether indulging or chastening her child,
Just so the World-Mother feels when overseeing our virtues and vices.

1.18. A son transgresses the limits of proper conduct at every step:
Who in the world forgives him except his mother?
1.19. Therefore go for refuge[6] to the supreme Mother without delay,
With sincere hearts. She will accomplish what you want.

Comment

As is typical in stories of the conflicts between the gods and demons, when the latter gain the upper hand, the gods seek refuge with some higher counselor, often one of the famous triumvirate (Trimūrti). This counselor, being less than the supreme power and physically not up to the task at hand, then defers to the ultimate supreme ruler, most commonly identified in the older epic and Purāṇic accounts with either Śiva or Viṣṇu, depending on the particular theistic leanings of the storyteller. That Viṣṇu is here cast into the role of the counselor is a clear rejection of the supremacy claimed for him by the Vaiṣṇavas. It is from Viṣṇu's own mouth that the supremacy of the Goddess as World-Mother is proclaimed.

Viṣṇu's counsel to the gods addresses one of the great paradoxical aspects of the Goddess, her great love for all her children and her seeming indifference. This paradox parallels in some ways the tension between her benevolent and horrific sides, the latter often manifesting in brutal violence, primarily in battle against demonic foes. In the *Devī-Bhāgavata* as a whole, the violent, martial nature of the Goddess, while much on display, is ultimately subordinated to her maternalistic compassion. Thus, even her bloody victories over the demons, who after all are still her offspring, are really meant simply to save them from their own evil ways. In the *Devī Gītā,* Viṣṇu explains that her compassion may manifest as indifference in order to teach. As Nīlakaṇṭha elucidates Viṣṇu's words in verse 1.16: "Her neglect is not for our destruction *(nāśāya),* but . . . for our instruction *(śikṣaṇāya).*"

Notes

1. *śivā;* "the auspicious one" (feminine form); a common name for Pārvatī, resonating with the sound of her husband's name Śiva. In the *Devī Gītā,* however,

the Goddess in her true nature is beyond all marital relationships: she is simply the auspicious energy that makes all life and prosperity possible, but is the consort of no one. Śivā is here a name applied to Bhuvaneśvarī, the Goddess who resides in the Jeweled Island.

2. *kāma-kalpa-druma;* a mythical tree in Indra's paradise able to grant all one's desires. See note 6 on 1.46 below.

3. Maṇidvīpa, the Jeweled Island, is the Devī's own celestial kingdom, high above all other heavenly worlds, including Viṣṇu's Vaikuṇṭha. For a brief description of this paradise, see the Introduction, pp. 24–25.

4. *bhuvaneśānī:* "Female Lord or Ruler of the Universe," a close synonym for Bhuvaneśvarī.

5. The maternal nature of the Goddess, expressed in such epithets as Jaganmātṛ, Jagadambikā, Amba, Parāmba, etc., is the most common characterization of the Goddess in the *Devī Gītā.*

6. *śaraṇa:* "refuge, or protection." The term also conveys a sense of extreme devotional commitment, of submitting or surrendering oneself, of turning one's life over to one's chosen deity, in this case the Goddess.

Translation

[The gods proceed to the Himālaya Mountain to worship the Goddess.]

Vyāsa continued:

1.20. Thus enjoining all the gods and accompanied by his wife, the great Viṣṇu,
As chief of the gods, set forth at once with his fellow lords.

1.21. He came to the great rocky crag, Himālaya, Lord of mountains,
And all the gods commenced the preliminary acts of worship.[1]

1.22. They then performed the Mother's sacrifice,[2] knowing well her ceremonial rites.
All the gods hastened to perform her ritual observances, including the third-day rites,[3] O King.

1.23. Some of the gods were fully absorbed in meditation; others were focused on her name.
Some concentrated on her hymn,[4] while others were intent on reciting her names.

1.24. Some were devoted to chanting mantras, or practicing severe austerities.
Some were absorbed in mental sacrifices,[5] and others implanted mystic powers in their bodies.[6]
1.25. Unwearied, they worshiped[7] the supreme Śakti with the mantra known as Hṛllekhā.[8]
Many years thus passed away, O Janamejaya.

Comment

The Mother's sacrifice or worship described above is similar to other invocatory scenes recounted elsewhere in the *Devī-Bhāgavata.* Of particular relevance here are two stories focusing on the humbling of the gods by the Goddess. The first story, regarding the humbling of Viṣṇu and Śiva (told, interestingly enough, just prior to the *Devī Gītā*),[9] finds its resolution when the sage Dakṣa and his peers go to the Himālaya Mountain to worship the Goddess. They practice austerities and meditate on the supreme Śakti, but the key practice is their repetition *(japa)* of the sacred mantric syllable of the Goddess, known as the Hṛllekhā or the Māyā-bīja (seed mantra of Māyā).[10] The protective nature of the Goddess as manifest in the Hṛllekhā is suggested by the etymology of its name. According to the commentator Nīlakaṇṭha, the syllable is called the Hṛllekhā because the Goddess "keeps watch in the furrow *(lekha)* of the heart *(hṛd)*."[11] The second story, the humbling of Agni, Vāyu, and Indra, is likewise resolved when Indra, instructed by the Goddess herself, recites the Māyā-bīja while fasting and meditating.[12] In both stories, the recitation of the sonic essence of the Goddess who resides in the heart brings about her visible presence. (For a brief account of these stories, see the Comment on verses 1.26–29 below.)

The general purposes of mantra recitation are threefold: propitiation of a god or goddess, acquisition of some material good or other desired end, and identification of the worshiper with the power/deity being invoked.[13] In the *Devī-Bhāgavata,* such ends are almost always mediated through a vision or revelation of the Goddess. Thus, the recitation of the Māyā-bīja in the two "humbling" narratives and in the *Devī Gītā* has for its immediate end an audience with the Goddess. Then, once she appears, a request for various worldly gains can be put to her, or she can give calming assurances of safety.

From the devotional, *bhaktic* point of view, receiving a vision *(darśana)* of the Goddess is in many ways its own end, as the *Devī Gītā* itself later suggests.[14] From the point of view of wisdom or knowledge *(jñāna),* the appearance of the Goddess is an occasion for revelation of the supreme truth that leads to union with that truth. In the *Devī Gītā,* the undertaking of the Mother's sacrifice with recitation of the Hṛllekhā is ostensibly for the purposes of propitiating the Goddess and acquiring victory against Tāraka. But as Himālaya's request in 1.73 makes clear, identification or union with the supreme Goddess is the final goal.

Notes

1. *puraścaraṇa:* "preparatory rite," often in Tantra involving the recitation of the name or mantra of the deity, accompanied by other ritual acts such as fire offerings and the observance of dietary restrictions.

2. *amba-yajña;* the word *yajña* means both "sacrifice" and "worship." Worship in this sense means a ritual act of devotion, to honor a deity with sacrifices and other material and immaterial offerings. In the *Devī Gītā, yajña* is basically synonymous with *pūjā* (translated as "worship"), a term appearing in 1.25ab.

3. *tṛtīyādi-vratāni;* this refers to those rites that are to be performed on the third day of the dark and bright fortnights of the lunar month. These third-day rites are dedicated especially to the Goddess or various goddesses. See 8.37–38 below for more on these rites.

Nīlakaṇṭha indicates that the various rituals are described in the third Skandha or Book of the *Devī-Bhāgavata.* In *Devī-Bhāgavata* 3.12, the Devī's sacrifice *(devyā yajña)* is explained at some length. Of special interest is the fourfold division of the types of worship according to the three *guṇa*s of nature (see 7.4–10 and the Comment thereon for an explanation of the *guṇa*s). The fourth type, beyond the *guṇa*s, is the mental worship (in contrast to the three preceding external forms), referred to in the *Devī Gītā* two verses down (1.24). In *Devī-Bhāgavata* 3.13, the Devī's sacrifice (also referred to as the *yāgam ambikāyāḥ,* "the Mother's sacrifice") that Viṣṇu performed after visiting the Devī in her Jeweled Island and following the creation of the world is briefly described.

4. *sūkta-parāḥ;* Nīlakaṇṭha glosses this: *"ahaṃ rudrebhir ity ādi devī-sūkta-jāpina ity arthaḥ."* ("The meaning is that they [the gods] were engaged in reciting the hymn of the Devī that begins with the words, 'I, with the Rudras. . . .' ") The words quoted by Nīlakaṇṭha are the first words of the famous "Devī Sūkta" of *Ṛg Veda* 10.125. In *Devī Gītā* 10.22, the Goddess explicitly recommends reciting the "Devī Sūkta" for her enjoyment. Interestingly, the *Devī Upaniṣad,* just prior to its own "Hymn to the Goddess," has the Devī herself recite the "Devī Sūkta." The *Devī Gītā* has borrowed many motifs and verses from this Upaniṣad (see the Comment on 1.42–53 below).

5. *antar-yāga,* "internal or mental worship." In the third book of the *Devī-Bhāgavata* (3.12.39–63ab), this mental sacrifice *(mānasa-yāga)* is described at length. The sacrificer visually creates in the imagination the worship hall and altar,

mentally provides the priests and material substances to be offered, etc. This internal sacrifice is for those who have no worldly desires, only desire for *mokṣa.* Specifically, it is said that it should not be performed by kings desiring victory (verse 63). This suggests that at least some of the gods, in the scene described in the *Devī Gītā,* are not particularly concerned with Tāraka, using him merely as an excuse to worship the Goddess! In any case, according to the *Devī-Bhāgavata,* the final result of successfully performing the mental sacrifice is said to be a vision of the Goddess as the embodiment of infinite being, consciousness, and bliss *(sac-cid-ānanda-rūpiṇī),* and the attainment of liberation while living *(jīvan-mukti)* (3.12.56 and 58). Cf. *Devī Gītā* 9.3; 9.44–45ab; and 10.12cd.

The *Mahānirvāṇa Tantra* says that a practitioner, having worshiped the supreme Brahman who is *sac-cit-svarūpam,* should "in order to attain union with Brahman, worship with offerings of his mind," before commencing external worship (3.50–51, Woodroffe's translation).

6. The implanting or installing of mystic powers in one's body is called *nyāsa,* literally, "placing, putting down." In Tantric ritual, it refers to the placing or assigning of various powers or deities to different parts of the body, by touching those parts using symbolic gestures *(mudrās),* accompanied by invocatory mantras. Through this process, the practitioner is fully protected in all his/her limbs and becomes the embodiment of those powers and deities. *Nyāsa* is discussed in *Devī Gītā* 10.6–8.

7. Literally, "performed the worship *(pūjā)*"; the types and procedures of *devī-pūjā* ("Goddess worship") are the primary topics of chapters 9 and 10 of the *Devī Gītā.*

8. As Nīlakaṇṭha points out here, the Hṛllekhā is the seed mantra of Bhuvaneśvarī (and later, commenting on verse 10.6, he indicates it is also known as the *māyā-bīja* or seed mantra of Māyā; see also his comment on 8.30, discussed in the note to that verse below). It is the sacred syllable Hrīṃ (see the Comment on 1.42–53 below for an explanation of Hrīṃ). The name Hṛllekhā itself literally means "mark or scratch on the heart," thus "anxiety, desire." As a name of the seed mantra, it may be thought of as the audible essence and sign of Bhuvaneśvarī's heart.

As for the general significance of seed mantras, Guy Beck writes with specific reference to the Hṛllekhā: "A Tantric mantra in the form of a syllable is . . . a very compact form of the god or power that it 'is' in essence. A single mantra may focus the energy of a deity into a grosser or more bodily representation. The heart mantra, for example, is known as HRĪM and is based on the Sanskrit word *hṛdaya* for heart, used when the heart energy of a deity is to be evoked" (*Sonic Theology,* p. 128). (For more on seed mantras, see the Introduction, p. 19.)

A contemporary Hindu explains the significance of Hṛllekhā as follows: "In Tantric lore, Bhuvaneswari is called, among others, by the name of Hrillekha. It means the Power which is resident in the heart of man in the form of a creeper holding fast to him and guiding him. . . . Now, competent authorities identify this Hrillekha with the *Kundalini Sakti* resident in man" (V. A. K.

Ayer, "Mother Bhuvaneswari," *Tattvāloka* 11, no. 4 [1988]:45). (For Kuṇḍalinī Śakti, see 5.33 below.) Thus, the Hṛllekhā is both the Goddess and her essential sonic form, as well as her power manifest within the human individual.

The Hṛllekhā is also regarded as the energizing point/sound from which the entire universe unfolds. As another contemporary Hindu affirms, this syllable is the essential, dynamic point of the universe containing the pattern for all manifest forms: "Paradoxically, the dynamic point is the perfect potential universe. This is *bindu* [the primal point]. Words in common parlance can never express the basic idea or pattern *(hṛllekhā)*. An aspect of the basic pattern is sought to be expressed in Tantra by the mystic syllable or formula *hrīṃ (māyābīja)*" (Swami Pratyagatmananda, "Philosophy of the Tantras," in *The Philosophies*, ed. Haridas Bhattacharyya, *The Cultural Heritage of India*, vol. 3, p. 442).

In the Vaiṣṇava *Lakṣmī Tantra*, the Hṛllekhā is said to be the seed mantra of the supreme goddess known variously as Śrī, Lakṣmī, or Tārā. In 27.7, Śrī declares, "hṛllekhā, the supreme vidyā . . . is identified with me; she is my divine, absolute śakti, perpetually endowed with all my attributes" (Sanjukta Gupta's translation).

9. *Devī-Bhāgavata* 7.29.23–7.30.17.

10. See note 8 above.

11. Nīlakaṇṭha, comment on *Devī Gītā* 8.30 (see note 1 on 8.30 below).

12. *Devī-Bhāgavata* 12.8.12–86.

13. This classification is given by Bharati, *The Tantric Tradition*, pp. 111–13.

14. See 10.38 below, and the Comment on 10.38–43ab.

Translation

[The Goddess appears before the gods as a blazing light.]

1.26. Suddenly, on the ninth lunar day in the month of Caitra, on a Friday,[1]
That lustrous power revealed in scripture appeared before the gods.[2]

1.27. Praised on all sides by the four Vedas incarnate,
It blazed like ten million suns, yet soothed like ten million moons.

1.28. Flashing like ten million streaks of lightning[3] tinged with red,[4] that supreme lustrous power
Shone forth unencompassed above, across, and in the middle.[5]

1.29. Without beginning or end, it had no body, no hands, no other limbs,[6]
Nor did it have a woman's form, a man's form, nor the two combined.[7]

Comment

The sudden appearance of the Goddess in the form of an infinite, blazing mass of light closely parallels the account of her manifestation in the famous story of the humbling of the gods Agni, Vāyu, and Indra as told near the end of the *Devī-Bhāgavata*.[8] The *Devī-Bhāgavata*'s account is itself an elaboration and interpretation of the same story as found in the *Kena Upaniṣad*.[9]

The basic myth as told in the *Kena* concerns the arrogance of the gods in claiming for themselves a victory that was actually achieved by Brahman, the supreme power, on their behalf. To curb their false pride, Brahman appeared before the gods in the form of a spirit or *yakṣa*. The gods were curious to know who or what this spirit was, and first sent the fire god Agni to find out. Agni, approaching the spirit, was suddenly asked by the *yakṣa* what power he possessed. The fire god replied that he had the power to burn anything on Earth. The spirit then placed before him a blade of grass, which Agni was unable to burn. Humiliated, Agni returned to the gods, who then sent the wind god Vāyu, who has the power to blow away anything on Earth. But Vāyu was unable to blow away the blade of grass placed before him by the spirit. Finally, Indra was sent to the *yakṣa*, but it disappeared in front of him. Then, in that same space in the sky, Indra came across a woman, the brilliant and beautiful Umā Haimavatī, who revealed the identity of the *yakṣa* as Brahman, to whom the victory was due. In the subsequent tradition, Umā Haimavatī came to be identified with Brahmavidyā, the knowledge revealing Brahman.

The *Devī-Bhāgavata*, in its elaborate recounting of the *Kena* story, explicitly identifies the World-Mother with the *yakṣa*, and thus with Brahman itself rather than just with a mediator of Brahman. Further, the *Devī-Bhāgavata* adds a number of other details. The *yakṣa* when it first appears is described as a mass of light *(tejas)* like ten million suns, soothing like ten million moons, without hands, feet, or other limbs. This spirit is also referred to as the supreme lustrous power *(paraṃ mahas)*. When it disappears before Indra, it instructs him to recite the Māyā-bīja. For one hundred thousand years Indra devoutly carries out the repetition of this mantra. Then suddenly, on the ninth lunar day in the month of Caitra, the light reappears, in the midst of which manifests a beautiful young woman, identified as Umā Haimavatī Śivā, while her description is that of Bhuvaneśvarī (the emergence of Bhuvaneśvarī out of the light in the *Devī Gītā* is described in the next several verses).

The *Devī Gītā*'s introduction of the Goddess clearly resembles, and seems consciously to have in mind, the story of the humbling of Agni, Vāyu, and Indra as a mythological backdrop. Nīlakaṇṭha immediately identifies the supreme lustrous power as Umā Haimavatī (see note 2 below), and the *Devī Gītā,* in its concluding chapter, refers to the Devī as Haimavatī (10.39). The introduction thus establishes by dramatic means the identity of the Goddess as the supreme Brahman of the Upaniṣads, an identification enhanced by the frequent use of Upaniṣadic terminology (verses 1.28–29). The blazing light symbolizes her nature as pure consciousness, her supreme, aniconic or formless form.

Of interest here also is the placement of the *Devī Gītā* in the *Devī-Bhāgavata.* In the preceding two chapters of the *Devī-Bhāgavata,*[10] Vyāsa narrates the story of the humbling of Viṣṇu and Śiva, a thoroughly Śāktacized transformation of the *Kena* motif. In this Śākta rendition, Śiva and Viṣṇu, the two most prominent deities in the older Purāṇas and members of the ruling triumvirate (Trimūrti), falsely claim credit for victory over a host of demons, a victory due in reality to the power of the Goddess. The consorts or energizing powers *(śaktis)* of the gods, Gaurī and Lakṣmī, offended by the arrogance of their husbands, abandon them and thereby render them unconscious. The third member of the triumvirate, Brahmā, is forced to carry out all three functions of creation, preservation, and destruction. To relieve the overburdened creator and revive the other two deities, Dakṣa and other sages retreat to the Himālaya Mountain to worship the Devī, reciting her Māyā-bīja. In time, she graciously appears before them in her form as Bhuvaneśvarī and promises to restore to Viṣṇu and Śiva their lost wives (cf. the Comment on 10.38–43ab). Śiva's wife is restored to him as Satī, whose death by fire and rebirth as Himālaya's daughter provides the lead-in for Vyāsa's narration of the *Devī Gītā.*

The *Devī Gītā*'s introductory frame story thus fully resonates with the mythic and theological motifs of the two "humbling" stories. The frame story thereby implicitly establishes the Goddess not only as the highest reality affirmed by the Upaniṣads, but also as the supreme power behind the primary gods of *bhakti*—Śiva and Viṣṇu—extolled in the earlier Purāṇas.

Notes

1. The bright or waxing half of the lunar month Caitra (March/April) marks the beginning of the lunar year in much of India. It is also the time for celebrating the vernal Navarātra or "Nine Night" ritual of the Goddess (see 8.42). The culmination of the celebration occurs on the last, or ninth lunar day (night). Although the *Devī Gītā* does not explicitly indicate that the ninth lunar day belongs to the bright half (rather than to the dark half) of Caitra, it seems clear that the bright ninth is intended, given the significance of the day.

The solar day Friday is generally auspicious, though with ambivalent qualities. It is regarded as highly appropriate for worshiping benevolent goddesses (cf. note 5 on 8.38, concerning Friday rites, and 10.18). The Goddess thus chose an especially powerful conjunction of lunar and solar days for her appearance (cf. Lawrence A. Babb, *The Divine Hierarchy,* p. 113, and Diana L. Eck, *Banaras: City of Light,* pp. 255–56, 258). It was also on the ninth lunar day of Caitra, according to the *Devī-Bhāgavata,* that the Goddess appeared before Indra in the story of his humbling (see the Comment above).

2. Nīlakaṇṭha quotes from the *śruti* {*Kena Upaniṣad* 3.12} in explaining the identity of the lustrous power: " 'In that same space [where the spirit had disappeared] he [Indra] came upon a woman brilliantly beautiful, Umā Haimavatī,' thus [says the *Kena*]. And so [Umā Haimavatī] is the 'lustrous power of Śakti revealed in scripture.' "

3. This description of the lustrous power, beginning with "It blazed like ten million suns . . . ," is identical to the description of the spirit/light that appeared before the gods in the *Devī-Bhāgavata*'s story of the humbling of Agni, Vāyu, and Indra (12.8.19cd–20a).

4. According to Nīlakaṇṭha, the red color is due to the lustrous power's assuming the quality of activity *(rajo-guṇa)* for the sake of showing favor *(anugraha).* (Red is especially the color associated with *rajas,* whereas white is associated with *sattva,* calming rest.) Nīlakaṇṭha's explanation is indirectly supported elsewhere in the *Devī-Bhāgavata.* In its story of the humbling of Agni, Vāyu, and Indra, the *Devī-Bhāgavata* says that the World-Mother appeared in the form of a blazing spirit *(yakṣa)* specifically to show favor *(anugraha)* to the gods (12.8.18–19).

5. This line closely resembles *Śvetāśvatara Upaniṣad* 4.19a: "Nothing encompasses that one above, across, or in the middle" *(nainam ūrdhvaṃ na tiryañcaṃ na madhye na parijagrabhat).* This latter line also occurs in the *Mahānārāyaṇa Upaniṣad* (1.10a). Cf. *Devī Upaniṣad* 3, where the Goddess declares: "I am below, above, and in the middle" *(adhaś cordhvam ca tiryak cāham).* (See the Comment on 1.42–53 below for discussion of the relation of the *Devī Gītā* and the *Devī Upaniṣad.*) Cf. also *Muṇḍaka Upaniṣad* 2.2.12, a verse quoted by the *Devī Gītā* in 6.14, which asserts that Brahman alone extends below and above, etc.

6. *Muṇḍaka* 1.1.6 describes the supreme as "without eyes or ears, without hands or feet." In the *Devī-Bhāgavata*'s account of the humbling of Agni, Vāyu, and Indra, the spirit/light that manifests itself before the gods is described as "lacking hands, feet, etc." (12.8.20).

7. In *Maitrī Upaniṣad* 6.5, the supreme is characterized as "woman, man, and eunuch," and in *Śvetāśvatara Upaniṣad* 4.3, as "woman, man, boy, and maiden." (This latter text, however, goes on to describe the individual self as "neither a woman, nor a man, nor a eunuch" [5.10].) Such gender-inclusive descriptions of the ultimate emphasize the all-encompassing nature of the highest reality, and are especially prominent in the more theistic descriptions of that ultimate, who appears in the form of a personal deity (*īśvara* or *īśvarī*) endowed with various sexual characteristics. The nontheistic Hindu perspective accents the transcendent/ineffable nature of the supreme, in the form of the neuter Brahman, which is "*neti neti*," neither this nor that, including neither male nor female. The *Devī Gītā* synthesizes the theistic and nontheistic perspectives: in her aspect as pure consciousness, the Devī is identical with Brahman and is symbolized by the aniconic form of dazzling light, without limbs, and without gender. In her most compassionate aspect as World-Mother, she is symbolized as the auspicious, four-armed Bhuvaneśvarī, who is about to emerge from the dazzling light.

8. *Devī-Bhāgavata* 12.8.12–86.

9. *Kena Upaniṣad* 3.1–4.3.

10. *Devī-Bhāgavata* 7.29.23–30.19.

Translation

[The light evolves into a beautiful, four-armed woman.]

1.30. The dazzling brilliance blinded the eyes of the gods, O King.
When again their vision returned, the gods beheld
1.31. That light appearing now in the form of a woman, charming and delightful.
She was exceedingly beautiful of limb, a maiden in the freshness of youth.
1.32. Her full, upraised breasts put to shame the swelling buds of the lotus.
Her girdle and anklets jingled with clusters of tinkling bells.

Figure 1.1 Bhuvaneśvarī Appearing in an Orb of Light before the Gods. The latter, including the Four Vedas, are symbolically represented by their standard symbolic emblems outside the perimeter of light. The orb of light is suggested by the encircling mandorla composed of lighted lamps. (Verses 1.30cd–41.) Pencil drawing by Dr. Bala Viswanathan.

1.33. She was adorned with a necklace, armlets, and bracelets of gold,
Her throat resplendent with a chain of priceless gems.
1.34. The locks on her cheeks shimmered like black bees swarming on delicate Ketaka blooms.
An exquisite line of down on her midriff enhanced the charm of her shapely hips.
1.35. She was chewing on Tāmbūla[1] mixed with bits of mint camphor.
Pendant earrings of shining gold graced her lotus face.
1.36. Above long eyebrows her forehead shone with an image of the crescent moon.
Her eyes were red lotus petals, her nose dignified, her lips like nectar.
1.37. Her teeth resembled buds of white jasmine; a string of pearls adorned her neck.
Her crescent-shaped crown sparkled with jewels; she was bedecked with ornaments shining like new moons.
1.38. A garland of jasmine flowers brightened her luxuriant hair.
Her forehead sported a saffron dot, while her three eyes reflected her playful mood.
1.39. Three-eyed and four-armed, she held a noose and goad while gesturing her beneficence and assurance of safety.[2]
She was dressed in red and appeared lustrous like blooms of the pomegranate.
1.40. Richly adorned in garments all suited for love,[3] she was worshiped by all the gods.
Satisfying all desires, she is the Mother of all, the Deluder of all.[4]
1.41. The Mother's kindly face, so gracious, displayed a tender smile on the lotus mouth.
This embodiment of unfeigned compassion the gods beheld in their presence.

Comment

In the *Devī-Bhāgavata,* the beautiful, four-armed form of the Goddess described in the preceding verses is her highest iconic manifestation, the wholly auspicious Bhuvaneśvarī (explicitly named in verse 1.50 below). The iconography of Bhuvaneśvarī is rich and complex. Her lavish adornments attest to her sovereignty over all wealth, beauty, and prosperity. While her luxurious and splendid attire, including her "garments all suited for love," points to an erotic element in the Goddess (discussed below), her wealth primarily emphasizes her maternal power, as World-Mother, to bestow all manner of comforts and pleasures on her children-devotees. She is endowed with three eyes, as she is ever awake and watchful, concerned with the well-being of her children. The crescent moon on her forehead symbolizes her power of renewal and regeneration that allows the Earth to replenish itself.[5] Her four hands, symbolizing various gifts to her devotees, will be discussed in detail in a moment.

This splendorous manifestation of the Goddess as Bhuvaneśvarī is the form she assumes in the beginning while undertaking the auspicious work of bringing the universe into existence. It is in her role as cosmic creatrix that her erotic side expresses itself. According to the *Devī-Bhāgavata,* the Goddess at the beginning of creation resides in her celestial paradise, the Jeweled Island, and for the sake of her own play (including amorous sport, we may assume), divides herself into two halves. One half becomes Bhuvaneśa (Śiva), the other half remaining as Bhuvaneśī or Bhuvaneśvarī herself, who takes her seat on Śiva's left thigh. Only by such contact with her, the text stresses, is Śiva able to become ruler of all.[6]

A parallel cosmogonic motif is briefly narrated in the story of the humbling of Agni, Vāyu, and Indra. When questioned by Indra as to what the Yakṣa/Light truly is, Devī responds: "That [Yakṣa] form of mine is Brahman. . . . The single-syllable Brahman is 'Oṃ';[7] it is composed of the syllable 'Hrīṃ' *(hrīṃ-mayam),* so they[8] say. These two seed syllables are my chief mantras. . . . I assume both parts in order to create the whole world. The former part is called infinite being, consciousness, and bliss. The second part is known as Māyā and Prakṛti—that Māyā endowed with supreme power is I, the Īśvarī (Ruler/Queen)."[9] The Īśvarī, of course, is Bhuvaneśvarī, whose seed mantra is Hrīṃ. (See 1.53 below.)

After the creation, the Goddess remains in her form as Bhuvaneśvarī while overseeing the universe from her Jeweled Island. This is also the form she assumes when she appears in the world to greet or show favor to devout petitioners. Bhuvaneśvarī's benevolent and compassionate nature toward her children, especially her devotees, is well indicated by her four hands with their emblems and gestures. In a general sense, they represent her ability to bestow the four primary ends of life *(puruṣārthas)*, that is, virtue, wealth, pleasure, and liberation (see the Introduction, p. 3).

The *Prapañcasāra Tantra* explains the four hands and emblems of the Goddess in more specific fashion.[10] The noose *(pāśa)* embodies and reveals her ability to protect *(pā)* and to pervade *(aś)* the universe, since she protects all, pervading all things by a portion of herself that is the Self in all beings. The goad *(aṅkuśa)* symbolizes her power to draw or drag physical bodies toward the Self or Ātman. The Ātman is represented by *aṅ*, the body both by *ku* (meaning "earth," or "body"), and by *śa* (for *śarīra*, "body"). The gesture of assurance (*abhaya*, literally, "fearlessness") reveals her capacity to free a person from fear arising from the thought of losing one's wealth, and from dismay when contemplating the inexorable cycle of rebirth. The gesture of beneficence (*vara*, "boon, blessing, or wish," in the *Devī Gītā*; *iṣṭa*, "wish, desire" in the *Prapañcasāra Tantra*) signals her power to give what is just merely desired in thought.

Contemporary sources suggest other symbolic meanings to Bhuvaneśvarī's four hands that stress her role in the binding and liberation of beings. The hands holding the noose and goad point to her ruling powers, especially her control over demonic and evil forces, both external and internal. With the noose, she binds, as it were, the Self or Ātman within the body, with its sensual cravings, and with the goad she disciplines the seeker to transcend the various obstacles to liberation, such as anger and lust. The noose also binds the very senses and cravings with which she has bound the Self, emphasizing her role not only as the enchanting and captivating Māyā, but also as the liberating knowledge that brings fearlessness and the full enjoyment of her bounty, symbolized by her gestures of *abhaya* and *vara*, respectively.[11]

At times Bhuvaneśvarī appears directly to her devotees, as in the story of the humbling of Śiva and Viṣṇu.[12] At other times, as in the story of the humbling of Agni, Vāyu, and Indra, and here in the *Devī Gītā*, the Devī appears as Bhuvaneśvarī only after first manifesting as a blazing orb of light. Figure 1.1, page 63 illustrates the emergence of the Goddess out of the brilliant *mahas*, appearing before the stunned gods assembled on Himālaya, and surrounded on each side by the four Vedas singing her praise.

Bhuvaneśvarī's emergence from the light closely resembles that of the beautiful Lalitā in the *Lalitā Māhātmya* of the *Brahmāṇḍa Purāṇa*. There, when the gods (tormented by demons, as per custom) worship the Goddess with human flesh, a huge mass of light first appears before them. Then in its midst they perceive the lovely Lalitā, lavishly adorned, the abode of love, gracious, with a noose, goad, sugarcane bow and five arrows in her four hands.[13] The close resemblance of these two thoroughly auspicious Tantric goddesses was noted in the Introduction (pp. 25–26).

The various manifestations of the Goddess out of the blinding brilliance parallels Śiva's emergence from the Emblem of Infinite Light (Jyotir-liṅga) in the famous myth of the origin of his Liṅga (see the Introduction, pp. 11–12). The motif of Devī's emergence from her own orb of infinite light serves as a counterpart to Śiva's self-manifestation, suggesting at once her superiority over one of her chief male rivals, as well as her identity with the supreme Brahman that is the infinite light of consciousness.

The lovely, four-armed Bhuvaneśvarī is not only the Devī's preferred form for auspicious manifestation, it is also one of three aspects of the Goddess that are prime objects of meditation. The other two are her aspects as infinite being, consciousness, and bliss *(sac-cid-ānanda),* and as the Cosmic Body (Virāj).[14] The latter we shall meet in chapter 3 of the *Devī Gītā.* The former, of course, is the Goddess as Brahman, that is, as pure consciousness, symbolized aniconically by the blazing light called *mahas.* These three forms as meditation objects are discussed in chapter 9 below. While in such meditative contexts, the iconic forms tend to be subordinated to the aniconic, the beautiful Bhuvaneśvarī is the object of loving description, rich in symbolic meaning, and the focus of the highest devotion throughout the text.

Notes

1. Tāmbūla is a mixture of betel nut, betel leaves, and several other spicy ingredients such as cardamom and clove, chewed after meals to freshen the breath. It is a standard offering to the gods in *pūjā* (cf. 10.21), and descriptions of the Goddess often describe her as chewing on Tāmbūla, as in the description of Lalitā in the *Lalitā-Māhātmya* of the *Brahmāṇḍa Purāṇa* (37.79). Cf. Pandurang Vaman Kane, *History of Dharmaśāstra,* vol. 2, pp. 734–35.

2. This line specifies the essential, identifying characteristics of the Goddess as Bhuvaneśvarī. The *Śāradā-Tilaka Tantra* catalogues the *dhyāna*s (iconic forms to be visualized in meditation) of a number of gods and goddesses. Chapter 9 of that work is devoted to describing Bhuvaneśvarī, introducing her as the World-Mother *(jagad-dhātrī).* Her *dhyāna* given there is as follows: "One should worship Bhuvaneśvarī as having the luster of the rising sun, with the moon in her crown, with prominent breasts, three-eyed, smiling, gesturing beneficence and assurance of safety while holding a noose and goad" (9.14). The *Devī Upaniṣad* (24) gives a similar meditation for Bhuvaneśvarī: "I worship her who resides in the lotus of the heart, shining like the sun, bearing the noose and goad, gentle, gesturing beneficence and assurance of safety, three-eyed,

dressed in red, a wish-fulfilling cow to her devotees." In the *Prapañcasāra Tantra,* a goddess called both Prakṛti ("Nature") and Prapañca-svarūpā ("Essence of the Universe"), and who appears to be identical with Bhuvaneśvarī, is described as having the brilliance of a thousand rising suns, ever radiating through the infinity of space, with a crescent moon on her head, and bearing in two of her hands the noose and goad, while gesturing her assurance and blessings with the other two (11.64; cf. 10.10 for a similar description). While other divergent *dhyānas* or descriptions of Bhuvaneśvarī exist, including even a twenty-armed form, the above four-armed form seems to be the classic standard.

3. *śṛṅgāra;* it is one of the nine poetic sentiments and refers specifically to erotic love and sexual passion. For the significance of the erotic aspect of the Goddess, see the Comment above.

4. The Goddess as the universal Mother fulfills the desires of her children, yet these very desires are due to the illusion of being separated from her, an illusion brought about by her own deluding power of Māyā.

5. The above observations regarding the significance of the three eyes and the crescent moon are based on an unpublished ms. on Bhuvaneśvarī ("Bhuvaneśvarī: Whose Body is the World," pp. 15–16), by David Kinsley. A complementary interpretation of the crescent moon is provided by Alain Daniélou, who quotes from a Hindi source: "With the ambrosia made from the lunar essence, that is, the seed, the sacrificial offering, *soma,* she [Bhuvaneśvarī] quenches the thirst of the world. This is why the all-powerful goddess has the moon, the cup of *soma,* as her diadem" (*Hindu Polytheism,* p. 279).

6. *Devī-Bhāgavata* 12.12.13–14, 17, 39.

7. Cf. *Bhagavad-Gītā* 8.13.

8. The Vedas, according to Nīlakaṇṭha.

9. *Devī-Bhāgavata* 12.8.62–66.

10. *Prapañcasāra Tantra* 10.11–14.

11. The interpretations given in this paragraph are derived from descriptions given by Kinsley in his unpublished manuscript on Bhuvaneśvarī (p. 16). His descriptions are based in part on interviews with Hindu informants in Varanasi.

12. *Devī-Bhāgavata* 7.30.1–3.

13. *Brahmāṇḍa Purāṇa* 3.4.12.68–73.

14. See e.g., *Devī-Bhāgavata* 7.30.15–16.

Translation

[The gods sing the praises of Bhuvaneśvarī, Ruler of the Universe.]

1.42. Seeing her, the embodiment of compassion, the entire host of gods bowed low,
Unable to speak, choking on tears in silence.

1.43. Struggling to regain their composure, their necks bending in devotion,
Their eyes brimming with tears of loving joy,[1] they glorified the World-Mother with hymns.

The gods spoke:

1.44. Hail to the Goddess, to the Great Goddess; to the Auspicious One always hail!
Hail to Nature,[2] to the Propitious One; we humble ourselves attentively before her.[3]

1.45. To her, the color of fire, blazing like the sun with ascetic power,[4] and who is worshiped for attaining the fruits of action,
To her, the Goddess Durgā, I go for refuge. Hail to that raft of swift crossing.[5]

1.46. The gods created the Goddess Speech, whom animals of all sorts speak.
This Speech is pleasing to us, this cow yielding food and strength. She is well praised; may she come to us.[6]

1.47. To Kālarātrī praised by Brahmā,[7] to Vaiṣṇavī,[8] to the Mother of Skanda,
To Sarasvatī, to Aditi, the Daughter of Dakṣa,[9] we bow, to the pure Auspicious One.[10]

1.48. We know you as Mahālakṣmī, we meditate on you as the Śakti of all.
May the Goddess inspire that knowledge and meditation of ours.[11]

1.49. Hail to her in the form of the Cosmic Body;[12] hail to her in the form of the Cosmic Soul;[13]
Hail to her in the Unmanifest State;[14] hail to her in the form of the glorious Brahman.[15]

1.50. Through her power of ignorance, she shows herself as the world, like a rope appearing as a serpent, wreath, and the like.[16]
Through her power of knowledge, she dissolves the world back into herself.[17] We glorify her, Ruler of the Universe.[18]

1.51. We glorify her whose essence is pure consciousness, represented by the word *Tat*,[19]
And whose nature is undiminished bliss. It is she to whom the Vedas refer as their goal.

1.52. Transcending the five sheaths,[20] witness of the three states of consciousness,[21]
She is also in essence the individual soul, represented by the word *Tvam*.[22]

1.53. Hail to her in the form of the syllable Oṃ;[23] hail to her embodied in the syllable Hrīṃ.[24]
To her composed of manifold mantras,[25] that is to you the compassionate Goddess, hail! Hail!"

Comment

This Hymn to the Goddess may be divided into three parts. The first, verses 44–48, uses Vedic or Vedicized mantras in praising the Goddess. These five verses have been borrowed from a "Devī Stuti" ("Hymn to the Goddess") in the Śākta *Devī Upaniṣad*.[26] The *Devī Upaniṣad*'s hymn represents a collection of more ancient mantras in honor of various female divinities (the original source of each is indicated in the notes to the verses). Well before the time of the *Devī Upaniṣad* (ninth to fourteenth centuries),[27] the different goddesses had come to be seen as simply diverse manifestations or aspects of the Great Goddess.[28] In any case, for the devout practitioner, these five verses resonate with the power of Vedic utterances and affirm the Vedic identity of the Goddess.

The second part of the hymn, verses 49–52, utilizes the teachings of Advaita Vedānta in order to establish the essential nature of the

Goddess as the nondual Brahman. She is identified with the four quarters or states of consciousness that constitute the four aspects of Brahman as delineated in the *Māṇḍūkya Upaniṣad.* As Brahman, she is the substrate of the universe, appearing as the world through her power of ignorance or Māyā, her relation to the world being illustrated by the famous Advaitic analogy of the rope appearing as a snake. At this point, the gods refer to her as Bhuvaneśvarī, the great Tantric goddess who rules the universe. And finally she is identified with both the "Tat" and the "Tvam" of the Upaniṣadic Great Saying, "Tat tvam asi" ("You are That"), an affirmation in itself of the essential unity of Brahman ("Tat") and the individual soul ("Tvam").

The third part, consisting of the final verse, 53, refers to the two chief mantras of the Goddess: Oṃ, the one-syllable mantra of Brahman; and Hrīṃ, the seed mantra of Bhuvaneśvarī, also known as the Hṛllekhā (see verse 1.25). The significance of Hrīṃ vis-a-vis Oṃ in Tantric practice is nicely set forth in the *Mahānirvāṇa Tantra.* According to that text, in the first three world ages, the recitation of mantras was preceded by the Praṇava (the syllable Oṃ), but in this Kali age, the same mantras are recited, but preceded by the Māyā-bīja (Hrīṃ).[29] The implication is that in this dangerous and degenerate age of Kali, the Tantric Hrīṃ is a more powerful and efficacious means of attaining the fruits of mantra recitation than is the Vedic Oṃ. Hrīṃ is referred to, in fact, as the Tantric Praṇava.[30]

The *Devī Gītā* in its practical and devotional side focuses much more on Hrīṃ than Oṃ, but here, in its theoretical and symbolical representation of the nature of the Goddess, balances the two. The *Devī Gītā*'s hymn thus concludes by fusing Vedic and Tantric sonic symbolizations of ultimate reality. The verse hereby points to the two highest modes of the Goddess: her formless, aniconic aspect as Brahman, and her supreme iconic manifestation as Ruler of the universe, Bhuvaneśvarī.

Regarding Hrīṃ itself, it is the sonic essence of the World-Mother reverberating throughout the universe and within the hearts of beings, uniting all opposites in peace and harmony. Such cosmic and salvific meanings are embedded in the very structure of the syllable itself, in its letters and parts, according to various esoteric, Tantric explanations. For instance, the Goddess is said to be the mother who shines within, or pervades (from *ī,* "to shine," and "to pervade") the heart of beings, removing (from *hṛ,* "to carry away") their pain.[31] Or, the *h* represents Śiva, the *r* Śakti, and *ī* their union that produces tranquillity.[32] The *Varadā Tantra* provides the following esoteric correspondences, synthesizing the above two interpretations: "The letter 'h' signifies Śiva; 'r' means Prakṛti; the 'ī' indicates Mahāmāyā; the *nāda* (the nasal sound of the 'm') represents the Mother of the universe; and the *bindu* (the dot of the 'm,' the silent reverberation of the syllable following its audible recitation) signifies that she is the remover of sorrow."[33] (For another set of esoteric correspondences, see note 5 on 1.45.)

Notes

1. *preman;* ecstatic love or loving joy, characterized by such signs as weeping, stammering, and hair standing on end. Such emotionalistic devotion is emphasized in the *Bhāgavata Purāṇa* and has roots in the *Bhagavad Gītā,* in Arjuna's response to the cosmic revelation of Kṛṣṇa (11.14,35). Cf. *Devī Gītā* 3.41–42ab, 7.20, and 10.24 below.

2. In Śākta theology, Nature (Prakṛti) is an aspect or form of the Goddess and is not simply unconscious matter as in the Sāṃkhya philosophy. She is, rather, the power behind all the manifest world, including the power of consciousness.

3. This verse is identical to the opening verse of the hymn of praise offered by the gods to the Goddess in the fifth chapter of the *Devī Māhātmya* (5.7). In the *Devī Māhātmya,* the gods have gone to Himālaya to praise the Goddess to obtain help against the demons Śumbha and Niśumbha, a somewhat parallel situation to that of the gods in the *Devī Gītā.*

Nīlakaṇṭha refers to this verse as a Vedic *(vaidika)* mantra, probably because it is also the first verse of the "Hymn to the Goddess" in the *Devī Upaniṣad* (8–13). The following four verses of the *Devī Gītā* are also found in the *Devī Upaniṣad*'s hymn, which is the immediate source of quotation for the *Devī Gītā*'s author. The *Devī Gītā* specifically mentions the *Devī Upaniṣad* (referred to as the *Devī Atharvaśiras*) in 10.22.

4. Nīlakaṇṭha interprets "ascetic power" *(tapas)* as "knowledge" *(jñāna),* indicating the omniscience *(sarva-jñā)* of the Goddess." In support of this explanation, Nīlakaṇṭha refers to the *Muṇḍaka Upaniṣad* {1.1.8–9}, where Brahman is called omniscient *(sarva-jña),* and whose ascetic power is said to be knowledge *(jñāna).*

5. "Swift crossing" refers to crossing over the ocean of troubles that is samsara. Cf. the praise of the Goddess in *Devī-Māhātmya* 4.11b: "You are Durgā, the boat that takes men across the difficult ocean of worldly existence" (Jagadisvarananda's translation).

Nīlakaṇṭha says the verse (*Devī Gītā* 1.45) is a "*Ṛg* mantra." In fact it is identical with the *Ṛg Veda*'s Rātrī Khila 4.2.12 (which repeats the final refrain) and recurs also in *Taittirīya Āraṇyaka* 10.1. In this latter passage, there occurs a series of Gāyatrī mantras invoking various deities, one of whom is the goddess Kātyāyanī/Durgī. The *Devī Gītā* has its own "Devī-Gāyatrī" three verses down (1.48). The *Taittirīya Āraṇyaka* then quotes *Ṛg Veda* 1.99, a one verse hymn to Agni (Fire) as a boat of safety, and then gives the verse quoted in the *Devī Gītā*. (For discussion of the *Taittirīya Āraṇyaka* passage, see Thomas B. Coburn, *Devī-Māhātmya: The Crystallization of the Goddess Tradition,* pp. 117–18. Coburn provides a translation of the whole of the Rātrī Khila on pp. 265–67. See also Kane, *History of Dharmaśāstra,* vol. 5, p. 1045.) The immediate source of the quotation on which the author of the *Devī Gītā* relied is almost certainly the *Devī Upaniṣad* (see Comment above).

Nīlakaṇṭha, citing the third and fourth chapters of the *Prapañcasāra Tantra* as authority, provides an esoteric, Tantric interpretation of the verse: the word *agni* (fire) represents the seed mantra of Agni, i.e., *raṃ,* or the letter *r;* the word *tapas* (ascetic power) signifies Māyā, which represents the letter *ī; virocana* (sun) represents the seed mantra of Sūrya, i.e., *haṃ,* or the letter *h;* and the sovereign power within the sun that is the essence of *h* is the *bindu* or *ṃ*. (Regarding the correlation of deities and *bījas*, see Bharati, *The Tantric Tradition,* pp. 117–18, and the Comment above.) Thus, Durgā is the embodiment of the Māyābīja, Hrīṃ. In other words, according to this Tantric-style interpretation, to take refuge in Durgā is to take refuge in the mantra of Bhuvaneśvarī.

6. As Nīlakaṇṭha points out once again, this verse is a *Ṛg* mantra, in this case being identical to *Ṛg Veda* 8.100.11. The immediate source, however, is the *Devī Upaniṣad* (see Comment above).

Speech, or Vāc, is one of the most important female deities of the Vedic texts. She is often portrayed as an all-pervading, cosmogonic principle, associated especially with the creative power of the waters. This verse reveals that "Vāc apparently also has a more nourishing, maternal dimension [in the Vedic literature], and, like other goddesses . . . , she is likened to a cow and is described as yielding food" (Tracy Pintchman, *The Rise of the Goddess in the Hindu Tradition,* p. 40). (See also André Padoux, *Vāc: The Concept of the Word in Selected Hindu Tantras,* p. 8.) The cow, in her aspect of providing the comforts and desires of life, came to be idealized in the image of a magical "wish-granting" cow, the *kāma-dughā,* similar to the notion of the "wish-fulfilling tree" *(kāma-kalpa-druma).* The Goddess in her beneficent mode is likened to both. (See 1.15 above, and 1.55, 3.22 below.)

7. This refers to Brahmā's eulogizing of the goddess Yoganidrā, on the occasion of the battle between Viṣṇu and the demons Madhu and Kaiṭabha, described in the first chapter of the *Devī-Māhātmya.* In his praise, Brahmā refers to the goddess as Kālarātrī (1.59), the "Night of destruction," signifying her role as the destroyer of all at the time of the cosmic dissolution. The *Devī Gītā,* while not denying the destructive power of the Goddess, emphasizes much more her creative and nurturing aspects.

8. According to Nīlakaṇṭha, "Vaiṣnavī" and the following two names of the Goddess, "Mother of Skanda," and "Sarasvatī," refer to the *śaktis* of the Trimūrti: Viṣṇu's Lakśmī, Śiva's Pārvatī, and Brahmā's Sarasvatī, respectively.

9. According to Nīlakaṇṭha, Aditi, the Mother of the gods, is the daughter of Dakṣa (following Vedic tradition), otherwise known as Satī.

10. The several goddesses named in this verse, according to Nīlakaṇṭha, are simply various forms of the Goddess Bhuvaneśvarī. He also indicates that this verse is a mantra from the *Devī Atharvaśiras* (the *Devī Upaniṣad*) (see Comment above).

11. This verse is in the form of the famous Gāyatrī mantra of *Ṛg Veda* 3.62.10. The Vedic original invokes the god Savitṛ or the Sun. In the later tradition, the power embodied in the mantra came to be seen as the goddess Gāyatrī. Further, the mantra itself has been much imitated, or rather recreated, with various other deities, male and female, being substituted for Savitṛ. Already in *Taittirīya Āraṇyaka* 10.1, we find a Gāyatrī to Kātyāyanī, also called Durgī. *Devī Gītā* 1.48 is a typical Śākta recreation, with Mahālakṣmī being the deity invoked. Cf. the following Durgā Gāyatrī: *mahādevyai ca vidmahe durgādevyai ca dhīmahi tanno devī pracodayāt* (quoted by I. K. Taimni, *Gāyatrī: The Daily Religious Practice of the Hindus,* p. 61). Nīlakaṇṭha notes that the *Devī Gītā*'s Gāyatrī occurs in the *Devī Atharvaśiras* (see Comment above).

Repetition of this "Devī Gāyatrī" not only prepares the devotee for meditation, but also invites the Goddess to appear in person before the reciter. It is also the first verse of the "Navaślokī Devī Gītā."

12. *virāj;* the Gross, Material Body of the Goddess, identified with the myriad parts of the physical universe. The word *virāj* comes from a verbal root meaning both to rule and to shine, be beautiful or eminent. For further explication of the Virāj, see chapter 3 (especially the Comment on 3.22–34), where the Goddess displays this magnificent, shining body to the gods.

13. The *sūtrātman* is the Subtle Body of the Goddess as the World or Cosmic Soul, pervading the whole universe like a thread *(sūtra)* running through a string of pearls. Cf. *Bhagavad Gītā* 7.7cd, where Kṛṣṇa says that the whole universe is strung on him like pearls on a string. Cf. also *Dhyānabindu Upaniṣad* 6ab: "All beings are established on the Self, like pearls on a thread."

14. The *avyākṛta* is the Unmanifest or Causal Body of the Goddess, identified with the Lord *(īśvara).*

15. As Nīlakaṇṭha indicates, the four forms mentioned here constitute the fourfold Brahman *(catuṣpād-brahma).* In the *Māṇḍūkya Upaniṣad* the four aspects or quarters of Brahman relating to the Self and its states of consciousness are given. These are the *vaiśvānara (viśva)* or waking state, the *taijasa* or dream state, the *prajña* or state of deep sleep, and the *caturtha (turīya)* or fourth, nondual state. According to later Advaita tradition, these four correspond to cosmic aspects of the supreme being: the *virāj,* the *sūtrātman,* the *īśvara* (the Causal Body or Lord in an unmanifest state), and the transcendent Brahman. The first three quarters or bodies, in their cosmic and individual aspects, are enumerated in *Devī Gītā* 2.47–48. (Cf. 3.13ab.) This verse is the second of the "Navaślokī Devī Gītā."

16. The example of the rope and snake is probably the most famous analogy utilized in Advaita for explaining the existence of multiplicity (the world) in relation to the absolute, nondual Brahman. The analogy specifically is meant to show that the world is not an evolution *(pariṇāma)* from Brahman, but is merely an appearance *(vivarta)* of it—Brahman undergoes no real change at all, just as the rope undergoes no real modification but is simply falsely perceived.

The usual explanation of this false perception is in terms of "superimposition" *(adhyāsa):* just as the notion of a snake may be falsely superimposed on a rope lying in the path at dusk, so is the notion of the world falsely superimposed on Brahman. The *Devī Gītā*'s use of the analogy, employing the verb *bhā,* meaning both "to appear" and to "shine forth" or "show oneself," may suggest a somewhat different, less illusionistic, aspect of the appearance: the single substrate (the Goddess/rope) "shines forth," "shows herself/itself," or "appears" *(bhāti)* as many different things (the world with its multiple souls/the serpent, wreath, etc.). From this perspective, the emphasis is on the creative, projecting power of the Devī's Māyā that shines forth, rather than merely on the deluded misperception of the universe on the part of the individual soul. Surendranath Dasgupta, utilizing the rope-snake analogy, nicely characterizes these two aspects of Māyā with reference to the two powers (obscuring/covering, and creative) of ignorance *(ajñāna):* "It is through this covering power of *ajñāna* that the self appears as an agent and an enjoyer of pleasures and pains and subject to ignorant fears of rebirth, like the illusory perception of a piece of rope in darkness as a snake. Just as through the creative power of ignorance a piece of rope, the real nature of which is hidden from view, appears as a snake, so does ignorance by its creative power create on the hidden self the manifold world-appearance" (*A History of Indian Philosophy,* vol. 2, pp. 73–74). The *Devī Gītā* repeats the same rope-wreath-snake analogy in 3.18.

As for the inclusion of the wreath in the analogy, there is some precedent in the *Naiṣkarmya Siddhi* of Sureṣvara (ninth century, C.E.), though he employs the wreath, or garland, as a substitute for the rope. The *Naiṣkarmya Siddhi* opens with the following invocation: "Reverence to that Hari, the destroyer of darkness and witness of the intellect, from whom the world consisting of ether, air, fire, water and earth has come forth in mere appearance—like the snake *(phaṇī)* which appears to exist in a garland *(srak)*" (Alston's translation). And in 2.31: "It is only he whose mind is afflicted by darkness who sees a snake in a rope through error. Therefore no one sees a snake in a garland except through error" (Alston's trans.). There were thus a number of versions of the rope-snake analogy. (*Naiṣkarmya Siddhi* 4.38 refers to a snake imagined in a stick *[daṇḍa-sarpa].*)

The *Devī Gītā* in this verse simply refers to the "rope-snake-wreath-etc. analogy." I have interpreted the rope as the substrate for both the serpent and wreath in conformity with the clearer statement in *Devī Gītā* 3.18. In addition, I have emphasized the role of the Goddess as the metaphysical substrate, in accord with the *Devī Gītā*'s basic understanding of the Goddess. This line

(1.50ab) could be rendered minimally as "Through her power of ignorance, the world appears, just as a snake or wreath may appear in a rope."

Sadānanda (*Vedāntasāra* 137) refers to the rope-snake analogy, then a few verses later (vv. 143 ff.) commences on an explication of "*Tat*" and "*Tvam*" ("That" and "You"), as does the *Devī Gītā* in the next two verses.

17. Again, I have emphasized the aspect of the Goddess as the metaphysical substrate, into which the world eventually dissolves. The line could simply be rendered, "Through her power of knowledge, the world becomes dissolved."

18. Bhuvaneśvarī ("Ruler of the Universe") is the name of the highest iconic form of the Goddess in the *Devī-Bhāgavata*. See Comment on 1.30–41, and the Introduction, pp. 3–4.

This verse is the third included in the "Navaślokī Devī Gītā."

19. *Tat* is the first word in the famous Great Saying of the Upaniṣads, "Tat tvam asi" ("You are That"). See note 22 below.

20. The five are: *ānanda-maya-kośa* (the bliss sheath), *vijñāna-maya-kośa* (the intelligence sheath), *mano-maya-kośa* (the mind sheath), *prāṇa-maya-kośa* (the breath sheath), and *anna-maya-kośa* (the food sheath). The five obscure the true Self that lies hidden within. The notion of the five sheaths first appears in the *Taittirīya Upaniṣad* (2.1–5). For further explanation of the five sheaths, see *Devī Gītā* 4.30–31.

In *Pañcadaśī* 3.22, it is said that when the five sheaths are discarded, what remains is the witness *(sākṣī)*, mentioned in the next half line of the *Devī Gītā*.

21. The three states are waking, dream, and deep sleep, beyond which is the fourth, nondual state of pure consciousness (cf. note 15 above). Cf. *Vivekacūḍāmaṇi* 125: "There is a certain, eternal substratum of the ego-consciousness, witness of the three states, different from the five sheaths." The witness *(sākṣin)* in Advaita is the self-luminous consciousness that illumines all else. Cf. also *Kaivalya Upaniṣad* 18, where Sadāśiva, identified with Brahman, declares that he is different from the three states of consciousness, being their witness.

In *Devī Gītā* 1.59 the witness-nature of the Goddess is equated with her omniscience.

22. *Tvam* is the second word of the Great Saying, "Tat tvam asi" ("You are That"). The saying points to the oneness *(aikyam)* of the ultimate reality, "Tat" or Brahman (here identified with the Goddess), and the "Tvam" or individual soul (*pratyag-ātman* or *jīva*). The *Devī Gītā* discusses the saying in more detail in 4.18–23.

23. The text here refers to Oṃ by the term *praṇava*, "humming," as the syllable "is recited with a nasalized hum" (Georg Feuerstein, *Encyclopedic Dictionary of Yoga*, p. 267). It is a common designation of this sacred Vedic

syllable. The *Devī Gītā* also uses the term *praṇava* to refer to Bhuvaneśvarī's seed mantra Hrīṃ, calling it the *devī-praṇava* (4.41).

24. *Devī Gītā* 3.45 also identifies the Goddess with Oṃ and Hrīṃ.

The *Devī Upaniṣad,* shortly after the verses in the hymn to the Goddess quoted by the *Devī Gītā,* refers to the seed mantra Hrīṃ in verses 20–21. The *Devī Upaniṣad* refers only to Hrīṃ, without mention of Oṃ. For an explanation of Hrīṃ, see the Comment above.

25. Cf. *Devī Upaniṣad* 27, where the Goddess is referred to as the Mother *(mātṛkā)* of mantras.

26. *Devī Upaniṣad* 8–12. The verses in the *Devī Gītā* are nearly identical, with only minor variations in a couple of lines. For more on the relation of the *Devī Gītā* and *Devī Upaniṣad,* see the Introduction, pp. 25–26.

27. See the Introduction, p. 25.

28. This process was largely completed by the time of the *Devī Māhātmya* (fifth or sixth century C.E.). See Coburn, *Devī-Māhātmya,* esp. pp. 53–56, 306.

29. *Mahānirvāṇa Tantra* 9.9–10. See Gonda, *Change and Continuity in Indian Religion,* p. 436.

30. Cf. note 23 above.

31. Cf. Douglas Renfrew Brooks, *Auspicious Wisdom,* p. 103.

32. See Beck, *Sonic Theology,* p. 138.

33. The *Varadā Tantra* text (from chapter 6) is quoted and translated in John Woodroffe, *The Garland of Letters,* p. 244. The translation is mine.

Another approach to interpreting the significance of seed mantras utilizes a less esoteric, more scientific and historical etymological analysis. Bharati, in arguing against an older scholarly notion that seed mantras are mere nonsense syllables, looks for a mythic or literary source underlying them. In the case of "Hṛīṃ," he writes: "it ['hṛīṃ'] is always used when a female deity is concerned, or extended to a male god when his image is to be conjured up together with his female counterpart. . . . Now the Indian root for 'modesty,' 'bashfulness,' etc., i.e. connoting the feminine virtue extolled as supreme since the Vedic period, is *hrī*" (*The Tantric Tradition,* p. 115). Bharati then cites as traditional support for his interpretation the following statement from Tarkalankara's commentary to the *Mahānirvāṇa: "Hrīṃ hrīrlajjārupatvāt"* (translated by Bharati as *"hrīṃ*—because of Her being of the form of modesty") (*The Tantric Tradition,* p. 156). While Bharati's interpretation seems sound on historical and mythic grounds, its relevance for the theological vision of the *Devī Gītā* is minimal. Bhuvaneśvarī, as she appears in the *Devī Gītā,* is subordinate to no male, and bashfulness or modesty is hardly her supreme feminine virtue.

Translation

[A dialogue ensues between the Goddess and the gods, and she promises her assistance.]

Vyāsa continued:

1.54. Thus praised by the gods, she who dwells in the Jeweled Island then
Answered in the sweet, joyous tones of the cuckoo.

The blessed Goddess spoke:

1.55. O wise gods, explain the reason that brings you together here.
I am ever the bestower of boons, a wish-yielding tree to devotees.
1.56. You shine with devotion, so why are you anxious when I stand nearby?
I rescue my devotees from the troubled ocean of samsara.
1.57. Know this promise of mine to be sincere, O best of gods.

Vyāsa continued:

Hearing these words infused with loving joy, the gods were satisfied in their hearts.
1.58. Freed from fear, the immortals described their own ordeal, O King.

The gods spoke:

Nothing here in the three worlds is unknown to you,
1.59. Who are omniscient, the incarnate witness of all,[1] O Supreme Ruler.
The demon chief Tāraka torments us day and night.
1.60. His death shall come only at the hands of Śiva's son—so has Brahmā arranged, O Auspicious One.
But as you know, Great Ruler, Śiva has no wife.

1.61. What can ignorant beings reveal to one who is omniscient?
Such is our situation in brief; you can infer the rest, O Mother.
1.62. May we always show unswerving devotion to your lotus feet;
This is our foremost wish. We also pray that you will assume a body.[2]

Vyāsa continued:

1.63. The Supreme Ruler listened to these words of theirs and gave reply.

The Goddess spoke:

My potency who is Gaurī will be born to Himālaya.
1.64. She will be given in marriage to Śiva and will furnish what you need.
You shall be devoted to my lotus feet due to your earnest desire.
1.65. Himālaya, moved by intense devotion, truly worships me in his heart.
Thus I consider it a pleasure to take birth in his house.[3]

Comment

In this dialogue between Bhuvaneśvarī and the gods, we see clearly the subordination of the ancient theme of the conflict between the gods and demons to the ideals of *bhakti* (see the Introduction, p. 6). The gods make two appeals, one for the Goddess to incarnate in order to marry Śiva and to bear his son who will slay Tāraka, but their prime request is for "unswerving devotion to her lotus feet." This latter symbolizes the highest devotion that has no ulterior motive *(niṣkāma)*.

The frame story of the *Devī Gītā* regarding the birth of Gaurī/Pārvatī is based on older Śākta *gītās* such as the *Kūrma Devī Gītā* of the *Kūrma Purāṇa* and the *Pārvatī Gītā* of the *Mahābhāgavata Purāṇa* (see the Introduction, pp. 9–11). In the *Kūrma Devī Gītā*, the divine teachings are given to Himālaya by Pārvatī immediately after her birth. The *Pārvatī Gītā* closely patterns its own frame story upon that of the *Kūrma Devī Gītā.*

The *Devī Gītā* makes a significant innovation in the traditional pattern. The Goddess here enters into the account, first as the supreme lustrous light symbolizing Brahman, and then as Bhuvaneśvarī, prior to the birth of Pārvatī. The birth of Pārvatī or Gaurī is only briefly narrated, at the close of the Gītā. The teachings of the *Devī Gītā,* then, are delivered not by Gaurī, but by the Goddess in her highest form as Bhuvaneśvarī, when she is queried about the highest truth by Himālaya. The older Pārvatī-Himālaya dialogue now becomes the Bhuvaneśvarī-Himālaya dialogue. Gaurī/Pārvatī, traditionally seen as the spouse of Śiva, might easily be regarded as at least partially subordinate to him. Such subordination is clearly present in the *Kūrma Devī Gītā.* The *Devī Gītā* explicitly refers to Gaurī as simply a potency *(śakti)* of the Goddess (1.63cd), thereby affirming the absolute supremacy of the Goddess herself: she is the consort of none, the Śakti of all.[4]

Notes

1. Cf. the *Devī Upaniṣad* (27), which refers to the Goddess as beyond all states of knowing and as witnessing the emptiness of nonentities *(śūnyānāṃ śūnya-sākṣiṇī).* See also note 21 on 1.52 above.

2. For the purpose of conceiving a son by Śiva.

3. Nīlakaṇṭha refers to this birth as an avatara of the Goddess. Cf. *Devī Gītā* 9.22cd–23ab, where the Goddess declares her avataric mission.

4. This felicitous phrase is Thomas B. Coburn's. See his "Consort of None, Śakti of All: The Vision of the *Devī Māhātmya.*"

Translation

[Himālaya expresses his gratitude to the Goddess, and makes a further request.]

Vyāsa spoke:

1.66. Hearing her exceedingly kind words, Himālaya on his part
Replied to the Great Sovereign Queen,[1] his eyes and throat congested with tears.

Himālaya spoke:

1.67. You greatly ennoble whomever you wish to favor,
For who am I, so dull and motionless, compared to you who embody infinite being and consciousness?[2]

1.68. That I should become your father in the course of hundreds of births is astonishing, O Faultless One,
Even with all the merits gained by performing horse sacrifices and other religious penances.[3]

1.69. Now I shall be renowned, for all the world will think: "The World-Mother has become the daughter
Of that Himālaya, wonder of wonders! How blessed and fortunate is he![4]

1.70. She whose womb contains tens of millions of worlds
Has been born as his daughter[5]—who on earth is his equal?"

1.71. I know not what heavenly realm has been prepared for my ancestors
To rest in, so blessed are they to have one such as myself born in their family.

1.72. As you have already granted me one favor through your loving compassion,
Would you also please describe for me your true nature as explained in all the Upaniṣads.

1.73. And further describe the paths of both yoga and knowledge combined with devotion, as approved by scripture.
Explain these, Supreme Ruler, so that I may become one with you.[6]

Vyāsa spoke:

1.74. Hearing these words of Himālaya, and with her lotus face kindly disposed,
The Mother undertook to reveal the mystic teachings[7] hidden in scripture.

Comment

Himālaya's request for Devī's instruction, inspired by her boon of becoming his daughter, sets the stage for the teachings proper of the *Devī Gītā*. In the following two chapters the Goddess expounds her own true nature and her relation to the world, and in the remaining seven chapters describes the various paths to the supreme goal through yoga, knowledge, and devotion. A noteworthy characteristic of the *gītā* genre is the fusion of the ideals of devotion and knowledge. In the case of the *Devī Gītā,* it is one's devotion to the Goddess that inspires her, as it were, to reveal the highest truths and deepest mysteries of life. Such knowledge leads to mergence into or oneness with the Goddess, as Himālaya's request makes clear.

Regarding the notion of the hidden or secret teachings *(rahasya)* of the *Devī Gītā,* see the Comments on 6.21cd–23ab, 10.34–37, and 10.43cd–45ab.

Notes

1. *mahā-rājñīm;* glossed by Nīlakaṇṭha as *sarveśvarīṃ bhuvaneśvarīm* ("Ruler of All, Bhuvaneśvarī").

2. The contrast here between the dull or unconscious *(jaḍa)* mountain and the pure consciousness *(cit)* of the supreme spirit suggests the Sāṃkhya-style dualism between the insentient Prakṛti (nature) and the sentient Puruṣa (spirit), except that here it is the Goddess, who is none other than Prakṛti, who is associated with consciousness. In any case, such a dualistic differentiation serves well the devotional outpourings of Himālaya at this point, but is soon transcended by his Advaita-style request for unity with the Goddess, in 1.73 below. The *Devī Gītā* discusses the term *jaḍa* and its relation to consciousness in 2.11–12, 2.19–20.

3. As Nīlakaṇṭha points out, the Goddess' becoming Himālaya's daughter is not due to his fitness *(yogyatā),* but is due solely to her wish or willingness *(icchā).* The *darśana* (revelation/manifestation) of the Goddess is purely an act of grace on her part. Cf. *Devī Gītā* 4.1–2.

4. *dhanya . . . bhāgyavat;* cf. *Pārvatī Gītā* (*Mahābhāgavata Purāṇa* 15.46), where Himālaya declares how blessed and completely fulfilled *(dhanya, kṛta-kṛtya)* he is, upon realizing that Pārvatī has been born as his daughter.

5. The paradox of the Mother's becoming the daughter is explained by the power of devotion: she who gives birth to all beings is herself willing to take birth in the home of those who are devoted to her.

6. *tvam evāhaṃ yato bhaveḥ:* literally, "so that you may become I." Nīlakaṇṭha renders: "whereby there will be no difference *(abheda)* between you and me."

7. *rahasya:* "mystery," "secret," or "esoteric doctrine." In the *Bhagavad Gītā,* Kṛṣṇa tells Arjuna that the yoga he is proclaiming is a supreme secret *(rahasya),* and is being revealed because Arjuna is a devotee and friend (4.3; cf. 18.63). Cf. *Devī Gītā* 6.21cd–22ab; 10.34–36; 43–44.

Chapter 2

The Goddess as the Supreme Cause of Creation

Translation

[The Goddess proclaims herself as the preexisting cause of the universe, from whom evolves the creative power of Māyā.]

The Goddess spoke:

2.1. May all the gods attend to what I have to say.
By merely hearing[1] these words of mine, one attains my essential nature.[2]

2.2. I alone existed in the beginning; there was nothing else at all,[3] O Mountain King.
My true Self is known as pure consciousness, the highest intelligence, the one supreme Brahman.

2.3. It is beyond reason, indescribable, incomparable, incorruptible.
From out of itself evolves a certain[4] power renowned as Māyā.

2.4. Neither real nor unreal is this Māyā, nor is it both, for that would be incongruous.[5]
Lacking such characteristics, this indefinite[6] entity has always subsisted.[7]

2.5. As heat inheres in fire, as brilliance in the sun,
As cool light in the moon, just so this Māyā inheres firmly in me.[8]

2.6. Into that Māyā the actions of souls, the souls themselves, and the ages eventually[9]
Dissolve without distinctions, as worldly concerns disappear in deep sleep.[10]

2.7. By uniting with this inherent power of mine, I become the cosmic seed.[11]
By obscuring me, its own basis, this power is prone to defects.[12]

2.8. Through its association with consciousness, Māyā is called the efficient cause of the world.[13]
Through its evolution into the visible realm, it is said to be the material cause.[14]

2.9. Some call this Māyā the power of austerity; others call it darkness; still others, dullness,
Or knowledge, illusion, matter, nature, energy, or the unborn.[15]

2.10. Those versed in Śaiva works call it intelligence,[16]
While the Vedāntins call it ignorance.[17]

2.11. Such are its various names found in the Vedic and other sacred texts.

Comment

The fundamental Vedāntic assumption regarding the nature of being prior to the first moment of creation is set forth in the famous verse of the *Chāndogya Upaniṣad*: "Just being existed in the beginning, one alone without a second."[18] This being in the Upaniṣads was soon identified with the Self, and in the later, theistic cosmogonies of the Purāṇas, with one or another personal, supreme being. Such notions are already associated with the Goddess in the *Devī Māhātmya*, but the martial context there, while suggestive of larger cosmological themes, largely ignores them.[19] The second verse above clearly identifies the Goddess as the primal, secondless being.

The process by which the primeval One becomes many is interpreted in terms of a mysterious power called Māyā. In Advaita, this

Māyā is typically defined as neither existent (*sat*), nor nonexistent (*asat*), nor both. Only Brahman is real (*sat*), in the sense that it alone is eternal and unchanging. The unreal (*asat*) refers to what absolutely does not exist (the example commonly given, and mentioned here by Nīlakaṇṭha in his commentary on 2.4, is the son of a barren woman, an example used by the *Devī Gītā* itself in 3.17). The world is an illusion (*mithyā*), in that it is not eternal and unchanging, but it is not unreal. Māyā, as the cause of the world, is also neither real nor unreal.[20]

In the theistic schools, this Māyā is wielded by the supreme being to create the world. Thus, the *Bhāgavata Purāṇa* declares: "That power of the all-seeing Lord is called Māyā, having the nature of being neither real nor unreal, by which he created this universe."[21] But whereas Viṣṇu is the controller and possessor of Māyā in the *Bhāgavata*, the Goddess in the *Devī Gītā* not only wields the power of Māyā, she also *is* Māyā.

The exact nature of the relationship between Māyā and the Goddess in the *Devī Gītā* is variously described. At times, the two are closely identified, or the two are said to be both different and nondifferent, a viewpoint also found in Advaita. As one Indian scholar puts it: "The Brahman is not the same as Māyā. If Māyā is what is neither existent, nor non-existent, nor both, nor neither, then the Brahman is a negation of all the four negations, a fifth negation. But if Māyā is thus different from the Brahman, should we not say that Māyā has its own being? No it cannot have its own being; its being is the same as the Being of the Brahman, just as the being of the power (*śakti*) to burn is the same as the being of fire."[22]

Such substance/attribute analogies as fire and heat, here used by the *Devī Gītā* (2.5) to illustrate the nonseparateness of the Goddess and Māyā, are especially fitting from a Śākta perspective. For Śāktas with their affirming cosmological orientation, Māyā is basically a positive, creative, magical energy of the Goddess that brings forth the universe, rather than a deceiving power that ensnares individuals in the false realm of the world and hinders their enlightenment—a common Advaita interpretation of Māyā.

The *Devī Gītā*, with its inclusivist approach, frequently conjoins Śākta and Advaita points of view. The Advaita perspective on the supreme Brahman as the one primal reality having the nature of infinite being, consciousness, and bliss, easily augments the Śākta perspective on the Goddess as supreme. Less accommodating is the Advaita view of the illusory world and of the power responsible for creating it. Yet such is the intellectual prestige of Advaita that the *Devī Gītā* does not hesitate to propound its teachings, even when there are tensions between the Advaita and Śākta perspectives. In this chapter, especially, the Goddess reveals herself to be quite conversant with

Advaita philosophy, particularly with its cosmological details. In the next section, the Goddess presents a thoroughgoing Advaita interpretation of her relation to Māyā.

Notes

1. The *bhaktic* ideal of listening (*śravaṇa*) is here raised to an extreme, being glorified as effective by itself in producing the supreme goal. This effusive idealization of hearing reflects a synthesis of devotional and Tantric notions about the transformative power of sacred names/sounds. Cf. note 2 on 1.2 above.

2. *mad-rūpatva;* this refers to the state of liberation known as *sārūpya:* assimilation of the form or essence of the supreme deity. This state is also mentioned in 4.19, 4.49, and 7.27, the latter defining her essence (*rūpa*) as pure consciousness. Somewhat paradoxically, all of existence is already a manifestation of the Devī's essence—as she herself declares in 7.16, the true devotee should look upon all beings "as embodying my own essence or form" (*mad-rūpatvena*). (Cf. 10.32.)

For other states of liberation, see 7.13 and 8.44.

3. Nīlakaṇṭha here cites a parallel passage from scripture {*Aitareya Upaniṣad* 1.1.1}: "The Self indeed was this universe, one alone in the beginning; there was nothing else at all." In the *Devī Māhātmya* (10.3ab), the Goddess declares, "I alone exist here in the world; what second, other than I, is there?" (Coburn's translation). Cf. *Bhāgavata Purāṇa* 2.9.32ab, where Viṣṇu declares: "Just I alone was in the beginning; there was nothing else existent or non-existent." Cf. also *Bhāgavata Purāṇa* 3.5.23ab.

4. *kā cit;* indefinite pronoun, glossed by Nīlakaṇṭha as *anirvacanīyā,* "indescribable, undefinable." In Vedānta, *anirvacanīyā* is used to describe Māyā, as Māyā cannot be defined as either real or unreal (see next verse). Cf. *Vedāntasāra* 34: "Ignorance (*ajñāna*) is undefinable (*anirvacanīya*) as either real or unreal." Ignorance is the manifestation of Māyā in the individual.

Cf. *Pañcadaśī* 3.38: "There is some sort (*kā cit*) of power (Māyā) belonging to the supreme."

5. Cf. *Vivekacūdāmaṇi* (traditionally ascribed to Śaṃkara), verse 109: "It [Māyā] is neither real nor unreal, nor does it have the character of both. . . . It is a great marvel, whose nature is indescribable (*anirvacanīya-rūpā*)."

According to the *Pañcadaśī* (6.128 and 130), Māyā is indefinable (*anirvācya, anirvacanīya*) from the logical point of view (in contrast to the popular and scriptural points of view; cf. *Devī Gītā* 3.2). Elaborating on this, one modern neo-Vedāntin scholar explains: "From the standpoint of reasoning, *māyā* is uncharacterizable either as real, or as unreal, or as both real and unreal" (T. M. P. Mahadevan, *The Pañcadaśī of Bhāratītīrtha-Vidyāraṇya,* p. xxv).

6. *kā cid;* again glossed by Nīlakaṇṭha as *anirvacanīyā.*

7. Nīlakaṇṭha adds: "It is beginningless, but endures only until *mokṣa.*" This accords with *Vivekacūdāmaṇi* 110: "It [Māyā] can be destroyed by realizing the pure, nondual Brahman." However, this interpretation is in some tension with the Śākta perspective that affirms the essential unity of the Goddess and Māyā (see next note).

8. Nīlakaṇṭha again qualifies the *Devī Gītā*'s statement by asserting that Māyā, while beginningless, inheres in the Goddess only until *mokṣa*. Nīlakaṇṭha thus presents a predominantly Advaitic interpretation in this and the preceding verse. From the Advaitic standpoint, Māyā, as ignorance or delusion, is not truly real (i.e., eternal) because it is destroyed by knowledge (as 2.11d below affirms). But Māyā is also the creative power of the Goddess, and in this sense, from a Śākta standpoint, it is not necessarily limited by time in any way, including *mokṣa*. The key word here in this verse is *sahajā*, translated as "inheres." Literally, it means "innate, natural"; that is, Māyā is innate or natural to the Goddess (with no suggestion of any temporal limitation). *Devī Gītā* 3.1 affirms the nonseparateness of the Goddess and Māyā. However, the *Devī Gītā* itself shifts back and forth between the Advaitic and Śākta perspectives.
For the significance of the analogies in the verse, see the Comment above.

9. *sañcare:* "in the course of time." Nīlakaṇṭha glosses as *pralaya-kāle,* "at the time of dissolution" (of the universe).

10. Nīlakaṇṭha takes the reference to the dissolution of the souls' actions (*karmāṇi*) into Māyā as an opportunity to acquit the Goddess of any blame for the inequality between souls. In producing souls of various conditions, the commentator maintains, the Goddess merely provides them with the fruits of their prior actions—for the souls and their actions are actually without beginning. And in any case, all distinctions disappear at the *pralaya.* Thus, he concludes, she is neither unjust nor cruel. Nīlakaṇṭha here may well have in mind the similar discussion occurring in Śaṃkara's commentary on the *Brahma Sūtras* (*Vedānta Sūtras*) 2.1.34–35, where the Lord is absolved of the defects of injustice and cruelty. Cf. *Devī-Bhāgavata* 4.25.69, where, following the statement that the Goddess sends forth souls in accord with their prior karma, the text says: "There is no injustice or cruelty ever on the part of the Goddess; Bhuvaneśvarī strives only for the liberation of souls."

11. *Pañcadaśī* 6.151 refers to *Māyā* as the seed (*bīja*) of the power of creation.

12. In post-Śaṃkara Advaita, obscuration or veiling (*āvaraṇa*) is one of two powers of Māyā, the other being projection (*vikṣepa*). These two powers of Māyā, which belong also to "ignorance," are discussed in *Vedāntasāra* 51–54. *Vikṣepa* projects the multiplicity of forms that constitute the world; *āvaraṇa* conceals the ultimate unity behind the multiplicity. The resulting error is to

mistake the multiplicity for the ultimate. See M. Hiriyanna, *Outlines of Indian Philosophy*, p. 366.

13. According to Nīlakaṇṭha, the association of Māyā with consciousness occurs when consciousness is reflected (*pratibimbita*) in Māyā. It is this reflection of consciousness (*cid-ābhāsa*), he explains, that is the instrumental or efficient cause (*nimitta-kāraṇa*) in bringing about the appearance (*vivarta*) of the multiplex and changing world.

14. Cf. *Vedāntasāra* 55, which refers to consciousness, in association with ignorance, as the efficient and material cause of the universe. The notion of efficient causality implies that the cause is not modified in producing its effect. The transformation of Brahman or consciousness into the world of multiplicity is apparent (*vivarta*) only, just as a snake seen in a rope is merely an appearance. Material causality, involving an evolution (*pariṇāma*) of the cause into its effect, implies actual change in the cause. Thus, Advaita subordinates the notion of evolution to that of appearance—that is, evolution is only an appearance—in order to maintain the ideal of the immutable, unitary Brahman.

15. Nīlakaṇṭha refers to a number of scriptural sources where these names are given: the *Muṇḍaka Upaniṣad* for the power of austerity {1.1.8, 9}; another scriptural text {the *Ṛg Veda*} for darkness {10.129.3}; the *Tāpanīya Upaniṣad* for dullness {9.4}; another scripture {the *Aitareya Upaniṣad*} for knowledge {3.1.2}; and the *Śvetāśvatara Upaniṣad* for matter {1.10 and 6.16}, for illusion and nature {4.10}, for energy {6.8}, and for the unborn {4.5}. Nīlakaṇṭha thus justifies the *Devī Gītā*'s statement in 2.11ab that these are some of the varied names of Māyā found in the Vedic texts (though Māyā is not explicitly mentioned in several of the passages cited above).

16. *vimarśa:* "creative vibration; intelligence, consciousness." The concept plays an important role in both Vīraśaivism and Kāśmīra Śaivism. It is a term applied to Śiva's Śakti, his dynamic aspect that is responsible both for self-consciousness and for bringing about the manifest world. The relation between Śiva and his Vimarśa Śakti is described in terms of attribute and substance, such as heat and fire, light and sun, analogies used by the *Devī Gītā* itself (2.5), to describe the Goddess' relation to Māyā. See Narendra Nath Bhattacharyya, *History of the Tantric Religion*, pp. 258–61.

17. *avidyā;* the individual aspect of the cosmic Māyā.

18. *Chāndogya Upaniṣad* 6.2.1.

19. See *Devī Māhātmya* 10.3ab. The Goddess had been challenged to single combat by her demon opponent, so by withdrawing her army, that is, her various manifestations of power back into herself, she could claim to be "alone, without a second."

20. See M. Hiriyanna, *The Essentials of Indian Philosophy*, pp. 155–56; also the same author's *Outlines of Indian Philosophy*, pp. 364–65.

21. *Bhāgavata Purāṇa* 3.5.25. Cf. *Bhāgavata Purāṇa* 2.9.32–33.

22. P. T. Raju, *Structural Depths of Indian Thought*, p. 397. Cf. Chatterjee, "Hindu Religious Thought," p. 239.

Translation

[The Goddess distinguishes between nonconscious Māyā and her own true Self as pure consciousness.]

2.11. [cont.] Since Māyā is something we can perceive, it has the nature of nonconscious matter; since knowledge destroys it, it is not truly existent.[1]

2.12. Consciousness is not something we can perceive; what we perceive is indeed nonconscious.
Consciousness is self-luminous; nothing else illuminates it.[2]

2.13. It does not even illuminate itself, for that would lead to the fallacy of infinite regress.[3]
As an agent and the object acted upon are distinct entities, so consciousness itself, like a lamp,

2.14. While shining brightly, illuminates what is other than itself. Know this, O Mountain,
For thus have I demonstrated that consciousness, belonging to my own nature, is eternal.[4]

2.15. The visible world appears and disappears constantly in the various states of waking, dream, and deep sleep.
Pure consciousness never experiences such fluctuation.[5]

2.16. Even if this consciousness itself became an object of perception, then the witness
Of that perception would abide as the real pure consciousness, as before.[6]

2.17. And so those versed in religious treatises regarding the real declare consciousness to be eternal.
Its nature is bliss, for it is the object of supreme love.
2.18. The feeling, 'Let me not cease to be; let me exist forever,' is rooted in love for the Self.[7]
Certainly there is no actual relation between me and all else, since all else is false.[8]
2.19. Therefore I am regarded truly as an undivided whole.
And that consciousness is not an attribute of the Self, for then the Self would be like an object.
2.20. In consciousness no possible trace of the object state can be found.
And so consciousness also has no attributes: consciousness is not a quality separable from consciousness itself.
2.21. Therefore the Self in essence is consciousness, and bliss as well, always.[9]
It is the real and complete, beyond all relation, and free from the illusion of duality.

Comment

In the Śākta view, Māyā is not simply an insentient force but a conscious and willful facet of the Goddess' personality. Somewhat paradoxically, it is the nondualist school of Advaita, emphasizing an acosmic view of reality and characterizing the realm of Māyā as false, that often stresses the greatest difference between Māyā and the supreme. Advaita objectifies Māyā, viewing it as inert and insentient (*jaḍa*), over against the supreme, conscious subject that is Brahman (or Ātman). By way of contrast, the *Devī-Bhāgavata*, more often than not presenting a Śākta viewpoint, asserts that Māyā is "the very essence of the supreme Brahman (*māyā para-brahma-svarūpiṇī*)," and that "the world without Māyā would ever be unconscious and inert (*jaḍa*)."[10]

The Goddess in the above verses of the *Devī Gītā* ignores for the moment the Śākta perspective, adopting a radical Advaita interpretation by drawing a sharp distinction between herself and Māyā. This distinction as characterized here is somewhat at odds with the earlier notion of "difference and nondifference" as suggested by the substance/attribute analogies of verse 5. The Goddess now denies the "nondifference," utilizing standard Advaitic visual images and metaphors that stress the "difference." As the pure subject or consciousness (variously called *caitanya, saṃvit, jñāna,* and *cit*), she likens herself to a lamp that is self-illuminating, revealing the visible realm that is Māyā, the realm of inert, material objects (referred to as *dṛśya,* "the seen," and as *jaḍa,* "inert, dull, insentient"). Pure consciousness itself is never an object of perception or knowledge, but is instead the eternal seer or witness (*sākṣin*), observing the ephemeral and false entities of empirical existence.

The Goddess here also denies that consciousness is an attribute of the Self—or herself—in accord with Advaitic principles affirming the radical oneness of the supreme subject, beyond all qualification or attribution (*neti neti*). Only objects have qualities or attributes. Thus the Goddess does not possess consciousness but rather *is* consciousness.

Notes

1. For Advaitins, whatever is an object of knowledge or perception (*dṛśya*) is considered inert and nonconscious (*jaḍa*), and is radically distinguished from the conscious knower or subject (Ātman). Cf. *Gauḍapāda's Kārikā* (2.4): "Different objects cognized in dream (are illusory) on account of their *being perceived to exist.* For the same reason, the objects seen in the waking state are illusory" (Nikhilananda's translation). Radhakrishnan, commenting on Śaṃkara's interpretation of this *Kārikā,* explains: "Śaṁkara holds that the distinction between reality and seeming, substance and show, is identical with that between subject and object. While the objects perceived are unreal, the Ātman, which perceives but is not itself perceived, is real. While distinguishing waking objects from dream ones, Śaṁkara urges that the two, insofar as they are objects of consciousness, are unreal" (*Indian Philosophy,* vol. 2, p. 562). The quality of being knowable belongs not only to the manifest world, but also to its cause, Māyā. However, even from the Advaita perspective, Māyā is not absolutely unreal, just as it is not absolutely existent, but rather is neither *sat* nor *asat* (cf. *Devī Gītā* 2.4 above). Cf. also Hiriyanna, *Outlines of Indian Philosophy,* pp. 364–65.)

2. Nīlakaṇṭha here quotes the famous Upaniṣadic verse {found in *Kaṭha Upaniṣad* 2.2.15, *Śvetāśvatara Upaniṣad* 6.14, and *Muṇḍaka Upaniṣad* 2.2.11}, regarding how neither the sun, moon, nor stars, etc., illuminate the highest. The *Devī Gītā* itself quotes the verse in 6.13.

3. That is, if it illuminated itself, this would imply that there is another consciousness to witness this illumination. Thus, as Mahadevan says in summarizing the first chapter of the *Pañcadaśī:* "Pure consciousness cannot

become the object of any other experience, and so it is self-luminous. To say that it is its own object is a manifest contradiction, and the assertion that there is another consciousness which cognizes it lands us in infinite regress" (*The Pañcadaśī of Bhāratītīrtha-Vidyāraṇya,* p. 4). Cf. Hiriyanna, *Outlines,* p. 343.

4. In *Pañcadaśī* 10.9–13, consciousness, referred to as the witness *(sākṣin),* is said to illuminate the agent, act, and objects acted upon, just as a lamp in a dance hall reveals the patron (agent or ego), audience (objects), and dancer (the intellect). Even when these are absent, the lamp (consciousness) continues to shine. Thus, pure consciousness endures even when the objects of consciousness disappear. The same notion is extended to the three states of consciousness in the next verse. Cf. Hiriyanna (*Outlines,* pp. 359–60) on the *sākṣin* as always present like an ever-luminous lamp, enduring in all three states. Cf. also Radhakrishnan, *Indian Philosophy,* vol. 2, p. 602.

5. Nīlakaṇṭha explains that some sense of "I" remains in all three states of consciousness: "That one, that I (*aham*) who perceives the waking state, is the very same one, the same I who perceives the dreaming state, and is the very same one, the same I who perceives the state of deep sleep." As for the sense of consciousness even in deep sleep, Mahadevan nicely summarizes the traditional Advaita argument: "Even in dreamless sleep there is consciousness, for when one rises from sleep one is aware of having had good sleep undisturbed by dreams. . . . There must be some one in sleep who is directly conscious of the absence of knowledge and is quiet, to whom this sleep and the consciousness of nothing are presented. . . . But this non-existence of the world [in sleep] does not affect the witnessing principle. It is witness even to the nescience of sleep" (*The Pañcadaśī of Bhāratītīrtha-Vidyāraṇya,* p. 4).

Pañcadaśī 1.3–7 analyzes the three states of consciousness or existence and concludes that it is the same consciousness that witnesses in all three states, and that consciousness itself is constant and self-revealing or self-luminous (*svayam prabhā*). See also *Vivekacūdāmaṇi* 217. Cf. Dasgupta, *History of Indian Philosophy,* vol. 2, p. 215, and Andrew O. Fort, *The Self and Its States,* p. 83.

6. Again, we are confronted with the fallacy of infinite regress. The problem addressed here is that if consciousness is something perceived, then like any other empirical object, it would not be constant or eternal. If, for the sake of argument, one maintains that consciousness could be perceived, there would still have to be an overarching witness to perceive this. And that overarching consciousness would be, then, the true, eternal witness.

7. *Devī Gītā* 2.17cd–18ab is close in wording to *Pañcadaśī* 1.8, which is an elaboration on the immutable consciousness existing in the three states discussed in *Pañcadaśī* 1.3–7 (cf. *Devī Gītā* 2.15 above). Commenting on *Pañcadaśī* 1.8, Mahadevan writes: "The experience of the desire 'Let me not go out of existence; let me live forever' proves that the love for the Self is direct, immediate, and unconditioned. Thus it is established from scriptural statements [e.g., *Bṛhadāraṇyaka Upaniṣad* I.4.8; II.4.5], reasoning, and the evidence of experience that the Self is the source of happiness and the locus of

love" (*The Pañcadaśī of Bhāratītīrtha-Vidyāraṇya,* p. 193). Cf. *Pañcadaśī* 12.31 and 72.

8. *mithyā:* "false, unreal." The term also appears in 4.26ab and 9.45cd. Cf. Mahadevan: "The *sat* [true being] has neither external relations nor internal differentiations. It is unrelated to anything, for there is nothing else with which it can be related" (*The Pañcadaśī of Bhāratītīrtha-Vidyāraṇya,* p. 12). Cf. Hiriyanna: "Brahman is the source of all; and neither the pot nor its material cause, which as part of the empirical world are false, can be in actual relation with it" (*Essentials,* p. 159).

9. Mahadevan, explaining the *Pañcadaśī*'s idea of the Self, writes: "Existence, consciousness, and bliss are not predicates which are attached to the *Ātman;* they are its self-nature *svarūpa-lakṣaṇa.* They are its essence, and not attributes. The *Ātman* is not *citdharma,* as the Naiyāyika thinks, it is *citsvabhāva.* It is not that the Ātman [*sic*] has existence, consciousness, and bliss; but it is *sat-cit-ānanda*" (*The Pañcadaśī of Bhāratītīrtha-Vidyāraṇya,* pp. 4–5).

10. *Devī-Bhāgavata* 4.25.68 and 70.

Translation

[The Goddess explains the initial impulse of the Self, in its aspect as the Unmanifest or Causal Body, to undertake the creation.]

2.22. This Self, however, by its own power of Māyā conjoined with desires, actions, and the like,[1]
Through the influence of prior experience ripening in time in accord with the law of karma,
2.23. And by confounding the primal elements,[2] being desirous to create, begins to bring forth.[3]
The resulting creation, devoid of intelligence,[4] will be further described to you, O Mountain King.
2.24. This extraordinary form of mine which I have mentioned
Is unevolved and unmanifest, yet becomes segmented through the power of Māyā.[5]
2.25. All the religious treatises declare it to be the cause of all causes,
The primal substance behind the elements, and as having the form of being, consciousness, bliss.

2.26. It is the condensation of all karma; it is the seat of will, knowledge, and action;[6]
It is expressed in the mantra Hrīṃ; it is the primal principle—so it is said.[7]

Comment

The creation of the universe in Advaita is seen as an apparent descent from the pure Brahman or Self down to the gross world of physical matter. The process is described using two rather different but overlapping models. One is an evolutionary model, based on the sequential unfolding of primary elements as outlined in classical Sāṃkhya. *Devī Gītā* 2.22–42ab presents this evolutionary scheme. The other model is one of reflection, whereby the one supreme reality, like an image in a mirror, appears reflected in Māyā as the manifold world. The *Devī Gītā* summarizes the reflection model in 2.42cd–49ab. Common to both models is the generation of the three bodies of the Self—Causal, Subtle, and Gross.

The above verses describe the first developmental phase in the evolutionary model, the generation of the Causal Body from which the primary elements arise. This process is here interpreted from a Śākta perspective. When the Goddess unites with her own Māyā, the latent powers of will, knowledge, and action become activated, and she becomes the Causal Body and unevolved seed of the universe. This seed, referred to as the primal substance or principle (*ādi-bhūta, ādi-tattva*), is roughly equivalent to the primary material element, Prakṛti, of the Sāṃkhya, from which the other elements evolve, except that it is not mere insentient matter. It is the supreme spiritual reality as well, that is, Brahman, indicated by its identification as being, consciousness, bliss. And from the Śākta-Tantric perspective, it is also identified with the primary sonic reverberation, Hrīṃ, seed syllable of Bhuvaneśvarī and source of all manifest creation.

Notes

1. Nīlakaṇṭha glosses *kāma* (desires) as *icchā* (will). The text here apparently refers to the three creative powers of Māyā known as *icchā, jñāna,* and *kriyā,* specifically mentioned in 2.26 below.

2. As Nīlakaṇṭha points out, these are the twenty-four elements (*tattvas*) of the Sāṃkhya. These twenty-four include Prakṛti and all its evolutes, but

exclude the twenty-fifth, the conscious Puruṣa. According to the Sāṃkhya, it is lack of discrimination (*aviveka*) between the elements, especially between Puruṣa and Prakṛti, that is said to be responsible for creation.

3. Cf. *Devī-Bhāgavata* 4.25.68: "In accord with their prior karma, Māyā, who is the essence of the supreme Brahman, sends forth beings unceasingly." In Advaita, the inherent nature (*svabhāva*) of the Lord is said to be Māyā conjoined with time and karma. (See Thibaut's comment in *The Vedānta Sūtras of Bādarāyana,* part 1, p. 357, note 1.)

4. For the Advaitins, since the creation springs from Māyā, regarded as nonintelligent, then creation too must be devoid of intelligence. The world thus arises not directly from Brahman, which is intelligence, but only from Brahman associated with Māyā. (Cf. Thibaut's comment in *The Vedānta Sūtras* of *Bādarāyana,* part 1, p. xciii.)

5. The extraordinary (*alaukika*) form is that aspect of the Goddess united with Māyā that forms the cosmic seed, mentioned in 2.7. This seed in Advaita is identified with the Causal Body, and is often called the unevolved and unmanifest *avyākṛta, avyakta.* See, e.g., Sureśvara, *Pañcīkaraṇa-Vārttika* (verse 2): "The supreme Brahman . . . through association with its own Māyā, becomes the cosmic seed, unevolved." The terms *avyākṛta* and *avyakta* can refer not only to the cosmic germ (*pradhāna* or *prakṛti*), but also to the supreme Brahman. In the *Devī Gītā,* these terms clearly refer to the Goddess both in her cosmogonic mode and in her aspect as Brahman: the next verse calls her unevolved form the cause of all causes, suggesting the Causal Body, and then identifies it as having the form of *sac-cid-ānanda,* the prime "qualities" of Brahman.

6. *icchā, jñāna,* and *kriyā;* in Śāktism, these are the three inherent powers of the supreme that become operative at the beginning of the creative process. They represent the willing or intending, the planning or formulating, and the executing or expressive powers of the highest. Nīlakaṇṭha quotes from the *Śvetāśvatara Upaniṣad* {6.8}, wherein an ancient, similar notion is affirmed: "His [the Lord's] supreme power (*śakti*) is manifold. . . . innate are his knowledge (*jñāna*), force (*bala*), and action (*kriyā*)." The commentator goes on to quote from "another Purāṇa": "Will, knowledge, and action are the goddesses Raudrī, Brāhmī, and Vaiṣṇavī. This threefold Śakti abides there in the supreme light that is Oṃ." The *Devī Gītā,* as seen in the next line, gives precedence to the syllable Hrīṃ as the sound form of the primal reality, from whose reverberation creation proceeds.

The *Devī Gītā* ascribes these three powers to the Causal Body of the Goddess. In later Advaita, these powers are ascribed to three sheaths of the Subtle Body: knowledge to the intelligence sheath, will to the mind sheath, and action to the breath sheath (*Vedāntasāra* 89; cf. 91).

7. The general structure of the *Devī Gītā*'s discussion here, beginning with the mention of the mantra Hrīṃ and continuing through the explanation

of the *pañcīkaraṇa* process, closely resembles that of Sureśvara's discourse on creation given in his *Vārttika* on Śaṃkara's *Pañcīkaraṇa*. Sureśvara begins with a reference to the syllable Oṃ as the essence of the Vedas and the revealer of the highest truth (verse 1). He then goes on (in verses 3–11) to expound the arising of the five elements and their subsequent fivefold evolution known as *pañcīkaraṇa*. The *Devī Gītā,* in its own description of these processes (2.27–35) follows, often verbatim, Sureśvara's account. The *Devī Gītā,* however, in accord with its Śākta-Tantric orientation, substitutes at the start the syllable Hrīm, the mantra of the Goddess, as the equivalent of the Vedic Oṃ.

Translation

[The Goddess recounts the creation of the five basic elements, the subsequent fivefold generative process known as Pañcīkaraṇa, and the compounding of the remaining two bodies—Subtle and Gross—of the Self.]

2.27. Out of that primal substance arose ether, endowed with the subtle quality of sound.[1]
Then arose air, characterized by the quality of touch, followed by fire, characterized by visible form.[2]

2.28. Next arose water, characterized by taste; then earth, characterized by smell.
Ether has the single quality of sound; air is endowed with touch and sound.

2.29. Fire has the qualities of sound, touch, and visible form, according to the wise;
Water has the four qualities of sound, touch, visible form, and taste, so they say.

2.30. Earth has the five qualities of sound, touch, visible form, taste, and smell.[3]
From those subtle elements came into being the great cosmic thread[4] which is called the Subtle Body.

2.31. It is proclaimed as all-pervading; this is the Subtle Body of the Self.
The Unmanifest is the Causal Body, which I mentioned earlier.[5]

2.32. In that lies the world seed,[6] from which evolves the Subtle Body.
From that, by the process of fivefold generation, the gross elements,
2.33. Five in number, arise.[7] I shall now describe this process.
Each of those elements previously mentioned shall be divided in half.
2.34. One half-part of each element shall be divided into four, O Mountain.
By joining the undivided half of each element with one of the quartered fractions from each of the other four, each element becomes fivefold.[8]
2.35. And they produce the Cosmic Body, or Gross Body, of the Self.[9]

Comment

The Goddess now explains the second and third developmental stages of cosmic evolution, namely, the generation of the Self's Subtle Body from the five subtle or uncompounded elements and the Gross Body from the gross or compounded elements. The three stages of evolution as outlined by the Goddess in the preceding two sections may be amplified and schematized as follows:

I. Goddess (Self) —> Māyā + Will-Knowledge-Action —> World Seed or Causal Body

II. World Seed —> The Uncompounded Elements:

sound —> ether
sound+touch —> air
sound+touch+form —> fire
sound+touch+form+taste —> water
sound+touch+form+taste+smell —> earth

} —> Subtle Body

III. The Uncompounded Elements	+ Quintuplication Process	—> Gross Elements	—> Gross Body

The specific model for the evolution of the elements and the fivefold generative process (*pañcīkaraṇa*) described above is found in the short Advaita work of Sureśvara, the *Pañcīkaraṇa-Vārttika*, a commentary on the *Pañcīkaraṇa* attributed to Śaṃkara. The *Pañcīkaraṇa* itself recounts the evolutionary process in order to show how liberation or Self-realization can be achieved by reversing the process through meditation on the syllable Oṃ. The *Devī Gītā* has a similar interest in Self-realization, but its corresponding meditation is directed to the syllable Hrīṃ and is given in a later chapter (4.46cd–48). Here in this chapter the Goddess is primarily concerned with her role as the overseer of creation, so she continues to provide details of the evolutionary process, details found in other Advaita works like the *Pañcadaśī* of Vidyāraṇya and *Vedāntasāra* of Sadānanda, as well as the *Pañcīkaraṇa-Vārttika*.

Notes

1. The evolution of the elements from a primal substance, such as the Self, is an idea found already in *Taittirīya Upaniṣad* 2.1.1 (this passage actually adds three more "elements": "herbs," "food," and "the person," to the basic five mentioned here in verses 2.27–28ab; the five are standard in the Sāṃkhya schema of evolution). In the classic Sāṃkhya, there is a basic, twofold distinction between the five gross elements (*bhūta*s) of ether, air, etc., and the five subtle qualities or elements (*tan-mātra*s) of sound, touch, etc. In Vedānta, with the added notion of the *pañcīkaraṇa* process (about to be described), a new distinction emerges between the original elements in their uncompounded state and in their compounded, quintuplicated state (see note 7 on 2.33 below).

2. As indicated in note 7 on 2.26, the *Devī Gītā*'s description of the arising of the gross and subtle elements and the subsequent fivefold evolution (in 2.27–35) closely follows Sureśvara's *Vārttika* on Śaṃkara's *Pañcīkaraṇa* 3–11. Cf. *Vedāntasara* 57–60, 98–100, and *Pañcadaśī* 1.18–27.

3. The successive elements combine more of the qualities, due to the nature of their evolution. Thus, from sound emerges ether, from sound combined with touch emerges air, and so on. Thus, each subsequent element, while having its own characteristic quality, also contains all the qualities of the preceding elements.

4. *mahat-sūtra;* also referred to as *sūtrātman,* the World or Cosmic Soul. See 1.49 above.

5. In 2.24–26 above.

6. *jagad-bīja;* Sureśvara refers to the world seed prior to his recounting the evolution of the elements (*Pañcīkaraṇa-Vārttika* 2). Cf. *Devī Gītā* 2.7ab.

7. As indicated in note 3 above, successive elements combine more of the subtle qualities, due to the nature of their evolution. But in classical Sāṃkhya there is no notion that the gross elements are themselves compounded with other elements. The *pañcīkaraṇa* process described in the following verses distinguishes between the original elements with their various qualities but in an uncompounded state, and those same elements each compounded with portions of the other elements. It is these compounded elements that are referred to here as the gross elements.

8. Thus, each compounded element is composed of one-half of its own original element and one-eighth of each of the other four original elements.

The *Devī Gītā,* in 2.34cd, departs from the *Pañcīkaraṇa-Vārttika,* inserting a line that is nearly identical with *Pañcadaśī* 1.27cd (which is also quoted in *Vedāntasāra* 100). The *Pañcadaśī* describes the *pañcīkaraṇa* process in 1.26–27.

9. The *Devī Gītā* reverts to the *Pañcīkaraṇa-Vārttika,* this line being very similar to 11bcd in the latter.

Translation

[The evolution of the Subtle Body is explained in greater detail.]

2.35. [cont.] From the aspects of lucidity[1] residing in the five elements arise hearing and the other

2.36. Organs of sense, each from a single element, O King.[2]
But from the lucid aspects of all the elements mixed together
Arises the internal organ, single, yet fourfold by reason of its different functions.

2.37. When it wills or wavers, it is known as mind.
When it knows decisively without doubts, it is called intellect.

2.38. When it remembers, it is known as recollection.[3]
When it functions to assert the sense of I, it becomes the principle of egoism.[4]

2.39. From the active aspects[5] of the elements arise in order the organs of action,[6]
Each from a single element; but from the active aspects of all the elements mixed together comes the fivefold breath.

2.40. The upward breath resides in the heart, the downward breath in the bowels, the middle breath in the navel,
The ascending breath in the throat, and the diffused breath throughout the body.[7]

2.41. The five organs of knowledge, the five organs of action,
And the five breaths, along with the mind accompanied by the intellect,[8]

2.42. These constitute the Subtle Body,[9] that is, my own rarefied form.[10]

Comment

The Goddess reexamines the second developmental stage, explaining in greater detail the generation of the Subtle Body in terms of the three qualities of primal matter. In the Sāṃkhya, Prakṛti (nature) is endowed with three qualities or *guṇas*: *sattva* (lucidity, brightness, lightness, goodness, virtue), *rajas* (activity, desire, passion), and *tamas* (dullness, darkness, inertness, ignorance). These qualities appear in various proportions in the diverse products of Prakṛti, beginning with the subtle elements. These qualities explain various details of the evolutionary process, on the principle that the qualities of the cause will appear in the effect. Thus, the mental and sensory faculties of the Subtle Body are said to arise from the *sattvic* aspects, since these faculties have the nature of luminosity.[11] The action faculties, including the five breaths, being characterized by their dynamic nature, arise from the *rajasic* aspects.[12] The Goddess in the *Devī Gītā* does not mention the *tamasic* aspects, but elsewhere these are said to give rise to the gross elements, characterized by inertness.[13] The evolution of the Subtle Body may be diagrammed thus:

Lucid aspects of elements, singly —>	five sense organs: hearing, touch, sight, taste, smell	
Lucid aspects of elements, mixed —>	internal organ: intellect, mind, recollection, ego	
Active aspects of elements, singly —>	five action organs: speech, hands, feet, evacuation, procreation	—> Subtle Body
Active aspects of elements, mixed —>	five breaths: upward, downward, middle, ascending, diffused	

In Advaita, the various bodies are considered as less than fully real, even false in a certain sense. Thus, Sureśvara, in his *Pañcīkaraṇa-Vārttika*, concludes his enumeration of the component elements of the Subtle Body with the words, "This Subtle Body is illusory (*māyika*), belonging to the innermost Self."[14] In Śāktism, the emphasis is not on the illusory nature of the bodies, but on their being manifestations of the Goddess. Accordingly, the *Devī Gītā* emends Sureśvara's conclusion, with the Goddess declaring that the Subtle Body is "my own rarefied form (*mama liṅgam*)."

Notes

1. *sattva;* see Comment above.

2. That is, the lucid (*sattva*) aspect or portion (*aṃśa*) in ether gives rise to hearing (or the ears), in air to touch (or skin), in fire to sight, (or the eyes), in water to taste (or the tongue), in earth to smell (or the nose).

These lines begin the description of the evolution of the seventeen component parts, starting with the five sense organs, that constitute the Subtle Body of the Self. A similar description is found in the *Pañcīkaraṇa-Vārttika* (31cd–37), but this work makes no mention of the *guṇa* aspects or portions (such as lucidity) of the elements that give rise to the different classes of organs. The role of the *guṇa* aspects in this evolution is explained both in the *Pañcadaśī* (1.19–23) and in the *Vedāntasāra* (61–89).

3. *anusandhāna-rūpaṃ tac-cittam;* of the four functions, that of *citta* (rendered as "recollection") is the least clear. It is said to have the form of *anusandhāna,* a term of rather broad meaning. The translators of the *Pañcīkaraṇa-Vārttika* (verse 34) and of the *Vedāntasāra* (verse 68) interpret *anusandhāna* as "contemplation" or "remembering." The basic meaning of its verbal root, *anusandhā,* is "to inquire into" or "investigate," and thus the *Vivekacūḍāmaṇi* refers to the function as *svārthānusandhāna,* "inquiring into or seeking one's own self-interest" (verse 94). In that case, *citta* might well be rendered "desire," rather than "recollection."

4. The *Vivekacūḍāmaṇi* (93–94) defines the internal organ (*antaḥkaraṇa*) as consisting of these same four functions: *manas, dhī* or *buddhi, ahaṃkṛti,* and *citta,* as does Sureśvara (*Pañcīkaraṇa-Vārttika* 33). The *Pañcadaśī* (1.20) defines the internal organ as twofold: mind (*manas*) and intellect (*buddhi*). The *Vedāntasāra* (67) explains that recollection (*citta*) and egoism (*ahaṃkāra*) are to be included in intellect and mind, respectively. Cf. *Devī Gītā* 2.41 below.

Interestingly, of the four psychic organs—*manas, buddhi, ahaṃkara,* and *citta*—that make up the internal organ (*antaḥkaraṇa*), only *citta* is not included in the classic Sāṃkhya scheme of evolution.

5. The aspects of *rajas;* see Comment above.

6. The organs of action, like those of sense, are five in number: speech, hands, feet, and the organs of evacuation and procreation.

7. The upward breath (*prāṇa*) is associated with respiration, the downward breath (*apāna*) with evacuation, the middle breath (*samāna*) with digestion, the ascending breath (*udāna*) with the vital air assisting the soul's exit from the body at death, and the diffused breath (*vyāna*) with the vital air enlivening the whole body. These five breaths are named in *Chāndogya Upaniṣad* 5.19–23.

8. The mind and intellect constitute the two main functions of the internal organ, and include egoism and recollection, mentioned in 2.38 above.

9. Both the *Vedāntasāra* (61–62) and *Pañcadaśī* (1.23) enumerate these same component parts of the Subtle Body and specify their number as seventeen. The *Vivekacūḍāmaṇi* (96) and *Pañcīkaraṇa-Vārttika* (35–37ab) add ignorance, desire, and action, and refer to the Subtle Body as consisting of eight cities: (1) the five sense organs, (2) the five action organs, (3) the five breaths, (4) the five subtle elements, (5) the internal organ, (6) ignorance, (7) desire, and (8) action. Cf. the introduction to the *Pañcīkaraṇa-Vārttika*, pp. xvi–xvii.

10. *liṅga;* short form of *liṅga-deha,* commonly translated as "subtle body." Here it is rendered as "rarefied form," to contrast with *sūkṣma-śarīra,* "Subtle Body." The two terms are synonymous.

11. See *Vedāntasāra* 71; *Pañcadaśī* 1.19–20.

12. See *Vedāntasāra* 88; cf. *Pañcadaśī* 21–22.

13. See *Vedāntasāra* 58; cf. *Pañcadaśī* 1.18.

14. *Pañcīkaraṇa-Vārttika* 37ab: *etat sūkṣmaśarīraṃ syān māyikaṃ pratyagātmanaḥ/*

Translation

[The Goddess describes the generation of the Lord and the soul, their three bodies, and their interrelationship.]

2.42. [cont.] Therein is the principle called nature,[1] O King.
It is twofold according to tradition.

2.43. One aspect, characterized by lucidity, is Māyā; the other aspect, mixed with all the qualities of nature, is nescience.[2]
That aspect which clearly reflects its own substrate is known as Māyā.

2.44. In that Māyā appears the reflected image of the universal ruler.[3]
He is called the supreme Lord; he is aware of his own substrate.

2.45. He is all-knowing and all-doing, the cause of all kindness.
But in nescience, the reflected image is partially obscured,[4] O Mountain King.
2.46. It is then known as the individual soul, and as the abode of all suffering.[5]
Now these two here, the Lord and the soul, are said to have three bodies through the power of nescience.
2.47. By identifying themselves with the three bodies, they also come to have three names.
The soul as the Causal Body is named the Intelligent; as the Subtle Body, the Brilliant;
2.48. And as the Gross Body, the All; thus are its three divisions known.[6]
In like manner the Lord is known by the terms the Lord, the Cosmic Soul, and the Cosmic Body.[7]
2.49. The soul is regarded as the individuated form, the Lord as the aggregated.[8]

Comment

In these verses the Goddess summarizes the second Advaitin model of creation to explain the arising of the three bodies of the supreme. This model, of manifestation through reflection, is informed by the Upaniṣadic notion of the three states of consciousness, rather than the Sāṃkhya notion of the elements. The three bodies, correlative to the three states, are said to arise simply through the power of *avidyā* or nescience. The model also emphasizes, in Upaniṣadic fashion, the basic correlations between the Lord and the individual soul, the macrocosmic and microcosmic planes, referred to here as the aggregated (*samaṣṭi*, the macrocosmic), and the individuated (*vyaṣṭi*, the microcosmic). This reflection model is preferred over the evolutionary model in Advaita, as it safeguards the immutable and unique nature of Brahman (or the Goddess, in the *Devī Gītā*), since change and duality are appearance only in this scheme. The process of creation through reflection as propounded in the *Devī Gītā*, along with the macro-microcosmic correlations, may be represented as follows:

	Macrocosmic (Samaṣṭi) Dimension	Microcosmic (Vyaṣṭi) Dimension
Reflection of the Goddess in →	Pure lucid aspect of Prakṛti (Māyā)	Mixed aspect of Prakṛti (Avidyā)
Manifests in the Image of →	Supreme Lord (Īśvara)	Individual soul (Jīva)
Subdivided into Three Bodies:		
a. Causal →	Lord (Īśa)	Intelligent (Prajña)
b. Subtle →	Cosmic Soul (Sūtrātman)	Brilliant (Taijasa)
c. Gross →	Cosmic Body (Virāj)	All (Viśva)

Among all these manifestations, the *Devī Gītā* has a special interest in the macrocosmic, Gross Body of the supreme, referred to as the Virāj. It is this form of the supreme, that is, of the Goddess, that is so splendidly revealed to the gods in the next chapter.

Notes

1. *prakṛti.*

2. *avidyā:* "ignorance, nescience." *Devī Gītā* 2.42cd–43ab follows *Pañcadaśī* 1.15–16. Cf. *Vedāntasāra* 37, 42, where it is ignorance (*ajñāna*) rather than Prakṛti that is twofold, according to whether it has a predominance of pure *sattva,* or of impure *sattva.*

3. In an Advaitic context, the image is implicitly understood to be the reflection of Brahman in Māyā. In the *Devī Gītā,* of course, since the Goddess is Brahman (see verse 2.2 above), the universal ruler is viewed as a reflection of the Devī herself.

4. That is, the image of ultimate reality (Brahman or the Goddess) is distorted when reflected in *avidyā.*

5. To explain the relation of the transpersonal Brahman to individual, conscious beings (including both the Lord and individual souls), Advaitins resort to two basic metaphors, reflection (*pratibimba*) and limitation (*avaccheda*). According to the latter, Brahman becomes limited by various adjuncts (*upādhis*), such as ignorance, just as space becomes limited by jars. But the space within the jars is not essentially different from that without, so that space at large is not truly affected, just as Brahman is not truly affected by ignorance. In this view, Brahman limited by ignorance characterized by pure *sattva* becomes the Lord, and when limited by ignorance

characterized by impure *sattva* becomes the soul. This is the approach of the *Vedāntasāra* (37, 42).

The *Pañcadaśī* (1.15–17) utilizes the reflection metaphor, of an image seen in a mirror. Here, Brahman is reflected in the mirror of Prakṛti, and any disturbances in the reflected image do not affect the prototype. The reflection of Brahman in pure *sattva* (that is, in Māyā) appears as the Lord, which remains transparent to, or does not obscure, its prototype (Brahman). The Lord thus remains omniscient. But when Brahman is reflected in impure *sattva* (that is, in *avidyā* or "nescience"), being mixed with the other two *guṇas*, the image is partially distorted and the prototype is obscured. This partial image is the soul, bound by ignorance. Cf. William M. Indich, *Consciousness in Advaita Vedānta,* pp. 50–52, and Raju, *Structural Depths of Indian Thought,* p. 396.

The *Devī Gītā* utilizes both metaphors at times, but here, in describing the origin of the Lord and soul from the Goddess (Brahman), follows the reflection theory as outlined in the *Pañcadaśī.*

6. These three bodies of the soul correspond to the three states of consciousness. The All (the *viśva*), also referred to as the *vaiśvānara,* is engrossed in the waking state, cognizing external objects. Śaṃkara explains its name: "He is called *Vaiśvānara* because he leads all creatures of the universe in diverse ways . . . ; or because he comprises all beings. . . . He is non-different from the totality of gross bodies (known as *Virāṭ*)" (Commentary on *Māṇḍukya Upaniṣad* 3 [Nikhilananda's translation]). The Brilliant (the *taijasa*) is involved in the dream state, cognizing internal objects. Śaṃkara explains: "He is called the *Taijasa* because he appears as the subject though this (dream) consciousness is without any (gross) object and is of the nature of the essence of light" (Commentary on *Māṇḍukya Upaniṣad* 4 [Nikhilananda's translation]). The Intelligent (the *prajña*) is immersed in deep sleep, as a mass of consciousness without cognizing external or internal objects. Again, Śaṃkara comments: "It is called *Prajña,* the knower *par excellence,* even in deep sleep, because of its having been so in the two previous states. Or it is called the *Prajña* because its peculiar feature is consciousness undifferentiated" (Commentary on *Māṇḍukya Upaniṣad* 5 [Nikhilananda's translation]).

7. Cf. *Pañcīkaraṇa-Vārttika* 44: "The one reality, having the nature of consciousness, through delusion appears as many: the All, the Brilliant, the Deeply Sleeping (*sauṣupta,* = *prajña,* the Intelligent), the Cosmic Body, the Cosmic Soul, and the Imperishable (*akṣara,* = *īśa,* the Lord)."

8. The individuated form is called *vyaṣṭi,* the aggregated or comprehensive form *samaṣṭi.* The *Vedāntasāra* (40, 47, 90) explains the difference between the two forms in terms of a forest (aggregated form) and its trees (individuated), or of a reservoir of water and the individual drops. Accordingly, the Lord is composed, as it were, of all the souls. Or as *Pañcadaśī* 1.25 explains, the Lord is comprehensive because he identifies himself with all souls, while the individual soul knows only itself. The two terms, *vyaṣṭi* and *samaṣṭi,* thus refer to

the individual and cosmic, or microcosmic and macrocosmic, aspects of the same reality that is the Self.

The *Vedāntasāra* provides the same basic correlations between the individual and cosmic forms of the three bodies. *Vedāntasāra* 35–48 explains the basic correlation between the individual and cosmic forms of the Causal Body, both forms being associated with deep sleep. *Vedāntasāra* 90–96 correlates the individual and cosmic forms of the Subtle Body, associated with dreaming. Verses 110–16 make the final set of correlations of the Gross Body, associated with waking.

Translation

[The Goddess concludes by summarizing the creative role of the Lord and his relation to herself.]

2.49. [cont.] That universal Lord himself, through his desire to favor the soul,

2.50. Creates the manifold world anew, with its store of various enjoyments.[1]
The Lord is ever sent forth by my power, having been conceived in me, O King.

Comment

In this chapter overall, the *Devī Gītā* presents an Advaitin analysis of the creative process. The Goddess here often sounds like a Śaṃkara, or more precisely, like post-Śaṃkara Advaitins such as Sureśvara or Vidyāraṇya. Thus, in 2.11cd, she affirms that Māyā is destroyed by knowledge, echoing the assertion in the *Vivekacūdāmaṇi* that Māyā is not eternal, for it "can be destroyed by realizing the pure, non-dual Brahman, just as the erroneous perception of a serpent is dispelled by correctly discriminating the rope."[2]

The Goddess provides hints, however, that the Advaitin analysis does not represent the final, or at least not the only, interpretation of creation. The illusionary aspect of Māyā, with the correlative notion of its eventual (future) destruction, is not infrequently overridden by a sense of Māyā's essential oneness with the Goddess. And due to this identity, Māyā is not "the power of the supreme Lord," as the

Vivekacūḍāmaṇi would have it,[3] but is rather the power that impels the Lord, as suggested in the last line above.

Moreover, while Advaitins talk of the Lord as the reflection of Brahman in Māyā, the Goddess concludes that the Lord is conceived (that is, imagined or fancied [*saṃkalpita*]) in herself. In one sense, then, she is reflected in her own self as Māyā. The commentator Nīlakaṇṭha interprets the last line, utilizing Śaṃkara's beloved analogy, as follows: "That Lord is conceived in me (the Goddess), who am Brahman in essence, as a snake is conceived in a rope. Therefore is he ever dependent on my power." While the commentator's remark can be interpreted in illusionistic terms, it also points to what the Goddess herself emphasizes, namely her enduring and absolute power of creative projection. This power, as indicated in 2.5 above and in the first verse of the next chapter, is inseparable from the Goddess. For Advaitins, Brahman does not possess attributes such as being, consciousness, and bliss, but rather *is* being, consciousness, and bliss. In a like manner, for Śāktas, the Goddess does not possess such attributes as Śakti and Māyā, for she *is* Śakti and Māyā.

Notes

1. Cf. *Pañcadaśī* 1.26.

2. *Vivekacūḍāmaṇi* 110.

3. *Vivekacūḍāmaṇi* 108.

Chapter 3

The Goddess Reveals Her Cosmic Body (The Virāj)

Translation

[The Goddess continues to explain the cosmogonic mysteries of Māyā, including her own entry into the creation.]

The Goddess spoke:

3.1. I imagine into being the whole world, moving and unmoving, through the power of my Māyā,
Yet that same Māyā is not separate from me; this is the highest truth.[1]

3.2. From the practical point of view, Māyā is regarded as self-evident.[2]
In reality, however, it does not exist—only the supreme exists, in an absolute sense.[3]

3.3. I, as Māyā, create the whole world and then enter within it,[4]
Accompanied by ignorance,[5] actions, and the like,[6] and preceded by the vital breath, O Mountain.

3.4. How else could souls be reborn into future lives?[7]
They take on various births in accord with modifications of Māyā.

Comment

By emphasizing her intrinsic involvement within the material realm, the Goddess begins to set the stage for the revelation of her cosmic form, known as the Virāj (see Comment on 3.22–34 below). Her entering within the world—in the form of souls or *jīvas*—gives a preliminary indication of her basic identity with all beings.

A mythological explanation for the cosmic nature of the Virāj is given in the *Bṛhadāraṇyaka Upaniṣad.*[8] There, the supreme reality (Puruṣa or Ātman) divides itself into male and female, and then in a devolving series of gendered pairs from human down through animal forms ending with ants, creates through copulation all sexual beings. The supreme Self, according to the text, then knew: "I am indeed this creation, for I have created all this." While the *Upaniṣad* does not specifically mention the term *Virāj,* Śaṃkara in commenting on the passage frequently applies the term to this transforming Puruṣa, an association already found in the *Ṛg Veda.*[9] The late Advaita text, the *Pañcadaśī,* in discussing the entry of the supreme Self into diverse bodies in the form of various souls, refers to the *Bṛhadāraṇyaka* myth and also names the Puruṣa as the Virāj.[10] The association of the world-pervading Self/Puruṣa with the Virāj is thus a well-established theme, which the Goddess assimilates to herself in the *Devī Gītā.*

Notes

1. *paramārthataḥ;* according to Advaita, there are two basic levels of truth, the supreme or higher (*paramārtha*), in which the ultimate unity of Self and Brahman is realized, and the empirical or worldly (*vyavahāra,* mentioned in the next verse), in which individuality and thus plurality are accepted as real. The unitary insight of the higher truth is here applied to the relationship between the Goddess and Māyā. Cf. 2.5 above.

2. *vidyā:* "knowledge, science." Māyā is said to be *vidyā* (from the practical point of view) in the sense that the realm of Māyā, the universe, is simply assumed to be true or real, the object of knowledge and needing no evidence for its own truth—thus "self-evident."

3. Cf. *Pañcadaśī* 6.130, which presents three perspectives on Māyā; from the viewpoint of scripture (*śrauta*), Māyā is unreal (*tucchā*); from the viewpoint of reasoning (*yauktika*), it is undefinable (*anirvacanīyā*); from the viewpoint of ordinary people (*laukika*), it is real (*vāstavī*). Cf. also *Pañcadaśī* 6.128–29, and *Devī Gītā* 2.4.

In translating the verb *exists* (*asti*), I have interpreted it as referring to absolute existence, in accord with common Advaita usage and the immediate context of the *Devī Gītā* itself.

4. On the notion of the supreme creating and then entering into the world, cf. *Chāndogya Upaniṣad* 6.2–3 and *Taittirīya Upaniṣad* 2.6.

Nīlakaṇṭha, in accord with Advaitic notions of the immutability of the ultimate, disavows any actual movement or activity on the part of the Goddess in "entering" into the world. Referring to her as the unchangeable Brahman (*kūṭastha-brahma-svarūpā*), and utilizing two famous Advaitic analogies, he argues that the Goddess means to say: "I enter within it (the world) as a reflection of consciousness (*cid-ābhāsa*), like space in a jar, like a reflection in a mirror." The Goddess herself below utilizes the space/jar analogy among others to indicate that her absolute nature is unaffected by her involvement in the material world.

5. *māyā;* glossed by Nīlakaṇṭha as "ignorance" (*avidyā*).

6. *ādi:* "and the like"; interpreted by Nīlakaṇṭha as referring to the various unconscious, psychic scars (*saṃskāras*) or impressions that one carries into a given life from actions performed in previous births.

7. The basic idea of this line and the preceding verse is that the ultimate, by entering into the world, takes on the form of individual souls (*jīvas*) with their karmic burdens and gives them their life force or vital breath (*prāṇa*). *Pañcadaśī* 4.10 states: "Assuming various soul-forms, the Lord entered into the body (of various beings). . . . The soul is so called as it supports the vital breath." Cf. *Pañcadaśī* 10.1: "Through his own Māyā, the supreme Self by himself became the world and then entered it in the form of the soul."

8. *Bṛhadāraṇyaka Upaniṣad* 1.4.3–5.

9. In *Ṛg Veda* 10.90.5, the Virāj is said to be born from Puruṣa, and Puruṣa from Virāj. Cf. Tracy Pintchman, *The Rise of the Goddess in the Hindu Tradition*, pp. 34–35.

10. *Pañcadaśī* 4.9–10. (Cf. note 7 above.)

Translation

[The Goddess affirms that she is not affected or tainted in any way by her differentiated manifestations.]

3.5. Modified by apparent limitations,[1] I become differentiated into parts, like space in different jars.[2]
The sun constantly illumines all objects however high or low,

3.6. Yet is not thereby stained; just so am I never stained by faults.[3]
Ordinary people superimpose[4] on me the active agency of the intellect[5] and the like:
3.7. "The Self is acting," say the bewildered, not the wise.[6]
Modifications of ignorance and modifications of Māyā
3.8. Divide the soul and the Lord into parts, respectively;[7] it is all contrived by Māyā.[8]
The contrived separation of the space within jars from space in general
3.9. Is like the contrived division between the individual soul and the supreme soul.[9]
Just as the multiple manifestations of the soul are due to ignorance,[10] not to the soul's inherent nature,
3.10. Just so are the multiple manifestations of the Lord[11] due to Māyā, not to his innate essence.
Creating divisions through the imagined distinctions of various bodies with all their senses,
3.11. Ignorance is the cause of the differentiation of souls; no other cause is revealed.[12]
Creating divisions through the imagined distinctions of the material qualities,[13] O Mountain,
3.12. Māyā is the cause of the differentiation of the supreme Lord into parts, and nothing else.[14]

Comment

The Goddess is about to expound a grand, cosmotheistic vision of the universe in which she identifies herself with the cosmos in all its myriad parts. But first she anticipates a possible misunderstanding. In identifying herself with the world, does she assume its various faults and limitations? Her answer is no, but how can this be? The world is finite, multiplex, changing, and subject to defects of various sorts, while the Goddess, from the Advaitic perspective, is infinite, one, immutable, and pure. How, then, can she identify herself with the world without compromising her absolute, pure, infinite nature?

The Goddess presents two analogies to elucidate the paradox of her involvement with and nondefilement by the world. The "illumination" analogy—of the sun not being stained by the objects it illumines—stresses the undefiled purity of the supreme. But the analogy presupposes a duality (between the sun and the illumined objects) and thus does little to illustrate or clarify the unity or identity of the Goddess and the world. The "limitation" analogy—of a jar that appears to limit or temporarily separate the space within it from infinite space, with which it remains fundamentally one—more adequately expresses the essential unity of the supreme with its phenomenally separate parts. This analogy is a favorite among certain Advaitins (the Bhāmatī school of *avacchedavādins* or "limitationists") to illustrate how the association of ignorance with pure consciousness, resulting in phenomenally separate souls, does not truly affect the essential unity of the supreme consciousness. With this analogy, then, the Goddess attempts to illustrate how the limiting conditions of Māyā or ignorance do not in reality effect a substantial change in her nature. All differentiations and their effects are merely imagined, or superimposed, upon her. Keeping these Advaitic qualifications in mind, the devotee is now ready to hear the cosmotheistic affirmations of the Goddess without misunderstanding.

It is worth noting here that verses 3.7cd–12ab are apparently based on the *Sūta Gītā*,[15] a Śaivite text. Frequently, as we have seen, the *Devī Gītā* incorporates earlier, Vaiṣṇava scriptural models, assimilating them into a Śākta theological framework. Here, it seems, the *Devī Gītā* has assimilated a few verses from a Śaivite Gītā. But whereas in the *Sūta Gītā*, ignorance and Māyā are distinct from the supreme Śiva,[16] here in the *Devī Gītā* the Goddess is not other than Māyā. Thus, the *Devī Gītā* does not reject the *Sūta Gītā*, but implicitly affirms aspects of the Śaivite view while providing a Śākta corrective, typical of the textual strategies of the *Devī Gītā*.

Notes

1. *upādhi:* a "limiting condition or adventitious adjunct" such as space, time, or matter. In Advaita, such finite limitations on the absolute are apparent only, since Brahman is unlimited.

2. This is a favorite analogy of the Advaitins (cf. note 4 on 3.3 above). An early example of the analogy occurs in the *Brahmabindu Upaniṣad* (13–14). Deussen suggests that this Upaniṣad appears to be "a link between the older Upaniṣads and Śaṁkara, whose favourite illustration of the space in the jar

and the universal space already appears here (verses 13–14)" (*Sixty Upaniṣads of the Veda*, p. 687). For the early Upaniṣads, see, for example, *Chāndogya Upaniṣad* 3.12.7–9, where space, identified with Brahman, whether outside a person, inside a person, or within the heart, is said to be the same space. The popularity of the analogy is attested to by its inclusion in a summary of the Vedāntic position on the nature of the universal Self that appears in the late (fourteenth century) *Sāṃkhya-pravacana Sūtra* (1.150; quoted in Sarvepalli Radhakrishnan and Charles A. Moore, eds., *A Source Book in Indian Philosophy*, p. 449). The *Pañcadaśī* utilizes and elaborates on the basic analogy in 6.18–21 and 6.237.

The analogy is apparently a favorite of the Goddess as well, as she repeats it in 3.8cd–9ab below.

3. A version of this analogy appears already in the *Kaṭha Upaniṣad* (2.2.11): "Just as the sun, the eye of the entire world, is not stained by the external faults seen by our eyes, so is the one Self residing within all beings, yet beyond, not stained by the world's suffering."

Cf. *Bhagavad Gītā* 13.31–32, where the Self is said not to be stained even though abiding in the body, just as space is not stained by contact with various objects. Interestingly, the following verse (13.33) likens the Self to the sun that illumines all the world. Cf. also *Vivekacūḍāmaṇi* 506: "As the sun is merely a witness of actions, . . . so am I the unaffected Self, pure consciousness."

4. *adhyasya;* a technical term in Advaita, used to explain the nature of misperception, in particular, of how humans fail to perceive the true nature of the world as Brahman. The famous definition given by Śaṃkara in the introduction to his commentary on the *Brahma Sūtras* (*Vedānta Sūtras*) is "the apparent presentation, in the form of remembrance, to consciousness of something previously observed, in some other thing" (Thibaut's translation). Specific examples that Śaṃkara offers are that of silver being superimposed on mother-of-pearl, and of two moons being superimposed (through faulty vision) on the one moon. The significant metaphysical error is superimposing upon the true Self things that are not-Self, such as the body, intellect, and the like, thereby obscuring the nondual Ātman that is identical with Brahman.

5. Cf. *Pañcadaśī* 6.23, which refers to the superimposition of intellect (*buddhi*) on the immutable (*kūṭastha*).

6. Nīlakaṇṭha elaborates: "Like the sun, I [the Goddess] am merely a witness, not an agent." *Vivekacūḍāmaṇi* 508 affirms: "Fools conclude that the movement of a reflection on a rippling surface [*upādhi*, literally, "adjunct"] is due to [the movement of] the object reflected, which is unwavering like the sun. They think, 'I am a doer, I am an enjoyer, I am slain, alas.' " Cf. *Bhāgavata Purāṇa* 3.27.1: "Though abiding in matter, spirit is unaffected by the *guṇa*s of nature, as it is beyond modification, beyond agency, beyond qualities, like the sun [reflected in] water." Cf. also *Bhagavad Gītā* 18.16: "One who sees the Self alone as agent due to distorted perception, such a person does not truly see, being deluded."

7. Māyā and ignornace (*ajñāna, avidyā*) in Advaita are commonly regarded as cosmic and individual aspects of the same basic power of manifestation: when the supreme Brahman is limited by the adjunct of Māyā, it becomes the Lord, Īśvara; when limited by ignorance, it becomes the individual *jīva* or soul. Cf. *Devī Gītā* 2.44–46ab. While in many Advaitic discussions, the Īśvara is regarded as a singular Lord of creation, the *Devī Gītā* sees both the Lord and the soul becoming multiple through the power of Māyā/ignorance (see also note 14 below).

8. Verse 3.7cd–8ab is a loose paraphrase of *Sūta Gītā* 2.8–9. The following four verses of the *Devī Gītā* are nearly identical with *Sūta Gītā* 2.10–11, 2.13–14.

9. While the preceding two lines (3.7cd–8ab) and the following six lines (3.9cd–12ab) deal with the contrived divisions of the soul and the Lord, respectively, into multiple parts, these two lines (3.8cd–9ab) deal with a more fundamental but equally contrived separation—of the individual soul from the supreme soul.

10. *māyā;* here it seems reasonable to take the term as signifying "ignorance," given what is stated in 3.7cd–8ab above, and repeated in 3.11 below.

11. According to Nīlakaṇṭha, these multiple manifestations consist of Brahmā, Viṣṇu, and the like.

12. Ignorance is a topic of prime importance in Advaita, not just in its cosmogonic aspect, discussed in this and preceding verses, but also, and more especially, in its psychological aspect and role in human bondage. The Goddess will return to such matters in the next chapter (4.3ff.), after the revelation of her Cosmic Body.

13. The *guṇa*s of nature (see the Comment on 2.35cd 42ab, for explanation of these qualities).

14. The idea implicit here is that the three *guṇa*s of Māyā or Prakṛti result in the division of the Lord into the *sattv*ic Viṣṇu, the *rajas*ic Brahmā, and the *tamas*ic Śiva. Nīlakaṇṭha (commenting on 3.11cd) indicates that the general notion is more fully explained in the *Sūta Gītā* of the *Sūta Saṃhitā,* and explicated there by Mādhavācārya. (The *Sūta Saṃhitā* is part of the *Skanda Purāṇa.*) S. Radhakrishnan, in explaining the relation of Māyā and *avidyā,* refers to a passage in the *Skanda Purāṇa* "where avidyā is regarded as the limiting adjunct of jīva, and māyā as the limiting adjunct of the Supreme viewed as Brahmā, Viṣṇu and Maheśvara" (*Indian Philosophy,* vol. 2, p. 589, n.2). He then quotes the Sanskrit text (without verse or chapter citation), which I translate as follows: "The *jīva* is limited by *avidyā,* not by Māyā. (The supreme, when) obscured by the effects of the *guṇa*s of Māyā, becomes Brahmā, Viṣṇu, and Maheśvara." (The lines are actually *Sūta Gītā* 2.52ab and 53ab.)

15. *Sūta Gītā* 2.8–14.

16. E.g., *Sūta Gītā* 2.5.

Translation

[The Goddess declares her identity with all cosmic and worldly entities.]

3.12. [cont.] In me this whole world is woven in all directions,[1] O Mountain.

3.13. I am the Lord and the Cosmic Soul; I am myself the Cosmic Body.[2]
I am Brahmā, Viṣṇu, and Rudra, as well as Gaurī, Brāhmī, and Vaiṣṇavī.[3]

3.14. I am the sun and the stars, and I am the Lord of the stars.[4]
I am the various species of beasts and birds; I am also the outcaste and thief.

3.15. I am the evil doer and the wicked deed; I am the righteous person and the virtuous deed.[5]
I am certainly female and male, and asexual as well.[6]

3.16. And whatever thing, anywhere,[7] you see or hear,
That entire thing I pervade, ever abiding inside it and outside.[8]

3.17. There is nothing at all, moving or unmoving, that is devoid of me;[9]
For if it were, it would be a nonentity,[10] like the son of a barren woman.[11]

3.18. Just as a single rope may appear variously as a serpent or wreath,
So also I may appear in the form of the Lord and the like; there is no doubt in this matter.[12]

3.19. The world cannot appear without an underlying basis.
Accordingly, the world comes to be only through my own being and in no other way.

Comment

The Goddess begins her cosmotheistic self-predications with reference to the Upaniṣadic notion that all the universe is woven upon the supreme, here identified, of course, with the Goddess herself. That is, everything is composed or tied together within the Goddess, who pervades all things. Then, resorting to the dramatic "I am . . ." formulations made famous by Kṛṣṇa in the *Bhagavad Gītā*, she proceeds to establish her identity with all beings and abstract entities in every dimension and at every level of the universe. Like Kṛṣṇa, she encompasses both good and evil. And like Kṛṣṇa, she is both female and male, but she is more thorough in elaborating on her gendered pairs—she goes beyond Kṛṣṇa in representing not only the male members of the Trimūrti, but the female as well.

In verse 16, echoing the *Muṇḍaka Upaniṣad*, the Goddess affirms that she exists both within and without all things. Such a statement clearly indicates the sort of cosmotheistic vision she is promulgating, a vision that definitively transcends simple pantheism. She explicitly denies here that she is *only* to be identified with the universe. Rather, she is both identical with *and different from* the cosmos.[13]

The famous Advaitic analogy of the rope and serpent (along with the wreath) presented in verse 18 appears also in *Devī Gītā* 1.50. A lengthy note (16) on that verse indicated that the *Devī Gītā*'s use of the verb *bhā* ("to shine forth," "to show oneself," as well as "to appear") suggests a more creative, less illusionistic aspect of Māyā than what we find in Advaita. In this verse here, the Goddess may be seen as shining forth (*vibhā/bhā*) or projecting an image of herself as the Lord and other aspects of the material world.

This less illusionistic emphasis would accord well with the surrounding cosmotheistic context, as well as with the general Tantric leanings of the *Devī Gītā*. As one contemporary scholar explains: "The peculiar metaphysical standpoint of the Tantras in the context of creation consists in its theory of Ābhāsa ["reflection"]. It rejects the Vivartavāda [mere-appearance school] of the Vedānta, as it is now-a-days interpreted. According to it the world is originally a false appearance due to error. The Tantras, on the other hand, hold that the world is real in the same way as an image is real but it has no existence apart from the medium in which it is manifested. The manifestation of the universe is thus a process of Ābhāsa and for the initiation of this process nothing beyond the play of the Will (the free will/Svātantrya of the Absolute) is needed. . . . To a Tantrist the world is real and it is the expression of the cit śakti/free will of the Lord and it is really spiritual in essence like the Lord Himself. In the last resort the world turns back into the cit śakti which is never withdrawn."[14] If one substitutes the Goddess for the Lord in this statement, we have a good summary of the general cosmogonic standpoint of the *Devī Gītā*. While at times the *Devī Gītā* presents a more Advaitic, acosmic view of the world, its general standpoint, as well as that of the *Devī-Bhāgavata* as a whole, seems to be much more world accepting and validating.

Notes

1. *protam otaṃ ca;* literally, "woven crosswise and lengthwise." Cf. *Bṛhadāraṇyaka Upaniṣad* 3.6, where Gārgī asks Yājñavalkya a series of questions regarding the ultimate basis of the universe. She first inquires, since this world is woven crosswise and lengthwise (*otaṃ ca protaṃ ca*) on water, on what is water woven crosswise and lengthwise? Yājñavalkya replies "air." Gārgī and Yājñavalkya then proceed from air, through the various worlds of the sky, sun, moon, stars, gods, etc., up to the worlds of Brahmā. When she asks on what are the worlds of Brahmā woven, Yājñavalkya tells Gārgī that her questioning may make her head fall off since she is asking too much about a divinity that is not to be excessively questioned. Gārgī desists for a while, but then, in 3.8, continues with two more questions. The first concerns the underlying basis of the entire spatial-temporal realm, to which Yajñavalkya answers "space." As to what space is woven upon, the answer is "the imperishable" (*akṣara,* that is, Brahman). In the *Devī Gītā* the imperishable is the Goddess.

2. Cf. 1.49, 2.47–48 above.

3. The self-predications in this and the following two verses are loosely modelled on the "I am . . ." sayings of the *Bhagavad Gītā* (7.8–11; 9.16–18; 10.20–38). In *Bhagavad Gītā* 10.21–29, Kṛṣṇa identifies himself with the best of a number of classes of beings and gods, including Viṣṇu and Śiva, but mentions no goddesses (though some female and feminine entities [in 10.34] are mentioned). The *Devī Gītā* in this verse, significantly, gives equal emphasis to the male and female aspects of the Trimūrti.

4. *tārakeśa;* literally, "lord of stars," i.e., "the moon."
In *Bhagavad Gītā* 10.21, Kṛṣṇa says, "I am the sun among radiant lights . . . I am the moon among the stars."

5. Cf. *Bhagavad Gītā* 10.36, where Kṛṣṇa declares: "I am the gambling of deceivers . . . I am the virtue of the righteous."

6. In *Bhagavad Gītā* 9.17, Kṛṣṇa asserts: "I am the father of the world, the mother. . . ." Cf. *Śvetāśvatara Upaniṣad* 4.3: "You (the supreme Lord) are woman, you are man, you are the young boy and young maiden too."

7. Cf. *Devī Māhātmya* 1.63: "And whatever thing, anywhere, exists, real or unreal . . . , of all that you [the Goddess] are its power."

8. Cf. *Muṇḍaka Upaniṣad* 2.1.2, where the formless Puruṣa is said to exist "inside and outside (all things)." The *Devī Gītā* in this chapter has utilized several verses from *Muṇḍaka* 2.1 (see verses 3.23cd–24, 46–51 below). Cf. *Bhagavad Gītā* 10.16, where Arjuna declares that Kṛṣṇa ever pervades the worlds with his supernal manifestations.

9. Cf. *Bhagavad Gītā* 10.39cd, where Kṛṣṇa declares: "There is nothing that exists, moving or unmoving, without me."

10. *śūnya;* glossed by Nīlakaṇṭha as "nonexistent" (*asat*), in contrast to the Goddess who is "existent" (*sat-rūpā*).

11. The analogy of the barren woman's son is commonly used in Advaita to illustrate the meaning of absolute nonexistence, over against the qualified existence of this somewhat real, somewhat illusory world. Cf. the Comment of *Devī Gītā* 2.1–11ab.

12. See note 16 on *Devī Gītā* 1.50, where this same rope-serpent-wreath analogy is also used, and see the Comment above.

13. The philosopher W. T. Stace defines the term *pantheistic* in a nontraditional way that could be applied to the teachings of the Goddess in the *Devī Gītā.* Stace rejects the more conventional notion of pantheism, that the universe as a whole is God and that God is nothing but the sum of all material energies and forces. Stace's definition reinterprets the term as affirming the paradox that the world is both "identical with God" and at the same time "distinct from, that is to say, *not* identical with God" (*Mysticism and Philosophy,* p. 212).

While I personally like Stace's redefinition, it is perhaps too unconventional and uncommon so that to use the term *pantheism* would be misleading to many readers. The term in its traditional sense does not apply to any Hindu text or viewpoint of which I am aware. Hindus frequently do assert that "God is the universe," but equally, and usually simultaneously, they add "and God is more." See, for instance, the famous "Puruṣa Sūkta" of the *Ṛg Veda* (10.90), where the Puruṣa who becomes the world is also said to extend "ten fingers beyond it," a marvelous poetic rejection of the traditional conception of pantheism (cf. Edgerton, The *Bhagavad Gītā,* pp. 148–49). Interestingly, Stace relies heavily on the Upaniṣads in justifying his definition of pantheism.

I have used the term *cosmotheism* to describe the attitude of the *Devī Gītā.* This term, while sometimes used as a synonym for pantheism, does not seem to me to carry the same absolute sense of total identification between God, or the Goddess, and the world. Cosmotheism refers to the view that the cosmos is divine and is the Goddess, but does not necessarily assume that the cosmos is all. Thus, room is left for the notion that the Goddess may be the cosmos and something else as well.

14. Basu, *Fundamentals of the Philosophy of Tantras,* pp. 211–12.

Translation

[Himālaya requests to see the aggregated form or Cosmic Body of the Goddess.]

Himālaya said:

3.20. Ruler of the Gods, since you have mentioned your aggregated cosmic form,[1]
I yearn to see it, O Goddess, if you would favor me.

Vyāsa said:

3.21. Hearing his request, all the gods including Viṣṇu
Rejoiced with gladdened hearts, praising Himālaya's words.

Comment

Himālaya, in using the term *aggregated form* (*samaṣṭy-ātma-vapus*) to refer to the Cosmic Body (Virāj) of the Goddess, is utilizing the technical terminology of relatively late Advaita philosophy. In the *Bhagavad Gītā* parallel, Arjuna simply asks Kṛṣṇa to reveal his majestic, lordly form (*rūpam aiśvaram*).[2] In the *Bhāgavata Purāṇa*, a somewhat more specialized vocabulary is used in naming the cosmic form of the Lord: it is referred to as both his gross body (*sthūlam rūpam*)[3] and as the cosmic man (*vairāja puruṣa*).[4] In late Advaitic primers like the *Pañcadaśī*, the concepts of aggregated and individuated forms of consciousness are briefly defined and explained.[5] The *Pañcadaśī* specifically connects the aggregated form with the gross body of the lord, and also refers to it as the Vaiśvānara.[6] The *Vedāntasāra* not only identifies the aggregated form with Vaiśvānara, but also explicitly refers to it as the Virāj.[7] Himālaya's request to the Goddess thus dramatizes a synthesis of the late cosmological elaborations of classical Advaita with the traditional mythic images regarding the cosmic Puruṣa or Virāj.

Notes

1. *samaṣṭy-ātma-vapus;* this comprehensive or aggregated body is glossed by Nīlakaṇṭha as "your [the Devī's] inherent form as the Virāj (Cosmic Body), regarding yourself as being all things." The Goddess mentioned her aggregated and individuated forms in 2.49.

2. *Bhagavad Gītā* 11.3; the same phrase is used in 11.9.

3. *Bhāgavata Purāṇa* 2.1.23.

4. *Bhāgavata Purāṇa* 2.1.25.

5. *Pañcadaśī* 1.24–25, 28. See note 8 on *Devī Gītā* 2.49.

6. *Pañcadaśī* 1.28. For a brief discussion of the term "Vaiśvānara," including Śaṃkara's definition of it, see note 6 on *Devī Gītā* 2.48.

7. *Vedāntasāra* 111.

Translation

[The Goddess manifests herself as the Virāj, revealing various macrocosmic and microcosmic correspondences.]

3.22. Then the Auspicious Goddess, who is a wish-granting cow to her devotees,[1] knowing the minds of the gods,
Revealed her own cosmic form, satisfying the desire of her devotees.
3.23. They beheld that Cosmic Body of the Great Goddess, that form beyond all other forms.
The sky is its head,[2] the moon and sun its eyes.[3]
3.24. The cardinal directions are its ears, the Vedas its speech, the wind its breath, so it is proclaimed;
The universe is its heart, they say; the earth its loins, so it is thought.[4]
3.25. The atmosphere is its navel, the stellar sphere its breast;
Maharloka is the neck, Janarloka its face, so it is thought.
3.26. Taparloka is the forehead, situated beneath Satyaloka.[5]
Indra and the gods are its arms, sound is the hearing of this Great Ruler.[6]
3.27. The twin Aśvins are its nostrils, scent its smelling, so think the wise.
Fire is proclaimed as its mouth, day and night as its two eyelids.

3.28. The abode of Brahmā is the play of its eyebrows; the waters are proclaimed as its palate.
Taste is proclaimed as its tongue, the God of Death as its fangs.
3.29. The various affections are its teeth; Māyā is proclaimed as its laughter.
Creation is its casting of sidelong glances; modesty is the upper lip of this Great Ruler.
3.30. Greed is its lower lip, the way of unrighteousness its back.[7]
And Prajāpati, the creator on earth, is its penis.[8]
3.31. The ocean is the belly, the mountains the bones of the Goddess,[9] the Great Ruler.
The rivers are proclaimed as her arteries, trees as her hair.
3.32. Childhood, youth, and old age are her excellent gaits;
Clouds are her hair, the two twilights the garments of the Lord.
3.33. O King, the moon is the mind of the holy World-Mother,
Viṣṇu is her power of discernment, and Śiva is the seat of her thoughts and feelings, so it is thought.
3.34. Horses and all the various species abide in the hips and loins of the Lord;
The great lower worlds such as Atala are situated below her buttocks.[10]

Comment

The *Devī Gītā*'s description of the Virāj or Cosmic Body of the Goddess consists of two basic parts. The first (verses 3.23cd–34 above) provides a relatively peaceful and benign portrayal of the Goddess, identifying her body in its various limbs and features with the manifold, material universe. The second (verses 3.35-38 below) transforms this peaceful image, endowing it with a powerful, terrifying, and destructive energy.

The first part, describing the various macrocosmic-microcosmic correspondences, illustrates a classic motif of Hindu cosmotheism, in which an essential unity is affirmed between God and the cosmos. Such cosmic theism has its roots in the famous "Puruṣa Sūkta" of the *Ṛg Veda*. There, the Cosmic Man (Puruṣa) gives birth to the Virāj, and the Virāj gives birth to the Puruṣa.[11] The Puruṣa is then dismembered in sacrifice, his parts forming the universe. This motif was much repeated and elaborated in the Upaniṣads. In the *Muṇḍaka Upaniṣad*, for instance, the Puruṣa, now identified with the transcendent ideals of Brahman and Ātman, is said to give birth to various cosmic elements that are correlated with his body parts, the specific correlations echoing those of the *Ṛg Veda*.[12] In later versions, these correspondences provide a blueprint for creating the universe: in the *Bhāgavata Purāṇa*, the Virāj form of Viṣṇu serves as an object of meditation for the creator Brahmā, allowing him to remember how to reconstitute the world after its previous dissolution.[13]

The *Devī Gītā*'s list of correspondences begins with three lines (23cd–24) largely based on the *Muṇḍaka Upaniṣad*,[14] thereby evoking the ancient Vedic and Vedāntic associations of the Virāj image. The remaining correlations closely follow the *Bhāgavata Purāṇa*'s description of Viṣṇu's cosmic form.[15] In this fashion the *Devī Gītā* takes over an important image of Vaiṣṇava cosmic theism and incorporates it into the theology of the Goddess.

A somewhat similar description of the cosmic correspondences belonging to the Virāj form of the Goddess Lalitā appears in the *Lalitā Māhātmya* of the *Brahmāṇḍa Purāṇa*. There, the description occurs as part of a hymn by the gods to the Goddess—no actual revelation of her Cosmic Body takes place.[16] (For the close resemblance of Lalitā and Bhuvaneśvarī, see the Introduction, pp. 25–26. See also the next Comment, for a significant difference.)

The cosmogonic overtones of the above correspondences in the *Devī Gītā* contrast sharply with the apocalyptic imagery that follows in the second part of the description of the Devī's Cosmic Body, given in the next few verses below.

Notes

1. See *Devī Gītā* 1.46, and its note 6.

2. Nīlakaṇṭha glosses *dyau* (sky) as "Satyaloka, above all." Satyaloka is the highest of the heavenly spheres, such as Maharloka, Janarloka, and Taparloka, mentioned in 3.25–26. This follows the *Bhāgavata Purāṇa*'s description of the Lord's cosmic form: "The Satya(loka) constitutes the heads of the thousand-headed (Puruṣa)" (2.1.28). *Muṇḍaka Upaniṣad* 2.1.4, on which *Devī Gītā* 3.23cd–24 is based, begins by stating "Fire is the head." Śaṃkara in his commentary identifies the fire with the world of the gods or heaven.

3. Cf. *Bhagavad Gītā* 11.19, where Arjuna describes Kṛṣṇa's cosmic form as having the moon and sun for its eyes (*śaśi-sūrya-netram*). The *Devī Gītā* uses the *Muṇḍaka*'s terminology, merely reversing its order: *cakṣuṣī candra-sūryau.*

4. Except for the first correspondence (sky = head, in verse 23) and this last (earth = loins), the other correspondences in 23cd–24 are exactly those of *Muṇḍaka Upaniṣad* 2.1.4 (the *Muṇḍaka* equates the earth with the feet of the cosmic being). In both exceptions, the *Devī Gītā* has followed the *Bhāgavata Purāṇa* (see *Bhāgavata* 2.1.27 for the earth = loins correspondence). Cf. *Ṛg Veda* 10.90.13–14.

5. According to *Vedāntasāra* 104, the five compounded elements (already discussed in *Devī Gītā* 2.33–35) evolved into fourteen realms, seven nether worlds and seven celestial. The latter in order are Bhūr (= earth, referred to as Bhūh in *Devī Gītā* 3.24), Bhuvar (= atmosphere), Svar (= stellar sphere), Mahar, Janas, Tapas, and Satyam. *Vedāntasāra* 111 then refers to the Virāj (Cosmic Body) arising from the compounded elements. Thus the *Vedāntasāra,* or a similar Vedāntic primer, may well have served as a general model for the *Devī Gītā*'s account of the Devī's Cosmic Body.

The *Vedāntasāra,* however, does not provide any of the specific correspondences of the worldly realms with the deity's body parts. For these, the *Devī Gītā* follows the *Bhāgavata Purāṇa* (2.1.26–28) in its description of the gross body of the Lord. The *Bhāgavata,* however, commences its correlations beginning with the feet up: the parts below the loins are matched with the seven lower worlds, from Pātala (the lowest) to Atala (just below the surface of the earth). The *Devī Gītā* merely summarizes these correlations of the lower half of the Goddess' body in 3.34.

6. *maheśitṛ;* such agent nouns are masculine in gender. But in verse 29, it is in apposition to *devī,* making clear that the Great Ruler is the Goddess.

The *Devī Gītā* conforms to the *Bhāgavata* not only in its correlations relating to the world spheres given in the preceding lines, but also in the more specific correspondences regarding the gods, abstract ideas, and concrete details of the physical universe, etc., dealt with here and in the following verses (3.26cd–34ab). Thus, *Devī Gītā* 3.24d–34 is closely based upon *Bhāgavata Purāṇa* 2.1.27cd–35, often using identical terminology, if somewhat rearranged, and with occasional elaborations or omissions.

7. The *Devī Gītā* has omitted from the *Bhāgavata Purāṇa*'s account the counterpart to unrighteousness: *dharmaḥ stano* ("righteousness is its breast") (2.1.32).

8. *meḍhra;* literally, "semen emitter." Prajāpati, the Lord of creatures and of procreation, produces the world through his cosmic emission. His identification with the penis of the Virāj is thus quite appropriate.

The *Devī Gītā* omits the next correspondence in the *Bhāgavata: vṛṣaṇau ca mitrau* ("and the two Mitras are its testicles") (2.1.32).

9. Needless to say, mention of the Goddess is a new element, not found in the *Bhāgavata Purāṇa*'s account. The *Devī Gītā*'s specific noting of the

Goddess at this point, immediately following the reference to Prajāpati and the Virāj's penis, presents an intriguing paradox, suggesting the androgynous nature of the Devī. The Virāj is *her* body, but in male form. Interestingly, Virāj itself has been of ambiguous gender, or androgynous. In the "Puruṣa Sūkta," its gender is unstated. "In the *Atharva Veda,* she [Virāj] is an independent creative principle, identified with the Spell (*brahma*), with Speech, and with Prajāpati" (Radhakrishnan and Moore, *A Sourcebook in Indian Philosophy,* p. 19). While Speech is female, Prajāpati is male. Cf. Pintchman, *The Rise of the Goddess in the Hindu Tradition,* pp. 34–37.

10. See note 5 on verse 3.26.

11. *Ṛg Veda* 10.90.5.

12. *Muṇḍaka Upaniṣad* 2.1.3–4.

13. *Bhāgavata Purāṇa* 2.1.3–4.

13. *Bhāgavata Purāṇa* 2.2.1.

14. *Muṇḍaka Upaniṣad* 2.1.4.

15. *Bhāgavata Purāṇa* 2.1.23–38.

16. *Brahmāṇḍa Purāṇa* 3.4.13.1–28.

Translation

[The Cosmic Body displays its fearsome aspect, causing the gods to swoon.]

3.35. Such was the massive form that the best of gods beheld,
With its thousands of blazing rays, licking with its tongue,[1]

3.36. Producing horrible crunching sounds with its teeth, spewing fire from its eyes,
Holding various weapons, heroic in stature, making mush of Brahmans and Kṣatriyas for its food.[2]

3.37. It had a thousand heads and eyes, and a thousand feet as well,[3]
Resembling millions of suns, radiant like millions of lightning streaks.

3.38. That fearful, horrific form, terrifying to heart and eye,
All the gods beheld and wailed, "Woe unto us, woe!"
3.39. With trembling hearts, they swooned helplessly.
Even the thought, "This is the World-Mother," escaped them.

Comment

In these verses the *Devī Gītā* shifts from the relatively static and benign description of the Virāj as found in the *Bhāgavata Purāṇa* with its cosmogonic overtones to the dynamic and terrifying imagery of the *Bhagavad Gītā*'s world-devouring Kṛṣṇa. But whereas Kṛṣṇa's grisly acts relate especially to the bloody tragedy about to unfold in the Mahābhārata war—as well as to the violent end of the current world cycle—the Goddess' ferocious gestures are divorced from any specific, epic-historic or mythic events.[4]

The Goddess' fierce, cosmic form is not always removed from dramatic, mythic encounters with violent foes. In the *Devī Māhātmya*, the Goddess arising from the massed energies of the gods bears a Virājlike form with a thousand arms.[5] The horrific aspect of the image is briefly indicated by its loud laughing and roaring[6] and is directly related to the Devī's heroic mission to slay the demon Mahiṣa. But there is no comparable mission for the *Devī Gītā*'s Virāj. Accordingly, the world-crunching Goddess in the *Devī Gītā* serves simply to highlight the horrific pole of the benevolent World-Mother, a paradox the gods cannot fathom or assimilate and who thus faint dead away.

The horrific aspect of the Virāj form of the Goddess is found not only in the *Devī Māhātmya*, but also in the early Śākta *gītās*, the *Kūrma Devī Gītā* and the *Pārvatī Gītā*.[7] Interestingly, the much-beloved tension between the horrific and the benign aspects of the Virāj in many Śākta texts is largely absent in the description of Lalitā's Cosmic Body in the *Lalitā Māhātmya*. There her Virāj form is described in almost exclusively benign terms. The thousand various limbs of the Virāj are commonly associated with the horrific side of the Goddess, as in the *Devī Gītā*. Lalitā's limbs, however, are wholly auspicious: her thousand hands and feet are described as lotuslike, and no mention is made of gnashing teeth in her thousand mouths.[8]

Notes

1. Nīlakaṇṭha elaborates: "Licking all the universe with its tongue, devouring it." Cf. *Bhagavad Gītā* 11.30, where Kṛṣṇa licks up all the worlds, devouring them with flaming mouths.

2. In the *Bhagavad Gītā*'s theophany (11.26–28), Arjuna in a prescient vision beholds Kṛṣṇa devouring the various heroes assembled for the great war. The *Devī Gītā*'s inclusion of Brahmans as well as Kṣatriyas evokes a passage from the *Kaṭha Upaniṣad* (1.2.25), quoted in part by Nīlakaṇṭha: "[The Self] for whom both Brahmans and Kṣatriyas are food (mush), with death as a sauce. . . ."

3. This is the well-known description of the cosmic Puruṣa in *Ṛg Veda* 10.90.1, also quoted in *Śvetāśvatara Upaniṣad* 3.14. Cf. *Bhagavad Gītā* 11.10, 16, 19, 23, 46.

4. See James William Laine, *The Theophany Narratives of the Mahābhārata*, pp. 303, 324–25, and my *Triumph of the Goddess*, pp. 189–90.

5. *Devī Māhātmya* 2.12–17, 37–38. Vasudeva S. Agrawala specifically identifies the form as the Virāj (*The Glorification of the Great Goddess*, pp. 192, 194).

6. *Devī Māhātmya* 2.31–32.

7. See the Introduction, p. 11, and also the Comment on 3.54–56 below.

8. *Brahmāṇḍa Purāṇa* 3.4.13.7.

Translation

[The gods, revived by the Vedas, sing the praises of the Goddess and request her to withdraw her fearsome form.]

3.40. Then the Vedas, stationed on the four sides of the Great Ruling Goddess,
With much effort awakened the unconscious gods from their swoon.

3.41. Then the gods, regaining their senses, received the supreme Vedic revelation.[1]
Tears of loving joy[2] filled the eyes of these immortals, while their throats tightened.

3.42. They began to offer praise, even as their voices faltered through the tears.[3]

The gods spoke:

Forgive our faults, O Mother; protect us who are wretched, as we are born of you.[4]

3.43. Remove your anger, O Ruler of the Gods; we have seen this form of yours and are frightened.
How can we poor immortals here offer adequate praise to you?[5]

3.44. The extent of your power is unknown even to yourself.[6]
How can it be comprehended by us who are born afterward?[7]

3.45. Hail to you, Ruler of the Universe;[8] hail to you, composed of the syllable Oṃ.
Hail to you, established in the whole of Vedānta, embodied in the syllable Hrīṃ.[9]

3.46. To the source from which fire has arisen, to the source of the sun and moon,
To the source of all plants, to that Self of all, hail![10]

3.47. And to the source from which the gods are born, as well as other celestial beings and birds,
And animals and men, to that Self of all, hail![11]

3.48. The in-breath and out-breath, rice and barley, asceticism, faith, and truth,
Self-restraint and sacred law, to the source of all these, hail! Hail![12]

3.49. To the source of the seven breaths and flames, and of the seven fuel sticks,
And of the seven oblations and worlds, to that Self of all, hail![13]

3.50. To the source from which issue the oceans, mountains, and rivers,
To the source of all plants and their sap, hail! Hail![14]

3.51. To the source from which arise the sacrifice, the consecration, the sacrificial post, and the gifts,
The verses, chants, and formulas, to that Self of all, hail![15]

3.52. Hail from in front and behind, hail to you on both sides;[16]
From below, from above, from the four directions, to you in the greatest degree, O Mother, hail! Hail!

3.53. Withdraw, O Ruler of the Gods, this extraordinary form;
Show us simply that exceedingly beautiful form of yours.[17]

Comment

The gods' hymn of praise here, like their praise in *Devī Gītā* 1.44–53, is largely based on older scriptural sources. The opening verses, 3.42cd–44, emphasizing the incapacity of mortals (including the so-called immortals or gods) to comprehend or praise her who is the source of all beings, reflect similar themes found in the *Devī Māhātmya*.

Verse 3.45, identifying the Goddess with the two sacred syllables Oṃ and Hrīṃ of Vedic and Tantric provenance, respectively, repeats this motif already found in the earlier hymn (*Devī Gītā* 1.53).

The major portion of the hymn, 3.46–51, is closely modeled on several verses from the *Muṇḍaka Upaniṣad*.[18] The Upaniṣadic verses affirm that the Lord is the source that gives birth (*samprasū*) to the material world, with no sense of the latter's illusory nature. Rather, the verses suggest an outpouring of the supreme reality from within itself to create the physical universe. The actual oneness of the supreme with the world is indicated in the preceding *Muṇḍaka* verse,[19] which identifies the Lord's body parts with aspects of the material cosmos. This verse is used by the author of the *Devī Gītā* to begin the description of the Goddess' cosmic form (3.23cd–24). The cosmic theism of the Upaniṣad is thus nicely utilized to frame the cosmic revelation of the Goddess.

The last verse and a half (3.52–53ab) shift back to themes from the *Bhagavad Gītā*, with the praise offered to the Goddess from all sides, and with the request for her to withdraw her fearsome form.

Four times in the hymn there occurs the refrain, "to that Self of all, hail! (*tasmai sarvātmane namaḥ*)." The epithet "Self of all" harmonizes both with the cosmic theism of the *Muṇḍaka* and with the nondualism of later Advaita. Similar epithets are common in all the scriptural sources of the *Devī Gītā*'s hymn. In the *Muṇḍaka* the Lord is called "the inner self of all beings (*sarva-bhūtāntarātmā*)."[20] In the *Devī Māhātmya* the Goddess is referred to as "the Self of all (*akhilātmikā, viśvātmikā*)."[21] In the *Bhagavad Gītā* Kṛṣṇa declares, "I am the Self abiding in the hearts of all beings."[22] And Arjuna, in offering praise to Kṛṣṇa from in front and behind, etc., addresses the Lord simply as "the all (*sarva*)."[23]

Notes

1. *śruti:* literally, "that which is heard," referring to the revelation of supreme truth as embodied in the Vedas. See Comment on 9.13cd–21ab below.

2. On loving joy, or *preman,* see 1.43 above, and its note 1.

3. The emotionalistic response of the gods to the Goddess is parallel to Arjuna's response to Kṛṣṇa's cosmic form in the *Bhagavad Gītā* (11.14, 35).

4. *tvad-udbhavān:* "having our birth or origin in you." Cf. *Devī Māhātmya* 1.65, where Brahmā declares that he, Śiva, and Viṣṇu have been made to assume bodies through her, and thus are incapable of adequately praising her, a theme also stressed in the following *Devī Gītā* verses.

5. Literally, "What praise of you [*kā te stutiḥ*] can be performed by us poor immortals?" Cf. *Devī Māhātmya* 11.5: "What praise of you [*kā te stutiḥ*] who are beyond praise (is possible)?" See also *Devī Māhātmya* 1.64: "Who here can adequately praise you?" Cf. 1.63 and 65.

6. Cf. *Bhāgavata Purāṇa* (3.6.39), where it is said of Viṣṇu's mysterious power: "The Māyā of the Lord deludes even those who wield Māyā; when he himself knows not the limits of his own self, how can others?"

7. Nīlakaṇṭha explains by referring to the scriptural passage {*Ṛg Veda* 10.129.6–7}: "The gods were born after the creation of this world. Who, then, knows from what it has arisen? The one who looks over this world from the highest heaven surely knows, or perhaps not!"

8. Bhuvaneśānī.

9. Cf. 1.53ab above. See the Comment on 1.42–53 for the symbolic significance of Oṃ and Hrīṃ in the Tantric tradition.

10. This verse is loosely based on *Muṇḍaka Upaniṣad* 2.1.5ab, where Puruṣa is said to be the source of fire, whose fuel is the sun, while the moon

is said to be the source of rain, giving rise to plants on earth. The following *Devī Gītā* verses, 3.47–51, are also based, quite closely at times, on *Muṇḍaka* verses 2.1.6–9, with some rearrangement. Interestingly, the preceding *Muṇḍaka* verse (2.1.4) was utilized by the *Devī Gītā* to begin the description of cosmic correspondences of the Devī's Virāj form (3.23cd–24).

11. Cf. *Muṇḍaka Upaniṣad* 2.1.7ab.

12. Cf. *Muṇḍaka Upaniṣad* 2.1.7cd.

13. Cf. *Muṇḍaka Upaniṣad* 2.1.8.

14. Cf. *Muṇḍaka Upaniṣad* 2.1.9.

15. Cf. *Muṇḍaka Upaniṣad* 2.1.6ab. On the verses, chant, and formulas (*ṛco yajūṃṣi sāmāni*), cf. also *Devī Māhātmya* 4.9 and *Bhagavad Gītā* 9.17.

16. Cf. Arjuna's words to Kṛṣṇa in *Bhagavad-Gītā* 11.40: "Hail to you from in front and from behind; hail to you from all sides, you who are all."

17. Cf. Arjuna's request to Kṛṣṇa in *Bhagavad-Gītā* 11.45. For a brief discussion of these two forms (extraordinary and beautiful) of the Goddess, see the Comment on 3.54–56.

18. Cf. *Muṇḍaka Upaniṣad* 2.1.5–9.

19. Cf. *Muṇḍaka Upaniṣad* 2.1.4.

20. Cf. *Muṇḍaka Upaniṣad* 2.1.4.

21. *Devī Māhātmya* 1.63 and 11.32.

22. *Bhagavad Gītā* 10.20.

23. *Bhagavad Gītā* 11.40.

Translation

[The Goddess grants the gods their wish and manifests once again her benign form as Bhuvaneśvarī.]

Vyāsa said:

3.54. Seeing the gods so frightened, the World-Mother, an ocean of compassion,
Withdrew her horrific form and revealed her beautiful aspect:

3.55. She held a noose and goad while gesturing her beneficence and assurance of safety;[1] delicate was she in all her limbs.
Her eyes overflowed with compassion as her lotus face gently smiled.
3.56. When the gods beheld that beautiful form, their fears dissolved
And their minds attained peace; inarticulate from joy, they bowed down in silence.

Comment

The Devī's horrific (*ghora*) appearance as the Virāj and her beautiful (*sundara*) manifestation as the four-armed Bhuvaneśvarī parallel the cosmic and ordinary forms of Kṛṣṇa in the *Bhagavad Gītā*. In the *Bhagavad Gītā* Kṛṣṇa's fearsome, thousand-armed, universal form (*viśvarūpa*) is contrasted with his benign, four-armed form that he bore prior to manifesting his cosmic body.[2] (Later Kṛṣṇaite tradition portrays Kṛṣṇa himself as two-armed, and Viṣṇu as four-armed, carrying a club and disc—both mentioned in the *Bhagavad Gītā*[3]—along with a conch and lotus.) The *Bhagavad Gītā* refers to the thousand-armed form as horrific (*ghora*), the four-armed as innate (*svaka*) to Kṛṣṇa, as pleasing or gentle (*saumya*), and as human (*mānuṣa*).[4] The *Devī Gītā* (3.53) refers to the Goddess' cosmic form not only as horrific, but also as extraordinary or unworldly (*alaukika*).

In earlier Śākta *gītās*, as mentioned above, there occur similar benign and horrific theophanies of the Goddess. In the *Kūrma Devī Gītā*, Pārvatī, originally eight-armed, reveals a frightening, multiple-armed Virāj form that embodies aspects of both Viṣṇu and Śiva, the two major male figures of the cosmic triumvirate. Then, she manifests a gracious, two-armed form at Himālaya's request. In the *Mahābhāgavata*'s *gītā*, which loosely follows the *Kūrma*, Pārvatī's horrific Virāj form divides into two, revealing a Śivalike and a Viṣṇulike cosmic form, before manifesting a third, benign, also Viṣṇulike form. The *Mahābhāgavata*, in splitting the Devī's horrific form into Śiva and Viṣṇu components, somewhat obscures the horrific/benign polarity. The *Devī Gītā* clearly prefers the model of the *Bhagavad Gītā* and *Kūrma Devī Gītā*, with their stark contrast of the horrific and benign. Going beyond the *Kūrma Devī Gītā*, however, the *Devī Gītā* replaces the gracious, two-armed form of Pārvatī with its own supreme feminine iconic form, that of the lovely, four-armed Bhuvaneśvarī.[5]

Notes

1. These are the primary signs of the lovely, four-armed Bhuvaneśvarī. See 1.39 above and the Comment on 1.30–41.

2. *Bhagavad Gītā* 11.46.

3. *Bhagavad Gītā* 11.46.

4. *Bhagavad Gītā* 11.49–51.

5. For more detailed discussion of the iconic forms in the earlier Śākta *gītās,* see my *Triumph of the Goddess,* pp. 190–91.

Chapter 4

Instruction in the Yoga of Knowledge

Translation

[The Goddess indicates the real reason behind the revelation of her cosmic form.]

The Goddess spoke:

4.1. How distant you are, so humble, from this form of mine, so magnificent!
Yet out of affection for my devotees, I have displayed such a form.

4.2. Not by study of the Vedas, nor by yoga, charity, austerity, or sacrifice
Can you see this form in any way, without my favor.[1]

Comment

These first two verses, forming the conclusion to the awesome manifestation of the Devī's Cosmic Body in the preceding chapter, emphasize the notion of divine grace. The ideal of grace is an integral aspect of the Hindu path of devotion (Bhakti Yoga). Here in the *Devī Gītā* the Goddess affirms that it is only through her loving affection for those devoted to her that she is moved to reveal her Cosmic Body. No human effort, no good works in themselves, can compel such a vision. This *bhaktic* doctrine of divine grace is first enunciated by Kṛṣṇa in the eleventh chapter of the *Bhagavad Gītā*, following the withdrawal of his own cosmic form. Kṛṣṇa declares to Arjuna: "As I am pleased with you, Arjuna, I have revealed this supreme form through my own great power. . . . Not by the Vedas, by sacrifice, by study, by gifts, by rites, nor by fierce austerities, can I be seen in the human world in such a form, except by you."[2]

Parallel to this devotional ideal of grace is the philosophical ideal of Self-realization. For instance, the *Vivekacūḍāmaṇi* affirms: "Not by yoga, nor by deliberation, nor by works, nor by learning, can one realize *mokṣa*, except by awakening to the oneness of Brahman and Ātman."[3] Thus, the paths of Self-realization or knowledge (Jñāna Yoga) and of devotion both radically subordinate the path of good works or action (Karma Yoga). In the next two sections, the Goddess explains in detail the subordinate role of action to knowledge in the attainment of liberation. The opening verses of this chapter, then, serve implicitly as a bridge between the *bhaktic* ideals of grace evoked by the cosmic vision and the ideals of wisdom or knowledge (*jñāna*) about to be discussed. The relation between knowledge and devotion is considered in chapter 7.

Notes

1. *kṛpā:* "compassion, pity, tenderness, or favor." Himālaya, we may recall, in asking to see the Devī's cosmic form, had qualified his request by adding, "if you would favor me (*yadi devi kṛpā mayi*)" (3.20d). For the significance of this notion of divine favor or grace, see the Comment above.

2. *Bhagavad Gītā* 11.47ab,48. Cf. 11.53–54.

3. *Vivekacūḍāmaṇi* 56. Cf. verse 6.

Translation

[The Goddess continues her discussion—interrupted by her cosmic manifestation—of the genesis of the individual soul due to ignorance and its subsequent karmic entanglements.]

4.3. Listen, O King, let us return to the original subject regarding the supreme Self and how it becomes the individual soul.
By combining with apparent limitations,[1] the Self seemingly assumes the role of an active agent and so on.

4.4. The soul performs diverse acts, the sole cause of virtue and vice.
Thereby it attains birth in various wombs and experiences happiness and sorrow.[2]

4.5. Again, under their determining influence,[3] ever intent on new actions of various sorts,
It attains new bodies of various kinds and experiences further happiness and sorrow.

4.6. Like a water wheel,[4] this cycling never ceases.
Ignorance alone is its root; from that springs desire, from that actions.[5]

4.7. Therefore a person should ever strive for the destruction of ignorance,
For one's birth is fruitful when ignorance is destroyed.

4.8. One thereby attains the ends of human existence[6] and the state of being liberated while living.[7]

Comment

The Goddess now returns to her earlier subject (introduced in 3.1–12ab) regarding the manifestation of individual souls through the power of ignorance. Her focus now, however, shifts from cosmogonic to soteriological concerns: how does ignorance bind the soul, so that one may learn how to undo its effects and attain liberation? She begins by outlining the basic law of karma according to the Advaita: desire gives rise to actions, which result in pleasure and pain. These in turn produce more desire, future births, and still more actions with their consequences. Even righteous action has its karmic consequences, resulting in future rewards or pleasures that entail samsaric involvement. The whole karmic cycle is an ironic one, for ultimately the individual self is not truly an actor at all. Thus ignorance, in the form of the false assumption of being an active agent, underlies the individual's desire to act, whether to gain happiness or to avoid sorrow. All acts, then, are bound to end in frustration, until the underlying ignorance is rooted out. With the destruction of ignorance, the Goddess concludes in verse 4.7, one's birth (life) finds its true fulfillment. In these verses, the Goddess closely reflects the teachings of the Advaitin Sureśvara in his *Naiṣkarmya Siddhi*.

This association of action with ignorance as its underlying cause is firmly rooted in the ancient Upaniṣads. Commenting on the above mentioned verse (4.7), Nīlakaṇṭha cites a line from scripture {the *Bṛhadāraṇyaka Upaniṣad*}, which concludes that one who knows not the eternal, departing this world, is helpless or pitiable.[8] The *Bṛhadāraṇyaka* verse from which Nīlakaṇṭha quotes begins by stating that the sacrifices, worship, and austerities of an ignorant person, even if carried on for a thousand years, all come to an end eventually. That is why such a person is to be pitied at death. Conversely, the *Bṛhadāraṇyaka* verse concludes, one who knows the imperishable is a Brāhmaṇa or a knower of Brahman. The clear inference is that a person's life is fruitful only when one attains knowledge of Brahman.

This knowledge, or rather the destruction of ignorance that obscures it, the Goddess proclaims, brings about the state of being liberated while still living (*jīvan-mukta*). She equates this state with the attainment or fulfillment of the ends of existence, as does Sureśvara. The implications of this equation are somewhat unclear. The four ends, beginning with pleasure and ending with liberation, are often hierarchically arranged with each successive end subordinated to the next. In the more extreme interpretations of this hierarchy, there is felt to be a considerable tension, if not outright incompatibility, between the last, *mokṣa*, and the first three. This radical hierarchical ordering of the ends is dominant in the ascetic traditions, including the Advaita, and is the perspective assumed by Sureśvara. That is, the first three ends are "fulfilled" in the sense of being left behind, renounced, no longer of concern to the liberated soul. In Tantric Śāktism, however, the fulfillment of all the ends simultaneously is upheld as an ideal, expressed in the notion that the Goddess provides her devotees with both *mukti* (the fourth end) and *bhukti* ("enjoyment," representing the first three), and not necessarily in a sequential order that would reintroduce the hierarchy. This Tantric perspective is confirmed elsewhere in the *Devī-Bhāgavata*,[9] but here in this chapter of the *Devī Gītā* the whole flavor of the Goddess' teaching is predominantly Advaitic.

Notes

1. *upādhi-yogāt*; for a brief explanation of *upādhi*, see *Devī Gītā* 3.5, note 1.

2. Cf. Sureśvara's statement in his *Naiṣkarmya Siddhi* (1.41): "The person whose mind is covered by a veil of ignorance accepts the idea of being an agent and so on. . . . [Such a person is] helpless: by good acts he becomes a god, by evil acts he attains hell; by good and evil acts, he becomes a human."

Cf. also *Bhāgavata Purāṇa* 3.27.2–3, where the person who imagines himself to be an agent becomes unhappy and helpless through the faults of actions, taking birth in good, bad, and mixed wombs.

3. *tat-saṃskṛti-vaśāt*; according to Nīlakaṇṭha, this refers to the psychic scars (*saṃskāras*) produced by the happiness and sorrow.

4. *ghaṭi-yantra*; a wheel with attached buckets for drawing water from a well, driven by oxen. Cf. the *Gheraṇḍa Saṃhitā* 1.7: "As the water wheel (set of buckets) moves up and down by the power of the oxen, so does the soul move through birth and death by the power of its karma." See also next note.

5. Cf. Sureśvara's *Naiṣkarmya Siddhi* (1.42): "In this terrible ocean of misery [an ignorant person] rises up and down like a water wheel, taking birth in various wombs, inferior, middling, and superior, providing momentary happiness, sorrow, and delusion. . . . In this way revolving torturously, the man of desire is bound by ignorance, desire and actions; he is born and dies filled with misery."

Cf. also *Sarvasiddhāntasaṃgraha* (*Patañjalipakṣa* 8cd): "One performs actions out of desire, arising from the sense of agency rooted in ignorance."

6. *puruṣārtha*; these goals of existence are four: pleasure (*kāma*), prosperity (*artha*), responsibility (*dharma*), and liberation (*mokṣa*). Cf. Sureśvara's *Naiṣkarmya Siddhi* (1.1): "When [ignorance] is entirely destroyed, it is the complete fulfillment of all the ends of human existence."

7. *jīvan-mukta*; this is the one occurrence of the term in the *Devī Gītā*, though its synonym, *kṛtya-kṛta*, occurs more frequently. See note 1 on *Devī Gītā* 1.3.

8. {*Bṛhadāraṇyaka Upaniṣad* 3.8.10.}

9. See my *Triumph of the Goddess*, pp. 172–75.

Translation

[The Goddess indicates that knowledge, not action, is the antidote to ignorance, and summarizes the preparatory stage for Jñāna Yoga.]

4.8. [cont.] Wisdom alone is competent for the destruction of ignorance.

4.9. Action, born of ignorance, is incompetent to destroy ignorance, since the two are not opposed, O Mountain.[1]
Rather, the hope that ignorance can be destroyed by action is futile.

4.10. Useless are actions with their fruits, which humans crave again and again.
From that arises passion, from that evil, from that great calamity.
4.11. Therefore a person should acquire knowledge with all-out effort.
Yet scripture itself seems to enjoin the necessity of action, as when it states: "Ever performing actions here. . . ."[2]
4.12. But scripture also states: "From knowledge indeed comes emancipation."[3] Thus some conclude that the two should be conjoined:[4]
Action should be a complement of knowledge, as its benefactor.
4.13. Others say that this is impossible, due to their opposition.
The knot of the heart is loosened through knowledge; when the knot is tight, action arises.[5]
4.14. Coexistence of the two together is thus impossible, due to their opposition,
Just as darkness and light cannot appear simultaneously.[6]
4.15. Therefore, high-minded one, all Vedic actions
Reach their end when the heart is purified;[7] perform them with diligence
4.16. Until tranquillity, restraint, patience, dispassion, and goodness arise.
Up to this point actions are fitting, but no further.[8]

Comment

Regarding the relative roles of knowledge and action in securing the highest end of human existence, the *Devī Gītā* closely follows the views of Śaṃkara and especially Sureśvara. The issue had long been debated in Hindu philosophical circles. The Mīmāṃsakas, stressing the ritual portion of the Vedas, argued for the necessity of action, specifically ritual action, for attaining liberation from the suffering of samsara.[9] As for the role of knowledge in performing Vedic rites, certain later Mīmāṃsakas argued that knowledge of the Self is an aid in avoiding the further accumulation of good and evil karma, and thus should be combined with Vedic action. Such a view is known as the conjunction of knowledge and action (*jñāna-karma-samuccaya*).[10]

The Vedāntins, relying on the knowledge portion of the Vedas (the Upaniṣads), give greater weight to knowledge than do the Mīmāṃsakas. Nonetheless, even among some Vedāntins various forms of the *jñāna-karma-samuccaya* view were advocated, a position rejected by Śaṃkara and other Advaitins like Sureśvara.[11] Their rejection was based on the conviction that Brahman, or realization of Brahman, is not something that can be acquired, as Brahman is one's very nature. Thus, it cannot be the fruit or result of any action. Yet even their denial of action as a means to realization or knowledge of Brahman needs some qualification. For action can be an indirect or mediate means for acquiring knowlege, by preparing the student through purifying his emotions and will.[12]

This purification of the mind or heart involves the mastering of various mental and psychological attitudes, specified in *Devī Gītā* 4.16. These, or almost identical qualities, are mentioned in the *Bṛhadāraṇyaka Upaniṣad*.[13] There, after stating that the greatness of a Brahman-knower is neither increased nor decreased by actions, the Upaniṣad goes on to affirm that "one who knows thus, having become calm (*sānta*), controlled (*dānta*), withdrawn from the world (*uparata*), patient (*titikṣu*), and composed (*samāhita*), sees the Self in oneself, and everything as the Self." These five qualities came to be seen as essential mental qualifications of a student desiring to undertake Jñāna Yoga. Advaitin writers typically list six, adding faith (*śraddhā*).[14] Faith, in this context, is defined as accepting the truths of scripture as taught by a guru (see next section). These five or six "mental treasures" constitute the third of four standard, indispensable qualifications: 1) discrimination of the eternal and noneternal; 2) nonattachment to things of this or the next world; 3) the five or six noble qualities such as tranquillity of mind; and 4) desire for liberation.[15]

The performance of appropriate actions in a spirit of detachment to purify the mind constitutes the preliminary or preparatory stage for the practice of Jñāna Yoga proper. Such psychological and mental attainment qualifies the student to commence upon the path to the immediate realization of Brahman. The steps along this path are outlined by the Goddess in the next section.

Notes

1. Regarding the relative roles of action and knowledge in liberation, the *Devī Gītā* follows the Advaita position of Sureśvara as outlined in the first book of his *Naiṣkarmya Siddhi*. On this particular line (4.9ab), cf. *Naiṣkarmya Siddhi* 1.35: "Action, since it is born of ignorance, cannot destroy ignorance; right knowledge [can destroy ignorance], being its opposite, just as the sun opposes darkness."

2. The *Devī Gītā* here quotes the first few words of *Īśā Upaniṣad* 2: "Ever performing actions here, one should wish to live a hundred years" (*kurvann eveha karmāṇi jijīviṣet śataṃ samāḥ*). Sureśvara, in *Naiṣkarmya Siddhi* 1.18, refers to this same *Īśā* verse. He uses it in a preliminary argument against his own position, the theoretical objector citing the verse to insist that actions are necessary and liberation through knowledge alone is not the right view. Sureśvara gives his own interpretation of the *Īśā* verse in 1.96, to the effect that the verse is addressed to one whose self-image is still that of an individual agent, not to one who recognizes the true, nondual and quiescent Self within. For the ignorant, constant performance of proper action is the only way to transcend hindering or evil karma and thereby attain the purity of mind necessary for the acquisition of spiritual knowledge (see Balasubramanian's comment on *Naiṣkarmya Siddhi* 1.96, in his translation).

Cf. *Bhagavad Gītā* 6.3, utilized by Sureśvara in *Naiṣkarmya Siddhi* 1.51, to support the same point.

3. *kaivalya*: "isolation, absolute unity, or emancipation." While many Upaniṣadic passages emphasize knowledge as the means to liberation, I have not been able to locate the specific citation.

4. *tat-samuccaya*; this is the doctrine of *jñana-karma-samuccaya-vāda*, explained in the Comment above.

5. Cf. *Muṇḍaka Upaniṣad* 2.2.9.

6. Cf. Sureśvara, *Naiṣkarmya Siddhi* 1.66: "One may also reject the conjunction of knowledge and action for this reason: the causes, nature, and effects of knowledge and action are opposed to each other, like light and darkness; therefore there is no possible association between the two." Cf. also *Naiṣkarmya Siddhi* 1.55–56.

7. Cf. Sureśvara, *Naiṣkarmya Siddhi* 1.47, 49: "Regarding the performance of daily and occasional rites: one's mind becomes pure through actions dedicated to the Lord, and then pure dispassion arises towards all objects. . . . Actions, having purified the intellect, their purpose achieved, disappear." And cf. *Vivekacūḍāmaṇi* 11: "Action is for purifying the mind, but not for perceiving the truth. Realization of truth comes through discrimination, not by millions of acts." Finally, cf. *Bhāgavata Purāṇa* 11.20.9: "One should carry out acts so long as aversion to the world does not arise, or yearning to listen to my (Kṛṣṇa's) stories does not arise."

8. Cf. Sureśvara, *Naiṣkarmya Siddhi* 1.45, where he argues that actions serve as an indirect cause (*ārādupakāraka*) of liberation. Such actions lead to the qualities of mind like tranquillity and dispassion, which are in turn the direct cause of knowledge, which constitutes liberation. Cf. also Śaṃkara's commentary on the *Brahma Sūtras,* 4.1.16: "Works . . . may subserve final release mediately. For in so far as furthering knowledge, work may be spoken of as an indirect cause of final release" (Thibaut's translation).

9. For the Mīmāṃsakas, optional (*kāmya*) and forbidden (*pratiṣiddha*) acts are to be avoided, while obligatory (*nitya*) acts as enjoined by the Veda are to be carried out. The former create new karmic effects, the latter do not, so when the effects of the former are exhausted, the person performing the Vedic injunctions will be free of all karma. Not to perform the obligatory Vedic acts is seen as a kind of forbidden act, a sin of omission, as it were, entailing further karmic consequences.

10. For discussions of the *jñāna-karma-samuccaya-vāda* and related issues, see M. Hiriyanna, *Outlines,* pp. 335, 378–79; S. Radhakrishnan, *Indian Philosophy,* vol. 2, pp. 423, 614–18; Surendranath Dasgupta, *A History of Indian Philosophy,* vol. 2, pp. 99–100 (specifically on Sureśvara's views).

11. For Śaṃkara's discussion of the problem, see especially his commentary on the *Brahma Sūtras,* 3.4. For Sureśvara's, see *Naiṣkarmya Siddhi* 1.

12. See notes 7 and 8 above.

13. *Bṛhadāraṇyaka Upaniṣad* 4.4.23. Cf. Śaṃkara's commentary on *Brahma Sūtras* 3.4.27.

14. The *Devī Gītā* itself refers to "the six virtues beginning with tranquillity" (7.40).

15. See *Vivekacūḍāmaṇi* 18–27; *Sarva-Vedānta-Siddhānta-Sārasaṃgraha* 14–15, 94; Sadānanda, *Vedāntasāra* 15–25.

Translation

[The Goddess describes the basic steps of Jñāna Yoga, with special reference to the great saying, "You are That."]

4.17. And then renouncing worldly attachments, being self-restrained, one should resort to a guru
Well-versed in the Veda and absorbed in Brahman, approaching with true devotion.[1]

4.18. One should listen to the Upaniṣads daily and with attention,
Reflecting constantly[2] on the meaning of such great sayings as "You are That."

4.19. The great saying, "You are That," indicates the oneness of the soul and Brahman.
When the identity is realized, one goes beyond fear and assumes my essential nature.[3]

4.20. First one should comprehend the meaning of the individual words, then the meaning of the sentence as a whole.
Now the word *That* refers to I myself, O Mountain; this is well proclaimed,

4.21. While the word *You* refers certainly to the individual soul.
The identity of the two is indicated by the word *are*, so say the wise.

4.22. Due to the opposed nature of the two expressed referents, their identity may not seem possible.
Thus one must adopt the secondary meaning of the terms *That* and *You*, as fixed in scripture.

4.23. Just pure consciousness is the secondary meaning implied by both terms: their essential oneness is thereby established.
Realizing their oneness by disregarding their nonessential differences, one transcends duality.

4.24. In the same manner, the sentence "This is that Devadatta" uses the secondary meanings, so it is taught.[4]

Comment

Having established that actions have only a provisional utility and must ultimately be transcended, the Goddess proceeds to outline the basic steps of Jñāna Yoga proper. These steps must proceed under the guidance of a guru or qualified teacher. It is the guru, well versed in Vedānta (the Upaniṣads), who can instruct the student in the Śruti (revealed) texts that establish the oneness of the Self and Brahman.

Listening (*śravaṇa*) to the texts thus expounded is the first of four traditional steps in Jñāna Yoga. (Sometimes only three steps are given, when the last step is regarded as the actual goal of the yoga.) The additional three are reflection (*manana* or *vicāra*), intense meditation (*nididhyāsana*), and absorption in the Absolute (*samādhi*). The *Pañcadaśī* defines the four steps as follows: "The inquiry into the meaning of that [identity of the Self and Brahman] by means of the great sayings is listening. The inquiry into its possible validity through reasoning is reflection. When, by these two inquiries, the mind knows the meaning without any doubt, that one-pointed concentration is intense meditation. When the mind abandons the notions of meditator and meditating and is immersed solely in the object of meditation, that is called absorption."[5] The *Devī Gītā* refrains from a precise enumeration of these steps, mentioning explicitly, in verses 4.18–19, only the first two and the final culminating step of absorption, interpreted here as assuming the essential nature of the Goddess. The third step, of intense meditation, is mentioned in 4.40.

The great sayings (*mahā-vākyas*) of the Upaniṣads are often said to be four: (1) Consciousness is Brahman; (2) Ātman is Brahman; (3) I am Brahman; and (4) You are That. All point to the essential identity of the individual and the ultimate. It is especially the last saying, "You are That," which has been favored by Advaitin philosophers to illustrate the process of Jñāna Yoga.[6] The saying may at first appear untrue, since "That" and "You" refer on the literal level to opposed entities: Brahman on the one hand, and the individual soul on the other. The former is supreme, unlimited, omniscient, while the latter is finite, limited, deluded. Yet common to each is the nature of pure consciousness, so by rejecting the nonessential differences between the two, one realizes the identity of their implied meaning.

Advaita texts frequently illustrate and explain the logical structure of this great saying by the sentence, "This is that Devadatta." The *Vedāntasāra* elucidates: ". . . in the sentence, 'This is that Devadatta', the word 'That' signifying Devadatta associated with the past, and the word 'This' signifying Devadatta associated with the present, both refer to one and the same person called Devadatta. Similarly in the sentence, 'Thou art That', the word 'That' signifying Consciousness characterized by remoteness etc., and the word 'Thou' signifying Consciousness characterized by immediacy etc., both refer to one and the same Consciousness, viz. Brahman."[7] One must simply eliminate the contradictory elements of each term, such as remoteness and immediacy, to recognize the fundamental essence of each as identical.

Such logical clarifications, part of the process of listening and reflection, bring one to a mediate knowledge of Brahman. But a merely intellectual conviction is not sufficient. Immediate knowledge requires an inner, direct realization, to be actualized through intense meditative practices. To such practices the Goddess now turns.

Notes

1. Cf. *Muṇḍaka Upaniṣad* 1.2.12: "Examining the worlds attained by work, a Brahman seeker should reach indifference, for the world that is not made (that is, the eternal world) is not attained by work. For the sake of knowledge, he should approach . . . a guru well-versed in the Veda and absorbed in Brahman." This passage is frequently quoted by Advaitin writers in stressing the necessity both of indifference to the world and of seeking out a qualified guru (see e.g., Śaṃkara, *Upadeśasāhasrī* 1.2–3; Sadānanda, *Vedāntasāra* 30). The passage also points to the nature of the guru as both scholar and spiritual master (see William Cenkner, *A Tradition of Teachers,* pp. 8–9).

Regarding "true devotion," Nīlakaṇṭha cites a *śruti* text {*Śvetāśvatara Upaniṣad* 6.23}, where it is said that the (secret Vedāntic) teachings will become clear to the noble soul who has supreme devotion for his guru as for God. This Upaniṣadic verse is quoted by the *Devī Gītā* in 6.22cd–23ab. Cf. *Vivekacūḍāmaṇi* 35: "Worshiping the guru with devotion, approaching him when pleased with bowing, respect, and service, one should ask about the Self."

2. *vicārayet*: "one ought to reflect, or reason." *Vicāra* is a synonym for *manana* ("thinking, reasoning"), the more usual term for the second step of Jñāna Yoga. Cf. *Vivekacūḍāmaṇi* 45: "Through reasoning (*vicāra*) on the meaning of the Vedānta texts, one attains the highest knowledge."

3. *mad-rūpa*; see *Devī Gītā* 2.1, note 2. Cf. 4.49 and 7.27 below.

4. This sentence regarding Devadatta, the John Doe of Vedānta, is frequently utilized by Advaitin writers to explain the sense of "You are That." See *Sarva-Vedanta-Siddhanta-Sarasaṃgraha,* verses 733–59, esp. 754–55; *Vivekacūḍāmaṇi* 241–49; *Vedāntasāra* 148–54. For discussions of the Advaitin interpretations of this great saying and their use of the Devadatta illustration, see T. M. P. Mahadevan, *Superimposition in Advaita Vedānta,* pp. 67–68; Hari Prasad Bhattacharyya, *Status of the World in Advaita Vedānta,* pp. 233–58, esp. pp. 240, 254; and Swami Satchidanandendra Sarasvati, *The Method of the Vedanta,* pp. 826–27. An explanation of the Devadatta example is given in the Comment above.

5. *Pañcadaśī* 1.53–55. Cf. *Vedāntasāra* 181–99 for more elaborate, and somewhat differing, definitions. Cf. also *Vivekacūḍāmaṇi* 70.

6. See, e.g., *Upadeśasāhasrī* 2.18 for Śaṃkara's detailed discussion of this great saying.

7. *Vedāntasāra* 151 (Nikhilananda's translation).

Translation

[The Goddess summarizes the nature of the Gross, Subtle, and Causal Bodies, and of the Self that lies beyond these three.]

4.24. [cont.] When freed from the three bodies beginning with the Gross, a person becomes absorbed in Brahman.[1]

4.25. The Gross Body arises from the fivefold compounded gross elements.[2]
It experiences the fruit of all its actions and is subject to old age and disease.[3]

4.26. In truth it is false,[4] yet it appears real, being full of Māyā.
This is the gross limiting condition[5] of my own Self, O Mountain King.

4.27. The union of the organs of knowledge and action, conjoined with the five breaths
And fused with the mind and intellect, produces the Subtle Body; this the wise discern.[6]

4.28. Arising from the uncompounded elements, this Subtle Body of the Self
Is my second limiting condition, experiencing pleasure and pain.[7]

4.29. Without beginning and indefinable, ignorance is the third limiting condition;
It is that Body of the Self which appears as Causal in nature, O Mountain Lord.[8]

4.30. When these limiting conditions are dissolved,[9] the Self alone remains.
The five sheaths ever reside within the three bodies.[10]

4.31. When the five sheaths are discarded, one attains the root that is Brahman,[11]
Described by such sayings as "Not this, not that,"[12] indicating my own essential form.

Comment

In these verses the Goddess recapitulates the evolution of the Causal, Subtle, and Gross Bodies of the Self detailed earlier in chapter 2. There the focus was on her cosmogonic role as the sole cause of creation. Here the Goddess turns her attention to liberation, a process frequently conceived of in Hindu thought as a reversal of creative evolution. The summary of the evolution of the three bodies thus points indirectly to the means by which liberation or Self-realization can be achieved.

The dissolution of the limiting factors (*upādhi-vilaya*) mentioned in verse 30 refers to the reversal of the evolution of the universe on the microcosmic scale, within one's own body. All effects—the three bodies and their corresponding states of waking, dream, and deep sleep—are sequentially resolved back into their cause. This *upādhi-vilaya* is referred to in Advaita as *apavāda* or the negation of the superimposition (*adhyāropa*, or *adhyāsa*) that is responsible for the appearance of the world. Thus, just as the snake falsely perceived in a rope is dissolved when the substrate of the rope is realized, so also the limiting factors of the three bodies falsely superimposed on the reality of the Self are dissolved when the true Self is recognized.

A specific contemplative practice for actualizing this dissolution or reversal of creation is provided by the Goddess in the final ten verses of the chapter (4.41–50), where she concludes her account of Jñāna Yoga by explaining the procedures for Laya Upāsanā (resorptive meditation). But first, she recites two well-known passages from the *Kaṭha Upaniṣad*, thereby demonstrating to the gods once again the first step of Jñāna Yoga: listening to the words of scripture to establish the nature of the Self or Brahman.

Notes

1. Nīlakaṇṭha connects the ensuing description of the three bodies with the prior discussion of "You are That" by affirming that through the direct realization (*anubhava*) of the truth of the Upaniṣadic great saying, one becomes free of the three bodies.

2. The fivefold compounding process and the evolution of the Gross Body have been described in detail in *Devī Gītā* 2.32cd–35ab. Cf. Śaṃkara, *Pañcīkaraṇa*, p. 1.

3. Cf. *Vivekacūḍāmaṇi* 91: "Birth, decay and death are the various characteristics of the gross body, as also stoutness, etc.; childhood, etc., are its different conditions; it has got various restrictions regarding caste and order of life; it is subject to various diseases, and meets with different kinds of treatment, such as worship, insult and high honours" (Swami Madhavananda's translation).

4. *mithyā*; cf. *Devī Gītā* 2.18cd and 9.45ab.

5. *sthūla upādhi*; the three bodies, the Gross (*sthūla*), etc., are here and in the next few verses regarded as limiting adjuncts or conditions (*upādhi*) of the unconditioned Self or Goddess. According to the Advaita, such limitations are apparent only, or false (*mithyā*). Cf. *Devī Gītā* 3.5.

6. The generation of the Subtle Body has been described in *Devī Gītā* 2.27–31ab. Cf. *Pañcīkaraṇa*, p. 2.

7. *sukhādi*: "pleasure and so forth," glossed by Nīlakaṇṭha as *sukha-duḥkhādi* ("pleasure and pain, etc."). Cf. *Vivekacūḍāmaṇi* 105: "When the sense-objects are favourable it becomes happy, and it becomes miserable when the case is contrary. So happiness (*sukha*) and misery (*duḥkha*) are the characteristics of egoism [a major component of the Subtle Body]" (S. Madhavananda's trans).

8. See *Devī Gītā* 2.22–26 for the development of the Causal Body. Cf. *Pañcīkaraṇa*, pp. 3–4.

Ignorance is here regarded as a limiting adjunct that allows Brahman to appear as the Causal Body. In Advaita, ignorance (*ajñāna*) is used interchangeably with Māyā, Avidyā, Avyakta (the unmanifested), Avyākṛta (the unevolved). They are commonly described as *anādi* (without beginning), and as *anirvācya* (indefinable), being neither existent, nonexistent, nor both. See Sureśvara, *Pañcīkaraṇa-Vārttika* 40; *Vivekacūḍāmaṇi* 108; and *Vedāntasāra* 33–39.

9. *upādhi-vilaya*; refers to the regressive dissolution of the adjuncts, or bodies, in the reverse order from the original sequence of manifestation, until only their ultimate source remains. Cf. *Vedāntasāra* 137–42, which describes the devolution of the cosmos, including the three bodies of the Self, back into Brahman.

10. The five sheaths have already been mentioned in *Devī Gītā* 1.52. In Advaita, beginning at least with Sureśvara, the five sheaths are distributed among the three bodies (cf. Sarvepalli Radhakrishnan, *The Principal Upaniṣads*, p. 542). The bliss sheath is identified with the Causal Body; the intelligence, mind, and breath sheaths with the Subtle Body; and the food

sheath with the Gross Body. See *Vedāntasāra* 39, 45, 72–74, 88–89, 92, 94, 112.

11. *brahma puccha*: literally, the "tail, or end point (root) that is Brahman." The *Devī Gītā* here evokes a passage from the *Taittirīya Upaniṣad* (2.1–5), where the concept of the five sheaths is first developed. The *Taittirīya* describes the evolution of the five sheaths and the ultimate root or basis of each. The innermost sheath of bliss is said to have Brahman as its root and basis (*brahma puccha pratiṣthā*) (2.5).

Pañcadaśī 1.37 states that by proper discrimination, one can extract the Self from the five sheaths and attain the supreme Brahman. Cf. *Pañcadaśī* 3.22: "When the five sheaths are discarded, there remains the witness."

12. *neti neti*: literally, "not thus, not thus." It is one of the famous sayings of the Upaniṣads describing Brahman or the Self. This particular saying occurs a number of times in the *Bṛhadāraṇyaka Upaniṣad*, referring to Ātman: *sa eṣa neti nety ātmā* (3.9.26; 4.2.4; 4.4.22; 4.5.15).

Translation

[Reciting from the *Kaṭha Upaniṣad*, the Goddess describes the immortal Self, likening it to the owner of a chariot.]

4.32. That Self is never born nor does it die; it did not come into existence, for nothing real comes into existence from nothing.[1]
It is unborn, eternal, everlasting, ancient. It is not slain when the body is slain.

4.33. If the slayer believes "I slay," if the slain believes "I am slain,"
Then neither understands that the Self does not slay and cannot be slain.[2]

4.34. Smaller than an atom, greater than the greatest is the Self dwelling in the heart of each being.
One who is free of desires, who is beyond sorrow, sees that Self and its greatness through the grace of the creator.[3]

4.35. Know the Self as the owner of a chariot, and the body as the chariot;
Know the intellect as the driver, and the mind as the reins.[4]

4.36. The senses are the horses, they say, the objects of sense their fields of forage.
The Self, united with the senses and mind, is an enjoyer, so say the wise.

4.37. Whoever, on the one hand, lacks knowledge becomes mindless and ever impure;
That person does not attain the highest goal but continues in samsara.

4.38. Whoever, on the other hand, has understanding becomes mindful and ever pure;
That person attains the highest goal, from which there is no return.

4.39. That person who has understanding for the driver and who controls the reins of the mind,
Arrives at the end of the journey, which is my own supreme state.[5]

4.40. Thus through hearing about, reflecting upon, and ascertaining[6] the Self by the Self,[7]
One should also, through intense meditation, realize that I am in essence the Self.

Comment

The Goddess has chosen two famous passages from the *Kaṭha Upaniṣad* in order to instruct the gods regarding the true nature of the Self. The first, regarding the Self as incapable either of slaying or of being slain, occurs also in the *Bhagavad Gītā,* where the unslayability of the soul directly relates to Kṛṣṇa's message to Arjuna to fight. Here, it simply reinforces the basic Advaitic notion that the Self is neither an actor nor an object acted upon. The second passage, on the metaphor of the Self as a chariot owner, stresses the need for understanding to control the mind and its hankering after sensual enjoyments. Detachment, as indicated earlier, is a necessary prerequisite for the acquisition of knowledge.

Following the recitation of the *Kaṭha* passages, in the final verse (40), the Goddess refers to the first three steps of Jñāna Yoga—hearing (*śruti*), reflection (*mati*), and intense meditation (*nididhyāsana*)—and inserts another stage, ascertainment or determination (*niściti*). Her purpose in reciting from the *Kaṭha Upaniṣad* is not only to illustrate the first steps of listening to scripture and reflecting thereon, but also to affirm that the real import of Upaniṣadic teaching and Vedāntic training is the realization of the Self as her own Self (cf. note 2 on *Devī Gītā* 1.2). One method of intense meditation, by which this realization can be actualized, is the subject of the last section of the chapter.

Notes

1. Verses 4.32–34 are based on *Kaṭha Upaniṣad* 1.2.18–20. However, the second part of this line (32ab) diverges somewhat from the *Kaṭha* text, incorporating some of the wording of *Bhagavad Gītā* 2.20 (which is also based on *Kaṭha* 1.2.18). The resulting mix is somewhat obscure in meaning, although the basic intent is clear enough. I have added the clarifying phrase, "from nothing." Cf. Edgerton's comment on *Bhagavad Gītā* 2.20 (*The Bhagavad Gītā*, p. 92, note 5).

2. Cf. *Bhagavad Gītā* 2.19. The *Bhagavad Gītā* (2.19–20) reverses, while the *Devī Gītā* (4.32–33) follows, the order of the *Kaṭha* verses (1.2.18–19). This same verse (*Devī Gītā* 4.33), with some variations, is also quoted in the *Mahābhāgavata Purāṇa* (16.17).

3. *dhātuḥ prasādāt*; glossed by Nīlakaṇṭha as "through the tranquillity of the mind" (*citti-prasādāt*), a meaning seemingly more consistent with a reading of *dhātu-prasādāt*, which is a variant of *Kaṭha Upaniṣad* 1.2.20. However, *Śvetāśvatara Upaniṣad* 3.20 has still another variant, including the phrase *dhātuḥ prasādāt*, that clearly intends the idea of the grace of the lord or creator. Certainly the idea of grace of the creator (identified with the Goddess) would not be inconsistent with the general teachings of the *Devī Gītā*.

4. Verses 4.35–39 are nearly identical with *Kaṭha Upaniṣad* 1.3.3–4, 7–9.

5. The verse is nearly identical with *Kaṭha Upaniṣad* 1.3.9, except that the latter designates the end of the journey as "the supreme abode of Viṣṇu."

Nīlakaṇṭha describes the supreme abode or state of the Goddess as "replete with being, consciousness, and bliss."

6. *niściti*: "ascertaining, investigating, resolving, coming to a firm conclusion about." This would seem to correspond to the *Pañcadaśī*'s definition of intense meditation (see the Comment on 4.17–24ab). The *Devī Gītā* apparently makes a slight distinction between ascertainment and intense meditation (*nididhyāsana*), referred to in the next line.

7. On realizing the Self by the Self, cf. *Bhagavad Gītā* 6.5; 10.15; 13.24.

Translation

[The Goddess prescribes meditation on her mystic syllable Hrīṃ for realizing the identity of oneself with her own supreme Self.]

4.41. Before attaining the final absorption,[1] one should contemplate within one's self the triad of letters
Known as the sacred syllable of the Goddess,[2] for the sake of meditating on the two meanings of the mantra.[3]

4.42. The letter *h* is the Gross Body, the letter *r* the Subtle Body,
The letter *ī* the Causal Body. The whole sound *hrīṃ* is I myself as the Transcendent Fourth.[4]

4.43. In this manner, recognizing sequentially the triadic elements of the seed mantra contained within the comprehensive whole,[5]
The wise person should reflect on the identity of the whole and the parts.[6]

4.44. Prior to the moment of total absorption, while concentrating earnestly in the above manner,
With the eyes closed, one should then meditate upon me, the Goddess, Ruler of the Universe.[7]

4.45. One should equalize the inhalations and exhalations flowing through the nose,[8]
Being unaffected by sensual desires, without faults, free from jealousy.

4.46. With sincere devotion, within the silent void of the heart,
One should dissolve the "All-pervading" gross aspect of the Self that is the letter *h* into the letter *r*.

4.47. One should dissolve the "Luminous" subtle aspect of the spirit that is the letter *r* into the letter *ī*.
One should dissolve the "Intelligent" causal aspect of the Self that is the letter *ī* into the sound *hrīṃ*.

4.48. It transcends the distinction of "name" and "named,"[9] beyond all dualities.
It is whole, infinite being, consciousness, and bliss. One should meditate on that reality within the flaming light of consciousness.[10]

4.49. By this meditation, O King, the noble person will perceive me directly
And then merge into my own essence,[11] since we two are one.

4.50. By practicing this yoga, one realizes me as the supreme Self.
In that instant, ignorance and its effects all perish.[12]

Comment

The third traditional step in Jñāna Yoga is the intense meditation (*nidhidhyāsana*) on the Self, leading to realization of and absorption into the supreme (*samādhi*). One such meditative practice, briefly outlined in the *Pañcīkaraṇa* attributed to Śaṃkara, involves contemplation on the syllable Oṃ, an ancient support or aid to spiritual reflection. The specific practice as expounded in the *Pañcīkaraṇa* entails, first, a comprehension of the correspondence between the three parts of Oṃ (Auṃ)[13] and the three bodies—Gross, Subtle, and Causal—of the Self, with their individual and cosmic counterparts, as well as their correlative states of consciousness. In a cosmogonic context, the three bodies are seen as progressively evolving one from the next: the Gross from the Subtle, the Subtle from the Causal, and finally—though not explicitly stated in the *Pañcīkaraṇa*—the Causal from the pure consciousness of Brahman/Ātman.

The second phase of this meditation, variously known as Laya Upāsanā (resorptive meditation) and Ahaṃ-graha Upāsanā (recovering-the-I meditation),[14] consists in reversing within oneself the cosmogonic process. This is accomplished by dissolving or reabsorbing in due order the three bodies, states, and so forth, back into their source, until the meditator finally merges into the supreme I or nondual Self. This resorption is actualized in the contemplative practice by regressively dissolving the letters of Oṃ (*a*, *u*, and *m*) back into their origin: *a* into *u*, *u* into *m*, and *m* into *Oṃ*, and finally *Oṃ* into the supreme *I* (the Ātman or Brahman). In such fashion the meditator is able to realize fully the identity of the individual soul with Ātman/Brahman.

Here, then, is the fruit of contemplating the Upaniṣadic teaching, "You are That."

This Laya Upāsanā of the *Pañcīkaraṇa*, especially as explained and elaborated on by Sureśvara in his commentary thereon, serves as a model for the Goddess' own concluding discussion of Jñāna Yoga. She replaces, naturally enough, the syllable Oṃ with Hrīṃ. Noteworthy is her reference to Hrīṃ as the Devī-Praṇava (see 4.41, note 2), for it is Oṃ that traditionally is called the Praṇava. And just as this prime Advaitic, sonic symbol has been sublated here by its Tantric counterpart, so it would seem has Brahman been largely sublated by the Goddess.

Underlying this intense meditation practice are various physical disciplines, such as breath control, briefly alluded to in verse 45. These physical disciplines and their relation to mental concentration are explained in the next chapter, on the Eight-limbed Yoga and Kuṇḍalinī Yoga.

Notes

1. Nīlakaṇṭha glosses *yoga-vṛtti* as *samādhi-vṛtti*, "the state (or attaining) of final absorption." Cf. *Devī Gītā* 4.44.

2. *devī-praṇava;* refers to the seed syllable of the Devī, Hrīṃ. The word *praṇava* is commonly used to designate the sacred Vedic syllable Oṃ. In the *Devī Gītā,* this is in fact the meaning of the term in three of its four occurrences (1.53, 3.45, and 6.6). In the first two of those occurrences (1.53 and 3.45), the *praṇava* is specifically paired with the Devī's sacred syllable, Hrīṃ. Here, Oṃ has been consciously supplanted by Hrīṃ, and to avoid any ambiguity, the latter is referred to as the *devī-praṇava.* Cf. *Devī Gītā* 1.53, note 23.

The Goddess refers to Hrīṃ in the first part of the verse as a "triad of letters" by ignoring the nasalization (ṃ).

3. Nīlakaṇṭha indicates that the two meanings refer to the *samaṣṭi* and *vyaṣṭi* (the "aggregated" or "comprehensive" and "individuated") aspects contained within the mantra (and specifically mentioned by the Devī in 4.43). These aspects are explained in the next two verses. The comprehensive aspect apparently refers to the syllable taken as a whole, the individuated to the parts, or letters, taken separately (but cf. note 6 on 4.43).

4. The correlations in this verse and the following description of the resorptive meditation on the component letters or sounds of Hrīṃ closely resembles the account of Oṃ given by Sureśvara in his *Pañcīkaraṇa-Vārttika* (verses 44–52).

Regarding the correlations, Sureśvara first notes the correspondences between the three individual or microcosmic and the three macrocosmic aspects of the Self or pure consciousness: the All-pervading (*viśva*) is identical with the Gross Body (*virāj*), the Shining (*taijasa*) with the Subtle Body (*sūtra*), and the Consciousness (*prājñā*, or *sauṣupta*) with the Causal Body or the Imperishable (*akṣara*) (44–45). He then identifies the entire universe as manifest in the three microcosmic aspects or states of consciousness with the three elements of the syllable Oṃ (the *o* is a dipthong, composed of *a* and *u*, and thus the three elements are *a*, *u*, and *m* [disregarding for the moment the fourth element represented by the dot, symbolizing the silence following the *m*]). That is, he equates the letter *a* with the All-pervading (*viśva*), *u* with the Shining (*taijasa*), and *m* with Consciousness (*prajña*) (verses 46–47).

5. That is, recognizing the three cosmic bodies symbolized by *h*, *r*, and *ī* as contained within the comprehensive Transcendent Fourth, symbolized by the entire syllable *hrīṃ* and identical with the Goddess.

6. The *Devī Gītā* here seems to be suggesting the identity of the Goddess in her comprehensive (*samaṣṭi*) aspect as the Transcendent Fourth, symbolized by the whole seed syllable Hrīṃ, with her individuated (*vyaṣṭi*) parts, the three cosmic bodies symbolized by the three letters *h*, *r*, and *ī*. Another possible interpretation of the identity of the comprehensive and individuated forms would be to equate the cosmic bodies of the Self (elsewhere regarded as aggregated forms) with the individual states of consciousness (regarded as individuated forms). Such an interpretation, while not fitting well the *Devī Gītā*'s preceding explanation, is suggested by the parallel text of Sureśvara's *Pañcīkaraṇa-Vārttika*. In discussing the various cosmic bodies and states of consciousness of the ultimate reality, Sureśvara develops these ideas somewhat differently. He stresses the identity of the three cosmic bodies and the three states of individual consciousness: "The three [individuated] forms, *vīśva*, etc., should be seen as identical with the three [aggregated] forms, the *virāj*, etc., to realize the absence of any difference" (*Pañcīkaraṇa-Vārttika* 45). For Sureśvara, as for the *Devī Gītā*, however, the different individual or seemingly separate parts (states/bodies) are regarded, ultimately, as identical with the one transcendent reality of pure consciousness (*Pañcīkaraṇa-Vārttika* 44).

7. The first half of the verse is nearly identical with *Pañcīkaraṇa-Vārttika* 48ab. According to the *Pañcīkaraṇa-Vārttika*, after reflecting on the macrocosmic and microcosmic correspondences of Oṃ and before the final moment of *samādhi*, one should begin the resorptive meditation that consists in merging or resolving the three bodies, beginning with the Gross, regressively back into their ultimate source, the pure consciousness of the Ātman. The *Devī Gītā*, before describing its own version of the resorptive meditation, emphasizes that such practice is in reality meditation upon the Goddess.

8. This line is identical to *Bhagavad-Gītā* 5.27cd. For further details on breath control, see *Devī Gītā* 5.15–21ab.

9. *Pañcīkaraṇa-Vārttika* 62 also describes the supreme reality as beyond name and named (*vācya-vācaka*). Cf. *Pañcīkaraṇa-Vārttika* 46, which states that Oṃ is the universe, there being no difference between the name and the named.

10. Nīlakaṇṭha glosses *śikhāntare* as "within the fiery light of consciousness" and cites a *śruti* text {*Mahānārāyaṇa Upaniṣad* 13.12}: "In the midst of that flame (*śikhā*) [within the heart] abides the supreme Self." The next line of the Upaniṣad identifies this Self with *parama svarāj*, the supreme, self-luminous consciousness. Cf. *Devī-Bhāgavata* 11.1.37: "One should meditate upon the Lord [identified with the Self] as a flame within the heart."

11. *mad-rūpa;* cf. 4.19, 7.27, and especially note 2 on 2.1.

12. Cf. *Pañcīkaraṇa-Vārttika* 53: "By thus practicing, the yogi, attaining final absorption, filled with faith and devotion, with his senses and anger conquered, sees the nondual Self."

13. See note 4 on 4.42.

14. See *Pañcīkaraṇa-Vārttika* 49, note 1. Cf. Swami Gambhirananda, "Upaniṣadic Meditation," pp. 384–85.

Chapter 5

Instruction in the Eight-limbed/Kuṇḍalinī Yoga

Translation

[Himālaya inquires about yoga, and the Goddess responds with a brief definition.]

Himālaya spoke:

5.1. O Great Queen, describe that yoga with all its limbs which bestows supreme understanding,[1]
So that by practicing it, I may become fit to see the truth.

The Goddess spoke:

5.2. The goal of yoga[2] is not found in the heavens, nor on earth, nor in the underworld,
But in the union of the individual soul and the supreme Self; thus do skilled adepts define yoga.[3]

Comment

The term *yoga* here encompasses the classical Yoga of Eight Limbs (*aṣṭāṅga-yoga*), expounded in the famous *Yoga Sūtras* of Patañjali (c. second century C.E.), conjoined with the Tantric discipline of

Kuṇḍalinī Yoga. The preceding chapter of the *Devī Gītā* details the Vedāntic path of knowledge, commonly referred to as Jñāna Yoga. At the end of that chapter (4.49–50), the Goddess describes the goal of Jñāna Yoga as the mergence of the individual practitioner in her own essence and the realization of herself as the supreme Self. The goal of the Eight-limbed/Kuṇḍalinī Yoga is here defined as the union or oneness (*aikya*) of the individual soul (*jīva*) and supreme Self (*ātman*). Thus the goals of the two yogas are seen as identical. They are distinguished by their specific means or techniques. The method of Jñāna Yoga may be characterized as intellectual-contemplative inquiry, that of Patañjali's yoga (conjoined with Kuṇḍalinī Yoga) as psychophysical experimentation. But as will be seen, even the methods of these yogas overlap to a considerable degree.

The definition of yoga given above and the subsequent description of the Eight-limbed/Kuṇḍalinī Yoga follows the summation of this discipline as provided in the *Śāradā-Tilaka Tantra*. The *Devī Gītā* adheres especially closely to the *Śāradā-Tilaka*'s account of the eight limbs. The *Śāradā-Tilaka* provides a fairly standard medieval elaboration and ramification of the simpler systematization of the eight limbs as given in the *Yoga Sūtras*. The *Śāradā-Tilaka* and the *Devī Gītā* both attest to the general Tantric affirmation of the basic complementary nature of the Eight-limbed Yoga and Kuṇḍalinī Yoga.

Notes

1. The description of the eight limbs of yoga in *Devī Gītā* 5.1–26 is very closely modeled on *Śāradā-Tilaka Tantra* 25.1–27. Except for the necessary changes to account for the different interlocutors in the two texts, *Devī Gītā* 5.1ab is almost identical to 25.1ab in the *Śāradā-Tilaka*. *Devī Gītā* 1cd–2ab is not found in the *Śāradā-Tilaka*, but the close parallels continue in 2cd ff.

2. The text simply reads "yoga." However, "yoga" refers both to "union" and "the means to that union," the discipline with its limbs. Given what follows in the next line, I have taken "yoga" here in the sense of the goal.

3. *Devī Gītā* 5.2cd is identical with *Śāradā-Tilaka Tantra* 25.1cd. I have supplied the words *But in* in the translation to complete the thought of 5.2ab, which has no parallel in the *Śāradā-Tilaka*. The latter text adds other definitions of yoga: the perception of the nondifference of Śiva and the Self; the knowledge of Śiva and Śakti; and the knowledge of the primal Puruṣa (25.2–3ab). These definitions reflect the perspectives of the Vedāntins (the one included in the *Devī Gītā*), Śaivas, Vaiṣṇavas, Sāṃkhyas, and others, according to the commentator Rāghava. The definition of yoga as the union or oneness of the individual and the supreme Self occurs also in the *Māyā Tantra*, according to Kālīcharana in his comment on *Ṣaṭcakra-Nirūpaṇa* 51.

Translation

[The Goddess provides an overview of yoga: its obstacles and limbs.]

5.3. Impeding the practice of yoga are the obstacles, said to be six, O Faultless One.
They are designated as desire and anger, greed and delusion, arrogance and jealousy.[1]

5.4. Adept yogis use the limbs of yoga to break through these obstacles and to reach the goal of union.
Restraint and observance, followed by posture, breath control,

5.5. Withdrawing the senses, concentration, meditation, and finally absorption—
These, they say, are the eight limbs practiced by adepts in pursuing yoga.[2]

Comment

Regarding the obstacles to spiritual practice, many lists of varying length occur in yogic literature. The first three obstacles (desire, *kāma*; anger, *krodha* or *kopa*; and greed, *lobha*) are standard in most. The *Bhagavad Gītā* refers to these as the "threefold gate to hell."[3] A common listing of five obstacles or defects includes, beyond the basic three, fear and sleep. Sometimes faulty breathing, excessive sleeping or waking or eating are included. These more behavioral faults/hindrances point to the yogic concern for physical training, as well as mental. But all of the impediments are generally agreed to stem ultimately from ignorance.[4] Thus, Jñāna Yoga and the Eight-limbed Yoga not only share a common goal, but also a common view of humankind's basic predicament.

By the time of the *Devī Gītā* and *Śāradā-Tilaka Tantra,* the list of six mental impediments as found in these works had become standard.[5] The latter text refers to them as the six enemies (*ari-ṣaḍ-varga*), as they cause affliction to oneself. Rāghava, the fifteenth-century commentator on the *Śāradā-Tilaka,* defines the six as follows: "Desire is the longing for the enjoyment of a woman, etc.; anger is the desire for revenge, etc.; greed is thirst for wealth; delusion is ignorance of the real; arrogance is pride in the form of the thought, 'I am happy, wealthy, wise'; jealousy is hatred of the fortune of others."[6] The eight limbs, next to be recounted, are intended to curtail the bodily disturbances and mental cravings that destroy peace in one's heart.

Notes

1. *Devī Gītā* 5.3–26 now follows closely, line by line, *Śāradā-Tilaka Tantra* 25.4–27.

The *Devī Gītā* refers to the six obstacles as *pratyūhas* (impediments) and as *yoga-vighna-kāras* (obstacles to yoga). The *Śāradā-Tilaka Tantra* calls them the "six enemies" (*ari-ṣad-varga*). The *Yoga Sūtras* (1.30) cites nine impediments, referred to as "foes of yoga" (*yoga-pratipakṣa, yogāntarāya*) in Vyāsa's commentary. The nine are: "Sickness, Incompetence, Doubt, Delusion, Sloth, Nonabstention, Erroneous Conception, Nonattainment of any Yogic Stage, And instability to Stay in a Yogic State" (Mukerji's translation). The *Yoga Sūtras* (2.3) also mentions a set of five afflictions (*kleśas*): ignorance (*avidyā*), egoism (*asmitā*), attachment (*rāga*), aversion (*dveṣa*), and clinging to life (*abhiniveśa*). These afflictions act as further impediments on the yogic path.

2. These eight are listed in the *Yoga Sūtras,* 2.29.

3. *Bhagavad Gītā* 16.21.

4. Cf. Georg Feuerstein, *Encyclopedic Dictionary of Yoga,* "dosha." Cf. also *Sarva-Siddhānta-Saṅgraha* (*Patañjalipakṣa* 9cd–10ab), where the five *kleśas* (*avidyā, rāga, dveṣa, asmitā, abhiniveśa*) are all said to have *avidyā* as their cause, in conformity with *Yoga Sūtras* 2.3–4.

5. See, for instance, the *Sarva-Vedānta-Siddhānta-Sārasaṃgraha* (101) which gives *kāmaḥ krodhaś ca lobhaś ca mado mohaś ca matsaraḥ*; and the *Prapañcasāra* (19.15): *kāma, kopa, lobha, pramoha, mada, matsaratā.* This latter text then proceeds to list and define the eight limbs of yoga, as do the *Devī Gītā* and *Śāradā-Tilaka Tantra.*

6. Rāghava, comment on verse 25.4 of the *Śāradā-Tilaka Tantra.*

Translation

[The Goddess enumerates the moral habits and dispositions involved in the first two limbs.]

5.6. Noninjury, truthfulness, nonstealing, abstinence, compassion, humility,
Patience, steadiness, moderation in eating, and purity, these are the ten restraints.[1]

5.7. Austerity, contentment, faith, charity, worshiping the deity,
Listening to established truth, shame, understanding, recitation, and sacrifice,
5.8. These I proclaim as the ten observances,[2] O Chief of Mountains.

Comment

In Patañjali's *Yoga Sūtras* the restraints and observances are five each (see notes 1 and 2 below), but the lists were eventually expanded to ten or more. The distinction between the "restraints" (*yamas*) and the "observances" (*niyamas*) is defined in various ways. An ancient tradition regards the restraints as obligatory practices requiring only one's own body as the means, the observances as optional practices depending on external means like water. Or the restraints are seen as concerned with others and as largely negative in character (e.g., do not hurt others), while the observances are seen as concerned with oneself and mainly positive in character (e.g., cultivate studiousness).[3] Again, the observances are sometimes regarded as more advanced than the restraints.[4] None of these distinctions is fully satisfactory, especially when applied to the extended lists beyond Patañjali's two sets of five. For example, the "negative" restraints are permeated by "positive" aspects and consequences.[5] Not suprisingly, then, in the later yoga texts the same practice or disposition may often be listed under either limb. What is clear, however, is that the restraints and observances taken as a whole represent a radical moral and spiritual training of the entire person in body, speech, and mind, involving attention both to inward intentions/motivations and to outward acts.

Rāghava, in his commentary on the *Śāradā-Tilaka Tantra,* correlates the ten restraints with the six obstacles: noninjury and abstinence overcome desire; compassion and patience subdue anger; nonstealing, truth, and humility defeat greed; moderate eating and purity prevail over delusion; patience and humility conquer arrogance; and finally noninjury, compassion, humility, and patience overcome jealousy.[6]

Nīlakaṇṭha gives the following traditional, and at times obvious, definitions of the restraints. Noninjury is not inflicting pain on others. Truthfulness is speaking the truth. Nonstealing is avoiding any kind of theft. Abstinence is renouncing the eight forms of sexual enjoyment: looking, touching, amorous playing, talking, secret confiding, resolving, persevering, and consummating. Compassion is kindness to beings. Humility is sincere recognition of one's own insignificance in relation to all others. Patience is enduring, like the Earth, all manner of disrespect. Steadiness is equanimity in the face of total disaster. Moderation in eating requires "filling two quarters of the stomach with food, one quarter with water, and leaving one quarter empty for air to move about."[7] And purity is both external (physical) and internal (mental).

As for the observances, Nīlakaṇṭha defines austerity as religious observances enjoined by established rules, but not including certain bodily mortifications.[8] Contentment is being satisfied in one's heart with whatever comes to one through fate. Faith is confidence in the Vedas, gods, Brahmans, and one's guru. Charity is giving away wealth to fit recipients in accord with one's ability. Worship of the deity is worshiping the supreme Lord. Listening to established truth is listening to the Vedāntic texts. Shame is a sense of disgrace in doing what is not proper. Understanding is knowledge of proper action according to the scriptures. Recitation is repetition of mantras beginning with the Gāyatrī, Praṇava, and Bhuvaneśvarī's mantra. Sacrifice is the prescribed fire offering.[9]

Notes

1. Patañjali (*Yoga-Sutras* 2.30) lists five restraints: noninjury (*ahiṃsa*), truth (*satya*), nonstealing (*asteya*), abstinence (*brahmacarya*), and absence of greed, or renunciation (*aparigrahā*).

2. Patañjali gives the following five (*Yoga Sūtras* 2.32): purity (*śauca*), contentment (*santoṣa*), austerity (*tapas*), study, (*svādhyāya*), and devotion to the lord (*īśvara-praṇidhānāni*).

The *Śāradā-Tilaka Tantra*'s and *Devī Gītā*'s list of the ten restraints and ten observances is quite common in later yogic literature. Svātmārāma's *Haṭhayoga Pradīpikā* (1.17) provides an identical list, and the *Śāṇḍilya Upaniṣad* (1.1.4; 1.2.1) (Aiyer's translation, in *Thirty Minor Upaniṣads*, pp. 173–74) has a nearly identical enumeration, making only the one substitution of *vratāni* (vows or rites) for *huta* (sacrifice) for the last observance.

3. Pandurang Vaman Kane, *History of Dharmaśāstra*, vol. 5, p. 1422.

4. Cf. Surendranath Dasgupta, *Yoga as Philosophy and Religion*, pp. 142–44.

5. See Jean Varenne, *Yoga and the Hindu Tradition*, pp. 101–102.

6. Rāghava, commentary on *Śāradā-Tilaka Tantra* 25.7.

7. Śrīdhara also quotes this same line, referring to it as a Smṛti text, in defining moderate eating (comment on *Bhāgavata Purāṇa* 3.28.3).

8. *na kṛcchrādi*; many older definitions of *tapas* mention the performance of the vows called *kṛcchra* and *cāndrāyana* (see Vyāsa's comment on *Yoga Sūtras* 2.32 and Rāghava's comment on *Śāradā-Tilaka Tantra* 25.8; see also *Śāṇḍilya Upaniṣad* 1.2.2). These vows are described in various ways but generally involve fasting, bodily and mental purifications, and other penances (for detailed descriptions, see Kane, *History of Dharmaśāstra*, vol. 4, pp. 120–21, 132–38). Nīlakaṇṭha, however, excludes these practices on the grounds that such austerities upset the body and are not conducive to the goal of yoga. The *Śiva Saṃhitā* (5.7–9) also includes *kṛcchra* and *cāndrāyana* in a long list of righteous acts that are actually obstacles to liberation.

9. Cf. the *Śāṇḍilya Upaniṣad*'s definitions of the restraints and observances (1.1.4–14; 1.2.2–11).

Translation

[The Goddess next describes five basic postures.]

5.8. [cont.] The Lotus Posture, the Happiness Posture, the Auspiciousness Posture, as well as the Diamond Posture,

5.9. And the Hero Posture, these in order are renowned as the five basic modes of sitting.
Duly placing the pure[1] soles of the feet upon the thighs,

5.10. One should catch hold of the big toes with one's hands crossed behind the back—
Such is the famous Lotus Posture,[2] beloved by yogis.

5.11. Duly putting the pure soles of the feet between the thighs and knees,
The yogi should sit with body straight[3]—such is deemed the Happiness Posture.[4]

5.12. Placing the heels firmly on either side of the perineum,
One should use the hands[5] to hold tight the heels of the feet beneath the genitals—

5.13. Such is the famous Auspiciousness Posture,[6] well honored by yogis.
Placing the feet alongside the outer thighs, with fingers cupping the knees,

5.14. One should firmly fix the hands—such is the unsurpassed Diamond Posture.[7]
Putting one foot under the opposite thigh and the other foot upon the remaining thigh,
5.15. The yogi should sit with body straight—such is the Hero Posture.[8]

Comment

Patañjali does not mention any specific postures (*āsanas*) in the *Yoga Sūtras*. In defining *āsana*, he merely says that the posture should be firm and comfortable (or held easily).[9] Vyāsa, in his commentary on the *Yoga Sūtras*, enumerates eleven *āsanas*, the first four—the Lotus, Hero, Auspiciousness, and Happiness postures—being included in the *Devī Gītā*'s list.[10] Later yogic literature extends the number of *āsanas* considerably. The *Śiva Saṃhitā* says there are eighty-four postures, with four main ones.[11] The *Gheraṇḍa Saṃhitā* says there are as many postures as there are living beings, that Śiva spoke of 8,400,000 postures, of which eighty-four (or 1600) are best but only thirty-two of which are useful in this world.[12] Commonly, it is said that one should practice the postures in a solitary and undisturbed place. While many of the later *āsanas* involve various positions other than sitting and have assorted therapeutic aims, the seated *āsanas* as described in the *Devī Gītā* have as their basic purpose comfortable and steady postures conducive to general well-being and suitable for prolonged meditation.

Notes

1. *śubhe*: "shining; beautiful; pure." I have taken the last meaning, on the assumption that the feet have been washed or purified before one begins the yoga. But the *Śāradā-Tilaka Tantra*, in its corresponding and nearly identical verse (25.10), simply has *ubhe*, "both."

2. The Lotus Posture described here is the variation known as the "Bound Lotus Posture" (*baddha-padmāsana*). The more common variation, with the hands not crossing behind the back but simply placed palm up in the lap, is referred to as the "Loosened Lotus Posture" (*mukta-padmāsana*). The latter is an all-purpose posture for worship and meditation. The former is especially utilized in purifying the subtle energy channels (*nāḍis*) of the body, which play an important role in Kuṇḍalinī Yoga, to be described later in the chapter. Woodroffe explains that by locking the feet with the hands in the Bound Lotus

Posture, "increased pressure is placed on the *mūlādhāra* [the "Root Support Center," described below in the *Devī Gītā*], and the nerves [*nāḍīs*] are braced with the tightening of the body" (*The Serpent Power*, p. 203, note).

3. *ṛju-kāya*. The *Bhagavad Gītā* recommends that the yogi should hold the body, neck, and head even (*sama*), unmoving, and steady (6.13ab). This steady, erect bearing (*ṛju-kāya*) is a basic mark of proper posture and often considered a requirement for further yogic practice. See, for instance, *Bhāgavata Purāṇa* 3.28.8 and *Yogatattva Upanishad* 36. Frequently the recommendation for holding the body straight is conjoined with the proviso that the posture be comfortable or easy (*samāsīna*). See again *Bhāgavata Purāṇa* 3.28.8, as well as *Darśana Upaniṣad* 3.6 and *Śāṇḍilya Upaniṣad* 1.3.1. The *Śiva-Saṃhitā* (3.113 [Ghosh ed.]) juxtaposes the terms *samakāya* (straight body) and *sukhāsīna* (comfortable sitting).

4. *svāstikāsana*. In this posture, the legs are crossed with one ankle on the ground, the other crossing on top, so that both feet rest between the calf and thigh muscles. The *Śiva-Saṃhitā* (3.115 [Ghosh ed.]) says that this posture destroys all afflictions and thus is also called the Posture of Well-being or Comfort (*sukhāsana*). Likewise, it is said to be an excellent means for maintaining good health. Similar claims are made for other *āsana*s as well. Thus, the *Haṭhayoga Pradīpikā* says that the Lotus and the Auspiciousness postures destroy all diseases (1.49 and 56).

5. The text has *pārṣṇibhyām*, "using the heels," but the *Śāradā-Tilaka Tantra* has *pāṇibhyām*, "using the hands," which makes better sense and is the standard formula for the posture. See, for instance, the *Śāṇḍilya Upaniṣad* 1.3.8; *Haṭhayoga Pradīpikā* 1.55–56. I have emended the translation in accord with the standard descriptions.

6. *bhadrāsana*. Here the soles of the feet press flat against each other beneath the genitals, with the knees wide to each side and on the ground. This posture, like the Lotus, has both bound (with arms crossed behind the back, hands grasping the big toes) and loosened (with hands holding the toes in front keeping the heels fixed tight next to the perineum) variations. The *Gheraṇḍa-Saṃhitā* (2.9) describes the bound posture, the *Darśana Upaniṣad* (3.7) and *Śāṇḍilya Upaniṣad* (1.3.8) the loosened form as found in the *Devī Gītā* and *Śāradā-Tilaka Tantra* (25.13–14ab).

7. *vajrāsana*. This is a kneeling posture, with the feet outside the buttocks rather than underneath (one variation does place the feet underneath), and with the hands resting comfortably on the top of each knee. The *Gheraṇḍa-Saṃhitā* (2.12) provides an etymological description of this posture: "Folding the legs, one should make the shanks hard like the diamond (*vajra-vat*)."

8. *vīrāsana*. This is a half-lotus.

9. *Yoga Sūtras* 2.46.

10. Vyāsa, commentary on *Yoga Sūtras* 2.46.

11. *Śiva Saṃhitā* 3.96.

12. *Gheraṇḍa Saṃhitā* 2.1–2.

Translation

[The Goddess recounts the basic practices of breath control.]

5.15 [cont.] Drawing in the breath through the left artery[1] for sixteen counts,[2]

5.16. The yogi should hold it fully for sixty-four counts,
Restraining it duly in the central artery;[3] then slowly, for thirty-two counts,

5.17. The excellent knower of yoga should exhale through the right artery[4]—
This is breath control,[5] so say those versed in the treatises on yoga.

5.18. Again and again, in proper order,[6] one should manipulate the breath.
Gradually, as is suitable, one should increase the count from twelve up to sixteen.[7]

5.19. When breath control is accompanied by mantric repetition[8] and meditations, the wise regard it as having a matrix.[9]
When breath control is not so accompanied, they regard it as without a matrix.

5.20. Through repeated practice, one progresses from the lowest level of accomplishment when a person's body begins to perspire,
Through the middle level when the body trembles, to the highest level when one levitates—so it is taught.[10]

5.21. One should strive constantly until one attains the fruits[11] of the highest level.

Comment

The fundamental purpose of breath control, according to the *Yoga Sūtras*, is purifying or calming the mind to make it fit for concentration (*dhāraṇā*).[12] Later yoga texts elaborate on this calming process, relating it to the purification of the subtle arteries (*nāḍīs*) through which the vital breath (*prāṇa*) flows within the body.[13] (The Tantric esoteric physiology of the body, including the *nāḍīs* and the main psycho-energetic centers of the central artery, is described below in verses 28–47.) Normally, in an untrained body with its *nāḍīs* impeded, the breath does not circulate freely, confined largely to flowing in and out the side arteries, the *iḍā* (beginning in the left nostril) and the *piṅgalā* (beginning in the right nostril), without entering the *suṣumnā* (the central artery running inside the spine). Such uncontrolled flow of breath eventually leads to death, without liberation. By purifying the arteries (*nāḍī-śuddhi*), especially the *suṣumnā*, the breath can be led into the latter, thereby bringing about the awakening of various psychosomatic and spiritual powers. According to some texts, purification of the arteries is brought about by physiological exercises or cleansings (*dhautis*) that must precede breath control proper, though certain preliminary breath control exercises may aid in the cleansing process.[14]

The basic technique of breath control, according to medieval yoga manuals, involves three phases: inhalation (*pūraka*), retention or supression (*kumbhaka*), and exhalation (*recaka*).[15] While the duration of the three phases as a whole may vary with the capacity of the practitioner, the ratio of the three to each other is a standard 1:4:2 (see note 7 below). In addition, the breath is alternated from left to right, and right to left, first inhaling through the left nostril and (after *kumbhaka*) exhaling through the right, then inhaling through the right and exhaling through the left, using the thumb and middle finger of the right hand to block the right or left nostril as necessary (see note 6 below).

To help concentrate the mind during the exercise, various aids may be adopted. The *Devī Gītā* specifically mentions the employment of mantric repetition (*japa*) and meditations (*dhyāna*), referred to as breath control with a matrix (*sagarbha*; verse 19). This meditation technique is explained in the *Gheraṇḍa Saṃhitā*.[16] It involves utilizing the three letters of the Praṇava (*a, u,* and *m*), correlated with the three *guṇa*s and the three gods of the Trimūrti, sequentially ordering them in accord with the three phases of inhalation, retention, and exhalation. Thus, while breathing in, one is to meditate on Brahmā, visualizing him as red in color, endowed with *rajas,* and embodying the letter *a.* The inhalation should extend for sixteen counts, measured by repetitions of the *a.* During the retention of sixty-four counts, one is to visualize Hari (Viṣṇu) as dark blue in color, endowed with *sattva,* and embodying *u.* Finally, one should exhale for thirty-two counts, meditating on Śiva as white, endowed with *tamas,* embodying *m.*

A Śākticized variant of the above *sagarbha* breath control is described in the *Śāṇḍilya Upaniṣad*.[17] The text says that the three phases of breath control "are in essence the letters (of Auṃ), and thus the Praṇava indeed is Prāṇāyāma."[18] The three goddesses Gāyatrī, Sāvitrī, and Sarasvatī are said to embody the three letters of Auṃ, respectively. During inhalation, one is to visualize Gāyatrī as a young girl, red in color, mounted on a goose, and holding a staff, while repeating *a* for sixteen counts. During retention, one meditates on Sāvitrī as a young woman, of white complexion, riding Tārkṣya (Garuḍa), and holding a disc, while repeating *u* for sixty-four counts. And during exhalation, one beholds Sarasvatī as an old woman, dark blue, riding a bull, and holding a trident, while reciting *m* for thirty-two counts. While the *Devī Gītā* does not give specific details for its *sagarbha* practice, an exercise such as the *Śāṇḍilya*'s utilizing goddess figures would seem quite fitting.[19]

Regarding the results or fruits of breath mastery, Nīlakaṇṭha points out a number of physiological benefits such as a beautiful, shining, and light body (see note 11 below). While some texts caution against seeking such fruits for their own ends, the *Devī Gītā* does not disparage such attainments—they are seen as clear indications of success in cleansing the *nāḍīs*, thus preparing the way for the following stages of yoga.

Notes

1. *iḍā*, the "Channel of Comfort." This artery or subtle channel (see lines 29cd–30ab below) runs along the left side of the body from the left nostril to the base of the spine. Thus, as Nīlakaṇṭha explains, to draw in air through the *iḍā* is to breathe in "through the cavity of the left nostril" (*vāma-nāsa-puṭena*).

2. Nīlakaṇṭha indicates the count (*mātrā*) is to be measured by uttering the Praṇava (Oṃ) sixteen times. In the following verses, similarly, according to the commentator, the counts are to be measured by repetitions of the Praṇava.

The *mātrā* is frequently used in regulating the duration of various breath control exercises, although the exact length of time of a *mātrā* is defined somewhat loosely. Thus, different texts define a *mātrā* as the time it takes to clap the hands three times, or to release an arrow or strike a bell, or to pull once on the udder of a cow in milking, or to open and shut the eyes, or to snap the thumb and middle finger three times, or to snap the fingers after circling the knee three times, or to fill and empty the lungs once (a complete respiration) (see Swami Digambarji and Mahajot Sahai, *Yoga Kośa*, p. 109, and Feuerstein, *Encyclopedic Dictionary of Yoga*, pp. 215–16). Regarding this last, Āraṇya calculates the time of a *mātrā* to be four seconds (on the assumption of fifteen respirations per minute). But he also cites another view, according to which a *mātrā* is one-third of the former measurement, i.e., one and one-third seconds (see his annotation on *Yoga Sūtras* 2.50, in *Yoga Philosophy of Patañjali*, p. 238). This latter duration seems to harmonize better with many of the above definitions. Ghosh comments: "The measure or unit of time is regulated in accordance with an individual's capacity and may range from one-quarter of a second, rising gradually to one second, then one minute—and even one hour in the case of adepts" (*The Original Yoga*, pp. 172–73).

3. *suṣumnā*. It is mentioned again in 5.29 and 5.31 below.

4. *piṅgalā*; this is the "Tawny-red Channel" referred to in 5.30 below. The idea is that one exhales through the right nostril, as Nīlakaṇṭha explains.

5. *prāṇāyāma*. Regarding the meaning of this term, Woodroffe points out:

> Prānāyāma is frequently translated "breath control". Having regard to the processes employed, the term is not altogether inappropriate if it is understood that "breath" means not only the Sthūla [gross] but the Sūkshma Vāyu [subtle breath]. But the word does not come from Prāna (breath) and Yāma (control), but from Prāna and Āyāma, which latter term, according to the Amarakosha, means length, rising, extensity, expansion; in other words, it is the process whereby the ordinary and comparatively slight manifestation of Prāna is lengthened and strengthened and developed. This takes place firstly in the Prāna as it courses in Idā and Pingalā, and then by its transference to the Sushumnā, when it is said to bloom (Sphurati) or to display itself in its fulness. When the body has been purified by constant practice, Prāna forces its way with ease through Sushumnā in their middle. From being the small path of daily experience, it becomes the "Royal Road" which is the Sushumnā. (*The Serpent Power*, pp. 212–13.)

6. As Nīlakaṇṭha points out, the proper order involves alternate nostril breathing, that is, drawing in the breath first through the left nostril and exhaling through the right, then inhaling through the right and exhaling through the left, repeatedly. This method of alternation is in accord with standard instructions for breath control as given, for instance, in the *Gheraṇḍa Saṃhitā* (5.38–44), *Haṭhayoga Pradīpikā* (2.7–10), and *Śiva Saṃhitā* (3.24–26).

7. That is, the count for the initial inhalation, with the counts for retention and exhalation adjusted proportionately. The ratio of inhalation, retention, and exhalation thus always remains 1:4:2. Accordingly, the *Devī Gītā* recommends that one begin with a count sequence of 12:48:24, eventually increasing to 16:64:32.

The *Gheraṇḍa Saṃhitā* (5.54) says that breath control is of three degrees of excellence; the lowest is of twelve counts (i.e., 12:48:24), the middling of sixteen counts, and the best of twenty counts. Woodroffe gives a different reckoning, whereby the three grades are said to be of 4:16:8, 8:32:16, and 16:64:32 counts respectively (*The Serpent Power*, p. 216).

8. *japa*: "recitation, repetition," often silently. It is glossed by Nīlakaṇṭha as *sveṣṭa-mantra-japa* ("repetition of one's favorite mantra").

9. *sagarbha*: "enwombed; with a matrix or support." For the general technique of *sagarbha* breath control, see the Comment above.

10. The three levels of accomplishment are mentioned in many texts. The *Gheraṇḍa Saṃhitā* (5.55) refers to them as marks of success (*siddhi-lakṣaṇa*) and correlates them with three levels of breath control practice according to the number of counts: twelve-inhalation practice results in perspiring, sixteen-inhalation practice in trembling along the spine, and twenty-inhalation practice in levitation. A similar scheme is given in the *Liṅga Purāṇa* (8.47–48), except that the counts for low, middle, and high practice are twelve, twenty-four, and thirty-six respectively. The *Śiva Saṃhitā* (3.47–49) adds that in the second stage, after trembling, the body jumps around like a frog, and then finally floats in the air. In rising off the ground, the yogi remains in Lotus Posture. This mastery of the breath (*vāyu-siddhi*), according to the text, destroys all ignorance about the world. The *Śāṇḍilya Upaniṣad* (1.7.3) also mentions retaining the Lotus Posture in levitation, and that the breath is fully suspended (*prāṇa-rodha*). The *Haṭhayoga Pradīpikā* (2.12) does not mention levitation, but only that at the highest level the yogi attains steadiness and holds the breath still.

11. Nīlakaṇṭha describes these fruits as attaining a brilliantly beautiful and shining body, needing little to eat, having lightness of body, and so forth. In similar fashion, the *Śāṇḍilya Upaniṣad* (1.5.4) declares that through practicing alternate nostril breathing for several months, the subtle arteries are cleansed and then the body becomes light and shining, with an increase in digestive fires, and a manifesting of the internal, spiritual sound. The *Śāṇḍilya* (1.7.4) also says that one should rub the body with the perspiration (arising in the first level of practice), and thus one's body becomes strong and light. In referring to the fruits of total breath suspension (retention without inhalation or exhalation), the *Śāṇḍilya* (1.7.13.6) adds that the body becomes lean, with shining countenance and clear eyes, with internal spiritual sound manifesting, free from diseases, with seminal fluid controlled, and with strong digestion. The *Haṭhayoga Pradīpikā* (2.78) gives the same basic fruits, seeing them as indications that the arteries are purified and as marks of success in *haṭha-yoga*.

12. *Yoga Sūtras* 1.34; 2.53.

13. See *Haṭhayoga Pradīpikā* 2.1–10; cf. *Śiva Saṃhitā* 3.22–29.

14. See, for instance, *Gheraṇḍa Saṃhitā* 5.32–44.

15. Patañjali mentions three operations (*vṛttis*) of the breath: external movement, internal movement, and suppression (*Yoga Sūtras* 2.50). These are similar to *recaka*, *pūraka*, and *kumbhaka*, but according to Āraṇya, they are not identical (*Yoga Philosophy of Patañjali*, pp. 230, 233). The *Bhagavad Gītā* (4.29) refers to the offering of the *prāṇa* (in-breath) in the *apāna* (out-breath), the

reverse, and the suppression of both the in- and out-breaths. Śaṃkara interprets these three as referring to *pūraka, recaka,* and *kumbhaka.*

16. *Gheraṇḍa Saṃhitā* 5.46–53.

17. *Śāṇḍilya Upaniṣad* 1.6.

18. *Śāṇḍilya Upaniṣad* 1.6.2.

19. Cf. *Devī-Bhāgavata* 11.1.38–42.

Translation

[The Goddess briefly summarizes the remaining limbs of yoga, from sense withdrawal to absorption.]

5.21 [cont.] The senses are wont to feed freely upon the objects of sense.
5.22. Seizing them back from those objects by force is called withdrawal of the senses.
On the toes, ankles, knees, thighs, anus,[1] sexual organ, navel,
5.23. On the heart, neck, throat, soft palate, and nose,
Between the brows, on the head, on the forehead, and on the crown of the head,[2] as prescribed,
5.24. Concentrating the vital breath on these points is called concentration.
Composing the mind and abiding inwardly in pure consciousness
5.25. While meditating on one's chosen deity within the Self is called meditation.
Ever realizing the identity of the individual Self and the supreme Self
5.26. Is absorption, sages avow. The nature of the eight limbs has thus been described.[3]

Comment

The last four limbs involve ever-deepening levels of mental concentration or absorption and flow naturally from the control of breath.

In the *Yoga Sūtras*, withdrawal of the senses (*pratyāhāra*) is defined as the separation of the senses from their objects, so that the senses conform to or follow the mind.[4] That is, instead of the mind following after the senses, the senses become obedient to the mind. So long as there is sensory input, the mind is disturbed. When the mind is focused or turned inward, the senses no longer wander externally, and the mind comes to rest. Withdrawal of the senses is thus part of a gradual process of mental training that begins in earlier limbs. Already in breath control, one calms the mind through concentration on the three phases, repetition of mantric syllables, and so forth, techniques that diminish the external activity of the senses. The overlap of breath control and concentration is well indicated in the *Śiva Saṃhitā*, according to which the total suppression of the breath for three hours is regarded as *pratyāhāra*.[5] Interestingly, the *Gheraṇḍa Saṃhitā* teaches sense withdrawal (chapter 4) prior to breath control (chapter 5), reversing the traditional order and thereby further suggesting the complementary nature of the two disciplines.

The *Śāṇḍilya Upaniṣad* indicates that *pratyāhāra* is of five kinds.[6] The first is described in almost the exact terms of the *Devī Gītā*'s definition. The other four are: (2) seeing all things as the Self; (3) renouncing the fruits of obligatory actions; (4) turning away from all sense objects; and (5) holding or concentrating (*dhāraṇa*) (the attention and breath) on eighteen vital points of the body (*marma-sthāna*) in ascending and then descending order. This last form of sense withdrawal in the *Śāṇḍilya* is taken by the *Devī Gītā* as the next limb, that of concentration (*dhāraṇā*).

The classical definition of *dhāraṇā* in the *Yoga Sūtras* is the binding of consciousness to a single point.[7] Vyāsa's comment on this definition indicates that the single point may be an external object, or any number of internal points or regions in the body. He mentions specifically the navel, the lotus of the heart, the shining head, the tip of the nose, and the tip of the tongue. Eventually, a system developed of concentrating the mind on a series of vital points (*marman*) in the body. The *Śāṇḍilya Upaniṣad* lists eighteen such regions, most of which correspond to the *Devī Gītā*'s list of sixteen given here.[8] It is not just the consciousness that is brought to these vital spots, but also the breath that is held or "concentrated" there, releasing the tensions in these points and allowing the *prāṇa* to circulate more freely.

The *Devī Gītā* in this chapter presents two different but overlapping forms of breath concentration. The first, described above and referred to as concentrating the vital winds of life (*dhāraṇaṃ prāṇa-marutaḥ*, in 5.24), is a more general and extended manipulation of the vital breath throughout the whole body. The second, described in 5.48-51 below and similarly called concentration of the life breath (*vāyu-dhāraṇa*, in 5.54), is a more specialized and focused manipulation of the breath, primarily in the central artery of the upper body and head. This latter form of breath concentration is elsewhere commonly referred to as Kuṇḍalinī Yoga.[9]

The *Devī Gītā* refers to yet another type of *dhāraṇā* in 5.55-58 below, involving the concentration of the mind or consciouness. While the text does not designate any special name for this third form of concentration, Nīlakaṇṭha refers to it as concentration of consciousness (*cittasya dhāraṇā*), in contrast to the *vāyu-dhāraṇā* described in the eight limbs.

Regarding meditation (*dhyāna*), in the *Yoga Sūtras* Patañjali describes this as a continuous flow of conscious awareness directed toward a single object.[10] Later texts distinguish various kinds of *dhyāna* according to the type of object focused upon. The *Śāṇḍilya Upaniṣad* refers to qualified (*saguṇa*) and nonqualified (*nirguṇa*) meditation.[11] The former involves focusing on a form (*mūrti*), the latter on the true nature of the Self.

The *Geraṇḍa Saṃhitā* gives a threefold typology of meditation: gross (*sthūla*), luminous (*jyotis*), and subtle (*sūkṣma*).[12] The first, meditating on concrete forms, includes a detailed visualization of one's chosen deity sitting on a jeweled throne on a heavenly island of gems in the midst of a nectar ocean (a description not unlike that of Bhuvaneśvarī in her Jeweled Island paradise). The luminous type involves meditating on the *jīvātman* (individual Self) that resides in the Root Support Center (see 5.36 below) as a flame of light, that is none other than Brahman. Or one may visualize a flaming Oṃ between the eyebrows. The subtle form requires intense, absorbed attention to the awakened Kuṇḍalinī, conjoined with the Ātman, as it leaves the body through the eyes, a subtle experience that defies ordinary perception. The *Gheraṇḍa Saṃhitā* sees the gross as quite inferior, the luminous as much better, and the subtle as extremely superior to the other types. The *Devī Gītā* offers a rather different and less systematic typology of various visualization practices (under mental concentration in verses 55-59 below), the common aim of all being mergence into the Goddess.

The description of absorption (*samādhi*) in the *Yoga Sūtras* is rather obscure and technical.[13] It is generally interpreted to mean a state of absorption beyond *dhyāna* in which consciousness of the self, and of the act of consciousness itself, are forgotten: only the object of consciousness remains. Thus absorption is also described as a state in which the subject-object dichotomy is transcended. There is a later trend to specify, as in the *Devī Gītā*, that *samādhi* is the realization of the oneness of the individual and supreme Self. The *Śāṇḍilya Upaniṣad* defines it as "abiding in the oneness of the individual Self and the supreme Self, devoid of the three aspects of knower, knowing and known,[14] supreme bliss, having the nature of pure consciousness."[15]

Notes

1. *mūlādhāra*, the mystic energy center (*cakra*) located in the anal region (cf. 5.36ab below). The *Śāṇḍilya Upaniṣad* (1.8.2) gives *pāyuḥ* (anus), and the *Śāradā-Tilaka Tantra* (25.24) *sīvanī* (perineum?).

2. *dvādaśānta*: literally, "having an end or limit of twelve." Rāghava (commenting on the parallel verse [25.25] in the *Śāradā-Tilaka Tantra*) glosses the terms as *brahma-randhra*, the crown of the head where resides the highest psychoenergetic center, the *sahasrāra cakra* (see 5.47 below). In some schools, this center is thought to lie twelve digits above the head.

3. The very close, often literal parallel with the *Śāradā-Tilaka Tantra* ends at this point. In discussing the subsequent topics of esoteric physiology and of arousing the Serpent Power, the *Devī Gītā* only loosely follows the general outline of the *Śāradā-Tilaka*.

4. *Yoga Sūtras* 2.54.

5. *Śiva Saṃhitā* 3.65.

6. *Śāṇḍilya Upaniṣad* 1.8.

7. *Yoga Sūtras* 3.1.

8. *Śāṇḍilya Upaniṣad* 1.8.

9. Regarding the general overlap and affiliation of the two forms of breath concentration, see the Comment on 5.52–54 below.

10. *Yoga Sūtras* 3.2.

11. *Śāṇḍilya Upaniṣad* 1.10.

12. *Gheraṇḍa Saṃhitā* 6.

13. *Yoga Sūtras* 3.3.

14. This interpretation of the three aspects (*tripuṭī*) is K. Nārāyaṇasvāmi Aiyar's according to his translation of the *Śāṇḍilya Upaniṣad*.

15. *Śāṇḍilya Upaniṣad* 1.11. Cf. *Haṭhayoga Pradīpikā* 4.7.

Translation

[The Goddess proceeds to the Kuṇḍalinī Yoga, here called Mantra Yoga; she first describes the esoteric physiology central to the Kuṇḍalinī Yoga, starting with the subtle channels that convey the life force.]

5.26 [cont.] Now I shall tell you about the excellent Mantra Yoga.[1]

5.27. The body is the cosmos,[2] composed of the five elements, so it is said, O Mountain.
It embodies the unity of the soul and Brahman, conjoined with the lustrous essence of the moon, sun, and fire.

5.28. There are reckoned to be thirty-five million subtle arteries[3] in the body.
Among these, ten are considered major and three are of special significance.[4]

5.29. The principal one[5] inside the spinal column[6] embodies the moon, sun, and fire.[7]
The "Channel of Comfort"[8] runs on the left side and shines white, embodying the moon;

5.30. This artery appears as Śakti herself visibly manifest, embodying the divine ambrosia.
The one on the right side is the "Tawny-red Channel,"[9] male in essence, embodying the sun.[10]

5.31. Composed of all brilliant light is the "Most Gracious Channel,"[11] embodying fire;
In its middle is the "Beautiful, Variegated Channel,"[12] characterized by will, knowledge, and action.[13]

Comment

The Goddess, while introducing her next topic as Mantra Yoga, has in mind what is commonly referred to as Kuṇḍalinī Yoga.[14] The *Devī Gītā* does not explain the exact relation between the Eight-limbed and Kuṇḍalinī yogas, but assumes the latter to flow naturally from the former. This latter involves the arousing of the Serpent Power (Kuṇḍalinī or Kuṇḍalī) that lies sleeping near the base of the spinal column within the human body (see verse 5.33 and the next Comment). The awakening of the Kuṇḍalinī and its further manipulations require the various skills of breath control and concentration developed in the practice of the eight limbs.

Kuṇḍalinī Yoga is based on an esoteric understanding of the body and presupposes a complex subtle physiology. Basic to this esoteric physiology is the conception that the body is an exact replica of the cosmos, often expressed in terms of the identity of the *piṇḍa* or *piṇḍāṇḍa* ("lump" or "lump-egg," referring to the body) and the *brahmāṇḍa* ("Brahma-egg," the universe).[15] The *Devī Gītā* largely assumes the various macro- and microcosmic correspondences that other texts spell out in detail. Thus, while the *Devī Gītā* simply refers to the spinal column as Meru, the *axis mundi*, the more complete body-world identification is brought out, for example, in the *Śiva Saṃhitā*: "In this body is Meru, surrounded by the seven islands with their rivers, oceans, mountains, fields and field-protecting gods."[16] The same text later identifies the three chief internal arteries (*nāḍīs*, discussed below) with the Gaṅgā, Yamunā, and Sarasvatī rivers, and affirms that one who bathes in the sacred place of their confluence (or meditates on the corresponding site in the body, at the mouth of the *suṣumnā*), attains liberation.[17]

The esoteric correspondences include not only physical entities but the transformative energies of the cosmos as well. The *Devī Gītā* mentions the lunar, solar, and fiery energies associated with the three chief arteries, the *iḍā* ("Channel of Comfort"), *piṅgalā* ("Tawny-red Channel"), and *suṣumnā* ("Most Gracious Channel"), respectively. The *suṣumnā* serves to unite the solar and lunar currents running in the *iḍā* and *piṅgalā*. As the *Śāradā-Tilaka Tantra* delcares: "The moon courses through the *iḍā,* the sun through the *piṅgalā,* and both course through the *suṣumnā*."[18] By uniting the lunar and solar energies, or breaths, in the central artery, the yogi transcends the basic polarity of time, night and day, and thereby attains immortality. The *Haṭhayoga Pradīpikā* represents this symbolically: "The sun and the moon create time in the form of night and day; the *suṣumnā* is the eater of time."[19] Accordingly, this chief, central artery is known as the path to liberation (*mokṣa-mārga*).

The underlying idea of Kuṇḍalinī Yoga, then, is that the truth of the universe can be realized in and through the body. The fundamental forces and processes at work in the universe are present within one's own body, and thus through understanding and mastery of the body, one achieves ultimate insight into the mysteries of the universe, including final liberation.[20] It is in the attitude toward the body and universe that we find perhaps the greatest contrast between the Tantric world view as expressed in Kuṇḍalinī Yoga and the Advaita Vedānta. Compare, for instance, the Tantric view just summarized with the statement in the *Vivekacūḍāmaṇi* that in order to realize the self-effulgent substratum of Brahman, one should reject the *brahmāṇḍa* and the *piṇḍāṇḍa* as filthy vessels.[21]

The subtle arteries or channels are already mentioned in the early Upaniṣads. They often speak of 101 *nāḍī*s, beginning in the heart, one of which leads up through the crown of the head. The life breath that circulates throughout these channels is thought to depart the body at death through one or another of these arteries. When the breath leaves through the artery that passes through the crown of the head, the person goes to immortality; when the breath exits by other arteries or apertures, one undergoes rebirth of various sorts.[22] While the *Maitrī Upaniṣad* refers to the *suṣumnā* by name,[23] the early Upaniṣads make no reference to the *iḍā* or *piṅgalā*. Nor do they conceive of the main or central artery as beginning at the base of the spine (but rather in the heart). They also make no mention of the various psychoenergetic centers (*cakra*s) situated along or within the *suṣumnā*, nor of the Kuṇḍalinī residing therein. The *cakra*s—among the most important aspects of the esoteric physiology of Kuṇḍalinī Yoga—are the subject of the next section.

Notes

1. Mantra Yoga basically involves the repetition of various sacred syllables and in a general sense is an aspect of many yoga practices, as seen above in the practice of *sagarbha prāṇāyāma.* Certain texts mention it specifically as one of various forms of yoga. The *Śiva Saṃhitā* (5.16–31) says there are four: Mantra Yoga, Laya Yoga, Haṭha Yoga, and Rāja Yoga. (The *Yogatattva Upaniṣad* [19] mentions the same four.) According to the *Śiva Saṃhitā,* each of these in order is appropriate for more and more advanced yogis. Mantra Yoga, in that text, is for the spiritual beginner, who is rather weak, ignorant, and ill-disciplined. But such a view hardly accords with the *Devī Gītā*'s.

The *Devī Gītā*'s use of the term *Mantra Yoga* is somewhat puzzling. Nīlakaṇṭha interprets it as that practice (yoga) bestowing success on mantras spoiled by various faults as described in the *Śāradā-Tilaka Tantra* {2.64–110}. This seemingly helps to explain verse 52 below, which affirms that the constant practice of this yoga will correct all improperly pronounced mantras. (Nīlakaṇṭha's comment on 5.52 again refers to the *Śāradā-Tilaka Tantra* passage.) But the puzzle remains, for the practice actually described—in verses 48–51, following the account of the esoteric physiology—involves the arousing of the

Serpent Power (*kuṇḍalinī*), and is elsewhere referred to as Kuṇḍalinī Yoga. This latter is an integral part of Haṭha Yoga (see, e.g., *Haṭhayoga Pradīpikā* 3), and is even at times, especially in Tantric circles, regarded as superior to Rāja Yoga, as it involves perfecting or illumining the body as well as transcending the mind.

Perhaps a key can be found in the *Śiva Saṃhitā*. After discussing the Haṭha and Rāja yogas (including an account of Kuṇḍalinī Yoga), the text refers to Mantra Sādhana (mantra practice) (5.236–56). This practice involves obtaining three seed mantras found in three of the esoteric energy centers (*cakras*). Sufficient repetition of the three will result in mergence into the supreme reality. Possibly the *Devī Gītā,* in referring to Mantra Yoga, has some such Mantra Sādhana in mind, focusing on the seed syllable Hrīṃ, the sonic manifestation or essence of both Bhuvaneśvarī and of the Kuṇḍalinī, found in the "Root Support Center" (5.32–33). Another key may lie in the presence of the various letters of the alphabet in the several esoteric energy centers. These letters are said to constitute the Mantra body of the Kuṇḍalinī. Regarding this Mantra body, see the Comment on 5.52–54 below.

2. *viśvam śarīram*; glossed by Nīlakaṇṭha as *piṇḍa-brahmāṇḍa.*

3. *naḍīs.*

4. Different texts give various numbers of *nāḍīs*. The *Śiva Saṃhitā* (2.13) says there are 350,000, with fourteen main arteries; the *Darśana Upaniṣad* (4.6) 72,000, with fourteen chief ones. The *Praśna Upaniṣad* (3.6) refers to 101 arteries, to each of which belong 100 smaller arteries, to each of which belong 72,000 still smaller, branching arteries. There is a general consensus in the later texts, however, that three are especially important for yogic purposes.

5. The *suṣumnā.*

6. *meru-daṇḍa*; in the macrocosm, Mt. Meru is the *axis mundi,* the supporting pillar of the earth, running from the underworlds to the heavens. In the microcosm (body), it is the spine, running from the "Root Support Center" to the cranium.

7. The *Śāradā-Tilaka Tantra* (25.31) similarly describes the *suṣumnā* as *soma-sūryāgni-rūpiṇī,* as does the *Ṣaṭcakra-Nirūpaṇa* (1): *candra-sūryāgni-rūpā.* The threefold symbolism may represent the three concentric tubes of the *suṣumnā*: the innermost *citriṇī* (pale like the moon), the middle *vajriṇī* (sunlike), and the outer, the *suṣumnā* itself (red and fiery) (see the commentary on *Ṣaṭcakra-Nirūpaṇa* 1).

8. The *iḍā nāḍī*. In translating, I here follow Feuerstein's suggestion: "The word [*iḍā*] is connected with the feminine noun *id,* one of whose meanings is 'comfort.' Thus the technical term *idā-nādī* could be interpreted to be the comforting channel—comforting because it cools the body during the heat of the day (*Encyclopedic Dictionary of Yoga,* p. 144). As the rest of the verse

indicates, the *iḍā* is associated with the moon, which in contrast to the sun is thought to possess cooling qualities.

9. The *piṅgalā nāḍī,* mentioned in 5.17 above as the right artery.

10. Verses 29cd–30 are very similar to *Sammohana Tantra* 4.5–6ab. The text is quoted by Kālīcharana in his commentary on *Ṣaṭcakra-Nirūpaṇa* 1. The two side channels, *iḍā* and *piṅgalā,* are often portrayed as twining back and forth around the *cakra*s, or as two bows lying on either side of the *suṣumnā.* (Cf. Woodroffe, *The Serpent Power,* p. 112.)

11. The *suṣumnā nāḍī.* Again, I follow Feuerstein in translating this technical term (*Encyclopedic Dictionary of Yoga,* p. 354). This is the central or principal channel mentioned in 5.16 and 5.29 above.

12. The *vicitrā,* also known as the *citriṇī* (*Ṣaṭcakra-Nirūpaṇa* 2) and the *citrā* (*Śāradā-Tilaka Tantra* 25.32; *Śiva Saṃhitā* 2.18). Nīlakaṇṭha glosses *vicitrā* as *citrā.* The *Śiva Saṃhitā* (2.19) says the *citrā,* running through the *suṣumnā,* is blazing with five colors (*pañcavarṇojjvalā*), thus explaining its name as bright and variegated. Cf. *Chāndogya Upaniṣad* 8.6.1, which refers to the arteries of the heart as reddish brown, white, blue, yellow, and red.

The *vicitrā* is the innermost channel within the *suṣumnā,* though the *Ṣaṭcakra-Nirūpaṇa* (2) refers to a *brahma-nāḍī* inside the *citriṇī.* The *brahma-nāḍī,* however, is merely the empty channel or space within the *citriṇī,* through which the Kuṇḍalinī moves. The *vicitrā* reaches from the area of the "Root Support Center" to the Brahmic aperture (*brahma-randhra*) in the crown of the head. The opening at its lower end is called the *brahma-dvāra* or door of Brahman, through which the Kuṇḍalinī enters to ascend to Brahman. Thus, it is called the divine path (*divya-mārga*) and the cause of immortal bliss (*amṛtānanda*) (*Śāradā-Tilaka Tantra* 25.33; *Śiva Saṃhitā* 2.20).

13. Will, knowledge, and action represent primal cosmogonic forces underlying creation. For a fuller explanation, see *Devī Gītā* 2.26, note 6.

14. See note 1 above.

15. Cf. note 2 above.

16. *Śiva Saṃhitā* 2.1. The following verses (2.2–12) give further details of the body-world identity.

17. *Śiva Saṃhitā* 170–72.

18. *Śāradā-Tilaka Tantra* 25.34.

19. *Haṭhayoga Pradīpikā* 4.17.

20. Cf. Shashi Bhusan Dasgupta, *Aspects of Indian Religious Thought,* pp. 149–50.

21. *Vivekacūḍāmaṇi* 289.

22. See *Praśna Upaniṣad* 3.8, *Chāndogya Upaniṣad* 8.6.6, and *Kaṭha Upaniṣad* 2.3.16. Cf. *Bṛhadāraṇyaka Upaniṣad* 4.4.2; *Maitrī Upaniṣad* 6.21, and *Taittirīya Upaniṣad* 1.6.1.

23. *Maitrī Upaniṣad* 6.21.

Translation

[The Goddess describes the Kuṇḍalinī and the psycho-energetic centers within the body.]

5.32. Inside[1] is the Svayambhū-liṅga,[2] shining like ten million suns.
Above that is the seed mantra of Māyā, which begins with *ha, ra,* and concludes with the nasal *m.*[3]

5.33. Above that is the the Coiled Serpent[4] appearing like a flame, blood-red in color.[5]
She is said to be the very essence of the Goddess, expanding with rapturous passion,[6] O Mountain Chief.

5.34. Outside her is the golden, four-petaled lotus[7] adorned with the letters *va* to *sa.*[8]
One should thus visualize this lotus, resembling molten gold.[9]

5.35. Above that is the six-petaled lotus, resembling fire and radiant like a diamond,
Adorned with the six letters *ba* to *la;*[10] this is the excellent "Own Abode Center."[11]

5.36. The lowest, root center supports all six lotuses,[12] and thus is known as the "Root Support Center."
Regarding the "Own Abode Center," it is so known since it is the "own abode" of the supreme Liṅga.[13]

5.37. Above that is the brightly shining "Jewel-filled Center"[14] in the area of the navel.[15]
It is brilliant like a cloud, like a flash of lightning, composed of great luster.

5.38. This lotus shines like a jewel, so it is called the "Jeweled Lotus."[16]
It is endowed with ten petals, adorned with the letters from *ḍa* to *pha*.[17]

5.39. Viṣṇu resides on this lotus, so that here one is able to attain a vision of Viṣṇu.[18]
Above that is the lotus of the "Unstruck Sound,"[19] shining like the stars and sun.[20]

5.40. Its petals are adorned with the letters from *ka* to *ṭha*.[21]
In its midst is the Bāṇa-liṅga[22] shining like ten thousand suns.

5.41. This center is composed of Brahman in the form of sound;[23] therein that sound, though unstruck, is perceived.
Thus sages call it the lotus of the "Unstruck Sound."[24]

5.42. It is the seat of bliss, wherein dwells the Supreme Person.[25]
Above that is the sixteen-petaled lotus known as the "Unstained."[26]

5.43. Conjoined with the sixteen vowels,[27] it is smoke-colored and highly effulgent.
Since the soul here attains purity by seeing the Supreme Self,[28]

5.44. It is known as the "Unstained Lotus." It is also known as ethereal and exceedingly marvelous.[29]
Above that is the "Command Center,"[30] wherein dwells the supreme Self.

5.45. Commands are received there; thus it is called the "Command Center."[31]
This lotus is two-petaled, adorned with the letters *ha* and *kṣa*, and very charming.

5.46. Above that is the "Kailāsa Center,"[32] and above that the "Blockade Center."[33]
Thus I have described the supporting centers[34] to you, who are of firm resolve.

5.47. Above them, it is said, is the seat of the primal point[35]
with its Lotus of a Thousand Petals.[36]
And so the entire, unexcelled pathway of yoga has
been disclosed.

Comment

The Kuṇḍalī, or Kuṇḍalinī, is the mysterious cosmic and psychospiritual power that is resident within the human body. She is a manifestation of the Goddess herself within us. In this form, she is called Kuṇḍalī (coiled) because she winds, like a serpent, three and a half times around the Self-existent Emblem (Svayambhū-liṅga) of Śiva, within the lowest of the psychoenergetic centers, the *mūlādhāra*. The *Ṣatcakra-Nirūpaṇa* describes her as the world deluder (*jagan-mohinī*), the cause or origin of speech, and the supporter of all beings by means of inspiration and expiration.[37] She is also described as "having the nature of creation itself, being in essence creation, preservation, and destruction, and she is also beyond the universe, having the nature of knowledge."[38] Though "serpentlike," she is typically visualized in the form of a beautiful young woman: "One should meditate upon the Kuṇḍalinī as one's chosen deity, ever sixteen years of age, with full, uplifted breasts, youthful, adorned with all ornaments, brilliant like the full moon, blood-red, with ever-restless [passionate] eyes."[39]

As the source and regulator of inspiration and expiration, the Kuṇḍalinī is the dynamic energy of the life-breath itself. In most humans, the Kuṇḍalinī lies asleep, wrapped around the Svayambhū-liṅga, and blocking with her mouth the opening or mouth of the central artery (the *suṣumnā*). This latter mouth is the *brahma-dvāra* or "Brahma-gate," and is the opening on top of the Svayambhū-liṅga. While she is sleeping, the energies of the individual—even when the individual is awake—lie largely dormant, or are dissipated, leading to successive births and deaths. The skilled yogi can arouse her through breath control, by causing the breath circulating in the lateral arteries of the *iḍā* and *piṅgalā* to enter the *suṣumnā*. By such means the yogi activates her to ascend the *suṣumnā,* resulting in the attainment of various physical, psychic, and spiritual powers as she enters or pierces the several psychoenergetic centers that lie along or within the central artery. (This awakening process is referred to briefly in verses 48-51 below and is the essence of the Kuṇḍalinī Yoga.)

The primary psychoenergetic centers (*cakra*s) or lotuses (*padma*s) are six in number. (Sometimes the number is given as seven, when the *sahasrāra* is included). These six, from the Root Support to the Command Center, are subtle focal points or confluences of consciousness and energy. They are identified with various bodily, cosmic, and divine powers. Specifically, the five lower *cakras* are identified with the five elements, earth, water, fire, air, and ether, in order; the sixth is identified with the "element" mind (*manas*). Each of the six centers is associated with a special protective divinity, representing various forms of vital activity such as smell, touch, and the like. Further, each lotus is inscribed with various letters, fifty in all, the number of letters in the Sanskrit alphabet and thus symbolizing the entirety of creation made manifest through sound. Each letter is itself a mantra, and a divinity. Taken as a whole, they represent the mantric body of the Kuṇḍalinī, who is none other than the Śabda-Brahman—the pure consciousness in the form of the primal, unarticulated sound that is in all beings and which emerges from the primal point (*bindu*).[40] As the *Śāradā-Tilaka Tantra* declares: "That (Śabda-Brahman), assuming the form of Kuṇḍalinī and entering into the body of all breathing beings, becomes manifest in the form of letters."[41]

The highest center, the Thousand-petaled Lotus (*sahasrāra*), is the original source or home of the Kuṇḍalinī, in the primal point. In Śaivite cosmology and yoga, the *sahasrāra* is commonly identified with Śiva's celestial paradise, Mt. Kailāsa, where he sports with Śakti. Just as it is the highest of all heavens, or even above the universe entirely, so the *sahasrāra* is envisioned as the crown of the head, or standing above it. Significantly, the *Devī Gītā* sees Kailāsa as merely a special locus above the Command Center, but inferior to the Thousand-petaled Lotus itself. One might suppose that the *Devī Gītā* would identify this highest realm with Maṇidvīpa, the Devī's celestial paradise, though such an explicit identification is not actually made. Interestingly, in the *Saundaryalaharī*, just prior to a brief description of the ascent of the Kuṇḍalinī to the *sahasrāra* where she sports in secret with her lord, the Goddess is described as sitting on the lap of Śiva in a jeweled hall, on the Jeweled Island (Maṇidvīpa), in the midst of the Nectar Ocean.[42] The association of nectar (*sudhā*) with both the Jeweled Island and the *sahasrāra* (see below) makes clear the correlation/identification of these two as the macrocosmic and microcosmic realms of bliss. In any case, in both Śaivite and Śākta yoga, the *sahasrāra* is the site for the reunion of Śiva and Śakti, as will be described shortly.

Much has been written on the exact nature of the esoteric physiology, in its several versions, described above. Often modern accounts are motivated by the desire to identify the different channels and centers with various anatomical features of the physical body as known to medical science. But such attempts may be beside the point. One contemporary scholar nicely summarizes what seems to be the essential point regarding this esoteric physiology:

> The plurality of yogic models is an indication of the fact that the *cakras* and *nādīs* are not altogether objective structures. Neither are they purely fictitious. A convenient way of looking at the different *cakra* models is that they are intended to be maps for the *yogin* on his inward odyssey, during which he discovers the psychosomatic structures of his being, only to transcend them in the unqualified radiance of original Being (*sat*), or transcendental Consciousness (*cit*). The purpose of yogic anatomy is thus to guide the *yogin* through and beyond the wonderland of the inner world of the psyche, which is interlinked with the physical vehicle.[43]

Notes

1. According to Nīlakaṇṭha, "inside" refers to inside the *citrā nāḍī* (the "Beautiful, Variegated Channel"). For discussion of the various views regarding whether the psychoenergetic centers are within or outside the *suṣumnā* and/or *citrā/citriṇī*, see Woodroffe, *The Serpent Power*, pp. 158–59.

2. According to the *Ṣatcakra-Nirūpaṇa* (8–11), the Svayambhū-liṅga (Self-existent mystic emblem) resides inside a downward-pointed triangle, the triangle and the Liṅga representing Śiva and Śakti, or the male and female powers of the universe, respectively. Wrapped around the Liṅga three and a half times is a more concrete manifestation of the female power, the Kuṇḍalinī herself. Her mouth covers the mouth of the Liṅga, which is the *brahma-dvāra* or opening to the *suṣumnā* leading up. All of these are located in the lowest center, the *mūlādhāra.*

The Liṅga, while in a shaftlike form that represents the phallus, as the prime emblem of Śiva transcends the sexual aspect. The *Śiva Saṃhitā* (5.88; cf. 5.117 and 5.132–33) refers to it as *tejas*, a brilliant, shining power. Regarding the significance of the Liṅga in the *mūlādhāra*, Woodroffe writes: "The *Svayambhu-Linga* in the Radical Centre [the *mūlādhāra*] round which Shakti or Power has coiled herself up in 'three coils and a half,' is the Self or *Ātman* in the Principle of solid matter which is sheathed by the coils of the 'Serpent Power' here immanent in Matter in its grossest form. All this signifies that Matter really involves Self or *Ātman* and the Power whereby this Self is sheathed is really Perfect Power, though 'asleep' " (*Mahāmāyā*, p. 157).

Various texts mention three or even four *liṅgas* in the different *cakras*. The *Śiva-Saṃhitā* mentions three: (1) the Svayambhū in the *mūlādhāra* (5.88, 90), meditation on which destroys one's sins (5.98); (2) the Bāṇa-liṅga in the *anāhata* (5.117), contemplation of which brings ability to move over earth and through the air at will (5.121); and (3) another *liṅga* simply called "the third," representing the transcendent state (*turīya*), identified with Śiva, and contemplation of which brings "sameness" with Śiva (5.133). The *Ṣatcakra-Nirūpaṇa* also refers to these three (see verses 25 and 33 for the last two), and calls the third *itara*, the "opposite." The *Devī Gītā* mentions by name only the first two (for the Bāṇa-liṅga, see verse 40). Cf. Woodroffe, *The Serpent Power*, p. 118.

3. The seed syllable, of course, is Hrīṃ. In Sanskrit orthography, convention adds a short *a* after a consonant to indicate its name. Thus, the verse supplies the *h*, *r*, and the *ṃ* of Hrīṃ. Nīlakaṇṭha makes explicit that the missing vowel is *ī*.

4. *kuṇḍalī.*

5. On the color of the Kuṇḍalī, see Woodroffe, *The Serpent Power*, p. 348.

6. *mada-bhinnā*; an alternative translation: "wild with intoxication or passion." According to the *Ṣatcakra-Nirūpaṇa* (11), the Kuṇḍalī makes a sweet humming sound like "love-mad bees" (Woodroffe's translation). This occurs when she is awakened. Thus, the image in the *Devī Gītā* verse here suggests that the Kuṇḍalī uncoils or expands when aroused, and is filled with passion as she begins her ascent to union with Śiva in the *brahma-randhra.*

7. The psychoenergetic centers are referred to both as *cakras* ("wheels") and as *padmas* (lotuses). Each center/lotus has its own, distinctive number of petals, with its own set of letters.

8. That is, the letters *va, śa, ṣa,* and *sa*. For the significance of the letters inscribed on the petals of the six lotus centers, see the Comment on 5.52–54 below.

9. This lotus is the *mūlādhāra* or "Root Support Center," located between the anus and the genitals. Its name is explained in verse 36.

10. That is, the letters *ba, bha, ma, ya, ra,* and *la.*

11. The *svādhiṣṭhāna*. It is located near the base of the genitals. For an explanation of the name, see the next verse and its note 13.

12. *ṣaṭ-koṇam*: literally, a "six-angled figure (i.e., a hexagon)," but this is confusing. The verse is almost identical to one quoted by Kālīcharana in his comment on *Ṣatcakra-Nirūpaṇa* 13, which has *ṣaṭ-kānām* (referring to a group of six, that is, the six major lotuses spaced along the *suṣumnā*) for *ṣaṭ-koṇam*. My interpretation follows Kālīcharana's clearer reading, which in any case provides the standard explanation for the name of this center.

13. Literally, the line reads: "The word 'sva' refers to the supreme Liṅga; thus it is known as the *svādhiṣṭhāna*." Various explanations of the name of the second center (the *svādhiṣṭhāna*) are given, depending on to whom or what

the *sva-* ("own") is thought to refer. Thus, it may be the "own abode" of the supreme Liṅga—as the text here indicates—or of Śakti (see Woodroffe, *The Serpent Power*, p. 118). The *Dhyānabindu Upaniṣad* (47) says that it is the resting place (*āśraya*) of breath (*prāṇa*). This same line is quoted by Kālīcharana in his comment on *Ṣatcakra-Nirūpaṇa* 18. According to Woodroffe's note (p. 362), this is from *Rudrayāmala* 27.58.

14. The *maṇi-pūra*. For the interpretation of this name, see verse 5.38 and its note 16 below.

15. Thus, this center is also referred to as the "Navel Center" (*nābhi-cakra*).

16. *maṇi-padma*. Various interpretations and translations of the name of this center (the *maṇi-pūra*) have been proposed. Feuerstein suggests "wheel of the jeweled city" (*Encyclopedic Dictionary of Yoga*, p. 210). Feuerstein notes, in addition: "The *Goraksha-Paddhati* (I.23) fancifully derives the name *mani-pura* from the fact that this is also the location of the 'bulb' (*kanda*), which is pierced by the central channel (*sushumnā-nādī*) 'like a gem [*maṇi*] by a string.' " The *Dhyānabindu Upaniṣad* (48cd–49ab) says: "Since the body is filled (or pierced, *pūrita*) by the breath like gems on a string, so the 'navel center' is called the Maṇipūra." Woodroffe offers "full of rays" (*The Serpent Power*, p. 247). Woodroffe also states that the center is "so called, according to the Guatamīya Tantra, because, owing to the presence of the fiery Tejas, it is lustrous as a gem (Mani)" (*The Serpent Power*, p. 119). The relevant text of the *Guatamīya Tantra* is quoted by Kālīcharana in his commentary on *Ṣatcakra-Nirūpaṇa* 21, and is nearly identical to *Devī Gītā* 5.38ab.

17. That is, the letters *ḍa, ḍha, ṇa, ta, tha, da, dha, na, pa,* and *pha.*

18. Through meditation on this center.

19. The *anāhata*. The name is explained in verse 5.41 and note 24 below.

20. It is located in the heart, and thus is also referred to as the "Heart Lotus" (*hṛt-padma*).

21. There are twelve petals, with the letters *ka, kha, ga, gha, ṅa, ca, cha, ja, jha, ña, ṭa,* and *ṭha.*

22. According to one tradition, the demon Bāṇa, a devotee of Śiva, established some one hundred and forty million mystic emblems (*liṅgas*) throughout the land, and these are thus called Bāṇa-liṅgas. (See Kane, *History of Dharmaśāstra*, vol. 2, p. 737). Vasant G. Rele claims that the Bāṇa-liṅga refers to a "Bulbous enlargement of the spinal cord in the cervical region." He explains: "The word Bana stands in Sanskrit literature for a symbolical expression for the number five and as this bulbous enlargement forms a subsidiary nerve centre for the five organs of sense it is called BA'NA-LINGA" (*The Mysterious Kundalini*, appendix, p. i).

The Bāṇa-liṅga and the Svayambhū-liṅga (v. 5.32 above), outside the context of the *cakras*, refer to two basic, natural emblems of Śiva. Svayambhū-liṅgas ("Self-existing emblems") are rough stones, perhaps slightly carved, in the shape of the *liṅga* of Śiva, and regarded as appearing spontaneously or descended from heaven. Bāṇā-liṅgas are small, white stones especially from the Nārmada River, rounded and polished by the natural action of the stream. (See Monier-Williams, *Brahmanism and Hinduism*, p. 69.) Both types of *liṅga*s are held to be so sacred by themselves, infused with the presence of Śiva, that no consecration of them for worship is needed.

In the *Ṣatcakra-Nirūpaṇa* (25), the Bāṇa-liṅga is described as residing within Śakti in the form of a (downward pointed) triangle, and to shine like gold. Cf. note 2 above.

23. *śabda-brahman*.

24. S. B. Dasgupta nicely describes the concept: "The word *anāhata* ["unstruck"] generally stands for *anāhata-dhvani*, which means the uncreated and unobstructed sound, which is all-pervading and eternal. In the process of *becoming* of the Being, the first stage is the *śakti* (power) and the next stage is the sound, the cosmic vibration from which evolves the visible world. It is the first music, the cosmic music, the divine music. The plexus in the heart is the seat of this *anāhata*. To listen to it, the yogin must withdraw his senses from outward objects, turn them inwards and then concentrate the mind on the centre in the heart; through such concentration and some accessory yogic practices, the mystery of *anāhata* becomes unfolded to the *sādhaka*, and he comes to be in tune with the cosmic rhythm, which arrests all the states and processes of the mind and draws the *sādhaka* near to God" (*Aspects of Indian Religious Thought*, pp. 164–65).

25. *puruṣa*, glossed by Nīlakaṇṭha as Rudra (Śiva). Cf. 5.39, where Viṣṇu is said to dwell in the *maṇipūra*.

26. The *viśuddha*. It is located at the throat. Its name is explained in verse 5.43cd–44ab.

27. These are *a, ā, i, ī, u, ū, ṛ, ṝ, ḷ, ḹ, e, ai, o, au, aṃ,* and *aḥ*.

28. *haṃsa*: "goose," but often representing the Self. I have followed Nīlakaṇṭha, who glosses *haṃsa* as "the supreme Self" (*paramātman*).

29. Kālīcharana, in commenting on *Ṣatcakra-Nirūpaṇa* 28, cites an anonymous verse that is nearly identical to *Devī Gītā* 5.43cd–44ab. Woodroffe, in describing the *cakra*, explains its name by refering to the *Devī Gītā*'s verse (*The Serpent Power*, p. 122), so perhaps Kālīcharana is quoting from our text. But Kālīcharana's text concludes with the phrase *mahat-param*, whereas the *Devī Gītā* verse ends with *mahādbhutam*.

30. The *ājñā*. It is located between the brows.

31. Kālīcharana, commenting on *Ṣatcakra-Nirūpaṇa* 32, explains that the center is called *ājñā* ("command") because it is here that the command of the guru is communicated from above. Woodroffe here cites similar statements from the *Guatamīya Tantra* and *Rudrayāmala* 27.68. Nīlakaṇṭha says it is the command of the Supreme Lord that is received in this *cakra*.

It is in this center that the third *liṅga*, the *itara* ("the remaining"), is found, according to such texts as the *Ṣatcakra-Nirūpaṇa* (33). The *Devī Gītā* refers to the first two (verses 5.32 and 40), though it does not mention this last. Cf. *Devī Gītā* 5.49 below.

32. According to Woodroffe, "the mystic mount Kailāsa is undoubtedly the upper brain" (*The Serpent Power*, p. 149). He also identifies it with the Thousand-petaled Lotus (the *sahasrāra*) (p. 153). The *Śiva Saṃhitā* (5.194–95) says: "Higher up [above the Moon, situated above the *ājñā*] is the *sahasrāra* . . . outside the cosmic universe of this body. It is called Kailāsa, where Śiva resides." The *Devī Gītā* situates the "Kailāsa Center" below the *sahasrāra*.

33. The *rodhinī*. Bhāskara Rāya, in his *Varivasyā-Rahasya*, describes this center as follows: "Rodhinī, which is immediately next [after Ardha-Candra], is triangular in shape and has the brightness of moonshine" (quoted in Beck, *Sonic Theology*, p. 142). Various centers of similar, if not identical name, are mentioned in other works. Silburn refers to a *nirodhikā* ("the obstructing one"), as an energy residing just above the brow center, in a list of about eight mystic centers or stages from the heart to the *brahma-randhra* (*Kuṇḍalinī*, p. 49). *Nirodhikā* also appears in a list of sixteen centers in the *Śārada-Tilaka Tantra* (12.122). A similar list is quoted by Kālīcharana, commenting on *Ṣaṭcakra-Nirūpaṇa* 33, where the term appears as *nibhodikā* ("enlightening"). Commenting on verse 40, he refers to a *bodhinī*, quoting from the *Sammohana Tantra*.

The six centers, from the *mūlādhāra* to the *ājñā*, are standard in almost all works dealing with the subject. But different texts refer to a variety of centers between (and/or within) the *ājñā* and the *sahasrāra*. (See Woodroffe, *The Serpent Power*, pp. 127–28, 148–49.) Regarding the two special centers mentioned in our text (the Kailāsa and *rodhinī*), Nīlakaṇṭha says that the nature of these two is explained in his great *ṭikā* (commentary) on the *Devī Gītā*—such a *ṭikā* apparently no longer exists.

34. *ādhāra-cakrāṇi*; by itself, *ādhāra* refers to the "Base Support Center," but in the plural may signify all the centers as "supports." Cf. Kālīcharana's comment on *Ṣaṭcakra-Nirūpaṇa* 33.

35. *bindu*, glossed by Nīlakaṇṭha as "Supreme Self" (*paramātman*). The term is a technical one, with many meanings in yoga. Here it refers to the original primal point from which emerges all manifest creation, beginning with sound (*nāda*).

36. This lotus is either at the crown of the head, or even above the head outside the body (cf. note 2 on 5.23). Nīlakaṇṭha simply points out that it is above all (other centers).

37. *Ṣaṭcakra-Nirūpaṇa* 10–11.

38. Quoted by Kālīcharana in his commentary to *Ṣatcakra-Nirūpaṇa* 10–11, citing merely "another Tantra."

39. Again quoted by Kālīcharana, commenting on *Ṣatcakra-Nirūpaṇa* 10–11, with no specific citation.

40. Cf. Woodroffe, *The Serpent Power,* pp. 116–17, and Varenne, *Yoga,* pp. 166–74.

41. *Śāradā-Tilaka Tantra* 1.14.

42. *Saundaryalaharī* 8–9.

43. Feuerstein, *Encyclopedic Dictionary of Yoga,* pp. 24–25.

Translation

[The Goddess briefly indicates the procedures for arousing and guiding the Kuṇḍalinī.]

5.48. First, breathing in with yogic control, one should bring the mind to focus on the Root Support.
There between the anus and the genitals resides the Śakti Kuṇḍalinī. Compressing her,[1] one should awaken her.

5.49. Then one should lead her to the highest center of the primal point by piercing the mystic emblems[2] in order.
One should visualize there that supreme Śakti as united with Śiva.

5.50. In that union is produced an ambrosial nectar[3] resembling molten red lac,[4]
Which should be given as a drink to the Śakti Māyā, who grants success in yoga.

5.51. Satisfying the presiding deities of the six centers by offering them that descending stream of nectar,
A wise person will then lead her back by the same path to the Root Support Center.[5]

Comment

The Goddess briefly summarizes the various procedures and stages of Kuṇḍalinī Yoga, describing only the key moments in the ascent and descent of the Serpent Power. Other Tantric texts provide many details merely assumed by the *Devī Gītā*. Though specifics may vary from one text to another, the general scheme of Kuṇḍalinī Yoga is as follows. The arousing of the Kuṇḍalinī is first brought about by focusing the mind on her dwelling in the Root Support, which aids in bringing the breath into the *suṣumnā*, thereby squeezing the sleeping serpent. Thus agitated, the Kuṇḍalinī uncoils herself from around the Svayambhū-liṅga and unblocks its opening—the Brahma-gate at its top. She then enters into the *suṣumnā* through the Brahma-gate, effectively "piercing" the *liṅga*, and begins her ascent through the other centers. In this manner, as she enters and pierces each successive *cakra*, she unites with the corresponding divinities and *liṅga*s of those centers, absorbing their energies into herself. Thus, her ascent is often referred to as *liṅga-bheda* (piercing the mystic emblems), or as *ṣaṭ-cakra-bheda* (piercing the six centers).

Pervading the traditional accounts of this Kuṇḍalinī Yoga is a multivalent sexual symbolism. Every union is a kind of dissolution; every dissolution a further mergence back toward the primordial reality and the supreme union. Even before the final merging into one (*ekībhūta*) of Śiva and Śakti in the *sahasrāra*, we see various other anticipatory unions, as the Kuṇḍalinī embraces the various *liṅga*s along her path. Further, the yogi at the beginning of the practice unites with the vital breath and then identifies himself or herself with the Kuṇḍalinī. The supreme union, in which the internal male and female principles are merged, is none other than the union of the individual *jīva* (as represented by the Kuṇḍalinī) and the supreme Self.

The symbolism of sexual union also involves both emission and absorption of vital fluids or energies. The uniting of the Kuṇḍalinī with the divinities in the lower centers emphasizes her absorption of their physical and psychic energies. The highest union accentuates the emission of the divine ambrosia, red in color due to being mixed with the menstrual flow. The Kuṇḍalinī drinks and reabsorbs the nectar, experiencing divine bliss. The flow of sexual energies thus symbolizes not only the production and exchange of various physical and cosmic powers, but also the blissful transformation of consciousness itself, from obscured awareness mired in duality to realization of the ultimate oneness.

It is noteworthy that Kuṇḍalinī Yoga does not end when the ascending process is completed. The descent or return of the Kuṇḍalinī to the Root Support is equally significant. The ascent is basically a dissolution of the universe, a resorption (*laya*) of all the cosmic entities and powers into the Kuṇḍalinī, culminating in a liberation that transcends or lies behind the manifest realm. In her descent, the Serpent revivifies and illumines what she had previously absorbed, infusing them with nectar. While her ascent is thus known as *laya-krama* (course of dissolution), her descent is called *sṛṣṭi-krama* (course of creation). In her upward course, she is said to be luminous, in her downward, ambrosial.[6] From the standpoint of the yogi, the revivification is not simply a recreation of the old order, for the new creation is superinfused with an abundance of nectar. Due to a fundamental change in the yogi's consciousness, the body with all its physical and psychic elements is now experienced as the body of the divine. The liberation attained through Kuṇḍalinī Yoga is thus not only transcendent, but also immanent, both beyond the cosmos and within one's own body.

Notes

1. Nīlakaṇṭha explains: "... squeezing her with the breath entered into the *mūlādhāra*."

2. *liṅga-bheda*; refers to the piercing of the three *liṅga*s, the Svayambhū-liṅga in the *mūlādhāra*, the Bāṇa-liṅga in the *anāhata*, and the Itara-liṅga in the *ājñā* (cf. note 31 on 5.45 above). These *liṅga*s are also referred to as knots (*granthi*s), and are known as Brahmā's knot, Viṣṇu's knot, and Rudra's knot, respectively. These knots form obstructions in the *suṣumnā*, blocking the passage of the Kuṇḍalinī, until great force is exerted against them, bursting open or piercing the knots. Cf. Woodroffe, *The Serpent Power*, p. 126, and *Ṣaṭcakra-Nirūpaṇa* 51.

3. *amṛta*; also called *sudhā*; indicates both "immortality" and "the divine ambrosia" or "nectar of immortality." According to the popular myth of "The Churning of the Milk Ocean," this nectar was one of the products to arise from the churning. In a yogic context, however, it is said to be produced in the crown of the head and to trickle down through the body, where it is wasted by ordinary people who do not understand how to increase its flow and use it properly. By uniting the female and male principles within oneself (the Kuṇḍalinī or Śakti and Śiva) in the crown of the head, the yogi causes an abundance of nectar to flow. When "drunk" by the yogi, the nectar produces feelings of supreme bliss, as well as immortality. The *Śāradā-Tilaka Tantra* (25.67) describes the Kuṇḍalinī, when united with Śiva, as "filled with an excess of blissful nectar (*sudhā*)." The same text (25.72) portrays the body of Kuṇḍalinī as "thoroughly moistened with oozing nectar as she passes through the *cakra*s."

4. Woodroffe, citing Śaṃkara, indicates that the nectar is red because it is mixed with menstrual blood. He adds that this is simply part of the erotic symbolism, the red representing the quality of *rajas* (activity) (*Ṣaṭcakra-Nirūpaṇa* 53, notes).

5. The ideas in *Devī Gītā* 5.50–51 closely parallel those of *Ṣaṭcakra-Nirūpaṇa* 53.

6. See *Ṣaṭcakra-Nirūpaṇa* 53, Kālīcharana's commentary thereon, and Woodroffe's notes.

Translation

[The Goddess describes the fruits of Kuṇḍalinī Yoga.]

5.52. It is certain that by such spiritual practice performed daily,
All mantras previously uttered incorrectly will become effective, without fail.[1]

5.53. One is freed from the bondage of worldly existence with its miseries of old age, death, and the like.
Just such qualities as belong to me, the divine World-mother,

5.54. Those very qualities will inhere in the accomplished adept, without fail.
Thus have I recounted the excellent practice of concentrating the breath,[2] my child.

Comment

The *Devī Gītā* is rather unconventional in its designation of the Kuṇḍalinī Yoga as Mantra Yoga (5.26), as suggested earlier. Here (5.52) the Goddess seems to propose a rationale for the term: the practice of this yoga corrects the faults of improperly pronounced mantras. Given that the esoteric centers or lotuses with their inscribed letters represent the mantric body of the Goddess, encompassing all mantras, it is hardly surprising that the successful manipulation of this body should result in the complete fruition of any prior partial or faulty mantric utterances. Such fruition, in view of the universal scope of mantric powers, naturally enough incorporates freedom from the bonds of samsara. And on the positive side, it includes assuming the virtues and attributes of the Goddess herself, a form of liberation known as *sārṣṭi*.

The Devī goes on to refer to the Kuṇḍalinī Yoga as *vāyu-dhāraṇa*, a designation that is quite understandable, given the role of breath manipulation in the discipline and the basic affinity between the life breath and the Kuṇḍalinī herself. Nīlakaṇṭha seems to assimilate this form of breath concentration involving the Kuṇḍalinī to the concentration of vital wind described earlier in the eight limbs of yoga, entailing concentration of breath on various vital points (*marman*) from the toes to the crown of the head.

Not infrequently in yogic texts, these two forms of breath concentration are closely affiliated and regarded either as successive or continuous manipulations of the breath. Thus, in the *Kṣurikā Upaniṣad*, the yogi is advised to concentrate the breath on the various vital points from the toes up to the navel, where the central artery (*suṣumnā*) is found. Then, at that point one is to enter the *suṣumnā* and continue to send upward the vital breath.[3] Similarly, in the *Yogatattva Upaniṣad*, following a brief description of forcing the breath in the form of the Kuṇḍalinī into the *suṣumnā*,[4] there ensues an elaborate account of a fivefold concentration (*dhāraṇā pañcadhā*) practice. This latter involves focusing on the five elements as distributed in five levels of the body: earth in the region from the feet to the knees, water from the knees to the anus, fire from the anus to the heart, wind from the heart to the middle of the brows, and ether from the middle of the brows to the crown of the head.[5] In Kuṇḍalinī Yoga, the elements are distributed in the five centers from the base support near the anus to the throat center, with the sixth "element" mind assigned to the center between the brows. As in the Kuṇḍalinī Yoga, the fivefold concentration involves leading the breath from the lower to the higher regions, resulting in immortality and bliss.

Notes

1. As in his earlier comment on 5.26, Nīlakaṇṭha here refers to the various faults mentioned in the *Śāradā-Tilaka Tantra* {2.64-110}. Now he quotes the next verse {2.111} of that work, to the effect that the defects can be corrected by Yoni-mudrā. This term, also known as Yoni-bandha ("locking the perineum"), is used in some texts as a synonym for Kuṇḍalinī Yoga. The *Yogatattva Upaniṣad* (120cd–121ab) explains Yoni-bandha as follows: "With the heel pressing the perineum (*yoni*), contracting it firmly, one should force upward the life breath (*apāna*)." The *Gheraṇḍa Saṃhitā* (3.37–42) is even more explicit in identifying the Yoni-mudrā with Kuṇḍalinī Yoga, defining Yoni-mudrā specifically as meditation on the six centers and the awakening of the Serpent Power. Thus is the Devī's statement in this verse justified, according to Nīlakaṇṭha.

2. *vāyu-dhāraṇa*. Cf. the explanation of *dhāraṇā* in the Comment on verses 5.21cd–26ab above.

3. *Kṣurikā Upaniṣad* 4–20.

4. *Yogatattva Upaniṣad* 81cd–83ab.

5. *Yogatattva Upaniṣad* 83cd–103ab.

Translation

[The Goddess describes other methods of concentration.]

5.55. Now listen attentively to me regarding another concentration practice.
Fixing the mind upon me as the Goddess transcending all space and time,[1]

5.56. One quickly merges with me through realizing the oneness of the soul and Brahman.
But if the mind is impure, one will not succeed at once.

5.57. Then the yogi should practice the Limb-by-limb Meditation:
On my charming limbs, on my hands, feet, and so on, O Mountain,

5.58. The adept well versed in mantras should focus the mind, mastering each member one by one.[2]
With the mind thus purified, the yogi should concentrate upon my whole form.

5.59. Until the mind dissolves into me, the Goddess who is divine consciousness, O Mountain,
The well-versed adept should continue reciting the approved mantra[3] accompanied by sacrificial offerings.[4]

Comment

The Goddess now turns from her description of breath concentration (*vāyu-dhāraṇa*, or Kuṇḍalinī Yoga) to another form of concentration, which Nīlakaṇṭha refers to as concentration of the mind (*cittasya dhāraṇā*). Given the intimate, interconnected functionings of the breath and the mind, the two types of concentration are not unrelated, but they do have rather different emphases, including the specific objects of concentration. Whereas the breath concentration focuses on the form of the Goddess within the body—in the form of the Serpent Power—the mind concentration fixates on the Goddess outside the body—in her lovely form (as Bhuvaneśvarī, we may assume) or as beyond all form.

In recounting the concentration of the mind, the Goddess suggests a three-step progression: the first and easiest step involves focusing one's mind on the various limbs and parts of her charming body; the next requires visualizing her body as an integrated whole; and the last fixing the mind in pure consciousness, into which it dissolves. This pure consciousness, of course, is that aspect of the Goddess which transcends all space and time, and is beyond any form. Concentrating the mind on such a formless "form" is rather challenging, and thus the Goddess offers the various preliminary visualization practices.

In chapters nine and ten of the *Devī Gītā*, the Goddess speaks of four kinds of worship (*pūjā*), which are somewhat parallel to the different kinds of concentration discussed in this chapter. The four kinds of worship focus on her basic forms: (1) the Virāj (external and Vedic), (2) the lovely four-armed form as Bhuvaneśvarī (also considered external and Vedic), (3) pure consciousness (internal, and what we may call Advaitic), and (4) the Kuṇḍalinī (Tantric). But in the present chapter, the corresponding first and second forms of concentration involve only the charming form of the Goddess (implicitly as Bhuvaneśvarī), either in her separate limbs or in integrated form, but with no reference to the Virāj.

The *Bhāgavata Purāṇa* has similar types of meditation (excluding the Kuṇḍalinī). This text refers to the Limb-by-limb Meditation on the four-armed Viṣṇu, and regards it as a more advanced form of meditation than concentration on the gross Puruṣa (the Virāj) form of Viṣṇu.[5] In the "Kapila Gītā" of the *Bhāgavata Purāṇa*, where a *bhakti*cized version of the eight limbs of yoga is recounted, *dhyāna* is explained as meditation on the Lord's body either as an integrated whole or as a limb-by-limb visualization.[6] The text dwells lovingly on the details of Viṣṇu's members, from his brilliant toenails, feet, knees, thighs, navel, nipples, and the like to his smiling face, with its shining cheeks, curly tresses, and lotuslike eyes. Meditation on these limbs leads to ecstatic devotion to Viṣṇu, culminating in *samādhi*, in which apparently the iconic forms of Viṣṇu are left behind as one perceives the Self in all beings and all beings in the Self.

The *Devī Gītā* glosses over the details of its Limb-by-limb Meditation, and subordinates more clearly than the *Bhāgavata* the iconic forms of meditation to the final realization, or dissolution into pure consciousness. Yet like the *Bhāgavata*, the *Devī Gītā*'s exposition of the Eight-limbed Yoga blends together Advaitic and *bhaktic* perspectives. Where the *Devī Gītā* most distinctly goes beyond the "Kapila Gītā" is in its inclusion of the Tantric perspective.

Notes

1. *dik-kālādy-anavacchinna*; a similar epithet (*dik-kālādi-vivarjita*) is found in the *Śāradā-Tilaka Tantra*'s account of the Kuṇḍalinī Yoga, but applied to Para-Śiva (25.82). The exact same form of the epithet, however, is applied to the Goddess, referred to as Para-Śakti and identified with the Kuṇḍalinī, in *Śāradā-Tilaka Tantra* 1.52.

2. That is, clearly visualizing each member in order. Cf. *Bhāgavata Purāṇa* 2.2.13 (describing the Limb-by-limb Meditation on the Lord Viṣṇu): "One should meditate on the limbs, one by one, from the feet to the smiling face of the mace-wielder (Viṣṇu). As one masters each member, one should leave it behind, fixing upon the next, and thus one's mind becomes ever purer."

3. *iṣṭa-manu*: "chosen or approved mantra," that is, the mantra of one's chosen deity, received from one's guru.

4. Cf. *Śiva Saṃhitā* 5.241–45, where the yogi is told to make one hundred thousand sacrificial offerings and to recite a threefold mantra obtained from his guru three hundred thousand times before the Goddess. (The threefold mantra consists of the three seed syllables found in the Base Support, Heart, and Command centers, according to the preceding verses.) Such practice is said to lead even an unlucky or slow yogi to success.

5. *Bhāgavata Purāṇa* 2.2.8–14.

6. *Bhāgavata Purāṇa* 3.28.

Translation

[The Goddess concludes by emphasizing the importance of both yoga and mantra.]

5.60. Through yoga accompanied by mantra practice, one
becomes fit to realize all that is to be known.
Mantra without yoga is ineffective; yoga without
mantra is also ineffective.

5.61. Integrating the two leads to realization of Brahman.
As a jar in a darkened house may be seen with a lamp,
5.62. So may the Self concealed by Māyā become evident through the mantra.[1]
Now I have explained the whole practice of yoga with its limbs.
5.63. This can be learned only from a teacher's instruction and not from millions of books.[2]

Comment

The Devī's declaration that yoga and mantra practice must be conjoined affirms on the one hand that mere repetition of sacred syllables, without the preparation, understanding, dedication, and guidance of a guru associated with spiritual discipline (yoga), is pointless (or even harmful, according to some texts). On the other, it points to the dependence of the practitioner upon the divine power embodied in the mantra.

In the context of this chapter, the Devī's statement seems also to suggest the complementary and interdependent nature of the Eight-limbed Yoga (referred to by the Goddess simply as yoga) and Kuṇḍalinī Yoga (referred to as Mantra Yoga, or mantra).[3] Whatever the particular yoga involved, the Goddess makes clear that the goals or final realization of all the practices described in the chapter are essentially the same. *Samādhi*, the culmination of the Eight-limbed Yoga, is the realization of the identity of the individual Self and the supreme Self (verse 25cd–26ab). The successful raising of the Serpent Power to the *sahasrāra* in Mantra or Kuṇḍalinī Yoga is the consummation of the union between Śakti and Śiva, that is, between the Serpent Power as the embodied energy of the individual soul and the supreme Godhead (verse 5.49). The final visualization and concentration practices terminate in the realization of the oneness of the soul and Brahman, and the dissolution of the practitioner into the supreme consciousness that is the Goddess (verses 5.56 and 5.59). All of these descriptions of the final goal are simply restatements or variations of the original definition of yoga offered by the Goddess (in verse 5.2): "the oneness of the individual soul and the supreme Self."[4]

Notes

1. In the *Yogakuṇḍalī Upaniṣad,* following its account of Kuṇḍalinī Yoga, a somewhat different set of metaphors is employed: "Just as fire hidden in wood does not blaze forth without rubbing, so does the light of knowledge not shine forth without the practice of yoga. Just as a light inside a jar does not shine outside until the jar is broken, when it blazes forth, so does the lamp (of knowledge) that is hidden in the jar of one's body shine forth as knowledge of Brahman when the body is burst by the words of the guru. . . . Think of the Self in the midst (of the body) like a lamp in a pot . . . deluded by Māyā" (3.14cd–17ab, 25cd, 27cd). Both the *Yogakuṇḍalī* and the *Devī Gītā* (see the following verse) stress the necessity of the guru's teaching.

2. This is a traditional Hindu proverb, stressing the oral as against the textual transmission of knowledge. The line is identical with *Sūta Saṃhitā* 5.9cd. Cf. *Amṛtabindu Upaniṣad* 18: "The learned wise person, having read many books, being intent on knowledge and wisdom, should abandon the whole corpus of books, as one throws out the chaff in seeking the grain."

Nīlakaṇṭha refrains from any specific comment on the last three and a half verses, but notes in conclusion to the chapter as a whole that the subject is explained at length in his great *Ṭīkā* on the *Devī Gītā*. Cf. note 33 on verse 5.46.

3. A similar kind of statement regarding Haṭha Yoga and Rāja Yoga is found in the *Śiva Saṃhitā* (5.226): "*Hatha-yoga* without *Rāja-yoga* and *Rāja-yoga* without *Hatha-yoga* are equally ineffective. Hence the yogi should first practice *Hatha-yoga* on the lines advised by a competent guru" (Ghosh's translation). While these two yogas are variously defined in different texts, there is a general consensus, when the two are contrasted, that Haṭha Yoga refers to the physical practices of bodily purification preparatory to the more mental disciplines (concentration and meditation) of Rāja Yoga.

4. For a detailed description of Kuṇḍalinī Yoga with attention to its relation to Patañjali's system within the Tantric tradition as a whole, see Sanjukta Gupta, Dirk Jan Hoens, and Teun Goudriaan, *Hindu Tantrism,* pp. 163–85.

Chapter 6

The Goal of the Yogas: Knowledge of Brahman

Translation

[The Goddess begins her summary of the goal of the yogic disciplines previously revealed.]

The Goddess spoke:

6.1. Cultivating the yogas just described, one should meditate on me as the true form of Brahman
With sincere devotion, assuming the proper posture, O King.

Comment

The Goddess is about to describe what is traditionally called Brahmavidyā, or knowledge of Brahman. Her introduction makes clear that this Brahmavidyā is knowledge of the Goddess herself, for she is "the true form of Brahman" (*brahma-svarūpinī*). Such knowledge is the goal both of Jñāna Yoga, explained in chapter four, and the Eight-limbed/ Kuṇḍalinī Yoga of chapter five. Thus, this sixth chapter serves as a kind of recapitulation of the preceding two, with their emphasis on meditative/intellectual practices as the path to the ultimate. Such practices, as this verse indicates, should be complemented by devotion. This emotional path, the way of Bhakti Yoga, will be the subject of the next chapter.

Translation

[The Goddess reveals the knowledge of Brahman as found in the *Muṇḍaka Upaniṣad.*]

6.2. It is manifest, well-fixed, pervading the hearts of beings, indeed; it is the great foundation.
Thereupon all that moves, breathes, and blinks is established.[1]

6.3. Know that[2] as existent and nonexistent,[3] as the most desirable, as supreme, as beyond the understanding of humankind.
What is luminous, what is smaller than the small, in which the worlds and their inhabitants are rooted,

6.4. That is this imperishable Brahman; it is the life principle, speech, and mind.
This is the real, the immortal; know, good sir, that this is what you are to pierce.[4]

6.5. Taking the great weapon of the Upaniṣads as the bow, nocked with the arrow honed by meditation,
Drawing it with a mind absorbed in contemplating that Brahman, know, good sir,[5] that imperishable reality is the target.

6.6. The syllable Oṃ[6] is the bow, while the Self is the arrow; Brahman is named as the target.
It will be pierced by one who concentrates. One will merge into it, like the arrow.

6.7. In it are woven the sky, earth, and atmosphere, as well as the mind along with all the breaths;
Know it alone as the one Self; let go of other notions,[7] as this is the bridge to immortality.[8]

6.8. Where the subtle channels of the body come together,[9] like the spokes in the nave of a wheel,
There this Self circulates within, manifesting in diverse modes.[10]

6.9. Meditate on Oṃ as the Self; may you fare well in crossing to the far shore beyond darkness.[11]
Within the space in the bright city of Brahman,[12] the Self is established.

6.10. Infused by the mind, directing the breaths and body, it abides in material form,[13] taking charge of the heart.
By their understanding the wise recognize this blissful immortal, which shines brightly.

6.11. The knot of the heart is untied,[14] all doubts are removed,
And the binding effects of one's deeds pass away when that Self is seen, both the higher and the lower.

6.12. In the highest golden sheath[15] resides the unstained, indivisible Brahman.
It is radiant, the light of lights; that is what Self-knowers know.

6.13. The sun shines not there, nor the moon and stars, nor do these lightenings shine, much less this fire.
All things shine only after it shines; by its light all this world becomes visible.[16]

6.14. Just this Brahman is immortal; in front is Brahman, behind is Brahman, on the right and the left;
It extends above and below. The whole universe is just this Brahman, the greatest.[17]

Comment

The *Devī Gītā* is quite indebted to the Upaniṣads in general, and to the *Muṇḍaka Upaniṣad* in particular. Already in chapter 3 of the *Devī Gītā*, following the revelation of the Devī's terrifying cosmic form, the gods praise her with verses (46–51) closely based on the *Muṇḍaka Upaniṣad* (2.1.5–9). Here in chapter 6, it is the Goddess who recites several verses (2–14) that are for the most part a verbatim recounting of *Muṇḍaka* 2.2.1–12. While the "borrowings" are often unacknowledged—typical of Purāṇic borrowings in general—the composer of the *Devī Gītā* could hardly have thought that no one would notice the near identity between the Goddess' revelation here in chapter 6 and the *Muṇḍaka Upaniṣad*. Indeed, such recognition was almost certainly anticipated and intended: the Goddess herself acknowledges (in 6.28cd–29ab, below) the prior transmission of this knowledge of Brahman. To argue that the *Devī Gītā* composer has plagiarized the *Muṇḍaka*, as one modern text critic has done,[18] is to impose quite irrelevant standards on the text, and to ignore or misunderstand its theological/philosophical assumptions and purposes.

Already the commentator Nīlakaṇṭha notes the textual borrowing and even supplies the half verse of the *Muṇḍaka* that the *Devī Gītā* omits.[19] Yet for Nīlakaṇṭha the Devī's recitation is not simply rote repetition. From his perspective, the Goddess is not so much reciting *from* the *Muṇḍaka*, but rather she is directly speaking *to* Himālaya and the gods. In the *Muṇḍaka*, the primary interlocutors are Aṅgiras and his disciple Śaunaka, while in the *Devī Gītā*, according to Nīlakaṇṭha's interpretation, the vocative "good sir" no longer refers to Śaunaka but to the Mountain King. Moreover, in this "Śākticized" context, the well-known scriptural verses are understood to be not just about Brahman per se, but rather about the Goddess herself. From the standpoint of the *Devī Gītā*, the Goddess' revelation herein to the gods thus provides new insight into and deeper understanding of the ancient Upaniṣadic text.

Notes

1. Verses 6.2–14 are nearly identical with *Muṇḍaka Upaniṣad* 2.2.1–12. Nīlakaṇṭha recognizes the correspondence, and indicates that he will utilize Śaṃkara's commentary on the *Muṇḍaka* in explaining the verses. Nīlakaṇṭha's strong Advaitic orientation, incidentally, is thus affirmed.

2. Nīlakaṇṭha here expands on the Upaniṣadic text to emphasize its significance within the *Devī Gītā*'s context: "The Goddess speaks these words, 'Know that,' [her meaning being:] 'O gods, know or understand that this Brahman is my own true nature (*mad-rūpam*)."

3. *sad asad*; these two terms are used in various senses in the scriptures and later philosophical schools. At one extreme, they represent the absolutely real and absolutely unreal. But they may also represent gross and subtle forms of existence, or formed and formless states. At times, the ultimate is represented as beyond both the existent and nonexistent; at other times, as including both, as I think is the case here.

Nīlakaṇṭha gives a different interpretation, according to which the existent refers to Māyā as cause, the nonexistent to the world as effect. Then, he joins these terms to the following word, *vareṇyam*, which I have rendered as "desireable," but which can also mean "best" or "beyond." Thus for Nīlakaṇṭha,

Brahman is the best, beyond both Māyā and the world. The general standpoint of the *Devī Gītā* seems closer to what I take to be the meaning of the Upaniṣadic original: like Brahman in the *Muṇḍaka*, the Goddess is both material cause (Māyā in the *Devī Gītā*'s terms) and the material effect (the world) in a more holistic or organic sense than Nīlakaṇṭha allows.

4. Pierce with the arrow of the mind in intense meditation, as Nīlakaṇṭha explains, anticipating the famous metaphor that follows.

5. This "good sir," Nīlakaṇṭha indicates, refers to the King of Mountains (Himālaya), thus transferring the Upaniṣadic context to that of the *Devī Gītā*.

6. *praṇava;* Nīlakaṇṭha glosses as the "the syllable Oṃ, or the Devī's *praṇava*," referring to the syllable "Hrīṃ." The former syllable is intended in the *Muṇḍaka Upaniṣad*, while the latter syllable would certainly be in line with the general views of the *Devī Gītā* (see, e.g., 1.53, and especially 4.41). However, the *Devī Gītā* here seems to mean Oṃ, as the text explicitly refers to "Oṃ" in 6.9a, in accord with the *Muṇḍaka*.

7. *vācas;* literally, "words, utterances." Nīlakaṇṭha, following Śaṃkara's commentary on the *Muṇḍaka*, glosses this as "words relating to lower knowledge (*apara-vidyā-rūpā*)."

8. *amṛta;* glossed by Nīlakaṇṭha as *mokṣa*.

9. That is, in the heart (Nīlakaṇṭha and Śaṃkara).

10. According to Nīlakaṇṭha, following Śaṃkara, the Self comes to dwell in the heart as the witness of various states of consciousness, these various states, joy, anger, etc., being as it were the diverse modes of manifestation of the Self, according to worldly opinion.

11. Nīlakaṇṭha emphasizes that this blessing is spoken by the Goddess, as she is a storehouse of compassion. He and Saṃkara gloss darkness (*tamas*) as ignorance (*avidyā*).

The *Devī Gītā* is missing one line of the *Muṇḍaka* (the first half of 2.2.7) at this point, a line supplied by Nīlakaṇṭha.

12. *brahma-pure;* glossed by Nīlakaṇṭha as "in the lotus of the heart." It is the space within the heart where Brahman resides.

13. *anna;* literally, "food"; by extension, what is composed of food, that is, material or bodily form.

14. That is, all the desires within the heart are destroyed; see *Kaṭha Upaniṣad* 2.3.14–15.

15. *hiraṇmaye pare kośe;* glossed by Nīlakaṇṭha as the sheath of bliss (*ānandamaye kośe*). The bliss sheath is the innermost of the five sheaths that cover the Ātman. See *Devī Gītā* 1.52, note 20.

16. This verse is a favorite among the Upaniṣadic seers. It appears verbatim in *Śvetāśvatara Upaniṣad* 6.14, *Muṇḍaka Upaniṣad* 2.2.11, and *Kaṭha Upaniṣad* 2.2.15. Cf. *Bhagavad Gītā* 15.6 and 12. According to Nīlakaṇṭha and Śaṃkara (commenting on the Upaniṣads), this verse explains how Brahman is "the light of lights." Secondary lights, such as the sun, can illumine other things with the light of Brahman, but cannot illumine Brahman itself, which is their own self-luminous Self.

17. Cf. *Devī Gītā* 1.28, where the supreme lustrous power of the Goddess is described in similar terms.

This verse concludes the second section of part two of the *Muṇḍaka Upaniṣad,* as well as the Goddess' citation from that scripture. It is also the eighth verse of the Navaślokī Devī Gītā.

18. R. C. Hazra, *Studies in the Upapurāṇas,* vol. 2, pp. 359–60.

19. See note 11 above.

Translation

[The Goddess sings the praise of the person who attains the knowledge of Brahman.]

6.15. Whoever realizes Brahman as such is the highest of humans, wholly fulfilled.[1]
Merged in Brahman and serene, that one neither grieves nor desires.[2]

6.16. Fear surely arises from another,[3] O King; in the absence of another, one does not fear.[4]
I am not separate from anyone, nor is anyone separate from me.

6.17. I, indeed, am that person, and that person truly is I; regard this as certain, O Mountain.
One sees me wherever one finds a person who knows me.[5]

6.18. I do not abide in any sacred site, not even in Kailāsa, nor in Vaikuṇṭha;[6]
Yet I dwell in the midst of the lotus-heart of one who knows me.[7]

6.19. Worshiping just once a person who knows me gives the same fruit as worshiping me millions of times.[8]
One's family is purified, one's mother is completely fulfilled,[9]
6.20. And the whole earth is blessed when one's heart dissolves into pure consciousness.[10]
The knowledge of Brahman that you inquired about, Best of Mountains,
6.21. I have described fully; there is nothing more to say.

Comment

The *Devī Gītā* praises the person who attains the knowledge of Brahman as fully realized, describing such a knower in the same terms Kṛṣṇa uses for the perfected being in the *Bhagavad Gītā*.[11] In both *gītā*s, this perfection leads to, or is the actual realization of, union with the deity. The *Devī Gītā* elaborates on this idea of unity drawing on the *Bṛhadāraṇyaka Upaniṣad*'s notion of fear arising only where there is another.[12] But in the *Bṛhadāraṇyaka*, the unity involved is prior to creation: when the primal being (Ātman, Puruṣa) recognized that there was no need to fear since there was no other, he was still unhappy being alone, and so desired a second. In the *Devī Gītā*, the insight that there is no other is the liberating awareness of the ultimate oneness of Brahman, that is, of the unity of the Goddess and her realized sage. Such insight results in the destruction not only of fear but also of desire.

The ultimate identity of the realized sage and the Goddess partially accounts for the extravagant praise of the former, who in some ways achieves a status greater even than that of the Goddess. This supreme stature of the devotee/sage, affirmed by the Goddess herself (verse 19ab), reveals her own love for those who truly know her, as well as her own self-effacing humility. Such deference on the part of the supreme deity toward devotees is a motif not uncommon in the medieval *bhakti*c movements.

Notes

1. *kṛtārtha*: "one whose purposes are realized or fulfilled." Cf. 7.45 and 10.33 below. The phrase is a synonym for *kṛta-kṛtya*, for which see note 1 on 1.3.

In *Śvetāśvatara Upaniṣad* 2.14, the person who has perceived the true nature of the Self is said to be *kṛthārtha*, and to be free of sorrow. The *Muṇḍaka Upaniṣad* (1.2.9–10) asserts that the ignorant who are attached to the performance of rituals falsely believe that they are *kṛtārtha*, but in fact, though they may achieve heaven, they will still reenter this world, being subject to the vagaries of rebirth.

2. The second half of this verse is identical with *Bhagavad Gītā* 18.54ab. In the *Bhagavad Gītā*, such a realized or perfected person is said to attain supreme devotion to Kṛṣṇa and to enter at once into him.

3. Cf. *Bṛhadāraṇyaka Upaniṣad* 1.4.2.

4. According to Nīlakaṇṭha, the knower of Brahman does not fear, since for him there is no other (all is Brahman). Cf. *Taittirīya Upaniṣad* 2.9.1: "One who knows the bliss of Brahman fears nothing at all."

5. Cf. *Bhagavad Gītā* 7.17cd–18ab, where Kṛṣṇa states: "I am extremely dear to the realized sage (*jñāni*), and he is dear to me. . . . The realized sage is my very Self."

6. The heavens of Śiva and Viṣṇu, respectively.

7. Cf. *Devī Gītā* 8.30, where the Goddess, after listing the several sacred sites of various of her forms, declares that the Supreme Ruler, Hṛllekhā, dwells in the lotus-hearts of realized sages. Cf. also *Brahmavaivarta Purāṇa* 2.6.55, where Kṛṣṇa declares "My real abode is not in Vaikuṇṭha or Goloka at the side of Rādhā. Where my *bhakta*s reside, there I dwell day and night" (quoted in my *God as Mother*, pp. 105–06).

8. Cf. *Muṇḍaka Upaniṣad* 3.1.10: "He who desires happiness should worship the realized knower of the Self." Cf. also *Devī Māhātmya* 11.32d: "Those who bow in devotion to you [the Goddess] are the refuge of the whole world."

9. *kṛta-kṛtyakā*; literally, "having done what is to be done." See note 1 on *Devī Gītā* 1.3.

10. *cil-layas*; glossed by Nīlakaṇṭha as dissolution in the supreme Ātman. It is a common Indian notion that the relatives of a holy person are thereby blessed, and even that merely being in the presence of a holy person has beatifying effects. Cf. *Brahmavaivarta Purāṇa* 2.10.86–87, where Kṛṣṇa affirms: "Those who are relatives of my devotees . . . go to my heaven Goloka. . . . Wherever they die, whether with *jñāna* or without, they are *jīvan-mukta*s, purified by the mere presence of my devotees" (quoted from my *God as Mother*, with slight modifications, p. 99).

11. See note 2 above.

12. See note 3 above.

Translation

[The Goddess indicates the proper recipients of this teaching.]

6.21. [cont.] This teaching, to an eldest son[1] filled with devotion and of good character,

6.22. And to a disciple of proper disposition,[2] is to be revealed, but not to anyone else at all.[3]

For one who is supremely devoted to God, and to the guru as to God,[4]

6.23. For such a noble soul these matters just described become clear.[5]

Comment

Regarding the qualities belonging to "a disciple of proper disposition," the *Śāradā-Tilaka Tantra* gives a long list. These include coming from a good family, having a pure heart, being intent on the four ends of life, being versed in the Veda, and wishing well of all creatures. Further, the disciple must be devoted to duty and to parents, and be willing to obey the guru in speech, mind, and body (cf. 6.27 below), even to the point of giving up life to honor the word of the guru. Such a student takes no pride in birth, learning, or wealth, and keeps hidden the mantra, rules of worship (*pūjā*), and secret teachings revealed by the guru.[6]

The motif of secrecy and the need for discretion pervades the guru-disciple relationship. In this regard, the famous compiler of religious law, Manu, tells an interesting metaphorical story about sacred knowledge: "Knowledge approached a Brahman and said to him, 'I am your treasure, protect me. Do not give me to a scorner, so that I may become most powerful. Tell me only to one who is pure, restrained, chaste, a Brahman, not negligent, who will protect the treasure [of knowledge].' "[7]

Manu here gives voice to an ancient and long-standing Indian tradition that the efficacy of mantra and certain other religious teachings/practices depends on their being kept secret. In part, this emphasizes the need for a certain spiritual bond and trust between the teacher and student, a bond that develops only gradually through a period of more or less extended service on the part of the student. Further, the secrecy presupposes the necessity of oral instruction, direct from teacher to disciple: what is learned merely from books is useless. The guru imparts a certain power to the teachings or mantra, on the one hand; and the disciple, on the other, if properly prepared and of right character, will be a fit receptacle for receiving and developing the spiritual power of the secret teaching.[8]

In the *bhaktic* movements, the traditional qualifications of the disciple such as self-control, good lineage, Brahmanical status, and the like are supplemented by, or even subordinated to, true devotion to the deity, as is the case in the *Devī Gītā*.[9] Devotion to the guru itself is an ancient theme. In affirming devotion to one's guru as to God, the Goddess is merely quoting from the *Śvetāśvatara Upaniṣad*.[10]

Notes

1. According to the first verse of the *Muṇḍaka Upaniṣad*, Brahmā first taught the knowledge of Brahman to his eldest son Atharvaṇa. See the Comment on 6.28cd–30 below.

2. *yathoktāya*; glossed by Nīlakaṇṭha as "to [a disciple] having the qualities described in the Śāstras." For such qualities as given in the famous Śāstra, *The Laws of Manu*, see the Comment above. In the *Muṇḍaka Upaniṣad* (1.2.13), the ideal disciple is said to be "of calm mind and controlled."

3. Cf. *Śvetāśvatara Upaniṣad* 6.22, which asserts that its secret teachings are not to be given to one who is not restrained, who is not a son or a disciple. Cf. also *Bṛhadāraṇyaka Upaniṣad* 6.3.12, *Maitrī Upaniṣad* 6.29, and *Devī Gītā* 8.50 and 10.36.

4. Cf. *Bhagavad Gītā* 18.67, where Kṛṣṇa warns Arjuna not to reveal his teaching to one not devoted. Śaṃkara comments: " 'Not devoted' means lacking devotion to guru and to God."

5. This verse (6.22cd–23ab) is identical with *Śvetāśvatara Upaniṣad* 6.23, except for not repeating the final refrain. Cf. note 1 on *Devī Gītā* 4.17.

6. *Śāradā-Tilaka Tantra* 2.145–52.

7. *The Laws of Manu*, 2.114–15.

8. The ideal of secrecy also is related to the establishment of a spiritual community. As Brooks notes, regarding Tantric secrecy: "it is a complex religious category that binds tradition . . . and lineage . . . together into a socioreligious community. Secret transmission of tradition is the way in which Tantrics cre-

ate a communal or 'family' . . . relationship which sets them apart from other Hindus. . . . Tantric secrecy, then, is a pact between generations and a method by which 'powerful' religious teachings are controlled and dispersed" (*Secret of the Three Cities*, p. 65).

9. See the Comment on *Devī Gītā* 10.34–37.

10. See note 5 above.

Translation

[The Goddess sings the praise of the guru who teaches this knowledge of Brahman.]

6.23. [cont.] One who teaches this knowledge is indeed the supreme Lord,[1]
6.24. Whose generosity the disciple can never repay.[2]
Greater even than the father, it is said, is the bestower of birth through spiritual knowledge,
6.25. For the birth engendered by the father perishes, but never what is engendered by the teacher.[3]
"Do no injury to the teacher," so says a sacred precept,[4] O Mountain.
6.26. Thus, the religious law concludes that the guru bestowing spiritual knowledge is supreme.[5]
When Śiva is provoked, the guru can save; when the guru is provoked, Śiva cannot save.[6]
6.27. Therefore, O Mountain, one should please the holy guru with all one's effort.
Dedicating all one does with body, mind, and speech to the guru,[7] one should remain thus focused.
6.28. Otherwise, one becomes ungrateful, and there is no expiation for ingratitude.

Comment

The importance of the guru from Upaniṣadic times on is almost universally stressed in Indian traditions.[8] The guru is responsible for the rebirth of the disciple into a higher, spiritual life, whether this involves the commencement of Vedic studies (in the traditional *upanayana* ceremony) or the undertaking of highly advanced and esoteric ritual practices, as in certain Tantric schools. Only with proper initiation, with the bestowing of the appropriate mantra or mantras, will the various endeavors of the disciple succeed. For such reasons, the teacher responsible for spiritual birth through knowledge (*brahma-janma*) is often elevated above the natural father who engenders only physical birth. The Goddess here in her praise of the guru seems to draw specifically upon *The Laws of Manu*.[9]

The qualifications of the guru are not explicitly mentioned here in the *Devī Gītā*, but were briefly referred to in 4.17: the teacher should be learned in the scriptures and absorbed or established in Brahman (*brahma-niṣṭha*).[10] This latter implies a considerable degree of spiritual insight, if not complete self-realization or liberation, on the part of the guru. In Advaita and in Tantra, the preferred guru is often said to be a *jīvan-mukta*.[11] However, in certain of the *bhakti* traditions such as Vaiṣṇavism, where direct, unmediated access to god is emphasized, the guru is not seen as a perfected human being (a *jīvan-mukta*), but as God incarnate. Some Tantras, in a grand synthesis of Advaitic and *bhakti*c ideals, regard the guru, mantra, deity (*devatā*) and devotee as ultimately one.[12] Such a view underlies the *Devī Gītā*'s ideal of the guru.[13]

Notes

1. In the *Devī Gītā*, as in many medieval *bhakti*c movements, the spiritual teacher is lavishly eulogized, being regarded as a representative or actual incarnation of the Lord (see Comment above). Such an attitude has its roots in the Upaniṣads (see *Śvetāśvatara Upaniṣad* 6.23, quoted in *Devī Gītā* 6.22cd–23ab above), and is elaborated in *The Laws of Manu*, where the teacher is said to be "the form of Brahman (*ācāryo brahmaṇo mūrtiḥ*)" (2.226), and to be "lord or master of the world of Brahmā (*brahmalokeśa*)" (4.182).

2. Manu, in a passage immediately following high praise for one's teacher, father, and mother, asserts that one's parents can never be compensated for all their troubles even in a hundred years (*The Laws of Manu*, 2.227). By implication, the teacher also cannot be adequately repaid.

3. Cf. *The Laws of Manu*, 2.146: "Between the giver of natural birth and the giver of spiritual knowledge (*brahma-dātṛ*), the giver of spiritual knowledge is the more venerable father; for a Brahman's birth through knowledge (*brahma-janma*) is everlasting, both here and after departing this world." For brief discussion of this verse in Tantrism, see S. C. Banerji, *A Brief History of Tantra Literature*, pp. 33, 249.

4. This apparently refers to *The Laws of Manu,* 2.144. Cf. 4.162.

5. This apparently refers to *The Laws of Manu,* 2.146, already closely paraphrased in lines 24cd–25ab above.

6. This is an oft-quoted proverb, appearing in the *Rudrayāmala Tantra* (Narendra Nath Bhattacharyya, *History of the Tantric Religion,* p. 77; Banerji, *A Brief History of Tantra Literature,* pp. 34, 398, 528; Pandurang Vaman Kane, *History of Dharmaśāstra,* vol. 5, p. 1101). Similarly, we find it said of Viṣṇu: "If Hari [Viṣṇu] is angry, the *guru* is our defence; but from the *guru*'s wrath there is no protection" (quoted from an unnamed text by Klostermaier, *A Survey of Hinduism,* p. 224).

7. The *Śāradā-Tilaka Tantra* says the disciple should delight in serving the guru with speech, mind, body, and wealth (2.147; cf. 2.150). Again, the *Śāradā-Tilaka* declares: "One should offer the guru everything: one's body, wealth, and life" (5.113). Cf. *The Laws of Manu,* 2.236.

8. See Kane, *History of Dharmaśāstra,* vol. 5, p. 1033, who quotes the *Śvetāśvatara Upaniṣad* 6.23 (quoted by the *Devī Gītā* in 6.22cd–23ab) as well as *Devī-Bhāgavata* 11.1.49 (quoted in note 2 to verse 10.1 below), to illustrate the continuity of stress on the importance of the guru. See also vol. 5, pp. 1071–72.

9. See especially notes 3–5 above.

10. Cf. *Muṇḍaka Upaniṣad* 1.2.12.

11. Cf. Bhattacharyya, *History of the Tantric Religion,* pp. 71–72.

12. Cf. *Śāradā-Tilaka Tantra* 5.112.

13. Cf. *Devī Gītā* 10.1, and note 2 thereon.

Translation

[To illustrate the difficulties and dangers of attaining knowledge of Brahman, the Goddess refers to the story of the beheading of the sage Atharvaṇa.]

6.28 [cont.] Indra revealed this knowledge to Atharvaṇa,
threatening to decapitate him.[1]

6.29. When Atharvaṇa revealed it to the two Aśvins, Indra
cut off his head.[2]
Seeing his horse head destroyed, the two Aśvins,
excellent, divine physicians,

6.30. Restored the sage's original head once again.
Thus is the knowledge of Brahman difficult to attain, Mountain Chief.
6.31 One who attains it is blessed and completely fulfilled,[3] O Mountain.

Comment

The story of the beheading of Atharvaṇa is based on an ancient myth in the *Śatapatha Brāhmaṇa*.[4] There, it is told how Viṣṇu, identified with the sacrifice, lost his head, and the gods, forced to work with the mutilated sacrifice, were totally frustrated. The sage Dadhyañc knew how to replace the head of the sacrifice, but was threatened by Indra with decapitation if he disclosed the restorative knowledge. The two Aśvins, previously excluded from the sacrifice and eager for its fruit, sought out Dadhyañc. On learning of Indra's threat against Dadhyañc, the Aśvins, famous for their physician's skill, offered to replace the sage's head with a horse head, holding the original in safekeeping. The horse head would then proclaim the esoteric knowledge, and when Indra would make good on his threat, the Aśvins would restore the original head of the sage. Dahyañc accepted the plan, which was duly executed.[5]

Dadhyañc's secret knowledge came to be known as Brahmavidyā, the knowledge of Brahman. Brahmavidyā is also the name given by the *Muṇḍaka Upaniṣad* to its own teachings. According to the opening verse of the *Muṇḍaka*, Brahmā taught this Brahmavidyā to his eldest son Atharvā (or Atharvaṇa), who in turn passed it on to a succession of qualified disciples. The Goddess in the *Devī Gītā*, having recited (in the first half of chapter 6) almost all the verses that appear in *Muṇḍaka* 2.2, dealing with Brahmavidyā, has implicitly identified Brahmā's eldest son with Dadhyañc of the *Śatapatha Brāhmaṇa*. Not surprisingly, Nīlakaṇṭha, in commenting on *Devī Gītā* 6.28, immediately refers to Atharvaṇa as Dadhyañc.

There are still further mythic resonances to this name Brahmavidyā. In the *Kena Upaniṣad* story of the humbling of Agni, Vāyu, and Indra,[6] Umā Haimavatī identifies the mysterious *yakṣa* as the supreme Brahman, and thus she is the revealer of Brahmavidyā. Eventually, Umā Haimavatī herself came to be known as Brahmavidyā. In the *Devī-Bhāgavata*, the Goddess is both the revealer of Brahmavidyā and the revealed, that is, Brahman itself.[7]

The Goddess explicitly acknowledges in verses 6.28cd–30 that the Brahmavidyā she has revealed to Himālaya and the gods is not something new. It is ancient, or rather, eternal, as she herself is eternal. Her self-revealing knowledge has been proclaimed on a number of occasions, both by herself—as Umā Haimavatī in the *Kena Upaniṣad* and as Bhuvaneśvarī in the *Devī Gītā*—and by sages such as Dadhyañc in the *Śatapatha Brāhmaṇa* and Atharvaṇa and his disciples in the *Muṇḍaka Upaniṣad*. Thus, the Goddess is hardly guilty of plagiarism. From the Śākta perspective, what the Goddess' recitation of the *Muṇḍaka* verses illustrates in dramatic fashion is the eternality of the truth of Śruti or Vedic scripture, in this case, even with regards to the very words in which that truth is expressed.

Notes

1. That is, Indra threatened to behead Atharvaṇa should he reveal the knowledge of Brahman to others.

2. This decapitated head was actually a horse head. Atharvaṇa's original head had previously been replaced with a substitute horse's head to meet just this exigency.

3. *kṛta-kṛtya*; see note 1 on *Devī Gītā* 1.3.

4. *Śatapatha Brāhmaṇa* 14.1.1.1ff.

5. See my *The Triumph of the Goddess*, pp. 41–44.

6. See Comment on *Devī Gītā* 1.26–29.

7. See *Triumph of the Goddess*, pp. 44–45.

Chapter 7

Instruction in the Yoga of Devotion

Translation

[Himālaya inquires about the path of devotion, and the Goddess indicates the ease of this yoga.]

Himālaya spoke:

7.1. Describe the path of devotion that focuses on you, O Mother. By such devotion, supreme knowledge easily
Develops in the ordinary person filled with passions.

The Goddess spoke:

7.2. There are three well-known paths of mine leading to liberation, Mountain King:
The yoga of action, the yoga of knowledge, and the yoga of devotion, my good sir.[1]

7.3. Of these three the latter is the easiest to practice in all respects,
Appealing naturally to the heart without distressing the body or mind.

Comment

The discussion of devotion in this chapter follows in many ways the account of Bhakti Yoga given in the *Kapila Gītā* of the *Bhāgavata Purāṇa*.[2] Both texts deal with the relation of devotion to knowledge and dispassion (*vairāgya*), but the *Devī Gītā* places greater emphasis on knowledge, and less on dispassion. These differences are already reflected in the initial queries of Himālaya and of his counterpart in the *Kapila Gītā*, Devahūti, mother of the Lord Kapila. Himālaya's opening question in 7.1 above echoes Devahūti's in the *Kapila Gītā*: "Tell me in full, Lord, the path of devotion, by which a person becomes entirely passionless."[3] While the *Bhāgavata* sees dispassion as the fruit of devotion and as an essential attribute of the true devotee, the *Devī Gītā* stresses that devotion leads even the person of passion to supreme knowledge, and that without knowledge, dispassion in itself is useless. The difference is one of nuance, but reflects the underlying attitudes of the two texts toward the life of the householder. The *Devī Gītā*, and the *Devī-Bhāgavata* as a whole, understand the householding stage, even with all its distractions and passions, as compatible with the highest spiritual attainment. The *Bhāgavata* generally regards householding as a severe spiritual obstacle.

Although there are many yogas as seen in chapter 5—Eight-limbed, Mantra, Kuṇḍalinī, Laya, Haṭha, Rāja, and the like—the Goddess indicates that three have come to be regarded as basic and as embracing all others: the yogas of action (*karma*), knowledge (*jñāna*), and devotion (*bhakti*). Similarly, Kṛṣṇa declares in the *Bhāgavata Purāṇa*: "Intending the highest good for humans, I have taught three yogas, knowledge, action, and devotion; there are no other means anywhere."[4] The relation between these three and the manner in which they subsume the other secondary yoga practices vary considerably from text to text, as already suggested in the preceding paragraph. This variation is facilitated by the fact that the different yogas for the most part do not have precise definitions and admit of considerable overlap. The techniques of the Eight-limbed Yoga, for example, are readily adapted to the practice of both the knowledge and devotion yogas. And the path of ritual action (Kriyā Yoga, sometimes identified with Karma Yoga; see note 1 below), is easily assimilated into Bhakti Yoga, as verses 7.22–26 below demonstrate.

Notes

1. Cf. *Umā-Saṃhitā* (*Śiva Purāṇa*) 51.7–11, where Kriyā Yoga, the performance of ritual acts, is included, along with the yogas of knowledge and devotion, as one of the three paths of the holy Mother, yielding both *bhukti*

and *mukti.* This text asserts that from ritual acts, devotion is born; from devotion, knowledge; and from knowledge, liberation.

2. *Bhāgavata Purāṇa* 3.29. In both the *Kapila Gītā* and the *Devī Gītā,* the discussion of Bhakti Yoga follows an account of the Eight-limbed Yoga. But in the *Bhāgavata,* the description of Bhakti Yoga immediately follows that of the Eight-limbed Yoga found in the preceding chapter (3.28). The *Devī Gīta* deals with the Eight-limbed Yoga in chapter 5, Bhakti Yoga in chapter 7, and inserts the discussion of the knowledge of Brahman in chapter 6.

3. *Bhāgavata Purāṇa* 3.29.2cd–3ab. My interpretation of these lines differs from that given by the commentator Śrīdhara and followed by most translators of the *Bhāgavata.* He takes the "by which" (*yena*) as referring ahead, to the account of the different destinies of the soul in samsara mentioned in 3cd. I have taken the "by which" as referring back to the Bhakti Yoga mentioned in 2cd, a rendering that is quite reasonable and fully parallel with the *Devī Gītā*'s version. But even if one takes Śrīdhara's interpretation, the fundamental emphasis on dispassion in the *Bhāgavata* remains.

4. *Bhāgavata Purāṇa* 11.20.6.

Translation

[The Goddess describes the first three grades of devotion according to the three *guṇas*, or qualities of nature.]

7.4. Devotion as practiced by human beings is of three kinds, in accord with the qualities of nature.
A person who intends harm to others while engaging in deceit,

7.5. And who is spiteful and irascible, practices devotion characterized by ignorance.[1]
One who intends no harm to others, being concerned simply with personal well-being,

7.6. Who is ever lustful, seeking fame and seizing pleasures,
Who worships me intently for the sake of obtaining this or that fruit,

7.7. Who foolishly assumes false distinctions,[2] thinking that I am other than one's own being,
Such a person practices devotion characterized by passionate yearning,[3] O Mountain Chief.

7.8. One who offers all karmic fruits to me, the Supreme Ruler, in order to be cleansed of evil,
Who thinks "I must carry out those acts enjoined by the Veda, without faltering,"
7.9. Who is thus convinced but who still clings to false distinctions,
Who performs all work out of a sense of love, such a person practices devotion characterized by virtue,[4] O Mountain.
7.10. This latter, though still clinging to false distinctions, leads to the highest devotion.
But the two former kinds of devotion do not lead to the highest, so it is understood.

Comment

The classification of devotional acts and motivations according to the three *guṇas* of nature is already found in the *Bhagavad Gītā*.[5] There Kṛṣṇa applies the standards of the *guṇas* to a variety of spiritual endeavors: worship (*yajña*), austerity (*tapas*), charity (*dāna*), renunciation (*tyāga*), knowledge (*jñāna*), and action in general (*karma*). Ignorant (*tāmasa*) actions are characterized by lack of faith, disregard for observing proper injunctions, delusion, incorrect understanding of the real nature of things, thoughtless unconcern for injury to oneself or others, stinginess, arrogance, dishonesty, and laziness. Actions of passionate yearning (*rājasa*) are marked by desire for the fruits, seeking honor and prestige, hypocrisy, emotional ups and downs, and seeing distinctions between all beings. Virtuous (*sāttvika*) actions conform to the proper injunctions, are motivated by faith and a sense of simply doing one's duty without regard for the fruits and with a serene mind that sees the unity of all beings.[6] The *Devī Gītā*'s classifications are clearly rooted in this ancient tradition of the *Bhagavad Gītā*. But the *Devī Gītā* elaborates a fourth type, supreme devotion, that transcends the three *guṇas*, to be discussed in the next section.[7]

Notes

1. *tāmasī*.

2. *bheda-buddhi*: "perceiving differences," or "believing in differences." The *Kapila Gītā* of the *Bhāgavata Purāṇa* uses the synonymous terms *bhinna-dṛś*

("perceiving as separate") and *pṛthag-bhāva* ("judging as distinct") (3.29.8 and 10). All are forms of *avidyā*, in which one sees oneself as distinct from others, and most critically, as separate from the supreme. Cf. *Devī-Bhāgavata* 1.18.41–43, where the wise King Janaka dismisses the notions of "friend" and "enemy" as ultimately delusions, arising from the sense of duality (*dvaita*) and the failure to realize the oneness of *jīva* and *brahman*. He concludes by saying that such belief in differences (*bheda-buddhi*) is *avidyā*.

3. *rājasī*.

4. *sāttvikī*.

5. *Bhagavad Gītā* 17.4, 11–22; 18.7–9, 20–40.

6. A similar, threefold classification of acts and motives according to the *guṇas* is found in *Bhāgavata Purāṇa* 11.25, with a fourth category beyond the *guṇas* briefly suggested.

7. The *Devī Gītā* follows the *Kapila Gītā* in its fourfold classification, as indicated below in the Comment on 7.11–27. The *Bhagavad Gītā* does present four types of worshipers, but without reference to the *guṇas* (7.16).

Translation

[The Goddess explains at length the supreme devotion, beyond the *guṇas*.]

7.11. Now be attentive while I explain the highest kind of devotion.[1]
One who constantly listens to my virtues[2] and recites my names,
7.12. Who is firmly intent on me, a treasury of auspicious qualities,
Whose concentration is ever steady like a continuous flow of oil,[3]
7.13. Who has no ulterior motive at all in these actions,[4]
Having no desire for liberation in any form—whether living in my presence, sharing my powers, merging into me, or dwelling in my heaven—[5]
7.14. Who knows absolutely nothing better than serving me,
Cherishing the notion of servant and master[6] and thus not aspiring even for liberation,

7.15. Who enthusiastically thinks of me alone with supreme affection,
Knowing me truly as never separate from oneself, not acknowledging any difference,[7]
7.16. Who thinks of beings as embodiments of myself,
Loving other selves as one's own Self;
7.17. Who makes no false distinctions, realizing the universality of pure consciousness,
My omnipresent essence manifested in all beings everywhere at all times,
7.18. Who honors and respects even the lowest outcaste,[8] O Lord,
Discarding any sense of difference and thus wishing harm to no one,
7.19. Who is eager to see my sacred sites[9] and to see my devotees,
And is eager to listen to scriptures that describe the mantras and rites used in worshiping me,[10] O Ruler,
7.20. Whose heart is overwhelmed with love for me, whose body ever thrills with joy,
Whose eyes are filled with tears of love, and whose voice falters,[11]
7.21. Who, with such enraptured feelings, O Mountain Chief, worships
Me as ruler, womb of the world, and cause of all causes,
7.22. Who performs my splendrous rites, both the regular and the occasional,[12]
Always with devotion and without miserly regard for cost,[13]
7.23. Who longs to see my festivals and to participate in them,[14]
Ever impelled by such desires arising spontaneously, O Mountain,
7.24. Who sings on high my names while dancing,
Unselfconscious and forgetful of the body,[15]

7.25. Who accepts the fruits of past karma as what must be,
Unconcerned with thoughts of preserving the body,
7.26. Such a person practices devotion deemed supreme,
In which there is no thought of anything except me, the Goddess.
7.27. The person in whom such supreme devotion truly arises, O Mountain,
Then dissolves into my essential nature of pure consciousness.

Comment

The ideal of devotion described in the above verses owes much to the *Bhāgavata Purāṇa*. Especially significant in this regard is the *Bhāgavata*'s combination of a detached devotion associated with knowledge, derived from the *Bhagavad Gītā*, and an emotional devotion of ecstatic abandon.[16] In the *Bhāgavata*, perhaps the most remarkable model of such detached or selfless devotion combined with emotional intensity is that of the cow maidens (*gopīs*) in their amorous sport with Kṛṣṇa. Such a model of amorous ecstasy, however, has no place in the *Devī Gītā*, where the supreme is the Mother. Aside from the obvious mother/child model, then, the *Devī Gītā* also offers that of the master/servant as its devotional ideal.

The *Devī Gītā*'s fourfold classification of Bhakti Yoga, culminating in supreme devotion transcending the *guṇas*, is directly based on the *Bhāgavata*'s *Kapila Gītā*.[17] Regarding the highest form of *bhakti*, both texts emphasize unceasing concentration on the supreme being, service without any selfish interest or motive, and a realization of the unity of all creatures in the ultimate reality. While disinterested service and recognition of the oneness of beings readily harmonize in the practical and social sphere, a certain tension between them arises on a metaphysical level. Service presupposes a dualism of master and servant, a dualism that seems contrary to the essential nondifference to be realized between the devotee and the supreme.

This tension is highlighted in both the *Devī Gītā* and the *Kapila Gītā* by their applying the ideal of disinterested service to the various traditional forms of liberation. Several of the forms— such as dwelling in the same world or having the same powers as the supreme—presuppose, or at least do not eradicate, a duality between God and the devotee.

They are therefore compatible with the idea of service, but are rejected by the highest devotees since their sole concern is to please the Lord or Goddess, regardless of whatever benefits may accrue to them. The remaining form of liberation, however, that of oneness with (*ekatva*) or mergence into (*sāyujya*) the supreme, would seem to abolish any distinction between the supreme and the devotee. Logically enough, then, such mergence would be spurned by those who wish to serve. Yet it is precisely such mergence that the *Devī Gītā*, at least, often affirms as the ultimate consequence and final goal. Thus, in *Devī Gītā* 8.43cd–44ab, the Goddess declares that the devotee who performs worshipful service simply with the desire to please her obtains mergence into her (*sāyujya*). A similar conclusion is drawn in the concluding verse above (7.27), where the supreme devotee is said to dissolve into the pure consciousness of the Devī. Given the frequency of such statements, final dissolution into the Goddess does not seem merely adventitious, a kind of unintended benefit for an unwilling devotee. It is rather a self-conscious goal that, in the end, transcends the master-servant relationship.

The *Kapila Gītā* is somewhat less clear in its account of the final goal of supreme *bhakti*, but Lord Kapila suggests there is some sort of union: he says simply that by such supreme devotion one attains to or is fit for "my state" (*mad-bhāva*).[18] The exact relation between this state and the state of oneness (*ekatva*) is left unexplained, though Śrīdhara glosses the phrase *mad-bhāva* as *brahmatva* ("state of Brahman").[19]

The idea that devotion culminates in some sort of mergence goes back to the *Bhagavad Gītā*. There, after describing the various kinds of actions and motivations according to the *guṇas*, Kṛṣṇa declares that the perfected person "is fit for becoming Brahman," and then, "having become Brahman . . . attains the highest devotion to me," and finally "realizes truly who I am . . . and enters into me."[20] Significantly, the *Bhagavad Gītā* here affirms the complementary nature of devotion and knowledge, without explaining their precise relationship. The exact nature of this relationship has important implications regarding the final state and is a topic much debated by later commentators. It is also the Devī's next topic of discussion.

Notes

1. *para-bhakti*; unlike the *Kapila Gītā* (*Bhāgavata Purāṇa* 3.29.12), the *Devī Gītā* does not use the term *nirguṇa* (without the *guṇas* of nature, unqualified) to describe this supreme devotion, perhaps because the supreme devotion described here includes various "qualified" ritual acts, that is, acts that are quite concrete and specific.

2. Cf. *Devī Gītā* 1.2, note 2.

3. An uninterrupted stream of oil is a common metaphor for truly advanced meditation where the mind is continuously focused on the object, in contrast to less focused, intermittent concentration that is likened to dripping water. The *Kapila Gītā* (*Bhāgavata Purāṇa* 3.29.11) compares the continuous flow of thoughts toward the Lord to the waters of the Ganges flowing to the ocean.

4. Cf. *Bhāgavata Purāṇa* 3.29.12, which refers to motiveless (*ahaitukya*) devotion.

5. *sāmīpya, sārṣṭī, sāyujya,* and *sālokya*. The *Kalipa Gītā* (*Bhāgavata Purāṇa* 3.29.13) refers to five kinds of liberation: dwelling in the same heaven as the supreme (*sālokya*), sharing the same powers (*sārṣṭi*), living in the presence of the supreme (*sāmīpya*), having the same form (*sārūpya*), and mergence into or unity with the supreme (*ekatva*, same as *sāyujya*). Cf. *Devī Gītā* 2.1, note 2, and 8.43cd–44ab.

6. Nīlakaṇṭha's Advaitic orientation leads him to reject the more natural reading of this verse, which seems to affirm the dualistic ideal of master and servant (*sevya-sevaka*). Nīlakaṇṭha assumes an implied negation, so he interprets the phrase to mean: "abandoning the idea of servant and master."

7. Nīlakaṇṭha comments that the devotee thinks, "I am the Goddess Bhagavatī, having the nature of *sac-cid-ānanda*."

This verse and the following, with their emphasis on nondifferentiation, together with the preceding verse, with its stress on the ideal of servant and master, nicely present the Advaitic-*bhaktic* tension that runs through much of the text.

8. This ideal of respect for all members of society regardless of class status is a hallmark of the *bhakti* of the *Bhāgavata Purāṇa*. In many ways it is the natural consequence both of Advaitic nondifferentiation and of *bhaktic* love for all God's creatures.

9. Many of these sites are listed in the next chapter (*Devī Gītā* 8.3–30).

10. *mantra-tantrādi*. Cf. *Kālikā Purāṇa* 62.131ff., where, following a description of sacred sites of the Goddess, Śiva is asked to explain the mantras and tantras relating to her various forms. Śiva responds by describing the use of various seed mantras used in worshiping the different forms of the Goddess, and the ritual procedures for worshiping her, as described in such works as the *Vaiṣṇavī Tantra, Tripurā Tantra, Uttara Tantra,* and *Kāmākhyā Tantra*.

11. Cf. *Devī Gītā* 1.42–43; 3.41–42ab above, and 10.24 below. Cf. also *Bhāgavata Purāṇa* 11.14.23–24.

12. *nitya-naimittika*; for explanation of these terms, see *Devī Gītā* 8.43, note 11.

13. *vitta-śāṭhya-vivarjitaḥ*: "devoid of deception regarding wealth." S. C. Banerji clarifies: "In the matter of offering various articles before deities, one

is warned against *vitta-śāṭhya* (deceitful economy). The idea is that one should give things in accordance with one's means, and should avoid niggardliness" (*Tantra in Bengal*, p. 144). Cf. *Devī Gītā* 8.48.

14. Several of these festivals are mentioned in *Devī Gītā* 8.44cd–46.

15. Cf. *Bhāgavata Purāṇa* 11.14.24cd: "One who unabashedly sings loudly and dances, filled with devotion to me, purifies the world." Cf. also *Devī Gītā* 10.24.

16. Cf. Daniel Sheridan, *The Advaitic Theism of the Bhāgavata Purāṇa*, pp. 96–97.

17. See *Bhāgavata Purāṇa* 3.29.7–27.

18. *Kapila Gītā* (*Bhāgavata Purāṇa*) 3.29.14.

19. For a discussion of the various forms of liberation in the *Bhāgavata Purāṇa*, see Sheridan, *The Advaitic Theism of the Bhāgavata Purāṇa*, pp. 93–96.

20. *Bhagavad Gītā* 18.53–55.

Translation

[The Goddess explains the relation between devotion and knowledge.]

7.28. Knowledge is proclaimed as the final goal of devotion,
And of dispassion as well, for both devotion and dispassion are fulfilled when knowledge arises.

7.29. Even when devotion is fully accomplished, O Mountain, if one's past karmic influences are not favorable,[1]
A person may fail to realize knowledge of me and so will depart to the Jeweled Island.

7.30. Going there, that person encounters enjoyments of all kinds, though remaining indifferent,
And in the end attains complete knowledge of my essence that is pure consciousness, O Mountain.

7.31. Thereby the person is forever liberated; liberation arises from knowledge and from nothing else.

Comment

In this section the Goddess makes a clear distinction between the limits and goals of devotion and knowledge. The highest reach of devotion, in and of itself, is the supreme heaven. Attainment of this blissful realm of the Jeweled Island constitutes the form of liberation known as *sālokya* and is largely adventitious, as demonstrated by the fact that the devotee residing there remains uninterested in its pleasures. Yet it is not without some real benefit, as it is a stepping stone to the Ultimate, for there one attains the knowledge that brings mergence.

The *Devī Gītā*'s subordination of devotion to knowledge differs from the perspective of the *Bhāgavata Purāṇa*. The *Kapila Gītā* generally regards devotion (in its highest, *nirguṇa* form) as the full equal of knowledge, both leading to the Lord.[2] Elsewhere, the *Bhāgavata* occasionally subordinates knowledge to devotion, as when Kṛṣṇa declares: "For a yogi who is filled with devotion to me and is focused on me, neither knowledge nor dispassion generally would be the best path here. What can be attained by action, by austerity, by knowledge and dispassion, by yoga, by charity, by other good means, all that my devotee attains directly through devotion to me . . . even though such a wise and steadfast devotee desires nothing."[3]

Notes

1. *prārabdha-vaśatas*: literally, "due to the force of fructifying karma."
2. *Bhāgavata Purāṇa* 3.32.32.
3. *Bhāgavata Purāṇa* 11.20.31–34.

Translation

[The Goddess affirms that knowledge may be attained in this world and explains the relation of knowledge to dispassion.]

7.31. [cont.] One who attains knowledge here in this world,
realizing the inner Self abiding in the heart,

7.32. Who is absorbed in my pure consciousness, loses not the vital breaths.[1]
Being Brahman, the person who knows Brahman attains Brahman.[2]

7.33. An object may vanish through ignorance, like gold forgotten on one's neck;
Through knowledge that destroys the ignorance, one may recover the desired object.[3]

7.34. My essence is different from the known and the unknown,[4] O Highest Mountain.
As in a mirror, so is that essence reflected clearly within the embodied Self; as in water, so is it reflected indistinctly in the world of ancestors.[5]

7.35. Just as the distinction between shadow and light is clear, just so
Is the knowledge, dispersing any sense of duality, that arises in my world.[6]

7.36. One who is dispassionate at death but who lacks knowledge
Will ever dwell in the world of Brahmā for an entire eon.

7.37. That person will be reborn in a virtuous and dignified family,[7]
And after practicing spiritual discipline, will thereby attain knowledge.

Comment

The Goddess once more proclaims the superiority of knowledge, utilizing various Upaniṣadic motifs to develop two interrelated themes. First, she argues that knowledge of Brahman (that is, of herself as pure consciousness) is most readily attained here in this world. Since Brahman is our true nature, realization of it is not dependent on the death of the body, or departure of the vital breaths. Such a person has "become" Brahman in this very life, and is free from rebirth. As the *Bṛhadāraṇyaka Upaniṣad* says, referring to one who is free from desire: "[That person's] vital breaths do not depart; being Brahman, one attains Brahman."[8] And the *Muṇḍaka Upaniṣad* adds: "One who knows Brahman becomes Brahman."[9] This describes the state of the *jīvanmukta,* who does not die when Brahman is realized. It is merely a realization of what one already has, or is, like remembering a gold necklace around one's neck that one has forgotten. Dying without the realization of Brahman generally leads to other worlds, such as that of the ancestors, where Brahman is less easily recognized. Here the Goddess draws upon the *Kaṭha Upaniṣad,* which likens the perception of the ultimate while in the body to seeing a clear image in a mirror, but if one has passed to the world of ancestors, it is like seeing a dream image; and in the world of Gandharvas, like seeing a distorted image in water.[10]

Second, there is one exceptional postmortem destination for the not-yet-realized which does produce clear knowledge. According to the *Kaṭha Upaniṣad* passage just referred to, that destination is the world of Brahmā. There one sees the Ultimate distinctly, like perceiving the difference between shadow and light.[11] The Goddess, however, departing from the *Kaṭha,* asserts that the world of Brahmā, attained by dispassion, does not lead to knowledge, at least not directly, but only to rebirth. While such rebirth is meritorious, having all the advantages necessary to gain final knowledge, it is still a bit of a spiritual detour. For the Devī, the one exceptional heavenly world, from which there is no rebirth, is her own Jeweled Island, where nondual knowledge arises spontaneously.

While the Goddess clearly exalts knowledge over dispassion, she implicitly elevates devotion over dispassion as well. As the preceding section (7.28–31ab) indicates, devotion leads to the highest celestial realm (the Jeweled Island), beyond the world of Brahmā. Both devotion and dispassion have knowledge as their final goal, but devotion, unlike dispassion, dispenses with the need for rebirth in the mundane realm.

Notes

1. That is, does not die upon attaining such realization and absorption.

2. Nīlakaṇṭha points out that this verse is based on *śruti* (*Bṛhadāraṇyaka Upaniṣad* 4.4.6). Cf. *Muṇḍaka Upaniṣad* 3.2.9. These passages are discussed in the Comment above.

3. As Nīlakaṇṭha explains, the metaphor illustrates how the Self may disappear through ignorance or forgetfulness, but later be discovered through knowledge that destroys the ignorance.

4. Nīlakaṇṭha glosses: "The perceived (or known) is the effect such as pots; the unperceived (unknown) is the cause in the form of *māyā*." He also points out that the line is based on *śruti* {*Kena Upaniṣad* 1.4}: "That [Ultimate] is other than the known and is also above the unknown." Nīlakaṇṭha goes on to say that he has explained the meaning of this statement in his commentary on the *Kena Upaniṣad*.

5. The line in Sanskrit is highly elliptical. Literally, it reads: "As in a mirror, so in the Self; as in water, so in the world of ancestors." The basic meaning is that the essence of the Goddess is more readily perceived while still embodied than when one has departed this life for the world of ancestors.

6. *Devī Gītā* 7.34cd–35 is a revision of *Kaṭha Upaniṣad* 2.3.5. See the above Comment for discussion of the *Kaṭha* passage.

7. Cf. *Bhagavad-Gītā* 6.41: "Attaining the heavens of the meritorious, dwelling there for endless years, one who has fallen from yoga will be reborn in a virtuous and dignified family."

8. *Bṛhadāraṇyaka Upaniṣad* 4.4.6.

9. *Muṇḍaka Upaniṣad* 3.2.9.

10. *Kaṭha Upaniṣad* 2.3.5. The interpretation follows that of Śaṃkara.

11. Again, this is according to Śaṃkara's interpretation. He adds that attaining Brahmaloka is difficult, and so one should strive to realize the Ultimate here in this world.

Translation

[The Goddess advises Himālaya that a life spent without seeking knowledge is wasted.]

7.38. In the course of many births does knowledge arise, O King, not in one;
Therefore with total commitment seek to acquire knowledge.[1]

7.39. Otherwise, it is a great loss, as this human birth is hard to attain.
Even if one is born a Brahman, access to the Vedas is hard to gain.[2]

7.40. Realizing the six virtues beginning with tranquillity,[3] achieving success in yoga as well,
And finding an excellent teacher, all these are hard to attain in life,

7.41. As are keen senses and sanctification of the body.[4]
By the merit gained in several births, one comes to desire liberation.

7.42. Even after attaining the fruits of spiritual discipline, the person who
Does not strive after knowledge squanders the opportunity provided by birth.

Comment

Rare is the person who seeks, let alone discovers, the supreme truth. This at least is the view of the *Bhagavad Gītā*. There Kṛṣṇa declares that among thousands of persons, perhaps one strives for perfection (*siddhi*), and among those, perhaps one truly comes to know the Lord.[5] Developing this theme into a grand hierarchy, the *Kapila Gītā* ranks beings from lower to higher according to their spiritual attainments, beginning with inanimate entities, then animals, and concluding with humans. Among the latter, Brahmans are the best, and among them, those who know the Vedas. Further refinements in subsequent groups finally culminate in those who surrender all actions, and their own selves as well, to the Lord, realizing no difference between themselves and the Supreme.[6] The *Devī Gītā* elaborates a similar scheme, stressing the increasing difficulty of each successive level of attainment. Birth is thus regarded, especially on the various human levels, as an opportunity not to be wasted. Ultimately, only those births are fruitful which lead toward knowledge, regardless of any benefits received through spiritual discipline (*sādhana*).

Notes

1. Cf. *Bhagavad Gītā* 7.19ab, where Kṛṣṇa declares: "At the end of many births, one who is endowed with knowledge resorts to me." Cf. also *Bhagavad Gītā* 6.45: "Striving with great effort, the yogi, cleansed of sin, is perfected through many births and goes to the supreme goal."

2. Nīlakaṇṭha here quotes from *śruti* {*Kena Upaniṣad* 2.5}: "If here in this body one knows, then that is good; if one here knows not, that is a great loss." Cf. *Bṛhadāraṇyaka Upaniṣad* 4.4.14.

3. Cf. *Devī Gītā* 4.16, where five virtues or "mental treasures" are mentioned. See also the Comment following 4.16.

4. According to Nīlakaṇṭha, the sanctification is achieved through Vedic rites.

5. *Bhagavad Gītā* 7.3.

6. *Kapila Gītā* (*Bhāgavata Purāṇa*) 3.29.28–33.

Translation

[The Goddess concludes by emphasizing that the realization of knowledge is the supreme self-fulfillment.]

7.43. Therefore, O King, one should strive for knowledge with all one's strength;
Then one surely obtains the fruits of the horse sacrifice at every moment.[1]

7.44. Like clarified butter hidden in milk, knowledge dwells in every being;
One should stir continuously, using the mind as the churning stick.[2]

7.45. Attaining knowledge, one is wholly fulfilled[3]—thus the Vedānta proclaims.
I have described everything in brief; what more do you wish to hear?

Comment

The Goddess in the concluding verse stresses that through knowledge a person is fulfilled (*kṛtārtha*), with no qualifications. While the chapter as a whole shows the important role devotion plays in the attainment of knowledge, devotion is ultimately subordinated, while the Advaitic notions of self-realization, of discovering one's true inner essence, are accented. By way of contrast, as pointed out above, the

Bhāgavata Purāṇa not infrequently subordinates knowledge to devotion: knowledge by itself does not lead to fulfillment. The *Bhāgavata* (1.5.3–4) makes this point in rather dramatic fashion, when it describes the initial depression of its own basic narrator, Vyāsa. Although Vyāsa has composed the great epic *Māhābhārata* dealing with all the objects of human longing, and has inquired about and realized (or studied: *adhīta*) Brahman, he nonetheless grieves like one who is not fulfilled (*akṛtārtha*). The reason for Vyāsa's dissatisfaction is that, despite his knowledge, he has not sufficiently sung the praises of the supreme Lord. Such glorification of devotion over mere knowledge of Brahman is not unusual in the *Bhāgavata Purāṇa*, while the *Devī Gītā* sees knowledge of Brahman as identical with the supreme goal of devotion. The *Devī Gītā* qualifies *bhakti*: if it is not conjoined with knowledge, it is deficient. It does not make a similar qualification of knowledge.

Although the *Devī Gītā* acknowledges the final supremacy of knowledge on the absolute level, one should remember that the text also asserts that the premier kind of devotion involves the Advaitic realization of unity. As 7.15 states, the highest devotee is one "Who enthusiastically thinks of me alone with supreme affection, knowing me truly as never separate from oneself, not acknowledging any difference." On the practical level, then, the *Devī Gītā* often treats the two paths as equals, as intertwining, or simply as different aspects of one path. Given the importance of devotion, then, it is hardly surprising that the final three chapters of the *Devī Gītā* are dedicated to explaining various details and practices of Bhakti Yoga.

Notes

1. Nīlakaṇṭha comments: "One who is engaged in such acts as *śravaṇa* [e.g., listening to the stories of the Goddess] attains the fruit of the horse sacrifice at every moment." Nīlakaṇṭha apparently assumes that such listening brings about knowledge of the supreme. In introducing the devotional ideal of *śravaṇa*, Nīlakaṇṭha also seems to offer an indirect explanation for the reference to the horse sacrifice in the *Devī Gītā*.

The horse sacrifice was long noted for its expiatory efficiency, absolving a sinner even of such horrendous deeds as killing a Brahman. (See *The Laws of Manu*, 11.73–75. Cf. Pandurang Vaman Kane, *History of Dharmaśāstra*, vol. 5. p. 1589.) The *Bhāgavata Purāṇa* takes over this notion and infuses it with devotional elements. In recounting the story of Indra's slaying of Vṛtra, the *Bhāgavata* (6.13.6–9) says that Indra will be absolved of the sin of murdering a Brahman (Vṛtra) by worshiping the Lord with a horse sacrifice. Indeed, by such means he could be absolved from the sin of murdering the whole world!

The *Bhāgavata* (6.13.22–23) concludes the account of Indra's victory over Vṛtra and his absolution of the sin of Brahmancide by asserting that this narrative washes away all sins and that the wise should daily listen to and recite the story, which brings wealth, fame, long life, and all good fortune. Thus, listening to the tale of Indra and Vṛtra is as beneficial as actually carrying out the horse sacrifice. Elsewhere, the *Bhāgavata Purāṇa* (2.8.4–6) indicates that Kṛṣṇa enters through the ears into the heart of the devotee who daily listens to and recites the stories of the Lord. The devotee's heart is thus cleansed of all impurities, and all worldly afflictions vanish. Listening to the stories of the Lord thus lies at the heart of the *Bhāgavata*'s devotional practice, fully replacing any need to perform the sacrificial rite. It is the assimilation of the expiatory fame of the horse sacrifice to such devotional acts as hearing the stories of the Lord (or Goddess) that apparently lies behind Nīlakaṇṭha's comment.

2. The Goddess here quotes this verse from the *Amṛtabindu Upaniṣad* (20). The knowledge spoken of is the realization of the Self within. Cf. *Śvetāśvatara Upaniṣad* 1.15, where the Self is said to be apprehended within the person like oil in sesame seeds, clarified butter in thickened milk, water in riverbeds, and fire in wood. (This *Śvetāśvatara* verse is quoted in the concluding, verse section of the *Brahma Upaniṣad*.) Cf. also *Dhyānabindu Upaniṣad* 5–6, where all beings are said to exist in the Self like fragrance in flowers, clarified butter in milk, oil in sesame seeds, gold in ore, and thread running through [a string of] beads. The next verse (7) adds that the spirit (*puruṣa*) resides in the body like oil in seeds and fragrance in flowers.

3. *kṛtārtha*; see note 1 on 6.15.

Chapter 8

Further Instruction in the Yoga of Devotion: The Sacred Sites, Rites, and Festivals of the Goddess

Translation

[Himālaya asks about important pilgrimage sites, rites, and festivals of the Goddess; she responds by stressing her all-pervasive nature.]

Himālaya spoke:

8.1. O Ruler of the Gods, what sacred dwelling places[1] here on earth should one see?
Which ones are preeminent, purifying, and most pleasing to the Goddess?

8.2. What rites provide satisfaction,[2] and also what festivals?[3]
Tell me all about these matters, Mother, whereby a person becomes completely fulfilled.[4]

The Goddess spoke:

8.3. Every site is my dwelling place and worth seeing, all moments are fit for observing rites,
And festivals may be held on any occasion, for I pervade all times and places.[5]

8.4. Yet loving my devotees as I do, I shall be more specific.
Listen attentively to my words, Mountain King.

Comment

In the preceding chapter, the Goddess introduced the yoga of devotion by classifying its various kinds according to the qualities of nature, including the supreme devotion transcending the qualities. In her description of this latter, she referred to various emotional and attitudinal qualities of the highest devotee, such as being wholly intent on the Goddess and seeing her as embodied in all beings. She also briefly mentioned several worshipful activities in which such a devotee is eager to engage, including seeing her sacred sites, reciting or singing her names, performing her splendrous rites, and participating in her festivals. But in that chapter she provided few details of these activities, elaborating instead upon the relation of devotion to knowledge and dispassion.

In this chapter, prompted by Himālaya, the Devī turns her attention back to the specifics of the devotional path in its supreme form. She now is about to recite long lists of sacred sites, names, rites, and the like. But first she qualifies her comments by indicating that all times and places are sacred and appropriate for worshiping her, since she is omnipresent. In providing her various lists, the Goddess largely ignores the actual procedures of worship (specifics of Devī-*pūjā* are explained in the last two chapters of the *Devī Gītā*).

In the following two sections, the Goddess recites a long list of sacred sites and associated goddesses (a total of seventy-three places, depending on how one interprets some of the verses, and if one includes the lotus hearts of Devī's knowers, as well as Kāśī, mentioned later). While such a lengthy listing may be tedious to modern readers, especially those not intimately familiar with Indian geography, the significance of this section should not be overlooked. It is profoundly revealing of a major facet of the Devī's character: her intimate association with the land, and with the particularity of specific places. As Mahā-Devī (the Great Goddess) or as Bhuvaneśvarī dwelling in her celestial Jeweled Island home, the Goddess appears as the one universal ruler, but she may also seem rather removed from the mundane plane of this world in all its multiplex concreteness. But as identified with the vast number of local and regional goddesses who are the immediate guardians of the good life in this realm, the Great Goddess becomes accessible to ordinary devotees in their everyday circumstances.

Her accessibility within this world is made clear by the terms used in Śākta texts to refer to her sacred sites, *pīṭha* and *sthāna* (this latter term is the one used by the *Devī Gītā*.)[6] The most general term for holy places in the Hindu tradition is *tīrtha,* literally, a "ford" or "crossing." While river crossings themselves are often sites manifesting sacred power, the term applies to any place where one can contact such power, or cross from this human realm to the divine, from this world to a higher plane. A *tīrtha* thus evokes the notion of a place of sacred power within samsara, but leading to the far shore of transcendence and liberation.

The terms *pīṭha* and *sthāna* have a different orientation. *Pīṭha* means a seat or bench, *sthāṇa* an abode, residence, or dwelling place.[7] Both point to the rootedness of the Goddess, and of her various forms, in the world. As one scholar explains: "The *pīṭha* is not a place of 'crossing beyond' this world. . . . The word *pīṭha,* rather, suggests to us that the goddess takes a seat in this world—a firm seat, a bench—under a tree, by the side of a pool, or at the edge of a village as the presiding mistress of the place. She is immanent. . . . And the prayers and concerns that one might bring to the goddess who takes a seat at the edge of the village are not the other-worldly concerns of the far shore; they are the prayers and concerns of this shore, having to do with birth and death, disease and health, food and water, fertility and longevity."[8]

The multiform Great Goddess not only dwells within this world, she is also embodied in it, thereby thoroughly sacralizing the world. Essential to such embodiment is the concrete specificity that characterizes the following list. While the Goddess is omnipresent, as she herself has already declared, such omnipresence is an abstraction that may obscure her concrete embodiment. This theme of embodiment will be further developed in the next Comment.

Notes

1. *sthāna:* "abode, residence." For comparison with the concept of *tīrtha,* see Comment above.

2. That is, provide satisfaction to the Goddess.

3. As Nīlaṇkaṇṭha points out in his comment on the preceding verse, these rites, festivals, and sacred sites have been mentioned by the Goddess earlier (*Devī Gītā* 7.19a, 7.22a, 7.23ab).

4. *kṛta-kṛtya;* see note 1 on *Devī Gītā* 1.3.

5. *sarva-rūpiṇī:* literally, "all-embodying." In the context, it indicates her all-pervasive nature in time and space. Cf. *Matsya Purāṇa* 13.23–25, where Dakṣa asks Satī just before her self-immolation to list the places *(tīrthas)* where he will be able to see her, and to indicate what names he is to use in praising her. She responds: "At all times, in all beings, in all places on earth, I am to be seen, for there is no place in all the worlds that is apart from me." She then proceeds, out of her compassion, to be more specific, giving one 108 places and corresponding names where worshiping her will be easy and fruitful.

6. *Sthāna* is also the word used by the *Kālikā Purāṇa* (18.40) to indicate the various places where the body parts of Satī fell to earth (see Comment on 8.5–18).

7. Subhendugopal Bagchi notes that *pīṭhas* are seats which "are supposed to be the dwelling places of the *Devī* . . . ; that is why they are also called *'Devīsthānas'* " (*Eminent Indian Śākta Centres in Eastern India,* p. 1). He goes on to say that all the *pīṭhas* are *sthānas*, but not vice versa. He also notes that *pīṭhas* not associated with the various body parts of the Devī are known as *upapīṭhas* (minor seats). (This association of body parts and seats will be discussed in detail in the next Comment.) The *Devī-Bhāgavata* seems to make no clear distinction between the terms *pīṭha* and *sthāna,* using the two more or less interchangeably (see, for instance, 7.30.47–54). In the *Devī Gītā* itself, the word *pīṭha* occurs three times (10.8,15,16), referring to the ritual altar upon which one invokes the Goddess.

8. Diana L. Eck, "Shiva and Shakti in the Land of India," p. 34.

Translation

[The Goddess commences to enumerate her sacred dwelling places and the names of the goddesses associated with them.]

8.5. Kolapuram is a great dwelling place, where Lakṣmī ever lives.
Matṛpuram is a second prime abode, where Reṇukā resides.

8.6. Tulajāpuram is a third, Saptaśṛṅga yet another.
Hiṅgulā is a great dwelling place, and so is Jvālāmukhī.

8.7. There is the prime dwelling place of Śākambharī, and the excellent dwelling place of Bhrāmarī.
There is Śrī Raktadantikā's dwelling place, and Durgā's is yet another.

8.8. The dwelling place of Vindhyācalanivāsinī is most excellent.[1]
There is Annapūrṇā's great dwelling place, and the unsurpassed Kāñcipuram.

8.9. There is Bhīmādevī's prime dwelling place, and Vimalā's dwelling place as well,
And the great dwelling place of Śrī Candralā, and Kauśikī's dwelling place too.

8.10. There is Nīlāmbā's prime dwelling place on the summit of Mt. Nīla,[2]
As well as Jāmbūnadeśvarī's dwelling place, and the beautiful Śrīnagara.

8.11. Guhyakālī's great dwelling place is established in Nepal,
While Mīnākṣī's supreme dwelling place is in Cidambaram, so it is proclaimed.

8.12. Sundarī resides in the great dwelling place of Vedāraṇya.
The Supreme Śakti has established her great dwelling place at Ekāmbaram.[3]

8.13. Mahālasā is a prime dwelling place, and that of Yogeśvarī is yet another.
And there is Nīlasarasvatī's dwelling place, famous among the Chinese.

8.14. Bagalā's dwelling place in Vaidyanātha is considered most excellent.
The Jeweled Island is my abode, where I dwell as the auspicious and glorious Bhuvaneśvarī, as tradition affirms.[4]

8.15. The sacred zone of the Devī's womb at Kāmākhyā is the site of the auspicious Tripurabhairavī.[5]
It is the best of hallowed places in this earthly realm, and here Mahāmāyā dwells.[6]

8.16. There is no better dwelling place on earth than here,
Where every month Devī herself resides during her menses.
8.17. All the deities of that place have assumed the form of mountains.
Even the great deities dwell within those mountains.[7]
8.18. The whole earth there is the very essence of the Devī, so think the wise.
There is no better dwelling place than this sacred zone of the womb at Kāmākhyā.

Comment

Underlying the conception of these many dwelling places of the Goddess is the myth of Satī's dismemberment, as her corpse was being carried all over India by her distraught husband Śiva. Satī herself is a former manifestation or incarnation of the Great Goddess. The *Devī-Bhāgavata* presents one version of Satī's myth immediately preceding the *Devī Gītā*.[8] The myth is summarized in the Comment on 1.3–13. There it was noted that Viṣṇu cut off the body of Satī, piece by piece, with his arrows, until Śiva was relieved of his burden. Śiva then took up residence in the various places where the body parts had fallen to earth and declared to the gods: "Whoever in these places (*sthānas*) worships the Auspicious Goddess with supreme devotion will attain everything. In her own body-parts the supreme Mother is forever present."[9] There follows a listing of 108 such places, along with the names of goddesses associated with each.[10]

This list of sacred sites and names provided in the *Devī-Bhāgavata* (7.30) does not furnish specific correlations of body parts with places, except in the very first instance: "In Vārāṇasī, where Gaurī's face fell, dwells Viśālākṣī."[11] Likewise, the list here in the *Devī Gītā* refrains from such correlations, with the notable exception of the Devī's womb (*yoni-maṇḍala,* or simply *yoni*) at Kāmākhyā, also known as Kāmarūpa, in Assam. As the commentator Nīlakaṇṭha points out, the account of the fall of the womb [and other limbs] is given in the *Kālikā Purāṇa*.[12]

In the *Kālikā Purāṇa*'s version of the dismemberment, the gods Brahmā and Viṣṇu, along with Saturn (Śanaiśvara), entered into the corpse of Satī to cut it to pieces. Her feet fell in Devīkūṭa, her thighs in Uḍḍīyāna, her womb *(yoni-maṇḍala)* as well as her navel on the mountain Kāmagiri in Kāmarūpa, her breasts adorned with a golden necklace in Jālandhara, her shoulders and neck on the mountain Pūrṇagiri, and her head beyond Kāmarūpa. The text adds, specifically in connection with the thighs but applicable to all the parts, that they fell to earth "for the welfare of the world."[13]

The *Kālikā Purāṇa* also refers to the Kāmagiri mountain where Satī's *yoni* fell as the Blue Mountain (*nīla-śaila* or *nīla-kūṭa*).[14] In this Blue Mountain, according to the *Kālikā,* is a cave in which the *yoni* lies in the form of a stone, twelve fingers wide (about nine inches) and twenty-one fingers long. It is reddened with vermilion and saffron (symbolizing blood), and is said to grant all wishes.[15] A mortal who touches the stone attains immortality and eventually *mokṣa.*[16] The menses of the Goddess is celebrated there each month.[17] Of all the body parts of Satī, the *yoni,* as the prime symbol of the creative power of the Goddess, is understandably singled out by the *Devī Gītā* for special attention.

Interestingly, in the *Devī Gītā,* the Goddess mentions her own supreme iconic form as Bhuvaneśvarī, dwelling in the celestial Jeweled Island,[18] in the line just prior to the verses on Kāmākhyā.[19] This juxtaposition reinforces the identity of the Goddess as both World-Mother and Earth-Mother, that is, as cosmic genetrix and as fecund earth. These two aspects of the Devī are delineated in chapters 3 and 8, respectively, of the *Devī Gītā.* In chapter 3 the revelation of the Cosmic Body of the Goddess emphasized her role as the material cause of the universe. The correlations of her body parts there with various entities were cosmic and abstract. Here in chapter 8, the correlations are place-specific, and the earth itself becomes the living mother. Her womb in the cave on the Blue Mountain is simply the most striking example of the concrete embodiment of the Goddess in all her limbs.

The physical earth thus unites all the limbs—and the various goddesses associated with them—in the one body of the Goddess. And the limbs of the one body further unite the land of India, called "Mother India" (Bhārat Mātā), since the sites mentioned span the length and breadth of the subcontinent.[20] The Śākta devotee, accordingly, lives in a sacralized world, that is, in the lap of the Goddess. As Śiva declared above, the supreme Mother is forever present in all her body parts.

Notes

1. This goddess and the four mentioned in the preceding verse, along with Bhīma Devī mentioned in verse 8.9 below, form a special group, being the specific incarnations of the Goddess that the Devī herself names in the *Devī Māhātmya* (11.37–51).

2. This "Blue Mountain" *(nīla-parvata)* may be the name of a hill near Kāmakhyā, where the Devī's *yoni* is said to have fallen. According to *Kālikā Purāṇa* (62.57), the mountain turned blue *(nīla-varṇaḥ śailo 'bhūt)* when the *yoni* fell on it, and is known as *nīla-śaila* (62.87). The same text (62.74; 79.75) refers to the mountain as *nīla-kūṭa*. Cf. Sircar, *Geography*, pp. 86–87. The *Devī Gītā* (8.15) associates the *yoni* with Kāmākhyā.

3. According to Nīlakaṇṭha, Ekāmbaram is another name for Bhuvaneśvara and is the seat of Bhuvaneśvarī herself. In explaining this verse, he thus adds these words of the Goddess: "In this dwelling place (Ekāmbaram), established by the Supreme Śakti Bhuvaneśvarī, I who am Bhuvaneśvarī dwell." Cf. *Devī Gītā* 8.14, which refers to Maṇidvīpa as Bhuvaneśvarī's abode.

4. *smṛtam;* literally, "as remembered." Nīlakaṇṭha interprets this as referring to the account of the Jeweled Island given in the third Skandha of the *Devī-Bhāgavata.* The third Skandha (chapters 2–6) describes how the gods of the Trimūrti, on a visit to the Jeweled Island, were turned into women by the Goddess.

5. The name "Tripurabhairavī" means "Fearful Goddess of the Three Cities." She is often referred to simply as Tripurā. According to the *Kālikā Purāṇa* (63.51), Tripurā is a form of the goddess Kāmākhyā (whose name also refers to the site itself). (See also verses 63.53–57, and 62.80cd–81ab.) Kāmākhyā herself is said to have taken up residence in the fallen womb of Satī, once it had turned to stone (*Kālikā Purāṇa* 62.74cd–75ab). See the Comment above for the story of Satī's dismemberment and the fall of her womb.

6. According to *Kālikā Purāṇa* 62.57, the goddess Mahāmāyā dissolved into the mountain on which Satī's womb had fallen.

7. *Kālikā Purāṇa* 62.82–86 narrates how the *yoni,* having fallen on the mountain, turned to stone, along with Śiva and all the other gods, all thus assuming the form of mountains. The gods, Brahmā, Viṣṇu, and others, all resided there in order to pay homage to Kāmākhyā.

8. The myth of Satī is given in *Devī-Bhāgavata* 7.30.26–50.

9. *Devī-Bhāgavata* 7.30.47d–48.

10. This list in *Devī-Bhāgavata* 7.30.55–83 is found in various other Purāṇas. According to D. C. Sircar, it appears probably for the first time in *Matsya Purāṇa* 13 [verses 26–53] (*The Śākta Pīṭhas,* p. 25). It also appears in the *Padma* and *Skanda Purāṇas* (Sircar gives the Purāṇic text with references in *The Śākta Pīṭhas,* pp. 67–70). Sircar argues that the list in *Devī-Bhāgavata* 7.30 is earlier than the one in the *Devī Gītā.* Sircar also notes that the earlier list does not mention Kāmākhyā (Kāmarūpa). He suggests that the compiler of the list had to stretch to find 108 sites, since many of the places named are imaginary, and yet he was surely familiar with Kāmākhyā. Thus, the omission was seemingly intentional, possibly due to the compiler's aversion to the "out-and-out Tantric" milieu of the Kāmākhyā site (*The Śākta Pīṭhas,* pp. 28–31). The *Devī Gītā* clearly has no such aversion.

11. *Devī-Bhāgavata* 7.30.55ab. The translation follows Nīlakaṇṭha's interpretation of the verse. Cf. 8.27 below, where it is said that Viśālākṣī is at Avimukta (Vārāṇasī).

12. The *Kālikā Purāṇa* seems to be the basis for several of the details found in the *Devī Gītā*'s description of Kāmākhyā, such as the notion that all the gods reside there in the form of mountains.

13. *Kālikā Purāṇa* 18.39–43.

14. *Kālikā Purāṇa* 62.66 and 74; 79.75. Cf. 8.10ab above and note 2 above.

15. *Kālikā Purāṇa* 62.88–90.

16. *Kālikā Purāṇa* 62.75cd–76ab.

17. See David Kinsley, *Hindu Goddesses,* p. 187.

18. While the celestial Jeweled Island has a terrestrial counterpart today in Vindhyācal, neither the *Devī Gītā* nor the *Devī-Bhāgavata* as a whole make reference to, or seem aware of, such an earthly counterpart.

19. In the *Kālikā Purāṇa* (62.93), Bhuvaneśvarī appears simply as one of Kāmākhyā's attendant deities or *yoginīs*.

20. While there are Purāṇic traditions that talk of fifty-one or even 108 *pīṭhas* (the *Devī-Gītā* lists c. 73), these figures are too circumscribed from a devotional perspective. As Eck points out, "the tradition of the *pīṭhas* extends far beyond any list of fifty-one or 108, for there are thousands of goddesses all over India, which people claim to be a part of the body of Shakti" ("Shiva and Shakti in the Land of India," p. 50). And the *Kālikā Purāṇa* (18.45) says, after mentioning the places where the main body parts of Satī fell, that the gods cut the rest of the body into small particles that were blown away by the wind and fell into the celestial Gaṅgā. Who, we may ask, knows where all those particles may have eventually ended up?

Translation

[The Goddess continues her enumeration of sacred dwelling places.]

8.19. And Gāyatrī's prime dwelling place is the auspicious Puṣkara, so it is proclaimed.
In Amareśa dwells Caṇḍikā; in Prabhāsa is Puṣkarekṣiṇī.

8.20. In the great dwelling place Naimiṣa is the Devī Liṅgadhāriṇī. Puruhūtā is in Puṣkarākṣa, just as Rati is in Aṣāḍhī.

8.21. In the great dwelling place Caṇḍamuṇḍī is Daṇḍinī Parameśvarī.
In Bhārabhūti dwells Bhūti, in Nākula Nakuleśvarī.
8.22. Candrikā is in Hariścandra, in Śrīgiri is Śāṅkarī, according to tradition.
In Japyeśvara is Triśūlā; Sūkṣmā is in Āmrātakeśvara.
8.23. Śāṃkarī is in Mahākala, Śarvāṇī in the place named Madhyamā.
In the hallowed site called Kedāra is the Devī Mārgadāyinī.
8.24. In a place called Bhairava is Bhairavī; in Gayā is Maṅgalā, according to tradition.
Sthāṇupriyā is in Kurukṣetra, and Svāyambhuvī in Nākula.
8.25. In Kanakhala dwells Ugrā, Viśveśā in Vimaleśvara.
In Aṭṭahāsa is Mahānandā; in Mahendra is Mahāntakā.
8.26. In Bhīma, Bhīmeśvarī is proclaimed to be; in the dwelling place called Vastrāpatha,
Bhavānī Śāṃkarī is proclaimed, while Rudrāṇī is in Ardhakoṭika.
8.27. In Avimukta dwells Viśālākṣī, Mahābhāgā in Mahālaya.
In Gokarṇa dwells Bhadrakarṇī; Bhadrā dwells in Bhadrakarṇaka.
8.28. Utpalākṣī is in Suvarṇākṣa, Sthānvīśā in a place called Sthānu.
In Kamalālaya is Kamalā; Pracaṇḍā is in Chagalaṇḍaka.
8.29. At Kuraṇḍala dwells Trisandhyā; at Mākoṭa, Mukuṭeśvarī.
In Maṇḍaleśa dwells Śāṇḍakī, and Kālī at Kālañjara.
8.30. In Śaṃkukarṇa, Dhvani is proclaimed; Sthūlā dwells in Sthūlakeśvara.
In the lotus-hearts of the wise dwells Hṛllekhā,[1] the Parameśvarī.[2]
8.31. These places proclaimed above are most dear to the Goddess.

Comment

Unlike certain other medieval lists of *pīṭha*s with their goddesses, the *Devī Gītā*'s list makes no mention of corresponding male consorts or counterparts known as Bhairavas, fierce forms of Śiva, associated with each site. The inclusion of the Bhairavas in many lists was part of a Tantric, esoteric elaboration and interpretation of the *pīṭha*s that expressed on the earthly plane the bipolarity of the Ultimate, symbolized in sexual terms.

The reasons for the *Devī Gītā*'s omission of the Bhairavas are not entirely clear. Possibly it was to avoid any implication of subordination of the Goddess to Śiva, or of any codependency of her various forms on the Bhairavas. For instance, in the *Kālikā Purāṇa,* Bhuvaneśvarī appears simply as one of eight attendant deities or *yoginī*s of Kāmākhyā.[3] These *yoginī*s, along with other forms of the Goddess, are associated with various manifestations of Śiva, at times referred to as Bhairavas. According to the *Kālikā Purāṇa,* the *yoginī* Siddharūpiṇī, known also as Mahāgaurī, who dwells on Brahmā Mountain, is identified as the extremely beautiful Bhuvaneśvarī.[4] The *Devī Gītā* makes no such connection of Bhuvaneśvarī with the *yoginī*s or any Bhairava, or with any mundane mountain home, locating her safely beyond the reach of the Bhairavas, as it were, in the supreme celestial realm of the Jeweled Island (8.14cd).

The inclusion of the Jeweled Island in the list of seats reveals an important theological perspective of the text. While the earthly embodiment of the Goddess in all its particularity is highly significant, the *Devī Gītā* ultimately subordinates it to her more celestial and ideal form as Bhuvaneśvarī. The earthly body of the Goddess, after all, is the body of Satī, an incarnation or manifestation of Bhuvaneśvarī. Bhuvaneśvarī, the supreme iconic form of Devī, is not associated with a specific locale in this world—rather, her supreme presence in this realm is found in her prime sonic manifestation, as the seed syllable Hrīṃ (known as Hṛllekhā) resonating in the inner consciousness of realized sages (*jñānis*) (8.30cd).

Ultimately, from the *Devī Gītā*'s perspective, even the various physical sites are simply manifestations of divine consciousness. Bhuvaneśvarī herself is supreme consciousness, and all the goddesses of particular places are manifestations of her. Thus, as the *Devī-Bhāgavata* concludes in its account of the 108 seats: "These fields, yielding liberation, are composed of consciousness *(saṃvid)* itself."[5] The various body parts, accordingly, would appear to be nothing other than the concrete embodiments of the pure consciousness of the Goddess.

Notes

1. Hṛllekhā, name of the seed mantra of Bhuvaneśvarī, is the supreme sonic manifestation of the Goddess. Nīlakaṇṭha cites here the etymology of the word as given, he says, in the *Bhuvaneśvarī Rahasya:* "That supreme power of life *(prāṇa-śakti)* keeps watch in the furrow *(lekha)* of the heart *(hṛd)*. Thus it is called the Hṛllekhā." See *Devī Gītā* 1.25, note 8.

2. Cf. *Devī-Bhāgavata* 7.30.83 (= *Matsya Purāṇa* 13.53d), where Vyāsa concludes his listing of the 108 sites/names of the Devī by declaring: "Śakti is in all embodied beings." Cf. also *Devī Gītā* 6.18.

3. *Kālikā Purāṇa* 62.93.

4. *Kālikā Purāṇa* 62.122–23.

5. *Devī-Bhāgavata* 7.30.101ab.

Translation

[The Goddess indicates special provisions for pilgrimage, including the benefits of reciting her names.]

8.31. [cont.] First one should listen[1] to the particular virtues[2] of these various sacred sites, Highest Mountain.

8.32. Afterward one should worship the Goddess in the prescribed manner.
Alternatively, Highest Mountain, since all sacred sites exist in Kāśī,[3]

8.33. One may wish to live there always, ever absorbed in serving the Goddess.
By seeing those dwelling places, by reciting the names of the Goddess[4] without pause,

8.34. By meditating on her lotus feet, one becomes freed from bondage.
Whoever, arising at dawn, should recite these names of the Goddess,

8.35. Burns to ashes all sins instantly, in that very moment, O Mountain.
At the time of offerings to the dead, one should recite these holy names in the presence of Brahmans;

8.36. All one's ancestors will be freed and go to the highest state.[5]

Comment

The recitation *(japa, paṭha)* of the names of a deity is regarded as one of the foremost acts of worship that one can offer to the divine. It represents a devotional elaboration of ancient mantric practices. As has been noted, a mantra is identical with the god or goddess it symbolizes or embodies. A seed mantra, the single syllable that is the quintessential element of a mantra, is thus the essence of a deity manifest in sound. Its significance lies not in any semantic meaning—often there is no ordinary semantic meaning—but in its sonic power. Its constituent sounds symbolically represent the various divine and cosmic forces integrated within a particular deity. Accordingly, the proper repetition of the seed mantra provides direct access to the deity's power, and even identification with the deity.

A divine name is also a mantra, a focus of divine power. But it has semantic meaning as well (thus Lakṣmī is "Wealth," Śākambharī is "She-who-bears-vegetables"). A name indicates in ordinary language a virtue, quality, or aspect of the god or goddess. Thus a name provides both a verbal description of the deity, as well as representing a sonic essence. As such, a name has a powerful appeal to the mind and heart of the devotee.[6] By reciting the seed mantra, one may become the deity. By reciting the names, one may lose oneself in love for the deity.

Further, the seed mantra stresses the idea of concentration, of power compacted, while the divine name accents the notion of expansion, of power unfolding. That is, a seed mantra emphasizes the power of the deity in its most concentrated form, as a unique manifest point of energy. The divine name, however, is frequently chanted as part of a long list of such names, often 108, or even a thousand, expressing the manifold energies of the deity that pervade all time and space. As one modern Hindu commentator explains, the concept of the thousand names "is a logical outcome of Upaniṣadic philosophy. It stems from the idea underlying the statement *'Ekam sad viprā bahudhā vadanti'* ['Truth is one; sages call it by many names']. The thousand names of the Deity describe the essential unity which becomes multiplicity in manifestation."[7]

The fruits of reciting the divine names may include various mundane rewards, but the spiritual benefits are especially emphasized. Aside from those mentioned above, the *Devī-Bhāgavata* elsewhere affirms: "Many persons have attained success through reciting the 108 names [of the Goddess]. . . . Nothing is hard to attain for one who recites the 108 names; such a person will become completely fulfilled *(kṛta-kṛtya),* absorbed in devotion to the Devī, and assuming her nature *(devī-rūpa).*"[8]

Notes

1. See note 1 on *Devī Gītā* 1.2.

2. *māhātmya:* "greatness" or "virtue"; specifically, the particular virtues or merits of a deity or sacred site, or a work describing such virtues.

3. Kāśī, or Vārāṇasī (Benares), is generally considered by Hindus to be the most holy of all India's cities. Kāśī, the City of Light, is the supreme world center, the initial spot of light and original point of creation, as well as the all-inclusive, comprehensive sacred circle within which all other sacred centers are said to exist (see Eck, "Shiva and Shakti in the Land of India," p. 15). In *Banaras,* Eck writes: "Spatial transposition is a fascinating fact of India's spiritual geography. Kāshī, of course, is present in a thousand places in India. . . . Kāshī is the paradigm of the sacred place, to which other places subscribe in their claims to sanctity. At the same time, Kāshī includes all the other *tīrthas* within it. According to Purānic commentators, these *tīrthas* exist only partially and in gross form in their separate places, but in their fullness and in subtle form, they exist in Kāshī" (pp. 283–84).

4. *japan devīṃ:* "invoking the Goddess." In the context, repetition or recitation of her names seems clearly intended, and is explicitly mentioned in the next two verses. The basic meaning of the root *jap* is to utter, repeat silently, or recite in a low voice.

5. A nearly identical statement to 8.35cd–36ab occurs in 10.37, but there it is recitation of the whole *Devī Gītā* itself that is said to benefit one's ancestors. In *Devī-Bhāgavata* 7.30.100, the same idea is repeated almost verbatim, but there with reference to repetition of the 108 names of the Goddess.

6. Cf. Chaganty Suryanarayanamurthy's comments in his introduction to the *Śrī Lalitā Sahasranāma:* "Each of the thousand names is a Mantra by itself, the contemplation of the meaning of which will reveal to the disciple pathways towards his spiritual goal. . . . Whether a worshipper is a Bhakta or a Yogi or a Māntrika or a Jñāni, be he a householder or a Sanyāsi he will find in this Sahasra Nāma names which will exercise an irresistible appeal" (pp. 44–45).

7. Suryanarayanamurthy, introduction to the *Śrī Lalitā Sahasranāma,* pp. 43–44.

8. *Devī-Bhāgavata* 7.30.96ab, 98–99ab.

Translation

[The Goddess enumerates various *vratas* or rites.]

8.36. [cont.] Now I shall describe the rites to you, who are of firm resolve.[1]

8.37. Both women and men should perform them with diligence.
The third-day observance called the Rite of Infinite Blessings,[2] along with the Rite of Happiness and Prosperity,

8.38. And also the rite named the Bestower of Refreshing Bliss,[3] should all be done on the third lunar day.[4]
Then there is the Friday Rite,[5] the Dark Fourteenth Rite,[6]

8.39. The Tuesday Rite,[7] and the Evening Rite as well.[8]
In this rite, the god Mahādeva places the Goddess on her seat

8.40. And dances before her, together with the other gods, at the beginning of the night.
In this rite, a person should fast at dusk, and during the evening should worship the Auspicious Goddess.

8.41. It should be observed once each fortnight, and is pleasing to the Goddess.
There is also the Monday Rite,[9] especially dear to me, O Mountain.

8.42. In this rite, one should take food at night after worshiping the Goddess.
And there are the two celebrations of the Rite of Nine Nights,[10] highly pleasing to me.

8.43. Likewise, O Lord, there are other rites, both regular and occasional.[11]
Whoever performs these rites unselfishly, just to please me,

8.44. Attains union with me.[12] Such a person is devoted to me, is dear to me.

Comment

The word *vrata* (translated as "rite" above) is a ritual observance involving a number of behavioral restrictions such as fasting, vigil, continence, and other abstentions. Also included are special acts such as daily bathing, worship of deities, feeding of Brahmans, maidens, and the poor, and the giving away of gifts. The observance may extend from a day to several weeks, months, or even years. Underlying the *vrata* is the mental resolve *(saṃkalpa)* on the part of the person undertaking the observance to carry out all of its provisions to the very end. Accordingly, *vrata* suggests something of a vow, a common translation for the word.

Of special note is the fact that *vratas* can be performed by all members of society, men, women (whether married, unmarried, widowed, or prostitutes), and Śūdras.[13] In fact, many seem especially intended for women, in order for them to secure the happiness and well-being of their husbands and families.[14]

Different times and periods are prescribed for the individual *vratas*. Every moment, for Hindus, represents a special convergence of auspicious and inauspicious forces. As one contemporary scholar puts it: "In India, all times are not qualitatively equal, but each day comes with its own complexion and characteristics. . . . Times are different from one another. Certain days are good for weddings, others for travel. Certain days are for Shiva, others for Vishnu. The textured nature of times makes every day special for something."[15]

The auspicious and inauspicious forces are governed by the interaction of the celestial bodies (stars, planets, sun, moon) as they manifest in the intertwining cycles of time. These rhythmic pulsations include everything from the progression of hours through the day to the advance of the seasons through the year. Prominent among these cycles are those of the lunar days (*tithis*) and solar days (*vāras*). The *tithis* follow the thirty-day cycle of the moon through its dark (waning) and bright (waxing) fortnights, and are referred to by the number of the day in the dark or bright half of the month (e.g., the bright third, or dark fourteenth). The *vāras* are the seven days of the week common to the Western calendar (e.g., Monday, Friday). Most of the *vratas* mentioned by the Devī are fixed according to the rhythms of these lunar and solar days. For example, Tuesdays are inauspicious days and thus appropriate for worshiping the more fierce forms of the Goddess, in order to gain her protection. Fridays are more ambivalent or even auspicious, and are suited to worshiping benevolent forms of the Goddess. Bright thirds are especially connected with Devī's auspicious forms.

While each day partakes of the particular qualities of its specific lunar and solar aspects, it is also shaped by the season. The times of the spring and autumn equinoxes, for instance, are considered particularly hazardous, seasons of disease and death. Thus, the first nine days of the bright fortnights of Caitra (March/April) and of Āśvina (September/October) are the prime seasons of the Goddess—who is responsible both for illness and health—and are dedicated to her greatest celebrations, the Nine Nights Rite.

There are various kinds of *vratas*: some are considered expiatory, others obligatory, and still others optional or self-imposed *(kāmya)*—for the purpose of gaining some specific end. The rites listed by the Devī above are voluntary for the most part.[16] The ends or purposes for undertaking a *vrata* are countless, including all sorts of material and spiritual benefits in this world and the next, in short, everything that can be included under the categories *bhukti* and *mukti* (enjoyments and liberation). When *vratas* are performed without any personal desire or self-interest, according to the *Devī Gītā,* one attains union with the Goddess herself.

Notes

1. *suvrata:* "one strict in the observance of vows." Mental resolve is an important part in observing the rites. To address Himālaya as *suvrata* in introducing the topic of rites or vows (*vratas*) is thus quite appropriate.

2. *ananta-tṛtīyā:* literally, "the infinite third." I have translated this third-day rite as "Infinite Blessings" on the basis of the *Matsya Purāṇa*'s account of this ritual. The *Matsya* introduces the rite by describing it as "providing infinite merit" (*ananta-puṇya-kṛt* [62.4]), and concludes by referring to it as "this third-day rite bestowing infinite fruit" (*imām ananta-phala-dām . . . tṛtīyāṃ* [62.36]).

3. *ārdrānandakarī;* the *Padma Purāṇa* (1.22.161–62) says that this rite bestows the bliss of the Self *(ātmānanda),* and that a man who performs it secures long life and bliss *(ānanda).* Similarly, a woman who performs it, whether she be married, widowed, a maiden, or a demoness, attains the same results. Cf. Pushpendra Kumar, *Śakti Cult in Ancient India,* pp. 217–18. For more on this rite, see note 4 below.

4. For explanation of the lunar days, see the Comment above.

Nīlakaṇṭha, in commenting on 8.37, indicates that these three rites (in 8.37cd–38ab) are explained in the *Matsya Purāṇa* (62–64). There, Śiva discloses to Pārvatī (Umā) the basic rules of these rites. The first two (Anantatṛtīyā and Rasakalyāṇinī) focus on the Goddess (as Gaurī, Pārvatī, etc.), while the last (Ārdrānanda) includes both the Goddess and her consort. All three are auspicious rites, providing health, wealth, and prosperity in this world, and bliss in the next. The *Matsya* makes clear that both men and women are to perform the rites, and specifically mentions the benefits to women, whether they are young maidens, married, or widowed. Sometimes, a different protocol is given for men and women. Thus, in the Anantatṛtīyā, men are to wear yellow garments, married women red, widows ocher, and maidens white.

All three rites, according to the *Matsya,* involve a lengthy sequence of rituals extending over the course of a year, with parts of the rituals being performed only on the bright (waxing) third day of each lunar month, other parts being done on the third day of both bright and dark (waning) fortnights. Some parts are to be done only in certain months, while certain acts or aspects proceed in a twelve-month sequence. For instance, twelve different kinds of flower offerings, twelve different kinds of gifts, twelve different forms of the Goddess to be honored, and twelve different kinds of foods to be avoided by the devotee rotate through the cycle of twelve months.

The various offerings to the Goddess, such as flowers, clothing, incense, and food items like sugar, spices, and fruits, are the usual sorts of gifts common in *pūjās*. The deity's image is to be bathed with various sanctified fluids such as milk and honey, and entertained by reciting or singing the names of the Goddess. One especially important part of the procedures in all three rites is the worshiping of the Goddess' body, limb by limb, part by part, from feet, ankles, knees, waist, stomach, breasts, etc., to her mouth, nose, forehead, and hair, all accompanied with appropriate mantras.

A brief description of the three rites can be found in Kane, *History of Dharmaśāstra,* vol. 5, pp. 258 (Anantatṛtīyā), 272 (Ārdrānandakara), and 390 (Rasakalyāninī). See also Kumar, *Śakti Cult in Ancient India,* pp. 215–18.

It is apparently such third-day rites that the gods performed in worshiping the Goddess in *Devī Gītā* 1.22.

5. Friday, along with Monday, Wednesday, and Thursday, is generally considered an auspicious day, while the other weekdays are generally inauspicious, though opinions differ (cf. Kane, *History of Dharmaśātra,* vol. 5, p. 682). Regarding Friday, Lawrence A. Babb writes: "Friday's planetary association is with Venus, an auspicious planet, and it is therefore generally an auspicious day. According to the *Saptavar Vrat Katha* Friday is a day especially appropriate for the worship of a benevolent goddess known as Santoshi Mata" (*The Divine Hierarchy,* p. 113). Eck indicates that in Banāras, at least, Friday is a mixed day: "The fortunes of Friday . . . are ambiguous and lead many to the temples of the Goddess" (*Banaras,* p. 256). She further mentions that goddesses like Santoshī Mātā are especially associated with Fridays (see also *Banaras,* pp. 169–70). We may recall that the benevolent Bhuvaneśvarī made her appearance before the gods on a Friday (*Devī Gītā* 1.26).

6. The Dark Fourteenth (Kṛṣṇa-Caturdaśī: the fourteenth day of the waning fortnight) belongs to Śiva. Since he and his *śakti*s are active in the dark hours, the appropriate time for the rite is at night. It is thus referred to as Śiva's Night (Śivarātri). The Dark Fourteenth occurring in the month of Phālguna (February/March) is especially sacred, and is known as the "Great Night of Śiva (Mahā-Śivarātri). According to Eck, it is the "greatest high holy day" in Banāras (*Banaras,* p. 276). The primary elements in the observance of Śivarātri are fasting, an all-night vigil during which devotional songs (*bhajan*s) are sung, and worship of the *liṅga* with offerings of flowers or *bilva* (wood-apple) leaves. The fruits, though manifold, focus especially on the removal of sin. For further details, see Kane, *History of Dharmaśāstra,* vol. 5, pp. 225–36.

7. Tuesday, associated with the ill-omened Mars, is generally regarded as an inauspicious day. It is a day when one needs protection, and thus the ferocious forms of the Goddess such as Kālī or Durgā, capable of dealing with the more violent and sinister aspects of life, are especially propitiated. Eck notes: "Tuesdays and Saturdays are the most dangerous days of the week, and on those days the deities most adept at dealing with the dangers of the world and the fears of the heart are propitiated with special vigor" (*Banaras,* p. 255). Cf. Babb, *The Divine Hierarchy,* pp. 111–12.

8. *pradoṣa;* in general, the term refers to the two hours or so immediately following sunset. Here it refers to a special ritual to the Goddess performed once every fortnight (see verse 8.41) during the early evening. The *Devī Gītā* does not specify on which day of the fortnight the rite is to be observed. According to Kane (*History of Dharmaśāstra,* vol. 5, p. 350), the *pradoṣa-vrata* as described in the *Bhaviṣya Purāṇa* is observed in the first quarter of the night on the thirteenth *tithi* of each fortnight, in honor of Śiva.

9. As indicated in note 5 above, Monday is an auspicious day. It is the day of the Moon, an auspicious body, and is especially suited for worshiping Śiva.

10. The Navarātra or Nine Nights festival is celebrated in both the spring and the autumn, roughly at the time of the equinoxes, which are the prime seasons of the Goddess. The vernal celebration, covering the first nine days of the bright half of Caitra, marks the beginning of the lunar year. The autumnal celebration in Āśvina, also referred to as Durgā Pūjā, is the more momentous of the two. At the end of each of the Nine Nights occur two important rites for Rāma. In the spring, Rāma's birth is celebrated on the ninth day (Rāma Navamī: Rāma's Ninth), and in the autumn Rāma's slaying of the demon Rāvaṇa on the tenth (Vijaya Daśamī: Victorious Tenth). These juxtapositions of the festivals of the Goddess and Rāma suggest important links between the two deities. Indeed, in the Śākta tradition, Rāma was able to slay Rāvaṇa only after performing the Nine Nights ritual of the Goddess. The *Devī-Bhāgavata* (3.28–30) recounts the story of Rāma, including his performance of the Navarātra in the month of Āśvina. The same text (3.30.25–26) also affirms that Indra performed this ritual in order to slay Vṛtra, Śiva to slay Tripura, and Viṣṇu to slay Madhu.

Immediately preceding the story of Rāma, the *Devī-Bhāgavata* (3.26–27) gives a detailed description of the Nine Nights rites. The spring and autumnal seasons are called the two teeth of Yama (God of Death), as they are difficult to get through, for they are the times of disease and death. Thus, the two Navarātras are to be performed with care and devotion. Aside from the usual kinds of ritual procedures and offerings, what is special to the Nine Nights celebration is the worship of nine virgins (*kumārīs*), ages two to ten, on each of the nine nights. Each virgin is the embodiment of a form of the Goddess, and bestows her own particular benefits, such as freedom from disease, destruction of enemies, or wealth.

According to R. C. Hazra, "The procedure of this Vrata [of Nine Nights], as given in this work [the *Devī-Bhāgavata*], agrees with that followed in Western and Southern India, but is quite different from the method of Durgā-pūjā . . . followed in present-day Bengal" (*Studies in the Upapurāṇas*, vol. 2, pp. 357–58). For a detailed account of a contemporary performance of the Nine Nights ritual in central India, see Babb, *The Divine Hierarchy*, pp. 128, 132–40. Cf. Eck, *Banaras*, pp. 258–59, 268–69; Kinsley, *Hindu Goddesses*, pp. 106–09. For a historical survey of the literature and history of the Navarātra, see Kane, *History of Dharmaśāstra*, vol. 5, pp. 154–87.

11. *nitya-naimittika; nitya* here refers to "regular, daily, or ordinary" acts, while *naimittika* refers to acts done on special occasions or for emergencies (see also *Devī Gītā* 7.22). But as Babb points out regarding the *naimittika* acts, "While it is true that there are certain ceremonial events that . . . may occur at any time, observation reveals that even these tend to occur at points within the ritual cycles that are regarded as especially appropriate for defined types of ritual activity, and thus even 'occasional' rites are contained within the more general pattern of temporal cycles" (*The Divine Hierarchy*, p. 69).

Nitya can also mean "required, obligatory," and then it contrasts with *kāmya*, "optional." The latter refers to acts performed with some specific, desired end in mind. Purāṇic *vrata*s are generally of the *kāmya* sort, including for the most part those listed by the Devī above. However, these two categories are also not always clear cut. As Mary McGee summarizes her findings on the ritual lives of contemporary Hindu women: "My conclusion is not to suggest that the compilers of the digests were wrong in classifying most votive rites observed by women as *kāmya* (that is, desire-born). . . . But their classification was based on superficial, *prima-facie* evidence. If we take into account the experience and testimonies of women who observe these rites, we find that they are motivated more by a sense of duty than by desire. When applied to these rites, therefore, the label of *kāmya* is inadequate. . . . The category of *nitya* (duty-born) seems more accurate when all the evidence is taken into account" ("Desired Fruits: Motive and Intention in the Votive Rites of Hindu Women," in *Roles and Rituals for Hindu Women*, p. 87).

12. *sāyujya:* "union with," or "mergence into." It is synonymous with *ekatva*, "oneness with." It is one of the four or five traditional forms of liberation. Cf. *Devī Gītā* 7.13.

13. Kane, *History of Dharmaśāstra*, vol. 5, p. 45.

14. See Kumar, *Śākti Cult in Ancient India*, pp. 213–14, and McGee, "Desired Fruits," esp. pp. 78–84.

15. Eck, *Banaras*, p. 252.

16. See Kane, *History of Dharmaśāstra*, vol. 5, p. 28. He says that the Durgā Pūjā (Navarātra, mentioned in *Devī Gītā* 8.42) "is nitya [obligatory] as well as kāmya [optional], it is the first because the Kālikāpurāṇa [61.12–13] prescribes that whoever, through laziness, hypocrisy, hatred or stupidity, does not celebrate the great festival of Durgā has all his desires frustrated by the angry

Devī; it is also kāmya because rewards are promised when one celebrates Durgotsava [the Durgā festival]" (*History of Dharmaśāstra*, vol. 5, p. 156).

As in all such matters, different authorities have different opinions, so one can make no absolute generalization regarding the obligatory or optional nature of any particular rite. Cf. note 11 above.

Translation

[The Goddess turns to her *utsava*s or festivals.]

8.44. [cont.] One should also celebrate prominent festivals such as the Swing Festival,[1] O Lord.

8.45. One should perform both the Going-to-sleep Festival and the Waking-up Festival.[2]
And one should perform my Chariot Festival,[3] and the Jasmine Festival,[4]

8.46. And likewise the pleasing Festival of the Thread-Offering in the month of Śrāvaṇa.[5]
So indeed should my devotee always perform the other great festivals.

8.47. One should gladly feed my devotees, and also well-dressed
Maidens and young boys,[6] regarding them as none other than me.[7]

8.48. Without miserly regard for cost,[8] one should worship them with flowers and the like.
Whoever carries out all these acts every year, tirelessly and with devotion,

8.49. Is blessed and completely fulfilled.[9] Such a person is truly worthy of my favor.
All this that is pleasing to me I have related in brief.

8.50. Never impart these instructions to one who is not a disciple or devotee.[10]

Comment

The word *utsava*, "festival," also means "joy, merriment, delight." Embedded within the merrymaking are serious and deeply religious concerns. The original and underlying meaning of *utsava* is the generation or production of divine power.[11] A festival celebration is intended to generate or stimulate the creative and nurturing powers of the cosmos, and to maintain the balance or harmony between the various, interlinked realms of the universe, between the divine and human communities.

Pūjā (worship) has similar cosmic functions and is a basic element in both *utsavas* and *vratas*. (The specific details of *pūjā* are given in chapters 9 and 10.) Accordingly, there is no clear-cut distinction between a *vrata* ("rite") and an *utsava* ("festival"). *Vrata* emphasizes those aspects of a ritual which concern the behavioral restrictions observed by the devotee, such as fasting and vigil. *Utsava* accentuates the notions of celebration, of entertaining and feasting both the human and divine participants. These aspects are not exclusive and readily intertwine. Not surprisingly, then, some rituals are referred to both as *vrata* and as *utsava*. For instance, what the *Devī Gītā* calls the Nine Nights Rite (Navarātra-Vrata) is widely known as the Durgā Festival (Durgotsava)—as well as Durgā Worship (Durgā Pūjā).[12]

As with the *vrata*, so with the *utsava*, the time set for its celebration is determined by the flow of auspicious and inauspicious forces. "As the divine becomes spatially available in the *mūrti* [image], according to its own will and decision, so it determines its temporal availability in the *utsava*, the feast celebrated at the auspicious and revealed time. . . . Fixing the right time for a religious action depends as little on the will of human beings as does the time for the ripening of a fruit or the course of the year. Grace and merit are insolubly and divinely linked with time. . . . Public festivals are also determined by the 'right time,' celebrated at such junctures as to ensure the full benefit of grace to those who participate in it."[13]

This "full benefit of grace," as bestowed by the Goddess on those devoted to her, encompasses both worldly and other-worldly goals. Here again there is little distinction between a *vrata* and an *utsava*. Regarding the latter, the cosmic and world-oriented religious concerns can be seen in a traditional, medieval definition of *utsava* as "the remover of inauspicious things"—that is, the festival serves to remove all obstacles to wealth, health, and happiness in this world. The more mystical religious concern of liberation is seen in another medieval definition of *utsava* as "that which takes away samsara."[14] In the case of the Goddess, this latter goal may be emended to "that which takes away the *pain and suffering* of samsara (but not necessarily samsara itself)," for liberation is not something wholly apart from this world. The joy and pleasure of the celebration is a foretaste of, or rather participation in, the divine bliss.

In any case, the two aims of prosperity in this world and of liberation are evoked in the closing promise of the Goddess, when she affirms that whoever carries out these festivals becomes both blessed and completely fulfilled. "Blessed," *dhanya,* refers especially to the enjoyment of health, wealth, and other forms of worldly well-being. "Completely fulfilled," *kṛta-kṛtya,* is a common characterization of the person liberated while still living.[15]

Notes

1. This festival is performed in honor of various deities, such as Viṣṇu, Kṛṣṇa, Rāma, and Gaurī (see Kane, *History of Dharmaśāstra,* vol. 5, p. 317). In this festival, an image of the deity is placed on a swing, bathed, and presented the usual *pūjā* offerings, while occasionally rocked back and forth. Nīlakaṇṭha, citing the *Devī Purāṇa,* provides the following details. The festival should be performed on the third day of the bright half of Caitra (March/April). Devī should be worshiped along with Śiva, by offerings of saffron, aloe, camphor, jewels, clothes, perfumes, garlands, scents, incense, and lamps. One should then rock the swing, to please Śiva and Umā (Devī). The *Śiva Purāṇa* (*Umā-Saṃhitā* 51.55–58) gives nearly identical instructions.

The motion of the swing, according to Benjamin Walker, "symbolizes bliss and the cessation of care; a flying motion away from things mundane. The gentle dizziness it causes has a soporific effect and helps to induce ecstatic and trance-like moods. . . . [It also can signify] the cycle of *saṁsāra,* the coming and going of man on the earthly plane, the formation and dissolution of the universe" (*The Hindu World,* vol. 2, p. 470).

2. Regarding these rites, Nīlakaṇṭha refers to details as given in the *Vāmana Purāṇa* {17.3–29}. The *Vāmana* says that on the eleventh day of the bright half of Āṣāḍha (June/July), the Lord of the universe (Viṣṇu), prepares to rest. Then a worshiper should make ready a bed, in the form of the hood of the serpent Śeṣa for Viṣṇu to lie down on. After worshiping the Lord and offering to the image the sacred thread (see next verse), the devotee should then put him to sleep. Over the next several days, various other gods, goddesses, and celestial beings also go to sleep. They stay sleeping through the four months of the rainy season, referred to as the night of the gods. At the end of the night, in the month of Kārttika (October/November), the gods wake up one by one. The *Varāha Purāṇa* (209.30) indicates that the day of awakening *(prabodhanī)* on the eleventh day of the bright half of Kārttika is conducive to both devotion and liberation.

According to Kane, the meaning behind the gods' sleep may lie in the fact that during the rainy season, little movement is possible, and so not much activity takes place. Accordingly, it would be a fitting time for the gods to lie down to rest (*History of Dharmaśāstra,* vol. 5, p. 109). Eck notes: "After the searing hot season, the monsoon season is known for its good sleeping weather. Accordingly, one of the popular notions about the *chaturmāsa* [four months of rain] is that this is a season when Vishnu goes to sleep (*Banaras,* p. 261). Charlotte Vaudeville suggests: "This 'going to sleep' of Viṣṇu most probably symbolizes his reentering the womb of the primeval Mother, who is the primordial Night, that is, Kālī. There the god will lie as an embryo within the dark waters of the womb until he is manifested again at the end of the rainy season" ("Krishna Gopāla, Rādhā, and The Great Goddess," in *The Divine Consort,* p. 3).

The notion of the divine sleep is a bit paradoxical, in as much as the gods, or at least the supreme god, is also considered ever wakeful. In *Devī Gītā* 1.15, Bhuvaneśvarī herself is said to be awake in the Jeweled Island, implying in the context that she is ever looking out for the well-being of her devotees. Also, she is the power of sleep, sleep personified, as the goddess Nidrā.

The *Kālikā Purāṇa* (60) perhaps provides some clues to the idea of divine sleep as applied to the Goddess. The text, in recounting the Great Festival of Durgā (*durgā-mahotsava,* another name for the Navarātra), places her wakening ceremony at the end of the Nine Night rites in Āśvina (September/October). The Goddess is to be awakened on the ninth day (see verses 60.9 and 20)—apparently with songs and instrumental music (see verses 60.14 and 18). She is to be worshiped with offerings *(bali),* and then dismissed on the tenth day. This is loosely tied in to the slaying of Rāvaṇa by Rāma, which also occurred on the same ninth day of Āśvina. The *Kālikā* relates how formerly the Great Goddess was awakened on the first day of the bright half of Āśvina by Brahmā to slay Rāvaṇa. She went to Laṅka to incite Rāma and Rāvaṇa to fight. After watching their battle for seven days, she caused Rāvaṇa to be slain on the ninth day. All the gods then worshiped her and dismissed her on the tenth.

In the same way, the *Kālikā* affirms, the Goddess appears in many other ages, in similar situations, to annihilate demons. Her being wakened *(bodhitā)* is explicitly linked, or even identified, with her becoming manifest *(prādurbhūtā)* (verse 78). Specific mention is made of her slaying of the famous buffalo demon Mahiṣa. She is awakened by the gods, takes on solid form through their energies on the seventh day of the bright half of Āśvina, and finally slays Mahiṣa on the ninth day. She is dismissed and disappears on the tenth. From the perspective of the *Devī Gītā,* one might suggest that the Great Goddess, in her supreme form as Bhuvaneśvarī, is ever awake in her Jeweled Island, but her various forms or incarnations are at rest or asleep until aroused for action in this world. At the same time, the idea of alternating periods of waking and sleeping suggests that the grace of the deity is itself more or less available at different times of the year.

3. The Chariot Festival generally involves taking an image of the deity out of the temple and carrying the god or goddess on a large car or chariot in a grand procession around the surrounding precincts. Such festivals attract large numbers of people, who come to receive the *darśana* or auspicious vision

of the deity, while the deity returns a protecting glance. At the end of the festival, the deity is returned to the temple.

Nīlakaṇṭha cites the instructions for the festival as provided in the *Umā-Saṃhitā* {51.63–69} of the *Śiva Purāṇa.* According to the Purāṇa, the festival is to be performed on the third day of the bright half of Āṣāḍha (June/July) and is very pleasing to the Goddess. The chariot is then given a cosmic identity: the chariot itself is the earth, its wheels the sun and moon, the horses the Vedas, the charioteer Brahmā. The chariot is to be decorated with jewels and flowers, and the Goddess installed thereon. She is to be regarded as surveying the world for the sake of protecting it. As the chariot moves, the devotees are to shout "victory," and to pray for her protection. With such words and with the playing of musical instruments, one is to entertain the Goddess. After proceeding to the boundaries of the district or village, the Mother of the Universe is worshiped and praised, and then returned home.

According to Hazra, the *Devī Purāṇa* (22) indicates that the Devī's chariot festival is to be performed on the ninth day of the bright half of Āśvina (that is, on the ninth day of the autumnal Nine Nights celebration) (*Studies in the Upapurāṇas,* vol. 2, p. 45). Kumar gives a brief summary of the rite as described in the *Devi Purāṇa* (*Śakti Cult in Ancient India,* pp. 189–91).

4. *damanotsava;* the *damana* plant is the *kunda,* a kind of jasmine with white, delicate flowers. It is apparently the same as the *damanaka* plant, and the festival is also known as *damanakotsava* or *damanakāropaṇa* (placing or giving of *damanaka*). See Kane, *History of Dharmaśāstra,* vol. 5, pp. 310–11.

Nīlakaṇṭha provides meager details for this festival, indicating only that it is to be celebrated on the full moon day of Caitra, and that it is described in various Dharmaśāstras and Tantras. The *Garuḍa Purāṇa* (135.2) says of it: "On the bright ninth lunar day of Caitra, one should worship the Devī with Damanaka blossoms; thereby one attains long life, health, prosperity, and victory over enemies. This is the 'Ninth called Damana' *(damanākhyā navamī).*" Teun Goudriaan describes it as "Worship of the *damana* creeper which originated from the tears of Rati and Prīti when their husband Kāma was burnt by a flash from Śiva's third eye" (*Hindu Tantric and Śākta Literature,* p. 68, note 38). According to Goudriaan, the *Tantrarāja Tantra* considers it, as well as the *pavitrāropaṇa* ("thread-offering"), to be an optional *(kāmya)* rite. But in Sanjukta Gupta, Dirk Jan Hoens, and Teun Goudriaan, *Hindu Tantrism* (p. 158), these two rites are regarded as occasional *(naimittika).* The two are often coupled, and indeed the Festival of the Thread-Offering is mentioned in the next verse of the *Devī Gītā* (cf. Jan Gonda, *Medieval Religious Literature in Sanskrit,* p. 214).

5. The Festival of the Thread-Offering (*pavitrotsava,* also referred to as *pavitrāropaṇa*), involves the placing of a necklace made of thread or cord upon the image or emblem of a deity. According to Kane (*History of Dharmaśāstra,* vol. 5, p. 339), the rite "is supposed to make good all defects and mistakes committed in all pūjās." The Thread-Offering ceremony for various deities is described in *Kālikā Purāṇa* 59.35cd–95. The rite for Durgā, to be performed on

the eighth day of Āṣāḍha (June/July) or Śrāvaṇa (July/August), is said to be especially pleasing to the Goddess (verse 35cd–36ab). The *Kālikā* provides minute details for the materials used and procedures for making the thread. The cord is to have various mantras uttered over it, and to be adorned with flowers and anointed with saffron, camphor, and other unguents. After worshiping of the deity, the devotee is to place the cord over the head of the image while reciting the deity's seed mantra. Performing this rite for all the deities brings fruit for a year (that is, makes effective the worship ceremonies performed throughout the succeeding year). A grand cord, consisting of 1008 strands, offered to the Great Goddess, is said to grant both enjoyment and liberation, and to allow the worshiper to reside in heaven for thousands of eons and to "become Śiva" (verses 56cd–58ab).

Goudriaan describes the *pavitrāropaṇa* as "Worship of Devī in a pot with threads wrapped around it" (*Hindu Tantric and Śākta Literature,* p. 68, note 37).

6. *kumārī*s and *baṭukas*; virgins and young boys or young Brahmacārins. They are also the names of various attendant deities waiting upon the Goddess. In the *Kālikā Purāṇa,* four such *baṭuka*s are named, and each is said to have a corresponding maiden *(kumārī).* A devotee is to worship these *baṭuka*s, along with their *kumārī*s (*Kālikā Purāṇa* 63.97–99). In the *Devī Gītā,* the maidens and young boys that are fed are human embodiments of the various forms of the Goddess and her attendants. As the last of this verse indicates, all are simply aspects or manifestations of the Devī.

7. Cf. *Devī-Bhāgavata* 7.30.88–90, where it is said that after worshiping Devī in her various *pīṭha*s one should feed all the Brahmans, as well as the well-dressed maidens and boys.

8. Cf. *Devī Gītā* 7.22.

9. *kṛta-kṛtya;* see *Devī Gītā* 1.3, note 1.

10. Cf. *Devī Gītā* 6.21cd–23ab and the Comment thereon. Cf. also *Devī Gītā* 10.36.

11. See Gonda, *Medieval Religious Literature in Sanskrit,* p. 78.

12. Another example: the *Vāmana Purāṇa* (17) describes a number of *vrata*s, in which are included the "Going-to-sleep" and "Waking" ceremonies; the *Devī Gītā* refers to these latter as festivals. Cf. Kane, *History of Dharmaśāstra,* vol. 5, pp. 57–58, 253.

13. Klaus Klostermaier, *A Survey of Hinduism,* p. 309.

14. These two medieval definitions are quoted by Gonda, *Medieval Religious Literature in Sanskrit,* p. 78, note 193. The first definition is from the *Ānanda-Saṃhitā* (20.1), the second from the *Puruṣottama-Saṃhitā* (23.5).

15. *Dhanya* and *kṛta-kṛtya* are linked together on two other occasions in the *Devī Gītā* : 1.3, and 6.30.

Chapter 9

Vedic and Internal Forms of Goddess Worship

Translation

[Himālaya queries the Goddess about the rules of *pūjā* or ritual worship; she outlines the basic types.]

Hīmālaya spoke:

9.1. O Goddess of the Gods, Great Ruler, Ocean of Compassion, Mother,
Proclaim now in detail the proper manner of your worship.[1]

The Goddess spoke:

9.2. I shall explain the manner of worship, O King, that pleases the Mother.
Listen with great reverence, Best of Mountains.[2]
9.3. My worship is of two kinds: external and internal;[3]
The external also is said to be of two kinds: Vedic and Tantric.[4]
9.4. Vedic worship is also of two kinds, according to the type of image used, O Mountain.[5]
Vedic ritual is to be performed by Vaidikas—those initiated into the Vedas.

9.5. Tantric ritual should be embraced by those initiated into Tantric lore.[6]
One who knows not this mystery regarding worship and who thus acts in a contrary manner,[7]
9.6. Such a person behaves foolishly and falls into utter misery.[8]

Comment

Earlier, in chapter 7, we encountered a typology of devotion *(bhakti)*, based on the *guṇa*s of nature. The distinguishing marks there were subjective, dealing with the motivations of the worshiper. Here we find a typology of the more objective aspects of worship *(pūjā)*, involving the different methods, procedures, and images used. Subjective considerations are not irrelevant, however, for the various methods are seen as more or less appropriate for worshipers of different training and stages of spiritual development.

Typologies of the methods of worship similar to those of the *Devī Gītā* are already found in the *Bhāgavata Purāṇa,* where Kṛṣṇa indicates that he may be worshiped by Vedic, Tantric, and mixed rites.[9] Kṛṣṇa goes on to describe various mental (internal) and external acts of worship, but does not refer to them explicitly as two formal types of *pūjā.* In the *Sūta Saṃhitā,* the brief fifth chapter on Śakti-*pūjā* presents a more elaborate typology of worship forms that includes both the internal/external and Vedic/Tantric divisions. The *Sūta Saṃhitā* may well have served as the model, with some revisions, for the *Devī Gītā.* The *Devī Gītā* goes beyond the *Sūta Saṃhitā* in subdividing the Vedic form into two, according to the two different images of the Goddess utilized. These two images, as explained later, are the cosmic or Virāj form of the Devī and her lovely four-armed form as Bhuvaneśvarī. These forms represent the major mythic and iconic manifestations of the Goddess in our text.

In the above verses the Goddess, like Kṛṣṇa in the *Bhāgavata Purāṇa,* gives her blessings to both the Vedic and the Tantric ways of practice, two paths often viewed as in conflict with each other. The ancient Vedic ideals of the *varṇāśrama-dharma* (social order based on class and stage of life), were for centuries promoted and protected by the Brahmanical, priestly class. By the seventh century C.E., Tantric teachings and practices were becoming sufficiently popular to pose a serious challenge to certain aspects of the Vedic ideals. Especially the

Left-Handed or Vāmācāra forms of Tantricism provoked the distrust of Brahmanical orthodoxy. The Vāmācāra espoused such antinomian practices as the rite of the five *makāras*, involving the drinking of wine, eating of meat, and intercourse between unmarried partners. These practices were based on the assumption that the physical world and the body with all its senses are, or can be under proper instruction and discipline, vehicles for liberation.

The same general assumption, interpreted in "less scandalous" fashion, underlies the Right-Handed Tantra, or Dakṣiṇācāra. The Kuṇḍalinī Yoga described in chapter 5, though fraught with erotic symbolism, can be readily accommodated in the Right-Handed path. The *Devī Gītā*, and the *Devī-Bhāgavata* as a whole, are deeply suspicious of the Vāmācāra, but quite open to the Dakṣiṇācāra. While some Śākta Purāṇas, like the *Mahābhāgavata*, accord more or less equal treatment to the Vedas and Tantras, the *Devī-Bhāgavata* accepts the Tantras only when they do not conflict with the Vedas (see verses 18, 26cd–28ab, and 31 below).[10]

Notes

1. *pūjā;* ritual worship involving the offering of several kinds of material objects (water, flowers, incense, food, clothing) and different kinds of service (a bath, entertainment) to the deity. Such specifics of worship are dealt with in the next chapter, while here the Goddess concentrates on the different forms or images of herself to be used in worship.

2. *Devī Gītā* 9.2–6ab closely parallels *Sūta Saṃhitā* 5.2–6ab. Cf. K. N. Subramanian, "Suta on Sakti Puja," *Tattvāloka* 11, no. 4 (1988): 49–50.

3. On the relation of internal and external worship, see the Comment on 9.38cd–43 below.

4. Cf. *Bhāgavata Purāṇa* 11.27.7, which refers to three types of worship: Vedic, Tantric, and mixed. Cf. also *Bhāgavata Purāṇa* 11.3.47.

5. The *Bhāgavata Purāṇa* (11.27.12) refers to eight kinds of images, according to the type of material used, such as stone, wood, metal, clay, or thought. The same text (11.27.13) also makes a basic twofold division, according to whether an image is movable or not. The *Devī Gītā*'s twofold division is of a different sort, depending on two distinct iconic forms of the Goddess herself, as the text explains below.

6. Cf. *Devī Gītā* 9.32.

7. That is, if a Vaidika worships a Tantric deity, or a Tantrika worships a Vedic deity, without the proper initiation, this is contrary to the proper

order. In commenting on this verse, Nīlakaṇṭha quotes from an unspecified scripture to the effect that whoever abandons one's own deity to worship another attains not the supreme goal but becomes evil.

8. *patati:* "falls into ruin, or misery." Nīlakaṇṭha specifies that the person "falls into hell."

9. See note 4 above.

10. See also *Devī-Bhāgavata* 11.1.24–25, and my *Triumph of the Goddess,* pp. 151–52. For a general discussion of the relative authority of Tantric and Vedic literature, see Chintaharan Chakravarti, *Tantras: Studies on Their Religion and Literature,* pp. 29–37. See also S. C. Banerji, *A Brief History of Tantra Literature,* pp. 110–21.

Translation

[The Goddess speaks of the first type of Vedic worship, focusing on her Virāj form.]

9.6. [cont.] I shall now describe the first kind of Vedic worship mentioned above.
9.7. With your own eyes, O Mountain, you have already seen that supreme form of mine,
So grand with its countless heads and eyes, its countless feet,[1]
9.8. Omnipotent, the impeller behind all action, that form beyond all other forms.[2]
One should constantly worship it, bow to it, contemplate and remember it.
9.9. Such is that form of mine belonging to the first type of worship, O Mountain.
Being calm and mentally composed, without arrogance or pride,
9.10. You should become fully focused on that image, adoring it, taking refuge in it alone.[3]
Behold it in your mind, invoke it, and contemplate it at all times.[4]

9.11. With undistracted devotion and joy, inclining your heart toward me in love,
You should worship with sacrificial rites, and satisfy me completely with austerities and gifts.

9.12. In this way, through my grace, you shall be freed from the bonds of worldly existence.
Those who are fully focused on me, their hearts bound to me, are deemed the best of devotees.

9.13. I promise to rescue them quickly from this worldly existence.[5]

Comment

The image or form involved in the first kind of Vedic worship is that of the Virāj or Cosmic Body of the Goddess, revealed to the gods and Himālaya earlier in chapter 3 (3.22–39). The image, with its renowned countless heads, eyes, and feet, is thoroughly Vedic, as its provenance lies in the famous "Puruṣa Sūkta" of the *Ṛg Veda.*[6]

The *Devī Gītā* in this section no longer follows the typological model of the *Sūta Saṃhitā* but reverts to an earlier Śākta *gītā,* the *Kūrma Devī Gītā.* In the latter, the Goddess Pārvatī reveals her terrifying form as the Virāj to her father (Himālaya), and then remanifests her lovely, two-armed form as Pārvatī. Himālaya, after effusively praising her, inquires what he should do. The Goddess replies, in words similar to the above verses of the *Devī Gītā,* to worship and meditate on her cosmic form. Both the *Kūrma Devī Gītā* and the *Devī Gītā* reflect the ideal of divine, saving grace propounded in the *Bhagavad Gītā.*

The next several verses below appear as something of a digression, leaving for the moment the types of Vedic worship and dealing instead with the authoritativeness of Vedic tradition. The topic is not wholly irrelevant at this point, as the question of the relationship between Vedic and Tantric practices was raised implicitly in the opening verses of the chapter, but was left largely unresolved. Interestingly, the *Kūrma Devī Gītā,* following Pārvatī's words to her father to worship the Virāj form, commences to deal with this very issue, asserting the superiority of Vedic tradition. The composer of the *Devī Gītā,* in his desire to bolster Brahmanical orthodoxy, found the *Kūrma Devī Gītā*'s account much to his liking, and apparently he has utilized many of its verses in his own work. The juxtaposition of the exhortation to worship the Virāj and the tackling of the Vedic/Tantric controversy in the *Kūrma Devī Gītā* was a happy coincidence for our composer.

Notes

1. Cf. *Devī Gītā* 3.37.

2. *parāt-para;* the same term is used to describe the Virāj form of the Goddess in 3.23.

This section of the *Devī Gītā,* beginning with 9.7 and ending with 9.37, is loosely based on the *Kūrma Devī Gītā* of the *Kūrma Purāṇa* (1.11). Lines 9.7ab and 9.8ab of the *Devī Gītā* are nearly identical to *Kūrma Devī Gītā* 259 (*Kūrma Purāṇa* 1.11.259). In the latter, the Goddess speaks these words while still in her Virāj form, and advises Himālaya to worship and meditate upon it. The *Kūrma Devī Gītā* has no explicit classes of worship or any iconic typology like that of the *Devī Gītā,* although it does mention different forms of the Goddess that a devotee may choose to worship (*Kūrma Devī Gītā* 292–94).

3. Lines 9.9cd–10ab reflect, often verbatim, *Kūrma Devī Gītā* 260. Lines 10–13ab also reflect, though more loosely, *Bhagavad Gītā* 18.65–66.

4. According to R. C. Hazra, this verse, as well as verses 22cd–23ab below, are "plagiarized" from the *Bhagavad Gītā* (*Studies in the Upapurāṇas,* vol. 2, pp. 359–60). On the question of plagiarism in the *Devī Gītā,* see the Comment on 6.2–14 above.

5. Cf. *Bhagavad Gītā* 18.65–66, where Kṛṣṇa promises Arjuna: "In this way [through devotion] you will come to me, truly, I promise you. . . . I shall relieve you from all evils."

6. *Ṛg Veda* 10.90. See the Comment on 3.22–34 above.

Translation

[The Goddess interrupts her description of the types of worship to affirm the authority of Vedic tradition regarding righteous action.]

9.13. [cont.] Through meditation accompanied by action,
or through knowledge accompanied by devotion,

9.14. One can always reach me, O King, but never through
actions by themselves.[1]

From righteous action arises devotion; from devotion arises supreme knowledge.[2]

9.15. Vedic revelation and sacred law[3] are recognized sources of righteous action.

Other religious works, it is said, propound merely a reflection of righteous action.

9.16. From me, omniscient and omnipotent, the Veda has arisen.

Since ignorance is absent in me, Vedic revelation lacks nothing in authority.[4]

9.17. The works of sacred law issue forth from Vedic revelation, comprehending its meaning.

Thus sacred law like Manu's, as well as Vedic revelation, is regarded as authoritative.

9.18. In some places on occasion, it is implied that the Tantras constitute another authority.

While the Tantras speak of righteous action, they do so only in part and thus are not relied upon by Vaidikas.

9.19. The teachings of other authors are rooted in ignorance.

Due to the corrupting defect of ignorance, their statements lack authority.

9.20. Therefore, one who desires liberation should depend entirely on the Veda with regard to righteous action.[5]

For just as a king's command in the world is never ignored,

9.21. So my own command in the form of Vedic revelation, proclaimed by me, the Universal Ruler, can hardly be shunned by humans.[6]

Comment

The Goddess above refers to two major categories of Hindu scripture, *śruti* and *smṛti. Śruti,* translated here as "Vedic revelation,"[7] literally means "that which is heard." That is, divine truth, reverberating eternally throughout space in the form of subtle syllables, was heard by ancient seers (*ṛṣis*). These subtle syllables constitute the revelation of supreme knowledge, or Veda. This Veda was later compiled into four collections, known as the four Vedas *(Ṛg, Sāma, Yajur, Atharva)*, yet the fundamental meaning of the term remains supreme knowledge, and thus often appears in the singular (see verses 16 and 20 above).[8] According to the *Devī Gītā* (9.16 and 21), it is the Goddess herself who is the ultimate source of this eternal revelation. Accordingly, since the Goddess is all-knowing, the Veda itself is an infallible and unquestionable source of truth.

While *śruti* is undebatable, it may be interpreted and commented upon by human authors. As long as the commentators are fully conversant with Vedic truth, their works are also considered authoritative. Such works are known as *smṛti*, "that which is remembered." *Smṛti* works are basically written texts—unlike the fundamentally oral nature of *śruti*. They are more accessible to the people at large, and thus play a significant role in day-to-day life, even if their authority is derivative rather than primary. In a broad sense, *smṛti* includes the various law codes, epics, and Purāṇas. Here, however, the sense seems more restricted to just the treatises on law or righteous action (*dharma-śāstras*), such as the famous *Laws of Manu* (see verse 17); thus the term is translated as "sacred law."

In the above verses, the Goddess largely discounts the authority of the Tantras, without completely discrediting them. As the first Comment in this chapter points out, the *Devī Gītā* (and the *Devī-Bhāgavata*) accepts the Tantras so long as they are not in conflict with Vedic tradition. It is the Tantras of the Left-Hand schools that are specifically denounced (cf. lines 27cd–28ab below). For more on the scriptural or revelatory status of the Tantras, see the Comment on verses 26cd–33 below.

Notes

1. Lines 9.13cd–14ab closely parallel *Kūrma Devī Gītā* 264.

2. *para;* literally, "supreme." According to Nīlakaṇṭha, *para* indicates *jñāna* (supreme knowledge), which accords with the basic standpoint of the *Devī Gītā*. One can also interpret the last half of the line to mean: "from devotion arises the supreme (goal)." The whole line (9.14cd) appears in nearly identical form in the *Kūrma Devī Gītā* (266ab).

3. *śruti* and *smṛti;* see Comment above.

4. The word *pramāṇa* ("authority") literally means "measure," or "standard of measure." It comes to signify authoritative testimony or proof, as well

as a means of arriving at correct knowledge. As applied to the Veda, it means undebatable, sacred authority.

5. This line is nearly identical to *Kūrma Devī Gītā* 237cd. Cf. *Mahā-Bhāgavata Purāṇa* 15.64cd.

6. Nīlakaṇṭha, commenting on this line, quotes Pārvatī's words from the *Kūrma Purāṇa* {*Kūrma Devī Gītā* 268}: "That ancient, supreme power of mine, called Veda, in the beginning of creation arose in the form of the *Ṛg*, *Yajur*, and *Sāma* Vedas.

7. In earlier chapters, where the distinction between Vedic and non-Vedic was not an issue, I have translated the term *śruti* most often simply as "scripture" (see 1.26; 1.73; 1.74; 4.22).

8. Cf. note 6 above.

Translation

[The Goddess explains the means by which she combats unrighteousness.]

9.21. [cont.] For the safeguarding of my command, the Brahman and Kṣatriya classes

9.22. I have created.[1] Thus, one should regard my command embodied in Vedic revelation as the secret of good conduct.

Whenever there is a decline in righteousness, O Mountain,

9.23. And a rising up of unrighteousness, then I assume various guises.[2]

And related to this are the different fortunes of the gods and the demons, O King.[3]

9.24. For the sake of teaching those who do not act righteously, I have at all times

Provided hells, terrifying to anyone who hears about them.[4]

9.25. Those who abandon Vedic righteousness to follow another path,

Such unrighteous persons a king should banish from his lands.

9.26. Brahmans should not talk with them; the twice-born should not sit with them at meals.[5]

Comment

The *Devī Gītā* largely follows the *Kūrma Devī Gītā* in recounting the means by which righteousness is maintained, with some significant emendations. First, while both texts identify the Veda with the supreme Śakti, in the *Kūrma Devī Gītā* the Goddess Pārvatī identifies her spouse, the "unborn Lord" (Śiva), as the agent responsible for protecting the Veda. It is he, according to Pārvatī, who created the social classes and provided hells to deter the evil-minded. In the *Devī Gītā,* the Goddess claims direct responsibility for safeguarding the Vedas. Second, and in accord with the more active role of the Goddess in the *Devī Gītā,* our text introduces another means of combating unrighteousness: the direct intervention of the Goddess in the world as an avatara. The *Kūrma Devī Gītā* makes no mention of the avatara doctrine.

The avatara notion, interposed in lines 9.22cd–23ab, closely echoes Kṛṣṇa's pronouncement of his own avataric activity in *Bhagavad Gītā* 4.7. In both *gītās*, the avataric enterprise is triggered by a decline in righteousness. In the *Bhagavad Gītā,* Kṛṣṇa describes his coming into the world by saying, "Then I send forth myself." In the *Devī Gītā,* the Goddess makes the corresponding statement, "Then I assume various guises (or disguises: *veṣān*)." The idea of the avatara as a kind of disguise is absent in the *Bhagavad Gītā,* though it is present in the *Bhāgavata Purāṇa.*[6] The notion of disguise suggests that, in one sense, the deity is merely play-acting in coming into the world and is ultimately unaffected by the mundane turmoil involved in the contest between good and evil.

The term *veṣa* also suggests that the true identity of an avatara may be missed. In this regard, Nīlakaṇṭha makes an interesting comment about *veṣa.* He explains that it refers to the various avataras of the Goddess such as Śākambharī, Rāma, and Kṛṣṇa. The story of Śākambharī ("She-who-bears-vegetables") is told in detail in the *Devī-Bhāgavata*[7] and is briefly mentioned in the *Devī Māhātmya* in its listing of the Goddess' avataras.[8] Śākambharī, thus, is traditionally recognized as an incarnation of the Goddess. The other two incarnations named by Nīlakaṇṭha, however, are usually considered, at least in Vaiṣṇava circles, to be the most famous of Viṣṇu's avataras, who fulfill thoroughly masculine role models as ideal husband and lover, respectively. According to Nīlakaṇṭha, it is the Goddess, not Viṣṇu, who lies beneath the deceptively masculine visages of Rāma and Kṛṣṇa. The disguises encompassed by *veṣa,* then, include the radical transformations of sexual identity.

Notes

1. In the *Kūrma Devī Gītā* (269), Pārvatī declares that "the unborn Lord" created the Brahmans and other classes to protect the Vedas.

2. *veṣa:* "dress, disguise, assumed appearance," referring to her various avataras.
Lines 22cd–23ab are nearly identical to *Bhagavad Gītā* 4.7. Cf. note 4 on *Devī Gītā* 9.10 above.

3. Nīlakaṇṭha clarifies by indicating that the gods are preservers of, and the demons destroyers of, the Vedas. He thus links the ascendancy and good fortune of the gods to times of waxing righteousness, the ascendancy of the demons to times of waning righteousness, due to the appearance or disappearance of the Vedas from earth.

4. In *Kūrma Devī Gītā* 270, Pārvatī ascribes the creation of the hells to the Lord.

5. *Kūrma Devī Gītā* 271cd simply states that one who rejoices in things other than the Veda should not be talked to by the twice-born.

6. The *Bhāgavata Purāṇa* occasionally uses the term *viḍambana* ("imitation, disguise, deception") to refer to Kṛṣṇa's incarnations. See my *Triumph of the Goddess,* pp. 50–51.

7. *Devī-Bhāgavata* 7.28.

8. *Devī Māhātmya* 11.42–45.

Translation

[The Goddess disparages those scriptures opposed to the Vedas.]

9.26. [cont.] The various other religious treatises in this world
9.27. Which are opposed to Vedic revelation and sacred law are entirely based on error.[1]
The scriptures[2] of the Vāmas, Kāpālakas, Kaulakas, and Bhairavas[3]

9.28. Were composed by Śiva for the sake of delusion, and for no other reason.[4]
Due to the curses of Dakṣa, Bhṛgu, and Dadhīca,
9.29. The most excellent of Brahmans were scorched and excluded from the Vedic path.[5]
For the sake of rescuing them step by step, at all times,
9.30. The Śaiva and Vaiṣṇava, the Saura as well as the Śākta,
And the Gāṇapatya scriptures[6] were composed by Śiva.[7]
9.31. In these, there are occasional passages not opposed to the Veda.
There is no fault whatsoever in Vaidikas accepting these.
9.32. A Brahman by all means is not entitled[8] to scriptures having different aims from the Veda;
One who is not entitled to the Veda may be entitled to those other scriptures.[9]
9.33. Therefore with whole-hearted effort a Vaidika should adhere to the Veda.
Knowledge assisted by righteous action will reveal the supreme Brahman.[10]

Comment

Earlier the Goddess referred to the two major classifications of Hindu scriptures known as *śruti* (Vedic revelation) and *smṛti* (sacred law). Another important classification is *āgama* (literally, "that which comes, or is received or acquired"; thus, "acquisition or accumulation [of knowledge], tradition"). *Āgama* as a textual category generally refers to any revealed scripture and may include the Vedas, but usually it is applied to non-Vedic texts that are regarded as revelation by one or another sect. At times, *āgama* is used specifically to refer to a genre of Śaivite texts (revelations of Śiva), while Tantra is used for comparable Śākta texts, but such distinctions are far from absolute or universal.

In *Devī Gītā* 9.27cd, the term *āgama* is used with specific reference to the scriptures of certain Śaivite schools, all belonging to the Left-Handed Tantra, and fully dismissed by the Goddess as delusory teachings. *Āgama* is also used, in 9.30, to refer to the sectarian scriptures of the five major theistic sects whose respective deities, Śiva, Viṣṇu, Sūrya (the Sun), Devī, and Gaṇeśa (or Gaṇapati), are comprehended in the notion of the *pañcāyatana-pūjā.* This ritual, according to tradition, was instituted by the teacher Śaṃkara. It involves the simultaneous worship of all five deities (on "five altars," the literal meaning of the term *pañcāyatana*), symbolizing the idea that they are all simply different manifestations of the one Absolute. All five of the sects, in their more moderate forms, are viewed by the *Devī Gītā* as at least to some degree on the right (Vedic) path. Thus, while Left-Handed Tantric texts lead people wholly astray, causing them to ignore totally the Vedic path and thereby putting them beyond hope of (immediate) salvation, the "*pañcāyatana*" scriptures, while partial or incomplete, are still helpful in leading people back toward the fold of full Vedic orthopraxy.

The interrelated motifs of a curse that induces people to follow scriptures that lead away from the Vedic path and of Śiva's composing such scriptures are not uncommon in the Purāṇic texts.[11] These texts stress that those who lose all contact with the Vedic tradition are bound to suffer in this life, to endure miserable rebirths, or even to descend into various hellish realms. Yet even these people are not wholly lost, for Śiva creates not only fully delusory treatises, but also rehabilitative texts. These latter, we should understand, are of necessity incomplete, for otherwise they would be at once rejected by those adverse to Vedic practice. The sufferings of such apostates, however, have prepared them to accept a watered-down version of the truth. Ultimately, Śiva's creation of both deluding and of rehabilitating texts is all part of his gracious, salvific activity. From the point of view of the *Devī Gītā,* of course, Śiva's saving grace is simply a channel for the Goddess' own divine compassion.

Notes

1. *tāmasa:* "relating to or derived from *tamas,* the quality of darkness, mental darkness, delusion, or error."

2. *āgamas*; see Comment above.

3. The four sects named here are all of the Left-Handed or Vāmācara tradition. The name of the first sect mentioned, the Vāmas, simply means "those of the left" or "left-handed." It is not clear to what specific Tantric

school this may have referred and may be merely a generic designation for Left-Handed schools. The Kāpālakas (or more usually, Kāpālikas) are a well-known Śaivite, Tantric school, now extinct, whose adherents were noted for carrying human skulls (*kapālas*), from which they ate and drank. They engaged in the practice of the five *makāras*. No texts of the school are extant, so that our knowledge of them comes largely from outside, often unsympathetic, sources. The Purāṇas generally disparage the sect as being outside the pale of Vedic orthodoxy. The available sources all agree that the sect worshipped Śiva in his form as Bhairava ("The Frightening One"), and thus the sect of Bhairavas mentioned in the verse may simply be a synonym for the Kāpālikas. (See David N. Lorenzen, *The Kāpālikas and Kālāmukhas,* for detailed information on the sect.) The Kaulakas or Kaulas are a distinct, but closely related school.

Cf. *Kūrma Devī Gītā* (273), where Pārvatī declares: "The scriptures of the Kāpālas, Pañcarātras, Yāmalas, Vāmas, Ārhatas, and various others exist simply in order to delude."

4. In the *Kūrma Devī Gītā* (274), Pārvatī herself takes credit for producing the evil, non-Vedic works, in order to delude those who delude others! According to Lorenzen, another passage in the *Kūrma Purāṇa,* like the *Devī Gītā,* attributes the production of the inferior works to Śiva: "I (Śiva) have declared other *śāstras* which are a source of confusion in this world and are opposed to the word of the Vedas. The Vāma, Pāśupata, Soma, Lāṅgala, and Bhairava *(śāstras)* are declared to be outside the Vedas and are not to be served" (*The Kāpālikas and Kālāmukhas,* p. 11).

The motif of Śiva's producing religious treatises in order to delude people is also found in *Varāha Purāṇa* 70. There a partial explanation is given for such deceptive revelations. The *Varāha* describes a time (the first three ages) when nearly everyone worshiped Viṣṇu, and thus salvation was widespread. This state of affairs worried the other gods, who protested to Viṣṇu: "All the people are on the path to *mukti* (liberation); how will creation continue, and who will dwell in the hells?" Viṣṇu responded by saying that he would introduce delusion in the Kali age, so that people would be confused and few would worship him. Further, Viṣṇu directed Śiva to create deluding treatises (*moha-śāstras*) that would be even more efficient in confusing the people! World order thus seems to demand a balance of the devout and the depraved.

5. Nīlakaṇṭha indicates that the story of the cursing is found in the *Kūrma Purāṇa,* the *Sūta Saṃhitā,* and in other Purāṇas. In the *Kūrma Purāṇa* {1.14}, shortly following the *Kūrma Devī Gītā* itself, there occurs an account of Dadhīca's cursing of Dakṣa and other sages that clearly underlies the *Devī Gītā*'s statement, though some details are obscure.

According to the *Kūrma* version, Dadhīca cursed Dakṣa and his party of fellow Brahman sages for ignoring Śiva as well as the Vedas. Dadhīca condemned them, somewhat redundantly, to be excluded from the Vedas, to be Śiva's enemies, and to be attached to evil treatises. Further, mired in ignorance, they would suffer the terrors of the Kali Yuga, and abandoning all (Vedic) penance, end up in various hells. Then, following the destruction of

Dakṣa's sacrifice by Śiva's emissary Vīrabhadra, Śiva and Pārvatī appeared before Dakṣa, who at last paid homage to them. At Pārvatī's request, Śiva then bestowed his grace upon Dakṣa, rewarding him with, among other things, devotion to Śiva himself. The story concludes by saying that all the sages, burnt by the curse of Dadhīca, were born in the Kali age and fell into hells, and would eventually be freed from the curse by their own former virtues and would be restored to their former positions by the grace of Śiva.

A similar story, relating to Gautama's curse of some jealous Brahmans, occurs in the *Devī-Bhāgavata* (12.9), where the role of Śiva is largely taken over by the Goddess. In that account, Gautama curses the jealous Brahmans to shun the Vedic way of life and to be adverse to the worship of the Devī. Lacking faith in the Vedas and in the Goddess Mūla-Prakṛti, they eventually become Kāpālikas, Kaulas, Buddhists, and Jains. A rather different version of Gautama's curse is found in *Varāha Purāṇa* 71.

6. *āgamas*; see Comment above.

7. The gods of the five schools referred to here constitute the five members of the famous *pañcāyatana-pūjā*. See Comment above.

8. *adhikārin:* "having authority for, qualified for, entitled to." Such authority or qualification is based on a number of considerations, such as social class, ability, spiritual maturity, and especially proper initiation by a worthy teacher, such initiation being based on the previous considerations. Cf. note 5 on *Devī Gītā* 10.33.

9. Cf. *Devī Gītā* 9.4cd–5ab.

10. This verse is nearly identical to *Kūrma Devī Gītā* 285.

11. See notes 4 and 5 above.

Translation

[The Goddess resumes her discussion of the first type of Vedic worship.]

9.34. Abandoning all desires, taking refuge in me alone,[1]
Showing kindness to all beings, leaving behind anger and self-conceit,

9.35. Giving their hearts to me, devoting their life-energies to me, delighting in accounts of my sacred places,[2]
Thus should renouncers, forest-dwellers, householders, and students

9.36. Always, with devotion, practice that yoga focused on my cosmic majesty.[3]
The mental darkness sprung from ignorance of those who are always so absorbed,[4]
9.37. I shall disperse with the sunlight of knowledge, without a doubt.[5]
Such, then, is the first form of Vedic worship, O Mountain,
9.38. Described briefly in its essence.

Comment

The Goddess now recounts the appropriate virtues of those devotees who worship her first Vedic form. These devotees may belong to any stage of life, from student to renouncer, and specifically including the householder. The description here follows closely that of the *Kūrma Devī Gītā.*

Regarding the first Vedic form of worship, the *Devī Gītā* refers to it as the "yoga known as majestic" *(yogam aiśvara-saṃjñitam).* This terminology resonates with the expressions surrounding Kṛṣṇa's display of his own Virāj form in the *Bhagavad Gītā.* The latter twice refers to Kṛṣṇa's cosmic manifestation as his "majestic form" *(rūpam aiśvaram),*[6] and Kṛṣṇa tells Arjuna after bestowing on him the divine eye with which to view the Virāj: "Behold my majestic power *(yogam aiśvaram).*"[7] In the *Bhagavad Gītā,* the phrase *yogam aiśvaram* denotes Kṛṣṇa's divine power by which he creates and sustains the world, and thus is the power reflected or manifested in his cosmic form.[8] The *Kūrma Devī Gītā* and *Devī Gītā* use the phrase to indicate the particular yogic practice in which the devotee focuses on the cosmic majesty of the Goddess, that is, on her Virāj form.

Notes

1. Cf. *Bhagavad Gītā* 18.66, where Kṛṣṇa advises Arjuna: "Abandoning all righteous actions, take refuge in me alone."

2. This line echoes *Bhagavad Gītā* 10.9.

3. *yogam aiśvara-saṃjñitam;* literally, "the yoga known as the lordly, or majestic." As Nīlakaṇṭha indicates, this refers to the meditation on the cosmic or Virāj form of the Goddess. See Comment above.

4. More literally, "ever unseparated [from me]." That is, their thoughts and emotions are always focused on the Goddess.

5. Lines 36cd–37ab echo *Bhagavad Gītā* 10.11.
The section up to this point (verses 9.34–37ab) follows *Kūrma Devī Gītā* 286–89, sometimes verbatim.

6. *Bhagavad Gītā* 11.3 and 11.9.

7. *Bhagavad Gītā* 11.8.

8. See *Bhagavad Gītā* 9.5 as well as 11.8.

Translation

[The Goddess describes the second type of Vedic worship, focusing on her form as Bhuvaneśvarī.]

9.38. [cont.] Hear now the second type.
Either in an icon, on prepared ground, in the orb of the sun or moon,
9.39. In water, in a Bāṇa-Liṅga,[1] on a sacred diagram,[2] on a cloth,
Or also in the auspicious lotus of one's own heart, one should meditate on the supreme Goddess.[3]
9.40. She is endowed with fine qualities, filled with compassion, youthful, red like the dawn,
The quintessence of beauty, lovely in every limb.
9.41. She is filled with the sentiment of passion and is ever distressed by the sorrows of her devotees;
Disposed to kindness, she is the Mother bearing a crescent moon in her locks.
9.42. She holds a noose and goad while gesturing her beneficence and assurance of safety;[4] she is bliss incarnate.
One should worship her with such offerings as one can afford.
9.43. Until one is prepared[5] for internal worship,
A person should continue to perform this external worship; only when prepared should one abandon it.[6]

Comment

The second type of Vedic worship involves the image of the beautiful, four-armed Bhuvaneśvarī, described at length in chapter 1. While historically Bhuvaneśvarī seems to have arisen within Tantric circles from the ten Mahāvidyās,[7] her Vedic pedigree is affirmed, in the mythic terms of the *Devī Gītā*, by the story of her manifestation out of the blazing circle of light known as *mahas*, identified with the supreme Brahman of the Upaniṣads.[8] The two Vedic forms of the Goddess, as the Virāj and as Bhuvaneśvarī, are also her two major iconic manifestations in the *Devī Gītā*.

The different media on which worship of the Goddess may be performed are quite varied. The *Kālikā Purāṇa* says *pūjā* is to be performed on prepared ground, on blazing fire, on water, on the rays of the sun, on icons, on the Śālagrama stones (sacred to Viṣṇu), on Śiva-liṅgas, or on any stones.[9] The same text elsewhere gives a somewhat different list of media: a *liṅga*, a book, prepared ground, sandals, icons, a painting, a trident, a sword, water, a stone, a mountain top, and a mountain cave.[10] Thus, both natural and artificial objects may be used to represent, or may manifest within themselves, the presence of the Goddess. Some, like fire, water, and the sun or moon, represent fundamental aspects of nature through which her power flows. Others, like the book, point to her watchful care over the various fields of human endeavor. Such external objects help to focus the mind, allowing one to visualize more clearly the beautiful form and/or qualities of Bhuvaneśvarī herself.

One important medium is one's own heart (chapter 10 of the *Devī Gītā* elaborates on this medium). At this point, the line between external and internal types of worship begins to break down, for here the image (Bhuvaneśvarī) apparently belongs to the external mode, but the medium is internal. According to the *Sūta Saṃhitā*, such worship is considered internal, but "with conceptual support" (see the Comment on 9.44–47 below).

Regarding the relation between internal (or mental) and external worship, one scholar notes: "Tantras . . . lay the greatest emphasis on mental worship *(mānasa-pūjā)*. In fact, this *pūjā* is regarded as far superior to external *pūjā*. Some Tantras go so far as to assert that without *mānasa pūjā*, external *pūjā* is futile. The *Śāktānanda-taraṅgiṇī* holds that the search for god outside, having disregarded god within one's ownself *[sic]*, is like the quest of glass after ignoring the *kaustabha* jewel within one's own hand."[11] At the same time, other Tantric texts, such as the *Mahānirvāṇa Tantra*, regard some form of internal worship as mental preparation for the external (see *Devī Gītā* 1.24, note 5). This is the approach of the *Devī Gītā* in the next chapter, dealing with Tantric worship, which according to 9.3 above, is considered an external form of worship. Here in this chapter, however, the *Devī Gītā* views external worship as a necessary prerequisite for the more advanced, internal practice, about to be described.

Notes

1. On the Bāṇa-liṅga, see *Devī Gītā* 5.40, note 22.

2. *yantra;* a geometrical design, utilizing triangles, squares, circles, lotus petals, and a central point to represent the physical and metaphysical levels of the cosmos, the human body, and one's chosen deity. The *yantra* serves as a device in Tantric worship whereby the devotee is able to identify his or her body with the body of the divine.

3. Cf. *Bhāgavata Purāṇa* 11.27.9, where Kṛṣṇa says: "One should worship me in an image, on prepared ground, in fire, in water, in the heart, in a Brahman. . . . "

4. These four emblems and gestures are the major identifying characteristics of the beautiful, four-armed Bhuvaneśvarī. See *Devī Gītā* 1.39, note 2, and the Comment on 1.30–41.

5. *adhikāra;* refers to the entitlement of a person to certain practices or teachings, based on spiritual fitness as well as appropriate initiation. Cf. *Devī Gītā* 9.32, note 8, and note 5 on 10.33.

6. Cf. *Sūta-Saṃhitā* 5.10: "If one is qualified for the internal worship, then the wise person will abandon this external worship and resort to the supreme (internal worship)."

7. See the Introduction, p. 23–26.

8. See *Devī Gītā* 1.26–41.

9. *Kālikā Purāṇa* 57.184–85ab.

10. *Kālikā Purāṇa* 58.31–33.

11. Banerji, *Tantra in Bengal,* p. 12.

Translation

[The Goddess describes internal worship.]

9.44. Internal worship, according to tradition, comprises dissolution into pure consciousness.[1]
Pure consciousness alone, devoid of finitude,[2] is my supreme form.

9.45. Thus, focus your awareness on my form that is pure consciousness, without using any conceptual support.[3]
What appears outside this pure consciousness as the world, composed of illusion, is false.[4]
9.46. Thus, to dispel the world-appearance, upon the supreme witness in the form of the Self,[5]
One should meditate without doubts and with a heart disciplined through yoga.[6]
9.47. Now, then, I shall describe at length the final type of external worship.
Listen with an attentive mind, Best of Mountains.

Comment

As mentioned in the Comment on verses 9.1–6ab, the *Sūta Saṃhitā* may well have served as the model for the *Devī Gītā*'s typology of worship modes, though there are some differences. The *Devī Gītā* subdivides the Vedic type into two (focusing on the Virāj and Bhuvaneśvarī, respectively), a distinction absent in the *Sūta Saṃhitā*. Further, the *Devī Gītā* makes only indirect reference to the *Sūta Saṃhitā*'s subdivision of the internal worship into two: with conceptual support *(sādhārā)* and without such support *(nirādhāra)*. This latter is defined in the *Sūta Saṃhitā* as focusing on pure consciousness, into which the mind dissolves, and is considered the highest form of worship.[7] It clearly is identical to the *Devī Gītā*'s internal worship, described as "without conceptual support" *(nirāśraya)*.

The *Sūta Saṃhitā* defines the internal worship with conceptual support as utilizing an imagined or visualized form *(varṇa-saṃkḷpta-vigraha)* of the supreme Goddess.[8] The *Devī Gītā* seems to include this type of *pūjā* under the category of external worship of Bhuvaneśvarī, even when the medium of worship is one's own heart (9.39) rather than an outward symbol. For the *Devī Gītā*, apparently, the form of the Goddess is the most important characteristic in determining the type of *pūjā*.

In any case, both the *Sūta Saṃhitā* and the *Devī Gītā* suggest a smooth progression of worship, proceeding from gross to subtle forms, and from external to internal focus. For the *Devī Gītā*, the devotee begins with the gross, Cosmic Body or Virāj, then moves on to the more benign and refined form of the Goddess as Bhuvaneśvarī, first using some external support such as an icon or *yantra,* before internalizing the image in his or her own heart. Finally, the worshiper does away with all images, all thoughts, concentrating on and merging into the pure consciousness that is the supreme form of the Goddess beyond all form.

The final type of external worship mentioned in the last verse is the Tantric, the main subject of the next and concluding chapter of the *Devī Gītā.*

Notes

1. Cf. *Sūta Saṃhitā* 5.13cd: "The [internal] worship is said to focus on pure consciousness, into which the mind dissolves."

2. *upādhi;* translated earlier (3.5; 4.3; 4.26; 4.28; 4.30) as "apparent limitation" or "limiting condition." The limiting conditions are those of finitude, such as space, time, and matter.

3. *nirāśraya:* "without support or dependence on anything." Specifically, it here refers to meditation on the infinite form of the Goddess as pure consciousness, without the aid even of a mental image or concept of her since pure consciousness is beyond all form and thought. The *Sūta Saṃhitā* (5.11–13) uses the synonymous term *nirādhārā* to refer to this type of worship.

4. *mithyā;* cf. *Devī Gītā* 2.18cd, 4.26ab.

5. Lines 9.45cd–46 summarize *Sūta Saṃhitā* 5.14–15: "Whatever appears outside pure consciousness is called the transmigrating world *(saṃsāra)* of all selves. Thus, to dispel the world, one should worship the supreme witness in the form of the Self, the supreme Śakti devoid of the enchanting world-appearance."

6. Nīlakaṇṭha interprets yoga here as *bhakti-yoga.*

7. *Sūta Saṃhitā* 5.12–13.

8. Cf. *Bhāgavata Purāṇa* 3.28, where the meditation on Viṣṇu's auspicious form is introduced as *sabīja yoga,* "yoga using a seed (support)" (3.28.1).

Chapter 10

The Tantric Form of Goddess Worship and the Disappearance of the Great Goddess

Translation

[The Goddess sets forth the preliminaries of Tantric worship.]

The Goddess spoke:

10.1. Rising at dawn, one should call to mind the radiant lotus on the top of the head,[1]
Shining like camphor. On that lotus one should recollect the form of one's own blessed guru,[2]
10.2. Kindly disposed, adorned with shining ornaments, conjoined with his consort.[3]
The wise person will bow to them, and then calling to mind the coiled Goddess Kuṇḍalī, will reflect:
10.3. "She shines brilliantly[4] in her ascent; she appears like nectar in her descent;
I take refuge in that woman[5] who wanders along the middle channel in the form of bliss."[6]

Figure 10.1 Bhuvaneśvarī on Her Throne of Five Corpses (verses 10.9–12ab). Pencil drawing by Dr. Bala Viswanathan.

10.4. Meditating in this manner, focusing on my form as infinite being, consciousness, and bliss that dwells in the internal flame,[7]
One should meditate on me. Next one should complete all those rites beginning with personal cleansing.[8]
10.5. The best of Brahmans should then offer oblations into the sacred fire[9] in order to please me.
After the fire offering one should take a firm seat and resolve to complete the worship ceremony.[10]

Comment

Tantric practice takes two basic forms: meditative yoga of the Kuṇḍalinī type (described in chapter five of the *Devī Gītā*), and ritual worship (*pūjā*), the main topic of this chapter. The two reinforce each other, and are regarded by Tantrics as equally important.[11] The explicit reference to Kuṇḍalinī Yoga at the beginning of the *pūjā* performance in verses 10.2cd–3 attests to the complementary nature of the two sets of practices.

The various preliminary steps in Tantric worship described above are part of what the *Devī-Bhāgavata Purāṇa* in its eleventh book refers to as "customary observances" or "proper conduct" (*ācāra, sad-ācāra*). The Purāṇa describes this *ācāra* as "the foremost duty (*dharma*) declared in the *śruti* and *smṛti*."[12] There are two fundamental sources of *ācāra*, the religious treatises (*śāstra*s) and popular custom (*laukika*), both of which are to be observed.[13] The *Devī-Bhāgavata* accepts as valid those statements about *dharma/ācāra* that one may find in various texts, including the Tantras, so long as they do not contradict the Veda.[14] Accordingly, then, the customary observances endorsed by the *Devī-Bhāgavata* may be referred to as Vedācāra (practices conforming to Vedic norms), although they encompass disciplines like Kuṇḍalinī Yoga that are of Tantric provenance.

The distinction between Tantric and Vedic is far from clear, for these two modes of religious observance "have not unoften been hopelessly intermixed making it difficult to separate the one from the other."[15] In addition to Kuṇḍalinī Yoga, such practices as "purification of the physical elements" (*bhūta-śuddhi*; see 10.6ab), "mystic installation" of letters and mantras on the body (*nyāsa*; see 10.6cd–8ab), the use of certain kinds of protective spells (*kavaca*; see 10.22ab), mantras and seed syllables like "Hrīṃ," and sacred diagrams (*yantras*; see 10.18ab) are regarded as Tantric, though these often have Vedic parallels or antecedents.[16] Further confusing the issue is the fact that certain Vedic rites, like the fire offering (*agni-hotra, homa*), have been assimilated into Tantra. The Tantric style of performance, in the case of the *homa*, emphasizes the identity of the worshiper, the fire, and the deity invoked (see note 20 on 10.26).[17]

Certain late Tantric texts refer to seven ways or sets of proper conduct, the first of which is Vedācāra. The next three ways still observe the Vedācāra, and all of the first four are part of the Dakṣiṇācāra (Right-Handed path). The last three are classified as Vāmācāra (Left-Handed path), going beyond the Vedic rituals and introducing the five *makāras* (eating meat, consuming wine, etc.).[18] The *Devī Gītā* wholly rejects the Left-Handed Tantra, while approving the Right-Handed.[19] The latter, permeated throughout by the Vedācāra, thus imbues its Tantric practices with the aura of Vedic orthopraxy dear to the author of the *Devī Gītā*.

The specific requirements of proper Vedic conduct or Vedācāra are set forth in the form of suitable daily routines. The eleventh book of the *Devī-Bhāgavata* provides the following general pattern for the first part of the day. One should rise at dawn and begin meditating on various subjects: the Self or Brahman, one's chosen deity, and one's guru.[20] The ideal of identification between the meditator and the subject of meditation is emphasized. As one passage states: "The wise person should rise at dawn and fully observe proper conduct. . . . For some time one should reflect on one's chosen deity and meditate on Brahman. . . . By this meditation, one quickly realizes the oneness of the *jīva* and Brahman, and one immediately becomes liberated while living (*jīvan-mukta*)."[21] Then one should answer the calls of nature and take care of personal hygiene. Following the morning prayers, *homa* is to be performed, and so on. The *Devī Gītā* here in the tenth chapter provides a brief outline of this daily routine.

Of particular relevance to the *Devī Gītā* is the description of the early morning meditation on the Goddess Kuṇḍalinī found in the eleventh book of the *Devī-Bhāgavata*. The latter presents an expanded form of the meditation summarized above in verse 10.3. The meditation as given in the eleventh book is as follows:

> She [the Kuṇḍalinī] resides on the ruddy lotus [the *mūlādhāra*].
> She is blood-red in color and has "Hrīṃ" for her symbol.
> She is like a lotus-filament.

Her face is the sun, her breasts the moon.
If she dwells just once in one's heart, one is liberated.
She is [all acts]: sitting, coming, going, understanding, reflecting, lauding, singing. I am universal and divine; all [my acts and] praise are worship of you [the Devī].
I am the Goddess; you are not other [than I]. I am Brahman, free of sorrow.
I am infinite being, consciousness, and bliss. Thus should one reflect on one's Self.
She shines brilliantly in her ascent; she appears like nectar in her descent;
I take refuge in that woman who wanders along the middle channel in the form of bliss.[22]

The last two lines are identical with 10.3 above. The more complete text from the eleventh book makes clear the underlying notion of identification and interpenetration between the worshiper and the Goddess. Such interpenetration is a much repeated theme of Tantric worship (see the Comment on 10.12cd–16ab below).

The fact that the various preliminaries discussed above are part of the Vedācāra also makes clear that Tantric worship should be a daily part of one's life. Daily worship of the Goddess in the prescribed, Tantric manner is thus regarded as part of the routine of proper living. Even the most spiritual, self-realized Tantric, who in one sense has transcended the necessity for ritual practice, remains committed to the daily fulfillment of such worship.[23]

In general terms, the various ritual acts of Tantric *pūjā* described above and continued below may be divided into three main groups, frequently overlapping. First are the purificatory rites involving cleansing of the self, the place of worship, the mantra and all materials used in the ritual, and the deity worshiped. Second are the protective rites to remove potential obstacles and to prevent the interference of malevolent spirits in the performance of the *pūjā*. And third, there are the actual offering of gifts and services to the Goddess.[24]

Notes

1. As Nīlakaṇṭha explains, this refers to the mystical Lotus of a Thousand Petals (the *sahasrāra*) situated on the Brahmic aperture (*brahmarandhra*).

2. Cf. *Devī-Bhāgavata* 11.1.48–49: "Within the top of one's skull (*brahmarandhra*) one should meditate on and worship the guru as the Lord. . . . The guru is Brahmā, the guru is Viṣṇu, the guru is the god Maheśvara (Śiva); the guru indeed is the supreme Brahman. Hail to that one, the blessed guru!" For the importance of the guru in the *Devī Gītā*, see 6.23cd–28ab.

3. *śakti*, glossed by Nīlakaṇṭha as *sva-patnī*. He adds: "If one's guru is the Mother, then one should meditate upon her conjoined with her consort."

4. In the form of consciousness (*cit*), according to Nīlakaṇṭha.

5. *abalā:* without strength; a woman. A paradoxical epithet, as indicated by Nīlakaṇṭha's gloss of the term as *parā śakti*. The early twentieth-century devotee, Vasishtha Ganapati Muni, in his poem *Umasahasram*, lauds the Goddess in a series of paradoxical qualities, such as her having the universe for her body yet being slender, dark yet fair, and including: being "the power of all, yet weak (*sarvasya śāktir abalā*)" (14.2) (in M. P. Pandit, ed., *Adoration of the Divine Mother; Gems from Umasahasram*, p. 98).

6. This verse refers to the ascent of the Goddess in her form as the Serpent Power (Kuṇḍalī or Kuṇḍalinī) from the Root Support Center (*mūlādhāra*) at the base of the spine through the central channel of the *suṣumṇā* to the Lotus of a Thousand Petals at the top of the head. There she unites with Śiva, producing ambrosial nectar, with which she then descends back to the Root Support Center. See *Devī Gītā* 5.27–51.

7. *śikhā;* Nīlakaṇṭha interprets the flame as the fire of consciousness of the Kuṇḍalinī dwelling internally in the Root Support Center. Nīlakaṇṭha quotes a passage from the "Taittirīya scripture" {*Mahānārāyaṇa Upaniṣad* 13.12}, which asserts that the supreme Self dwells in the midst of the flame (near the heart, or in the *suṣumnā*).

8. *śauca:* "purity." Here, it refers to the purifying or cleansing rites performed after attending to the calls of nature. Nīlakaṇṭha adds that the set of rites referred to here end with the morning prayers (*sandhyā-vandana*).

9. *agni-hotra;* the sacrificial fire into which various offerings, especially clarified butter (*ghee*), are made. Cf. 10.26, note 20, below.

10. *pūjā-saṃkalpam;* this resolution, once made, commits the worshiper to completing the *pūjā*, allowing no interruptions until the final mantras are said. A contemporary manual giving instructions for the worship of the modern woman saint and incarnation of the Goddess, Mata Amritanandamayi, provides the following resolution: "Now, at this auspicious moment, in the time of Eternity, in the place of Omnipresence, on this auspicious day, may I please You, O . . . Devi. That I may attain devotion, wisdom and dispassion, I undertake to perform this worship of the Supreme Goddess" (*Puja: The Process of Ritualistic Worship*, p. 8).

11. See Sanjukta Gupta, Dirk Jan Hoens, and Teun Goudriaan, *Hindu Tantrism*, p. 123.

12. *Devī Bhāgavata* 11.1.9ab.

13. *Devī Bhāgavata* 11.1.16.

14. Cf. *Devī Gītā* 9.13cd–33, especially verses 26cd–31.

15. Chintaharan Chakravarti, *Tantras: Studies on Their Religion and Literature,* p. 80.

16. For an excellent discussion of what constitutes Tantric doctrine and ritual practice, see Douglas Renfrew Brooks, *The Secret of the Three Cities,* pp. 54–72. See also Gupta, Hoens, and Goudriaan, *Hindu Tantrism,* pp. 121–24.

17. It is tempting to see Vedic and Purāṇic worship as emphasizing a distinction between the worshiper and the worshiped, while Tantric emphasizes their identity. Thus, S. C. Banerji writes: "The Tāntric mode of worship, full of *mantras* and *kavacas,* is similar to the Purāṇic [Vedic-Purāṇic] mode. The difference is that the Tāntric worshipper identifies himself with the deity worshipped. But, the follower of the Purāṇa does not do so; he is ever conscious that he is finite with limited capacity whereas God is infinite with unlimited power" (*A Brief History of Tantra Literature*). (Banerji expresses the same view in his *Tantra in Bengal,* p. 23.) But such a view oversimplifies a complex situation, for many Purāṇas, influenced by Advaita as well as by Tantra, stress the unity and/or identity of the devotee and God.

18. The seven *ācāras* are Vedācāra, Vaiṣṇavācāra, Śaivācāra, Dakṣiṇācāra, Vāmācāra, Siddhāntācāra, and Kulācāra. For discussion of these *ācāras,* see Banerji, *Tantra in Bengal,* pp. 186–90; and Narendra Nath Bhattacharyya, *History of the Tantric Religion,* pp. 341–47.

19. See the Comment on 9.26cd–33.

20. Cf. *Mahānirvāṇa Tantra* chapter 5 for a lengthy description of these preliminary rites.

21. *Devī-Bhāgavata* 11.2.2–4.

22. *Devī-Bhāgavata* 11.1.44–47.

23. Cf. Gupta, Hoens, and Goudriaan: "The importance of *pūjā* [for Tantrics] cannot be exaggerated. From the time of his initiation till the end of his life, every Tantric is bound by the duty of performing his daily pūjā" (*Hindu Tantrism,* p. 121).

24. For discussion of this threefold division of rites, see Gupta, Hoens, and Goudriaan, *Hindu Tantrism,* pp. 134–36. Chapter 5 of their *Hindu Tantrism,* on "Tantric Sādhanā: Pūjā," includes an excellent overview of the basic steps in the Tantric daily worship of the Goddess (pp. 121–57). Their overview supplements many of my own Comments in explaining the details of Tantric *pūjā* referred to in the *Devī Gītā.*

Translation

[The Goddess summarizes the procedures for transforming the physical body into a divine body.]

10.6. First one should purify the material elements within oneself.[1] Then install upon the body the maternal powers embedded in the alphabet.[2]
One should always install next the maternal powers embedded in the Hṛllekhā mantra.[3]

10.7. Fix the letter *H* in the Root Support Center, the letter *r* in the heart,
The letter *ī* between the brows, and install the entire syllable *Hrīṃ*[4] on the top of the head.

10.8. One should then finish all other mystic installations, which will be empowered by this mantra.

Comment

The Goddess here briefly outlines two interrelated and overlapping Tantric procedures for realizing the identity of oneself with the supreme—the purification of material elements within the body, or *bhūta-śuddhi*, and the installation of the maternal powers, or *mātṛkā-nyāsa*. She merely mentions the first procedure, *bhūta-śuddhi*, but a full description of this meditative ritual is found later in the *Devī-Bhāgavata*.[5] As explained there, the process is similar to Kuṇḍalinī Yoga and involves the dissolution or destruction of the old body and the creation of a new, purified and divine body. The Kuṇḍalinī is visualized as ascending the central channel to the Brahmic aperture, while the material elements associated with the different levels of the body are progressively dissolved back into the preceding element (earth into water, water into fire, etc.), and eventually all is merged back into the supreme Self. Becoming pure consciousness, one then visualizes within the body a symbolic person representing all one's evil tendencies (the *pāpa-puruṣa*). This sinful person is then burnt with the fire of breath control, and the ashes are then revived with divine nectar and transformed into a new, divine body. This body, infused with the life-breath of the Devī, is now the body of the Goddess herself.[6]

The process of infusing the life-breath or life (*jīva*) of the deity into one's body is called *jīva-nyāsa* ("installation of life"). It is the first in a series of infusions or installations of various psychospiritual powers into the new body and ties the procedures of *bhūta-śuddhi* together with the following rites of *mātṛkā-nyāsa* and the more specialized *hṛllekhā-mātṛkā-nyāsa*. *Mātṛkā-nyāsa* involves the installation of the mystic powers of all fifty letters of the Sanskrit alphabet, referred to as "Mothers" (*mātṛkās*). The installation of these powers is done by touching various parts of the body with the fingertips and palms of the hands, while pronouncing appropriate mantras. The identification of the letters with the *mātṛkās* is explained by a contemporary Indian scholar in the following way:

> All sounds are made up of the fifty letters (*varṇa*) of the alphabet (Sanskrit alphabet, including the vowels and the consonants), and all the sounds are modes and modifications of the one power of the Mother. These letters are therefore called the *mātṛkās* (diminutive forms of *mātṛ*, mother). A common practice in Tāntric worship is to make *mantras* out of each one of the letters and associate them with different parts of the body; the idea behind it is to feel that the different parts of our body are but the objectification of the different aspects of the great Mother, i.e., the whole body, with all its biological and psychological processes, is but an instrument in and through which the divine power is having its display. This actually is a process of self-surrender, surrender both of body and mind.[7]

The *hṛllekhā-mātṛkā-nyāsa*, from the point of view of the *Devī Gītā*, is simply the infusion of the most powerful set of all letters, those of the seed syllable Hrīṃ of the Goddess Bhuvaneśvarī herself. This syllable, manifesting the essential or heart energy of the Goddess, once infused into the central axis of one's body, empowers all further infusions.

There are many other kinds of installations, such as *aṅga-nyāsa* (installation of letters on the limbs of the body) and *kara-nyāsa* (installation on the hands and fingers). The *Śāradā-Tilaka Tantra* mentions a number of different *nyāsas*, including *mātṛkā-nyāsa*, *mantra-nyāsa*, and concluding with *pīṭha-nyāsa*.[8] This latter is the installation within the body of the sacred seat or altar of one's chosen deity. The installation of Bhuvaneśvarī's altar or sacred throne is the Devī's next topic of discussion.

Notes

1. *bhūta-śuddhi.* See Comment above, and cf. Agehananda Bharati, *The Tantric Tradition*, p. 112, and Wade T. Wheelock, "The Mantra in Vedic and Tantric Ritual," pp. 102–103.

2. *mātṛkā-nyāsa:* literally, "installation of the 'Mothers'." These "Mothers" (*mātṛkās*) represent the fifty letters of the Sanskrit alphabet, symbolizing various deities and/or powers, all of which derive from the supreme Goddess or World-Mother. Accordingly, I have translated *mātṛikās* as "maternal powers embedded in the alphabet." For the specific procedures and significance of installing these alphabetic powers, see the Comment above.

3. This is the seed syllable Hrīṃ. For discussion of the Hṛllekhā, see *Devī Gītā* 1.25, note 8.

4. For a discussion of this syllable, see *Devī Gītā* 1.53, note 24.

5. *Devī-Bhāgavata* 11.8.

6. Cf. *Mahānirvāṇa Tantra,* 5.93–105.

7. Shashi Bhusan Dasgupta, *Aspects of Indian Religious Thought,* p. 36.

8. *Śāradā-Tilaka Tantra* 4.31–42.

Translation

[The Goddess describes the installation of her sacred throne.]

10.8. [cont.] One should further visualize within the body my sacred throne with its legs consisting of righteousness and the like.[1]

10.9. The wise person should then meditate upon the Great Goddess, visualizing me in the breath-expanded Lotus of the heart,[2] on my sacred resting place that is the seat of the five corpses:[3]

10.10. Brahmā, Viṣṇu, Rudra, Īśvara, and Sadāśiva. These five great corpses reside under my feet.

10.11. They have the nature of the five elements, and also the nature of the five states of consciousness.[4] But I, in the form of unmanifest consciousness, transcend them altogether.[5]

10.12. Thus they have come to constitute my throne forever, according to the Tantras of Śakti.

Comment

The *Devī Gītā*'s description of the sacred throne of the Goddess is a bit puzzling at first. On the one hand, the throne is said to have righteousness (*dharma*) and the like for its legs, and on the other it is said to be the seat of the five corpses (*pañca-pretas*). How do these two notions relate?

The image of the throne with legs consisting of righteousness and the like is explained more fully in the twelfth book of the *Devī-Bhāgavata*, in an account of the rules for initiation (*dīkṣā*). The procedures for initiation loosely parallel those described here in the *Devī Gītā* as preliminaries for worship. According to the twelfth book, the teacher, after performing the morning rituals, including *bhūta-śuddhi* and *mātṛkā-nyāsa*, installs the mystic throne within the body in the following manner. On the right shoulder the guru installs righteousness (*dharma*), on the left shoulder knowledge (*jñāna*), on the left thigh dispassion (*vairāgya*), and on the right thigh prosperity (*aiśvarya*). Then the opposites of these four qualities, unrighteousness (*adharma*), etc., are installed on the mouth, left side, navel, and right side, respectively. The four positive qualities are to be considered as the legs of the throne, the four negative ones as the limbs or sides. In the midst of this seat, in the heart, one installs the serpent Ananta as a soft cushion, on which one places a lotus symbolizing the universe of five elements (*prapañca-padma*). Further installations are named, and then the account concludes: "One should worship this throne, and visualize upon it the supreme Mother."[6]

The *Devī-Bhāgavata*'s description of this throne composed of abstract qualities is likely based on the *Śāradā-Tilaka Tantra*. The latter, in its rules of initiation, provides a nearly identical explanation, but concludes with a more general prescription: one is to visualize one's chosen deity (*iṣṭa-devatā*) on the throne (rather than the supreme Mother, unless she is one's chosen deity).

Both the *Devī-Bhāgavata* and the *Śāradā-Tilaka*, after dealing with further preparatory rituals, go on to describe the actual worship of the sacred throne. The *Devī-Bhāgavata*'s account is much abbreviated,[7] while the *Śāradā-Tilaka* provides the following details.[8] One is to visualize the throne as situated on top of an ascending series of cosmic supports, beginning with the foundational Ādhāra-śakti (supporting power of the universe), upon which rests the world-supporting tortoise, then the serpent Ananta, and the Earth. The Earth is surrounded by oceans [including the Ocean of Nectar, though this is not explicitly mentioned], in which is a Jeweled Island. On the Island is a chamber of gems (*cintāmaṇi-maṇḍapa*), surrounded by celestial Kalpa trees. Beneath the trees is a brilliant altar, on which rests the throne of abstract qualities.[9]

The symbolic setting of the sacred throne on the Jeweled Island at the pinnacle of the cosmic supports helps to explain the connection of the throne with the five corpses. The Jeweled Island, of course, is Bhuvaneśvarī's supreme celestial paradise. In book twelve of the *Devī-Bhāgavata*, there is an extended account of this island paradise, with its magnificent mansions. The chief of all these mansions is the Devī's own palace, known as the chamber of gems (*cintāmaṇi-gṛha*). Within this is a splendorous sofa (*mañca*),[10] on which the Goddess sports while residing in her celestial home. This sofa is described as having ten stairs composed of the elemental powers (*śakti-tattvas*),[11] and with Brahmā, Viṣṇu, Rudra, and Iśvara for its legs, and Sadāśiva for its seat. The *Devī Gītā* has thus identified the throne of abstract qualities that is to be installed in one's body with the luxurious sofa on which the Goddess reclines in her supreme paradise.

This motif of the Devī's heavenly throne composed of the five gods or corpses (*pañca-pretāsana*) is a common one within the Śākta/Tantric tradition.[12] In the *Tripurā-Rahasya*, following a brief description of the Jeweled Island, the Goddess Tripurā claims for her throne a sofa "composed of the five Brahmā-gods" (*pañca-brahma-maya muñca*).[13] In the *Lalitā Sahasranāma*, among the thousand names of the Goddess are the epithets, "She-who-is-seated-on-the-throne-composed-of-the-five-corpses" (*pañca-pretāsanāsīnā*), "She-whose-forms-are-the-five-Brahmās" (*pañca-brahma-svarūpiṇī*), and "She-who-reclines-upon-the-couch-of-the-five-corpses" (*pañca-preta-mañcādhiśāyinī*).[14] And in the *Saundaryalaharī*, there is reference to the throne, situated in the chamber of gems on the Jeweled Island, as the "sofa in the form of Śiva" (*śivākāre*).[15] The same text also affirms that the gods Brahmā, Hari, Rudra, and Īśvara have merged into the sofa of the Goddess.[16] Finally, in the "Lalitopākhyāna" of the *Brahmāṇḍa Purāṇa*, the Goddess Lalitā rests on a sofa "composed of the five Brahmā-gods," with the usual identification of its legs and seat with the five gods.[17] The sofa is said to be the root of the whole universe.

The sofa of five corpses is perhaps a younger notion than the throne of abstract qualities. In any case, the latter throne was not an exclusive endowment of the Goddess. In the *Śāradā-Tilaka*, as already noted, it was regarded as the seat for one's chosen deity, whoever that might be. And in the *Bhāgavata Purāṇa*, Kṛṣṇa advises: "One should visualize my seat with righteousness and the like [for its legs]."[18]

The sofa or seat of the five corpses situated in the Jeweled Island, unlike the throne of abstract qualities, is associated with the Goddess alone. It dramatically illustrates her utter supremacy over all other gods. The five gods of the sofa represent the chief male deities who oversee the functioning of the cosmos. These five, reduced to "sofahood," not only symbolize her various functions and subservient powers, but also are mere ghosts (*pretas*) or corpses until empowered by her *śakti*. One commentator on the *Saundaryalaharī* nicely captures the theological point of the mythological image: "Only when frolicking with the Śakti (His consort, Haimavatī, seated on his lap) would Śiva . . . be capable of procreating . . . ; otherwise, the Deva (though self-effulgent) becomes powerless even of stirring. . . . While so, how dares one . . . either to make obeisance . . . before, or to glorify Thee (O Goddess!) that art served by Hari, Hara, Viriñca (and Īśvara, as the four legs of Thy couch, by Sadāśiva as Thy mattress, Mahendra as Thy spittoon and so on)?"[19]

In summary, the *Devī Gītā* has apparently fused together two traditions regarding the Devī's divine throne. The resulting synthetic conception nicely illustrates and affirms the nature of Bhuvaneśvarī as both supreme overlord of the universe and as transcendent beyond all the gods. And it is this cosmic and transcendent Goddess that one is to install on her sacred throne in one's heart!

Notes

1. The text's description of the throne as "having righteousness and the like" refers to a traditional conceptualization of the divine seat of one's chosen deity. As Nīlakaṇṭha points out, the throne has four legs consisting of righteousness (*dharma*), knowledge (*jñāna*), dispassion (*vairāgya*), and supremacy (*aiśvarya*) for its legs, unrighteousness, ignorance, passion, and inferiority for its sides. In addition, there are various deities and *śaktis* surrounding or surmounting the throne that are to be worshiped. He indicates that these matters are explained in the *Śāradā-Tilaka Tantra*. Interestingly, this line of the *Devī Gītā* (10.8ab) is nearly identical with *Śāradā-Tilaka Tantra* 4.38ab. The *Śāradā-Tilaka* account of the *pīṭha-nyāsa* (4.38–43ab) is probably the model on which the *Devī-Bhāgavata* (12.12.31–39) bases its own description of this ritual, discussed in the Comment above.

2. That is, the heart lotus is made to bloom or open through the practice of breath control.

3. *pañca-pretāsana;* a *preta* is literally "one who is departed (from this world)," and thus "a departed spirit or ghost." The seat is composed of the bodies left behind by the departed spirits, as explained in the Comment above.

4. The five states are, according to Nīlakaṇṭha, waking (*jagrat*), dreaming (*svapna*), deep sleep (*suṣupti*), the fourth (*turya*), and the beyond (*atīta*). The first four are the traditional states of consciousness as found in the *Māṇḍūkya Upaniṣad* (see note 15 on *Devī Gītā* 1.49). Late Advaita added still more refined and subtle states of consciousness, such as the *atīta* mentioned by Nīlakaṇṭha.

5. Cf. *Kaivalya Upaniṣad* 18, where Sadāśiva, identifying himself as pure consciousness, affirms that he is different from the three (lower) states of consciousness.

6. *Devī-Bhāgavata* 12.12.39cd. The account of the throne begins in verse 31.

7. The *Devī-Bhāgavata* summarizes this worship in just one line, 12.12.58cd.

8. *Śāradā-Tilaka Tantra* 4.57–63.

9. Cf. *Mahānirvāṇa Tantra* 5.128–135, which provides a similar description of the *pīṭha-nyāsa,* with the same ascending series of cosmic supports.

10. The word *mañca* can mean a bed or sofa, as well as a dais or throne. In *Devī-Bhāgavata* 3.3.35, the Devī's celestial seat in the Jeweled Island is referred to as a "sofa in the form of Śiva" (*śivākāraḥ paryaṅkaḥ*). (Cf. *Devī-Bhāgavata* 7.29.7, where it is called *pañca-brahmāsana.*)

11. In the "Lalitopākhyāna" of the *Brahmāṇḍa Purāṇa* (3.4.37.56–61), the stairs of the sofa are said to be thirty-six, and are identified with the thirty-six *tattva*s or elements, beginning with earth, water, fire, etc. of Śaivite theology. The ten *śakti-tattva*s of the *Devī Bhāgavata* probably refer to the five gross elements and their subtle corresponding elements. The "Lalitopākhyāna" adds an interesting detail: the legs are in the form of pillars in their upper and lower parts, but in the middle have the form of *puruṣa*s (persons) (3.4.37.53cd).

12. See, for instance, John Woodroffe, ed., *Hymn to Kālī,* p. 63, note 5; he writes: "Similarly [to Devī being pictured astride two corpses of Śiva] the Devī is represented as reclining on a couch made of five corpses, which are the Mahāpreta[s]. . . . Sadāśiva, Īśāna, Rudra, Viṣṇu, and Brahmā." See also John Woodroffe, ed., *Principles of Tantra,* vol. 2, pp. 388–92. And see Goudriaan and Gupta, *Hindu Tantric and Śākta Literature,* p. 68.

13. *Tripurā-Rahasya, Jñāna-Khaṇḍa* 20.37.

14. *Lalitā Sahasranāma,* verses 249, 250, and 947. Chaganthy Suryanarayanamurthy, in commenting on the last epithet (in 947) interprets the couch in terms of the esoteric physiology of the Kuṇḍalinī Yoga. The five male deities are identified with five of the *cakra*s, Sadāśiva being seen as resting in the *sahasrāra.* Above that is the supreme Śiva, in whose lap the Goddess sits. Thus, according to Suryanarayanamurthy, "She is seated above [*adhiśāyinī*] these five Pretās."

15. *Saundaryalaharī* verse 8. Cf. R. G. Bhandarkar, *Vaiṣṇavism, Śaivism, and Minor Religious Systems,* pp. 144–45.

16. *Saundaryalaharī* 92a.

17. "Lalitopākhyāna" of the *Brahmāṇḍa Purāṇa,* 3.4.37.48–64.

18. *Bhāgavata Purāṇa* 11.27.25. Chapter 27 of the eleventh book of the *Bhāgavata,* incidentally, provides an account of Vedic-Tantric procedures of worship, in this case directed to Kṛṣṇa, that is very similar to the *Devī Gītā*'s description of Devī worship. One of the major differences between the two is the latter's inclusion of the motif of the *pañca-pretāsana.*

19. Kāmeśvarasūri's commentary on verse 1 of the *Saundaryalaharī*, quoted in Śāstrī and Ayyaṅgar, ed. and trans., *Saundarya-Laharī*, pp. 11–12.

Translation

[The Goddess summarizes the preparatory stages for external worship.]

10.12. [cont.] After completing the above meditations, one should worship me with mental offerings[1] and practice recitation.[2]

10.13. One should surrender the fruits of this recitation to me, the blessed Goddess. Then one should prepare the general water offering.[3]
Setting out next the sprinkling vessel[4] and purifying the materials for worship

10.14. With that water while intoning the protective missile mantra,[5] the worshiper
Should secure at once the surrounding space.[6] Then bowing to the teacher

10.15. And receiving the latter's consent, one should focus on the external altar.
Recalling that divine and pleasing form of mine visualized in the heart,

10.16. One should then summon[7] me to that altar, using the life-infusing incantation.[8]

Comment

In chapter 9, the internal worship of the Goddess as pure consciousness into which one merges is presented as higher than external types of *pūjā*. The internal worship described in chapter 9 is thoroughly Advaitic in nature, relying on no material or even conceptual supports, as these are deemed apparent limitations imposed on the Ultimate and—in the final stages of meditation—obstacles to its realization. In the Advaitic path, the seeker begins with external forms and eventually goes beyond them, culminating in the realization of the one Brahman without a second.

The goal of Tantric worship as described in this chapter also seeks unity or identification with the Supreme, but the approach is quite different. Physical substances and one's own body are regarded as extraordinarily powerful tools for spiritual transformation. In the Tantric path, the practitioner first prepares the mind with internal worship, in order to realize the interpenetration of all material and spiritual realities, the One Goddess in all things. In sum, the worshiper is to realize the identity of the divine power or Śakti present in one's own body, in the articles of worship, and in the Goddess herself.

In Tantra, material entities are thus seen as forms or vessels waiting to be filled with, or infused by, physical, emotional, mental, and spiritual energies. Without such material vessels, these energies remain dispersed and incapable of being fully utilized.

Two important substances or vessels in the worship described in this section are water and the external altar with its icon (or sacred diagram). The preparation of the water offering (*arghya-sthāpana*) involves infusing into the water itself the presence of the sacred rivers such as the Ganges, themselves manifestations of the Goddess in liquid form. By this means, the powerfully purifying waters of such rivers are made available to sanctify all the articles and materials used in the service.

The icon on the altar is not a mere idol of inanimate stone or metal, or a mere painting, but rather serves as the vessel containing the presence of the Goddess once she is led out from within one's heart. The infusion of the Devī's life and spirit into one's body (*jīva-nyāsa*, described earlier) is similar to the infusion of her presence into the body of the icon (*prāṇa-sthāpana*). Of particular interest is the process (merely alluded to in the *Devī Gītā*) of bringing the Goddess out from the heart and leading it to the altar, a process involving yet another infusion—of the Devī's spirit into a flower. According to the *Kālikā Purāṇa*, after performing the mental worship of the Goddess in one's heart, one leads her out of the body through the right nostril, and summons or invokes her to be present in a flower, which is placed on the external altar.[9] The *Mahānirvāṇa Tantra* further details the process: one leads the Goddess from the heart up through the central channel (*suṣumṇā*) to the *sahasrāra*, then out through the nostrils onto a flower, which is finally placed on the *yantra* or altar.[10] The presence of the Goddess then is transferred from the flower to the image, if an icon is being used.

The choice of a flower as the vehicle for the last stage of the Devī's journey is quite fitting. The spiritual significance of flowers is explained by the *Kālikā Purāṇa* as follows: "Flowers delight the gods.

The gods reside in flowers. . . . The supreme light manifests itself in flowers and is delighted by flowers."[11]

Notes

1. *mānasair bhogaiḥ:* literally, "with mental enjoyments." The word *bhoga* refers to the usual offerings (*upacāras*) made to a deity, such as a seat, foot water, and the like, for his or her enjoyment (see the Comment on 10.16cd–27 below). In the *Mahānirvāṇa Tantra* (5.142–46), the following articles for mental worship are listed (based on Woodroffe's translation): one's lotus heart for the seat of the Goddess, the nectar from the *sahasrāra* for the foot washing, one's mind for the respect offering, the same nectar for the mouth rinsing and body bathing, the essences of ether and smell for the clothes and perfume, one's heart for flowers, one's life-breath for incense, fire for light, the Ocean of Nectar for food, the sound of the unstruck sound of Brahman in the *anāhata* center for the bell ringing, the essence of air for the fan and fly whisk, and the roving senses and mind for the dance before the Goddess. The text goes on to describe other offerings, including symbolic representations of the five *makāras* of the Left-Handed path, which the *Devī Gītā* would hardly commend.

2. Recitation of the deity's root mantra (*mūla-mantra*) is understood: as Nīlakaṇṭha indicates, after making the mental offerings to the Goddess, one is to recite the *śakti-mūla-mantra.* A root mantra is longer than a seed mantra; it is a brief expansion or sprouting of the latter. Neither the *Devī Gītā* nor Nīlakaṇṭha in his commentary thereon specifies what the root mantra of Bhuvaneśvarī is. However, in *Devī-Bhāgavata* 11.18.21, there is reference to the Devī's mantra "known to begin with the Māyā-bīja (Hrīṃ)." Nīlakaṇṭha there provides the mantra as "Hrīṃ Bhuvaneśvaryai Namaḥ" ("Hrīṃ, Obeisance to Bhuvaneśvarī"), which apparently is her root mantra. Nagaraja Sharma, temple priest at the Hindu Temple of San Antonio, confirmed that the mantra provided by Nīlakaṇṭha is Bhuvaneśvarī's root mantra, but added that her root mantra as given by gurus today is "Auṃ, Hrīṃ, Aiṃ, Klīṃ, Bhuvaneśvaryai Namaḥ." (Cf. *Mahānirvāṇa Tantra* 5.152–55, which states that after the mental worship of the Goddess, one should recite her *mūla-mantra* in combination with all the letters of the alphabet. Woodroffe indicates that the root mantra of the Goddess [Ādyā Kālī] is "Hrīṃ, Śrīṃ, Krīṃ, Parameśvari Svāhā.")

3. *arghya-sthāpana:* "establishing or fixing the (general) water offering." Nīlakaṇṭha says that due to the cumbersome nature of the procedure, it is not described here, but that it is explained in the *Śāradā-Tilaka Tantra* (4.43cd–48). The *Devī-Bhāgavata* also describes the procedure in 12.12.42–55ab. It involves setting a conch shell on a special *yantra,* filling the conch with water (perfumed with sandal flowers and the like, according to the *Śāradā-Tilaka* [5.45ab]), uttering the appropriate mantras, and invoking into the water the presence of

the sacred rivers (*tīrthas*). Thus prepared, the *arghya* is a powerful purifying force, used to sanctify other parts of the *pūjā*. But first, some of the water from the conch will be put in the "sprinkling vessel" (*prokṣaṇī-pātra*), already partly filled with water. Water needed to perform other acts in the worship will be taken from the *prokṣaṇī-pātra,* now infused with the power of the *arghya* (see the next two lines). This *arghya* is thus referred to as the "general water offering" (*sāmānyārghya*). Cf. *Devī-Bhāgavata* 11.18.4, which prescribes: "The wise person, having established the conch shell (*śaṅkhasya sthāpana*) and prepared the general water offering (*sāmānyārghya*), should sprinkle the materials of worship, using the missile (-mantra)."

4. *pātra,* "vessel"; this here refers specifically to the *prokṣaṇī-pātra* ("sprinkling vessel"), which contains some of the prepared *arghya* water. See preceding note.

5. *astra-mantra;* it is the single syllable *phaṭ,* used repeatedly in the preparation of the *pūjā* in all its aspects to ward off evil influences or spirits.

6. *dig-bandhaṃ:* "securing or fencing in the directions." Nīlakaṇṭha explains: "One should visualize a wall of fire surrounding oneself, while reciting the mantra *phaṭ.*" The *Mahānirvāṇa Tantra* (5.90, 92) also calls for visualizing the wall of fire, and then provides these instructions for the actual securing of the directions: "Then in the following manner let him [the worshiper] fence all the quarters so that no obstructions proceed from them. Join the first and second fingers of the right hand, and tap the palm of the left hand three times, each time after the first with greater force, thus making a loud sound, and then snap the fingers while uttering the Weapon-Mantra" (Woodroffe's trans.).

7. *āvāhayet;* this refers to the invocation of the deity to dwell within the image on the altar. See Comment above for details of the process, and the next note.

8. *prāṇa-sthāpana-vidyā;* the *Śāradā-Tilaka Tantra* (5.82–84) gives the general form of the incantation: "May the life-breaths of such and such a deity, as well as its soul (*jīva*) abide here [in the icon]; further, may all the senses and organs, speech, mind, eyes, ears, etc., of such and such a deity come here and remain for a long time." Cf. the similar incantation in the *Mahānirvāṇa Tantra* (6.72–74).

See John Woodroffe and Pramatha Nātha Mukhyopādhyāya, *Mahāmāyā,* pp. 142–45, for an interpretation of this ritual and its relation to the preceding rites.

9. *Kālikā Purāṇa* 65.29–30ab.

10. *Mahānirvāṇa Tantra* 6.65–66. The same process is described in *Śāradā-Tilaka Tantra* 4.88–89.

11. *Kālikā Purāṇa* 69.106ab, 107cd.

Translation

[The Goddess enumerates the various services and offerings to be rendered during external worship.]

10.16. [cont.] A seat, an invitation,[1] a respect offering,[2] water for washing the feet, and for rinsing the mouth,

10.17. A bath,[3] a set of clothes,[4] ornaments of all kinds,
Perfume, and flowers,[5] all these as is proper one should present to the Goddess, inspired by one's own devotion.

10.18. One should duly perform the worship of the protective deities abiding in the sacred diagram;[6]
If unable to worship them every day, one should set aside Friday[7] to do so.

10.19. One should regard the attendant deities as manifesting the splendor of the chief goddess;
And one should consider the whole universe, including the nether regions, as pervaded by her splendor.

10.20. Again, one should worship the chief goddess accompanied by her surrounding deities
With perfumes, fragrances and the like, including sweet-scented flowers,

10.21. As well as with food and refreshing water,[8] along with Tāmbūla[9] and various gifts.
Then one should please me by reciting the hymn of my thousand names that you composed.[10]

10.22. Recite my protective mantra[11] and my hymn beginning "I, with the Rudras . . . ,"[12] O Lord,
Along with the mantras from the *Hṛllekhā Upaniṣad*, otherwise known as the *Devī-Atharva-Śiras*.[13]

10.23. With those great mystic spells and great mantras one should please me again and again.
The person whose heart overflows with ecstatic love should seek absolution[14] from the World-Mother.[15]

10.24. Trembling with thrills of joy in all limbs, speechless, with eyes flooded by tears,[16]
One should please me again and again with the tumultuous sounds of dancing, singing,[17] and other celebrations.
10.25. In the whole of the Vedas and in all the Purāṇas
I am truly proclaimed;[18] thus by reciting these one will please me.
10.26. One should offer to me daily all possessions, including the body.[19]
Next one should perform the daily fire offering.[20]
And then to Brahmans, to well-dressed virgins,
10.27. To young boys, to the poor and others, one should give food with the conviction that they are none other than the Goddess.[21]
One should bow down and then bid her farewell,[22] leading her back again into one's heart.[23]

Comment

The offerings (*upacāras*) presented to the deity in *pūjā* are modeled on the services and gifts of hospitality provided to an honored guest in one's home. This symbolism is made explicit in two common offerings, not mentioned by the *Devī Gītā* but often included after the invocation or invitation: the "welcoming" (*svāgata*) of the deity, and "asking about his or her welfare" (*kuśala-praśna*).[24] Thus, just as for a guest, one furnishes the Goddess with rest, refreshment, and entertainment, providing for her physical and mental comfort in every conceivable way. Noteworthy is the sensual nature of these offerings, appealing to all five physical senses as well as the mind. The gods and the Goddess herself, like human beings, take great delight in such "worldly" pleasures. From the devotional Śākta point of view, all such pleasures are gifts from the Goddess in the first place, and thus it is quite fitting to share them with her.

Lists of offerings became fairly standardized, sixteen different items being commonly mentioned, with many minor variations. Often the lists conclude with a variety of different reverential actions that, if counted separately, would extend the number well beyond sixteen, as in the *Devī Gītā*. One extremely common item not mentioned in the *Devī Gītā* is the offering of a lamp or light (*dīpa*). Given the nearly universal inclusion of this offering elsewhere, its absence in the *Devī Gītā* is surprising and should probably be added.[25] The *Devī-Bhāgavata* itself, in an account of the *upacāras*, advises: "With intense devotion one should offer a hundred or even a thousand lights to the Goddess."[26] And as the *Kālikā Purāṇa* says, in propitiating a deity, excluding all other offerings, one should at least offer a lamp.[27]

The absolution (*kṣamā*) mentioned in verse 23 involves asking the World-Mother for forgiveness regarding any shortcomings in the worship service itself and in the worshiper. The devotee often asserts ignorance of the basic procedures of worship, but affirms the great compassion of the Mother who will overlook these failings. An interesting example of such a petition is found in the following hymn of absolution by Śaṃkara, who emphasizes the forgiving and ever kind nature of a mother to a son:

> I know not mantra nor yantra nor hymn of praise, alas!
> Neither invocation, meditation, nor even stories of praise,
> Nor your mudras, nor lamentations do I know.
> O Mother, I know that following you is the supreme means for removing affliction.
> Through ignorance of the rules, through want of wealth, through laziness,
> Through inability to do what should be done, one is deprived of your feet.
> Please forgive all that, O Mother, Auspicious, who rescues all.
> A wicked son may be born at times, but never a wicked mother.
>
> . . . .
>
> O World-Mother, Mother, I have failed to serve your feet,
> Or to offer you much wealth.
> Even so, the affection you show me is without equal.
> A wicked son may be born at times, but never a wicked mother.[28]

The dismissal or bidding farewell to the Goddess is the last of the set of hospitable acts. This gesture completes her journey from one's heart, up to the top of one's head, down and out through the nose, conveyed by breath onto a flower, then onto the image, and finally back in reverse order into one's heart (see preceding Comment). In this manner, also, the cycle of ritual, from internal to external, and back to internal, is fulfilled.

Notes

1. *āvahana;* the summoning of the deity to the altar, the invocation.

2. *arghya;* this is variously interpreted, but in any case is different from the *arghya* (water offering) mentioned in 10.13. Dev sees it as offerings of flowers, food, etc. (*The Concept of Śakti in the Purāṇas,* p. 21). The *Śāradā-Tilaka Tantra* (4.95–96ab) says that this *arghya* is made up of sandal and flowers, pounded rice, barley, kuśa grass, sesamum, mustard, and panic grass. Sometimes it is simply regarded as part of three water offerings, as water for washing the hands, in addition to the water for washing the feet and rinsing the mouth (see *Pūjā; The Process of Ritualistic Worship,* p. 11).

3. The *Kālikā Purāṇa* (68.54–55) describes the water used for the bath as being mixed with a number of pleasant and sweet-smelling ingredients, including honey, milk, sesame oil, ghee, and the like. The bath (*snāna, abhiṣekha*) involves pouring or sprinkling these consecrated fluids over the image of the deity.

4. *vāso-dvayam;* literally, a "pair of clothes." The *Sūta Saṃhitā* (5.6), in its list of offerings, includes *vāsottarīyam,* the "upper garment." The *Kālikā Purāṇa* (69.4cd–5ab), refers to five different items of clothing, including the upper garment and the lower (*paridhānam*). The *Devī Gītā* may be referring to the set of upper and lower garments.

5. *Devī Gītā* 10.16cd–17abc is nearly identical to *Sūta Saṃhitā* 9.5cd–7a. The latter text continues to list other offerings: incense (*dhūpa*), light (*dīpa*), refreshing water along with food (*annena tarpaṇa*), and the like. It appears as though the *Devī Gītā* list is abruptly interrupted in order to include consideration of the attendant deities. In the process, the very important offering of the lamp or light has been left out in the *Devī Gītā*'s list.

Cynthia Humes has suggested that the omission of the *dīpa* was deliberate, that the Goddess herself may be represented by light or flame (as in the *homa* sacrifice below, and in accord with her original appearance in the *Devī Gītā* as a blazing orb of light), and thus the light is to be worshiped rather than offered. Humes finds such an explanation plausible "especially since in the modern worship with the *Devī Māhātmya,* . . . *dīpas* are not offered to the Goddess but represent her during recitation" (personal communication, November 30, 1996). While Humes' suggestion is very reasonable, I am inclined to think the omission is inadvertent, as the *Devī-Bhāgavata* elsewhere strongly recommends the offering of *dīpas* to the Goddess (see the Comment above).

6. *yantra;* the sacred, geometric design symbolizing the universe, in the center of which the altar or seat of the Goddess is placed. The protective deities occupy various points or angles in the diagram, surrounding and protecting the center.

7. Regarding the nature of Friday as a special time for worshiping the Goddess, see note 5 on *Devī Gītā* 8.38.

8. *tarpana:* literally, "satisfaction."

9. See *Devī Gītā* 1.35, note 1.

10. As Nīlakaṇṭha points out, the hymn of the Devī's thousand (or thousand and eight) names composed by Himālaya appears not in the *Devī-Bhāgavata* but in the twelfth chapter of the *Kūrma Purāṇa* (= eleventh chapter in the critical ed., which is the *Kūrma Devī Gītā*). Himālaya composed it in response to viewing the Devī's Virāj form.

11. *kavaca:* "armor, coat of mail." In this context, *kavaca* refers to a mantra or prayer addressed to a deity asking protection for the various parts of one's body. The prayer is inscribed on birch bark, paper, etc., and placed in a metal case worn on one's arm or around the neck, as an amulet. The recitation of the protective mantra is often placed in conjunction with the recitation of the names of the deity. See, for instance, *Mahānirvāṇa Tantra* 7.55–68, where the protective mantra of Ādyā Kālikā is given, following her hymn of a hundred names. Cf. *Kālikā Purāṇa* 75.28–72, for the *kavaca* of the Goddess Tripurā. The *Devī Gītā,* short on details as usual, does not provide any specifics regarding the particular *kavaca* recommended. Nīlakaṇṭha simply says the *kavaca* is stated in various Tantras. We can imagine its form to be something like: "Hrīṃ, may Bhuvaneśvarī protect my head; may the supreme Śakti protect my mouth; may the World-Mother protect my heart, etc."

12. This is the beginning of the famous "Devī Sūkta" from the *Ṛg Veda* (10.125). It is also found in the *Devī-Atharva-Śiras Upaniṣad,* mentioned in the next line.

13. Nīlakaṇṭha glosses this line: "The *Hṛllekhā Upaniṣad,* that is, the Upaniṣad of Bhuvaneśvarī, known as the *Devī-Atharva-Śiras,* begins with the words, 'All the gods approached the Goddess.' " This is the opening line of what is called the *Devī Upaniṣad* in the Adyar Library series of Śākta Upaniṣads. In this Upaniṣad, when the gods approach the Devī, they ask her who she is. After she identifies herself as the all-pervading Brahman, she then recites the "Devī Sūkta" (see preceding note). The gods respond with a hymn of praise to the Goddess, composed of a number of verses drawn from the Vedic corpus. This hymn, incidentally, is recited by the gods in *Devī Gītā* 1.44–48. The Upaniṣad goes on to describe certain mystic spells (*vidyās*) and mantras (see the next verse), gives the esoteric construction of the syllable "Hrīṃ" (the Hṛllekhā), and provides a visual meditation of the Goddess in her form as Bhuvaneśvarī.

14. *kṣamā;* Woodroffe explains the act of absolution in this way: "He [the worshiper] asks to be forgiven both because of the trouble he has given Her [the Devī] as also for his shortcomings in worship" (*Mahānirvāṇa Tantra* p. 185, note 5).

A contemporary formula for this absolution, used in the worship of Mata Amritanandamayi, runs as follows: "O Supreme Goddess, I know not the proper means of invoking You or communicating with You as You are. A full knowledge of priestly rites has not been imparted, so kindly overlook and forgive any mistakes or omissions. I know little of mantras or pious conduct, and I am a stranger to true devotion. Nonetheless forgive me, and whatsoever worship I have been able to do, accept it as full and complete because You are my only refuge, my Supreme Empress. For me there is no other. Because of this have mercy, O Mother, and protect me who prays to You" (*Puja; the Process of Ritualistic Worship*, pp. 20–21).

15. *Devī-Bhāgavata* 11.18.46cd gives a similar provision. Immediately before, the text mentions two other common *upacāras*: circumambulation (*pradakṣiṇa*) and reverential salutation (*namaskāra*). The absolution is often uttered while performing the salutation.

16. Such physical symptoms are typical manifestations of *preman* (ecstatic love), mentioned in the preceding verse. Cf. *Devī Gītā* 1.43, note 1.

17. Cf. *Devī Gītā* 7.24, and *Bhāgavata Purāṇa* 11.27.35cd.

18. Cf. *Bhagavad Gītā* 15.15c, where Kṛṣṇa affirms: "And by all the Vedas I alone am to be known."

19. Cf. *Devī Bhāgavata* 12.7.147, where, at the end of the initiation ritual, the student offers to the guru all possessions for life.

20. *homa;* the *Śāradā-Tilaka Tantra* (4.118cd–120) briefly describes this fire offering, indicating that the oblation should consist of *pāyasa* (rice boiled in milk with sugar), dressed with clarified butter. The offering is to be repeated twenty-five times, with the appropriate mantras being recited. A detailed description is given in *Mahānirvāṇa Tantra* 6.119–64. The worshiper is to regard the Self as identical with the fire, which itself is identical with the Goddess.

Regarding this Tantricized Vedic rite, Banerji writes: "Tantra emphasises [*sic*] self-surrender which indeed is the inner significance of *homa*" (*Tantra in Bengal*, p. 22).

21. Cf. *Devī-Gītā* 8.47. Cf. also *Devī-Bhāgavata* 12.7.147cd–148.

22. *visarjayet;* "one should dismiss or allow to go." It is the counterpart to the invitation or invocation of the deity into the icon.

23. *vyutkrameṇa visarjayet:* "send away or dismiss by the reversal (of the invocatory rite)." Nīlakaṇṭha explains that the reversal is to be done by means of the *saṃhāra-mudrā* ("the gesture of withdrawal"). In the *Mahānirvāṇa Tantra* (6.162), the dismissal of the deity is part of the conclusion to the fire offering. The worshiper utilizes the *saṃhāra-mudrā* to transfer the Goddess from the fire (see note 20 above) back to the heart lotus within the body. The gesture of

withdrawal involves holding the hands in a special position with which one picks up from the altar a flower, regarded as containing the presence of the Devī. One then brings the flower to the nose and smells it. With the inhalation, one absorbs back into oneself the Devī's spirit, which resides once again in the heart. Cf. *Śāradā-Tilaka Tantra* 4.121cd. Cf. also the procedure for dismissal given in *Puja; The Process of Ritualistic Worship,* p. 21.

24. See *Śāradā-Tilaka Tantra* 4.92cd and *Devī-Bhāgavata* 12.7.65cd.

25. But see Humes' suggestion in note 5 above.

26. *Devī-Bhāgavata* 11.18.37cd.

27. *Kālikā Purāṇa* 69.133.

28. Śāṃkara, *devyaparādhakṣamāpanastotram,* verses 1–2, 4. Cf. note 14 above.

Translation

[The Goddess sings the praises of her special mantra, the Hṛllekhā.]

10.28. One should perform the whole of my worship with the Hṛllekhā mantra,[1] O you of firm resolve.
The Hṛllekhā is regarded as the supreme director of all mantras.

10.29. I am ever reflected in the Hṛllekhā as in a mirror.
Therefore, whatever one gives while reciting the Hṛllekhā is offered with all mantras.

Comment

As indicated in the Introduction, there are many similarities between Bhuvaneśvarī and the goddess Lalitā.[2] One of these similarities concerns the chief mantra of each, the Hṛllekhā of Bhuvaneśvarī and the Śrī Vidyā of Lalitā. In the *Brahmāṇḍa Purāṇa,* in the "Lalitophākhyāna" ("Story of the Goddess Lalitā"), the Śrī Vidyā, or Auspicious Mantra of Lalitā, is ranked above all other mantras, including those belonging to Viṣṇu, Durgā, Gaṇapati, Sūrya, Śiva, Lakṣmī, Sarasvatī, Pārvatī, and others.[3] It is also referred to as the "supreme director,"[4] similar to the statement in *Devī Gītā* 10.28cd regarding the Hṛllekhā. The Śrī Vidyā, however, is not a seed mantra, being composed of fifteen (or sixteen) seed syllables, in three sets, each set ending with the Hṛllekhā ("Hrīṃ").

The notion of the Hṛllekhā as the director of all mantras is perhaps best explained by the Goddess' own words in 10.8ab above, where she indicates that after installing Hrīṃ in one's body, all other installations (with their requisite mantras) will be empowered by it. And verse 10.29 implies that the Hṛllekhā not only empowers all other mantras, it is in effect all other mantras. The Hṛllekhā itself is so empowered as it directly reflects, like a mirror, the divine *śakti* of the Goddess. The Goddess, as it were, has visually infused herself into this most powerful of all sounds.

Notes

1. That is, one should utter the Hṛllekhā (Hrīṃ) while offering each of the just mentioned *upacāras*, according to Nīlakaṇṭha.

2. See pp. 24–26.

3. *Brahmāṇḍa Purāṇa* 3.4.38.3–10.

4. *śrī-vidyaiṣā parā nāyikā; Brahmāṇḍa Purāṇa* 3.4.41.15cd.

Translation

[The Goddess concludes her description of Devī *pūjā*, briefly enumerating the fruits of performing it.]

10.30. After honoring one's teacher with ornaments and the like, one will attain complete fulfillment.[1]
Whoever in such manner worships the Goddess, the auspicious, world-charming beauty,[2]

10.31. For that person nothing is difficult to attain anytime, anywhere.
Upon leaving the body, that one most certainly will go to my Jeweled Island.[3]

10.32. Such a person may be recognized as bearing the form of the Goddess herself.[4] The gods constantly bow before that one.
Thus, O King, I have narrated to you the procedures of worship for the Great Goddess.

10.33. Consider all this in detail. And in accord with your qualifications,[5]
Perform my worship. Thereby you will be wholly fulfilled.[6]

Comment

The above account of the procedures of Devī *pūjā* is quite similar to the description given in the eleventh book of the *Devī-Bhāgavata*. The latter account, in its conclusion to the acts of offering (*upacāras*), nicely evokes the devotional mood motivating the faithful worshiper: "As the Goddess is pleased when one remembers her just once, what wonder is there that she is pleased when worshiped with all these services and gifts?"[7]

Such gifts and acts earn for oneself, as it were, the celestial paradise of the Goddess, her Jeweled Island. And there, one attains the essential form of the Goddess (*devī-svarūpa*). As the *Devī Gītā* has previously affirmed, this essential form is none other than her nature as pure consciousness, and thus devotion eventually reaches its fulfillment in this nondual state.[8] From a Śākta-Advaitic perspective, wherein the worshiper and the Goddess are already one, there is no need to wait for death and ascension to the Jeweled Island to attain supreme satisfaction. From the Tantric, devotional perspective emphasized in this chapter of the *Devī Gītā*, such satisfaction is available in the very act of worship. In an interesting synthesis of Advaitic, Tantric, and *bhaktic* ideals, the *Devī-Bhāgavata* affirms (following a description of the various *upacāras*), "The satisfaction of the auspicious Great Goddess is the satisfaction of the whole world, for everything has her for its essence, just like a snake in a rope."[9]

Notes

1. *kṛta-kṛtya-tva:* "the condition of having done what is to be done." See note 1 on *Devī Gītā* 1.3.

2. *bhavana-sundarī;* this is an interesting epithet for Bhuvaneśvarī, as it parallels that of Lalitā as Tripura-sundarī.

3. Cf. *Devī-Bhāgavata* 11.18.33–34ab: "The best of practitioners [who perform Devī *pūjā*], even if a great sinner, is freed from all sins, and upon leaving the body attains the lotus feet of the Auspicious Goddess, hard to obtain even by the gods."

4. *devī-svarūpa:* "having the same form or essence as the Devī" (cf. note 2 on *Devī Gītā* 2.1).

5. *adhikāra;* cf. note 8 on *Devī Gītā* 9.32 and note 5 on 9.43. Brooks, in listing various descriptive criteria of Tantrism, includes as the tenth and last: *"Perhaps Tantrism's most distinctive feature . . . is initiation (dīkṣā) in which the established criteria of caste and gender are not the primary tests of qualification (adhikāra) for sādhana."* He elaborates: "Caste and gender are not unimportant criteria for determining Tantric qualification. . . . Tantrics, however, depend more upon physical and mental dispositions, such as personal self-discipline and a commitment to undertake the rigors of the spiritual disciplines of daily practice" (*The Secret of the Three Cities,* p. 71).

6. *kṛtārtha;* see note 1 on *Devī Gītā* 6.15.

7. *Devī-Bhāgavata* 11.18.47.

8. See *Devī Gītā* 7.27.

9. *Devī-Bhāgavata* 11.18.40.

Translation

[The Goddess cautions against the indiscriminate dissemination of the *Devī Gītā* and indicates its appropriate recipients.]

10.34. One should never utter the teachings of my *Song* to one who is not a disciple;
Nor should it be given to one who lacks devotion, or is deceitful and wicked-hearted.[1]

10.35. Displaying this publicly is like exposing the breasts of a mother.
Therefore by all means this is to be diligently guarded always.

10.36. It may be given to an ardent disciple and to an eldest son,
If they are well behaved, properly dressed, and devoted to the Goddess.[2]

10.37. At the time of offerings to the dead, one should recite this in the presence of Brahmans;
All one's ancestors will be satisfied and go to the supreme abode.[3]

Comment

Stipulation of the proper recipients of religious instructions is an ancient Hindu concern and became a standard part of the concluding counsel of any important teaching. Such sets of restrictions, for instance, appear near the end of both the *Bhagavad Gītā* and the *Kapila Gītā*.[4] Of particular interest is the latter's exclusion of those whose hearts are fixed on the home. This exclusion is in full accord with the general suspicion of the *Bhāgavata Purāṇa* toward the householding state. By contrast, the *Devī Gītā* has no concern over the qualifications of householders, so long as they are devoted to the Goddess.

The motif of secrecy and discretion in the transmission of esoteric teachings has already been discussed in the Comment on 6.21cd–23ab. There it was noted that without the requisite initiation from a guru, one is not properly prepared to take advantage of the teachings and practices (such as the use of mantras). Indeed, without such preparation, these practices may be dangerous to oneself and others. At the same time, the notion of futility and even danger for the uninitiated in carrying out various spiritual disciplines is in tension with the *bhaktic* ideal of the grace of the supreme.

From this devotional perspective, acts of worship are regarded as inherently pleasing to the deity, so pleasing, in fact, that even the unconscious performance of them, without any proper initiation, can lead to extraordinarily beneficent results through the grace of the god or goddess. For example, the *Devī-Bhāgavata* in concluding another discussion of Devī *pūjā* tells the following story of King Bṛhadratha. In a former life as a bird, he went searching for scraps of food in the temple courtyard of the Goddess Annapūrṇā in Kāśī. Unconsciously, through the force of prior karma, he circumambulated her image in the center of the temple. As a consequence, when he died, he went to heaven, and in his next birth became a great king, with knowledge of all his previous births. Such is the power of the Goddess.[5]

The *bhaktic* ideal of the graciousness of the Goddess that overflows the bounds of orthodox formality and rigid procedure, as reflected in the story of King Bṛhadratha, should be kept in mind while considering the strictures against indiscriminate dissemination of the *Devī Gītā*. These strictures, then, given by the Goddess herself and echoed by Vyāsa below (in lines 43cd–44ab), ultimately stress that the primary qualification for receiving the *Devī Gītā* is devotion to the Goddess. Such devotion, clearly, is enhanced and deepened by appropriate instruction (and initiation). But without devotion, no other qualifying criteria are sufficient.

Notes

1. Cf. *Bhagavad Gītā* 18.67, where Kṛṣṇa tells Arjuna: "Do not reveal this to anyone lacking austerities or devotion, or to one who does not wish to listen, or who talks against me." Cf. also Kapila's words to his mother in the *Kapila Gītā* (*Bhāgavata Purāṇa* 3.32.39–40): "One should never teach this to a wicked person, or to one who is arrogant, hard-hearted, vicious, hypocritical. Nor should one teach it to a sensual person, or to one attached to the home, or lacking devotion, or hating my devotees."

2. Cf. *Devī Gītā,* 6.21cd–23ab, and 8.50. Cf. also Kapila's advice in the *Kapila Gītā* (*Bhāgavata Purāṇa* 3.32.41–42), that his teachings may be given to one who is "reverent and devoted, modest, free of malice, friendly to all beings, desirous of listening, detached from external objects, calm in mind, free of jealousy, pure, and holding me dear beyond all else."

3. Cf. *Devī Gītā* 8.35cd–36ab.

4. See notes 1 and 2 above.

5. *Devī-Bhāgavata* 11.18,49–71.

Translation

[The Goddess disappears, and Vyāsa briefly reverts to the frame story regarding the birth of Gaurī and the slaying of Tāraka.]

Vyāsa spoke:

10.38. The glorious one finished her speech and then vanished from sight,
While all the gods rejoiced for having seen the Goddess.[1]

10.39. Later she was born to Himālaya as the goddess Haimavatī,[2]
Who would be renowned as Gaurī. She was given in marriage to Śīva.[3]

10.40. Afterward Skanda was born, who slew Tāraka.[4]
Earlier, during the churning of the ocean, precious jewels arose,[5] O King.

10.41. On that occasion the gods, eager to gain prosperity in the form of Lakṣmī, praised the Goddess.
Then, to favor the gods, Lakṣmī herself came forth.
10.42. The gods gave her in marriage to Viṣṇu, who thereby attained peace of mind.
Thus I have recounted to you, O King, this sublime glorification of the Goddess,[6]
10.43. Dealing with the births of Gaurī and Lakṣmī, and granting all desires.

Comment

When the Goddess disappears, the gods rejoice, for they have just received the holy and auspicious sight of the Goddess (*devī-darśana*). To receive the "vision" (*darśana*) or sight of a deity, or holy person, is considered to be an extremely auspicious event. This sight involves not only seeing, but also being seen by, the deity. The devotee visually touches the god, and is touched in return, thereby absorbing something of the divine, auspicious power.[7] For instance, the effect of the powerful glance of the Goddess Lalitā is nicely described in the *Lalitā Mahātmya*. When the gods, in their usual predicament with the demons, successfully attain Lalitā's *darśana*, receiving her propitious glance, "they are all immediately free from ailments, their limbs become full and firm, their bodies hard like diamonds, endowed with great power."[8] No wonder the gods in the *Devī Gītā* rejoice when they realize they have been touched by, and infused with, a portion of the World-Mother's *śakti*.

With the Goddess vanished, Vyāsa proceeds to tie up the loose ends of the frame story. We may recall from chapter 1 that the victory of the demon Tāraka over the gods provided the occasion for the appearance of the Goddess. The tormented gods sought out the assistance of the Devī, who promised to send her Śakti Gaurī to be born to Himālaya. Gaurī, with Śiva, would produce Skanda, the only being capable of slaying Tāraka. Vyāsa here briefly indicates the fulfillment of these predictions.

In addition to the birth of Gaurī, Vyāsa refers to the arising of Lakṣmī from the Milk Ocean. This detail relates back to the story of the humbling of Viṣṇu and Śiva found in the *Devī-Bhāgavata*, in the two chapters immediately preceding the *Devī Gītā*. (This story is summarized in the Comment on 1.26–29.) When the two gods, due to their arrogance, lost their wives, Gaurī and Lakṣmī, they went out of their minds and became unconscious. The Goddess eventually restored their wives/Śaktis, promising that one Śakti would be born in Dakṣa's house (Satī/Gaurī, Śiva's spouse), and the other in the Milk Ocean (Lakṣmī, Viṣṇu's spouse).

It is noteworthy that Vyāsa refers to the whole of the *Devī Gītā*—with its brief mention of the stories of the births of Gaurī and Lakṣmī—as a glorification of the Goddess (*devī-māhātmya*). This title often refers specifically to the famous *Devī Māhātmya* of the *Mārkaṇḍeya Purāṇa*, but in a generic sense it refers to any glorification of the Goddess. This self-reference on the part of the *Devī Gītā* is interesting, for it reveals a continuity between *māhātmya*-type literature, emphasizing praise for a deity, and *gītā*-type literature, focusing on revelations by a deity.[9] The bulk of the *Devī Gītā*, of course, consists of the teachings of the Goddess. But it also contains two important hymns of praise to the Devī (in the first and third chapters), and thus may easily be considered a *māhātmya* as well.

Notes

1. *devī-darśana:* "the seeing or vision of the Goddess." See Comment above.

2. See the Comment on 1.26–29.

3. Thus the promise made by the Goddess in 1.63–64 is fulfilled.

4. See *Matsya Purāṇa* 146–59 for a lengthy account of the birth of Tāraka, his battle with the gods, and his eventual destruction by Skanda. The *Devī Gītā* here summarizes this famous myth in exactly two lines—clearly the author of the text has little interest in the story, except as a frame for introducing the Goddess.

5. This refers to the famous myth of the churning of the Milk Ocean. As a result of the churning, various items and entities arose out of the ocean, like butter from milk, including the jewels mentioned here, and the goddess Lakṣmī mentioned in the next verse.

6. *devī-māhātmya;* see Comment above. The sage Medhas in the *Devī Māhātmya* (13.2) concludes his account of the great deeds of the Goddess in almost identical words.

7. See Diana L. Eck, *Darśan*, pp. 3–9.

8. *Lalitā Mahātmya* (*Brahmāṇḍa Purāṇa*) 3.4.12.75.

9. The *Kūrma Devī Gītā,* which appears to be the earliest Śākta *gītā,* also refers to itself as a glorification of the Goddess (*devyā-māhātmya; Kūrma Purāṇa* 1.11.336). Cf. my *The Triumph of the Goddess,* pp. 180–82.

Translation

[Vyāsa in conclusion, like the Goddess, cautions against the indiscriminate dissemination of the secret teachings of the *Devī Gītā.*]

10.43. [cont.] Do not reveal this secret mystery that I have narrated to just anyone, anywhere.

10.44. Diligently guard the secret mystery of this *Song.* I have briefly answered all your questions, Faultless One.

10.45 This account is purifying, sanctifying, and divine. What further do you wish to hear?

Comment

In the first chapter, Vyāsa referred to the teachings of the Goddess as a mystery hidden in scripture (1.74), a notion repeated here. Such a mystery, as we have seen on a number of occasions, is to be revealed only to those properly qualified. From the perspective of the *Devī Gītā,* the basic qualification is quite straightforward: devotion to the Goddess. As Vyāsa himself told Janamejaya, the Faultless One, shortly before narrating to him the *Devī Gītā,* "There is nothing that cannot be revealed to you, as you are devoted to the Goddess."[1]

The *Devī Gītā* now comes to a close, with Vyāsa patiently asking if Janamejaya has further questions. The king, insatiable in his quest for knowledge about the Goddess, in the next book (eight) of the *Devī-Bhāgavata,* continues with a query about how the World-Mother was worshiped in ages past.

Note

1. *Devī Bhāgavata* 7.29.23cd.

Afterword

It is beyond the scope of this book to examine in detail the ways in which the *Devī Gītā* has been received, perceived, and utilized in the centuries since its composition. But these are important and intriguing issues, and they deserve at least some consideration. Many of the issues relate to the complex question of what "scripture" itself is, a question that depends in large part on how a "sacred text" is approached by those for whom it functions as scripture.

Many scholars of Indian religions today appreciate the fact that Hindus approach the holy words of their scriptural traditions from two rather distinct perspectives. One concerns itself with the content or meaning (*artha*) of a text, an approach with which most readers of this translation are quite familiar and which reflects their main motivation in picking up this book in the first place. Concern for the meaning of the text was also the main reason why I undertook the task of translating the *Devī Gītā*. This content-oriented approach has dominated Western scholarly understanding of scriptures (both written and oral) from the various religious traditions of the world, at least until fairly recently. The other approach concentrates on the form or sound (*śabda*) of the words, in an attempt to unlock and tap their sonic power. The former emphasizes intelligibility and understanding, the latter mantric-style recitation or chanting.[1]

Probably most Hindu scriptural texts inspire both kinds of response to some degree, but often with a strong leaning toward one or the other. The ancient Vedic oral texts generally elicit a response focusing on the mantric side, with understanding radically subordinated. Purāṇic texts largely reverse the relative emphasis. A few texts, such as the *Mārkaṇḍeya Purāṇa*'s *Devī Māhātmya*, inspire significant responses of both types.

The *Devī Gītā*, embedded in its own Purāṇic setting, has probably been interpreted and received through the centuries primarily as a text focusing on *artha*. Its very genre as a *gītā*, underscoring the instruction or *upadeśa* of the Goddess, indicates that its original function was to teach, to provide intellectual insight and understanding. That is, its philosophical and polemical orientation, along with its many explanatory quotations from the Upaniṣads, points to its basic concern with the meaning of its words, not with (or not primarily with) their form or sound. Nīlakaṇṭha himself, the erudite commentator on the *Devī Gītā*, understood and interpreted the text as belonging chiefly to the *artha* tradition, judging by the nature of his comments. Such an approach is also reflected in the prefaces of modern editions of the *Devī Gītā* text. For example, Gangadhar Dvivedi, in his Hindi preface to a recent edition, compares the teachings of the *Bhagavad Gītā* with those of the *Devī Gītā* and concludes: "There is excellence and much that is worthy of meditation in almost all of both *gītās*. From critical study of [them], one can understand many deep matters about questions of self. Because of the similarities [of the two texts], much from the *Bhagavad Gītā* has been clarified and simplified for me."[2]

As a text long interpreted in terms of its meaning and content, the *Devī Gītā* has provided important delineations of the character of the Goddess and her relationship to humankind. Perhaps the text's most significant contribution to the Śākta theological tradition is the ideal of a Goddess both single and benign. The specific impact or influence of the *Devī Gītā*'s vision on various Śākta thinkers and schools is not well researched. There are many opportunities here for further investigations, and hopefully this translation with commentary will both inspire and facilitate such efforts.

While the *Devī Gītā* has been approached historically primarily as a text to be understood, its mantric potential has not been entirely neglected. Nīlakaṇṭha points out a number of verses in the *Devī Gītā* that are Vedic mantras.[3] (This inclusion of Vedic mantras in a Purāṇic text, of course, raises a number of complex issues about exactly what kind of text it is, and who is qualified to receive or hear it.) He also quotes a verse at least as old as the sixteenth century that urges: "One should recite the *Devī-Bhāgavata* [which, of course, includes the *Devī Gītā*] daily with devotion and concentration, especially in Navarātra, with joy, for the pleasure of Śrī Devī."[4] Cynthia A. Humes, who has spent considerable time in India studying the ritual recitation of the

Devī Māhātmya, reports that the *Devī-Bhāgavata* as a whole is recited on occasion at the Devī temple in Vindhyācal, especially during the Navarātra.[5] The shift to, or rather inclusion of, a more mantric interpretation of the text was perhaps inevitable, given the prestige of the *śabda* tradition in India.

The inclusion of the "Navaślokī Devī Gītā" ("The Essential Devī Gītā in Nine Verses") in a recent printed edition of the *Devī Gītā*[6] represents in all probability a modern attempt to encourage further the use of the text in a mantric fashion, parallel to the ritual uses of the *Devī Māhātmya* (or *Durgā Saptaśatī*, as it is also known). (The "Navaślokī Devī Gītā" appears at the beginning of this translation, along with commentary.) The Navaśloki Devī Gītā may well have been composed in imitation of similar selected sets of seven or nine verses from the *Devī Māhātmya,* such as "the well-known 'Saptaślokī Durgā,' . . . [that represents] the power of the text in condensed or abridged form."[7] Such abridged versions are clearly intended for more convenient recitation.

There is some question concerning the age of the "Navaślokī Devī Gītā." Humes contends:

> I doubt very much that it [the prefixing of the nine verses] is hundreds of years old. I am inclined to believe it is a modern invention deliberately modeled on most editions of the *Devī Māhātmya*'s inclusion of a nine verse Navaślokī Saptaśatī. . . . The author's teacher [Ramadhin Caturvedi] writes in the Hindi preface, "It is my fullest hope that, like the *Durgā Saptaśatī,* from the recitation of this *Devī Gītā* as well as [this] investigation into its meaning, faithful and curious devotees may have all of their heart's desires fulfilled, and that they may experience feelings of the greatest bliss."[8] By providing the Navaślokī [for the *Devī Gītā*], the author allows for the creation of a daily ritual which incorporates stronger philosophical ties to the Goddess in replacement of the less philosophical and perhaps more devotional/tantric use of mantra, promised by those who have discussed the ritual efficacy of the *Devī Māhātmya.*[9]

We may note the encouragement above, by Caturvedi, of both "investigation" and "recitation," encompassing both the *artha* and *śabda* perspectives.

The promotion of the mantric aspect of the *Devī Gītā* as attested by the inclusion of the "Navaślokī" represents a significant broadening of the way this text has been perceived and used, especially as an independent scripture apart from its Purāṇic context. Humes argues that although the author of the "Navaślokī" edition and his teacher

> are deliberately stressing the text's mantric capacity . . . the *Devī Gītā* has not functioned in a ritual manner, as far as I know, on a popular level. For instance, when the text is found in ritual manuals, no description of how it is to be used is given. This is unusual, because most ritual manuals give elaborate descriptions of how a mantra should be used. Thus, the Navaślokī edition appears to be a deliberate attempt to refashion practice of the *Devī Gītā* on the model of the *Devī Māhātmya*. It may or may not be successful; that it is published suggests that some believe there may be a market for a more philosophically sophisticated exposition of the Goddess in mantric form.[10]

Humes suggests, however, that the *Devī Gītā*'s philosophical bent, especially its strong Advaitin flavor that many Goddess devotees do not embrace, combined with its sectarian outlook (the *Devī-Bhāgavata* is well known to be anti-Vaiṣṇava), will limit the appeal of the text, especially as a rival to the popular *Devī Māhātmya* with its more inclusive spirit and vivid mythic imagery.[11]

It is interesting to note that the *Devī Māhātmya* itself may have undergone a similar process of transformation—from an *artha* text to one inclusive of *artha* and *śabda*—centuries earlier. Thomas B. Coburn summarizes the views of A. N. Jani, a contemporary devotee of the Goddess, regarding the *Devī Māhātmya*: "In Jani's estimation, the verses that comprise the *Devī-Māhātmya* were, in all likelihood, originally Purāṇic compositions. . . . However, surmises Jani, over time these words were found to have—like lots of other words in India—a potency that transcended their semantic sense. They came to function as *mantra*, their power turned to a variety of ends, and so they came to have an independent life of their own, outside the Purāṇic context."[12]

It is significant that Jani sees the *śabda* dimension of a text as "transcending" its semantic or *artha* aspect. What is it about a text, we may ask, that allows it, sooner or later, to transcend its semantic sense? To what extent is the sacred authority of a text augmented if it is fully explored in both its *śabda* and *artha* aspects? And what is the relationship between the *śabda* and *artha* dimensions of a single text? These are all questions worthy of further study. It is clear enough that the two approaches easily complement each other. The complementarity of the two was brought home to me as I studied the text of the *Devī Gītā* with Nagaraja Sharma, the associate priest at the Hindu Temple of San Antonio. He was delighted to find a Westerner interested in translating the *Devī Gītā*, and we discussed for hours the meanings of this or that verse. I would often read out a line, in my usual speaking or reading voice. When he would read aloud a verse, he almost always chanted the lines. It was clear to me that the sound of the *Devī Gītā* was as important to him as its meaning. Thus, whatever one has learned about the Goddess from this translation of her *Song*, we must remember that it is only part of what this scripture conveys in its fullness to Hindus. As the second verse of the *Devī Gītā* itself affirms: "What thoughtful person would ever tire of drinking the nectarine tales of Śakti? Death comes even to those who drink divine ambrosia, but not to one who hears this act of hers."

Notes

1. For discussions of these two approaches to scripture, see my "Purāṇa as Scripture," *History of Religions* 26 (1986):68–86; Thomas B. Coburn, *Encountering the Goddess*, pp. 150–56; and Lawrence A. Babb, *The Divine Hierarchy*, p. 218.

2. Gangadhar Dvivedi, preface to the Śrī Hari Śāstrī Dādhīca edition of the *Devī Gītā*, p. 3. I have slightly edited the translation of the preface provided to me by Cynthia A. Humes.

3. See his comments on verses 1.44–48.

4. Nīlakaṇṭha, in the introduction to his commentary on the *Devī-Bhāgavata*, attributes the verse to the *Devī-Yāmala*, as quoted by Maheśa Ṭhakkura (sixteenth century). See my *Triumph of the Goddess*, p. 291.

5. Personal communication from Humes. See my *Triumph of the Goddess*, pp. 291–92, for a summary of her comments on contemporary recitation of the *Devī-Bhāgavata*.

6. The Vārāṇasī edition translated into Hindi by Upendra Pāṇḍeya, with a preface by his teacher, Ramadhin Caturvedi.

7. Coburn, *Encountering the Goddess*, p. 152. While Coburn refers to a set of seven verses, the "Saptaślokī Durgā," Cynthia A. Humes refers to a nine-verse set, the "Navaślokī Saptaśatī."

8. Quoted from Ramadhin Caturvedi's preface (p. iv) to Upendra Pandey's translation of the *Devī Gītā*.

9. Personal correspondence from Cynthia Ann Humes (slightly edited with her permission), September 5 and 7, 1995. I am especially grateful for her translation of parts of the Hindi preface, as I do not know Hindi.

10. Personal correspondence with Humes, September 7, 1995.

11. Personal correspondences with Humes, September 26, 1995, and July 24, 1996.

12. Coburn, *Encountering the Goddess*, p. 146. Cf. p. 162.

Appendix

Verse Index of the Epithets and Names of the Goddess

The list below includes the various Sanskrit proper names, identifications, and epithets of the Goddess and of some of her major manifestations or incarnations (such as Satī and Gaurī) that appear in the text of the *Devī Gītā*. The distinction between a proper name and an epithet is not a sharp one in Sanskrit, nor is the distinction between the generic use of a term (such as *śakti*, "power") and its use as a name or epithet. Thus the inclusion or exclusion of a term in a given context is often a matter of judgment. The self-predications of the Goddess in *Devī Gītā* 3.3.13–16, where she identifies herself with various parts of the universe, are not included. Also excluded are the epithets of Brahman in 6.2–14, quoted from the *Muṇḍaka Upaniṣad*. Only the most important names/manifestations of the Goddess mentioned in the catalogue of holy sites and their associated goddesses in chapter 8 (8.5–30) are included.

The translations of the names and epithets of the Goddess given in parentheses generally correspond to their rendering in the main text, but there are several exceptions. For instance, some proper names, like Aditi, Durgā, and Satī, are left untranslated in the text. In other cases, the translations here have been modified so that they can stand alone, outside the grammatical and semantic context of the verses in which they appear.

Compounded names or epithets are given separately both in their full and in their simple or uncompounded forms. In the latter case, the compound forms are indicated in parentheses following the verse citation, e.g., Ambā: 1.19 (Para-), indicating that the form Parāmbā occurs in the cited verse (Parāmbā also has its own entry).

Aditi (The Boundless [Mother of the Gods]): 1.47

Ādyantarahita (Without Beginning or End): 1.29 (applied to the supreme lustrous light of the Goddess)

Agnivarṇā (Having the Color of Fire): 1.45

Akhaṇḍa (Whole): 4.48 (applied to Hrīṃ)

Akhaṇḍānandarūpā (Having the Nature of Undiminished Bliss): 1.51

Ambā (Mother): 1.19 (Para-), 22 (twice), 41, 74; 3.33 (Jagad-), 39 (Jagad-), 42, 54 (Jagad-); 7.1; 9.41

Ambikā (Mother): 1.43 (Jagad-), 61; 9.1, 2

Anaghā (Faultless One): 1.68

Anāmaya (Incorruptible): 2.3 (applied to the Goddess as Brahman)

Ānandarūpiṇī (She Who Is Bliss Incarnate): 9.42

Anaupamya (Incomparable): 2.3 (applied to the Goddess as Brahman)

Anirdeśya (Indescribable): 2.3 (applied to the Goddess as Brahman)

Aparycchinnatā (Having Undivided Wholeness): 2.19

Apratarkya (Beyond Reason): 2.3 (applied to the Goddess as Brahman)

Asaṅga (Beyond All Relation): 2.21 (applied to the Goddess as the Self)

Atītā (Gone Beyond, Transcending [the lower states of consciousness]): 10.11

Ātman Parātpara (The Supreme Self): 4.50

Ātmarūpā (She Who in Essence Is the Self): 4.40

Avasthātrayasākṣiṇī (Witness of the Three States of Consciousness): 1.52

Avyājakaruṇāmūrti (Embodiment of Unfeigned Compassion): 1.41 (see also Karuṇā and Karuṇāmūrti)

Avyākṛta (Unmanifest): 2.24 (applied to the Cosmic Seed form of the Goddess)

Avyākṛtarūpiṇī (She Who Resides in the Unmanifest State): 1.49

Avyakta (Unevolved): 2.24 (applied to the Cosmic Seed form of the Goddess)

Avyaktacidrūpā (Having the Form of Unmanifest Consciousness): 10.11 (see also Cit)

Bhadrā (The Propitious One): 1.44

Bhagavatī (The Glorious One): 10.38

Bhaktakāmadughā (She Who Is a Wish-granting Cow to Devotees): 3.22

Bhaktakāmakalpadrumā (She Who Is a Wish-yielding Tree to Devotees): 1.55 (see also Kāmakalpadrumā)

Bhaktakāmaprapūriṇī (She Who Satisfies the Desire of Her Devotees): 3.22

Bhaktārtikātarā (She Who Is Distressed by the Sorrows of Her Devotees): 9.41

Bhuvanasundarī (World-Charming Beauty): 10.30

Bhuvaneśānī (Ruler of the Universe): 1.15; 3.45 (see also Īśānī)

Bhuvaneśvarī (Ruler of the Universe): 1.50; 8.14 (Śrīmacchrī-) (see also Īśvarī)

Bījātmatā (Having the Nature of the Cosmic Seed): 2.7

Brahmaika (The One Brahman): 2.2 (Para-)

Brahmamūrti (She Who Resides in the Form of Brahman): 1.49

Brahmarūpiṇī (She Who Is the True Form of Brahman): 6.1

Caturbāhu (Four-Armed): 1.39

Cidekarasarūpiṇī (She Whose Essence Is Pure Consciousness): 1.51 (see also Cit)

Cidrūpa (She Whose Essence Is Consciousness) 7.30

Cinmātra (Pure Consciousness): 7.26 (see also Cit)

Cit (Pure Consciousness): 1.51 (-ekarasarūpiṇī); 2.2; 7.26 (-mātra), 30 (-rūpa); 10.11 (Avyakta- -rūpā)

Dakṣaduhitṛ (Daughter of Dakśa [the Goddess Satī, aka Aditi]): 1.47

Devadevī (Goddess of the Gods): 9.1 (see also Devī)

Deveṣī (Ruler of the Gods): 3.20, 43, 53; 8.1

Devī (Goddess): 1.3, 5, 44, 44 (Mahā-), 45, 46, 48; 3.20, 23 (Mahā-),31; 4.41 (-praṇava), 44; 5.33, 53, 55 (Dikkālādyanavacchinna-),59; 7.26; 8.1, 16, 18, 31, 32, 33 (twice), 34, 39, 41, 42; 9.1 (Deva-),39 (Parātparā); 10.9 (Mahā-), 13 (Śrī-), 17, 19 (Mūla-),20 (Mūla-), 27, 30, 32, 32 (Mahā-), 36 (-bhakti), 38 (-darśana), 41, 42 (-māhātmya)

Dhenu ([Wish-yielding] Cow): 1.46 (see also Bhaktakāmadughā)

Dikkālādyanavacchinnadevī (The Goddess Transcending All Space and Time): 5.55 (see also Devī)

Divya(-ā) (Divine): 1.31 (applied to the Goddess as Bhuvaneśvarī); 10.15 (applied to the Goddess visualized within one's heart)

Durgā (The Unassailable): 1.45

Dvaitajālavivarjita (Free from the Illusion of Duality): 2.21 (applied to the Self that is identified with the Goddess)

Gaurī (The Brilliant One [a Śakti of the Goddess]): 1.63; 10.39, 43

Haimavatī (She Who Is Born of the Snowy One [the Goddess Pāravatī, aka Umā, Gaurī]): 10.39

Hrīṃkāra (The Sound or Syllable Hrīṃ): 4.42

Hrīṃkāramantravācya (That Which Is Expressed in the Mantra Hrīṃ): 2.26 (applied to the Cosmic Seed manifestion of the Goddess)

Hrīṃkāramūrti (She Who Is Embodied in the Syllable Hrīṃ): 1.53; 3.45

Icchājñānakriyāśraya (The Seat of Will, Knowledge, and Action): 2.26 (applied to the Cosmic Seed manifestion of the Goddess)

Īśā (Ruler): 7.8 (Parama-)

Īśānī (Ruler or Queen): 1.15 (Bhuvana-), 73 (Parama-); 3.45 (Bhuvana); 5.1 (Mahā-); 9.1 (Mahā-), 21 (Sarva-)

Īśvarī ([Female] Ruler): 1.50 (Bhuvana-), 59 (Parama-), 60 (Mahā-), 63 (Parama-); 4.44 (Jagad-); 7.21; 8.14 (Śrīmacchrībhuvana-), 30 (Parama)

Jagadambā (World-Mother): 3.33, 39, 54 (see also Ambā)

Jagadambikā (World-Mother): 1.43 (see also Ambikā)

Jagaddhātrī (World-Mother): 10.23

Jagadīśvarī (Ruler of the Universe): 4.44 (see also Īśvarī)

Jagadyoni (Womb of the World): 7.21

Jaganmātṛ (World-Mother): 1.16, 17, 69; 5.53 (see also Mātṛ)

Jāgartī (She Who Is Attentive): 1.15

Kālarātri (She Who Is the Dark Night of Destruction): 1.47

Kalyāṇaguṇaratnānām Ākara (A Treasury of Auspicious Qualities): 7.12

Kāmakalpadrumā (She Who Is a Wish-fulfilling Tree): 1.15, 55 (Bhakta-)

Karuṇā (The Compassionate One): 1.53

Karuṇāmūrti (The Embodiment of Compassion): 1.41 (Avyāja-), 42

Karuṇāpūrṇā (Filled with Compassion): 9.40

Karuṇāpūrṇanayana (She Whose Eyes Overflow with Compassion): 3.55

Karuṇāsāgarā (Ocean of Compassion): 9.1

Kṛpārṇavā (Ocean of Compassion): 3.54

Kumārī (Maiden): 1.31

Kuṇḍalī (Coiled Serpent): 5.33 (said to be the essence of the Goddess)

Lakṣmī (The Goddess of Fortune): 10.41, 43

Mahādevī (The Great Goddess): 1.44; 3.23; 10.9, 32 (see also Devī)

Mahālakṣmī (The Great Goddess of Fortune): 1.48;

Mahāmāyā (The Great Power of Creation/Illusion): 8.15

Mahārājñī (Great Sovereign Queen): 1.66

Mahas (Lustrous Power): 1.1 (Paraṃ), 26, 28 (Paraṃ)

Mahāvibhu (Great Ruling Lord/Goddess): 3.40 (see also Vibhu)

Maheśānī (Great Ruler or Queen): 5.1; 9.1 (see also Īśānī)

Maheśitṛ (Great Ruler): 3.26, 29, 31

Maheśvarī (Great Ruler): 1.60

Mandasmitamukhāmbujā (She Who Displays a Tender Smile on her Lotus Mouth/Face): 1.41; 3.55

Maṇīdvīpādhivāsinī (She Who Dwells in the Jeweled Island): 1.15, 54

Manohara(-ā) (Delightful): 1.31; 10.15 (applied to the Goddess visualized within one's heart)

Mātṛ (Mother): 1.16 (Jagan-), 17 (Jagan-), 40 (Sarva-), 47 (Skanda-), 69 (Jagan-); 3.52; 5.53 (Jagan-); 8.2

Māyā (Power of Creation and Delusion): 2.3 (as evolute of the Goddess); 3.1 (as not separate from the Goddess); 5.50 (refers to the Kuṇḍalinī)

Mūladevī (Chief Goddess): 10.19, 20 (see also Devī)

Nānāmantrātmikā (She Who Is Composed of Manifold Mantras): 1.53

Navayauvanā (Having the Freshness of Youth): 1.31

Neti Neti ("Not This, Not That"): 4.31

Netratrayavilāsinī (She Whose Three Eyes Shine Playfully): 1.38

Pañcakoṣātiriktā (She Who Transcends the Five Sheaths): 1.52

Parabrahmaika (The One Supreme Brahman): 2.2

Paraṃ Mahas (Supreme Lustrous Power): 1.1,28 (see also Mahas)

Parāmbā (Supreme Mother): 1.19 (see also Ambā)

Parameśā (Supreme Ruler): 7.8

Parameśānī (Supreme Ruler): 1.73 (see also Īśānī)

Parameśvarī (Supreme Ruler): 1.59, 63; 8.30 (refers to Hṛllekhā) (see also Īśvarī)

Para(-ā)śakti (Supreme Power): 1.25; 8.12 (see also Śakti)

Pāśāṃkuśavarābhīti (She Who Holds a Noose and Goad while Gesturing Her Beneficence and Assurance of Safety) 1.39 (-caturbāhu); 3.55 (-dhara); 9.42 (-dharā)

Pāvanā (The Pure One): 1.47

Prakṛti ([Mother] Nature): 1.44

Praṇavarūpā (She Who Has the Form of the Syllable Oṃ): 1.53

Praṇavātmikā (She Who Is Composed of the Syllable Oṃ): 3.45

Prasādasumukhī (She of Gracious and Kindly Face, Disposed to Kindness): 1.41; 9.41

Prasannamukhapaṅkajā (She with a Lotus Face Kindly Disposed): 1.74

Pratyagātmasvarūpiṇī (She Who in Essence Is the Individual Soul): 1.52

Pūrṇa (Complete): 2.21 (applied to the Self that Is identified with the Goddess)

Ramaṇīyāṅgī (Beautiful of Limb): 1.31

Saccidānanda (Infinite Being, Consciousness, Bliss): 4.48 (applied to Hrīṃ)

Saccidānandarūpiṇī (Having the Form of Infinite Being, Consciousness, and Bliss): 10.4

Saccidānandavigraha (Having the Form of Being, Consciousness, and Bliss): 2.25 (applied to the Cosmic Seed manifestation of the Goddess)

Saccitsvarūpinī (She Who Embodies Infinite Being and Consciousness): 1.67

Saguṇā (Endowed with Fine Qualities): 9.40

Sākṣinī (Witness): 1.52 (Avasthātraya-); 9.46

Śakti (Power, Energy): 1.2, 6, 25 (Parā-), 48 (Sarva-), 63 (refers to Gaurī); 2.3 (refers to Māyā); 5.49 (Parā) (refers to the Kuṇḍalinī), 5.50 (refers to the Kuṇḍalinī); 8.12 (Para-); 9.16 (Sarva-)

Saṃvit (Intelligence, Consciousness): 2.2, 14; 5.59; 7.32; 9.44, 45 (twice)

Sarasvatī (Goddess of Speech): 1.47

Sarvadevanamaskṛtā (She Who Is Worshiped by All the Gods): 1.40

Sarvajñā (Omniscient): 1.59, 61; 9.16

Sarvakāraṇakāraṇa(-ā) (Cause of All Causes): 2.25 (applied to the Cosmic Seed manifestation of the Goddess); 7.21

Sarvamātṛ (Mother of All): 1.40 (see also Mātṛ)

Sarvamohinī (Deluder of All): 1.40

Sarvāṅgakomala (She Who Is Delicate in All Her Limbs): 3.55

Sarvasākṣirūpiṇī (Incarnate Witness of All): 1.59

Sarvaśakti (Power of All, Omnipotent): 1.48; 9.16 (see also Śakti)

Sarvāśāpūrikā (She Who Fulfills All Desires): 1.40

Sarvaśṛṅgāraveśāḍhyā (She Who Is Richly Adorned in Garments All Suited for Love): 1.40

Sarvātmā (Self of all): 3.46, 47, 49, 51

Sarvāvayavasundarī (Lovely in Every Limb): 9.40

Sarvavedāntasaṃsiddhā (She Who Is Established in the Whole of Vedānta): 3.45 (cf. Vedatātparyabhūmikā)

Sarveśānī (Universal Ruler): 9.21 (see also Īśānī)

Satī (The Virtuous One [a Śakti of the Goddess]): 1.4,9

Satya (Real): 2.21 (applied to the Self that Is identified with the Goddess)

Saundaryasārasīmā (The Quintessence of Beauty): 9.40

Śivā (The Auspicious One): 1.15, 44, 47, 60; 3.22; 8.40

Skandamātṛ (Mother of Skanda): 1.47 (see also Mātṛ)

Śrīdevī (Blessed Goddess): 10.13

Śrīmacchrībhuvaneśvarī (The Auspicious and Glorious Bhuvaneśvarī): 8.14 (see also Bhuvaneśvarī)

Śṛṅgārarasasampūrṇā (Filled with the Sentiment of Passion): 9.41

Sukharūpa (Having the Nature of Bliss): 2.21 (applied to the Self that Is identified with the Goddess)

Sūtrātmamūrti (She Who Has the Form of the Cosmic Soul): 1.49

Taruṇī (Youthful): 9.40

Tat (That [in the phrase, "You Are That"]): 4.20

Trilocanā (Three-Eyed): 1.39 (cf. Netratrayavilāsinī)

Turīyaka (The Transcendent Fourth): 4.42

Upādhirahita (Devoid of Finitude): 9.44 (applied to the Goddess as Pure Consciousness)

Vāc (Speech): 1.46 (twice)

Vairocanī (She Who Blazes Like the Sun): 1.45

Vaiṣṇavī (She Who Empowers Viṣṇu): 1.47

Varadā (Bestower of Boons): 1.55

Vedatātparyabhūmikā (She to Whom the Vedas Refer as Their Goal): 1.51 (cf. Sarvavedāntasaṃsiddhā)

Vibhu (Lord): 3.32, 34, 40 (Mahā-)

Viditāviditād Anya (Different from the Known and the Unknown): 7.34

Virāṭsvarūpiṇī (She Who Assumes the Form of the Cosmic Body): 1.49

Vyākṛtarūpiṇī (She Who Assumes the Form of the Unmanifest): 1.49

Yogasiddhidā (She Who Grants Success in Yoga): 5.50 (refers to the Śakti Kuṇḍalinī)

देवीगीता

प्रथमो ऽध्यायः

जनमेजय उवाच ।

धराधराधीश मौलावाविरासीत्परं महः । यदुक्तं भवता पूर्वं विस्तरात्तद्वदस्व मे ॥१॥
को विरज्येत मतिमान्पिबञ्छक्तिकथामृतम् । सुधां तु पिबतां मृत्युः स नैतच्छृण्वतो भवेत् ॥२॥

व्यास उवाच ।

धन्यो ऽसि कृतकृत्यो ऽसि शिक्षितो ऽसि महात्मभिः ।
भाग्यवानसि यद्देव्यां निर्व्याजा भक्तिरस्ति ते ॥३॥
शृणु राजन्पुरा वृत्तं सतीदेहे ऽग्निभर्जिते । भ्रान्तः शिवस्तु बभ्राम क्वचिद्देशे स्थिरो ऽभवत् ॥४॥
प्रपञ्चभानरहितः समाधिगतमानसः । ध्यायन्देवीस्वरूपं तु कालं निन्ये स आत्मवान् ॥५॥
सौभाग्यरहितं जातं त्रैलोक्यं सचराचरम् । शक्तिहीनं जगत्सर्वं साब्धिद्वीपं सपर्वतम् ॥६॥
आनन्दः शुष्कतां यातः सर्वेषां हृदयान्तरे । उदासीनाः सर्वलोकाश्चिन्ताजर्जरचेतसः ॥७॥
सदा दुःखोदधौ मग्ना रोगग्रस्तास्तदा ऽभवन् । ग्रहाणां देवतानां च वैपरीत्येन वर्तनम् ॥८॥
अधिभूताधिदैवानां सत्यभावान्नृपा ऽभवन् । अथा ऽस्मिन्नेव काले तु तारकाख्यो महसुरः ॥९॥
ब्रह्मदत्तवरो दैत्यो ऽभवत्त्रैलोक्यनायकः । शिवौरसस्तु यः पुत्रः स ते हन्ता भविष्यति ॥१०॥
इति कल्पितमृत्युः स देवदेवैर्महासुरः । शिवौरससुताभावाज्जगर्ज च ननन्द च ॥११॥
तेन चोपद्रुताः सर्वे स्वस्थानात्प्रच्युताः सुराः । शिवौरससुताभावाच्चिन्तामापुर्दुरत्ययाम् ॥१२॥
नाङ्गना शङ्करस्यास्ति कथं तत्सुतसम्भावः । अस्माकं भाग्यहीनानां कथं कार्यं भविष्यति ॥१३॥
इति चिन्तातुराः सर्वे जग्मुर्वैकुण्ठमण्डले । शशंसुर्हरिमेकान्ते स चोपायं जगाद ह ॥१४॥
कुतश्चिन्तातुराः सर्वे कामकल्पद्रुमा शिवा । जागर्ति भुवनेशानी मणिद्वीपाधिवासिनी ॥१५॥
अस्माकमनयादेव तदुपेक्षा ऽस्ति नान्यथा । शिक्षैवेयं जगन्मात्रा कृता ऽस्मच्छिक्षणाय च ॥१६॥
लालने ताडने मातुर्नाकारुण्यं यथा ऽर्भके । तद्वदेव जगन्मातुर्नियन्त्रा गुणदोषयोः ॥१७॥
अपराधो भवत्येव तनयस्य पदे पदे । को ऽपरः सहते लोके केवलं मातरं विना ॥१८॥
तस्माद्यूयं पराम्बां तां शरणं यात मा चिरम् । निर्व्याजया चित्तवृत्त्या सा वः कार्यं विधास्यति ॥१९॥
इत्यादिश्य सुरान्सर्वान्महाविष्णुः स्वजायया । संयुतो निर्जगामा ऽशु देवैः सह सुराधिपः ॥२०॥
आजगाम महाशैलं हिमवन्तं नगाधिपम् । अभवंश्च सुराः सर्वे पुरश्चरणकर्मिणः ॥२१॥
अम्बायज्ञविधानज्ञा अम्बायज्ञं च चक्रिरे । तृतीयादिव्रतान्याशु चक्रुः सर्वे सुरा नृप ॥२२॥

देवीगीतायां प्रथमो ऽध्यायः

केचित्समाधिनिष्णाताः केचिन्नामपरायणाः । केचित्सूक्तपराः केचिन्नामपारायणोत्सुकाः ॥२३॥
मन्त्रपारायणपराः केचित्कृच्छ्रादि कारिणः । अन्तर्यागपराः केचित्केचिन्न्यासपरायणाः ॥२४॥
हृल्लेखया पराशक्तेः पूजां चक्रुरतन्द्रिताः । इत्येवं बहुवर्षाणि कालो ऽगाज्जनमेजय ॥२५॥
अकस्माच्चैत्रमासीयनवम्यां च भृगोर्दिने । प्रादुर्बभूव पुरतस्तन्महः श्रुतिबोधितम् ॥२६॥
चतुर्दिक्षु चतुर्वेदैर्मूर्तिमद्भिरभिष्टुतम् । कोटिसूर्यप्रतीकाशं चन्द्रकोटिसुशीतलम् ॥२७॥
विद्युत्कोटिसमानाभमरुणं तत्परं महः । नैव चोर्ध्वं न तिर्यक्च न मध्ये परिजग्रभत् ॥२८॥
आद्यन्तरहितं तत्तु न हस्ताद्यङ्गसंयुतम् । न च स्त्रीरूपमथवा न पुंरूपमथोभयम् ॥२९॥
दीप्त्या पिधानं नेत्राणां तेषामासीन्महीपते । पुनश्च धैर्यमालम्ब्य यावत्ते ददृशुः सुराः ॥३०॥
तावत्तदेव स्त्रीरूपेणा ऽभाद्दिव्यं मनोहरम् । अतीव रमणीयाङ्गीं कुमारीं नवयौवनाम् ॥३१॥
उद्यत्पीनकुचद्वन्द्वनिन्दिताम्भोजकुड्मलाम् । रणत्किङ्किणिकाजालसिञ्जन्मञ्जीरमेखलाम् ॥३२॥
कनकाङ्गदकेयूरग्रैवेयकविभूषिताम् । अनर्घ्यमणिसम्भिन्नगलबन्धविराजिताम् ॥३३॥
तनुकेतकसंराजन्नीलभ्रमरकुन्तलाम् । नितम्बबिम्बसुभगां रोमराजिविराजिताम् ॥३४॥
कर्पूरशकलोन्मिश्रताम्बूलपूरिताननाम् । कनत्कनकताटङ्कविटङ्कवदनाम्बुजाम् ॥३५॥
अष्टमीचन्द्रबिम्बाभललाटामायतभ्रुवम् । रक्तारविन्दनयनामुन्नसां मधुराधराम् ॥३६॥
कुन्दकुड्मलदन्ताग्रां मुक्ताहारविराजिताम् । रत्नसम्भिन्नमुकुटां चन्द्ररेखावतंसिनीम् ॥३७॥
मल्लिकामालतीमालाकेशपाशविराजिताम् । काश्मीरबिन्दुनिटिलां नेत्रत्रयविलासिनीम् ॥३८॥
पाशाङ्कुशवराभीतिचतुर्बाहुं त्रिलोचनाम् । रक्तवस्त्रपरीधानां दाडिमीकुसुमप्रभाम् ॥३९॥
सर्वशृङ्गारवेषाढ्यां सर्वदेवनमस्कृताम् । सर्वाशापूरिकां सर्वमातरं सर्वमोहिनीम् ॥४०॥
प्रसादसुमुखीमम्बां मन्दस्मितमुखाम्बुजाम् । अव्याजकरुणामूर्तिं ददृशुः पुरतः सुराः ॥४१॥
दृष्ट्वा तां करुणामूर्तिं प्रणेमुः सकलाः सुराः । वक्तुं नाशक्नुवन्किंचिद्बाष्पसंरुद्धनिःस्वनाः ॥४२॥
कथंचित्स्थैर्यमालम्ब्य भक्त्या चानतकन्धराः । प्रेमाश्रुपूर्णनयनास्तुष्टुवुर्जगदम्बिकाम् ॥४३॥

देवा ऊचुः ।

नमो देव्यै महादेव्यै शिवायै सततं नमः । नमः प्रकृत्यै भद्रायै नियताः प्रणताः स्म ताम् ॥४४॥
तामग्निवर्णां तपसा ज्वलन्तीं वैरोचनीं कर्मफलेषु जुष्टाम् ।
दुर्गां देवीं शरणमहं प्रपद्ये सुतरसि तरसे नमः ॥४५॥
देवीं वाचमजनयन्त देवास्तां विश्वरूपाः पशवो वदन्ति ।
सा नो मन्द्रेषमूर्जं दुहाना धेनुर्वागस्मानुपसुष्टुतैतु ॥४६॥

कालरात्रीं ब्रह्मस्तुतां वैष्णवीं स्कन्दमातरम् ।

सरस्वतीमदितिं दक्षदुहितरं नमामः पावनां शिवाम् ॥४७॥

महालक्ष्म्यै च विद्महे सर्वशक्त्यै च धीमहि । तन्नो देवी प्रचोदयात् ॥४८॥

नमो विराट्स्वरूपिण्यै नमः सूत्रात्ममूर्तये । नमो ऽव्याकृतरूपिण्यै नमः श्रीब्रह्म मूर्तये ॥४९॥

यदज्ञानाज्जगद्भाति रज्जुसर्पस्त्रगादिवत् । यज्ज्ञानाल्लयमाप्नोति नुमस्तां भुवनेश्वरीम् ॥५०॥

नुमस्तत्पदलक्ष्यार्थां चिदेकरसरूपिणीम् । अखण्डानन्दरूपां तां वेदतात्पर्यभूमिकाम् ॥५१॥

पञ्चकोशातिरिक्तां तामवस्थात्रयसाक्षिणीम् । पुनस्त्वम्पदलक्ष्यार्थां प्रत्यगात्मस्वरूपिणीम् ॥५२॥

नमः प्रणवरूपायै नमो ह्रींकारमूर्तये । नानामन्त्रात्मिकायै ते करुणायै नमो नमः ॥५३॥

इति स्तुता तदा देवैर्मणिद्वीपाधिवासिनी । प्राह वाचा मधुरया मत्तकोकिलनिःस्वना ॥५४॥

श्रीदेव्युवाच ।

वदन्तु विबुधाः कार्यं यदर्थमिह सङ्गताः । वरदाहं सदा भक्तकामकल्पद्रुमा ऽस्मि च ॥५५॥

तिष्ठन्त्यां मयि का चिन्ता युष्माकं भक्तिशालिनाम् । समुद्धरामि मद्भक्तान्दुःखसंसारसागरात् ॥

इति प्रतिज्ञां मे सत्यां जानीथ विबुधोत्तमाः । इति प्रेमाकुलां वाणीं श्रुत्वा सन्तुष्टमानसाः ॥५७॥

निर्भया निर्जरा राजन्नूचुर्दुःखं स्वकीयकम् ।

देवा ऊचुः ।

ना ऽज्ञातं किञ्चिदप्यत्र भवत्या ऽस्ति जगत्त्रये ॥५८॥

सर्वज्ञया सर्वसाक्षिरूपिण्या परमेश्वरि । तारकेणा ऽसुरेन्द्रेण पीडिताः स्मो दिवानिशम् ॥५९॥

शिवाङ्गजाद्वधस्तस्य निर्मितो ब्रह्मणाशिवे । शिवाङ्गना तु नैवास्ति जानासि त्वं महेश्वरि ॥६०॥

सर्वज्ञपुरतः किं वा वक्तव्यं पामरैर्जनैः । एतदुद्देशतः प्रोक्तमपरं तर्कयाम्बिके ॥६१॥

सर्वदा चरणाम्भोजे भक्तिः स्यात्तव निश्चला । प्रार्थनीयमिदं मुख्यमपरं देहहेतवे ॥६२॥

इति तेषां वचः श्रुत्वा प्रोवाच परमेश्वरी । मम शक्तिस्तु या गौरी भविष्यति हिमालये ॥६३॥

शिवाय सा प्रदेया स्यात्सा वः कार्यं विधास्यति । भक्तिर्मच्चरणाम्भोजे भूयाद्युष्माकमादरात् ॥६४॥

हिमालयो हि मनसा मामुपास्ते ऽतिभक्तितः । ततस्तस्य गृहे जन्म मम प्रियकरं मतम् ॥६५॥

व्यास उवाच ।

हिमालयो ऽपि तच्छ्रुत्वा ऽत्यनुग्रहकरं वचः । बाष्पैः संरुद्धकण्ठाक्षो महाराज्ञीं वचो ऽब्रवीत् ॥

महत्तरं तं कुरुषे यस्यानुग्रहमिच्छसि । नोचेत्क्वाहं जडः स्थाणुः क्व त्वं सच्चित्स्वरूपिणी ॥६७॥

असम्भाव्यं जन्मशतैस्त्वत्पितृत्वं ममा ऽनघे । अश्वमेधादि पुण्यैर्वा पुण्यैर्वा तत्समाधिजैः ॥६८॥

देवीगीतायां प्रथमो ऽध्याय:

अद्य प्रपञ्चे कीर्तिः स्याज्जगन्माता सुता ऽभवत्।

अहो हिमालयस्यास्य धन्यो ऽसौ भाग्यवानिति ॥६९॥

यस्यास्तु जठरे सन्ति ब्रह्माण्डानां च कोटयः। सैव यस्य सुता जाता को वा स्यात्तत्समो भुवि ॥

न जाने ऽस्मत्पितृणां किं स्थानं स्यान्निर्मितं परम्। एतादृशानां वासाय येषां वंशे ऽस्ति मादृशः ॥

इदं यथा च दत्तं मे कृपया प्रेमपूर्णया। सर्ववेदान्तसिद्धं च त्वद्रूपं ब्रूहि मे तथा ॥७२॥

योगं च भक्तिसहितं ज्ञानं च श्रुतिसम्मतम्। वदस्व परमेशानि त्वमेवाहं यतो भवेः ॥७३॥

व्यास उवाच।

इति तस्य वचः श्रुत्वा प्रसन्नमुखपङ्कजा। वक्तुमारभथा ऽम्बा सा रहस्यं श्रुतिगूहितम् ॥७४॥

इति देवीगीतायां प्रथमो ऽध्याय:

द्वितीयो ऽध्याय:

श्रीदेव्युवाच।

शृण्वन्तु निर्जराः सर्वे व्याहरन्त्या वचो मम। यस्य श्रवणमात्रेण मद्रूपत्वं प्रपद्यते ॥१॥

अहमेवा ऽऽस पूर्वं तु नान्यत्किञ्चिन्नगाधिप। तदात्मरूपं चित्संवित्परब्रह्मैकनामकम् ॥२॥

अप्रतर्क्यमनिर्देश्यमनौपम्यमनामयम्। तस्य काचित्स्वतः सिद्धा शक्तिर्मायेति विश्रुता ॥३॥

न सती सा ना ऽसती सा नोभयात्मा विरोधतः। एतद्विलक्षणा काचिद्वस्तुभूता ऽस्ति सर्वदा ॥४॥

पावकस्योष्ण्यतेवेयमुष्णांशोरिव दीधितिः। चन्द्रस्य चन्द्रिकेवेयं ममेयं सहजा ध्रुवा ॥५॥

तस्यां कर्माणि जीवानां जीवाः कालाश्च सञ्चरे। अभेदेन विलीनाः स्युः सुषुप्तौ व्यवहारवत् ॥६॥

स्वशक्तेश्च समायोगादहं बीजात्मतां गता। स्वाधारावरणात्तस्या दोषत्वं च समागतम् ॥७॥

चैतन्यस्य समायोगान्निमित्तत्वं च कथ्यते। प्रपञ्चपरिणामाच्च समवायित्वमुच्यते ॥८॥

केचित्तां तप इत्याहुस्तमः केचिज्जडं परे। ज्ञानं मायां प्रधानं च प्रकृतिं शक्तिमप्यजाम् ॥९॥

विमर्श इति तां प्राहुः शैवशास्त्रविशारदाः। अविद्यामितरे प्राहुर्वेदतत्त्वार्थचिन्तकाः ॥१०॥

एवं नानाविधानि स्युर्नामानि निगमादिषु। तस्या जडत्वं दृश्यत्वाज्ज्ञाननाशात्ततो ऽसती ॥११॥

चैतन्यस्य न दृश्यत्वं दृश्यत्वे जडमेव तत्। स्वप्रकाशं च चैतन्यं न परेण प्रकाशितम् ॥१२॥

अनवस्थादोषसत्त्वान्न स्वेना ऽपि प्रकाशितम्। कर्मकर्त्रीविरोधः स्यात्तस्मात्तद्दीपवत्स्वयम् ॥१३॥

प्रकाशमानमन्येषां भासकं विद्धि पर्वत। अत एव च नित्यत्वं सिद्धसंवित्तनोर्मम ॥१४॥

जाग्रत्स्वप्नसुषुप्त्यादौ दृश्यस्य व्यभिचारतः। संविदो व्यभिचारश्च नानुभूतो ऽस्ति कर्हिचित् ॥१५॥

देवीगीतायां द्वितीयो ऽध्याय:

यदि तस्या ऽप्यनुभवस्तर्ह्ययं येन साक्षिणा। अनुभूत: स एवा ऽत्र शिष्ट: संविद्वपु: पुरा॥१६॥
अत एव च नित्यत्वं प्रोक्तं सच्छास्त्रकोविदै:। आनन्दरूपता चा ऽस्या: परप्रेमास्पदत्वत:॥१७॥
मा न भूवं हि भूयासमिति प्रेमात्मनि स्थितम्। सर्वस्या ऽन्यस्य मिथ्यात्वादसङ्गत्वं स्फुटं मम।१८।
अपरिच्छिन्नताप्येवमत एव मता मम। तच्च ज्ञानं नात्मधर्मो धर्मत्वे जडतात्मन:॥१९॥
ज्ञानस्य जडशेषत्वं न दृष्टं न च सम्भवि। चिद्धर्मत्वं तथा नास्ति चितश्चिन्न हि भिद्यते॥२०॥
तस्मादात्मा ज्ञानरूप: सुखरूपश्च सर्वदा। सत्य: पूर्णो ऽप्यसङ्गश्च द्वैतजालविवर्जित:॥२१॥
स पुन: कामकर्मादियुक्तया स्वीयमायया। पूर्वानुभूतसंस्कारात्कालकर्मविपाकत:॥२२॥
अविवेकाच्च तत्त्वस्य सिसृक्षावान्प्रजायते। अबुद्धिपूर्व: सर्गो ऽयं कथितस्ते नगाधिप॥२३॥
एतद्धि यन्मया प्रोक्तं मम रूपमलौकिकम्। अव्याकृतं तदव्यक्तं मायाशबलमित्यपि॥२४॥
प्रोच्यते सर्वशास्त्रेषु सर्वकारणकारणम्। तत्त्वानामादिभूतं च सच्चिदानन्दविग्रहम्॥२५॥
सर्वकर्मघनीभूतमिच्छाज्ञानक्रियाश्रयम्। ह्रींकारमन्त्रवाच्यं तदादितत्त्वं तदुच्यते॥२६॥
तस्मादाकाश उत्पन्न: शब्दतन्मात्ररूपक:। भवेत्स्पर्शात्मको वायुस्तेजोरूपात्मकं पुन:॥२७॥
जलं रसात्मकं पश्चात्ततो गन्धात्मिका धरा। शब्दैकगुण आकाशो वायु: स्पर्शरवान्वित:॥२८॥
शब्दस्पर्शरूपगुणं तेज इत्युच्यते बुधै:। शब्दस्पर्शरूपरसैरापो वेदगुणा: स्मृता:॥२९॥
शब्दस्पर्शरूपरसगन्धै: पञ्चगुणा धरा। तेभ्यो ऽभवन्महत्सूत्रं यल्लिङ्गं परिचक्षते॥३०॥
सर्वात्मकं तत्सम्प्रोक्तं सूक्ष्मदेहो ऽयमात्मन:। अव्यक्तं कारणो देह: स चोक्त: पूर्वमेव हि॥३१॥
यस्मिञ्जगद्बीजरूपं स्थितं लिङ्गोद्भवो यत:। तत: स्थूलानि भूतानि पञ्चीकरणमार्गत:॥३२॥
पञ्चसंख्यानि जायन्ते तत्प्रकारस्त्वथोच्यते। पूर्वोक्तानि च भूतानि प्रत्येकं विभजेद् द्विधा॥३३॥
एकैकं भागमेकस्य चतुर्धा विभजेद्गिरे। स्वस्वेतरद्वितीयांशे योजनात्पञ्च पञ्च ते॥३४॥
तत्कार्यं च विराड्देह: स्थूलदेहो ऽयमात्मन:। पञ्चभूतस्थसत्त्वांशै: श्रोत्रादीनां समुद्भव:॥३५॥
ज्ञानेन्द्रियाणां राजेन्द्र प्रत्येकं मिलितैस्तु तै:। अन्त:करणमेकं स्याद् वृत्तिभेदाच्चतुर्विधम्॥३६॥
यदा तु सङ्कल्पविकल्पकृत्यं तदा भवेत्तन्मन इत्यभिख्यम्।
स्याद् बुद्धिसंज्ञं च यदा प्रवेत्ति सुनिश्चितं संशयहीनरूपम्॥३७॥
अनुसन्धानरूपं तच्चित्तं च परिकीर्तितम्। अहंकृत्यात्मवृत्त्या तु तदहङ्कारतां गतम्॥३८॥
तेषां रजोंशैर्जातानि क्रमात्कर्मेन्द्रियाणि च। प्रत्येकं मिलितैस्तैस्तु प्राणो भवति पञ्चधा॥३९॥
हृदि प्राणो गुदे ऽपानो नाभिस्थस्तु समानक:। कण्ठदेशे ऽप्युदान: स्याद्व्यान: सर्वशरीरग:।४०।
ज्ञानेन्द्रियाणि पञ्चैव पञ्च कर्मेन्द्रियाणि च। प्राणादिपञ्चकं चैव धिया च सहितं मन:॥४१॥

५

देवीगीतायां द्वितीयो ऽध्याय:

एतत्सूक्ष्मशरीरं स्यान्मम लिङ्गं यदुच्यते। तत्र या प्रकृति: प्रोक्ता सा राजन्द्विविधा स्मृता ॥४२॥
सत्त्वात्मिका तु माया स्यादविद्या गुणमिश्रिता। स्वाश्रयं या तु संरक्षेत्सा मायेति निगद्यते ॥४३॥
तस्यां यत्प्रतिबिम्बं स्याद्बिम्बभूतस्य चेशितु:। स ईश्वर: समाख्यात: स्वाश्रयज्ञानवान्पर: ॥४४॥
सर्वज्ञ: सर्वकर्ता च सर्वानुग्रहकारक:। अविद्यायां तु यत्किंचित्प्रतिबिम्बं नगाधिप ॥४५॥
तदेव जीवसंज्ञं स्यात्सर्वदु:खाश्रयं पुन:। द्वयोरपीह सम्प्रोक्तं देहत्रयमविद्यया ॥४६॥
देहत्रयाभिमानाच्चाप्यभून्नामत्रयं पुन:। प्राज्ञस्तु कारणात्मा स्यात्सूक्ष्मदेही तु तैजस: ॥४७॥
स्थूलदेही तु विश्वाख्यस्त्रिविध: परिकीर्तित:। एवमीशो ऽपि सम्प्रोक्त ईशसूत्रविराट्पदै: ॥४८॥
प्रथमो व्यष्टिरूपस्तु समष्ट्यात्मा पर: स्मृत:। स हि सर्वेश्वर: साक्षाज्जीवानुग्रहकाम्यया ॥४९॥
करोति विविधं विश्वं नानाभोगाश्रयं पुन:। मच्छक्तिप्रेरितो नित्यं मयि राजन्प्रकल्पित: ॥५०॥

इति देवीगीतायां द्वितीयो ऽध्याय:

तृतीयो ऽध्याय:

देव्युवाच।

मन्मायाशक्तिसंक्लृप्तं जगत्सर्वं चराचरम्। सा ऽपि मत्त: पृथङ् माया नास्त्येव परमार्थत: ॥१॥
व्यवहारदृशा सेयं विद्या मायेति विश्रुता। तत्त्वदृष्ट्या तु नास्त्येव तत्त्वमेवा ऽस्ति केवलम् ॥२॥
सा ऽहं सर्वं जगत्सृष्ट्वा तदन्त: प्रविशाम्यहम्। मायाकर्मादिसहिता गिरे प्राणपुर:सरा ॥३॥
लोकान्तरगतिर्नो चेत्कथं स्यादिति हेतुना। यथा यथा भवन्त्येव मायाभेदास्तथा तथा ॥४॥
उपाधिभेदाद्भिन्ना ऽहं घटाकाशादयो यथा। उच्चनीचादिवस्तूनि भासयन्भास्कर: सदा ॥५॥
न दुष्यति तथैवा ऽहं दोषैर्लिप्ता कदा ऽपि न। मयि बुद्ध्यादिकर्तृत्वमध्यस्यैवापरे जना: ॥६॥
वदन्ति चा ऽऽत्मा कर्मेति विमूढा न सुबुद्धय:। अज्ञानभेदतस्तद्वन्मायाया भेदतस्तथा ॥७॥
जीवेश्वरविभागश्च कल्पितो माययैव तु। घटाकाशमहाकाशविभाग: कल्पितो यथा ॥८॥
तथैव कल्पितो भेदो जीवात्मपरमात्मनो:। यथा जीवबहुत्वं च माययैव न च स्वत: ॥९॥
तथेश्वरबहुत्वं च मायया न स्वभावत:। देहेन्द्रियादिसङ्घातवासनाभेदभेदिता ॥१०॥
अविद्या जीवभेदस्य हेतुर्नान्य: प्रकीर्तित:। गुणानां वासनाभेदभेदिता या धराधर ॥११॥
माया सा परभेदस्य हेतुर्नान्य: कदाचन। मयि सर्वमिदं प्रोतमोतं च धरणीधर ॥१२॥
ईश्वरो ऽहं च सूत्रात्मा विराडात्मा ऽहमस्मि च। ब्रह्मा ऽहं विष्णुरुद्रौ च गौरी ब्राह्मी च वैष्णवी ॥

देवीगीतायां तृतीयो ऽध्याय:

सूर्यो ऽहं तारकाश्चा ऽहं तारकेशस्तथा ऽस्म्यहम्।
पशुपक्षिस्वरूपा ऽहं चाण्डालो ऽहं च तस्कर: ॥१४॥
व्याधो ऽहं क्रूरकर्मा ऽहं सत्कर्मा ऽहं महाजन: । स्त्रीपुन्नपुंसकाकारो ऽप्यहमेव न संशय: ॥१५॥
यच्च किञ्चित्क्वचिद्वस्तु दृश्यते श्रूयते ऽपि वा। अन्तर्बहिश्च तत्सर्वं व्याप्या ऽहं सर्वदा स्थिता ॥
न तदस्ति मया त्यक्तं वस्तु किञ्चिच्चराचरम्। यद्यस्ति चेत्तच्छून्यं स्याद्वन्ध्यापुत्रोपमं हि तत् ॥१७॥
रज्जुर्यथा सर्पमालाभेदैरेका विभाति हि। तथैवेशादिरूपेण भाम्यहं ना ऽत्र संशय: ॥१८॥
अधिष्ठानातिरेकेण कल्पितं तन्न भासते। तस्मान्मत्सत्तयैवैतत् सत्तावन्नान्यथा भवेत् ॥१९॥

हिमालय उवाच।

यथा वदसि देवेशि समष्ट्यात्मवपुस्त्विदम्। तथैव द्रष्टुमिच्छामि यदि देवि कृपा मयि ॥२०॥

व्यास उवाच।

इति तस्य वच: श्रुत्वा सर्वे देवा: सविष्णव: । ननन्दुर्मुदितात्मान: पूजयन्तश्च तद्वच: ॥२१॥
अथ देवमतं ज्ञात्वा भक्तकामदुघा शिवा। अदर्शयन्निजं रूपं भक्तकामप्रपूरिणी ॥२२॥
अपश्यंस्ते महादेव्या विराड्रूपं परात्परम्। द्यौर्मस्तकं भवेद्यस्य चन्द्रसूर्यौ च चक्षुषी ॥२३॥
दिश: श्रोत्रे वचो वेदा: प्राणो वायु: प्रकीर्तित: । विश्वं हृदयमित्याहु: पृथिवी जघनं स्मृतम् ॥२४॥
नभस्तलं नाभिसरो ज्योतिश्चक्रमुर: स्थलम्। महर्लोकस्तु ग्रीवा स्याज्जनोलोको मुखं स्मृतम्।२५॥
तपोलोको रराटिस्तु सत्यलोकादध: स्थित: । इन्द्रादयो बाहव: स्यु: शब्द: श्रोत्रं महेशितु: ॥२६॥
नासत्यदस्रौ नासे स्तो गन्धो घ्राणं स्मृतो बुधै: । मुखमग्नि: समाख्यातो दिवारात्री च पक्ष्मणी ।२७॥
ब्रह्मस्थानं भ्रूविजृम्भो ऽप्यापस्तालु: प्रकीर्तिता: । रसो जिह्वा समाख्याता यमो दंष्ट्रा: प्रकीर्तिता: ॥
दन्ता: स्नेहकला यस्य हासो माया प्रकीर्तिता। सर्गस्त्वपाङ्गमोक्ष: स्याद्व्रीडोर्ध्वोष्ठो महेशितु: ॥२९॥
लोभ: स्यादधरोष्ठो ऽस्या धर्ममार्गस्तु पृष्ठभू: । प्रजापतिश्च मेढ्रं स्याद्य: स्रष्टा जगतीतले ॥३०॥
कुक्षि: समुद्रा गिरयो ऽस्थीनि देव्या महेशितु: ।
नद्यो नाड्य: समाख्याता वृक्षा: केश: प्रकीर्तिता: ॥३१॥
कौमारयौवनजरावयो ऽस्य गतिरुत्तमा। बलाहकास्तु केशा: स्यु: सन्ध्ये ते वाससी विभो: ॥३२॥
राजञ्छ्रीजगदम्बायाश्चन्द्रमास्तु मन: स्मृत: । विज्ञानशक्तिस्तु हरी रुद्रो ऽन्त:करणं स्मृतम् ॥३३॥
अश्वा हि जातय: सर्वा: श्रोणिदेशे स्थिता विभो: । अतलादिमहालोका: कट्यधोभागतां गता: ॥
एतादृशं महारूपं ददृशु: सुरपुङ्गवा: । ज्वालामालासहस्राढ्यं लेलिहानं च जिह्वया ॥३५॥
दंष्ट्राकटकटारावं वमन्तं वह्निमक्षिभि: । नानायुधधरं वीरं ब्रह्मक्षत्रौदनं च यत् ॥३६॥

देवीगीतायां तृतीयो ऽध्याय:

सहस्रशीर्षनयनं सहस्रचरणं तथा। कोटिसूर्यप्रतीकाशं विद्युत्कोटिसमप्रभम् ॥३७॥
भयङ्करं महाघोरं हृदक्ष्णोस्त्रासकारकम्। ददृशुस्ते सुरा: सर्वे हाहाकारं च चक्रिरे ॥३८॥
विकम्पमानहृदया मूर्च्छामापुर्दुरत्ययाम्। स्मरणं च गतं तेषां जगदम्बेयमित्यपि ॥३९॥
अथ ते ये स्थिता वेदाश्चतुर्दिक्षु महाविभो:। बोधयामासुरत्युग्रं मूर्छातो मूर्च्छितान्सुरान् ॥४०॥
अथ ते धैर्यमालम्ब्य लब्ध्वा च श्रुतिमुत्तमाम्। प्रेमाश्रुपूर्णनयना रुद्धकण्ठास्तु निर्जरा: ॥४१॥
बाष्पगद्गदया वाचा स्तोतुं समुपचक्रिरे।

देवा ऊचु:।

अपराधं क्षमस्वाम्ब पाहि दीनांस्त्वदुद्भवान् ॥४२॥
कोपं संहर देवेशि सभया रूपदर्शनात्। का ते स्तुति: प्रकर्तव्या पामरैर्निर्जरैरिह ॥४३॥
स्वस्याप्यज्ञेय एवा ऽसौ यावान्यश्च स्वविक्रम:। तदर्वाग्जायमानानां कथं स विषयो भवेत् ॥४४॥
नमस्ते भुवनेशानि नमस्ते प्रणवात्मिके। सर्ववेदान्तसंसिद्धे नमो ह्रींकारमूर्तये ॥४५॥
यस्मादग्नि: समुत्पन्नो यस्मात्सूर्यश्च चन्द्रमा:। यस्मादोषधय: सर्वास्तस्मै सर्वात्मने नम: ॥४६॥
यस्माच्च देवा: सम्भूता: साध्या:पक्षिण एव च। पशवश्च मनुष्याश्च तस्मै सर्वात्मने नम: ॥४७॥
प्राणापानौ व्रीहियवौ तप: श्रद्धा ऋतं तथा। ब्रह्मचर्यं विधिश्चैव यस्मात्तस्मै नमो नम: ॥४८॥
सप्त प्राणार्चिषो यस्मात्समिध: सप्त एव च। होमा: सप्त तथा लोकास्तस्मै सर्वात्मने नम: ॥४९॥
यस्मात्समुद्रा गिरय: सिन्धव: प्रचरन्ति च। यस्मादोषधय: सर्वा रसास्तस्मै नमो नम: ॥५०॥
यस्माद्यज्ञ: समुद्भूतो दीक्षा यूपश्च दक्षिणा:। ऋचो यजूंषि सामानि तस्मै सर्वात्मने नम: ॥५१॥
नम: पुरस्तात्पृष्ठे च नमस्ते पार्श्वयोर्द्वयो:। अध ऊर्ध्वं चतुर्दिक्षु मातर्भूयो नमो नम: ॥५२॥
उपसंहर देवेशि रूपमेतदलौकिकम्। तदेव दर्शया ऽस्माकं रूपं सुन्दरसुन्दरम् ॥५३॥

व्यास उवाच।

इति भीतान्सुरान्दृष्ट्वा जगदम्बा कृपार्णवा। संहृत्य रूपं घोरं तद्दर्शयामास सुन्दरम् ॥५४॥
पाशाङ्कुशवराभीतिधरं सर्वाङ्गकोमलम्। करुणापूर्णनयनं मन्दस्मितमुखाम्बुजम् ॥५५॥
दृष्ट्वा तत्सुन्दरं रूपं तदा भीतिविवर्जिता:। शान्तचित्ता: प्रणेमुस्ते हर्षगद्गदनि:स्वना: ॥५६॥

इति देवीगीतायां तृतीयो ऽध्याय:

चतुर्थोऽध्यायः

श्रीदेव्युवाच।

क्व यूयं मन्दभाग्या वै क्वेदं रूपं महाद्भुतम्। तथापि भक्तवात्सल्यादीदृशं दर्शितं मया ॥१॥
न वेदाध्ययनैर्योगैर्न दानैस्तपसेज्यया। रूपं द्रष्टुमिदं शक्यं केवलं मत्कृपां विना ॥२॥
प्रकृतं शृणु राजेन्द्र परमात्मा ऽत्र जीवताम्। उपाधियोगात्सम्प्राप्तः कर्तृत्वादिकमप्युत ॥३॥
क्रियाः करोति विविधा धर्माधर्मैकहेतवः। नानायोनीस्ततः प्राप्य सुखदुःखैश्च युज्यते ॥४॥
पुनस्तत्संस्कृतिवशान्नानाकर्मरतः सदा। नानादेहान्समाप्नोति सुखदुःखैश्च युज्यते ॥५॥
घटीयन्त्रवदेतस्य न विरामः कदापि हि। अज्ञानमेव मूलं स्यात्ततः कामः क्रियास्ततः ॥६॥
तस्मादज्ञाननाशाय यतेत नियतं नरः। एतद्धि जन्मसाफल्यं यदज्ञानस्य नाशनम् ॥७॥
पुरुषार्थसमाप्तिश्च जीवन्मुक्तदशा ऽपि च। अज्ञाननाशने शक्ता विद्यैव तु पटीयसी ॥८॥
न कर्म तज्जन्नोपास्तिर्विरोधाभावतो गिरे। प्रत्युताशा ऽज्ञाननाशे कर्मणा नैव भाव्यताम् ॥९॥
अनर्थदानि कर्माणि पुनः पुनरुशन्ति हि। ततो रागस्ततो दोषस्ततो ऽनर्थो महान्भवेत् ॥१०॥
तस्मात्सर्वप्रयत्नेन ज्ञानं सम्पादयेन्नरः। कुर्वन्नेवेह कर्माणीत्यतः कर्मा ऽप्यवश्यकम् ॥११॥
ज्ञानादेव हि कैवल्यमतः स्यात्तत्समुच्चयः। सहायतां व्रजेत्कर्म ज्ञानस्य हितकारि च ॥१२॥
इति केचिद्वदन्त्यत्र तद्विरोधान्न सम्भवेत्। ज्ञानाद्धृद्ग्रन्थिभेदः स्याद्धृद्ग्रन्थौ कर्मसम्भवः ॥१३॥
यौगपद्यं न सम्भाव्यं विरोधात्तु ततस्तयोः। तमः प्रकाशयोर्यद्वद्यौगपद्यं न सम्भवि ॥१४॥
तस्मात्सर्वाणि कर्माणि वैदिकानि महामते। चित्तशुद्ध्यन्तमेव स्युस्तानि कुर्यात्प्रयत्नतः ॥१५॥
शमो दमस्तितिक्षा च वैराग्यं सत्त्वसम्भवः। तावत्पर्यन्तमेव स्युः कर्माणि न ततः परम् ॥१६॥
तदन्ते चैव संन्यस्य संश्रयेद्गुरुमात्मवान्। श्रोत्रियं ब्रह्मनिष्ठं च भक्त्या निर्व्याजया पुनः ॥१७॥
वेदान्तश्रवणं कुर्यान्नित्यमेवमतन्द्रितः। तत्त्वमस्यादिवाक्यस्य नित्यमर्थं विचारयेत् ॥१८॥
तत्त्वमस्यादिवाक्यं तु जीवब्रह्मैक्यबोधकम्। ऐक्ये ज्ञाते निर्भयस्तु मद्रूपो हि प्रजायते ॥१९॥
पदार्थावगतिः पूर्वं वाक्यार्थावगतिस्ततः। तत्पदस्य च वाक्यार्थो गिरे ऽहं परिकीर्तितः ॥२०॥
त्वंपदस्य च वाच्यार्थो जीव एव न संशयः। उभयोरैक्यमसिना पदेन प्रोच्यते बुधैः ॥२१॥
वाच्यार्थयोर्विरुद्धत्वादैक्यं नैव घटेत ह। लक्षणा ऽतः प्रकर्तव्या तत्त्वमोः श्रुतिसंस्थयोः ॥२२॥
चिन्मात्रं तु तयोर्लक्ष्यं तयोरैक्यस्य सम्भवः। तयोरैक्यं तथा ज्ञात्वा स्वाभेदेनाद्वयो भवेत् ॥२३॥
देवदत्तः स एवा ऽयमितिवल्लक्षणा स्मृता। स्थूलादिदेहरहितो ब्रह्म सम्पद्यते नरः ॥२४॥

देवीगीतायां चतुर्थो ऽध्यायः

पञ्चीकृतमहाभूतसम्भूतः स्थूलदेहकः । भोगालयो जराव्याधिसंयुतः सर्वकर्मणाम् ॥२५॥
मिथ्याभूतो ऽयमाभाति स्फुटं मायामयत्वतः । सो ऽयं स्थूल उपाधिः स्यादात्मनो मे नगेश्वर ॥२६॥
ज्ञानकर्मेन्द्रिययुतं प्राणपञ्चकसंयुतम् । मनोबुद्धियुतं चैतत्सूक्ष्मं तत्कवयो विदुः ॥२७॥
अपञ्चीकृतभूतोत्थं सूक्ष्मदेहो ऽयमात्मनः । द्वितीयो ऽयमुपाधिः स्यात्सुखादेरवबोधकः ॥२८॥
अनाद्यनिर्वाच्यमिदमज्ञानं तु तृतीयकः । देहो ऽयमात्मनो भाति कारणात्मा नगेश्वर ॥२९॥
उपाधिविलये जाते केवलात्मा ऽवशिष्यते । देहत्रये पञ्चकोशा अन्तःस्थाः सन्ति सर्वदा ॥३०॥
पञ्चकोशपरित्यागे ब्रह्मपुच्छं हि लभ्यते । नेति नेतीत्यादिवाक्यैर्मम रूपं यदुच्यते ॥३१॥
न जायते म्रियते तत्कदाचिन्ना ऽयं भूत्वा न बभूव कश्चित् ।
अजो नित्यः शाश्वतो ऽयं पुराणो न हन्यते हन्यमाने शरीरे ॥३२॥
हतं चेन्मन्यते हन्तुं हतश्चेन्मन्यते हतम् । उभौ तौ न विजानीतो ना ऽयं हन्ति न हन्यते ॥३३॥
अणोरणीयान्महतो महीयानात्मा ऽस्य जन्तोर्निहितो गुहायाम् ।
तमक्रतुः पश्यति वीतशोको धातुः प्रसादान्महिमानमस्य ॥३४॥
आत्मानं रथिनं विद्धि शरीरं रथमेव तु । बुद्धिं तु सारथिं विद्धि मनः प्रग्रहमेव च ॥३५॥
इन्द्रियाणि हयानाहुर्विषयांस्तेषु गोचरान् । आत्मेन्द्रियमनोयुक्तं भोक्तेत्याहुर्मनीषिणः ॥३६॥
यस्त्वविद्वान्भवति चा ऽमनस्कश्च सदा ऽशुचिः । न तत्पदमवाप्नोति संसारं चाधिगच्छति ॥३७॥
यस्तु विज्ञानवान्भवति समनस्कः सदा शुचिः । स तु तत्पदमाप्नोति यस्माद्भूयो न जायते ॥३८॥
विज्ञानसारथिर्यस्तु मनः प्रग्रहवान्नरः । सो ऽध्वनः पारमाप्नोति मदीयं यत्परं पदम् ॥३९॥
इत्थं श्रुत्या च मत्या च निश्चित्या ऽऽत्मानमात्मना ।
भावयेन्मामात्मरूपां निदिध्यासनतो ऽपि च ॥४०॥
योगवृत्तेः पुरा स्वस्मिन्भावयेदक्षरत्रयम् । देवीप्रणवसञ्ज्ञस्य ध्यानार्थं मन्त्रवाच्ययोः ॥४१॥
हकारः स्थूलदेहः स्याद्रकारः सूक्ष्मदेहकः । ईकारः कारणात्मासौ ह्रींकारो ऽहं तुरीयकम् ॥४२॥
एवं समष्टिदेहे ऽपि ज्ञात्वा बीजत्रयं क्रमात् । समष्टिव्यष्ट्योरेकत्वं भावयेन्मतिमान्नरः ॥४३॥
समाधिकालात्पूर्वं तु भावयित्वैवमादृतः । ततो ध्यायेन्निलीनाक्षो देवीं मां जगदीश्वरीम् ॥४४॥
प्राणापानौ समौ कृत्वा नासाभ्यन्तरचारिणौ । निवृत्तविषयाकांक्षो वीतदोषो विमत्सरः ॥४५॥
भक्त्या निर्व्याजया युक्तो गुहायां निःस्वने स्थले । हकारं विश्वमात्मानं रकारे प्रविलापयेत् ॥४६॥
रकारं तैजसं देवमीकारे प्रविलापयेत् । ईकारं प्राज्ञमात्मानं ह्रींकारे प्रविलापयेत् ॥४७॥
वाच्यवाचकताहीनं द्वैतभावविवर्जितम् । अखण्डं सच्चिदानन्दं भावयेत्तच्छिखान्तरे ॥४८॥

इति ध्यानेन मां राजन्साक्षात्कृत्य नरोत्तम: । मद्रूप एव भवति द्वयोरप्येकता यत: ॥४९॥
योगयुक्त्या ऽनया दृष्ट्वा मामात्मानं परात्परम् । अज्ञानस्य सकार्यस्य तत्क्षणे नाशको भवेत् ॥५०॥
इति देवीगीतायां चतुर्थो ऽध्याय:

पञ्चमो ऽध्याय:

हिमालय उवाच ।
योगं वद महेशानि साङ्गं संवित्प्रदायकम् । कृतेन येन योग्यो ऽहं भवेयं तत्त्वदर्शने ॥१॥
श्रीदेव्युवाच ।
न योगो नभस: पृष्ठे न भूमौ न रसातले । ऐक्यं जीवात्मनोराहुर्योगं योगविशारदा: ॥२॥
तत्प्रत्यूहा: षडाख्याता योगविघ्नकरानघ । कामक्रोधौ लोभमोहौ मदमात्सर्यसञ्ज्ञकौ ॥३॥
योगाङ्गैरेव भित्त्वा तान्योगिनो योगमाप्नुयु: । यमं नियममासनप्राणायामौ तत: परम् ॥४॥
प्रत्याहारं धारणाख्यं ध्यानं सार्धं समाधिना । अष्टाङ्गान्याहुरेतानि योगिनां योगसाधने ॥५॥
अहिंसा सत्यमस्तेयं ब्रह्मचर्यं दया ऽऽर्जवम् । क्षमा धृतिर्मिताहार: शौचं चेति यमा दश ॥६॥
तप: सन्तोष आस्तिक्यं दानं देवस्य पूजनम् । सिद्धान्तश्रवणं चैव ह्रीर्मतिश्च जपो हुतम् ॥७॥
दशैते नियमा: प्रोक्ता मया पर्वतनायक । पद्मासनं स्वस्तिकं च भद्रं वज्रासनं तथा ॥८॥
वीरासनमिति प्रोक्तं क्रमादासनपञ्चकम् । ऊर्वोरुपरि विन्यस्य सम्यक्पादतले शुभे ॥९॥
अङ्गुष्ठौ च निबध्नीयाद्धस्ताभ्यां व्युत्क्रमात्तत: । पद्मासनमिति प्रोक्तं योगिनां हृदयङ्गमम् ॥१०॥
जानूर्वोरन्तरे सम्यक्कृत्वा पादतले शुभे । ऋजुकायो विशेद्योगी स्वस्तिकं तत्प्रचक्षते ॥११॥
सीवन्या: पार्श्वयोर्न्यस्य गुल्फयुग्मं सुनिश्चितम् । वृषणाध: पादपार्ष्णी पार्ष्णिभ्यां परिबन्धयेत् ।१२।
भद्रासनमिति प्रोक्तं योगिभि: परिपूजितम् । ऊर्वो: पादौ क्रमान्न्यस्यजान्वो: प्रत्यङ्मुखाङ्गुली ॥१३॥
करौ विदध्यादाख्यातं वज्रासनमनुत्तमम् । एकं पादमध: कृत्वा विन्यस्योरुं तथोत्तरे ॥१४॥
ऋजुकायो विशेद्योगी वीरासनमितीरितम् । इडया ऽऽकर्षयेद्वायुं बाह्यं षोडशमात्रया ॥१५॥
धारयेत्पूरितं योगी चतु:षष्ट्या तु मात्रया । सुषुम्नामध्यगं सम्यग्द्वात्रिंशन्मात्रया शनै: ॥१६॥
नाड्या पिङ्गलया चैव रेचयेद्योगवित्तम: । प्राणायाममिमं प्राहुर्योगशास्त्रविशारदा: ॥१७॥
भूयोभूय: क्रमात्तस्य बाह्यमेवं समाचरेत् । मात्रावृद्धि: क्रमेणैव सम्यग्द्वादश षोडश ॥१८॥
जपध्यानादिभि: सार्धं सगर्भं तं विदुर्बुधा: । तदपेतं विगर्भं च प्राणायामं परे विदु: ॥१९॥
क्रमादभ्यस्यत: पुंसो देहे स्वेदोद्गमो ऽधम: । मध्यम: कम्पसंयुक्तो भूमित्याग: परो मत: ॥२०॥

देवीगीतायां पञ्चमो ऽध्याय:

उत्तमस्य गुणावाप्तिर्यविच्छीलनमिष्यते। इन्द्रियाणां विचरतां विषयेषु निरर्गलम् ॥२१॥
बलादाहरणं तेभ्य: प्रत्याहारो ऽभिधीयते। अङ्गुष्ठगुल्फजानूरुमूलाधारलिङ्गनाभिषु ॥२२॥
हृद्ग्रीवाकण्ठदेशेषु लम्बिकायां ततो नसि। भ्रूमध्ये मस्तके मूर्ध्नि द्वादशान्ते यथाविधि ॥२३॥
धारणं प्राणमरुतो धारणेति निगद्यते। समाहितेन मनसा चैतन्यान्तरवर्तिना ॥२४॥
आत्मन्यभीष्टदेवानां ध्यानं ध्यानमिहोच्यते। समत्वभावना नित्यं जीवात्मपरमात्मनो: ॥२५॥
समाधिमाहुर्मुनय: प्रोक्तमष्टाङ्गलक्षणम्। इदानीं कथये ते ऽहं मन्त्रयोगमनुत्तमम् ॥२६॥
विश्वं शरीरमित्युक्तं पञ्चभूतात्मकं नग। चन्द्रसूर्याग्नितेजोभिर्जीवब्रह्मैक्यरूपकम् ॥२७॥
तिस्र: कोट्यस्तदर्धेन शरीरे नाड्यो मता:। तासु मुख्या दश प्रोक्तास्ताभ्यस्तिस्रो व्यवस्थिता: ।२८।
प्रधाना मेरुदण्डे ऽत्र चन्द्रसूर्याग्निरूपिणी। इडा वामे स्थिता नाडी शुभ्रा तु चन्द्ररूपिणी ॥२९॥
शक्तिरूपा तु सा नाडी साक्षादमृतविग्रहा। दक्षिणे या पिङ्गलाख्या पुंरूपा सूर्यविग्रहा ॥३०॥
सर्वतेजोमयी सा तु सुषुम्ना वह्निरूपिणी। तस्या मध्ये विचित्राख्ये इच्छाज्ञानक्रियात्मकम् ॥३१॥
मध्ये स्वयंभूलिङ्गं तु कोटिसूर्यसमप्रभम्। तदूर्ध्वं मायाबीजं तु हरात्मा बिन्दुनादकम् ॥३२॥
तदूर्ध्वं तु शिखाकारा कुण्डली रक्तविग्रहा। देव्यात्मिका तु सा प्रोक्ता मदभिन्ना नगाधिप ॥३३॥
तद्बाह्ये हेमरूपाभं वादिसान्तचतुर्दलम्। द्रुतहेमसमप्रख्यं पद्मं तत्र विचिन्तयेत् ॥३४॥
तदूर्ध्वं त्वनलप्रख्यं षड्दलं हीरकप्रभम्। बादिलान्तषड्वर्णेन स्वाधिष्ठानमनुत्तमम् ॥३५॥
मूलमाधारषट्कोणं मूलाधारं ततो विदु:। स्वशब्देन परं लिंगं स्वाधिष्ठानं ततो विदु: ॥३६॥
तदूर्ध्वं नाभिदेशे तु मणिपूरं महाप्रभम्। मेघाभं विद्युदाभं च बहुतेजोमयं तत: ॥३७॥
मणिवद्भिन्नं तत्पद्मं मणिपद्मं तथोच्यते। दशभिश्च दलैर्युक्तं डादिफान्ताक्षरान्वितम् ॥३८॥
विष्णुनाधिष्ठितं पद्मं विष्ण्वालोकनकारणम्। तदूर्ध्वेनाहतं पद्ममुद्यदादित्यसन्निभम् ॥३९॥
कादिठान्तदलैरेकं पत्रैश्च समधिष्ठितम्। तन्मध्ये बाणलिङ्गं तु सूर्यायुतसमप्रभम् ॥४०॥
शब्दब्रह्ममयं शब्दानाहतं तत्र दृश्यते। अनाहताख्यं तत्पद्मं मुनिभि: परिकीर्तितम् ॥४१॥
आनन्दसदनं तत्तु पुरुषाधिष्ठितं परम्। तदूर्ध्वं तु विशुद्धाख्यं दलं षोडशपङ्कजम् ॥४२॥
स्वरै: षोडशभिर्युक्तं धूम्रवर्णं महाप्रभम्। विशुद्धं तनुते यस्माज्जीवस्य हंसलोकनात् ॥४३॥
विशुद्धं पद्ममाख्यातमाकाशाख्यं महाद्भुतम्। आज्ञाचक्रं तदुर्ध्वे तु आत्मनाधिष्ठितं परम् ॥४४॥
आज्ञासंक्रमणं तत्र तेनाज्ञेति प्रकीर्तितम्। द्विदलं हक्षसंयुक्तं पद्मं तत्सुमनोहरम् ॥४५॥
कैलासाख्यं तदूर्ध्वं तु रोधिनी तु तदूर्ध्वत:। एवं त्वाधारचक्राणि प्रोक्तानि तव सुव्रत ॥४६॥
सहस्त्रारयुतं बिन्दुस्थानं तदूर्ध्वमीरितम्। इत्येतत्कथितं सर्वं योगमार्गमनुत्तमम् ॥४७॥

आदौ पूरकयोगेनाप्याधारे योजयेन्मनः। गुदमेढ्रान्तरे शक्तिस्तामाकुञ्च्य प्रबोधयेत् ॥४८॥
लिङ्गभेदक्रमेणैव बिन्दुचक्रं च प्रापयेत्। शम्भुना तां परां शक्तिमेकीभूतां विचिन्तयेत् ॥४९॥
तत्रोत्थितामृतं यत्तु द्रुतलाक्षारसोपमम्। पाययित्वा तु तां शक्तिं मायाख्यां योगसिद्धिदम् ॥५०॥
षट्चक्रदेवतास्तत्र सन्तर्प्यामृतधारया। आनयेत्तेन मार्गेण मूलाधारं ततः सुधी ॥५१॥
एवमभ्यस्यमानस्या ऽप्यहन्यहनि निश्चितम्। पूर्वोक्तदूषिता मन्त्राः सर्वे सिध्यन्ति नान्यथा ॥५२॥
जरामरणदुःखाद्यैर्मुच्यते भवबन्धनात्। ये गुणाः सन्ति देव्या मे जगन्मातुर्यथा तथा ॥५३॥
ते गुणाः साधकवरे भवन्त्येव न चान्यथा। इत्येवं कथितं तात वायुधारणमुत्तमम् ॥५४॥
इदानीं धारणाख्यं तु शृणुष्वावहितो मम। दिक्कालाद्यनवच्छिन्नदेव्यां चेतो विधाय च ॥५५॥
तन्मयो भवति क्षिप्रं जीवब्रह्मैक्ययोजनात्। अथवा समलं चेतो यदि क्षिप्रं न सिद्ध्यति ॥५६॥
तदा ऽवयवयोगेन योगी योगान्समभ्यसेत्। मदीयहस्तपादादावङ्गे तु मधुरे नग ॥५७॥
चित्तं संस्थापयेन्मन्त्री स्थानस्थानजयात्पुनः। विशुद्धचित्तः सर्वस्मिन्रूपे संस्थापयेन्मनः ॥५८॥
यावन्मनो लयं याति देव्यां संविदि पर्वत। तावदिष्टमनुं मन्त्री जपहोमैः समभ्यसेत् ॥५९॥
मन्त्राभ्यासेन योगेन ज्ञेयज्ञानाय कल्पते। न योगेन विना मन्त्रो न मन्त्रेण विना हि सः ॥६०॥
द्वयोरभ्यासयोगो हि ब्रह्मसंसिद्धिकारणम्। तमः परिवृते गेहे घटो दीपेन दृश्यते ॥६१॥
एवं मायावृतो ह्यात्मा मनुना गोचरीकृतः। इति योगविधिः कृत्स्नः साङ्गः प्रोक्तो मया ऽधुना ।६२॥
गुरूपदेशतो ज्ञेयो नान्यथा शास्त्रकोटिभिः ॥६३॥

इति देवीगीतायां पञ्चमो ऽध्यायः

षष्ठो ऽध्यायः

देव्युवाच।

इत्यादियोगयुक्तात्मा ध्यायेन्मां ब्रह्मरूपिणीम्। भक्त्या निर्व्याजया राजन्नासने समुपस्थितः ॥१॥
आविः सन्निहितं गुहाचरं नाम महत्पदम्। अत्रैतत्सर्वमर्पितमेजत्प्राणन्निमिषच्च यत् ॥२॥
एतज्जानथ सदसद्वरेण्यं परं विज्ञानाद्यद्वरिष्ठं प्रजानाम्।
यदर्चिमद्यदणुभ्यो ऽणु च यस्मिँल्लोका निहिता लोकिनश्च ॥३॥
तदेतदक्षरं ब्रह्म स प्राणस्तदु वाङ्मनः। तदेतत्सत्यममृतं तद्वेद्धव्यं सौम्य विद्धि ॥४॥
धनुर्गृहीत्वौपनिषदं महास्त्रं शरं ह्युपासानिशितं सन्धयीत।
आयम्य तद्भावगतेन चेतसा लक्ष्यं तदेवाक्षरं सौम्य विद्धि ॥५॥

देवीगीतायां षष्ठो ऽध्यायः

प्रणवो धनुः शरो ह्यात्मा ब्रह्म तल्लक्ष्यमुच्यते। अप्रमत्तेन वेद्धव्यं शरवत्तन्मयो भवेत् ॥६॥
यस्मिन्द्यौश्च पृथिवी चान्तरिक्षमोतं मनः सह प्राणैश्च सर्वैः।
तमेवैकं जानथात्मानमन्या वाचो विमुञ्चथामृतस्यैष सेतुः ॥७॥
अरा इव रथनाभौ संहता यत्र नाड्यः। स एषो ऽन्तश्चरते बहुधा जायमानः ॥८॥
ओमित्येवं ध्यायथात्मानं स्वस्ति वः पाराय तमसः परस्तात्।
दिव्ये ब्रह्मपुरे व्योम्नि आत्मा सम्प्रतिष्ठतिः ॥९॥
मनोमयः प्राणशरीरनेता प्रतिष्ठितो ऽन्ने हृदयं सन्निधाय।
तद्विज्ञानेन परिपश्यन्ति धीरा आनन्दरूपममृतं यद्विभाति ॥१०॥
भिद्यते हृदयग्रन्थिश्छिद्यन्ते सर्वसंशयाः। क्षीयन्ते चा ऽस्य कर्माणि तस्मिन्दृष्टे परावरे ॥११॥
हिरण्मये परे कोशे विराजं ब्रह्म निष्कलम्। तच्छुभ्रं ज्योतिषां ज्योतिस्तद्यदात्मविदो विदुः ॥१२॥
न तत्र सूर्यो भाति न चन्द्रतारकं नेमा विद्युतो भान्ति कुतो ऽयमग्निः।
तमेव भान्तमनुभाति सर्वं तस्य भासा सर्वमिदं विभाति ॥१३॥
ब्रह्मैवेदममृतं पुरस्ताद्ब्रह्म पश्चाद्ब्रह्म दक्षिणतश्चोत्तरेण। अधश्चोर्ध्वं च प्रसृतं ब्रह्मैवेदं विश्वं वरिष्ठम् ॥
एतादृगनुभवो यस्य स कृतार्थो नरोत्तमः। ब्रह्मभूतः प्रसन्नात्मा न शोचति न काङ्क्षति॥१५॥
द्वितीयाद्वै भयं राजंस्तदभावाद्बिभेति न। न तद्वियोगो मे ऽप्यस्ति मद्वियोगो ऽपि तस्य न ॥१६॥
अहमेव स सो ऽहं वै निश्चितं विद्धि पर्वत। मद्दर्शनं तु तत्र स्याद्यत्र ज्ञानी स्थितो मम ॥१७॥
ना ऽहं तीर्थे न कैलासे वैकुण्ठे वा न कर्हिचित्। वसामि किन्तु मज्ज्ञानिहृदयाम्भोजमध्यमे ।१८।
मत्पूजाकोटिफलदं सकृन्मज्ज्ञानिनो ऽर्चनम्। कुलं पवित्रं तस्या ऽस्ति जननी कृतकृत्यका ।१९।
विश्वम्भरा पुण्यवती चिल्लयो यस्य चेतसः। ब्रह्मज्ञानं तु यत्पृष्टं त्वया पर्वतसत्तम ॥२०॥
कथितं तन्मया सर्वं ना ऽतो वक्तव्यमस्ति हि। इदं ज्येष्ठाय पुत्राय भक्तियुक्ताय शीलिने ॥२१॥
शिष्याय च यथोक्ताय वक्तव्यं ना ऽन्यथा क्वचित्। यस्य देवे परा भक्तिर्यथा देवे तथा गुरौ ।२२॥
तस्यैते कथिता ह्यर्थाः प्रकाशन्ते महात्मनः। येनोपदिष्टाविद्येयं स एव परमेश्वरः ॥२३॥
यस्यायं सुकृतं कर्तुमसमर्थस्ततो ऋणी। पित्रोरप्यधिकः प्रोक्तो ब्रह्मजन्मप्रदायकः ॥२४॥
पितृजातं जन्म नष्टं नेत्थं जातं कदाचन। तस्मै न द्रुह्येदित्यादि निगमो ऽप्यवदन्नग ॥२५॥
तस्माच्छास्त्रस्य सिद्धान्तो ब्रह्मदाता गुरुः परः। शिवे रुष्टे गुरुस्त्राता गुरौ रुष्टे न शङ्करः ॥२६॥
तस्मात्सर्वप्रयत्नेन श्रीगुरुं तोषयेन्नग। कायेन मनसा वाचा सर्वदा तत्परो भवेत् ॥२७॥
अन्यथा तु कृतघ्नः स्यात्कृतघ्ने नास्ति निष्कृतिः। इन्द्रेणा ऽथर्वणायोक्ता शिरश्छेदप्रतिज्ञया ॥२८॥

अश्विभ्यां कथने तस्य शिरश्छिन्नं च वज्रिणा। अश्वीयं तच्छिरो नष्टं दृष्ट्वा वैद्यौ सुरोत्तमौ ॥२९॥
पुन: संयोजितं स्वीयं ताभ्यां मुनिशिरस्तदा। इति सङ्कटसम्पाद्या ब्रह्मविद्या नगाधिप ॥३०॥
लाब्धा येन स धन्य: स्यात्कृतकृत्यश्च भूधर ॥३१॥

इति देवीगीतायां षष्ठो ऽध्याय:

सप्तमो ऽध्याय:

हिमालय उवाच।

स्वीयां भक्तिं वदस्वा ऽम्ब येन ज्ञानं सुखेन हि। जायेत मनुजस्या ऽस्य मध्यमस्या ऽविरागिण: ।१॥

देव्युवाच।

मार्गास्त्रयो मे विख्याता मोक्षप्राप्तौ नगाधिप। कर्मयोगो ज्ञानयोगो भक्तियोगश्च सत्तम ॥२॥
त्रयाणामप्ययं योग्य: कर्तुं शक्यो ऽस्ति सर्वथा। सुलभत्वान्मानसत्वात्कायचित्ताद्यपीडनात् ॥३॥
गुणभेदान्मनुष्याणां सा भक्तिस्त्रिविधा मता। परपीडां समुद्दिश्य दम्भं कृत्वा पुर:सरम् ॥४॥
मात्सर्यक्रोधयुक्तो यस्तस्य भक्तिस्तु तामसी। परपीडादिरहित: स्वकल्याणार्थमेवच ॥५॥
नित्यं सकामो हृदयं यशोर्थी भोगलोलुप:। तत्तत्फलसमावाप्त्यै मामुपास्ते ऽतिभक्तित: ॥६॥
भेदबुद्ध्या तु मां स्वस्मादन्यां जानाति पामर:। तस्य भक्ति: समाख्याता नगाधिप तु राजसी ॥७॥
परमेशार्पणं कर्म पापसङ्क्षालनाय च। वेदोक्तत्वादवश्यं तत्कर्तव्यं तु मया ऽनिशम् ॥८॥
इति निश्चितबुद्धिस्तु भेदबुद्धिमुपाश्रित:। करोति प्रीतये कर्म भक्ति: सा नग सात्त्विकी ॥९॥
परभक्ते: प्रापिकेयं भेदबुद्ध्यवलम्बनात्। पूर्वप्रोक्ते ह्युभे भक्ती न परप्रापिके मते ॥१०॥
अधुना परभक्तिं तु प्रोच्यमानां निबोध मे। मद्गुणश्रवणं नित्यं मम नामानुकीर्तनम् ॥११॥
कल्याणगुणरत्नानामाकरायां मयि स्थिरम्। चेतसो वर्तनं चैव तैलधारासमं सदा ॥१२॥
हेतुस्तु तत्र को वापि न कदाचिद्भवेदपि। सामीप्यसार्ष्टिसायुज्यसालोक्यानां न चैषणा ॥१३॥
मत्सेवातो ऽधिकं किञ्चिन्नैव जानाति कर्हिचित्। सेव्यसेवकताभावात्तत्र मोक्षं न वाञ्छति ॥१४॥
परानुरक्त्या मामेव चिन्तयेद्यो ह्यतन्द्रित:। स्वाभेदेनैव मां नित्यं जानाति न विभेदत: ॥१५॥
मद्रूपत्वेन जीवानां चिन्तनं कुरुते तु य:। यथा स्वस्यात्मनि प्रीतिस्तथैव च परात्मनि ॥१६॥
चैतन्यस्य समानत्वान्न भेदं कुरुते तु य:। सर्वत्र वर्तमानानां सर्वरूपां च सर्वदा ॥१७॥
नमते यजते चैवा ऽप्याचाण्डालान्तमीश्वर। न कुत्रापि द्रोहबुद्धिं कुरुते भेदवर्जनात् ॥१८॥
मत्स्थानदर्शने श्रद्धा मद्भक्तदर्शने तथा। मच्छास्त्रश्रवणे श्रद्धा मन्त्रतन्त्रादिषु प्रभो ॥१९॥

देवीगीतायां सप्तमो ऽध्यायः

मयि प्रेमाकुलमती रोमाञ्चिततनुः सदा । प्रेमाश्रुजलपूर्णाक्षः कण्ठगद्गदनिस्वनः ॥२०॥
अनन्येनैव भावेन पूजयेद्यो नगाधिप । मामीश्वरीं जगद्योनिं सर्वकारणकारणम् ॥२१॥
व्रतानि मम दिव्यानि नित्यनैमित्तिकान्यपि । नित्यं यः कुरुते भक्त्या वित्तशाठ्यविवर्जितः ॥२२॥
मदुत्सवदिदृक्षा च मदुत्सवकृतिस्तथा । जायते यस्य नियतं स्वभावादेव भूधर ॥२३॥
उच्चैर्गायंश्च नामानि ममैव खलु नृत्यति । अहङ्कारादिरहितो देहतादात्म्यवर्जितः ॥२४॥
प्रारब्धेन यथा यच्च क्रियते तत्तथा भवेत् । न मे चिन्ता ऽस्ति तत्रापि देहसंरक्षणादिषु ॥२५॥
इति भक्तिस्तु या प्रोक्ता परभक्तिस्तु सा स्मृता । यस्यां देव्यतिरिक्तं तु न किञ्चिदपि भाव्यते ॥२६॥
इत्थं जाता परा भक्तिर्यस्य भूधर तत्त्वतः । तदैव तस्य चिन्मात्रे मद्रूपे विलयो भवेत् ॥२७॥
भक्तेस्तु या परा काष्ठा सैव ज्ञानं प्रकीर्तितम् । वैराग्यस्य च सीमा सा ज्ञाने तदुभयं यतः ॥२८॥
भक्तौ कृतायां यस्यापि प्रारब्धवशतो नग । न जायते मम ज्ञानं मणिद्वीपं स गच्छति ॥२९॥
तत्र गत्वा ऽखिलान्भोगाननिच्छन्नपि चर्च्छति । तदन्ते मम चिद्रूपज्ञानं सम्यग्भवेन्नग ॥३०॥
तेन मुक्तः सदैव स्याज्ज्ञानान्मुक्तिर्न चान्यथा । इहैव यस्य ज्ञानं स्याद्धृद्गतप्रत्यगात्मनः ॥३१॥
मम संवित्परतनोस्तस्य प्राणा व्रजन्ति न । ब्रह्मैव संस्तदाप्नोति ब्रह्मैव ब्रह्म वेद यः ॥३२॥
कण्ठचामीकरसममज्ञानात्तु तिरोहितम् । ज्ञानादज्ञाननाशेन लब्धमेव हि लभ्यते ॥३३॥
विदिताविदितादन्यन्नगोत्तम वपुर्मम । यथा ऽऽदर्शे तथा ऽऽत्मनि यथा जले तथा पितृलोके ॥
छायातपौ यथा स्वच्छौ विविक्तौ तद्वदेव हि । मम लोके भवेज्ज्ञानं द्वैतभावविवर्जितम् ॥३५॥
यस्तु वैराग्यवानेव ज्ञानहीनो म्रियेत चेत् । ब्रह्मलोके वसेन्नित्यं यावत्कल्पं ततः परम् ॥३६॥
शुचीनां श्रीमतां गेहे भवेत्तस्य जनिः पुनः । करोति साधनं पश्चात्ततो ज्ञानं हि जायते ॥३७॥
अनेकजन्मभी राजञ्ज्ञानं स्यान्नैकजन्मना । ततः सर्वप्रयत्नेन ज्ञानार्थं यत्नमाश्रयेत् ॥३८॥
नोचेन्महान्विनाशः स्याज्जन्मैतद्दुर्लभं पुनः । तत्रा ऽपि प्रथमे वर्णे वेदप्राप्तिश्च दुर्लभा ॥३९॥
शमादिषट्कसम्पत्तिर्योगसिद्धिस्तथैव च । तथोत्तमगुरुप्राप्तिः सर्वमेवा ऽत्र दुर्लभम् ॥४०॥
तथेन्द्रियाणां पटुता संस्कृतत्वं तनोस्तथा । अनेकजन्मपुण्यैस्तु मोक्षेच्छा जायते ततः ॥४१॥
साधने सफले ऽप्येवं जायमाने ऽपि यो नरः । ज्ञानार्थं नैव यतते तस्य जन्म निरर्थकम् ॥४२॥
तस्माद्राजन्यथाशक्त्या ज्ञानार्थं यत्नमाश्रयेत् । पदेपदे ऽश्वमेधस्य फलमाप्नोति निश्चितम् ॥४३॥
घृतमिव पयसि निगूढं भूते भूते च वसति विज्ञानम् । सततं मन्थयितव्यं मनसा मन्थानभूतेन ॥
ज्ञानं लब्ध्वा कृतार्थः स्यादिति वेदान्तडिण्डिमः । सर्वमुक्तं समासेन किं भूयः श्रोतुमिच्छसि ।४५॥

इति देवीगीतायां सप्तमो ऽध्यायः

१६

अष्टमो ऽध्याय:

हिमालय उवाच ।

कति स्थानानि देवेशि द्रष्टव्यानि महीतले । मुख्यानि च पवित्राणि देवीप्रियतमानि च ॥१॥

व्रतान्यपि तथा यानि तुष्टिदान्युत्सवा अपि । तत्सर्वं वद मे मात: कृतकृत्यो यतो नर: ॥२॥

श्रीदेव्युवाच ।

सर्वं दृश्यं मम स्थानं सर्वे काला व्रतात्मका: । उत्सवा: सर्वकालेषु यतो ऽहं सर्वरूपिणी ॥३॥

तथापि भक्तवात्सल्यात्किञ्चित्किञ्चिदथोच्यते । शृणुष्वा ऽवहितो भूत्वा नगराज वचो मम ॥४॥

कोलापुरं महास्थानं यत्र लक्ष्मी: सदा स्थिता । मातु: पुरं द्वितीयं च रेणुकाधिष्ठितं परम् ॥५॥

तुलजापुरं तृतीयं स्यात्सप्तशृङ्गं तथैव च । हिङ्गुलाया महास्थानं ज्वालामुख्यास्तथैव च ॥६॥

शकम्भर्या: परं स्थानं भ्रामर्या: स्थानमुत्तमम् । श्रीरक्तदन्तिकास्थानं दुर्गास्थानं तथैव च ॥७॥

विन्ध्याचलनिवासिन्या: स्थानं सर्वोत्तमोत्तमम् । अन्नपूर्णामहास्थानं काञ्चीपुरमनुत्तमम् ॥८॥

भीमादेव्या: परं स्थानं विमलास्थानमेव च । श्रीचन्द्रलामहास्थानं कौशिकीस्थानमेव च ॥९॥

नीलाम्बाया: परं स्थानं नीलपर्वतमस्तके । जाम्बूनदेश्वरीस्थानं तथा श्रीनगरं शुभम् ॥१०॥

गुह्यकाल्या महास्थानं नेपाले यत्प्रतिष्ठितम् । मीनाक्ष्या: परमं स्थानं यच्च प्रोक्तं चिदम्बरे ॥११॥

वेदारण्यं महास्थानं सुन्दर्या: समधिष्ठितम् । एकाम्बरं महास्थानं परशक्त्या प्रतिष्ठितम् ॥१२॥

महालसापरं स्थानं योगेश्वर्यास्तथैव च । तथा नीलसरस्वत्या: स्थानं चीनेषु विश्रुतम् ॥१३॥

वैद्यनाथे तु बगलास्थानं सर्वोत्तमं मतम् । श्रीमच्छ्रीभुवनेश्वर्या मणिद्वीपं मम स्मृतम् ॥१४॥

श्रीमत्त्रिपुरभैरव्या: कामाख्यायोनिमण्डलम् । भूमण्डले क्षेत्ररत्नं महामायाधिवासितम् ॥१५॥

नात: परतरं स्थानं क्वचिदस्ति धरातले । प्रतिमासं भवेद्देवी यत्र साक्षाद्रजस्वला ॥१६॥

तत्रत्या देवता: सर्वा: पर्वतात्मकतां गता: । पर्वतेषु वसन्त्येव महत्यो देवता अपि ॥१७॥

तत्रत्या पृथिवी सर्वा देवीरूपा स्मृता बुधै: । नात: परतरं स्थानं कामाख्यायोनिमण्डलात् ॥१८॥

गायत्र्याश्च परं स्थानं श्रीमत्पुष्करमीरितम् । अमरेशे चण्डिका स्यात्प्रभासे पुष्करेक्षिणी ॥१९॥

नैमिषे तु महास्थाने देवी सा लिङ्गधारिणी । पुरुहूता पुष्कराक्षे अषाढौ च रतिस्तथा ॥२०॥

चण्डमुण्डीमहास्थाने दण्डिनी परमेश्वरी । भारभूतौ भवेद्भूतिर्नाकुले नकुलेश्वरी ॥२१॥

चन्द्रिका तु हरिश्चन्द्रे श्रीगिरौ शाङ्करी स्मृता । जप्येश्वरे त्रिशूला स्यात्सूक्ष्मा चाम्रातकेश्वरे ॥२२॥

शाङ्करी तु महाकाले शर्वाणी मध्यमाभिधे । केदाराख्ये महाक्षेत्रे देवी सा मार्गदायिनी ॥२३॥

भैरवाख्ये भैरवी सा गयायां मङ्गला स्मृता । स्थाणुप्रिया कुरुक्षेत्रे स्वायम्भुव्यपि नाकुले ॥२४॥

देवीगीतायामष्टमो ऽध्याय:

कनखले भवेदुग्रा विश्वेशा विमलेश्वरे। अट्टहासे महानन्दा महेन्द्रे तु महान्तका ॥२५॥
भीमे भीमेश्वरी प्रोक्ता स्थाने वस्त्रापथे पुनः। भवानी शाङ्करी प्रोक्ता रुद्राणी त्वर्धकोटिके ॥२६॥
अविमुक्ते विशालाक्षी महाभागा महालये। गोकर्णे भद्रकर्णी स्याद्भद्रा स्याद्भद्रकर्णके ॥२७॥
उत्पलाक्षी सुवर्णाक्षे स्थाण्वीशा स्थाणुसञ्ज्ञिके। कमलालये तु कमला प्रचण्डा छगलण्डके ॥
कुरण्डले त्रिसन्ध्या स्यान्माकोटे मुकुटेश्वरी। मण्डलेशे शाण्डकी स्यात्काली कालञ्जरे पुनः ॥२९॥
शङ्कुर्णे ध्वनिः प्रोक्ता स्थूला स्यात्स्थूलकेश्वरे। ज्ञानिनां हृदयाम्भोजे हृल्लेखा परमेश्वरी ॥३०॥
प्रोक्तानीमानि स्थानानि देव्याः प्रियतमानि च। तत्तत्क्षेत्रस्य माहात्म्यं श्रुत्वा पूर्वं नगोत्तम ॥३१॥
तदुक्तेन विधानेन पश्चाद्देवीं प्रपूजयेत्। अथवा सर्वक्षेत्राणि काश्यां सन्ति नगोत्तम ॥३२॥
तत्र नित्यं वसेन्नित्यं देवीभक्तिपरायणः। तानि स्थानानि सम्पश्यञ्जपन्देवीं निरन्तरम् ॥३३॥
ध्यायंस्तच्चरणाम्भोजं मुक्तो भवति बन्धनात्। इमानि देवीनामानि प्रातरुत्थाय यः पठेत् ॥३४॥
भस्मीभवन्ति पापानि तत्क्षणान्नग सत्वरम्। श्राद्धकाले पठेदेतान्यमलानि द्विजाग्रतः ॥३५॥
मुक्तास्तत्पितरः सर्वे प्रयान्ति परमां गतिम्। अधुना कथयिष्यामि व्रतानि तव सुव्रत ॥३६॥
नारीभिश्च नरैश्चैव कर्तव्यानि प्रयत्नतः। व्रतमनन्ततृतीयाख्यं रसकल्याणिनीव्रतम् ॥३७॥
आर्द्रानन्दकरं नाम्ना तृतीयाया व्रतं च यत्। शुक्रवारव्रतं चैव तथा कृष्णचतुर्दशी ॥३८॥
भौमवारव्रतं चैव प्रदोषव्रतमेव च। यत्र देवो महादेवो देवीं संस्थाप्य विष्टरे ॥३९॥
नृत्यं करोति पुरतः सार्धं देवैर्निशामुखे। तत्रोपोष्य रजन्यादौ प्रदोषे पूजयेच्छिवाम् ॥४०॥
प्रतिपक्षं विशेषेण तद्देवीप्रीतिकारकम्। सोमवारव्रतं चैव ममा ऽतिप्रियकृन्नग ॥४१॥
तत्रापि देवीं सम्पूज्य रात्रौ भोजनमाचरेत्। नवरात्रद्वयं चैव व्रतं प्रीतिकरं मम ॥४२॥
एवमन्यान्यपि विभो नित्यनैमित्तिकानि च। व्रतानि कुरुते यो वै मत्प्रीत्यर्थं विमत्सरः ॥४३॥
प्राप्नोति मम सायुज्यं स मे भक्तः स मे प्रियः। उत्सवानपि कुर्वीत दोलोत्सवसुखान्विभो ॥४४॥
शयनोत्सवं यथा कुर्यात्तथा जागरणोत्सवम्। रथोत्सवं च मे कुर्याद्दमनोत्सवमेव च ॥४५॥
पवित्रोत्सवमेवापि श्रावणे प्रीतिकारकम्। मम भक्तः सदा कुर्यादेवमन्यान्महोत्सवान् ॥४६॥
मद्भक्तान्भोजयेत्प्रीत्या तथा चैव सुवासिनीः। कुमारीर्बटुकांश्चापि मद्बुद्ध्या तद्गतान्तरः ॥४७॥
वित्तशाठ्येन रहितो यजेदेतान्सुमादिभिः। य एवं कुरुते भक्त्या प्रतिवर्षमतन्द्रितः ॥४८॥
स धन्यः कृतकृत्यो ऽसौ मत्प्रीतेः पात्रमञ्जसा। सर्वमुक्तं समासेन मम प्रीतिप्रदायकम् ॥४९॥
ना ऽशिष्याय प्रदातव्यं ना ऽभक्ताय कदाचन ॥५०॥

इति देवीगीतायामष्टमो ऽध्याय

१८

नवमो ऽध्यायः

हिमालय उवाच ।

देवदेवि महेशानि करुणासागरे ऽम्बिके । ब्रूहि पूजाविधिं सम्यग्यथावदधुना निजम् ॥१॥

श्रीदेव्युवाच ।

वक्ष्ये पूजाविधिं राजन्नम्बिकाया यथा प्रियम् । अत्यन्तश्रद्धया सार्धं शृणु पर्वतपुङ्गव ॥२॥
द्विविधा मम पूजा स्याद्बाह्या चा ऽऽभ्यन्तरा ऽपि च ।
बाह्या ऽपि द्विविधा प्रोक्ता वैदिकी तान्त्रिकी तथा ॥३॥
वैदिक्यर्चा ऽपि द्विविधा मूर्तिभेदेन भूधर । वैदिकी वैदिकैः कार्या वेददीक्षासमन्वितैः ॥४॥
तन्त्रोक्तदीक्षावद्भिस्तु तान्त्रिकी संश्रिता भवेत् । इत्थं पूजारहस्यं च न ज्ञात्वा विपरीतकम् ॥५॥
करोति यो नरो मूढः स पतत्येवसर्वथा । तत्र या वैदिकी प्रोक्ता प्रथमा तां वदाम्यहम् ॥६॥
यन्मे साक्षात्परं रूपं दृष्टवानसि भूधर । अनन्तशीर्षनयनमनन्तचरणं महत् ॥७॥
सर्वशक्तिसमायुक्तं प्रेरकं यत्परात्परम् । तदेव पूजयेन्नित्यं नमेद्ध्यायेत्स्मरेदपि ॥८॥
इत्येतत्प्रथमार्चायाः स्वरूपं कथितं नग । शान्तः समाहितमना दम्भाहङ्कारवर्जितः ॥९॥
तत्परो भव तद्याजी तदेव शरणं व्रज । तदेव चेतसा पश्य जप ध्यायस्व सर्वदा ॥१०॥
अनन्यया प्रेमयुक्तभक्त्या मद्भावमाश्रितः । यज्ञैर्यज तपोदानैर्मामेव परितोषय ॥११॥
इत्थं ममा ऽनुग्रहतो मोक्ष्यसे भवबन्धनात् । मत्परा ये मदासक्तचित्ता भक्तवरा मताः ॥१२॥
प्रतिजाने भवादस्मादुद्धराम्यचिरेण तु । ध्यानेन कर्मयुक्तेन भक्तिज्ञानेन वा पुनः ॥१३॥
प्राप्या ऽहं सर्वथा राजन्न तु केवलकर्मभिः । धर्मात्सञ्जायते भक्तिर्भक्त्या सञ्जायते परम् ॥१४॥
श्रुतिस्मृतिभ्यामुदितं यत्स धर्मः प्रकीर्तितः । अन्यशास्त्रेण यः प्रोक्तो धर्माभासः स उच्यते ॥१५॥
सर्वज्ञात्सर्वशक्तेश्च मत्तो वेदः समुत्थितः । अज्ञानस्य ममा ऽभावादप्रमाणा न च श्रुतिः ॥१६॥
स्मृतयश्च श्रुतेरर्थं गृहीत्वैव च निर्गताः । मन्वादीनां श्रुतीनां च ततः प्रामाण्यमिष्यते ॥१७॥
क्वचित्कदाचित्तन्त्रार्थकटाक्षेण परोदितम् । धर्मं वदन्ति सोंशस्तु नैवग्राह्यो ऽस्ति वैदिकैः ॥१८॥
अन्येषां शास्त्रकर्तृणामज्ञानप्रभवत्वतः । अज्ञानदोषदुष्टत्वात्तदुक्तेर्न प्रमाणता ॥१९॥
तस्मान्मुमुक्षुर्धर्मार्थं सर्वथा वेदमाश्रयेत् । राजाज्ञा च यथा लोके हन्यते न कदाचन ॥२०॥
सर्वेशान्या ममाज्ञा सा श्रुतिस्त्याज्या कथं नृभिः । मदाज्ञारक्षणार्थं तु ब्रह्मक्षत्रियजातयः ॥२१॥
मया सृष्टास्ततो ज्ञेयं रहस्यं मे श्रुतेर्वचः । यदा यदा हि धर्मस्य ग्लानिर्भवति भूधर ॥२२॥
अभ्युत्थानमधर्मस्य तदा वेषान्बिभर्म्यहम् । देवदैत्यविभागश्चा ऽप्यत एवा ऽभवन्नृप ॥२३॥

देवीगीतायां नवमो ऽध्याय:

ये न कुर्वन्ति तद्धर्मं तच्छिक्षार्थं मया सदा। सम्पादितास्तु नरकास्त्रासो यच्छ्रवणाद्भवेत् ॥२४॥
यो वेदधर्ममुज्झित्य धर्ममन्यं समाश्रयेत्। राजा प्रवासयेद्देशान्निजादेतानधर्मिण: ॥२५॥
ब्राह्मणैर्न च सम्भाष्या: पङ्क्तिग्राह्या न च द्विजै:।
अन्यानि यानि शास्त्राणि लोके ऽस्मिन्विविधानि च ॥२६॥
श्रुतिस्मृतिविरुद्धानि तामसान्येव सर्वश:। वामं कापालकं चैव कौलकं भैरवागम: ॥२७॥
शिवेन मोहनार्थाय प्रणीतो नान्यहेतुक:। दक्षशापाद् भृगो: शापाद्दधीचस्य च शापत: ॥२८॥
दग्धा ये ब्राह्मणवरा वेदमार्गबहिष्कृता:। तेषामुद्धरणार्थाय सोपानक्रमत: सदा ॥२९॥
शैवाश्च वैष्णवाश्चैव सौरा: शाक्तास्तथैव च। गाणपत्या आगमाश्च प्रणीता: शङ्करेण तु ॥३०॥
तत्र वेदाविरुद्धोंशो ऽप्युक्त एव क्वचित्क्वचित्। वैदिकैस्तद्ग्रहे दोषो न भवत्येव कर्हिचित् ॥३१॥
सर्वथा वेदभिन्नार्थे नाधिकारी द्विजो भवेत्। वेदाधिकारहीनस्तु भवेत्तत्राधिकारवान् ॥३२॥
तस्मात्सर्वप्रयत्नेन वैदिको वेदमाश्रयेत्। धर्मेण सहितं ज्ञानं परं ब्रह्म प्रकाशयेत् ॥३३॥
सर्वैषणा: परित्यज्य मामेव शरणं गता:। सर्वभूतदयावन्तो मानाहङ्कारवर्जिता: ॥३४॥
मच्चित्ता मद्गतप्राणा मत्स्थानकथने रता:। संन्यासिनो वनस्थाश्च गृहस्था ब्रह्मचारिण: ॥३५॥
उपासन्ते सदा भक्त्या योगमैश्वरसञ्ज्ञितम्। तेषां नित्यावियुक्तानामहमज्ञानजं तम: ॥३६॥
ज्ञानसूर्यप्रकाशेन नाशयामि न संशय:। इत्थं वैदिकपूजाया: प्रथमाया नगाधिप ॥३७॥
स्वरूपमुक्तं संक्षेपाद् द्वितीयाया अथो ब्रुवे। मूर्तौ वा स्थण्डिले वा ऽपि तथा सूर्येन्दुमण्डले ॥३८॥
जले ऽथवा बाणलिङ्गे यन्त्रे वा ऽपि महापटे। तथा श्रीहृदयाम्भोजे ध्यात्वा देवीं परात्पराम् ॥३९॥
सगुणां करुणापूर्णां तरुणीमरुणारुणाम्। सौन्दर्यसारसीमान्तां सर्वावयवसुन्दराम् ॥४०॥
शृङ्गाररससम्पूर्णां सदा भक्तार्तिकातराम्। प्रसादसुमुखीमम्बां चन्द्रखण्डशिखण्डिनीम् ॥४१॥
पाशाङ्कुशवराभीतिधरामानन्दरूपिणीम्। पूजयेदुपचारैश्च यथावित्तानुसारत: ॥४२॥
यावदान्तरपूजायामधिकारो भवेन्न हि। तावद्बाह्यामिमां पूजां श्रयेज्जाते तु तां त्यजेत् ॥४३॥
आभ्यन्तरा तु या पूजा सा तु संविल्लय: स्मृत:। संविदेव परं रूपमुपाधिरहितं मम ॥४४॥
अत: संविदि मद्रूपे चेत: स्थाप्यं निराश्रयम्। संविद्रूपातिरिक्तं तु मिथ्या मायामयं जगत् ॥४५॥
अत: संसारनाशाय साक्षिणीमात्मरूपिणीम्। भावयेन्निर्मनस्केन योगयुक्तेन चेतसा ॥४६॥
अत: परं बाह्यपूजाविस्तार: कथ्यते मया। सावधानेन मनसा शृणु पर्वतसत्तम ॥४७॥

इति देवीगीतायां नवमो ऽध्याय:

दशमो ऽध्यायः

श्रीदेव्युवाच ।

प्रातरुत्थाय शिरसि संस्मरेत्पद्ममुज्ज्वलम् । कर्पूराभं स्मरेत्तत्र श्रीगुरुं निजरूपिणम् ॥१॥
सुप्रसन्नं लसद्भूषाभूषितं शक्तिसंयुतम् । नमस्कृत्य ततो देवीं कुण्डलीं संस्मरेद्बुधः ॥२॥
प्रकाशमानां प्रथमे प्रयाणे प्रतिप्रयाणे ऽप्यमृतायमानाम् ।
अन्तः पदव्यामनुसञ्चरन्तीमानन्दरूपामबलां प्रपद्ये ॥३॥
ध्यात्वैवं तच्छिखामध्ये सच्चिदानन्दरूपिणीम् । मां ध्यायेदथ शौचादिक्रियाः सर्वाः समापयेत् ॥४॥
अग्निहोत्रं ततो हुत्वा मत्प्रीत्यर्थं द्विजोत्तमः । होमान्ते स्वासने स्थित्वा पूजासङ्कल्पमाचरेत् ॥५॥
भूतशुद्धिं पुरा कृत्वा मातृकान्यासमेव च । हृल्लेखामातृकान्यासं नित्यमेव समाचरेत् ॥६॥
मूलाधारे हकारं च हृदये च रकारकम् । भ्रूमध्ये तद्वदीकारं ह्रींकारं मस्तके न्यसेत् ॥७॥
तत्तन्मन्त्रोदितानन्यान्न्यासान्सर्वान्समाचरेत् । कल्पयेत्स्वात्मनो देहे पीठं धर्मादिभिः पुनः ॥८॥
ततो ध्यायेन्महादेवीं प्राणायामैर्विजृम्भिते । हृदम्भोजे मम स्थाने पञ्चप्रेतासने बुधः ॥९॥
ब्रह्मा विष्णुश्च रुद्रश्च ईश्वरश्च सदाशिवः । एते पञ्च महाप्रेताः पादमूले मम स्थिताः ॥१०॥
पञ्चभूतात्मका ह्येते पञ्चावस्थात्मका अपि । अहं त्वव्यक्तचिद्रूपा तदतीता ऽस्मि सर्वथा ॥११॥
ततो विष्टरतां याताः शक्तितन्त्रेषु सर्वदा । ध्यात्वैवं मानसैर्भोगैः पूजयेन्मां जपेदपि ॥१२॥
जपं समर्प्य श्रीदेव्यै ततो ऽर्घ्यस्थापनं चरेत् । पात्रासादनकं कृत्वा पूजाद्रव्याणि शोधयेत् ॥१३॥
जलेन तेन मनुना चास्त्रमन्त्रेण देशिकः । दिग्बन्धं च पुरा कृत्वा गुरून्नत्वा ततः परम् ॥१४॥
तदनुज्ञां समादाय बाह्यपीठे ततः परम् । हृदिस्थां भावितां मूर्तिं मम दिव्यां मनोहराम् ॥१५॥
आवाहयेत्ततः पीठे प्राणस्थापनविद्यया । आसनावाहने चा ऽर्घ्यं पाद्याद्याचमनं तथा ॥१६॥
स्नानं वासोद्वयं चैव भूषणानि च सर्वशः । गन्धपुष्पं यथायोग्यं दत्त्वा देव्यै स्वभक्तितः ॥१७॥
यन्त्रस्थानामावृतीनां पूजनं सम्यगाचरेत् । प्रतिवारमशक्तानां शुक्रवारो नियम्यते ॥१८॥
मूलदेवीप्रभारूपाः स्मर्तव्या अङ्गदेवताः । तत्प्रभापटलव्याप्तं त्रैलोक्यं च विचिन्तयेत् ॥१९॥
पुनरावृत्तिसहितां मूलदेवीं च पूजयेत् । गन्धादिभिः सुगन्धैस्तु तथा पुष्पैः सुवासितैः ॥२०॥
नैवेद्यैस्तर्पणैश्चैव ताम्बूलैर्दक्षिणादिभिः । तोषयेन्मां त्वत्कृतेन नाम्नां साहस्रकेण च ॥२१॥
कवचेन च सूक्तेना ऽहं रुद्रेभिरिति प्रभो । देव्यथर्वशिरोमन्त्रैर्हृल्लेखोपनिषद्भवैः ॥२२॥
महाविद्यामहामन्त्रैस्तोषयेन्मां मुहुर्मुहुः । क्षमापयेज्जगद्धात्रीं प्रेमार्द्रहृदयो नरः ॥२३॥
पुलकाङ्कितसर्वाङ्गैर्बाष्परुद्धाक्षिनिःस्वनः । नृत्यगीतादिघोषेण तोषयेन्मां मुहुर्मुहुः ॥२४॥

देवीगीतायां दशमो ऽध्याय:

वेदपारायणैश्चैव पुराणै: सकलैरपि। प्रतिपाद्या यतो ऽहं वै तस्मात्तैस्तोषयेत्तु माम् ॥२५॥
निजं सर्वस्वमपि मे सदेहं नित्यशो ऽर्पयेत्। नित्यहोमं तत: कुर्याद् ब्राह्मणांश्च सुवासिनी: ॥२६॥
बटुकान्पामरानन्यान्देवीबुद्ध्या तु भोजयेत्। नत्वा पुन: स्वहृदये व्युत्क्रमेण विसर्जयेत् ॥२७॥
सर्वं हृल्लेखया कुर्यात्पूजनं मम सुव्रत। हृल्लेखा सर्वमन्त्राणां नायिका परमा स्मृता ॥२८॥
हृल्लेखादर्पणे नित्यमहं तत्प्रतिबिम्बिता। तस्माद् हृल्लेखया दत्तं सर्वमन्त्रै: समर्पितम् ॥२९॥
गुरुं सम्पूज्य भूषाद्यै: कृतकृत्यत्वमावहेत्। य एवं पूजयेद्देवीं श्रीमद्भुवनसुन्दरीम् ॥३०॥
न तस्य दुरलभं किञ्चित्कदाचित्क्वचिदस्ति हि। देहान्ते तु मणिद्वीपं मम यात्येव सर्वथा ॥३१॥
ज्ञेयो देवीस्वरूपो ऽसौ देवा नित्यं नमन्ति तम्। इति ते कथितं राजन्महादेव्या: प्रपूजनम् ॥३२॥
विमृश्यैतदशेषेणाप्यधिकारानुरूपत:। कुरु मे पूजनं तेन कृतार्थस्त्वं भविष्यसि ॥३३॥
इदं तु गीताशास्त्रं मे ना ऽशिष्याय वदेत्क्वचित्। ना ऽभक्ताय प्रदातव्यं न धूर्ताय च दुर्हृदे ॥३४॥
एतत्प्रकाशनं मातुरुद्घाटनमुरोजयो:। तस्मादवश्यं यत्नेन गोपनीयमिदं सदा ॥३५॥
देयं भक्ताय शिष्याय ज्येष्ठपुत्राय चैव हि। सुशीलाय सुवेषाय देवीभक्तियुताय च ॥३६॥
श्राद्धकाले पठेदेतद् ब्राह्मणानां समीपत:। तृप्तास्तत्पितर: सर्वे प्रयान्ति परमं पदम् ॥३७॥

व्यास उवाच।

इत्युक्त्वा सा भगवती तत्रैवान्तरधीयत। देवाश्च मुदिता: सर्वे देवीदर्शनतो ऽभवन् ॥३८॥

व्यास उवाच।

ततो हिमालये जज्ञे देवी हैमवती तु सा। या गौरीति प्रसिद्धा ऽसीद्दत्ता सा शङ्कराय च ॥३९॥
तत: स्कन्द: समुद्भूतस्तारकस्तेन पातित:। समुद्रमन्थने पूर्वं रत्नान्यासुर्नराधिप ॥४०॥
तत्र देवै: स्तुता देवी लक्ष्मीप्राप्त्यर्थमादरात्। तेषामनुग्रहार्थाय निर्गता तु रमा तत: ॥४१॥
वैकुण्ठाय सुरैर्दत्ता तेन तस्य शमो ऽभवत्। इति ते कथितं राजन्देवीमाहात्म्यमुत्तमम् ॥४२॥
गौरीलक्ष्म्यो: समुद्भूतिविषयं सर्वकामदम्। न वाच्यं त्वेतदन्यस्मै रहस्यं कथितं यत: ॥४३॥
गीता रहस्यभूतेयं गोपनीया प्रयत्नत:। सर्वमुक्तं समसेन यत्पृष्टं तत्त्वया ऽनघ ॥४४॥
पवित्रं पावनं दिव्यं किं भूय: श्रोतुमिच्छसि ॥४५॥

इति देवीगीतायां दशमो ऽध्याय:

देवीगीता समाप्ता

Bibliography

Primary Sources with Translations

Aitareya Upaniṣad. In *Eight Upaniṣads, with the Commentary of Śaṅkarācārya* [with Sanskrit text of the Upaniṣad], trans. Swāmī Gambhīrānanda, vol. 2, pp. 1–75. 2d ed. Calcutta: Advaita Ashrama, 1965.

Amṛtabindu Upaniṣad

amṛtabindūpaniṣat. In *The Yoga Upaniṣad-s, with the Commentary of Śrī Upaniṣad-Brahmayogin*, ed. A. Mahadeva Sastri, pp. 26–36. 1920. Reprint. Madras: Adyar Library Research Center, 1968.

Amṛṭabinḍu-Upaniṣaḍ of Kṛshṇa-Yajurveḍa. In *Thirty Minor Upanishaḍs*, trans. K. Nārāyaṇasvāmi Aiyar, pp. 34–36. Madras: Vasanṭā Press, 1914.

[Bādarāyaṇa] Bādarāyana. *The Vedānta Sūtras of Bādarāyana, with the Commentary by Śaṅkara*. Trans. George Thibaut. Sacred Books of the East, vols. 34 and 38. 1890 and 1896. Reprint. 2 parts. New York: Dover, 1962.

Bhagavad Gītā

The Bhagavad-Gītā with the Commentary of Śrī Śankarācārya. Crit. ed. Dinkar Vishnu Gokhale. 2d rev. ed. Poona Oriental Series, no. 1. Poona: Oriental Book Agency, 1950.

The Bhagavad-Gītā with the Commentary of Śrī Sankarāchārya. Trans. A. Mahādeva Śāstri. 4th ed. Madras: V. Ramaswamy Sastrulu, 1929.

The Bhagavad Gītā. Trans. Franklin Edgerton. Rev. ed. Cambridge: Harvard University Press, 1972.

The Bhagavad-Gita; Krishna's Counsel in Time of War. Trans. Barbara Stoler Miller. New York: Bantam, 1986.

Bhāgavata Purāṇa

Bhāgavata Purāṇa of Kṛṣṇa Dvaipāyana Vyāsa, with Sanskrit Commentary Bhāvārthabodhinī of Śrīdharasvāmin. Ed. J. L. Shastri. Delhi: Motilal Banarsidass, 1983.

Srimad Bhāgavata Mahāpurāṇa (with Sanskrit Text and English Translation). 2 vols. Trans. C. L. Goswami. Gorakhpur: Motilal Jalan, 1971.

Brahma Upaniṣad

Brahmopanishad. In *Minor Upaniṣads, with Original Text, Introduction, English Rendering, and Comments*, ed. and trans. Swami Madhavananda, pp. 45–64. Calcutta: Advaita Ashrama, 1973.

Brahmopaniṣad of Kṛshṇa-Yajurveḍa. In *Thirty Minor Upanishaḍs*, trans. K. Nārāyaṇasvāmi Aiyar, pp. 106–109. Madras: Vasanṭā Press, 1914.

Brahmabindu Upaniṣad. In *Sixty Upaniṣads of the Veda*, translated from the German translation of Paul Deussen by V. M. Bedekar and G. B. Palsule, pp. 687–90. Delhi: Motilal Banarsidass, 1980.

Brahmāṇḍa Purāṇa

Brahmāṇḍa Purāṇa of Sage Kṛṣṇa Dvaipāyana Vyāsa (with Introduction in Sanskrit and English and an Alphabetical Index of Verses). Ed. J. L. Shastri. Delhi: Motilal Banarsidass, 1973.

The Brahmāṇḍa Purāṇa. 5 vols. Trans. Ganesh Vasudeo Tagare. Ancient Indian Tradition and Mythology Series, vols. 22–26. Delhi: Motilal Banarsidass, 1983–1984.

The Bṛhadāraṇyaka Upaniṣad with the Commentary of Śaṅkarācārya [with Sanskrit text of the Upaniṣad]. Trans. Swāmī Mādhavānanda. 4th ed. Calcutta: Advaita Ashrama, 1965.

Chāndogya Upaniṣad. In *The Principal Upaniṣads: Edited with Introduction, Text, Translation and Notes*, ed. and trans. S. Radhakrishnan, pp. 335–512. London: George Allen & Unwin, 1953.

[*Darśana Upaniṣad*] *darśanopaniṣat*. In *The Yoga Upaniṣad-s, with the Commentary of Śrī Upaniṣad-Brahmayogin*, ed. A. Mahadeva Sastri, pp. 152–85. 1920. Reprint. Madras: Adyar Library Research Center, 1968.

Devī-Bhāgavata Purāṇa

śrīmaddevībhāgavataṃ saṭīkaṃ samāhātmyam [Sanskrit commentary by Nīlakaṇṭha]. [Bombay:] Veṅkaṭeśvara Press, n.d.

śrīmaddevībhāgavatam; mahāpurāṇam. Varanasi: Thākur, Prasad, n.d.

śrīmaddevībhāgavatam (mahāpurāṇam). Ed. Rāmatejapāṇḍeya. Kāśī: Paṇḍita-Pustakālaya, 1969.

The Srimad Devi Bhagawatam. Trans. Hari Prasanna Chatterji [Swami Vijnananda]. Sacred Books of the Hindus, vol. 26. Allahabad: Panini Office, 1921–23. Reprint, New Delhi: Oriental Books, 1977.

Devī Gītā (constitutes chaps. 31–40 of the 7th Skandha of the *Devī-Bhāgavata Purāṇa*, for which see above. It has also been published separately):

śrī bhagavatī-gītā. Hindi trans. and comm. Śrī Hari Śāstrī Dādhīca. Ilāhābād: Śrī Ramādatta Śukla, *saṃvat* 2007 [1951].

devīgītā; arcanāvyākhyāsahitā. Hindi trans. and comm. Upendra Pāṇḍeya. Vārāṇasī: Vārāṇaseya Saṃskṛta śaṃsthāna, 1986.

Devī Gītā. Trans. Swami Satyananda Saraswati. Napa, California and Delhi: Devi Mandir Publications and Motilal Banarsidass, 1991.

Devī Māhātmya

The Devī-Māhātmyam or Śrī Durgā-Saptaśatī (700 Mantras on Śrī Durgā) [with Sanskrit text]. Trans. Jagadīśvarānanda. Madras: Sri Ramakrishna Math, 1969.

Encountering the Goddess: A Translation of the Devī-Māhātmya *and a Study of Its Interpretation*. See under Thomas B. Coburn, in the Secondary Sources below.

Devī Upaniṣad

devyupaniṣat. In *The Śākta Upaniṣads, with the Commentary of Śrī Upaniṣad-Brahma-Yogin*, ed. A. Mahadeva Sastri, pp. 53–60. Adyar Library Series, no. 10. Madras: Adyar Library, 1950.

Devī Upaniṣad. In *The Śākta Upaniṣad-s: Translated into English (Based Mainly on the Commentary of Upaniṣad-Brahmayogin)*, trans. A. G. Krishna Warrier, pp. 77–84. Adyar Library Series, vol. 89. Madras: Adyar Library, 1967.

Dhyānabindu Upaniṣad

dhyānabindūpaniṣat. In *The Yoga Upaniṣad-s, with the Commentary of Śrī Upaniṣad-Brahmayogin*, ed. A. Mahadeva Sastri, pp. 186–213. 1920. Reprint. Madras: Adyar Library Research Center, 1968.

Ḍhyānabinḍu-Upanishaḍ of the Sāmaveḍa. In *Thirty Minor Upanishaḍs*, trans. K. Nārāyaṇasvāmi Aiyar, pp. 202–11. Madras: Vasanṭā Press, 1914.

Garuḍa Purāṇa

śrīgaruḍamahāpurāṇam. Ed. Rāmatejapāṇḍeya. Kashi: Paṇḍita-Pustakālaya, 1963.

The Garuḍa-Purāṇam: A Prose English Translation. Trans. Manmatha Nath Dutt Shastrī. Chowkhamba Sanskrit Studies, vol. 67. Varanasī: Chowkhamba Sanskrit Series Office, 1968.

Gauḍapāda [*Māṇḍūkya-Kārikās*]. *The Āgamaśāstra of Gauḍapāda*. Ed. and trans. Vidhushekhara Bhattacharya. 1943. Reprint. Delhi: Motilal Banarsidass, 1989.

Gheraṇḍa Saṃhitā

The Gheranda Samhita [with Sanskrit text]. Trans. Rai Bahadur Srisa Chandra Vasu. Sacred Books of the Hindus, vol. 15, part 2. 1914. Reprint. New York: AMS Press, 1974.

The Gheraṇḍa Saṃhitā: A Treatise on Haṭha Yoga. Trans. Śrī Chandra Vasu. 3d ed. London: Theosophical Publishing House, 1976.

Haṭhayoga Pradīpikā

The Hathayogapradīpikā of Svātmārāma with the Commentary Jyotsnā *of Brahmānanda and English Translation*. Trans. Srinivasa Iyangar, rev. Radha Burnier and A. A. Ramanathan. Adyar Library General Series, no. 4. Madras: Adyar Library and Research Centre, 1972.

The Hatha Yoga Pradipika, Translated into English [with Sanskrit text]. Trans. Pancham Sinh. Sacred Books of the Hindus, vol. 15, part 3. 1915. Reprint. New York: AMS Press, 1974.

Īśā Upaniṣad. In *Eight Upaniṣads, with the Commentary of Śaṅkarācārya* [with Sanskrit text of the Upaniṣad], trans. Swāmī Gambhīrānanda, vol. 1, pp. 1–31. 2d ed. Calcutta: Advaita Ashrama, 1965.

Kaivalya Upaniṣad. In *The Principal Upaniṣads: Edited with Introduction, Text, Translation and Notes*, ed. and trans. S. Radhakrishnan, pp. 925–32. London: George Allen & Unwin, 1953.

The Kālikāpurāṇā (Text, Introduction, and Translation in English). 3 vols. Ed. and trans. Biswa Narayan Shastri. Delhi: Nag Publishers, 1991–92.

Kaṭha Upaniṣad. In *Eight Upaniṣads, with the Commentary of Śaṅkarācārya* [with Sanskrit text of the Upaniṣad], trans. Swāmī Gambhīrānanda, vol. 1, pp. 97–229. 2d ed. Calcutta: Advaita Ashrama, 1965.

Kena Upaniṣad. In *Eight Upaniṣads, with the Commentary of Śaṅkarācārya* [with Sanskrit text of the Upaniṣad], trans. Swāmī Gambhīrānanda, vol. 1, pp. 33–96. 2d ed. Calcutta: Advaita Ashrama, 1965.

Kṣurika Upaniṣad

kṣurikopaniṣat. In *The Yoga Upaniṣad-s, with the Commentary of Śrī Upaniṣad-Brahmayogin*, ed. A. Mahadeva Sastri, pp. 36–44. 1920. Reprint. Madras: Adyar Library Research Center, 1968.

Kṣurikā Upaniṣad. In *Sixty Upaniṣads of the Veda*, translated from the German translation of Paul Deussen by V. M. Bedekar and G. B. Palsule, pp. 671–75. Delhi: Motilal Banarsidass, 1980.

[*Kūrma Devī Gītā*] (constitutes chap. 11 of the 1st Skandha of the *Kūrma Purāṇa*, for which see below).

The Kūrma Purāṇa (with English Translation). Crit. ed. Anand Swarup Gupta. Trans. Ahibhushan Bhattacharya et al. Varanasi: All-India Kashiraj Trust, 1972.

Lakṣmī Tantra: A Pāñcarātra Text; Translation and Notes. Trans. Sanjukta Gupta. Leiden: E. J. Brill, 1972.

[*Lalitā Sahasranāma*] *Śri Lalitā Sahasranāmaṁ: With Introduction and Commentary*. Ed. Chaganty Suryanarayanamurthy. 2d rev. ed. Bombay: Bharatiya Vidya Bhavan, 1975.

Laws of Manu

The Laws of Manu, Translated with Extracts from Seven Commentaries. Trans. Georg Bühler. Sacred Books of the East, vol. 25. 1886. Reprint. New York: Dover, 1969.

The Laws of Manu, with an Introduction and Notes. Trans. Wendy Doniger with Brian K. Smith. London: Penguin Books, 1991.

manusmṛtiḥ (medhātithibhāṣya samalaṅkṛtā). 2 vols. Ed. Manasukharay More. Gurumaṇḍal Series, no. 24. Calcutta: 1967, 1971.

The Mahābhāgavata Purāṇa (An Ancient Treatise on Śakti Cult). Crit. ed. by Pushpendra Kumar. Delhi: Eastern Book Linkers, 1983.

[*Mahānārāyaṇa Upaniṣad*] *Mahānārāyaṇopaniṣad (with Accented Text): Introduction, Translation, Interpretation in Sanskrit, and Critical and Explanatory Notes*. Trans. Swāmī Vimalānanda. Madras: Sri Ramakrishna Math, 1979.

[*Mahānirvāṇa Tantra*] *Tantra of the Great Liberation (Mahānirvāna Tantra): A Translation from the Sanskrit, with Introduction and Commentary*. Trans. John Woodroffe [Arthur Avalon]. London: Luzac, 1913.

Maitrī Upaniṣad. In *The Principal Upaniṣads: Edited with Introduction, Text, Translation and Notes*, ed. and trans. S. Radhakrishnan, pp. 793–859. London: George Allen & Unwin, 1953.

Māṇḍūkya Upaniṣad and Kārikā. In *Eight Upaniṣads, with the Commentary of Śaṅkarācārya* [with Sanskrit text of the Upaniṣad and Kārikā], trans. Swāmī Gambhīrānanda, vol. 2, pp. 173–404. 2nd ed. Calcutta: Advaita Ashram, 1966.

Manu. See under Laws of Manu.

Mārkaṇḍeya Purāṇa

The Mārkaṇḍeyamahāpurāṇam. [Bombay:] Veṅkaṭeśvara Press. Reprint, arranged by Nag Sharma Singh, Delhi: Nag Publishers, n.d.

The Mārkaṇḍeya Purāṇa. Trans. F. Eden Pargiter. Calcutta: Asiatic Society of Bengal, 1904. Bibliotheca Indica, New Series nos. 700, 706, etc. Reprint, Delhi: Indological Book House, 1969.

Matsya Purāṇa

The Matsya Puranam. Ed. Nandalal More. Gurumandal Series, no. 13. Calcutta; 1954.

The Matsya Purāṇam. Ed. and trans. Jamna Das Akhtar. Sacred Books of the Aryans, vol. 1. Delhi: Oriental Publishers, 1972.

Muṇḍaka Upaniṣad. In *Eight Upaniṣads, with the Commentary of Śaṅkarācārya* [with Sanskrit text of the Upaniṣad], vol. 2, pp. 77–172. Trans. Swāmī Gambhīrānanda. 2d ed. Calcutta: Advaita Ashrama, 1966.

Muni, Vasishtha Ganapati. [*Umasahasram*] *Adoration of the Divine Mother; Gems from* Umasahasram. Ed. M. P. Pandit. Madras: Ganesh, 1973.

[*Padma Purāṇa*] *Padma Puranam* 5 vols. Ed. Manasukharay More. Gurumandal Series, no. 18. Calcutta: 1957–1959.

Padmapāda. [*Pañcapādikā*] *The Pañcapādikā of Padmapāda (translated into English).* Trans. D. Venkataramiah. Gaekwad's Oriental Series, 107. Baroda, Oriental Institute, 1948.

Pañcadaśī

Panchadasi, with English Translation and Notes . . . and an Introduction. Trans. Sri Jnanananda Bharathi Svaminah. Madras: Sri Abhinava Vidyatheertha Mahaswamigal Educational Trust, 1983.

Pañcadaśī of Śrī Vidyāraṇya Swāmī: English Translation and Notes . . . with an Introduction. [with Sanskrit text]. Trans. Swāmī Swāhānanda. Intro. T. M. P. Mahadevan. Madras: Sri Ramakrishna Math, 1967.

Pañcīkaraṇa. See under Śaṃkara.

Pañcīkaraṇa-Vārttika. See under Sureśvara.

[*Pārvatī Gītā*] (constitutes chaps. 15–19 of the *Mahābhāgavata Purāṇa*, for which see above).

Patañjali. [*Yoga Sūtras*] *Yoga Philosophy of Patañjali: Containing His Yoga Aphorisms with Vyāsa's Commentary in Sanskrit and a Translation with Annotations Including Many Suggestions for the Practice of Yoga, by Sāṁkhya-yogāchārya Swāmi Hariharānanda Āraṇya*. Trans. P. N. Mukerji. Albany: State University of New York Press, 1983.

———. *The Yoga-Sūtra of Patañjali: A New Translation and Commentary*. Trans. Georg Feverstein, Kent, England: Wm. Dawson, 1979.

[*Prapañcasāra Tantra*] *Prapancasāra Tantra of Śaṅkarācārya: With the Commentary Vivaraṇa by Padmapādācārya and Prayogakramadīpikā—a Vṛtti on the Vivaraṇa*. Ed. John Woodroffe [Arthur Avalon] and Aṭalānanda Sarasvatī. Tantric Text Series, vol. 19. 1935. Reprint. Delhi: Motilal Banarsidass, 1981.

Praśna Upaniṣad. In *Eight Upaniṣads, with the Commentary of Śaṅkarācārya* [with Sanskrit text of the Upaniṣad], trans. Swāmī Gambhīrānanda, vol. 2, pp. 405–506. 2d ed. Calcutta: Advaita Ashrama, 1965.

Puja: The Process of Ritualistic Worship. San Ramon, Calif.: Mata Amritanandamayi Center, 1992.

Ṛg Veda

Ṛg-Veda Saṁhitā: Text in Nagari, English Translation Notes and Appendices, etc. Trans. H. H. Wilson. Enlarged and arranged by Nag Sharan Singh. N. P. Series, no. 17. Delhi: Nag Publishers, 1977–78.

Der Rig Veda. 4 vols. Trans. Karl Friedrich Geldner. Harvard Oriental Series, vols. 33–36. Cambridge: Harvard University Press, 1951–57.

Sadānanda. See under *Vedāntasāra*.

Śaṃkara. *Commentaries on the* [short] *Upanishads*. Complete Works of Sri Sankaracharya in the Original Sanskrit, vol. 8. Rev. ed. Madras: Samata Books, 1983.

———. [Commentary on the *Brahma-Sūtras*] *Brahmasutra Bhashya*. Complete Works of Sri Sankaracharya in the Original Sanskrit, vol. 7. Rev. ed. Madras: Samata Books, 1983.

———. [Commentary on the *Kaṭha Upaniṣad*]. In *The Katha and Prasna Upanishads and Sri Sankara's Commentary*, trans. S. Sitarama Sastri. The Upanishads, vol. 2. Madras: V. C. Seshacharri, 1923.

———. [Commentary on the *Māṇḍukya Upaniṣad*]. In *The Māṇḍūkyopaniṣad with Gauḍapāda's Kārikā and Saṅkara's Commentary*, trans. Swāmī Nikhilānanda. 4th ed. Mysore: Sri Ramakrishna Ashrama, 1955.

———. [Commentary on the *Muṇḍaka Upaniṣad*]. See under *Muṇḍaka Upaniṣad* above.

———. [*Pañcīkaraṇa*] *Pañcīkaraṇam: Text and the Vārttika with Word for Word Translation, English Rendering, Comments, and the Glossary*. No trans. 3d rev. ed. Calcutta: Advaita Ashrama, 1976.

———. [*Upadeśasāhasrī*] *A Thousand Teachings in Two Parts—Prose and Poetry—of Śrī Sankārachārya* [with Sanskrit text]. Trans. Swāmi Jagadānanda. 3d ed. Madras: Sri Ramakrishna Math, 1961.

Śāṇḍilya Upaniṣad

śāṇḍilyopaniṣat. In *The Yoga Upaniṣad-s, with the Commentary of Śrī Upaniṣad-Brahmayogin*, ed. A. Mahadeva Sastri, pp. 518–58. Adyar Library Series, vol. 6. 1920. Reprint. Madras, Adyar Library and Research Centre, 1968.

Śāṇdilya-Upanishaḍ of Aṭharvaṇaveḍa. In *Thirty Minor Upanishaḍs*, trans. K. Nārāyaṇasvāmi Aiyar, pp. 173–91. Madras: Vasanṭā Press, 1914.

Śāradā-Tilaka Tantra

Śāradā-Tilaka Tantram: Text with Introduction [with Rāghava's commentary]. Ed. John Woodroffe [Arthur Avalon]. Tantrik Text Series vol. 17. 1933. Reprint. Delhi: Motilal Banarsidass, 1982.

The Śārdā-Tilaka [*sic*] *Tantram: English Translation with Notes and Yantras*. Translated by a Board of Scholars. Sri Garibdas Oriental Series, no. 82. Delhi: Sri Satguru Publicatons, 1988.

[*Sarva-Siddhānta-Saṃgraha*] *The Sarva-Siddhānta-Sangraha of Śaṅkarācārya: Text with English Translation, Introduction, Notes & Glossary*. Trans. M. Raṅgācārya. New Delhi: Ajay Book Service, 1983.

[*Sarva-Vedānta-Siddhānta-Sārasaṃgraha*] *The Quintessence of Vedanta: A Translation of the Sarva-Vedanta-Siddhanta-Sarasangraha of Acharya Sankara*. Trans. Swami Tattwananda. 2d ed. Kerala: Sri Ramakrishna Advaita Ashrama, 1970.

[*Ṣaṭcakra-Nirūpaṇa*] Shatchakranirūpana *and Pādukāpanchaka*. Ed. Tārānātha Vidyāratna. Tantrik Texts, vol. 2. 3d rev. ed. Madras: Ganesh, 1931. In *The Serpent Power: Being the* Shat-Chakra-Nirūpana *and Pādukā-Panchaka; Two Works on Laya Yoga, Translated from the Sanskrit, with Introduction and Commentary*, trans. John Woodroffe [Arthur Avalon]. 3d rev. ed. Madras: Ganesh, 1931.

Saundaryalaharī

Saundaryalaharī (The Ocean of Divine Beauty) of Śaṅkarācārya: Sanskrit Text in Devanāgarī with Roman Transliteration, English Translation, Explanatory Notes, Yantric Diagrams and Index. Ed. and trans. V. K. Subramanian. Delhi: Motilal Banarsidass, 1977.

Saundarya-Laharī (The Ocean of Beauty) of Śrī Śaṃkara-Bhagavat-Pāda: With Transliteration, English Translation, Commentary, Diagrams and an Appendix on Prayoga. 2d ed. Ed. and trans. S. Subrahmaṇya Śāstrī and T. R. Śrīnivāsa Ayyaṅgār. Madras: Theosophical Publishing House, 1948.

Śiva Purāṇa

The Śiva Mahāpurāṇa. Crit. ed. Pushpendra Kumar. NP Series, no. 48. Delhi: Nag Publishers, 1981.

The Śiva Purāṇa. 4 vols. Translated by a Board of Scholars. Ancient Indian Tradition and Mythology Series, vols. 1–4. Delhi: Motilal Banarsidass, 1970.

[*Śiva-Saṃhitā*].

The Siva Samhita [with Sanskrit text]. Trans. Rai Bahadur Srisa Chandra Vasu. Sacred Books of the Hindus, vol. 15, part 1. 1914. Reprint. New York: AMS Press, 1974.

Śiva-Samhita. In *The Original Yoga as Expounded in Śiva-Samhitā, Gheraṇḍa-Samhitā and Pātañjala Yoga-sūtra: Original Text in Sanskrit, Translated, Edited and Annotated with an Introduction*, ed. and trans. Shyam Ghosh, pp. 1–118. New Delhi: Munshiram Manoharlal, 1980.

Sureśvara. *The Naiṣkarmyasiddhi of Sureśvara: Edited with Introduction, English Translation Annotation, and Indices*. Ed. and trans. R. Balasubramanian. Madras University Philosophical Series, no. 47. Madras: University of Madras, 1988.

______. [*Naiṣkarmya Siddhi*] *The Realization of the Absolute: The "Naiṣkarmya Siddhi" of Śrī Sureśvara*. Trans. A. J. Alston. 2d ed. London: Shanti Sadan, 1971.

______. [*Pañcīkaraṇa-Vārttika*]. *Śrī Sureśvarācārya's Vārttika on Pañcīkaraṇam*. In Śrī Śaṅkarācārya [Śaṃkara], *Pañcīkaraṇam: Text and the Vārttika with Word for Word Trans., English Rendering, Comments, and the Glossary*, pp. 9–59. 3d rev. ed. Calcutta: Advaita Ashrama, 1976.

Sūta Gītā. [This constitutes eight chapters in the fourth section of the Yajñavaibhava Khaṇḍa in the *Sūta Saṃhitā* edition cited below, pp. 991–1066. The *Sūta Saṃhitā* is part of the *Skanda Purāṇa*.]

[*Sūta Saṃhitā*]. *Sūtasamhitā with Tatparyadeepika of Srimad Vidyaranya, Mainly Based on the Various South Indian Texts.* Ed. S. Ramachandra Sastri and K. Kuppuswamy Sastri. Madras: K. R. Sastry, 1916.

Svātmārāma. See under *Haṭhayoga Pradīpikā.*

Śvetāśvatara Upaniṣad. In *The Principal Upaniṣads: Edited with Introduction, Text, Translation and Notes,* ed. and trans. S. Radhakrishnan, pp. 707–50. London: George Allen & Unwin, 1953.

Taittirīya Upaniṣad. In *Eight Upaniṣads, with the Commentary of Śaṅkarācārya* [with Sanskrit text of the Upaniṣad], vol. 1, pp. 231–416. Trans. Swāmī Gambhīrānanda. 2d ed. Calcutta: Advaita Ashrama, 1965.

[Tāpanīya Upaniṣad] nṛsiṃhatāpinyām uttaratāpinyupaniṣat. In *The Vaishnava-Upanishads with the Commentary of Sri Upanishad-Brahma-Yogin,* ed. A. Mahadeva Sastri, pp. 223–304. Madras: Adyar Library, 1923.

Tripurā-Rahasya

Tripurā Rahasyam (Jñāna Khaṇḍa): With Commentary Tātparyadīpikā of Śrīnivāsa. Sarasvatī Bhavana Granthamālā, vol. 15. Varanasi: Varanaseya Sanskrit Vishvavidyalaya, 1965.

Tripurā-Rahasya (Jñānakhanda): English Translation and a Comparative Study of the Process of Individuation. Trans. A. U. Vasavada. Chowkhamba Sanskrit Studies vol. 50. Varanasi: Chowkhamba Sanskrit Series Office, 1965.

Uddhārakośa. In *Devī Rahasya with Pariśishṭas,* ed. Ram Chandra Kak and Harabhatta Shastri, pp. 522–74. 1941. Reprint. Delhi: Butala, 1985.

[*Vāmana Purāṇa*] *The Vāmana Purāṇa: with English Translation.* Ed. Anand Swarup Gupta and trans. Satyamsu Mohan Mukhopadhyaya, et al. Varanasi: All India Kashiraj Trust, 1968.

[*Varāha Purāṇa*] *The Varāha-Purāṇa (with English Translation).* Ed. Anand Swarup Gupta and trans. Ahibhushan Bhattacharya. Varanasi: All India Kashiraj Trust, 1981.

[*Vedāntasāra*] *Vedantasara; Or, The Essence of Vedanta of Sadananda Yogindra* [with Sanskrit text]. Trans. Swami Nikhilananda. 3d ed. Calcutta: Advaita Ashrama, 1949.

Vedānta Sūtras. See under Śaṃkara [Commentary on the *Brahma-Sūtras*].

Vidyārāṇya. See under *Pañcadaśī.*

[*Vivekacūḍāmaṇi*]. *Vivekachudamani of Sri Sankaracharya: Text, with English Translation, Notes and Index.* Trans. Swami Madhavananda. 3d ed. Mayavati, U.P.: Advaita Ashrama, 1932.

Yogakuṇḍalī Upaniṣad

Yogakuṇḍalī Upaniṣad. In *The Yoga Upaniṣad-s, with the Commentary of Śrī Upaniṣad-Brahmayogin*, ed. A. Mahadeva Sastri, pp. 307–36. 1920. Reprint. Madras: Adyar Library Research Center, 1968.

Yogakuṇḍalī-Upaniṣaḍ of Kṛshṇa-Yajurveḍa. In *Thirty Minor Upanishaḍs*, trans. K. Nārāyaṇasvāmi Aiyar, pp. 260–72. Madras: Vasanṭā Press, 1914.

Yogatattva Upaniṣad

yogatattvopaniṣat. In *The Yoga Upaniṣad-s, with the Commentary of Śrī Upaniṣad-Brahmayogin*, ed. A. Mahadeva Sastri, pp. 363–89. 1920. Reprint. Madras: Adyar Library Research Center, 1968.

Yogaṭaṭṭva-Upanishaḍ of Kṛshṇa-Yajurveḍa. In *Thirty Minor Upanishaḍs*, trans. K. Nārāyaṇasvāmi Aiyar, pp. 192–201. Madras: Vasanṭā Press, 1914.

Secondary Sources

Agrawala, Vasudeva S. *The Glorification of the Great Goddess*. Varanasi: All-India Kashiraj Trust, 1963.

Alston, A. J. *Śaṃkara on Enlightenment*. A Śaṃkara Source Book, vol. 6. London: Shanti Sadan. 1989.

Ayer, V. A. K. "Mother Bhuvaneswari." *Tattvāloka: The Splendour of Truth* 11, no. 4 (1988):45–46.

Babb, Lawrence A. *The Divine Hierarchy: Popular Hinduism in Central India*. New York: Columbia University Press, 1975.

Bagchi, Subhendugopal. *Eminent Indian Śākta Centres in Eastern India (An Interdisciplinary Study in the Background of the Pīṭhas of Kālīghāṭa, Vakreśvara and Kāmākhyā)*. Calcutta: Punthi Pustak, 1980.

Banerji, S. C. *A Brief History of Tantra Literature*. Calcutta: Naya Prokash, 1988.

———. *Tantra in Bengal: A Study in Its Origin, Development and Influence*. Calcutta: Naya Prokash, 1977.

Barua, B. K., and H. V. Sreenivasa Murthy. *Temples and Legends of Assam*. Bombay: Bharatiya Vidya Bhavan, 1988.

Basu, Manoranjan. *Fundamentals of the Philosophy of Tantras*. Calcutta: Mira Basu, 1986.

Beck, Guy. *Sonic Theology: Hinduism and Sacred Sound*. Columbia: University of South Carolina, 1993.

Bhandarkar, R. G. *Vaiṣṇavism, Śaivism, and Minor Religious Systems*. Varanasi: Indological Book House, 1965.

Bharany, Chhote. *Images of Devi in Pahari Paintings*. New Delhi: Clarion Books, 1984.

Bharati, Agehananda. *The Tantric Tradition*. London: Rider, 1965.

Bhardwaj, Surinder Mohan. *Hindu Places of Pilgrimage in India (A Study in Cultural Geography)*. Berkeley, Los Angeles, London: University of California Press, 1973.

Bhattacharya, Batuknath. "Festivals and Sacred Days." In *The Religions*, ed. Haridas Bhattacharyya, pp. 479–94. *The Cultural Heritage of India*, vol. 4. Calcutta: Ramakrishnan Mission Institute of Culture, 1956.

Bhattacharya, D. C. "An Unknown Form of Tārā." In *The Śakti Cult and Tārā*, ed. D. C. Sircar, pp. 134–42. Calcutta: University of Calcutta, 1967.

Bhattacharyya, Hari Prasad. *Status of the World in Advaita Vedānta*. Bharata Manisha Research Series, no. 12. Varanasi: Bharata Manisha, 1979.

Bhattacharyya, Narendra Nath. *History of the Śākta Religion*. New Delhi: Munshiram Manoharlal, 1973.

———. *History of the Tantric Religion (A Historical, Ritualistic and Philosophical Study)*. New Delhi: Manohar, 1982.

Brooks, Douglas Renfrew. *Auspicious Wisdom: The Texts and Traditions of Śrīvidyā Śākta Tantrism in South India*. Albany: State University of New York Press, 1992.

———. *The Secret of the Three Cities: An Introduction to Hindu Śākta Tantrism*. Chicago: University of Chicago Press, 1990.

Brown, C. Mackenzie. *God as Mother: A Feminine Theology in India; An Historical and Theological Study of the Brahmavaivarta Purāṇa*. Hartford, Vt.: Claude Stark, 1974.

———. "Purāṇa as Scripture: From Sound to Image of the Holy Word in the Hindu Tradition." *History of Religions* 26 no. 1 (August 1986):68–86.

———. *The Triumph of the Goddess: The Canonical Models and Theological Visions of the* Devī-Bhāgavata Purāṇa. Albany: State University of New York Press, 1990.

Cenkner, William. *A Tradition of Teachers: Śaṅkara and the Jagadgurus Today*. Delhi: Motilal Banarsidass, 1983.

Chakravarti, Chintaharan. "Nīlakaṇṭha the Śaiva." *Indian Historical Quarterly* 16 (1940):574–79.

———. *Tantras: Studies on Their Religion and Literature*. Calcutta: Punthi Pustak, 1963.

Chatterjee, Satis Chandra. "Hindu Religious Thought." In *The Religion of the Hindus*, ed. Kenneth W. Morgan, pp. 206–61. New York: Ronald Press, 1953.

Coburn, Thomas B. "Consort of None, Śakti of All: The Vision of the *Devī Māhātmya*." In *The Divine Consort: Rādhā and the Goddesses of India*, ed. John Stratton Hawley and Donna Marie Wulff, pp. 153–65. Berkeley: Graduate Theological Union, 1982.

———. *Devī-Māhātmya: The Crystallization of the Goddess Tradition*. Delhi: Motilal Banarsidass, 1984.

———. *Encountering the Goddess: A Translation of the* Devī-Māhātmya *and a Study of Its Interpretation*. Albany: State University of New York Press, 1991.

Daniélou, Alain. *Hindu Polytheism*. Bollingen Series 73. New York: Bollingen Foundation, 1964.

Dasgupta, Shashi Bhusan. *Aspects of Indian Religious Thought*. Calcutta: A. Mukherjee, 1957.

Dasgupta, Surendranath. *A History of Indian Philosophy*. 5 vols. Cambridge: Cambridge University Press, 1922–55.

———. *Yoga as Philosophy and Religion*. 1924. Reprint. Delhi: Motilal Banarsidass, 1973.

Dev, Usha. *The Concept of Śakti in the Purāṇas*. Purāṇa Vidya Series, no. 2. Delhi: Nag Publishers, 1987.

Digambarji, Swami, and Mahajot Sahai. *Yoga Kośa: Yoga Terms Explained with Reference to Context*. Vol. 1. Poona: Kaivalyadhama S. M. Y. M. Samiti, 1973.

Eck, Diana L. *Banaras: City of Light*. New York: Alfred A. Knopf, 1982.

———. *Darśan: Seeing the Divine Image in India*. 2d rev. ed. Chambersburg, Pa.: Anima Books, 1985.

———. "Shiva and Shakti in the Land of India." Paper presented for the Larwill Lectures in Religion, Kenyon College, 1982. Photocopied.

Farquhar, J. N. *An Outline of the Religious Literature of India*. 1920. Reprint. Delhi: Motilal Banarsidass, 1967.

Feuerstein, Georg. *Encyclopedic Dictionary of Yoga*. New York: Paragon House, 1990.

Fiorenza, Elisabeth Schüssler. *In Memory of Her: A Feminist Theological Reconstruction of Christian Origins*. New York: Crossroad, 1983.

Fort, Andrew O. *The Self and Its States: A States of Consciousness Doctrine in Advaita Vedānta*. Delhi: Motilal Banarsidass, 1990.

Gambhirananda, Swami. "Upaniṣadic Meditation." In *The Early Phases (Prehistoric, Vedic and Upaniṣadic, Jaina, and Buddhist)*, rev. ed., ed. S. K. Chatterji et al., pp. 375–85. Cultural Heritage of India, vol. 1. Calcutta: Ramakrishna Mission Institute of Culture, 1958.

Ghosh, Shyam. *The Original Yoga as Expounded in Śiva-Samhitā, Gheraṇḍa-Samhitā and Pātañjala Yoga-sūtra; Original Text in Sanskrit, Translated, Edited and Annotated with an Introduction*. New Delhi: Munshiram Manoharlal, 1980.

Gonda, J. *Change and Continuity in Indian Religion*. The Hague: Mouton, 1965.

———. *Medieval Religious Literature in Sanskrit*. A History of Indian Literature, vol. 2, fasc. 1. Wiesbaden: Otto Harrassowitz, 1977.

Goudriaan, Teun, and Sanjukta Gupta. *Hindu Tantric and Śākta Literature*. A History of Indian Literature, vol. 2, fasc. 2. Wiesbaden: Otto Harrassowitz, 1981.

Gupta, Sanjukta, Dirk Jan Hoens, and Teun Goudriaan. *Hindu Tantrism*. Handbuch der Orientalistik, 2. Abt.: Indien, 4. Band, 2. Abschnitt. Leiden/Cologne: E. J. Brill, 1979.

Hazra, R. C. *Studies in the Upapurāṇas*. 2 vols. Calcutta: Sanskrit College, 1958, 1963.

Hiriyanna, M. *The Essentials of Indian Philosophy*. London: George Allen & Unwin, 1949.

———. *Outlines of Indian Philosophy*. London: George Allen & Unwin, 1932.

Indich, William M. *Consciousness in Advaita Vedānta*. Varanasi: Motilal Banarsidass, 1980.

Kane, Pandurang Vaman. *History of Dharmaśāstra (Ancient and Mediaeval Religious and Civil Law in India)*. 5 vols. Poona: Bhandarkar Oriental Institute, 1930–62.

Kinsley, David. "Bhuvaneśvarī: Whose Body Is the World." Unpublished ms. N.d.

———. *Hindu Goddesses: Visions of the Divine Feminine in the Hindu Religious Tradition*. Berkeley and Los Angeles: University of California Press, 1986.

———. *Tantric Visions of the Divine Feminine: The Ten Mahāvidyās*. Berkeley and Los Angleles: University of California Press, 1997.

Klostermaier, Klaus. *Mythologies and Philosophies of Salvation in the Theistic Traditions of India.* (Vol. 5, Editions in the study of religion.) Waterloo, Ont.: Wilfred Laurier University Press, 1984.

———. *A Survey of Hinduism.* Albany: State University of New York Press, 1989.

Kumar, Pushpendra. *Śakti Cult in Ancient India (with Special Reference to the Purāṇic Literature).* Varanasi: Bhartiya, 1974.

Laine, James William. *The Theophany Narratives of the* Mahābhārata. Ann Arbor, Mich.: University Microfilms International, 1984.

Lorenzen, David N. *The Kāpālikas and Kālāmukhas: Two Lost Śaivite Sects.* Berkeley and Los Angeles: University of California Press, 1972.

Mahadevan, T. M. P. *Gauḍapāda: A Study in Early Advaita.* 4th ed. Madras: University of Madras, 1975.

———. *The Pañcadaśī of Bhāratītīrtha-Vidyāraṇya: An Interpretive Exposition.* Madras University Philosophical Series, no. 13. Madras: University of Madras, 1969.

———. *Superimposition in Advaita Vedānta.* New Delhi: Sterling, 1985.

McGee, Mary. "Desired Fruits: Motive and Intention in the Votive Rites of Hindu Women." In *Roles and Rituals for Hindu Women,* ed. Julia Leslie, pp. 71–88. Delhi: Motilal Banarsidass, 1992.

Monier-Williams, Monier. *Brāhmanism and Hindūism; Or, Religious Thought and Life in India, as Based on the Veda and Other Sacred Books of the Hindūs.* 4th ed. London: John Murray, 1891.

Müller-Ortega, Paul Eduardo. *The Triadic Heart of Śiva; Kaula Tantricism of Abhinavagupta in the Non-Dual Shaivism of Kashmir.* Albany: State University of New York Press, 1989.

Nilkantan, R. *Gītās in the Mahābhārata and the Purāṇas.* Delhi: Nag Publishers, 1989.

Padoux, André. *Vāc: The Concept of the Word in Selected Hindu Tantras.* Trans. Jacques Gontier. Albany: State University of New York Press, 1990.

Pal, Pratapaditya. *Hindu Religion and Iconology According to the* Tantrasāra. Los Angeles: Vichitra Press, 1981.

Pintchman, Tracy. *The Rise of the Goddess in the Hindu Tradition.* Albany: State University of New York Press, 1994.

Pratyagatmananda, Swami. "Philosophy of the Tantras." In *The Philosophies,* ed. Haridas Bhattacharyya. *The Cultural Heritage of India,* vol. 3, pp. 437–48. 2d ed., rev. and enl. Calcutta: Ramakrishna Mission Institute of Culture, 1953.

Punjani, Shakuntala. *Pañcadaśī: A Critical Study*. Delhi: Parimal, 1985.

Radhakrishnan, S. *Indian Philosophy*. 2 vols. 2d ed. London: George Allen & Unwin, 1931.

Radhakrishnan, Sarvepalli, and Charles A. Moore, eds. *A Source Book in Indian Philosophy*. Princeton, N.J.: Princeton University Press, 1957.

Raju, P. T. *Structural Depths of Indian Thought*. New Delhi: South Asian Publishers, 1985.

Rao, S. K. Ramachandra. *Tantra Mantra Yantra: The Tantra Psychology*. New Delhi: Arnold-Heinemann, 1979.

Rele, Vasant G. *The Mysterious Kundalini (The Physical Basis of the "Kundali (Hatha) Yoga" According to Our Present Knowledge of Western Anatomy and Physiology)*. Bombay: D. B. Taraporevala, 1927.

Sarasvati, Swami Satchidanandendra. *The Method of the Vedanta: A Critical Account of the Advaita Tradition*. Trans. A. J. Alston. London: Kegan Paul International, 1989.

Sheridan, P. Daniel. *The Advaitic Theism of the Bhāgavata Purāṇa*. Delhi: Motilal Banarsidass, 1986.

Silburn, Lilian. *Kuṇḍalinī: The Energy of the Depths; A Comprehensive Study Based on the Scriptures of Nondualistic Kaśmir Śaivism*. Trans. Jacques Gontier. Albany: State University of New York Press, 1988.

Sircar, D. C. *The Śākta Pīṭhas*. 2d rev. ed. Delhi: Motilal Banarsidass, 1973.

———. *Studies in the Geography of Ancient and Medieval India*. Delhi: Motilal Banarsidass, 1960.

Smith, Frederick M. "Indra's Curse, Varuṇa's Noose, and the Suppression of the Woman in the Vedic *Śrauta* Ritual." In *Roles and Rituals for Hindu Women*, ed. Julia Leslie, pp. 17–45. Delhi: Motilal Banarsidass, 1992.

Stace, W. T. *Mysticism and Philosophy*. London: Macmillan, 1960.

Subramanian, K. N. "Suta on Sakti Puja." *Tattvāloka: The Splendour of Truth* 11, no. 4 (1988):49–50.

Taimni, I. K. *Gāyatrī: The Daily Religious Practice of the Hindus*. 3d rev. ed. Madras: Theosophical Publishing House, 1978.

Varenne, Jean. *Yoga and the Hindu Tradition*. Trans. Derek Coltman. Chicago: University of Chicago Press, 1973.

Vaudeville, Charlotte. "Krishna Gopāla, Rādhā, and The Great Goddess." In *The Divine Consort: Rādhā and the Goddesses of India*, ed. John Stratton Hawley and Donna Marie Wulff, pp. 1–12. Berkeley: Graduate Theological Union, 1982.

Wadley, Susan S. "Women and the Hindu Tradition." In Doranne Jacobson and Susan S. Wadley, *Women in India: Two Perspectives*, pp. 111–35. 2d enl. ed. Columbia, Mo.: South Asia Publications, 1992.

Walker, Benjamin. *The Hindu World: An Encyclopedic Survey of Hinduism*. 2 vols. New York: Frederick A. Praeger, 1968.

Wheelock, Wade T. "The Mantra in Vedic and Tantric Ritual." In *Mantra*, ed. Harvey P. Alper, pp. 96–122. Albany: State University of New York Press, 1989.

Winternitz, Maurice. *A History of Indian Literature*. Vol. 1. Trans. S. V. Ketkar and rev. by the author. Calcutta: University of Calcutta, 1927.

Woodroffe, John. *The Garland of Letters (Varnamālā): Studies in the Mantra-Shāstra*. Madras: Ganesh, 1922.

——— [Arthur Avalon], ed. *Hymn to Kālī: Karpūrādi-Stotra, with Introduction and Commentary by Vimalānanda-Svāmī*. 2d rev. ed. Madras: Ganesh, 1953.

———, ed. *Principles of Tantra: The Tantratattva of Ṣhrīyukta Ṣhiva Chandra Vidyārnava Bhattāchāryya Mahodaya*. 2 vols. London: Luzac, 1914.

———, trans. *The Serpent Power*. See *Ṣaṭcakra-Nirūpaṇa* under primary sources.

Woodroffe, John, and Pramatha Nātha Mukhyopādhyāya. *Mahāmāyā: The World as Power: Power as Consciousness (Chit-Shakti)*. 1929. Reprint. Madras: Ganesh, 1964.

Index

Numbers in bold indicate the page reference is to the translation.

Absorption (*samādhi*): as culmination of the Eight-limbed yoga, **175**, 177–78, 201; as culmination of Limb-by-limb Meditation, 199; in Jñāna Yoga, 14, 147; and resorptive meditation, **155**, 156; and Śiva's response to Śatī's death, **48**, 51n

Activity (*rajas, rajo guṇa,* active aspects) (see also *Guṇas*), **101**, 102, 195n

Adhyāsa (superimposition), 75n, **114**, 115, 116n, 150

Advaita Vedānta (see also under *Devī Gītā*): and filthiness of physical world, 181; general summary of, 12–16; and hierarchical ordering of ends of life, 140; in the hymn to Bhuvaneśvarī, 70–71; and internal/external forms of worship, 299; and *kṛta-kṛtya*, 50–51n; and late or post-Śaṃkara developments, 15, 89n, 97n, 108, 122, 297n; and Māyā, 15, 86–87, 89n, 92–93, 117n, 119; and reality of physical world, 75n, 87, 90n, 103, 105, 119–20

Advaitic theism (blending/synthesis of Advaitic and *bhaktic* perspectives), 17, 200, 291n, 311

Agāma/Āgamas, 21, 274–75

Aggregated (*samaṣṭi*) form of the Devī as the Virāj, **122**, 122, 122n

Aggregated (*samaṣṭi*) and individuated (*vyaṣṭi*) forms/aspects: of the supreme Lord and the individual soul, **105**, 105, 106, 107–108n; of the mantra Hrīṃ, 157n, 158n

Aiśvarya (sovereignty), 24, 51n

Aitareya Upaniṣad, 88n

Amṛtabindu Upaniṣad, 202n, 236n

Analogies: of a barren woman's son, 15, 87, **118**, 121n; of a bow, arrow, and target, **204**; of butter in milk, **43**, **234**, 236n; of a chariot and its driver, **152–53**, 153; of darkness and light not appearing together, **142**, 144n; of disappearance of concerns in deep sleep, **86**; of exposing the

Analogies *(continued)*
breasts of a mother, **312**; of fire hidden in wood, 202n, 236n; of gold forgotten on one's neck, **230**, 231; of jars and space, 106n, 113n, **113**, **114**, 115, 115–16n; of a jar in a darkened house, **201**; of a king's command, **269**; of a lamp inside a jar, 202n; of a lamp, self-illuminating, **91**, 93, 94n; of a mirror and reflected image, 107n, 113n, **309**, 310; of oil flowing continuously, **223**, 227n; of a rope and snake/wreath, **42**, 43, **70**, 71, 75n, 76n, 90n, 108, 109, **118**, 119, 150, 311; of space not stained by contact with objects, 116n; of substance and attribute (fire and heat, etc.), **86**, 87, 90n, 92–93, 236n; of the sun, unstained/unwavering, **113–114**, 115, 116n; of sunlight and darkness, **278**; of a thread running through a string of beads/pearls, 74n, 236n

Ancestors, **81**, **248**, 250n, **312**

Androcentrism, 34–37

Anirvacanīya (*anirvācya*, indescribable), 88n, 151n

Appearance of world (*vivarta*) (*see also* Cosmogony), 75n, 90n, 119

Arjuna: and Kṛṣṇa's cosmic form/revelation, 72n, 122, 126n, 129n, 132, 132n, 133n; as Kṛṣṇa's disciple/devotee, 2–3, 83n, 138

Aśvins, and the beheading of Atharvaṇa, **215–16**, 216

Atharvaṇa, **215–16**, 216, 217

Atharva Veda, 127n

Ātman (Self): in Advaita, 14, 153; in all beings, and all beings in, 199; as being (existence), consciousness, and bliss, 95n; as concealed by Māyā, **201**; as dwelling in the flame of consciousness, 290n; and the goad of Bhuvaneśvarī, 66; and goal of yoga, **161**, 162, **175**, 201; as identified with the Kuṇḍalinī, 177; as identified with the Svayambhū-liṅga, 188n; in the *Kaṭha Upaniṣad*, **152–53**; in the *Muṇḍaka Upaniṣad*, **204–205**; as *"neti, neti,"* 152n; as non-agent, **114**, **138**, 139, 153; as not perceived, 93n; as object of love, **92**, 94–95n; as one alone, 88n; and process of becoming the individual soul, **138**; as self-luminous, 208n; as Self of all, identified with the Devī (or Devī as supreme Self), **130–31**, **156**; three bodies of, **149**; as witness, 207n, **282**, 283n

Auṃ. *See under* Oṃ

Auspiciousness (*saubhāgya*, *śivā*), 49, 51n, 53–54n; and time, 252, 254n, 255n, 258

Austerities (*tapas*, asceticism), as practiced by demons, 49; in Goddess worship, **55**, **267**; as synonym for knowledge, 72n; and the vows *kṛccha* and *cāndrayāna*, 167n

Avatara(s). *See* Devī, avataras of; Devī, avataric mission of; Kṛṣṇa, avataric mission of; Viṣṇu, avataras of

Bāṇa-liṅga, **185**, 188n, 190–91n, 195n, **279**

Base Support Center. *See* Centers of energy, Base (Root) Support Center

Being, consciousness, and bliss (*sac-cid-ānanda*), as "attributes" of: the Ātman/Self, 95n, 289; Brahman, 13, 87, 109; the cosmic

seed, **95**, 96, 97n; the Devī in the *Devī Gītā*, 16, 57n, 67, 227n, **286**; the Devī in the *Pārvatī Gitā*, 11; the Devī's supreme state, 154n; Hrīṃ, **42**, **156**; Oṃ, 65
Bhagavad Gītā (see also *Devī Gītā*, and the *Bhagavad Gītā*): and Arjuna's response to/praise of Kṛṣṇa's cosmic form, 132, 132n, 133n; and the *bhakti* tradition, 6; on breath control, 174–75n; and detached devotion combined with knowledge, 225; and divine grace, 138, 267; and "imitations" of, 8–9; and Kṛṣṇa's avataric mission, 272; and Kṛṣṇa's cosmic or lordly form, 4, 122, 126n, 128, 129n, 134; and Kṛṣṇa as proclaimed by the Vedas, 308n; on *kṛta-kṛtya*, 51n; on obstacles to yoga, 163; on the perfected or realized being, 209, 210n, 226, 233n; and *preman*, 72n; on promise of salvation, 268n; on rarity of person who seeks truth, 233; on rebirth, 232n; on refuge, 278n; on secret teachings, 83n, 212n, 313, 314n; on the Self as neither actor nor object, 153; on the Self as unstained, 116n; and the self-predications of Kṛṣṇa, 119, 120n, 132; on talking about Kṛṣṇa, 47n; on types of devotional acts, 222, 223n; on the universe as strung on Kṛṣṇa, 74n; on the world-pervading nature of Kṛṣṇa, 121n; on yogic posture, 169n
Bhāgavata Purāṇa (see also *Devī Gītā*, and the *Bhāgavata Purāṇa*): and Advaitic theism, 17; on the avatara doctrine, 272, 273n; on the cosmic form (Virāj) of the Lord/Viṣṇu, 122, 125, 125n, 128; and the *Devī-Bhāgavata Purāṇa*, 5, 7–8; and the *Kapila Gītā*, 9; on Kṛṣṇa's throne, 296; on listening (*śravaṇa*), 47n; on love for all creatures, 227n; on Māyā, 87; on media of worship, 281n; on *preman*, 72n; on provisional role of acts, 144n; on the self's deluded sense of agency, 140n; on spirit as beyond *guṇas*, 116n; and the story of Indra's Bramancide, 235–36n; on types of acts, according to the *guṇas*, 223n; on types of images, 265n; on types of meditation, including the Limb-by-limb, 199, 200n; on Viṣṇu as "one alone," 88n
Bhairava(s) (form[s] of Śiva), 247, 276n
Bhairavas (sect), **273**, 276n
Bhakti. See Devotion
Bhakti Yoga (path of devotion) (*see also* Devotion): and doctrine of divine grace, 137–38; as easiest of three paths, **219**; and Eight-limbed Yoga, 220; fourfold classiification of, 225; as means to supreme knowledge, **219**, 220, 221n; as one of three paths, **219**, 220, 220–21n; and path of good works, 138; and path of knowledge, 16, **81**, 82, 138, 203–204, 235; and surrendering fruits of action, 9
Bhāmatī school of Advaita, 115
Bhāskara Rāya, 192n
Bhuta-śuddhi. See Tantric worship, rites included in: cleansing rites
Bhuvaneśvarī. *See also* Devī
and *aiśvarya*, 24
binding and liberating aspects of, 66
and Brahman, 23, 43, 71, 280
and emergence from orb of light, 11–12, 60, 62n, **62**, 63 (fig.), **64**, 66–67, 280

Bhuvaneśvarī *(continued)*
as ever wakeful/attentive, 1, **52**, 260n
hymn to, 4, **69–70**, 70–71
iconic form of: in the *Devī Gītā*, general portrayal of, 3, 51n, **62**, 63 (fig.), **64**, 65–67, **133–34**, 134–35, 286 (fig.); in the *Devī Gītā*, in Vedic worship, 26, 199, 264, **279**, 280, 282; in the *Devī Upaniṣad*, 25–26, 67; in the *Prapañcasāra Tantra*, 66, 68n; in the *Śāradā-Tilaka Tantra*, 67n
and Lalitā, 24, 25–26, 309
in list of names of goddesses and pilgrimage sites, **241**, 243
as revealer of the *Devī Gītā*, 3, 10, 80, 217
root mantra of, 301n
and the Seat of Five Corpses, 1–2, 286 (fig.), 296
seed mantra of (*see* Hrīṃ, Hṛllekhā)
subordinate status of, in the *Kālikā Purāṇa*, 245n, 247
as supreme goddess/Śakti/universal ruler: in the *Devī Gītā*, 1–2, 10, 16, 23, 238–39, 244n, 247, 297; in the *Devī Upaniṣad*, 25
Tantric origins of, 23–26, 280
and translation of name, 37–38
Bhuvaneśvarī Rahasya, 248n
Bīja-mantras. *See* Seed mantra(s)
Bindu (energizing point, primal point), 58n, 72, 73n, **186**, 187,192n, **193**
Birth, human, **232–33**, 233
Blissful nature: of Brahman, 210n; of the Devī, **279**, of the immortal, **205**; of the Kuṇḍalinī, **285**, 289; of the Self, 14, **92**
Bliss, sheath of, 207n
Bodies, the three cosmic (Gross Body [Cosmic Body, Virāj], Subtle [Cosmic Soul, *sūtrātman*], and Causal Body [*avyākṛta*, the Unmanifest, Unmanifest State]): in the cosmogonic process, **95**, 96, 97n, **98–99**, 99, **101–102**, 102–103, 103n, 104n, **105**, 106; and the elements of Oṃ, 156, 157–58n; and the five sheaths, 151–52n; freedom from, **149**, 150n; as part of the fourfold Brahman, **42**, **70**, 74n; resorption of, 150, **155**, 156, 157–58n; and states of consciousness, 107n
Body, one's own, to be dedicated/given: to the Devī, **303**; to the guru, 211, **213**, 215n
Boon(s), **48**, 49–50, 82
Brahmā (*see also* Trimūrti, the), 11, 125; and awakening of the Devī, 260n; and dismemberment of Satī, 242; as granter of boons, **48**, 49–50, **78**; as teacher of Brahmavidyā, 216
Brahmaloka (world of Brahmā), **230**, 231, 232n
Brahmabindu Upaniṣad, 115n
Brahma-dvāra (Brahma-gate, door of Brahman), 183n, 186, 188n, 194
Brahman (*see also* Liberation/highest spiritual goals of life, with reference to Brahman): in Advaita, 13–17, 181; city of (*brahma-pura*), **205**, 207n; as existent and nonexistent, **204**, 206–207n; and evolution or appearance of the world, 75n, 90n, 96, 97n, 105, 106–107n; four quarters of, 13–14, **42**, 43, 71, 74n; and gender, 62n; and the great saying, "Tat tvam asi," **146**, 147; higher and lower (aniconic and iconic) aspects, 12, 13; as identified with the Goddess (*see under* Devī, and Brahman; Bhuvaneśvarī, and

Brahman); as identified with the guru, 290n; as identified with I, 147, 289; as identified with the individual Self or soul, **43**, 71, **146**, 177, **179**, **198**, 210, 223n, 288; as identified with one who knows Brahman, **230**; as identified with the self-luminous Self, 208n; as identified with Śiva, 12; in the *Kena Upaniṣad*, 59; knowledge of, vs. works, 140, 143; and Māyā/ignorance, 15, 86–87, 92, 109, 117n, 151n; in the *Muṇḍaka Upaniṣad*, **204–205**; omnipresence of, **43**; as root of the five sheaths, **150**, 152n; as *Śabdabrahman* (Brahman in the form of sound), 47n, **185**, 187; in Tantra, 18; and tension with Bhuvaneśvarī, 23

Brahman(s) (priestly class): as best of humans, 233; and access to the Vedas, **232**; as entitled only to scriptures of Vedic aims, **274**; feeding of, 251, 262n, **304**; and the fire offering, **287**; Kṛṣṇa worshiped in, 281n; and Kṣatriyas, as food for the Devī, **127**, 129n; and Kṣatriyas, as protectors of the Devī's command/Vedas, **271**, 273n; recitation in presence of, **248**, **312**; and tragedy of being excluded from the Vedic path, **274**, 276–77n; and the unrighteous, **272**; and *varṇāśrama-dharma*, 18

Brahmāṇḍa and *piṇḍāṇḍa*, 180, 181

Brahmāṇḍa Purāṇa, 25, 66, 67n, 296

Brahmanical authority/orthodoxy, and Tantric tradition, 18, 21, 36, 264–65, 267

Brahma-randhra (Brahmic aperture), 178n, 183n, 189n, 192n, 289n, 290n, 292

Brahma Sūtras, Śaṃkara's commentary on, 89n, 116n, 145n

Brahmavaivarta Purāṇa, 210n

Brahmavidyā (knowledge of Brahman), 59, 203, 206, **209**, 209, 221n, 230; and the beheading of Arthavaṇa, **215–16**, 216–17

Breath(s) (*see also* Breath control), **204**, **205**

- the five (fivefold), **101–102**, 102, 104n, **149**
- the vital or life-breath(s) (*prāṇa*, *vāyu*): associated/identified with the Kuṇḍalinī, 186, 197; departing of, through the arteries, 181; not lost when absorption in pure consciousness attained, **230**, 230–31; and rebirth, **111**, 113n; united with, by the yogi, 194

Breath control (*prāṇāyāma*): according to count, **170**, 170–72, 172–73n; and breath concentration (*vāyu-dhāraṇa*) in Kuṇḍalinī Yoga, 177, 180, 186, **196**, 196–97, 198–99; definition of, 173n; and equalizing the inhalations and exhalations, **155**; fruits of, **170**, 172, 174n; relation to other limbs of yoga, 175–77; role of, in Jñāna Yoga, 157; the three phases of, **170**, 171, 174–75n; with a matrix (*sagarbha*), **170**, 171, 172, 181n

Bṛhadāraṇyaka Upaniṣad, 16; and fear of another, 209; and knowledge of Brahman, 140; and mental qualifications of a student, 143; and "*neti, neti*," 152n; and non-departing of vital breaths when Brahman realized, 230–31; and the Virāj, 112; and the warp and woof of the universe, 120n

Bṛhadāraṇyaka Upaniṣad, Śaṃkara's commentary on, 112

Cakras. *See* Centers of energy
Caturvedi, Ramadhin, 321
Causal Body. *See* Bodies, the three cosmic
Centers of energy (*cakra*s, *padma*s, lotuses)
all the centers, collectively, 20, 182n, 189n, 192n, 197n; absence of, in early Upaniṣads, 181; description of, **184–86**, 186–87; and the energy channels, 183n; and *liṅga*s in, 188–89n; objective reality of, 188; piercing of, 186, **193**, 194, 195n
Base (Root) Support Center (*mūlādhāra*): as base of the *vicitrā*, 183n; and the Bound Lotus Posture, 169n; and infusion of the Hṛllekhā, **292**; as lowest/support of all centers, **184**, 186, 187, 188n, 189n; as resting place of the individual Self, 177; as resting place of the Kuṇḍalinī, 20, 182n, 186, **193**, 194, 288, 290n
Blockade Center (*rodhinī*), **185**, 192n
Command Center (*ājñā*), **185**, 187, 191–92n, 195n
Jewel-filled Center (*maṇi-padma*), **184–85**, 190n
Kailāsa Center, **185**, 187, 192n
Lotus of a Thousand Petals/Thousand-petaled Lotus (*sahasrāra*), 178n, **186**, 187, 192n, 194, 201, **285**, 289n, 290n, 300
Own Abode Center (*svādhiṣṭhāna*), **184**, 189–90n
Unstained Center (*viśuddha*), **184**
Unstruck Sound Center (*anāhata*), **185**, 188n, 191n, 195n
Chāndogya Upaniṣad, 86, 104n, 116n, 183n
Channels of energy (*nāḍī*s, arteries)
all the channels, collectively, 20; and the Bound Lotus Posture, 169n; in the *Muṇḍaka Upaniṣad*, **204**; numbers of, **179**, 182n; objective reality of, 188; purification of (*nāḍī-śuddhi*), 171, 172, 174n; in the early Upaniṣads, 181
Beautiful, Variegated Channel (*vicitrā*), **179**, 183n, 188n
Central artery (*suṣumnā*/Sushumnā, Most Gracious Channel, middle channel): ascent of the Kuṇḍalinī within, 194, 195n, 197, **285**, 289, 290n; description of, **179**, 180, 182n, 183n; leading the Kuṇḍalinī out of the body through, 300; in the *Maitrī Upaniṣad*, 181; mouth of, 188n; restraining breath within, **170**, 171, 173n, 177, 186, 194, 197; and the Self residing in, 290n
Left artery (*iḍā*/Idā, Channel of Comfort) and Right artery (*piṅgalā*/Pingalā, Tawny-red Channel), **170**, 171, 172n, 173n, **179**, 180, 181, 182–83n, 186
Chosen (or one's own) deity, **175**, 177, 186, 266n, 288, 295, 296, 297n
Churning of the Milk Ocean, 195n, **314–15**, 315–16, 316n
Cleansings (*dhauti*s), 171
Coburn, Thomas B., 322
Concentration (*dhāraṇa/dhāraṇā*, concentration of breath or mind), 170–71, 176–77, 180, 191, **196**, 196–97, **198**, 198–99
Conduct, proper (*ācāra*, *sad-ācāra*, Vedācāra), 287, 288, 289
Consciousness (*cit*) (*see also* Devī, as consciousness)
and Brahman, 13–14

and the great saying, *"Tat tvam asi,"* **146**, 147
nature of, **91**, **92**, 93–94n
as reflected (*cid-abhāsa, pratibimbita*), 90n, 113n
and Śabda Brahman, 187
as the Self, **92**, 178
states of, **91**, **294**; in Advaita, 13–14, 74n, 76n, 94n, 297n; and Devī as witness of, **70**; as identified with the Devī, 71; and *mahas*, 46n; and resorptive meditation, 150, 156, 158n; Śaṃkara's description of, 107n; and Self as witness of, 207n; Upaniṣadic notion of, 74n, 105; and unconsciousness (*jaḍa-tva*), 82n, 92–93
Cosmic Body. *See* Bodies, the three cosmic; Virāj
Cosmic order, 6, 23
Cosmic seed (extraordinary form, world seed), **86**, 89n, **95**, 96, 97n, **99**, 99, 100n
Cosmic Soul. *See* Bodies, the three cosmic
Cosmogony (creation): evolutionary model of, 75n, 90n, **95–96**, 96, **98–99**, 99, 100, 100n, **101–102**, 103, 103n, 105, **149**; limitation model of, 106n, 115; in the Purāṇas, 5, 86; reflection/appearance model of, 75n, 90n, 96, **104–105**, 105–106, 106n, 119; reversal/dissolution of, as liberation, 15–16, 100, 150, 151n; and revivification of, in Kuṇḍalinī Yoga, 194–95
Cosmotheism (cosmotheistic perspective or vision): in the *Muṇḍaka Upaniṣad*, 131, 132; and pantheism, 121n; and the self-predications of the Devī, 114–15, 119; in the Upaniṣads, 13, 17; and the Virāj, 4, 124–25
Curse(s), **274**, 275, 276–77n

Dadhīca, **274**, 276–77n
Dadhyañc, 216, 217
Dakṣa, 10, 23, 49, 55, 60, 240n; curse/cursing of, **274**, 276–77n
Dance/dancing, **224**, 228n, **251**, 301n, **304**
Darśana (appearance; iconic manifestation; revelation of form; vision of), 9, 10, 60, 82n, 260–61n; as aim of mantra recitation/worship, 55–56, 57n; of the Devī in the Cosmic Body (Virāj), **123–24**, **137**, 137–38; of the Devī in the orb of light (*see* Bhuvaneśvarī, and emergence from orb of light); explanation of, 315; and rejoicing of the gods, **314**, 315; in relation to teachings and hymns, 3–4
Darśana Upaniṣad, 169n, 182n
Demons, and conflict with the gods (*see also* Tāraka), 6, 49–50, 53, 60, 66, 79; and decline of righteousness, **271**, 273n
Devadatta, **146**, 147, 148n
Devī (the Goddess; the Great Goddess; Mahā-devī) (*See also* Bhuvaneśvarī, Śākti)
accessibility of, 239
androgynous nature of, 22, **118**, 119, 127n
aniconic form of, as lustrous power (*mahas*), 60, 67; and description of, **58–59**
asexual nature of, **59**, 62n, **118**,
avataras (births, incarnations) of, 2, 10, 11, **79**, 80n, 243n, 260n; and the Mahāvidyās, 23, 25
avataric mission of (assuming avataric guises), 2, **271**, 272–73, 273n

Devī *(continued)*
as being, consciousness, bliss (*saccid-ānanda*), 16, 57n, 65, 67, 227n, **286**
benign and/or horrific aspects of: in the *Devī Māhātmya* 8; as manifested in her cosmic forms, 9, 124, **127–28**, 128, **131**, **133–34**, 134–35; as manifested in the Mahāvidyās, 23; in Śākta Tantrism, 22; and worship of, according to days of the week, 252, 254n, 255n
benign aspect of, emphasized in the *Devī-Bhāgavata Purāṇa* and *Devī Gītā*, 1, 3, 22, 53
binding and liberating aspects of, 66
and Brahman: in the *Devī Upaniṣad*, 26; as embodiment, nature, or form of, 16, 17, **42**, 43, **70**, **85**, **150**, **203**, 203, 206n; in the hymn to Bhuvaneśvarī, 70–71; as the imperishable of the *Bṛhadāraṇyaka Upaniṣad*, 120n; in the myth of emergence from the orb of light, 11–12, 67; in the *Pārvatī Gītā*, 10; as represented by Oṃ, 19, 65, 157; in the story of Umā Haimavatī, 59–60, 216; as the supreme of the *Muṇḍaka Upaniṣad*, 206; as symbolized by the lustrous power (*mahas*), 46, 46–47n, 59–60, 62n, 80; as unchangeable, 113n
compared to other Hindu goddesses, 1
as compassion: embodiment, storehouse, or ocean of, **64**, **69**, **133**, 207n, **263**
as consciousness (*cit*, *saṃvit*), 2, **85**, **198**, 199, **224**, **225**, 226, **228**, 311; and internal worship, **281–82**, 283, 283n, 299; and lustrous power (*mahas*), 11, 12, 46n, 60, 62n, 67; as manifested in her sacred sites, 247; and self-luminosity, **91**, 93; and the states of, 71, **294**; and the unconscious, 82n
as creatrix (overseer of creation), 2, 65, 100
and devotees: her compassion/concern for, 1, 2, **52–53**, 62, 65–66, **78**, **81**, **137**, **238**, 240n; her deference to, 209; her distress over sorrows of, **279**; her satisfying desires of, **123**; her seeming indifference to, **52**, 53
as dwelling in the hearts of her knower/realized sages/the wise, **208**, 210n, **246**, 247
erotic aspect of, **64**, 65,
historical development of, 7
iconic and aniconic forms of: interconnected in the myth of emergence from the orb of light, 11–12, 59–60, 62n, **62**, 63 (fig.), 66–67; in the hymn to Bhuvaneśvarī, 71
iconic forms of (*see also under* Bhuvaneśvarī, iconic form of; Virāj, as cosmic manifestation of the Devī), and types of Goddess worship, 26, 67, 199, **263**, 264
as independent of any consort, 1, 7, 26, 53–54n, 77n, 247
as manifest in virgins/young boys, **257**, 262n, **304**
maternal apsect of: as beneficent World-Mother, 1, 2, 8, 65; and epithets for, 54n; and human motherhood, **52–53**, 305; as forgiving of faults, **130**, 305; as Mother of the gods, **130**; as opposed to amorous ecstasy, 225
menses of, 2, 21, **242**, 243

as neither known nor unknown, **230**
omniscience of, 72n, 76n,
as one alone, **85**, 86, 88n, 90n
as opposed to the false, **92**, **282**
paradoxes of, 2
possible cruelty or injustice of, 89n
as punisher of the unrighteous, **271**
as source of the Veda, **269**, 270
as Self (Self of all), **131–32**,132, **153**
as not separate from anyone, **208**, **224**, 235
and Śiva: amorous sport with, 2, 65; subordinated to, as spouse, 10, 22, 80; superiority over, 2, 10, 11–12, 22–23, 60, 65, 67; worshiped by, **251**, 255n
superiority of, over the gods in general (*see also* Humbling of the gods, stories of), 1–2; and the birth of the gods from her, **130**, 132n; in the *Devī-Bhāgavata Purāṇa* and *Devī Gītā*, 7–8, 10, 11; and her granting of victory to the gods, 255n, 260n; and the swooning of the gods before her cosmic form, **128**, **129**
as teacher of wisdom, 8, 10, **81**, 82
and the universe: Devī's body parts identified with parts of this world, 239, 240n, 242–43, 247; Devī's Cosmic Body identified with parts of the universe, **123–124**, 124, 243; Devī's entering into, identifying with, or pervading the world, **111**, 112, 113n, 114–15, **118**, 119, 207n, **303**
Vedic identity of, 70
Virāj/cosmic form of (*see under* Virāj)
and Viṣṇu/Kṛṣṇa: similarity to, 8; superiority over, 8, 53, 60; worshiped by, 255n
Devī-Bhāgavata Purāṇa: and the *Bhāgavata Purāṇa*, 5, 7–8, 17; and the *Devī Gītā*, general relationship between, 4–8, 50, 60; and the *Devī Māhātmya*, 8; on gender of the supreme, 22; and the *Kena Upaniṣad*, 59—60; as a Mahā-Purāṇa, 7; and the Mahāvidyās, 24; and Nīlakaṇṭha's commentary, 32; and the *Śāradā-Tilaka Tantra*, 295, 297n; and synthesis of Advaitic, Tantric, and *bhaktic* ideals, 311; and Tantra, Left- and Right-Handed, 265, 270
Devī Gītā
and Advaita Vedānta: on the four ends of life, 140; general comparison with, 16–17; on knowledge and action, 144n; on Māyā, 92–93, 108–109, 119; on the reality of the world, 75n, 87–88, 89n, 120
Advaitin flavor of, 322
and androcentrism, 34–37
and the *Bhagavad Gītā*: on the avatara doctrine, 272; on divine grace, 267; general comparison with, 2–4, 320; and historical developments between, 12; on the horrific and pleasing forms of the supreme, 134; as model for, 8; on the perfected being, 209; on the self-predications of the supreme, 119, 120n; on types of devotion, according to the *guṇas*, 222; on the world-devouring, fearsome Virāj, 128, 129n, 131
and the *Bhāgavata Purāṇa*: and Advaitic theism/*bhakti*, 17, 200; and amorous sport, 225; on

Devī Gītā (continued)
detached devotion, 225; on devotion and knowledge, 234–35; on devotion, knowledge, and dispassion, 229; on the householder, 220, 313; on Māyā, 87; on passion/dispassion, 220, 221n; on the supreme not knowing its own power/limits, 132n; on types of meditation, 199–200; on Vedic-Tantric rites/worship, 264, 298n; on the Virāj (Cosmic Body), 125, 126n 128
contribution of, to Śākta tradition, 320
date of, 4
and the *Devī-Bhāgavata Purāṇa*, general relationship between, 4–8, 50, 60
and the *Devī Māhātmya*: character of the Goddess in each, 8, 73n; and common verses or motifs, 72n, 88n, 90n, 131, 132, 132n; and ritual uses of, 321–22
and the *Devī Upaniṣad* (*Devī Atharvaśiras*, *Hṛllekhā Upaniṣad*), 26, 70, 72n, **303**, 307n
frame story of, 6, 10–11, 50, 60, 79–80, 315, 316n
and gender of the supreme, 22–23, **59**, 62n
as an independent text, 4, 321–22
and the *Kālikā Purāṇa*, 245n
and the *Kapila Gītā*, 9, 199–200; and Bhakti Yoga, 220, 221n, 223n, 225–26, 226n, 227n, 229
and the *Kaṭha Upaniṣad*, 150, **152–53**, 153–54, 154n, 231
and the *Kūrma Devī Gītā*, 9–11, 79–80, 267–68, 268n, 272, 278, 279n
and the *Muṇḍaka Upaniṣad*: on Brahmavidyā, **204–205**, 205–206, 206n, 207n, 208n, 216, 217; on the cosmotheistic vision of the Puruṣa/Virāj, 119, 121n, 125, 125n, 126n, 131–32, 132–33n
originality of, 26–27
and plagiarism, 205–206, 217
and the *Pañcadaśī*, 101n
and the *Pañcīkaraṇa-Vārttika* of Sureśvara, 97–98n, 100, 100n, 101n, 157, 157n, 158n
and the *Pārvatī Gītā*, 9–11, 79–80
and recitation of, **312**, 320–23
and the *Śāradā-Tilaka Tantra*, 162, 162n, 166n, 178n, 297n
sectarian nature of, 322
summary of, 1–4
and the *Sūta Gītā*, 9, 115, 117n
and the *Sūta Saṃhitā*, 264, 282, 283n, 306n
synthetic/inclusive character of, 44, 62n, 71, 87
and Tantra, 17–26, 265, 288
and the Upaniṣads/Vedic scripture, 205, 217, 320
and use/reception of the text, 319–323; as an "*artha*" text, 320; as a mantric text, 320–23
Devī-māhātmya (glorification of the Goddess), generic sense of, **315**, 316, 317n
Devī Māhātmya (of the *Mārkaṇḍeya Purāṇa*) (see also *Devī Gītā*, and the *Devī Māhātmya*): and avataras of the Devī, 243n, 272; and the Devī as "alone, without a second," 88n, 90n; and the Devī as "Self of all," 132; and the *Devī-Bhāgavata Purāṇa*, 8; and *devī-māhātmya*, 316; and the devotee of the Devī as refuge, 210n; and the emergence of the Great Goddess, 7, 86; and the Mahāvidyās, 24; mantric aspects (*śabda*) and meaning aspects (*artha*) of, 319–20, 322; recitation of, 320–21; and the

Virāj, 128; and worship of the Devī with, 306n
Devī Māhātmya (of the *Kūrma Purāṇa*). See *Kūrma Devī Gītā*
Devī Purāṇa, 7, 259n, 261n
Devī Stuti (of the *Devī Upaniṣad*), 26, 70
Devī Sūkta (Hymn of the Devī), 26, **54**, 56n, **303**, 307n
Devī Upaniṣad (*Devī Atharvaśiras*, *Devī-Atharvā-Śiras*, *Hṛllekhā Upaniṣad*) (see also *Devī Gītā*, and the *Devī Upaniṣad*): convergence of Bhuvaneśvarī and Tripurā in, 25–26; and the Devī Sūkta, 56n, 307n; and Hrīṃ, 77n, 307n; and its Devī Stuti, 26, 70; on the omnipresence of the Devī, 61n
Devotee(s) (*bhakta*[s]) (*see also* Devī, and devotees: her compassion/concern for; Devotion): characteristics of, as a topic in the Purāṇas, 7; characteristics of, in the *Devī Gītā*, 88n, 220, **267**, **277–78**, 278; deference of the Devī towards, 209; eagerness to see, **224**; feeding of, **257**; as fit recipient of secret knowledge, 83n, **257**; as one with guru, mantra, and deity, 214; purifying power of, 210n, 228n
Devotion (*see also* Bhakti Yoga; Devotee[s]): acts of, 47n, **223–25**, 226n; and Advaita, 16, 82n, 227n, 234–35; and *darśana*, 55; to the Devī as Brahman, **203**; and dispassion, 220, **228**, 229, 231; and ecstatic joy, 69, **224**; and the god-demon conflict, 6, 79; and indifference to all forms of liberation, **223**, 225–26; as inspiration for offerings, **303**; and knowledge, **81**, 82, 220, 225, 226, **228**, 229, 231, 234–35, **268–69**; to the lotus feet of the Devī, **79**, 79, 305; and offering fruits of action to the Devī, **222**; as primary qualification for discipleship/receiving the *Devī Gītā*, 36–37, **211**, 212, **312**, 313, 317; in the Purāṇas 6–7; as qualification of Janamejaya, **47**, 317; role of, in the path of knowledge, **145**, 148n; role of, in resorptive meditation, **155**; role of, in the yogas, **203**, 203, **278**; supreme/highest, 79, **222**, **223–25**, 225–26, 226n, 238; typologies of, 9, **221–22**, 222, 225, 264; undistracted, **267**
Dharma, 38, 287; as righteous action (righteousness), **269**, **271**, **274**
Dhyāna. *See* Meditation
Dhyānabindu Upaniṣad, 74n, 190n, 236n
Dispassion (*vairāgya*), 220, **228**, 229, **230**, 231
Dullness (*tamas*, darkness, error) (see also *Guṇas*), 102, 207n, **273**
Durgā, 1, 73n, **241**, 255n, 261n, 309
Durgā Pūjā. *See* Rites, specific: Rite of Nine Nights
Durgama, 23, 24
Durgā Saptaśatī (see also *Devī Māhātmya* [of the *Mārkaṇḍeya Purāṇa*]), 321
Dvivedi, Gangadhar, 320

Ecstatic/loving joy (*preman*), **69**, 72n, **78**, **129**, **303–304**
Efficient cause, **86**, 90n
Eight-limbed Yoga (*aṣṭāṅga-yoga*) of Patañjali
  *bhakti*cized versions of, 199–200
  and Bhakti Yoga, 220
  definition/goal of, **161**, 162, 162n, **163**, 201
  the eight limbs of, defined, **163:** (1) restraints and (2) observances,

Eight-limbed Yoga *(continued)*
164–65, 165–66; 166n; (3) postures, **167–68**, 168, 168–69n; (4) breath control, **170**, 170–172, 172n–75n; (5) withdrawal of the senses, **175**, 176; (6) concentration of vital breath, **175**, 176–77, **196**, 197; (7) meditation, **175**, 177, 200; (8) absorption, **175**, 177–78, 200
and Jñāna Yoga, 162, 163, 203, 220
relation to Kuṇḍalinī Yoga, 20, 161–62, 201
the six obstacles to, **163**, 163–64, 164n
and women, 36
Embodiment, and the body, view of: in Advaita and the *Devī Gītā*, 17; in the *Devī Gītā*, 21; in Tantra/Kuṇḍalinī Yoga, 19, 180–81, 195, 265, 300
Evening Rite (*pradoṣa*), **251**, 255n
Evolution of world. *See* Cosmogony (creation), evolutionary model of

False perception of distinctions/differences/separateness, 15, **221**, **222**, 222–23n
Festivals (*utsavas*)
and devotion, **224**
general description of, 257–59
Himālaya's query about, **237–38**
and rites *(vratas)*, 258, 262n
specific: Chariot Festival, **257**, 260–61n; Festival of the Thread-Offering, **257**, 261–62n; Going-to-sleep and Waking-up Festivals, **257**, 259–60n, 262n; Jasmine Festival, **257**, 261n; Swing Festival, **257**, 259n
Four ends/goals of life (*puruṣārthas*) (*see also* Liberation/highest spiritual goals of life), 3, 66, **139**, 140, 141n
Four stages of life (student, householder, etc.), **277**, 278

Garuḍa Purāṇa, 261n
Gauḍapāda's Kārikā, 93n
Gaurī. *See* Pārvatī
Gautama, 277n
Gautamīya Tantra, 190n, 191n
Gāyatrī mantra, 43, 72–73n, 74n, 166
Gender (*see also* Androcentrism; Women): and conceptions of the supreme 22–23, **59**, 62n, **118**, 119, 127n; and initiation, 21, 312n; and liberation, 35–36
Gheraṇḍa Saṃhitā, 141n, 168, 169n, 171, 173n, 174n, 176, 177, 197n
Gītās (*see also specific titles*): devotion and knowledge conjoined in, 82; as "imitations" of the *Bhagavad Gītā*, 8–9; and *māhātmyas*, 9, 316; and the Śaivite and Vaiṣṇava *gītās*, 9; and Śākta *gītās*, 9–11, 79, 128, 134, 317n; as songs, 2
Goals of life, worldly, 2, 20, 239, 253n, 255n, 258–59, 261n
Goddess, the. *See* Devī
Grace (*anugraha*, favor), of the Devī, 61n, 65, **81**, 258, **267**, 267; not attained by merit, **81**, 82n, **137**, 137–38; variable availability of, 260n; and Śiva's, 275
Great Goddess, the (Mahā-Devī). *See* Devī
Gross Body. *See* Bodies, the three cosmic
Guṇas (*guṇa* aspects; ignorance, passionate yearning, virtue; three *guṇas*) (*see also* Activity; Dullness; Lucidity), 102, 103n, 117n, 171, 238; and types of devotion, **221–22**, 222, 223n, 225, 226, 264

Guru (teacher): devotion/obedience/obligations to, **211**, 211, **213**, 308n, **310**; difficulty in attaining of, **233**; importance of, 213–14, 313; as incarnation/manifestation of the Lord or Brahman, 214, 214n, 290n; and installation of the Devī's throne, 295; and knowledge from books, **201**, 202n, 212; meditation on, 285; as more venerable than the father, **213**, 214, 214n; as one with mantra, deity, and devotee, 214; qualifications of, **145**, 146–47, 214; role of, in Eight-limbed Yoga, 201; role of, in Jñāna Yoga, **145**, 146–47, 148n; role of, in Tantric practice, 20–21, 214; as superior to Śivạ/Viṣṇu, **213**, 215n

Haimavatī. *See* Umā Haimavatī
Haṭha Yoga, 181n, 182n, 202n
Haṭhayoga Pradīpikā, 166n, 169n, 174n, 180
Hell(s), 5, 140n, 163, 266n, **271**, 272, 273n, 275, 276–77n
Hidden (*rahasya*, mystic, secret) teachings, 20, **81**, 83n, 211–212, 212–213n, **271**, **312**, 313, 314n, **317**, 317
Himālaya: and Devī's cosmic form, **122**, 122, 267, 268n; as devotee/disciple of the Devī, 3, 5, 9–11, 56, **79**, 80, **80**, 82, 206, 217, 220; as father of Gaurī/Pārvatī, 9–11, 46, 50, 60, **79**, **81**, 267, **314**, 315; as pilgrimage site for performing Devī worship, 11, **54**, 55, 60, 66, 72n; as site of Devī's manifestation, 5, **45**, 46, 60
Horse sacrifice, **81**, **234**, 235–36n
Hrīṃ (Bhuvaneśvarī's mantra, the Māyā-bīja) (*see also* Hṛllekhā): aggregated and individuated aspects of, 157n, 158n; Bharati's interpretation of, 77n; character of, **42**, **156**; as the Devī-Praṇava, 77n, 157, 157n; in the *Devī Upaniṣad*, 26, 307n; as emodiment of the Devī, **70**, **130**, 131; as expression of the primal principle or cosmic seed, **96**, 96; and the protective mantra of the Devī, 307n; relation to Oṃ, 65, 71, 77n, 97n, 98n, 131, 157, 157n, 207n; and reversal of evolution through meditation on, 100, **155–56**; and root mantra of Bhuvaneśvarī, 301n; as seed mantra of Bhuvaneśvarī 19, 71, 182n; as seed mantra of the Kuṇḍalinī, 182n, 288; Tantric interpretation of, 71, 73n; use of, in the Eight-limbed Yoga, 166; within the body, **184**, 189n
Hṛllekhā (Bhuvaneśvarī's mantra, the Māyā-bīja) (*see also* Hrīṃ): as director of all mantras, **309**, 309–310; as dwelling in the hearts of realized sages/the wise 210n, **246**, 247; etymology of, 248n; general significance of, 57–58n; identified with the Kuṇḍalinī, 57n; and infusion of its letters, 20, **292**, 293; as name of Hrīṃ, 19, 71; recited by gods and sages, **55**, 55–56, 59, 60; and the Śrī Vidyā, 309–310; use of, as obligatory in Devī worship, **309**, 310n
Hṛllekhā Upaniṣad. See *Devī-Upaniṣad*
Humbling of the gods, stories of, 55, 59–60, 61n, 62n, 65, 66, 216, 315–16
Humes, Cynthia A., 320–22

Hymn(s) (*stotras, stūtis)*: to Bhuvaneśvarī, **69–70**, 70–71; in the *Devī Gītā*, 4, 316; and the Devī Sūkta of the *Ṛg Veda*, 26, **54**, 56n, **303**, 307n; Himālaya's, of one thousand (and eight) names, 9, **303**, 307n; in the Purāṇas, 6; and the Puruṣa Sūkta of the *Ṛg Veda*, 125, 127n, 267; to the Virāj form of the Devī, **130–31**, 131–32

Icon, use of, in Tantric worship, 300
Idā. See under Channels of energy
Ignorance (*ajñāna, avidyā, tamas,* delusion, nescience): as aspect of Prakṛti, **104–105**, 106; as cause of differentiation of souls, **114**, 117n; destruction of, and attainment of liberation, 140, **156**, **230**; and perception of duality/separateness, 223n; as power of the Devī: **42**, **70**, 71, 75n, 76n; as power of Māyā, 43, 89n; and reflection of Brahman in, 107n; as root of desire and/or actions, 14, 139, 140n, **141**, 144n, 163; as root of mental darkness, **278**; as root of non-authoritative teachings, **269**, **273**; and *tamas*, 207n; as undefinable, 88n, 151n; as an *upādhi*, 106n, **149**, 151
Indra, **215**, 216, 235–36n, 255n
Initiation (*dīkṣā*): and gender, 21, 312n; procedures of, 295; qualifications of a disciple for, 20–21; subordinated to ritual action of Devī *pūjā*, 313; in Tantra, 20–21; into the Vedas or Tantras, **263–64**, 265–66n
Internal organ (*antaḥkaraṇa*, mind and intellect), **101**, 102, 103n, 104n, **149**
Iśa Upaniṣad, 144n
Īśvara. See Lord
Īśvarī ("Female Lord"), 37, 62n, 65

Jaḍa (inert, unconscious), 82n, 92, 93, 93n
Janamejaya, 4–5, 45–46, 317
Jani, A. N., 322
Japa. See Recitation
Jeweled Island (Maṇidvīpa): as celestial home of the Devī, 1, **52**, 54n, 65, 239, 247, 260n; as destination of the saved, 5, 17, **228**, 229, **310**; detailed description of, 24–25; and the Lotus of a Thousand Petals, 187; as object of meditation, 177; as one of the sacred sites of the Devī, **241**, 243, 244n, 245n; and the throne of the Devī, 295–96, 298n
Jīva(s). *See* Soul(s), individual
Jīvan-mukta(s) (liberated while living), 35, 50n, **139**, 140, 141n, 210n, 214, 230–31, 259, 288
Jīvan-mukti (*see also* Liberation/highest spiritual goals of life), 57n
Jñāna. See Knowledge.
Jñāna-karma-samuccaya (conjunction of knowledge and action), 143, 144n
Jñāna Yoga (path of knowledge) (*see also* Knowledge): and the Eight-limbed/Kuṇḍalinī Yoga, 162, 163, 203, 220; as one of three paths, **219**, 220, 220–21n; and path of devotion, 16, **81**, 82, 138, 203–204, 235; and path of good works or action, 138, **141–42**; preparatory stage for, **141–42**, 143; qualifications of a student for, 143; and resorptive meditation, **155–56**, 156–57; stages/steps of, 14, 47n, **145–46**, 146–47, **153**, 153–54

Jyotis (light) (*see also* Lustrous power of the Devī), 11–12, 177

Kailāsa (*see also* Centers of energy, Kailāsa Center), **208**
Kaivalya Upaniṣad, 75n, 297n
Kālī, 1, 255n, 260n
Kali age/Kali Yuga, 71, 276n
Kālīcharana (commentator on the *Ṣaṭcakra-Nirūpaṇa*), 162n, 183n, 189n, 190n, 191n, 192n
Kālikā Purāṇa, 7; as basis for *Devī Gītā*'s description of Kāmākhyā, 245n; on bathing of the deity, 306n; on Bhuvaneśvarī, 245n, 247; on the fall of Satī's body parts, 240n, 242–43, 244n, 245n; on the Festival of the Thread-Offering, 261–62n; on flowers, 300–301; on invocation of the Devī, 300; and the *kavaca* of Tripurā, 307n; on the lamp offering, 305; on mantras and tantras, 227n; on the media for Goddess worship, 280; on Navarātra, 256–57n; on offerings of clothes, 306n; on Śiva's grief, 51n; on sleep/awakening of the Devī, 260n; on worship of virgins/young boys, 262n
Kāmākhyā (the goddess), 244n, 247
Kāmākhyā/Kāmarūpa (the site), 2, 21, **241–42**, 242–43, 244n, 245n
Kane, Vaman Pandurang, 32
Kāpālakas/Kāpālikas, **273**, 276n, 277n
Kapila Gītā: on devotion and knowledge, 229; and the Eight-limbed Yoga, 199, 200; as imitation of the *Bhagavad Gītā*, 9; as model for the *Devī Gītā*'s discussion of Bhakti Yoga, 220, 221n, 223n, 225–26, 226n, 227n, 233; on proper recipient of teachings, 313, 314n; on spiritual hierarchy of beings, 233
Karma (acts, actions, deeds, karmic influences, rituals) (*see also* Dharma, as righteous action; Rites): disregard for fruits of, 222; dissolution of, into Māyā, **86**; indifferent acceptance of, **225**; and knowledge, **142**, 142–43, 144n, **268–69**; law of (being bound by, reaping fruits of), 89n, **95**, 139, **149**, **205**, **228**, 313; and meditation, **268**; as rooted in ignorance, **139**, 139–40, 140n, **141**; surrendering fruits of, to the Devī, 9, **222**, **299**
Karma Yoga (Kriyā Yoga): as one of three paths, **219**, 220, 220–21n; and paths of devotion and knowledge, 138
Kāśī, 238, **248**, 250n
Kaṭha Upaniṣad, 16, 93n, 116n, 129n; and the *Devī Gītā*, 150, **152–53**, 153–54, 154n, 231
Kaulakas/Kaulas, **273**, 276n, 277n
Kavaca(s) (protective mantra), 287, 291n, **303**, 307n
Kena Upaniṣad, 59–60, 61n, 216–17, 232n
Knower(s) of the supreme (*jñānis*, sages, the wise), **208**, 209, 210n, **246**, 247
Knowledge (*jñāna*, wisdom) (See also Brahmavidyā; Jñāna Yoga; *Veda*): and action, 14, **142**, 142–43, 144n, **268**, **274**; attained through many births, **232**; and *darśana*, 55–56; and detachment, 153; and devotion, **81**, 82, **219**, 220, 221n, 225, 226, **228**, 229, 231, 234–35, **268–69**; and dispassion, **228**, **229–30**, 231; as fulfillment of human birth, **233**, 233, **234**; giver of, superior to giver of birth, **213**, 214; and

Knowledge *(continued)*
ignorance, **152–53**; as inherent in all beings, **43**; and the *jīvanmukta*, 230–31; and the Mahāvidyās, 23; and Māyā, 44, 89n; as power/attribute of the Devī, **42**, **70**, 76n; as *tapas*, 72n; as unnecessary for relatives of devotees, 210n

Kriyā Yoga (*see also* Karma Yoga), 220, 220n

Kṛṣṇa: and amorous sport, 225; as avatara of the Devī, 272; avataric mission of, 272, 273n; benign and horrific forms of, 134; in the *Bhāgavata Purāṇa*, 8; and the *bhakti* tradition, 6; cosmic or lordly (Virāj) form of 4, 9, 122, 126n, 128, 129n, 132n, 134, 278; listening to deeds of, 47n, 144n; and the realized sage, 210n; and self-predications in the *Bhagavad Gītā*, 119, 120n, 132; as teacher of the *Bhagavad Gītā*, 2–3

Kṣurikā Upaniṣad, 197

Kuṇḍalī/Kuṇḍalinī (Coiled One, Serpent Power): absence of, in early Upaniṣads, 181; and affinity with the life breath, 186, 197; ascent and descent of, 20, **193**, 193–95, **285**, 289, 290n; awakening/arousing/ascending of, 20, 180, 181–82n, 183n, 186, 189n, **193**, 197n, 292; as the Goddess within, 2, 21, 186; as identified with Hrīṃ/Hṛllekhā, 57n, 288; mantric body of, 187, 196; as object of concentration or meditation, 177, 199, **285**; and obstacles to her ascent, 195n; as one of the forms for Goddess worship/meditation, 26; as residing in the Base Support, 20, **184**, 188n, 290n; united with Śiva, 187, 189n, **193**, 195n, 201, 290n; as "woman" (*abalā*), **285**, 290n

Kuṇḍalinī Yoga (*see also* Kuṇḍalinī): and ascent and descent of the Kuṇḍalinī, 20, **193**, 193–95, **285**, 289, 290n; and bipolar/sexual symbolism, 22–23, 194; and breath control (*prāṇāyāma*) or concentration (*vāyu-dhāraṇa*), 177, 180, 186, **196**, 196–97; and the Eight-limbed Yoga of Patañjali, 20, 161–62, 179–80, 201; esoteric physiology of, **179**, 180–81, 182–83n, **184–86**, 186–88, 298n; fruits/goal of, 20, 180, 186, 188–89n, **193**, 194–95, **196**, 196; and Jñāna Yoga, 203; and Mantra Yoga, **179**, 179, 181–82n, 196; and purification of the channels, 168n; and recreation of the body, 19, 292; and Right-Handed Tantra, 265; and Tantric worship, 287; and Yonibandha/Yoni-mudrā, 197n

Kūrma Devī Gītā (*devī māhātmya* of the *Kūrma Purāṇa*) (See also *Devī Gītā*, and the *Kūrma Devī Gītā*), 7, 128, 134, 271n, 273n, 276n, 307n, 317n

Kūrma Purāṇa (see also *Kūrma Devī Gītā*), 7, 9, 276n

Lakṣmī (Viṣṇu's wife), 1, 36, **54**, 58n, 60, **240**, 249, 309; birth/arising of, **315**, 315–16, 316n

Lakṣmī Tantra, 58n

Lalitā, 22, 25–26, 66–67, 67n, 296, 309, 315; and the Virāj form of the Goddess, 125, 128

Lalitā Māhātmya, of the *Brahmāṇḍa Purāṇa*, 66, 67n, 125, 128, 315

Lalitā Sahasranāma, 250n, 296

Lalitopākhyāna, of the *Brahmāṇḍa Purāṇa*, 296, 298n, 309

Laws of Manu, 50–51n, 211, 214, 214n, **269**, 270
Left artery. *See under* Channels of energy
Left-Handed Tantra (Vāmācāra), 18, 265, 270, 275, 275–76n, 288, 301n
Liberation/highest spiritual goals of life (*see also* Four ends/goals of life; Goals of life, worldly; *Jīvan-mukta*[s]; *Jīvan-mukti*)
 and complete fulfillment (*kṛta-kṛtya/kṛtārtha*), **47**, **237**; basic definition of, 50–51n, 209–10n; as fruit of Devī *pūjā*, **310**, **311**; as fruit of knowledge, **216**, **234**, 234; as fruit of observing the Devī's festivals, **257**, 259; as fruit of realizing Brahman, **208**; as fruit of reciting the divine names, 249; and the *jīvan-mukta*, 50n; and liberating one's mother through worshiping a knower, **209**; in the *Pārvatī Gītā*, 82n; whether possible for women, 35
 and gender, 35–36
 general descriptions of, as attaining: bliss, 14, 194, 195n, 197, 253n, 258, 321; dissolution into pure consciousness, 199–200, **209**, **281**, 282, 283, 292; freedom from bondage/samsara, 14, 143, **153**, **196**, 196, 258, **248**, **267**, 289; immortality, **45**, 180, 181, 195n, 197, **204**, 243; removal of sins **248**, 254, 311n; the supreme state/abode, **153**, 226, **248**, **312**; transformation into the deity, 249
 in the practice of: Advaita, 14–16, 150; Kuṇḍalinī Yoga, 20, 180, 182n, **193**, 194–95; Tantric worship, **310–11**, 311, 311n
 with reference to Brahman and realization of (union with/dissolution into), 14, 16, 47n, 57n, **149**, **150**, 156, 181, **201**, 201, **204**, **208**, 209, **230**, **274**, 288, 299
 with reference to the Devī and attaining/assuming her essential nature/form (*rūpatva, sārūpya*), **85**, 87n, **146**, 147, 249, **310**, 311; as facilitated by dwelling in the Jeweled Island, 17, **228**, 229, 231; as fruit of devotion, **225**; as fruit of internal worship, 299; as fruit of knowledge, 82; as fruit of listening (*śravaṇa*), 47n; as fruit of realizing oneness of soul and Brahman, **198**, 201; as fruit of resorptive meditation, **155–56**; as fruit of ritual observances, **251**, 253; as a prime concern of Himālaya, 11, 56, **81**, 83n; as realization of identity of Śakti within oneself, the Devī, and the articles of worship, 300; as recognition of the Self as the Self of the Devī, 154; in tension with service, 225–26; as transforming one's own body into the divine body of the Devī, 292
 with reference to the Devī and attaining her same qualities (*sārṣṭi*), **196**, 196
 with reference to the Devī and devotion/service to, 17, **223**, 225–26, **248**; and attaining/worshiping her lotus feet, **79**, 79, 311n; and *darśana*, 57n; and dwelling in the Jeweled Island, 2, 17, **310**, 311
 with reference to the Devī and knowledge of, **228**
 with reference to the Devī and realization of (union with, dissolution into), 2, 20, **43**, 44, 201, **230**; as aim of visualization practice, 177

Liberation/highest spiritual goals of life *(continued)*
with reference to Kṛṣṇa and union with, 209, 210n, 226
with reference to Śiva and union with, 262n
with reference to the supreme Self and realization of (union with/dissolution into), 150, 159n, **161**, 162, **175**, 194, 210n, **229**, 292
and rejection of traditional forms of, **223**, 225–26
as reversal/dissolution of cosmogony, 15–16, 100, 150, 151n
and worldly goals (*bhukti* and *mukti*, worldly enjoyments and liberation), 25, 57n, 140, 220–21n; 253, 258–59, 262n
Liṅga(s) (emblems of Śiva), in the energy centers, **184**, 188–89n, 189–90n, 190–91n, 192n; of light (Jyotir-liṅga), 11–12, 67; piercing of, in the energy centers, **193**, 194, 195n
Liṅga Purāṇa, 174n
Listening (*śravaṇa*, hearing): benefits of, for one who hears the *Devī Gītā*, **45**, **85**, 323; in Bhakti Yoga, 47n, 88n, **223**, **224**, 235–36n; in Jñāna Yoga, 14, 47n, **146**, 147, 150, **153**, 153–54; as superceding the performance of acts, 144n; to virtues of sacred sites, **248**
Lord (*Īśvara*): and *aiśvarya*, 24; and the Causal Body, 74n; as deluded by his own Māyā, 132n; as differentiated into parts by Māyā, **114**, 117n; as empowered by the Devī, **108**, 108–109; free will of, 119–20; and giving birth to the world, 131; and *īśvarī*, 37, 62n; and possible injustice of, 89n; powers of, 97n; as projected image of the Devī, 119; as reflected in Māyā, **104–105**, 106, 106–107n; three aspects of, **105**, 106, **118**
Lucidity (*sattva*, *sattva guṇa*, lucid aspects) (see also *Guṇas*), **101**, 102, 103n, **104**, 106, 106–107n
Lustrous power of the Devī (*mahas*) (see also *Tejas*): definition of, 46n; as implicit identifier of the Devī as Brahman, 16, 46, 47n, 59–60, 80, 208n, 280; and Janamejaya's query about, 5, 46; and the lamp offering to the Devī, 306n; as primal manifestation of the Devī, 11, **45**, **58–59**, 66, 67; in the *Śāradā-Tilaka Tantra*, 47n; in the *Taittirīya Upaniṣad*, 16, 46n; as transformation of the *yakṣa* in the *Kena Upaniṣad*, 59–60, 61n

Mahābhāgavata Purāṇa (See also *Pārvatī Gītā*), 7, 10, 23, 265
Mahābhārata, 2, 5, 6, 9, 49, 235
Mahā-Devī. *See* Devī
Mahālakṣmī, 43, 74n
Mahānārāyaṇa Upaniṣad, 61n, 159n, 290n
Mahānirvāṇa Tantra, 57n, 71, 280, 298n, 300, 301n, 302n, 307n, 308n
Mahā-Purāṇas, 7–8
Mahas. See Lustrous power of the Devī
Māhātmya(s) (glorifications) (*see also specific titles*), 6–7, 9, 250n, 316
Mahāvidyā(s), 23–26, 28n, 280
Maitrī Upaniṣad, 62n, 181
Majestic Yoga, **278**, 278, 278n
Makāras, the five, 265, 276n, 301n
Māṇḍūkya Upaniṣad, 71, 74n, 297n
Māṇḍūkya Upaniṣad, Śaṃkara's commentary on, 107n

Maṇidvīpa. *See* Jeweled Island
Mantra(s) (*see also* Gāyatrī mantra; Seed mantra[s]): as composing the body of the Devī, **70**; dependence of, on yoga, **200–201**, 201; and divine names, 249; efficacy of, and secrecy, 211–212; faults in uttering, corrected by Kuṇḍalinī Yoga, **196**, 196, 197n; and the mantric body of the Kuṇḍalinī, 187, 196; and the Navaślokī Devī Gītā, 41; recitation/chanting of, **55**, 55,181n, 182n, **198**, 200n, 201; in Tantric worship, 287–88; Vedic/ *Ṛg* Vedic, 43, 70, 72n, 73n
Mantra Yoga. *See* Kuṇḍalinī Yoga
Manu. See *Laws of Manu*
Mārkaṇḍeya Purāṇa, 7, 8
Marman/marma-sthāna (vital points), 176, 197
Material cause, **86**, 90n, 207n, 243
Mātrā (count), 172–73n
Matsya Purāṇa, 50, 240n, 253n, 316n
Māyā: in Advaita, 15, 86–87, 89n, 92–93, 117n, 119; as beginningless but with an end, 89n; as cause of differentiation of Lord into parts, **114**; as creative power of Brahman, 15, 86–87, 97n; as creative power of the Devī, 17, 75n, **85**, 89n, 96, 99, **111**, 119; as creative power of the Self, **95**; as deluding/ concealing power (power of ignorance), 43, 44, 66, 68n, 71, 75n, 87, 89n, **201**, 202n; destroyed by knowledge, 89n, **91**, 108; as distinct from the Devī, 92–93; as efficient and material cause, **86**, 90n; as essence of Brahman, 92, 97n; as existent cause of non-existent world, 206–207n; and Gross Body, **149**; as identified with the Devī, 17, 21, 65, 66, **86**, 87, 89n; 108–109, **111**, 115; as identified with the Kuṇḍalinī, **193**; as the laughter of Devī's Cosmic Body, **124**; names of, **42**, **86**, 90n; as neither real nor unreal, 15, **85**, 87, 88n, 93n, 151n; as perceivable, **91**; as Prakṛti, aspect of, **104**, 106; and reflection of Brahman in, 107n, 109; as self-evident, **111**, 112n; translation of, 38; two powers of, 75n, 89n; as wielded by the supreme, 87; and world-dissolution, **86**
Māyā-bīja. See Hrīṃ; Hṛllekhā
Meditation(s) (*dhyāna*): and action, **268**; in breath control, **170**, 171; in Goddess worship, **54**; and iconic forms of Bhuvaneśvarī, 67–68n; Limb-by-limb, **198**, 199, 200n; on lotus feet of the Devī, **248**; resorptive (Lāyā Upāsanā, meditative dissolution), 15–16, 150, **155–56**, 156–57; as the seventh limb of yoga, **175**, 177; on three forms of the Devī, 67; on the Virāj form of the Devī, 278n; and visualization, 19
Menses (menstruation, menstral blood): of the Goddess, 2, 21, **242**, 243; and the nectar of Kuṇḍalinī Yoga, 195; of women, and ritual impurity, 21
Meru, 180, 182n
Mīmāṃsakas, 142–43, 145n
Mithyā (the false, unreal), **92**, 95n, **149**
Mokṣa (*mukti*, liberation) (*see also* Liberation/highest spiritual goals of life): and the destruction of Māyā, 89n; and one desirous of, dependent on the Veda, **269**; as result of knowledge, **142**, 142–43, 144n, **228**; as

Mokṣa (continued)
result of touching the Devī's yoni-stone, 243; and too many people attaining, 276n; traditional forms of, rejected in devotion, **223**, 225–26, 227n
Mudrā(s), 20, 305, 308n
Mūlādhāra. *See* Centers of energy, Base (Root) Support Center
Muṇḍaka Upaniṣad (see also *Devī Gītā*, and the *Muṇḍaka Upaniṣad*), 16; on aniconic form of the supreme, 62n; on Brahmavidyā, 216; on the ideal disciple, 212n; on the ignorant, 210n; on the knower of the Self, 210n; on knowing Brahman, 231; on the Lord who gives birth to the world, 131; on need for indifference to the world and for a qualified guru, 148n; on omnipresence of Brahman, 61n; on omniscience of Brahman, 72n
Muṇḍaka Upaniṣad, Śaṃkara's commentary on, 206n, 207n

Nāḍīs. *See* Channels of energy
Naiṣkarmya Siddhi of Sureśvara, 16; on knowledge, ignorance, and action, 139, 140n, 141n, 144n, 145n; on the rope/snake analogy, 75n
Name(s): recitation/singing of, **54**, **223**, **224**, **248**, 249; of goddesses and associated sacred sites, 238, 240n, **240–41**, **245–46**
Navarātra. *See* Rites, specific, Rite of Nine Nights
Navaślokī Devī Gītā, 41, 43–44, 321–22
Navaślokī Saptaśatī, 321
Nectar (*amṛta, sudhā*), **193**, 194,195n, **285**, 289
Nīlakaṇṭha: Advaitic leanings of, 89n, 206n, 227n; commentary of, on the *Devī-Bhāgavata Purāṇa*, 32–33, 38n; commentary of, on the *Devī Gītā*, 32, 192n, 202n
"Not this, not that" ("*neti, neti*,"), **150**, 152n
Nyāsa. *See under* Tantric worship, rites included in

Oṃ (Auṃ): as abode of the threefold Śakti, 97n; as bow of meditation, **204**; as essence of the Vedas, 98n; as form of the Devī, **70**, **130**, 131; and four quarters of, 14; meditation on, as the Self, **205**; relation to Hrīṃ, 65, 71, 77n, 97n, 98n, 131, 157, 157n, 207n; and reversal of evolution through meditation on, 100, 156–57; as seed mantra of Brahman, 19, 71; as seed mantra of the Devī, 65; and Śiva, 12; and the term *praṇava*, 76–77n, 157, 157n, 207n ; as the universe, 159n; use of, in breath control, 171, 172, 172n; visualization of, between the brows, 177
Organs of sense (knowledge) and action, **101–102**, 102, 104n, **149**
Outcaste, **118**, **224**

Padma Purāṇa, 253n
Padmas. *See* Centers of energy
Pañcadaśī of Vidyāraṇya, 16; on aggregated and individuated forms, 107n, 122; on the evolutionary process, 100, 101n, 103n, 104n; on the five sheaths, 76n, 152n; on the four steps of Jñāna Yoga, 147; on intense meditation, 154; on *kṛta-kṛtya*, 50–51n; on the Lord's assuming soul-forms, 113n; on Māyā, 88n, 112n; on the nature of con-

sciousness, 93–95n; on the Puruṣa/Virāj, 112; on the reflection model of creation, 107n
Pañca-Pretāsana. *See* Seat/throne of Five Corpses
Pañcāyatana-pūjā, 275
Pañcāyatana scriptures (of the Śaiva, Vaiṣṇava, Saura, Śākta, Gāṇapatya sects), **274**, 275
Pañcīkaraṇa (work attributed to Śaṃkara), 16, 100, 156–57
Pañcīkaraṇa (the fivefold generative process), 98n, **98–99**, 99–100, 100n, 101n
Pañcīkaraṇa-Vārttika of Sureśvara (see also *Devī Gītā*, and the *Pañcīkaraṇa-Vārttika*), 16; on Oṃ as the universe, 159n; on the process of evolution, 97n, 98n, 100, 100n, 103, 103n, 104n; on resorptive meditation, 157, 157n, 158n, 159n; on the states of consciousness, 107n
Pariṇāma. *See* Cosmogony (creation), evolutionary model of
Pārvatī (Gaurī): as author of non-Vedic works, 276n; benign and horrific forms of, 134–35; compared with the Devī, 1; as focus of third-day rites, 253n; identified with lustrous power of the Devī, 46; as incarnation/*śakti* of the Goddess, 9–11, 46, **79**, 79–80, 82n, 267, **315**, 315–16; mantra of, 309; and Śiva, 7, 10, 11, 49, 50, 60, **79**, 80, 253n, 272, 277n, **314**, 315–16
Pārvatī Gītā of the *Mahābhāgavata Purāṇa*, 9–11, 79–80, 82n, 128, 134
Pilgrimage sites (*pīṭhas*, *sthānas*, sacred sites/dwelling places): all, existing in Kāśī, **248**, 250n; delighting in accounts of, **277**; and devotion, **224**; and dispersal/fall of Satī's body parts, 49, 240n, 242–43, 245n; enumerated by the Devī, **240–42**, **245–46**; and feeding of Brahmans, 262n; Himālaya's query about, **237–38**; lists of, 238, 244n, 247; as manifestations of divine consciousness, 247; and *tīrtha*, in contrast to *pīṭha/sthāna*, 239; as a topic in the Purāṇas, 6
Piṇḍāṇḍā and *brahmāṇḍa*, 180, 181
Piṅgalā. *See under* Channels of energy
Pīṭhas. *See* Pilgrimage sites
Postures. *See under* Eight-limbed Yoga of Patañjali, the eight limbs of, defined
Prajāpati, as the penis of Devī's Cosmic Body, **124**, 126n, 127n
Prakṛti (Nature): as identified with the Devī, 21, 65, 68n, **69**, 82n; and material evolution, 96, 96–97n, 102; as mirror reflecting Brahman, 107n; in Sāṃkhya 15, 72n; twofold aspect of, **104–105**, 106; and the unmanifest, 97n
Pramāṇa (authority), 270–71
Praṇava/*praṇava*, 71, 76–77n, 166, 171, 172, 172n, 207n
Prapañcasāra Tantra, 66, 68n, 73n
Praśna Upaniṣad, 182n
Preman. *See* Ecstatic/loving joy
Pūjā. *See* Worship
Purāṇas (Purāṇic literature) (*see also specific titles*): and the *bhakti* tradition, 6–7; and the canon of eighteen Mahā-Purāṇas, 7–8; and emphasis on meaning (*artha*), 319; general nature of, 4, 5–7; and the god-demon conflict theme, 6, 53; and "imitation" *gītās*, 9; as intended for all, 36; and the Kāpālakas, 276n; as proclaiming the Devī,

Purāṇas (continued)
304; and prominence of Śiva and Viṣṇu in, 6–7, 60; and *smṛti*, 270; and Tantric worship, 291n; and textual borrowings, 205; and *vratas*, 256n
Purāṇic pantheon, and Bhuvaneśvarī, 23
Puruṣa (Spirit): in Sāṃkhya, 15; and the Virāj, 112, 113n, 122, 125, 200
Puruṣārthas. *See* Four ends/goals of life
Puruṣa Sūkta of the *Ṛg Veda*, 125, 127n, 267

Qualification(s): and/or duties of a student, **211**, 211, 212, 212n, **213**, 215n, 308n; and entitlement to the Vedas, **274**, 277n; and the mental treasures/virtues (tranquillity, etc.), **142**, 143, **233**; of a guru, **145**, 146–47, 148n; for receiving the *Devī Gītā*, 36–37, **211**, 212, **312**, 313, 317; for Tantric worship, **311**, 312n

Rāghava (commentator on the *Śāradā-Tilaka Tantra*), 47n, 162n, 163, 167n, 178n
Rāja Yoga, 181n, 182n, 202n
Rajo guṇa. *See* Activity
Raktadantikā, 24, **241**
Rāma, 255n, 259n, 260n, 272
Rāma Navamī, 255n
Recitation (*japa*, chanting, repetition) (*see also under* Name[s]): in breath control, **170**, 171, 174n; of the *Devī-Bhāgavata Purāṇa*, 320–21; of the *Devī Māhātmya*, 320–21; of the Gāyatrī, 43, 74n; of the Hṛllekhā (Māyā-bīja), **55**, 55–56, 59–60, 71; of mantras, **55**, 55,181n, 182n, **198**, 200n, 201; of names of the Devī, **54**, **223**, **248**, 249, 250n, 307n; of the root mantra of the Devī, **299**, 301n; of the *Song* of the Devī, **312**, 320–23
Refuge (*śaraṇa*): in the Devī, **277**; devotees of the Devī, as 210n; in Durgā, **69**, 73n; explanation of, 54n; in Kṛṣṇa, 278n; in the Kuṇḍalinī, **285**, 289; in the mantra of Bhuvaneśvarī, 73n; Mata Amritanadamayi, Supreme Goddess, as, 308n; in the supreme Mother, **53**; in the Virāj image of the Devī, **266**
Renunciation (detachment), **145**, 153
Ṛg Veda (*see also* Puruṣa Sūkta), 26, 43, 72–73n, 74n, 132n
Right-handed Tantra (Dakṣinācāra), 36, 265, 288
Right artery. *See under* Channels of energy
Rites (*vratas*, rituals, ritual acts, vows) (*see also* Karma)
  attacment to, by the ignorant, 210n
  enumerated by the Devī, **250–51**
  and festivals (*utsavas*), 258, 262n
  general description of, 238, 251–53
  Himālaya's query about, **237–38**
  specific (*see also* Tantric worship, rites included in): the austerities *kṛccha* and *cāndrayāna*, 167n; Dark Fourteenth Rite (Śivarātri), **251**, 254n; Evening Rite (*pradoṣa*), **251**, 255n; Rite of Nine Nights (Navarātra), 60n, **251**, 252, 255–57n, 258, 260n, 261n, 320, 321; third-day rites, **54**, 56n, **251**, 252, 253–54n, 259n, 261n; week-day rites, **251**, 252, 254n, 255n
  and supreme devotion, **224**, 226n
  types of: daily/regular and occasional, 144n, **224**, **251**, 256n, 261n; optional, forbidden, and

obligatory, 145n, 253, 256–57n, 261n
Vedic: necessity of, 142–43; to be performed only by Vaidikas, **263**, 265–66n
and women, 36, **251**, 252, 253n, 256n
Root mantra (*mūla-mantra*), 301n
Rudrayāmala Tantra, 215n

Śabda-brahman (Brahman in the form of sound), 47n, **185**, 187
Sac-cid-ānanda. See Being, consciousness, and bliss
Śaiva (Śaivite) literature or schools, **42**, **86**, 90n, 162n, **274**, 276n; and the Āgamas, 21, 274–75; and the *Sūta Gītā*, 9, 115
Śakambharī, 24, **241**, 249, 272
Sākṣin/sākṣinī. See Witness
Śākta literature: *gītās*, 9, 79, 128, 134, 317n; Purāṇas, 8, 265; Tantras, 274; Upaniṣads, 25
Śāktas and the *Devī-Bhāgavata Purāṇa*, 7
Śakti (as identified with the supreme Devī) (*see also* Bhuvaneśvarī; Devī; *Śakti*[s]/Śakti[s])
in all embodied beings, 248n
as identical with, rather than an attribute of, the Devī, 109
identified with Mahālakṣmī in the Gāyatrī, 43
identified with the Self as supreme witness, 283n
identified with the Veda, 272
as the Kuṇḍalinī, 21, **193**, 200n
as manifesting in the "Channel of Comfort," **179**
and Śiva: general relation to, 22–23, 90n, 297; in Kuṇḍalinī Yoga, 187, 188n, 189n, **193**, 194, 195n, 201, 290n; union of, symbolized by Hrīṃ, 71
as supreme cosmic energy or power: in the *Devī-Bhāgavata Purāṇa*, 7; in the *Devī Gītā*, 2, 22, 46, **69**, 80
translation of term, 38
Śakti(s)/Śakti(s): of the Devī, reflected in the Hṛllekhā, 310; as lower manifestation(s) of the Devī, 10–11,46, 50, 60, 80, 297n, 315–16; and the Mahāvidyās, 24; and state of world when deprived of, **48**, 49; as sustaining/energizing power of world, 51–52n, 315; of the Trimūrti, 73n
Śāktism (Śākta perspective/tradition, Śākta Tantrism): and Advaita perspectives, 87, 89n, 92, 103, 140; and the *Devī Gītā*, 21–26; and the Devī's recitation of the *Muṇḍaka Upaniṣad*, 217; and the motif of the Devī's throne, 296; and Prakṛti, 72n; on Rāma, 255n; as a theistic world view, 16; and world-affirmation/worldly pleasures, 87, 304
Samādhi. See Absorption
Samaṣṭi. See Aggregated (*samaṣṭi*) form of the Devī; Aggregated (*samaṣṭi*) and individuated (*vyaṣṭi*) forms/aspects
Saṃkalpa (mental resolve), 252, 253n, **287**, 290n
Śaṃkara (*see also works by*): and Advaita, 13; on Brahman as the light of lights, 208n; on breath control, 174n; on devotion of a disciple, 212n; hymn of absolution by, 305; on knowledge and action, 142–43; on nectar, 195; and the *pañcāyatana-pūjā*, 275; on possible injustice of the Lord, 89n; on the real and the unreal, 93n; on realization in

Śaṃkara *(continued)*
this world, 232n; on the states of consciousness, 107n; on superimposition, 116n; views of, compared with the *Devī Gītā*, 16, 17, 108
Sāṃkhya: and Advaita, 15, 82n; and evolution of elements, 96, 96–97n, 100n, 101n, 102, 103n, 105; and Prakṛti, 72n
Sammohana Tantra, 183n
Samsara/*saṃsāra* (*bhava*, rebirth, world-appearance, wordly existence)
in Advaita, 14
continutation in, due to: lack of knowledge, **153**, 210n; lack of Vedic tradition, 275
devotees rescued from, **78**, **267**
dispelling appearance of, **282**, 283n
liberation from: in this life, 230; its pain and suffering, 258; through attaining the Jeweled Island, 231; through Kuṇḍalinī Yoga, **196**, 196; through ritual action, 143
soul's entanglement in, **139**
symbolized in the swing festival, 259
and *tīrtha*, 239
Śāṇḍilya Upaniṣad, 166n, 167n, 169n, 174n, 176, 177, 178
Śāradā-Tilaka Tantra: and the channels of energy, 180, 182n; and correction of faults in mantras, 181n, 197n; and the *Devī Gītā*, 162, 162n, 166n, 178n, 297n; and *dhyāna* of Bhuvaneśvarī, 67n; and *mahas*, 47n; and the mantric body of the Kuṇḍalinī, 187; and *nyāsas*, 293; and Para-Śiva and Para-Śakti, 200n; and the postures, 169n; and the qualifications of a student, 211, 215n; and the six obstacles to yoga, 163n; and the ten restraints and observances, 166n; and the throne of the Devī, 295, 296, 297n; and the union of Śiva and the Kuṇḍalinī, 195n; and the water offering, 301n
Śaraṇa. *See* Refuge
Sarasvatī, 23, 172, 309
Śatapatha Brāhmaṇa, 216, 217
Ṣaṭcakra Nirūpaṇa: on the energy channels, 182n, 183n; on the Kuṇḍalinī, 186; on the *liṅga*s in the energy centers, 188n, 189n, 191n, 192n
Satī: and dismemberment/dispersal/fall of body parts, 49, 240n, 242–43, 244n; as incarnation of the Devī, 10, 247; meaning of name, 51n; as source of the ten Mahāvidyās, 23; suicide of, 11, 46, **48**, 49–50, 60, 240n
Sattva guṇa. *See* Lucidity
Saubhāgya. *See* Auspiciousness
Saundaryalaharī, 187, 296, 297
Sāvitrī, 172
Schüssler Fiorenza, Elisabeth, 35
Scripture, mantric aspects (*śabda*) and meaning aspects (*artha*) of, 319–20, 322
Scriptures opposed to the Vedas, **273–74**, 275
Seat/throne of Five Corpses (Bhuvaneśvarī's throne; Pañca-Pretāsana), 1–2, 286 (fig.), **294**, 294–97, 297n, 298n
Secret teachings. *See* Hidden teachings
Seed mantra(s) (*bīja-mantras*, seed syllables) (*see also* Hrīm; Hṛllekhā; Oṃ): definition/explanation of, 19, 249; in the energy centers, 182n, 200n; and root mantras, 301n; in Tantra, 19–20, 57n, 287–88

Serpent Power. *See* Kuṇḍalī/Kuṇḍalinī
Servant, ideal of, **223**, 225–26, 227n
Sharma, Nagaraja, 322–23
Sheaths (*kośas*), the five, 70, 76n, **149–50**, 151n, 152n
Sin(s), 235–36n, **248**, 254n, 311n
Singing, **224**, 228n, **304**
Śiva (Mahādeva, Maheśvara) (*see also* Devī, and Śiva; Pārvatī, and Śiva; Śakti, and Śiva; Trimūrti, the): as author of non-Vedic texts, **274**, 275, 276n; and the *bhakti* tradition, 6; as half of Devī's body, 2, 65; and Liṅga(s)/Jyotir-liṅga, 11–12, 67, 188–89n, 190–91n; mantra of, 309; as part of Devī's Cosmic Body, **124**; in the Purāṇas, 7; and Satī, 10, 11, 23, 46, **48**, 49–50, 51n, **78**, 242, 243; as subordinate to the guru, **213**
Śivā, 53–54n, 60
Śiva Purāṇa (see also *Umā Saṃhitā*), 11, 23, 24
Śivarātri (Dark Fourteenth Rite), **251**, 254n
Śiva Saṃhitā: on the austerities *kṛccha* and *cāndrayāna*, 167n; on breath control, 174n, 176; on the channels of energy, 182n, 183n; on forms of yoga, 181n, 182n; on *liṅgas* in the *cakras*, 188n; on Meru in the body, 180; on the postures,168, 169n; on practices for a slow yogi, 200n; on relation of Haṭha and Rāja Yoga, 202n; on the *sahasrāra*, 192n
Skanda (Śiva's son), 49, 50, **314**, 315, 316n
Skanda Purāṇa. See *Sūta Gītā*; *Sūta Saṃhitā*
Smṛti (sacred law), **269**, 269–70, **273**, 274, 287
Song of the Goddess. See *Devī Gītā*
Soul(s), individual (*jīva*, *jīvātman*, *pratyagātman*, individual Self): in Advaita, 14–15; dissolution of, into Māyā, **86**, 89n; divided, by ignorance, **114**, 117n; as forms of the Devī in the world, **111**, 112, 113n; genesis of, from the Self, **138–39**, 139; as reflected image in Māyā, **105**, 106; unity with Brahman or Self, **43**, 71, **146**, 147, **161**, 162, 177, 178, **179**, 194, **198**, 201, 223n, 288; unity with the Devī, **70**, 76n
Sovereignty (*Aiśvarya*), 24, 51n
Śravaṇa. *See* Listening
Śrīdhara (commentator on the *Bhāgavata Purāṇa*), 166n, 221n, 226
Śrī Vidyā (mantra), 309–310
Śrī Vidyā (school), 22
Śruti/*śruti* (revealed texts, Vedic revelation/scripture): and *āgama*, 274; authority of, **269**, 269–70, 271n; defined, 132n; as the Devī's command, **271**; and dharma, 287; eternality of, 217; and the guru, 147; received by the gods, **129**; and scriptures opposed to, **273**
Stages of life (student, householder, etc.), **277**, 278
Sthānas. *See* Pilgrimage sites
Stotras. *See* Hymns
Student, qualifications and/or duties of. *See under* Qualification(s)
Subtle Body. *See* Bodies, the three cosmic
Śūdras, 36, 252
Superimposition (*adhyāsa*), 75n, **114**, 115, 116n, 150
Sureśvara (see also *Naiṣkarmya Siddhi*, *Pañcīkaraṇa-Vārttika*), 16, 108, 139–40, 142–43, 151n

Suṣumnā. See under Channels of energy
Sūta Gītā (of the *Sūta Saṃhitā* of the *Skanda Purāṇa*), 9, 115, 117n
Sūta Saṃhitā (of the *Skanda Purāṇa*) 264, 267, 276n, 280, 281n, 282, 283n, 306n
Sūtrātman. See Bodies, the three cosmic
Svarūpa (true form) of the Devī, **48**, 51n
Svayambhū-liṅga, **184**, 186, 188n, 190–91n, 194, 195n
Śvetāśvatara Upaniṣad: on devotion to one's guru, 148n, 212; on the gender-inclusive nature of the supreme, 62n, 120n; on the grace of the creator, 154n; on the highest light, 93n; on the knower of the Self, 210n; on knowledge, force, and action, 97n; on omnipresence of the supreme, 61n; on the proper recipient of secret teachings, 212n; on the Self within, 236n

Taittirīya Āraṇyaka, 72–73n, 74n
Taittirīya Upaniṣad, 76n, 152n,100n, 210n; and *mahas*, 16, 46n
Tāmbūla, **64**, 67n, **303**
Tamo guṇa. See Dullness
Tantra (Tantric perspective/tradition, Tantrism) (*see also* Śāktism): and Advaita, 18–19, 119, 180–81, 299–300; and Advaitic and *bhaktic* ideals synthesized, 214, 311; basic world view and practices of, 18–21, 265; and bipolar/sexual symbolism, 22–23, 194, 247; definition of, 17; and the *Devī Gītā*, 17–21, 200; and interpretations of Hrīṃ, 71–72, 73n; and secrecy, 212–213n; and the Vedic tradition, 18, 26, 44, 71, **263–64**, 264–65, 267–68, **269**, 270, 275, 276n, 287–89, 291n; and women, 36
Tantras (*see also specific titles*): as Śākta works, 21, 274; of Śakti, **294**
Tantric worship:
- external and internal forms of, 56–57n, 280–81, 299–300, 305
- fruits of, **310–11**, 311, 311n, 313
- offerings/sacrifices (*upacāras*) in, 289: material gifts and services, **303–304**, 304–305, 306n, 308n, 311; mental, **55**, **299**, 301n
- preliminaries of, **285**, **287**, 287–89, 295
- relation to Kuṇḍalinī Yoga, 287
- rites included in: absolution (*kṣamā*), **303**, 305, 307–308n; cleansing rites/rites of personal hygiene (*bhūta-śuddhi, śauca*), 19, 202n, **287**, 287, 288, 289, 290n, **292**, 292–93, 295; dismissal of the Devī, **304**, 305, 308–309n; fire offering (*agni-hotra, homa*), **287**, 290n, **304**, 308n; infusion of life-breath (*jīva-nyāsa, prāṇa-sthāpana*), 292–93, **299**, 300, 302n; infusion of mystic powers (*mātṛka-nyāsa, nyāsa*, installing or implanting of divine energies in the body); 19–20, **55**, 57n, 287, **292**, 292, 293, 294n; installation within the body of the the deity's altar (*pīṭha-nyāsa*), 293, **294**, 295, 297, 297n; invocation (invitation/summoning) of the Devī, **299**, 300, 302n, **303**, 304; protective rites/securing space, 289, **299**, 302n; water offering (*arghya*), **299**, 300, 301–302n, 306n; worship of protective deities, **303**
- and use of the Hṛllekhā in, **309**
- and Vedic worship (*see under* Tantra, and the Vedic tradition)

Tapas. See Austerities
Tārā, 23, 24
Tāraka: and boon from Brahmā, **48**, **78**; role in *Devī Gītā*, 3, 6, 11, 49–50, 56, 57, 79, 315, 316n; slain by Skanda, **314**, 316n
Tat, **70**, 76n
Tat tvam asi ("You are That"), 14, 71, 76n, **146**, 148n, 150n, 157
Teaching(s) (*upadeśa*) of the *Devī Gītā*, 3, 11, 82, 316, 320
Tejas/Tejas (light/power) (*see also* Lustrous power of the Devī), 59, 188n, 190n
Theism (theistic or *bhaktic* perspective): and cosmogonies in the Purāṇas, 86; of the *Devī Gītā*, and Advaita, 16–17, 200; and gender of the supreme, 62n; and Māyā, 87; and Tantra, 18; in the Upaniṣads 13
Third-day rites, **54**, 56n, **251**, 252, 253–54n, 259n, 261n
Times, auspicious and inauspicious, 252, 254n, 255n, 258; and appearance of Bhuvaneśvarī, **58**, 60, 61n, 254n; and Friday as favorable for Devī-worship, 252, 254n, **303**
Trimūrti, the (Brahmā, Viṣṇu, and Śiva/Rudra; the male triumvirate) (*see also the individual gods*): as derived or born from the Goddess, 10, 132n; and the god-demon conflict, 53, 60; the Goddess identified with, **118**, 119; the guru identified with, 290n; humbled by the Devī, 60; *śaktis*/spouses/female aspects of (Brahmī, Vaiṣṇavī, Gaurī, or Sarasvatī, Lakṣmī, Pārvatī), 73n, **118**, 119, 120n; and the seat/throne/couch of five corpses, 1–2, **294**, 296–97, 298n; and the three *guṇas*, 117n; and the three knots in the energy centers, 195n; turned into women, 244n; as visualized in breath control with a matrix, 171
Tripurā, 23, 24, 25–26, 244n, 296, 307n
Tripurā-Rahasya, 25, 296
Truth, two levels of, 112n
Tvam, **70**, 76n

Uddārakośa, 23
Umā Haimavatī (Haimavatī), 59–60, 61n, 216, 217, 297, **314**,
Umā-Saṃhitā (of the *Śiva Purāṇa*), 220n, 259n, 261n
Unmanifest, the (Causal Body). *See* Bodies, the three cosmic
Upādhi(s) (apparent limitation, finitude, limiting adjuncts), 106, **113**, 115n, 117n, **138**, **281**, 283n; dissolution of (*upādhi-vilaya*), **149**, 150, 151n
Upaniṣad(s) (*see also specific titles*): and (cosmo-)theistic perspective, 13, 17, 121n, 125, 131; and doctrine of Brahman/ultimate being, 12, 13, 60, 86; and doctrine of ignorance as cause of action, 139–40; as explaining true nature of the Devī, **81**; great sayings of, 14, **146**, 147, 150n; as the great weapon of meditation, **204**; as knowledge portion of the Vedas, 143; listening to (*śravaṇa*), 47n, **146**; Śākta, 25; and *veda*, 13
Upa-Purāṇas, 7

Vāc (Speech), **69**, 73n
Vaidikas, **263**, **269**, **274**; and Vaidika Tantrics, 18
Vaikuṇṭha (Viṣṇu's heaven/supreme abode), **52**, 54n, 154n, **208**, 210n

Vaiṣṇava scriptures, qualified acceptance of, in the *Devī Gītā*, **274**
Vaiṣṇava views and perspectives: and avataras, 23, 272; and the *Bhāgavata Purāṇa*, 7–8, 17; and *gītās*, 9; and nature of the guru, 214; rejection of, regarding Viṣṇu's supremacy, in *Devī Gītā*, 53; and Tantras, 21
Vāmana Purāṇa, 259n, 262n
Vāmas, **273**, 275–76n
Varadā Tantra, 71
Varāha Purāṇa, 259n, 276n
Varṇāśrama-dharma, 18, 264
Veda (knowledge) (see also knowledge), 12–13, 270
Veda(s): access to, **232**; as arising from the Devī, **269**, 270, 271n; as blueprint of the universe, 18; dependence on/adherence to, **269**, **274**; the four, personified, **58**, 66, **129**; as having the Devī as their goal, **70**; as identified with the supreme Śakti, 272; known by best of Brahmans, 233; mantric nature of, 319; and non-Vedic scriptures/non-Vedic ways of life, **273–74**, 274–75, 277n, 287; as part of the Devī's Cosmic Body, **123**; and *pramāṇa*, 270–71n; as proclaiming Devī, **304**; as proclaiming Kṛṣṇa, 308n; protection of, **271**, 272, 273n; ritual and knowledge portions of, 142–43; as *śruti*, 269–70; study of, vs. grace of the supreme, **137**, 138; and *veda*, 13
Vedācāra, 287–89
Vedānta/*vedānta* (*see also* Advaita Vedānta), 12–13; and the Devī as the established truth of, **130**; and fulfillment, **234**
Vedāntasāra of Sadānanda, 16; on aggregated and individuated forms, 107–108n, 122; on *anirvacanīya*, 88n; on causality, 90n; on devolution of the cosmos back into Brahman, 151n; on the evolutionary process, 100, 103n, 104n, 126n; on the rope-snake analogy, 76n; on the great saying, "*Tat tvam asi*," 76n, 148n; on the twofold nature of ignorance, 106n, 107n; on the two powers of ignorance, 89n; on the Virāj, 126n
Vedāntins (*see also* Advaita Vedānta), **86**
Vedic tradition, and Tantra. *See* Tantra, and the Vedic tradition
Vicitrā ("Beautiful, Variegated Channel"). *See under* Channels of energy
Vidyāraṇya (see also *Pañcadaśī*), 108
Vijaya Daśamī, 255n
Vimarśa (intelligence), **86**, 90n
Virāj (Cosmic/Gross Body, cosmic form) (*see also* Bodies, the three cosmic)
as cosmic manifestation of the Devī, 4, 112, **122**, 122, 122n, **123–24**, 126n, 205, 243; androgynous aspect of, 127n; cosmogonic and apocalyptic aspects of, 125; as her Cosmic Body and one of four forms of Brahman, **42**, **70**; and Himālaya's hymn of her thousand names, 307n; horrific aspects of, 124, **127–28**, 128, **133**, 134; and hymn to the Devī as, 4, **130–31**, 131–32; as one of various forms for worship/meditation, 26, 67, 199, **266**, 267–68, 268n, **278**, 278, 278n, 280, 282; revealed by grace of the Devī, **137**, 137–38

definition of, 74n
as form of Kṛṣṇa/Viṣṇu, 4, 9, 122, 125, 126n, 128, 129n, 132n, 134, 278
and Puruṣa, 112, 113n, 125
Virgins (*kumārīs*, maidens), 255n; and young boys (*baṭukas*), **257**, 262n, **304**
Viṣṇu (*see also* Trimūrti, the): as adviser to the gods, 11, **52**, 53, **54**; avataras of, 8, 23, 272; beheading of, 216; and the *bhakti* tradition, 6; as creator of delusion, 276n; in the *Devī-Bhāgavata Purāṇa*, 8; eagerness of, to see the Devī's cosmic form, **122**; humiliated by the Devī, 60; in the Jeweled Lotus, **185**; Limb-by-limb Meditation on, 199, 200n; mantra of, 309; as part of Devī's Cosmic Body, **124**; and Pārvatī's Virāj form, 134; as proclaimer of Devī's superiority, 53; in the Purāṇas, 7; and Satī, 49, 242; and Śiva, 11; sleep of, 259–60n; as subordinate to the guru, 215n; Virāj form of, 125, 199; as wielder of Māyā, 87
Vivarta. *See* Cosmogony (creation), reflection/appearance model of
Vivekacūdāmaṇi: on consciousness, 76n; on devotion to one's guru, 148n; on the evolutionary process, 103, 104n; on the gross and subtle bodies, 151n; on Māyā, 88n, 89n, 108–109; on realization not attained by works, 138, 144n; on reasoning, 148n; on rejection of the world, 181; on the Self as non-agent, 116n
Vows. *See* Rites
Vratas. *See* Rites
Vyāsa (compiler of the Purāṇas), 5, 46, 49, 235, 315–16, 317
Vyāsa (commentator on the *Yoga Sūtras*), 167n, 168, 176
Vyaṣṭi. *See* Aggregated (*samaṣṭi*) and individuated (*vyaṣṭi*) forms/aspects

Will, knowledge, and action (*icchā, jñāna, kriyā*), **96**, 96, 96n, 97n, 99, **179**
Witness (*sākṣin/sākṣinī*): as the Devī, **70**, **78**, **282**, 283n; as pure consciousness, **91**, 93, 94n; of the states of consciousness, **70**, 76n, 207n
Womb (*yoni*): of the Devī, **81**, **224**; of the Devī at Kāmākhyā, **241**, **242**, 242–43, 244n; and Viṣṇu as embryo within, 260n
Women (*see also* Androcentrism; Gender; Menses): and auspicious state of marriage, 49; benevolent through marriage, 22; *Devī Gītā* intended for, 36; and liberation while embodied, 35; and rites (*vratas*), 36, **251**, 252, 253n, 256n
World-Mother: as daughter of Himālaya, **81**, 82n; likened to human mother, **52–53**; role in the *Devī-Bhāgavata Purāṇa*, 24, 65; role in the *Devī Gītā*, 1, 3, 8, 10, 26, 53
Worship (*pūjā, yāga, yajña*, sacrifice) (*see also* Rites; Tantric worship)
definitions of and terms for, 56n, 265n
of the Goddess, **54–55**, **248**: for rescuing a person from hell, 5; for success against demons 11, 66; and flesh offerings, 66; limb-by-limb, 254n
invocatory aspects of, 55–56

offerings in (*upācāras*) (*see also* Tantric worship, offerings/ sacrifices in), 254n, 259n
and recitation of divine names, 249
and relation to *utsavas* and *vratas*, 258
as a topic in Purāṇas, 6
types of, 26, 56n, 199, **263–64**, 264; external, **279**, 280–81, 282–83, **299**, 299–300, **303–304**, 305; internal, 56–57n, **279**, 280–81, **281–82**, 282–83, 299–300, 301n, 305; Tantric (*see* Tantric worship); Vedic, **266–67**, 267, **277–78**, 278, **279**, 280

Yantra(s) (sacred diagram[s]), **279**, 281n, 283, 288, 300, **303**, 306n
Yoga(s) (*see also specific yogas*), **81**, 82, **203**, **233**, **282**; as generic term for the Eight-limbed Yoga, 161–62, **200–201**; as "union," 162; and dependence on mantra/Mantra Yoga, **200–201**, 201
Yogakuṇḍalī Upaniṣad, 202n
Yogam aiśvaram. See Majestic Yoga
Yoga Sūtras of Patañjali (*see also* Eight-limbed Yoga), 20; on absorption, 177; on breath control, 170–71, 174n; on concentration, 176; on meditation, 177; on nine impediments to yoga, 164; on the postures, 168; on the restraints and observances, 166n; and the *Śāradā-Tilaka Tantra*, 162; on withdrawal of the senses, 176
Yogatattva Upaniṣad, 197, 197n
Yoni. See Womb
Yoni-bandha/Yoni-mudrā, 197n